OEDIPUS ON A PALE HORSE

Journey through Greece
in Search of a Personal Mythology

by

David Sheppard

FOR

My parents, Raymond (1916 – 1999) and Josephine Sheppard
and my daughter and son, Bear (Cynthia) and Richard, and
Elizabeth (1944 – 2007)

NOTES:

1. While on this journey through Greece, I took forty rolls of slide film with an Olympus OM-1 SLR. I have scanned these slides and presented them, segregated by location, at the following web address:

www.oedipusonapalehorse.com

2. Word spellings in Greek are not as standardized as are English words. Compounding the problem is that we have no recognized standard for transliterating Greek letters into English equivalents. Also, traditionally Greek words were Latinized before being Anglicized, which changed the spelling once again, or perhaps introduced a new word altogether, e.g., Herakles became Hercules. This practice is generally no longer followed; therefore, I have stayed with all things Greek as much as possible. Thus, you will see Zeus and not Jupiter, Hera and not Juno, Athena and not Minerva, etc. With all the spelling variations from guide books, scholarly works, and archaeological publications, it is difficult to standarize it for a work for the general reader. I have tried to maintain some consistency in the narrative but have, of course, left quotations as presented in the original documents.

3. This book is based on actual events; however, I have changed and rearranged some of it for rhetorical purposes. In particular, I have inserted archaeological and mythical material in places where I might not have had the thought in the actual setting. But I can assure you that all my interactions with people, both flashbacks and current events, are real, that my family history is as factual as I can make it, and that my journey through Greece, and the revelations concerning my life, are factual. To give you and idea of the magnitude of my effort on the road, I wrote 120,000 words during my ten weeks in Greece. I used this as a baseline for rewriting the material several times, and in doing so, I attained a truer reflection of my actual experience than I would have ever imagined possible.

Table of Contents

Prologue

Part I: Mainland Greece

1	Athens	3
2	Thebes	26
3	Delphi	48
4	Ithaca	74
5	Olympia	97
6	Sparta	112
7	Mycenae	124
8	Corinth, Epidaurus, Argos	140

Part II : Greek Islands

9	Mykonos, Delos	164
10	Santorini	178
11	Crete	192
12	Rhodes	219
13	Patmos	234

PART III: Turkey

14	Turkey: Ephesus I	275
15	Turkey: Troy	299
16	Turkey: Pergamon	319
17	Turkey: Ephesus II	334

PART IV : Greek Islands and Attica

18	Samos	346
19	Lesbos	358
20	Sounion	373
21	Aulis	387
22	Eleusis	401
23	Colonus	419

Epilogue	438
Afterward	441
Endnotes	444
Bibliography	465
Index of Ancient Greek Names	473

ACKNOWLEDGEMENTS

First of all, a big thank you to Ball Aerospace Corporation for laying me off on January 1, 1993. My work as an astronautical engineer had seemed repetitious for several years, but I could never come to terms with my problem. They solved it for me, and in so doing, changed my life immeasurably for the better. The next thing I knew, I was in Greece. I would like to express my gratitude to Kerry and Ken, who first encouraged me to take this journey through Greece and read the initial manuscript. A special thank you to Kerry for her repeated readings and assistance with it. Also, thanks to all the members of the Rocky Mountain Writers Guild in Boulder, Colorado for their critiques and favorable responses to this material. Dr. James Hutchinson was especially supportive. Thank you to my sister-in-law, Nancy Sheppard, who read the initial manuscript and encouraged me to get it published. A special thanks to Marilyn Mueller, my editor, for her hard work and expertise, and to Richard Sheppard for the cover illustration and layout, and drawings and maps.

Finally, I hardly know how to thank the people of Greece. They are a friendly, welcoming people, who open their borders and doors to the lonely traveler.

And I looked, and behold a pale horse:
and his name that sat on him was Death,
and Hell followed with him.

Revelation 6:8

Know Thyself.

The Delphic Oracle

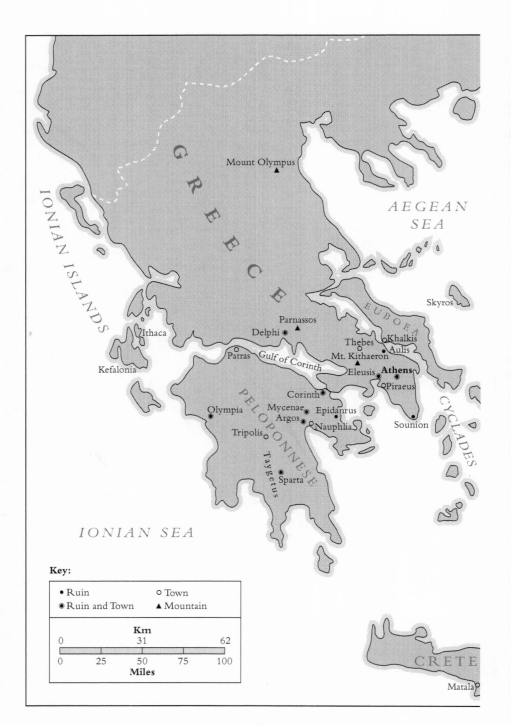

Key:

- Ruin ○ Town
- ⊛ Ruin and Town ▲ Mountain

Km		
0	31	62

0	25	50	75	100

Miles

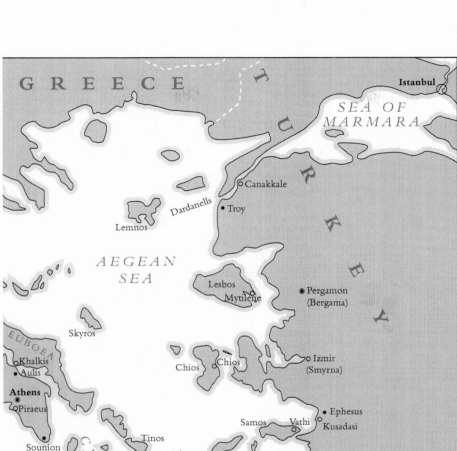

GREECE

TURKEY

Istanbul

SEA OF
MARMARA

○ Canakkale

Dardanells

• Troy

Lemnos

AEGEAN
SEA

Lesbos
Mytilene

• Pergamon
(Bergama)

Skyros

EUBOEA

○ Khalkis
• Aulis

Chios ○ Chios

○ Izmir
(Smyrna)

Athens
○ Piraeus

• Ephesus
○ Kusadasi

Samos Vathi
○

Sounion

CYCLADES

Tinos

Mykonos

Delos

Patmos

DODECANESE

Kos

Santorini
(Thera)

RHODES

○ Rhodes

Linos

Karpathos

CRETE

Iraklion
• Knossos

Matala • Phaestos

PROLOGUE

Since the age of nineteen when I first encountered Greek myths, I wanted to visit the land of King Oedipus, but the possibility always seemed remote until a recent job loss left me with unlimited free time. My purpose in going was to bring myself closer to the myths of our civilization, to grasp a deeper understanding of the forces working within our society. According to Thornton Wilder:

> ...myth-making is one of the means whereby the generalized truths of human knowledge finds expression and particularly the disavowed impulses of the mind escape the 'censor' of acquired social control and find their way into indirect confession. Myths constitute the dreaming subconscious soul of the race telling its story.[1]

In the same spirit, I was building a personal mythology that I hoped would lead to recognition and deeper understanding of the truths of my own life. I wanted to use the Greek myths as a catalyst to precipitate truth from confrontation. I went alone to Greece to confront myself with the ruins of my own past.

I had a little money stashed and enough frequent-flyer mileage for a free ticket to Greece. I also knew I couldn't afford to go through a travel agency, but then I wasn't looking for the usual tourist fast-in-and-fast-out cruise. I would be on my own. I looked into the feasibility of going to Greece as a traveler instead of a tourist and picked up a copy of *Let's Go: Greece & Turkey* to estimate expenses. I learned it was possible to spend two and one half months in Greece for $35 a day, or right at $2,500. Instead of selecting a couple of places to spend my days, I decided on an odyssey about the Greek mainland and islands, even to the western coast of Turkey. I couldn't afford a rental car and would use the public transportation system instead—buses, trains and ferries—to get from city to city and island to island. I read travel guides and the recently published *Balkan Ghosts* by Robert D. Kaplan on the history and politics of the region.

I wanted to carry my own weight during my journey, and to me that meant more than my backpack. I hired a tutor and bought a stack of books, many more than I needed, and dived into the language, Ελληνικα, Modern Greek. Since I couldn't use my frequent-flyer mileage during the summer, I had several months to prepare for my trip and scheduled my departure for the 1st of October. I went without hotel reservations, trusting to luck to find accommodations.

I dislike heavy luggage and opted for a travel pack, a combination backpack and suitcase with a zip-off daypack, which I promptly overloaded in an attempt to satisfy all contingencies. I was traveling the off-season during the months of October, November and early December and would experience both hot and cold weather. I took a security pouch, not so much to prevent the theft of my passport, international driver's license, traveler's checks and return airline ticket, as to provide a safe place for those valuables. I wanted to isolate them from my own idiocy and absentmindedness, and I tied the pouch around my neck and took it off only to shower.

★

On the 1st of October as the University clock tower tolled noon, I completed packing and was nearly ready for the five-block walk to the Boulder bus station. I first sat down on the couch staring at the Rocky Mountains trying to remember any last minute tasks. At the request of my landlady, the thermostat in my apartment was set at 68 F to prevent the plumbing from freezing, my furniture was pulled away from the electric heat radiators, and I had my apartment key in my wallet so I could get in upon my return. Was that everything? Never before had I been on the road for two and one half months. I was going alone.

Quite suddenly I was overcome with the loneliness of leaving. I looked out my front window and in the old elm tree saw the nervous squirrel and heard the fussy chatter of the magpies who had kept me company during all my summer studies on Greece. The trees were turning golden and dropping leaves. Two weeks before, we had received our first smattering of snow. I would miss fall in Colorado, my favorite time of year. Taking a deep breath, I shouldered my pack, locked the front door, and clumped heavily down the stairs.

PART I: Mainland Greece

CHAPTER 1: Athens

3 Oct, Sunday

A little after 3:00 AM, we descend through darkness into the airport just south of Athens, on schedule. The air inside the jetliner is thick with muffled voices and the clang and whir of the deploying flaps and landing gear. We've just been told to return our seat backs and tray tables to the full upright and locked position. In spite of sleeping only an hour in the last thirty-six, I'm not tired but hyper. From the airport in Denver, I had flown to Chicago, where I scurried to an adjacent concourse for my night flight to London. During the brutal twelve-hour layover at Heathrow, I had managed only an hour of sleep stretched out on a row of terminal seats, before boarding this night flight to Greece.

I talk to an American woman, JoAnn, between flight attendant announcements. She and I are in a flurry of activity getting out our journals to write down each other's names, addresses and telephone numbers. We want to compare notes when we get back to the States. As we descend through the night air, we quickly agree to meet again in Athens, before I leave on my journey around the mainland. She had befriended a Greek woman in Athens on her first trip twelve years ago and has been back every summer since. She passes a business card to me, and as I ogle her picture on the front, she tells me to turn it over so she can interpret the Athens address she's scrawled on the back.

I observe JoAnn, who is the essence of womanliness, long brown hair, round smiling face. She enjoys straightening her hair and freshening her makeup. She's from southern California. Suddenly the airplane smashes the ground with such force that it's another five seconds before we rebound, finally staying in contact with Greek soil. JoAnn catches her breath, and a chorus of raised voices expresses our distress.

Even at this ungodly hour, passport control is logjammed. We walk together to baggage claim, where JoAnn introduces me to three more Americans she met on the flight. "I envy you," she says. "God, I wish I had the courage to do what you're doing." Then she says good-bye and scurries off to find her Greek friend.

3

Athens

The arrivals terminal is a small one-story structure that reminds me of a bus station. The closed car rental and information booths are bathed in yellowish light. Along with the three Americans JoAnn passed me off to, I walk around the corner to the arrivals lounge and write in my journal while waiting for the sun to rise, eager for my first view of the land inhabited by the ancient Greeks. Four young people are stretched out in sleeping bags in a dark corner, their backpacks stacked against the wall of windows looking out over the runway. A plane takes off with its night-lights flashing. In the distance, a line of rocky hills along a small peninsula gradually becomes visible, then finally, I can see the Aegean lapping the ancient coast of Attica and enveloped in an ocean of haze. A row of white homes and businesses crowds to the edge of the sea.

I'm intimidated by the sight. Suddenly Greece, the ancient land of war, murder and suicide, has stepped out of my imagination. It's real and I'm here.

In the chair next to mine, a woman with fuzzy brown hair and dressed in a warm-up suit scrounges through her bag then beats it to the nearby toilette. She and the other two Americans have to report in with their tour group at one o'clock, and then they'll be free until six tonight when they'll board their cruise boat. After talking to me about my months of preparation, they're feeling a little disorganized.

The woman in the warm-up suit comes back expressing her envy of my journey. "I traveled Western Europe alone for two weeks last year," she tells me, "and I can't believe I've booked myself with a tour group this time." She stands expectantly over me, as if it would only take a word for her to join me. I have to remind myself that I've purposely come to Greece alone. I'm on a mission.

I hoist my pack, and we walk to the front of the airport to catch a bus. I lumber along the sidewalk behind them, minding my own business, when a sudden honk startles me. I look back to see an army tank bearing down on me, the long barrel of its cannon pointed just over my head. That's right, I say to myself, this is not America. Just north of here, a war rages in Bosnia, to the east a war rages in Turkey, to the south Qadafi rules Libya. I hurry to catch up with the others.

As we exit the red double-decker bus, I feel disoriented, don't quite know what direction to take. I'd like to tag along with them but realize I have my own agenda. Finally, I say good-bye to my newly found American friends, take a deep breath, and unload my pack on a bench at the side of the street. I'm at Σύνταγμα Πλατεία, Syntagma (Constitution) Square. Behind me, an iron fence and a row of evergreen trees casts a shade across me, blocking the heat of the morning sun. The auto exhaust down ΛΕΩΦ. ΒΑΣ. ΑΜΑΛΙΑΣ is suffocating, the blaring horns and squealing tires unsettling, and the scurry of people disrupting. All of these Greek signs are also going to take some getting used to.

Truly alone for the first time, I feel my journey through Greece has come as a series of false starts. It first began when I left Boulder, again when I boarded the plane in London for Athens, and now with the departure of the three Americans. I'm finding being alone in a foreign country, where I don't speak the language, a little intimidating. But I've planned to find a hotel in Plaka, the old part of the city just north of the Acropolis, a little less than a kilometer from here.

Time to get on with it.

From Syntagma, I walk south, lumbering beneath my forty-five pound pack and under assault from traffic noise and fumes, realizing I've over packed. I turn off the main street, looking for Hotel Phaedra. The din of city noise and smell of exhaust fades. Taking a deep breath is no longer painful. Plaka is the oldest continuously inhabited town in Europe. It's peaceful, shaded, quiet. I wander through the maze of shoulder-width streets and multistory buildings crowding in on me. I experience a hush, a sense of serenity.

An old man sits on a bench in the shade of a maple tree. "Συγγνομι." I say, excuse me. "Μιλατε Αγγλικα;" Do you speak English? "Οχι," no, he replies followed by a few Greek words I don't understand. He's chubby in an old withered way and has a tooth missing. "Το Ξενοδοχειο Φεδρα?" I ask. He smiles broadly, points down the street at a yellow sign, "Hotel Phaedra," in English. "Ευχαριστω," I say, feeling foolish for not seeing it myself.

The desk clerk is pleasant, an aristocratic presence in a small man with a big smile and smooth manner. A cool breeze blows through the open window and choral music wafts from the domed Byzantine church next door. A room will cost me 3800 drachmes ($16.67). More than I expected, but still quite a bargain.

After dumping my backpack on the floor, I inspect my room. Its old walls form a pieced-together pentagon with uneven length sides. The ceiling is very high. A glass of water with four red roses sits before the mirror above the leaking sink. The toilette is down the hall.

I'm suffering from the weight of my pack and lack of sleep, so I grab one of the thin white towels, a small bar of soap and head for the community toilette, which has a douche (shower) with no curtain. The tiles are beige and some have been chipped away so plumbing can stick through. It's all old but roomy. To the right of the toilette door is a white porcelain commode with a lidded basket beside it for toilet paper. Greek toilets cannot handle paper. Yes, even the real stinky stuff goes in the basket. I step out of my sweaty clothes onto the cold floor for my first shower in two days.

Athens

Afterward, I stand out on my patio in the bright sun staring up at the Acropolis looming over the hotel. Today's going to be a real scorcher. I'm tempted to stay in my room, take a little nap to help me over the jetlag, and go out this evening. The truth is, I'm a little afraid of what I've come here to accomplish. Previous frightening travel experiences have left me unsure I'm ready for this type of confrontation with myself.

I sit on my bed with my head in my hands, staring at the floor. I don't know where to start. How can I sit here whining like this? I'm in Greece! Good god, get over it, I think. Okay, to hell with this "traveler" business. I'm just a tourist looking at archaeological sites. Time to see the Acropolis.

My hotel is just southeast of the Acropolis, so I follow the street out front for two blocks until the noise and auto exhaust consume me. I look up to see the Arch of Hadrian on the other side of the busy street. The Arch was built in 130 AD, and looks as if it has been painted with a fresh coat of motor oil every summer since. I'm not really all that interested in the arch, but on the other side of it, I see ruins through some trees, and something strange takes hold of me. A surge of courage? This could be the confrontation I'm both seeking and trying to avoid. The Acropolis can wait a while. I walk on past the arch and enter the gate to the temple of Olympian Zeus.

Zeus was the natural ruler, the father of both gods and mortals. He was heavy-thundering and mighty voiced, known as the god of sky and weather. He hurled lightning bolts. Religion in ancient Greece was a Zeus religion, the meaning that gave light to life and birth to a civilization. His oracle to the north at Dodona, where he spoke to his priests through the rustle of the leaves of an old oak tree, was the oldest in Greece.

His temple here in Athens was the largest. The tall Corinthian columns are in the center of a large flat field where my feet raise dust as I walk. The temple was started sometime before 550 BC, but work was suspended and resumed several times and not completed until 700 years later when Hadrian finished it. The huge columns lay tumbled about the site, the few still standing jut up from the ground to sixty feet in the air. They're a stark sight against the deep-blue sky with the Acropolis in the background. In Greek mythology, Zeus was a very human-like father, a regal-looking man in midlife, kind, benevolent at times, but could be ruthlessly brutal, violent in his wrath.

I'm finding a little courage out here in the heat and dust, so I sit on a stone fence at the edge of the field to consider the reason I came to Greece in the first place, the reason a personal mythology is so important to me. Thirty-two years ago I had a run-in with my father. It occurred during the summer of 1961, the first year of John Kennedy's presidency.

Athens

I had just turned twenty and was home from college, working for my father on the cotton farm. We locked horns one day over something that seemed petty to me, but I wouldn't back down. I wasn't a kid anymore and wanted him to know it. We shouted at each other, and I told him if he was going to be like that, I'd just leave. "Okay, by God," he thundered, "get the hell out."

I'd been thinking about Greece anyway. Over a few beers, a friend of mine and I had talked about delaying college and working our way to Greece on a merchant ship. He had an uncle who'd done that. I needed a push to get me started, which my father had just provided. I walked down the hall away from him, thinking I'd pack and make my exit a quick one. I felt relieved really, wanted to be out from under his scrutiny. I heard his footsteps heavy on the hardwood floor behind me. I turned right into my bedroom, and he turned left into the one where he and my mother shared a bed.

My mother had witnessed the explosion between us, and I heard her footsteps down the hall at the same time I heard him slipping cartridges into the magazine of the deer rifle, heard the bolt action close. I'd fallen on my unmade bed, the cool sheets up against my face, my fingers clutching the edge of the soft bedspread. "What are you doing?" she asked him calmly, as if maybe he was getting ready to go sit on the porch for a while, as if we hadn't argued, and he didn't have a deer rifle in his hands. "I'm going to end it all," he said.

I wasn't afraid, just calm, calm in the extreme. I wondered if he planned to kill himself or me. Him or me? Him or me? The words kept echoing. I imagined how I'd feel when he blew his head off or how I'd feel when the bullet ripped through my body. The question was intellectual, theoretical. I heard the deer rifle click again and the cartridges hit the floor, heard the rifle go back in the closet, the closet door close, heard him crying. She closed their bedroom door, and I don't know what else passed between them except that later she told me that he had planned to kill himself.

I'm not sure how I expect to come to terms with this on my journey. In the thirty-two years since, I've never been conscious it's had an effect on me. I just find myself talking about it after I've had a few beers, or I avoid confrontations when I should stand my ground. I've noticed patterns in my life, an unnatural order. What seems unusual about my reaction is that I had no feelings. How could I have no feelings about my father almost killing himself?

I don't expect to find some Greek seer with the answer. I just thought I'd take that journey to Greece I contemplated thirty-two years ago, maybe recover something I lost when I heard him clicking the deer rifle. I'm on a journey in search of a feeling. Haphazard stumbling about the ruins of ancient Greece is a strange approach. But I've tried all the others. This personal mythology business seems a little trite also in this context. I don't know quite how to go about it. After stating the problem, I'll leave it at that. Just let it fester.

On the way back to the hotel, I stop at a street-side restaurant and have stuffed eggplant, bread and a Sprite accompanied by car exhaust and the blare of motorbikes. My first food in thirteen hours. I eat it greedily, growing duller of mind by the minute. I've had an hour of sleep in the last forty-eight.

Time to call it a day.

4 Oct, Monday

I rise early and walk along Λεοφ. Βασ. Αμαλιας Street to the National Archeological Museum, recovered somewhat from jetlag. Traffic in Athens is frightening. Every horn in the city blows at once. I have to dodge a motorbike doing forty on the crowded sidewalk, hide behind the waist-high metal poles that prevent cars from hitting pedestrians. The museum is overwhelming, echoing rooms full of ancient Greek sculptures, all masterpieces. Most are made of marble, but one stands out: the huge bronze statue of Zeus throwing a lightning bolt.

All this is from the Iron Age, after 1200 BC. Downstairs I run into the Mycenaean exhibit from the Bronze Age, prior to 1200 BC. On the wall across from the gold "Mask of Agamemnon" is a huge, blown-up photograph taken in 1876 of Heinrich Schliemann and his wife at the dig at Mycenae, his archeological crew posed about the site. Before Schliemann, few believed a Bronze Age civilization of any significance really existed. Most scholars had for centuries thought Homer's epic poetry an elaborately developed fiction, but Schliemann, an amateur archeologist, believed Homer wrote about the exploits of real people. He was so bold as to suggest he could find the ruins of their ancient kingdoms using Homer's text.

By 1873 Schliemann had uncovered the ancient city of Troy and located what he believed to be the gravesite of Agamemnon at Mycenae. Schliemann's archeological finds rocked not only the world of archaeology but classical literature as well. Legends of the ancient Greeks were viewed with a new respect. The names Theseus, Oedipus, Odysseus, Agamemnon took on a dimension heretofore realized only by those of the Bible. And ancient Greek religion took on a new respectability as well.

I walk through the exhibit of gold death masks, emerald-studded jewelry, shields, bronze spears inlaid with gold and silver and blackened with age, decorated vases. The Bronze Age came to an abrupt end during the years following the Trojan War, around 1200 BC. War spread, palaces burned throughout the region. The people were uprooted, and a great migration to the eastern coast of Asia

8

Athens

Minor (Turkey) occurred.

The cause of the end of the ancient Greek civilization in the Aegean is still a mystery. A four hundred year "Dark Age" followed in which people lived in poverty and lost the ability to write. Out of this period emerged classical Greece: Homer, Hesiod, and later Sappho, Sophocles, Socrates, Plato, Aristotle.

I'm not sure what to make of all this. The ancient myths are not literally true in all respects, but Schliemann's archaeological finds have me convinced it all fits together. Myth is married to the landscape and the Bronze Age civilization. Classical Greece, seven hundred years later, accepted the myths as truth. They have heavily influenced our modern civilization. But Schliemann has become somewhat of a mythical character himself. The biographical details of his early years have come under question, and some even believe the gold he supposedly found at Troy and Mycenae were counterfeits made from gold he picked up in the hills of California during the gold rush. He was rather low on ethics, making much of his money from shady dealings during the Crimean War. No one is quite sure who he was or what he did, how much of his own life he fabricated to gain publicity. Still, his impact on archaeology was profound. The ruins of Mycenae, Agamemnon's kingdom, are in the Peloponnese not far from here.

★

I sit on my patio eating a peach and a bunch of grapes while mountainous thunderheads move in from the Aegean. Zeus, god of weather, is on the move this morning. In the hotel lobby, I watch a CNN broadcast with a Greek voice-over of Boris Yeltsin, moving on the Russian white house to clear out the 100 parliament members holed up there. I ask the man at the desk what happened, and he tells me what he can, about the gunshots and some of those inside dying. Yeltsin is in control and all is quiet. The clerk can't tell me more, he says, because he doesn't know enough English. My Greek certainly isn't up to the task, but I wish it were. Russia isn't so far from Greece.

The Greek national election is this Sunday. Posters posted on top of posters are everywhere. The wind distributes them. Three parties are in the running: the New Democrats, the Socialists, and the Communists, the KKE (Kappa Kappa Epsilon). Their insignia is the red hammer and sickle. The New Democrats are currently in power but have lost the necessary votes in Parliament to govern. The New Democrats came to power when the previous Socialist president, Andreas Papandreou, was accused of embezzling $200 million. But Papandreou has cleared himself and is again the Socialist candidate.[2] He's seventy-four and has a young wife, Dimitra Liani, half his age. She used to be an Olympic Airlines hostess but is referred to now as the "official mistress." Supporters of Papandreou see this young lady as a sign of his vigor and manliness. I hear people arguing

9

about politics everywhere I go. Greeks take their sexy politics seriously.

★

In the evening, I descend into the dull dreamy world of jetlag but still manage the energy to take my first βολτα (volta, evening promenade) in Plaka. The volta is popular throughout Europe and was invented here in Greece thousands of years ago. The narrow streets are filled with foreign shoppers (Germans, English, Japanese, American) buying Greek vases, leather purses, T-shirts, jewelry. The shop owners stand out front of their stores inviting the tourists inside. And now I know why I feel that my hotel is on the corner of Motorbike and Truck streets. I'm staying at the entrance to Plaka. In the evening, taxies drop off their customers in the little courtyard beneath my window. Not only do I get the sounds of the vehicles, I also get the voices. In spite of all else Greeks have given western civilization, they didn't invent the whisper.

For dinner, I buy a feta cheese and tomato crepe at a little pastry shop and watch the woman make it in front of the open service window. She must know how fascinated I am with her because she smiles continuously but never looks at me as she pours the thick pale batter and spreads it on the circular grill. Her dark-brown hair hangs straight and curls forward on her cheek. She bites her bottom lip.

The dark-haired Greek women in Athens are gorgeous. They have smooth olive skin, wear dark skirts, white blouses. I'll be walking down the street under attack from exhaust fumes when a beautiful woman, one of these gorgeous dark-haired brunettes, will pass by, and a whiff of perfume, sweet as candy cane at Christmas, will surface through the ocean of smoke and soot. I feel drawn to these women. I was married for eighteen years, and after my wife left I felt like a boat without a steering oar. I'm drawn to women as though I'm seeking a sense of direction from them. When I met JoAnn aboard the flight into Athens, I latched onto her, let her pass me off to the others she'd met when she left me. Strange. I'll see her again before leaving Athens.

I can't get to sleep. I'm still thinking about the Greek girl, thinking about the difference between the dark-haired, olive-skinned Greeks of today and those of mythology, the fair-haired, light-complexioned Achaeans.

5 Oct, Tuesday

On my third morning in Athens, I wake slowly but with renewed excitement, and step out of my room with my camera for a walk around Plaka. Jet lag still has a death grip on me. The air is thick with humidity, the dark-gray buildings and streets slick with moisture. No one is out except shopkeepers sweeping trash and putting out produce, boxes of vegetables and fruit. The sounds are the swish of brooms and the rustling, fussy noises of sparrows and finches in trees. I pick up a kilo of peaches and grapes. Occasionally a Greek walks by purposefully with head down. My good-natured "καλημερα" doesn't get even a blink.

A monk sits in a chair in front of the 14th Century Byzantine Church of St. Catherine next to the hotel. The domed church is in a small park with palm trees and the ruins of a Roman colonnade. The monk has a long gray fan of a beard and wears the gray smock of the clergy over black pants cinched tight with a black belt. His expression is severe, but he straightens while I take his picture.

I decide to visit the Akropolis, which I've been avoiding because of the tourists. As I approach it, I walk off the road through evergreens and up a rocky path to the ruins of the theatre of Dionysus, which lies in a natural hollow in the side of the hill. I rest on a large hot stone shaped by the hands of some ancient Greek, wishing I had on cutoffs instead of Levis. The touch of fall in Colorado is definitely absent in Athens.

The theatre is 2500 years old and lies before me like a section of a gigantic eggshell. The birth of European theatre occurred in Athens in the 6th Century BC. Thespis was the first playwright. Then, theatre was not entertainment as we view it today but religious, a metaphor of the divine experience whose richly varied play was mythology. It was also political, the new democracy's method of educating the populace on being good citizens. The tragedy, even today, holds for the human imagination a tension between that which is morally acceptable and the destructive, darkly fascinating.[3]

Each spring during the 5th Century BC, the eight-day Festival of Dionysus was held in this theatre. Aeschylus, Sophocles and Euripides, among others, presented their tragedies in the competition. Before the festivities began, a goat was sacrificed. The word "tragedy" means "song of the goat." Shedding the goat's blood set the tone for the murder and suicide that followed on stage. The festivities started at sunup and continued all day. The theatre seated 17,000, enough for the entire Athenian population and any others who might flock to the festival. Women were only permitted to sit in the last few rows.

Dionysus was the patron deity of theatre and god of the mask. In vase paintings, other gods were more frequently shown in profile, whereas Dionysus was shown face-on, his entire large-eyed terrible face staring down the viewer. His face was the mask donned by the actors for their performance. Behind the mask dwelled the world of spirits,[4] everything creative and destructive, infinite rapture and terror. When he came, he brought pandemonium, bloodthirsty madness.

But the single most important aspect of Dionysus was his ability to simultaneously hold in suspension illusion and reality. That is the essence of theatre. For the audience to make anything at all of a play, it must deal with the reality of their lives as they sit there, and at the same time believe in the illusion on stage. This phenomenon is Dionysus. The concept has an extension. Shakespeare wrote:

> All the world's a stage
> And all the men and women merely players:
> They have their exits and their entrances;
> And one man in his time plays many parts...
> (As You Like It Act 2, Scene 7)

The ancient Greeks also knew that life itself has its realities and illusions. We're never quite sure which is which. The Greeks presented myth on stage. Thus myth was the illusion, yet it was based on the reality of the lives of the heroes they portrayed. I've heard it said that we are mythical beings. At times then, our lives must parallel myth. That being true, the personal mythology I'm searching for on this journey is the illusion, the myth my life was following when my father loaded the deer rifle.

The gods of old are illusive now. Yet, the ancient Greek encountered them as a highly personal experience, forces in the "now of life" shaping his own will. To know them was to know himself.[5] For us to experience the ancient Greek gods, we must reassemble them from what we see of their ancient temples and the words of those who wrote about them, work similar to that of an archaeologist. We then learn to recognize the presence of the god, and perhaps realize in retrospect, the impact he has had on our lives. It is essential that we bring these ancient gods to us as we create our own personal mythology.[6] You can't get there without divine influence.

Thirty-two years ago at a two-year college in Bakersfield, California in a small theatre patterned after this great theatre, I watched Sophocles' *Oedipus Tyrannus*, a play about a king who unknowingly killed his father and married his mother. The confrontation with my father followed close on the heels of seeing that play, my near tragedy echoing elements of Oedipus' tragedy. I came close to causing the death of my father, and the bizarre life of Oedipus has haunted me ever since. You might say that Dionysus had visited me. Thinking about the events of my life in juxtaposition with the ancient myths gives them a new weight. I feel a little better now about what I'm doing here in Greece. Perhaps something will come of it after all.

I reluctantly leave the theatre and trudge through the hot sun, belly-to-belly and shoulder-to-shoulder with tourists in shorts and tanktops, up the winding footpath of the huge Acropolis crag, and sit on a stone wall at the precipitous edge overlooking Athens.

The first inhabitants of the Acropolis came here around 3000 BC. Originally the Acropolis was a royal fortress, but through the centuries became a religious stronghold, a tribute to Athena, patron goddess of the city. The Akropolis is a flat limestone rock standing 160 meters above the plain, 270 meters in length, almost three football fields, and 160 meters wide. The surface is hard and covered with chips and crumblings of marble and stone. No vegetation grows here. It's a tribute to sunlight. The October heat on the Acropolis is startling. I'm very tired and dripping sweat, but I dry in the hot breeze whipping about me as it swirls tourists' voices.

My guidebooks talk about the massive architecture, the creamy-marble Parthenon, the Erechtheion with its tribune of caryatids that stand before me, but the view of Athens behind stretching to the horizon is simply mind-blowing, the tan buildings swallowing the landscape, overrunning the hills and merging into the pastel sea of pollution. Athens is a city of four million. Yet, a quietness sits on this flat mountain, broken by a whisper coming from below, a murmur, an echo of the city's voice returned by the rocky peaks jutting up in the distance.

Athens was the domain of Athena. She was a virgin goddess, daughter of Zeus and Metis, wisest of all gods and mortals. Zeus was afraid of Metis' wisdom and coerced her into making herself small and swallowed her. Zeus then gave birth to Athena through his head, a rather bizarre act accomplished by the blow of an ax. Since she was not born of a woman, she bonded with her father and, in addition to being the protectress of cities, gray-eyed Athena was the "weariless leader of armies, dreaded and mighty goddess, who stirs men to battle and is thrilled by the clash of arms."[7] Athena carried the aegis, the shield of Zeus, and had his courage and her mother's wise counsel. She forever remained a virgin. Athena's favorite animal was the wise old owl, a remnant of her mother, the wisest of all immortals.

To become the patron deity of Athens, she competed with Poseidon, the bellicose, trident-bearing god of the sea, who wanted the city for himself. Kekrops, the first king of Athens who was an earth-born primordial being with a man's body and a snake's tail for legs, judged the competition. Poseidon struck his trident on the Akropolis and a saltwater spring gushed forth. But Athena caused the first olive tree to grow. Understandably, Kekrops judged the olive tree more useful and awarded the city to her. She also invented the plow and was known as the bringer of civilization.

Athens

Parthenon, the most prominent and famous building on the Acropolis, took nine years to build and was completed in 431 BC. "Parthenon," or in ancient Greek, Παρθενος, means maiden, virgin. It is Athena's most important temple and the site of the great Panathenic festival honoring her birthday, Hekatombaeon 28 (mid August). Inside was one of the most glorious statues in all Greece. Pausanias, a doctor who traveled 2nd Century Greece for twenty years while all the temples were still intact, described the twelve-meter, ivory and gold statue:

> She has a sphinx in the middle of her helmet, and griffins worked on either side of it. ...Athene stands upright in an ankle-length tunic with the head of Medusa carved in ivory on her breast. She has a Victory about eight feet high, and a spear in her hand and a shield at her feet, and a snake beside the shield...The plinth of the statue is carved with the birth of Pandora the first woman.[8]

I stand at the northern edge of the Acropolis and look down over the city. Just to the west, I see the jumbled ruins of the ancient Agora, the market place, and beyond it, the Dipylon, the double-gated exit through the wall that surrounded the city. The Panathenic festival started there, came through the Agora along the Panathenic Way and ended here on the Acropolis at the Erechtheion, which was also originally a temple of Athena.

The Erechtheion housed a wooden statue of the goddess that had fallen from heaven. The purpose of the procession was to bring the peplos, a cloak or long robe, to the wood statue and dress her in it. The procession consisted of maidens carrying vessels followed by sacrificial animals, youths, musicians, and old men carrying olive branches. The woven, saffron-colored peplos, embroidered with scenes from the gods' battle with the giants, was in a chariot bringing up the rear.[9]

The woven peplos was a symbol of Athena's civilizing influence, which the Greeks saw as coming not from confrontation but through a weaving of differing wills. This city is a tribute to the goddess's civilizing influence. Yet Athena's love of the battle cry and the clash of arms led men on bloody paths. I'll not ignore Athena and her civilizing influence. That she invented the plow reminds me of my own upbringing on the farm. She championed Odysseus, the man of many wiles who fought at Troy and wandered the Mediterranean for ten years. Perhaps I should visit his home on Ithaca. If I do, I'll deal with Athena again.

I look off to the southwest through the haze to Piraeus, the seaport that has been in use since ancient times. The smog is so thick, I can barely make out the coastline. By the end of the month, after a wide swing around the Greek mainland, I hope to be in Piraeus on my way to the islands.

★

In the evening, I walk the streets of Plaka and have a feta cheese and tomato crepe again at the same shop where I ate last night. I'm in love with the girl who waits on me. It's her dark eyes, olive skin, dark hair and beautiful smile. I've never seen so many clear-skinned people. They're immune to blemishes. I wonder if a connection exists between all this noise, all this pollution, and the olive skin, the smooth complexions, the gorgeous women. Is there something organic, healthy about all this carelessness?

6 Oct, Wednesday

I wake during the early morning hours and watch the sparkling stars of Orion slowly traverse the heavens. I have insomnia. Quietness has finally come to the plateia. I hear my first Greek cricket. He's persistent. A car followed by quiet, the screech of a cat.

I came to Greece with a rough plan for the places I'd visit. I even thought of going north to Mt. Olympus and hiking its summit. But that seems too risky now. What if I stumbled and sprained an ankle? I'm still trying to get my bearings, find the settings that will foster this personal mythology. Perhaps I should move on to Thebes. After visiting the ancient theatre, I've grown more and more interested in Dionysus. He was born there. Oedipus, who killed his father and married his mother, was also King of Thebes. Sounds like the perfect place for me.

I rise at daybreak and walk the cold stone streets to a little cafe, have my first Greek coffee, which comes in a tiny white ceramic cup. Even though the woman asks and I say, "Οχι," my coffee is still sweet. Greek coffee is strong as motor oil. The fine sand-like grounds sit in a glob at the bottom. Since the coffee is so thick to begin with, you don't know you're drinking grounds until you notice a fine grit in your teeth. That means you didn't quit soon enough. My greasy cheese omelet comes with warmed white bread, pepper and sea salt.

While having breakfast, I mull over my comfortability here in Athens. I must move on to Thebes tomorrow. If I get settled in here with all my insecurities, I may never leave. I decide to hike to the tourist office near Syntagma for information on the bus and to visit JoAnn, the American woman with the bushy-brown hair, round face and rosy red lips I met on my flight into Athens. Her friend's family owns the Pericles Bead Shop in the Monastiraki district just north of the ruins of the ancient Agora.

JoAnn and her Greek friend have just returned from a quick car trip to Corinth. JoAnn walks me to a taverna. "Watch," she says, "I'll be the only woman in the place." We talk of her plans for the next two weeks here in Athens and my journey through Greece. "Tomorrow afternoon I leave for Thebes," I tell her, testing my own resolve. "But I am feeling a little insecure." She smiles, "No wonder. You're brave to be traveling alone." Her concern adds to mine. "Athens seems safe," I protest, "and it's supposed to have the most problems of any city in Greece." She shakes her head. "I mean the loneliness. Look, if you do run into trouble, trouble of any kind, come here to the Pericles Bead Shop. My friends will help."

How right she is. Loneliness is the central issue. And already I'm dreading leaving her. How great it would be to have a traveling companion. She senses that I've misread her. She asks the waiter for our bill, looks at me straight. "I'm paying and won't even discuss it." She knows I've been out of work since the first of the year. She is right about being the only woman in the taverna. "Greek women don't invade the male world," she says. As we part she says one more time, "Don't forget, if you need any help..."

I can't believe how much I like that married woman from Southern California, and I feel sad, lonely after leaving her. But my loneliness is short-lived. After I return to my room, I hear English mixed with laughter out in the plateia below my balcony and run down to see who's making all the noise. It's a young American couple, Chris and Janine. They're Christian evangelists from Bucharest, Romania where they've lived for the past year but are now vacationing with their two kids and another young American missionary, Justin. They are on their way to speak to a travel agent. I can't resist being with all these people, so I walk along with them, glad to delay the inevitable solitude.

While they talk to an agent about a short cruise in the Saronic Gulf, I talk to a man about going by ferry from Crete to Rhodes and Rhodes to Patmos in mid November. Seeing Patmos is important because I promised my mother a picture of the Cave of the Apocalypse where St. John spent eighteen months in exile. The man is emphatic. "No," he says. "It can't be done. You can't go from Crete to the Dodecanese without returning to Athens." I may have to rethink my trip to the islands. Even though I don't expect a straight answer, I ask him about a ferry from Samos to Turkey. I'm concerned about going to Turkey because political relations between the two countries are not good. "The ferries to Turkey are all Turkish, very unreliable," he tells me. "And in late November... Oχι."

The missionaries would like for me to join them for dinner, and in my current unsettled condition I'm more than happy to oblige. After scouring Plaka, we settle on an old restaurant beneath the Acropolis and eat upstairs overlooking city lights. Our waiter pushes three card-tables together, and we sit in folding chairs. He brings a huge platter with plates of meatballs, stuffed vine leaves, stuffed tomatoes, stuffed eggplant, fish, kalamari, large salatas with tomato wedges, cucumbers, olives, and big blocks of feta cheese. The dark-blue fish has been gutted and scaled but not decapitated.

Sitting here at this mini banquet, all gathered around the creaky card table in uncomfortable chairs, we seem one large family. Reminds me of family get-togethers at Thanksgiving and Christmas. I think about the ancient Greeks, their spirited conversation while reclining comfortably, and their table manners. Our table is set with knives and forks with a dispenser of white napkins. Etiquette in Athens has changed considerably in 2500 years:

> ...the reclining guests having neither knives nor forks, Aeschylus, Sophocles and Euripides ate with their fingers; and though neither fingers nor cupped hands could replace spoons for dealing with sauces and gravies, the spoon most in use at table was a piece of bread hollowed out as occasion required. There being no napkins, bread was used also for wiping the fingers, and then tossed to dogs awaiting their share at the diners' elbows. Remembering the garbage-littered alleys we shall not be astonished that the bare floor of the banqueting chamber was the regular depository for the scraps. I hasten to add that they were not left there indefinitely, but before the meal was over were punctiliously swept out--probably into the street.[10]

We have another man with us tonight. The missionaries have known him only a few days. He's originally from Romania. He tells an unsettling story. Fifteen years ago when he was eight, his father was a Romanian diplomat who got into trouble with the government and felt compelled to flee his life of privilege. He came to the United States with his wife and daughter and left his son behind in Romania, so as not to raise the suspicions of the authorities. They told everyone, including their son, that they were leaving on a one-week vacation to England. As the days passed and they didn't return, the son realized he had been abandoned. He was devastated. An entire year passed without word. He was laughed at, cursed, beat up, and suffered other indignities because he didn't have a family. Meanwhile, his parents were frantically working with US authorities to get him released by the Romanian government. It took a year.

The Romanian, a huge healthy-looking guy, has the fish. It swims in oil, which the waiter flamboyantly lights with a cigarette lighter. It sizzles and pops in the blue and yellow flame. As I watch the Romanian eat, I consider the abandonment he suffered, and it brings to mind the loneliness I felt after my confrontation with my father. That one incident seemed to separate me not only from my own feelings, but also from my family. I never felt the same afterward. I felt like a stranger among them, a stranger to myself.

After dinner we climb through the dark up Areopagos (Ares Hill) with the illuminated Acropolis just to the east, the marble Parthenon a glowing beacon in the darkness. The Areopagos has been the hill of judgment since prehistoric times and is where the ancient council of Athens tried murderers. It was named for Ares, the Greek god of war, who was the first tried for murder here. St. Paul was also here and preached to the heathen in the Agora below.

I sit on a rock still warm from the sun, using my flashlight to write in my journal while listening to the murmur of voices from the host of sightseers scattered about in the magnificent darkness. The hill is one rock, jagged and slick as glass, forcing us from the edge and into a tight little group. How cozy it seems. City lights surround us. I try to imagine Athens at night during the time of Sophocles. Lights would have come from fires. I imagine a strong smell of smoke. Athens in antiquity was not a plush utopia, but a slum. The lofty temples of marble on the majestic Acropolis stood in stark contrast to "the wilderness of crooked, narrow streets, squalid alleys, and expressionless houses"[11] where the common people lived.

The first king of Athens who really claims a prominent place in Greek mythology is Theseus who was king around 1300 BC, one hundred years before the Trojan War. Theseus united all the townships of Attica into one city-state by promising "a commonwealth without monarchy, a democracy or people's government."[12] Thus according to legend, the oldest experiment with democracy started with him.

Though Poseidon lost Athens to Athena, one of the ways he maintained a presence here was through Theseus. Theseus was of illegitimate and uncertain parentage, his mother Aethra having laid with both Aegeus, the king of Athens for whom the Aegean is named, and Poseidon on the night Theseus was conceived.[13] His mother and his grandfather in Troezen, in the southeastern Peloponnese, raised Theseus. When he grew to manhood, his mother sent him to Athens to meet his earthly father for the first time, and he eventually became king.

Athens lies before us in a huge valley covered by a bowl of stars, an absolute sea of light glowing neon with the eight or so hills dressed in black about us, the apex of each lit with a startling spray of luminescence. The haze of pollution spreads the glow. The Areopagos is a site a goddess would seek, a high promontory to view her city. Athens has a voice, a murmur that mixes with the gentle sounds of a soft breeze, the sweet-smelling breath of the city. The daytime mask of Athens has been removed, and the city has come alive, its incandescence revealing a raw lustiness.

After leaving Areopagos, we walk Plaka. Justin, the young missionary, keeps up a continuous stream of words about Jesus, how close He wants us to be to Him. We return to our hotel, and just as we top the stairs on the second floor, Justin asks an embarrassing question. "Are you a Christian?" I'm not that interested in organized religion and get defensive when someone questions me about my beliefs. "Yes," I say, finally, "I am a Christian." Immediately I wonder if I've told the truth, or if I've lied to save face. Justin loans me a book I'm to return tomorrow morning. Its title: *With Christ in the School of Obedience. Becoming a Faithful Follower*, written by Andrew Murray. "Obedience" and "following" are not two of my favorite words.

Years ago, I had a confrontation with my mother. My father was always the practical one, hard work and determination I got from him. My mother provided a philosophical framework for my intellectual development, and much of what she taught came wrapped in Christianity. I was receptive and tried hard to live up to her standards. But one day, she came to me carrying her big black Bible and told me to sit beside her. She read the story of Abraham and Isaac, of God asking Abraham to kill his beloved son as proof of faith. To my horror, Abraham didn't protest but took his son into the mountains and drew his knife to slit Isaac's throat, at which point God sent an angel to stay Abraham's hand. When I complained about Abraham to my mother, she got mad, told me I needed a revelation. I've had mixed feelings about religion ever since. What kind of God would ask a man to sacrifice his innocent son? What kind of father would grant such a request, and what kind of mother would read such a story to her own son? This event created a distance between both of my parents and me. I was eight years old. I wasn't literally abandoned like the man from Romania, but I felt a remoteness from that point forward that never went away.

I've been planning to visit Patmos, where St. John wrote Revelations, for my mother, but now I have my own reason for going. I'm looking for an answer to a question that's been simmering for forty-four years. I didn't plan to get into this on my journey, but here it is. It came to me, as if it's been stalking me.

★

The evening air from the Aegean enters my bedroom, cool and refreshing, without a hint of fumes. I listen to dogs barking out front while I mull over the guilt I've felt from the confrontation with my father, his near suicide. I feel as though I almost killed him myself. But I did something else right afterward, during that same hot summer day, that worries me even more.

This is the end of my fourth day in Athens, and I'm more reluctant than ever to leave. I dread trying to find the right bus to Thebes. What if I get on the wrong one? But I must move on. The sights of Athens could fill a lifetime. Perhaps at the end of my journey, I'll return for a few days.

It's almost midnight. I hear girls giggling in the courtyard.

7 Oct, Thursday

I wake before sunrise and burn a trail to the International Telephone Exchange. I walk past Hadrian's Arch with the morning star burning brightly as the first golden fingertips of dawn rise through the deep-blue Aegean sky. I haven't seen a cloud in days. The sidewalks are vacant of pedestrians, if not the trash from yesterday and the day before, and the day before that. The pedestrian lights have been turned off and stare with dark blank faces. I'm always irritable in the morning and that seems to help a little with my insecurity.

I tell my brother I've made it to Greece and that today I'll leave for Thebes. I pump him for information about our family, our elderly parents. My father has been to the doctor about his arthritic hip but the doctor told him he was a long way from needing it replaced. He's doing fine in spite of his complaints. My mother's heart problem, which she kept from us for months, is also under control. My older brother's heart, which had unaccountably accelerated on him, has stabilized. All the health problems in my family seem magnified this far from home. I feel like I'm holding my breath, sort of a deathwatch.

I have breakfast with Justin, the young single man who kept pressuring me about Jesus last night, and I return his book without comment. The Carter family joins us a little later, the bright faces of the kids looking shiny clean. We don't see the guy from Romania.

After breakfast, though I should be on my way to Thebes, I can't let these Americans go, and walk with them to the ancient Agora where the Apostle Paul preached to the multitude. The entrance is in the Monastiraki district where I met JoAnn yesterday. During the Bronze Age, it was a cemetery but was converted to a market place in the 6th Century BC. This site is different from any other I've seen in Athens. Trees make the difference. They stand throughout the Agora: pines, oaks, maples. They absorb sound and leave a sense of serenity, the giant stones standing stark and quiet among them.

Chris is a preacher, and now he stands on the same spot where Paul preached and preaches a little himself while Justin harasses him from the audience.

But the big attraction is the temple of Hephaestus, a large marble structure standing on a hill overlooking the ruins and rivaling the Parthenon on the

Akropolis. Of all the ancient Greek gods and goddesses, Hephaestus is my favorite, the god who fell to Earth. He is the god of fire. His birth was motivated by jealousy.

Zeus' first wife was Metis, but after he swallowed her, he married his sister, Hera. Hera was jealous of Zeus giving birth to Athena, so she contrived to have a child by herself. But when she gave birth to Hephaestus, his legs were deformed, the soles of his feet turned front to back. He walked with a limp, his body executing a forward rolling motion.[14] Hera was ashamed of him. When Zeus and Hera quarreled, Hephaestus took the side of his mother. This irritated Zeus so much that he threw Hephaestus out of heaven. He fell for an entire day, landing on the island of Lemnos at sunset.

According to Homer, Hephaestus was actually a son of Zeus, who wouldn't claim him because of his deformity. Thus, born of a critical mother and a rejecting father, he makes his life on Earth instead of on Olympus with the other gods. He is an artisan and blacksmith and has many workshops, the most famous located in the volcano of ever-smoking Mt. Aetna in Sicily where he works with the monstrous, one-eyed Cyclops. He is the only god who works, a master craftsman and consummate artist. When Zeus wished to punish Prometheus for stealing Hephaestus' fire and giving it to mankind, he turned to Hephaestus and asked him to form the first woman, Pandora, out of water and clay. He asked Aphrodite, goddess of erotic love, to give her "stinging desire and limb-gnawing passion," and Hermes, herald of the gods, to give her "the mind of a bitch and a thievish nature."[15]

But Hephaestus first shaped the beautiful form of woman. The god of fire, though crippled, was no dud when it came to women. He was married to the beautiful, but unfaithful, Aphrodite.

Athena has a dual nature, one not so well known, but closely associated with Hephaestus. In addition to the virgin hotheaded warrior woman, lover of the sound of clashing arms, protectress of cities, she is a mother goddess, the gentle nurse of children. Her nurturing nature is further revealed as the goddess of crafts, weavers and the arts. The origin of this second nature is told in the little-known story about the marriage of Athena, generally a virgin goddess, to Hephaestus.

Hephaestus first enters Athena's life as the "midwife" of Zeus at Athena's birth. Hephaestus was the god who split Zeus' head with an ax so Athena could be born. Later Athena came to him for forged weapons. Hephaestus had been abandoned by Aphrodite and was filled with desire for Athena. He chased her and even though hindered by his lameness, he caught her on the Akropolis. But Athena didn't wish to lose her virginity and wouldn't submit. Hephaestus ejaculated prematurely on her leg. Repulsed, Athena wiped off his sperm with a piece of wool and threw it on the ground. A son was then born from the earth, and Athena raised him but kept him hidden in a basket. Thus Athena and Hephaestus had a son, but she remained a virgin. Her son was named Erichthonius. He became king of Athens. The temple of Erichthonius on the Akropolis, where Athena's temple once stood, is his burial site. The Panathenic Procession ended there. But Athena was a virgin goddess and this episode with Hephaestus was an aberration not often mentioned. She was associated with the moon, her birthday always at the new or hidden moon. Thus she was perpetually renewed, her virginity restored.

I hope to pay tribute to Hephaestus by visiting a volcano, the island of Santorini. I hope to be there by the end of the month. As hotheaded as I am, visiting a place that blows its stack once in a while will be appropriate.

After shaking hands and saying farewell to the missionaries, I sit in the Agora in the shade of an old oak tree, once again feeling lost and alone in a foreign country. Just to my right are the ruins of the temple of Ares, god of war. Ares wasn't much appreciated by the other gods and goddesses or the ancient Greeks. This is one of the few temples dedicated to him. He loved war, the flow of blood, the butchery. Since the ancient Greeks dedicated few temples to Ares, he is the sleeping god who wakes suddenly and unexpectedly to heap destruction on the civilized world. Once set into motion, he's not easily put back to sleep. No one wants to believe he resides inside them. But the ancient Greeks knew he was inside all of us.

I've finally decided on a plan for my journey, and Ares will fit into it well. I'll pay tribute to him by visiting the most famous battlefield in history, Troy. Perhaps the travel agent we talked to yesterday will be right, and I won't be able to get into Turkey, but I'll still give it a shot. The plan I've formulated for this journey is to first visit Thebes and Delphi, the most famous oracle in antiquity, and then visit many of the homes of those who fought at Troy, round them up, and go to war.

It's ten o'clock, and all the tourists are gone from the Agora. I'm alone again, sitting in the shadow of the giant oak sacred to Zeus, its leaves whispering to me as the gentle breeze rustles them. As I leave Athens, I can't help but think again of Theseus, the ancient king of this marvelous city, his ruin. He lost favor in Athens because he kidnapped and raped a twelve-year-old girl from Sparta: Helen, the woman who would one day cause the Trojan War. She was the most beautiful woman in the world, the face that launched a thousand ships. A war with Sparta resulted that filled Athens with blood. Theseus was exiled and went to the island of Scyrus where his paternal grandfather had once ruled.

Athens

There he was murdered. Not far from here at the center of the ancient city is a gymnasium where Theseus' bones lie. They were returned to Athens in 469 BC after his ghost was seen leading the Athenian army at the battle of Marathon.

★

After checking out of my room and hiking back to Syntagma, I board a bus for Terminal B in north Athens where I must change to an intra-city bus for the ride to Thebes. Finding the right bus was a struggle because of the uncooperative ticket agents, but finally I'm aboard. At least that fear is behind me. The city bus is crammed with people standing in the aisles around the overflowing bench seats. Everyone is either working or shopping, and here I am, the old tourista, sweating profusely from the uphill walk, my big pack creating a nuisance.

As time passes and the passengers thin, I worry that I don't know where to get off for Terminal B. I try to ask some of my fellow passengers but can make none of them understand my question. Sure enough, the next thing I know the bus is almost empty, and we're out in the country at the end of the line, feels like the end of the world. I get off with the two remaining passengers, astounded at the mistake I've made. What does this say about my ability to get around in Greece by myself?

I stand at the side of the road in the hot sun waiting to be mugged. What am I to do now? This journey is a mistake. How could I possibly hope to get along alone? Just then I notice a group of men sitting at an outdoor table under a tree not far from me. How could I have missed seeing them before? If they find out I'm lost, will they mug me? I take the big chance and try a little of my Greek. The men are charmed with this lost, very confused American. What will they do to me when their amusement is satisfied?

And then the miraculous happens. One of them is a bus driver. He smiles, motions for me to follow him. He takes me to his bus and makes a special run back through town just for me, picking up a few passengers along the way. He talks to one of them and motions for me to get off with him. I thank the driver profusely but he brushes me aside. Then I follow the other guy, humping it as fast as I can with my heavy pack. He gradually puts some distance between us, and I lose sight of him just as I see Terminal B. He doesn't even give me the opportunity to thank him.

The terminal is a huge, drab, barn-like building with a drab waiting room, and a dark hanger-like enclosure with rows of fume-belching buses and hordes of milling Greeks. I enter it, out of breath and sweating profusely. The young woman behind the counter is full of smiles, as if she's been waiting just for me, and shortly I have my ticket in hand. I'm the only tourist in the place. I have only five minutes to catch my bus to Thebes, but I enter the snack bar anyway. If

Athens

I don't get something to drink, I won't live to see Thebes. I buy two cold Sprites, and down each of them in one long gulp.

The intra-city bus out of Athens is clean, nicely furnished, large and comfortable. The individual seatbacks have a white bra-like cloth covering, anchored with metal screws. Smoking is not allowed and it's quiet. I sit back in my seat, astonished at how rapidly I've recovered from my "life-threatening" mistake. I feel as though someone must be looking out for me. I check my guidebook, *Let's Go*, to see what it says about Thebes. It advises me not to go there at all, says it's "noisy and inelegant." I hope I'm not making another mistake.

A few kilometers from Athens, we pass the turnoff to Aphidnae, the town where Theseus held young, freshly-raped Helen captive in the care of his mother. Aphidnae is in the foothills to the south of the Parnitha Mountains. I see it from the freeway, a small town with white buildings shining brightly in the afternoon sun. The countryside is sparsely populated with an occasional cultivated field. Off to the right is the town of Marathon, which I cannot see from the road. During the battle of Marathon in 490 BC, the ghost of Theseus was seen leading the battle against the Persians. In that battle, the badly outnumbered Athenians killed 6,400 Persians while only losing 192 of their own.[16] This sighting of Theseus, 800 years after his death, prompted a search for his bones on the island of Skyrus, and their return to Athens in 469 BC. A motorist could detour to both these places, but if I rented a car, I couldn't afford to stay in Greece for ten weeks. Still, I want to scream as I pass up these ancient sites.

What impresses me most about the countryside is that I can see off into the distance, see rolling hills and mountain ranges rising up through the haze. I like the sense of freedom after being in a crowded city. The freeway is wide, well-constructed and well-traveled. To the west, I see a pale blue mountain in the distance, Mt. Kithaeron. In antiquity, Greeks commonly left sick and injured infants to die on Mt. Kithaeron.

When Oedipus came to Thebes as a young man, he didn't know he'd been born there. He'd been raised in Corinth, but his biological parents were the king and queen of Thebes. The oracle at Delphi had told Oedipus' father, Laios, that if he had a son by his wife, Jocasta, the son would grow up to kill him. When the baby was born, Laios drove a pin through the baby's ankles to keep him from walking even after death, and Jocasta gave him to a trusted shepherd to abandon on the slopes of Mt. Kithaeron. But the shepherd felt sorry for the infant and passed him off to another shepherd, who took him to Corinth where the childless king and queen raised him as their own. As a young man, Oedipus was told by the oracle at Delphi that he would one day kill his father and defile his mother's bed. Fearing he would fulfill the oracle, Oedipus wouldn't return to Corinth and instead turned toward Thebes, thus setting the stage for all his woes.

The freeway is modern, clean. I see olive orchards, grape vineyards, potato fields; and as we get closer to the orange-tile roofs of Thebes, something surprising: cotton fields. Already, I have a personal connection with this tragic city: cotton, and all the memories of home it resurrects.

CHAPTER 2: Thebes

The bus winds through the deserted streets of Thebes, and drops us off at a corner in the shade of the bus station, a brown nondescript building in the center of town. I step off the bus into a lazy afternoon and grab my black travel pack from the stack of suitcases thrown on the ground.

A woman standing next to me screams, and as I try to move away from her, she grabs me by the sleeve as if she expects me to help her. The man she's with steps forward to confront the ticket agent, who shouts back at both of them, then looks me off. The bus driver jumps out and shouts at the man. The woman, who's dressed in a loose plain smock and sandals, closes her eyes and screams again, her toothless mouth gaping. I jerk my sleeve from her and back away. I'm expecting an exchange of fists, but the driver gets back into the bus and pulls out with the ticket agent standing in the doorway, refusing to let them aboard. The woman's third scream sends a shiver through me, then she turns on me and shouts what I interpret to be an obscenity. I move on down the street away from this ominous beginning to my stay in Thebes.

Around the corner from the bus station, I drop my pack to the sidewalk and plop down on a cement step in the shade of a closed clothing store. I feel like crawling into a hole. My heart is still pounding. After a quiet, pleasant bus ride, now this. My insecurity has returned with new vigor. I've never seen a woman so distraught.

While I try to recover and assess my predicament, I survey the town. I have half a mind to give up on Thebes and move on to Delphi, but I'm afraid to return to the bus station. Thebes is located on a long, sloping plateau overlooking an agricultural valley. I see a tractor parked on the main street. All of the businesses are closed. No tourist shop in sight. The light traffic along Pindarou Street isn't bothersome, and I get a feeling of being in a sleepy village. No sign of the distraught woman and her companion. The air is clean, quite a change from Athens. Thebes seems strangely familiar. It isn't just the cotton fields on the way here. Something elusive, I'm not sure what.

When Oedipus arrived in Thebes, he'd come from the oracle at Delphi, just ninety kilometers to the west. He had killed four men on the way. One of them, unbeknownst to him, was his father, the king of Thebes. Another got away and would cause him untold trouble years later. Oedipus cleansed himself in a spring at the edge of town and met the Sphinx, a monster with the body of a winged lion and the head and bosom of a woman. The Sphinx held the city under siege. She had positioned herself on a mountain to the west and when someone approached, she'd swoop down, ask a riddle and if they didn't answer correctly, she would kill and eat them. Her question was: "What animal walks on four legs in the morning, two at noon and three in the evening but speaks with one voice?" Oedipus answered, "Man. He crawls on all fours as a child, walks upright as an adult, and walks with a cane in old age."

My favorite image of Oedipus' encounter with the Sphinx is an 1864 painting by Gustave Moreau.[17] It shows a long-haired Oedipus, naked except for a cloth wrapped once across his chest, into which the Sphinx has sunk both front claws. Her back paws are planted over his groin, and her bare breasts are pressed firmly against his chest. Her feathered angel-like wings extend from her shoulders to high above her head. She and Oedipus are peering deeply, penetratingly into each other's eyes, her tail coiled tightly, her posture expressing a rather sexual anticipation of her feast. Oedipus' head is bent downward, unintimidated. When Oedipus answered her riddle correctly, the Sphinx killed herself by plummeting from the city wall. In the Moreau painting, his feet are bare but show no sign of the famous injuries of childhood from which he got his name, Oedipus, meaning "swell-foot."

This single event, a bizarre happenstance much like a scene from a fairy tale inserted at a key point in a story otherwise marked by its real-life qualities, asks us to look deeper into Oedipus. The Sphinx's riddle was a restatement of an inscription above the door of the temple of Apollo at Delphi from where Oedipus had just come, "Know Thyself." The meaning of the inscription is "to know you are a man and not a god, to understand the limitations of mortal life." To put yourself on par with an immortal was highly offensive to the Greek gods, and they punished this presumptuousness swiftly and dramatically. Oedipus' answer showed he knew the lot of mankind, and by inference, his own limitations. But what followed also showed that having that much self-knowledge is not enough.

By answering the Sphinx's question, Oedipus opened the gateway to his own ruin. He won the hand of the queen of Thebes, who was his biological mother. When Oedipus' parents gave him as a child to the shepherd to be exposed on Mt. Kithaeron, Oedipus was essentially born again, the mystery-shrouded mountain becoming his second mother. From that time forth, he had a dual nature. The first was the way he presented himself to the world, his persona as the prince of Corinth where he was raised, and all his self-knowledge. His second nature was biological, hidden, more truly him. He was the biological child of the queen of Thebes, the woman who became his wife.

Oedipus is the Rosetta stone, which allows us to go beyond the limits of traditional self-knowledge. Sophocles' chorus of Theban elders says as much in his play *Oedipus Tyrannus*:

> You Oedipus are my great example, you, your life
> your destiny, Oedipus, man of misery—I count no man blest.[18]

Sophocles' actual words are even more specific. He uses the ancient Greek, παραδειγμ, paradeigm. Sophocles saw Oedipus as a lesson or warning for all men. Knowing this, two things we can say immediately. Firstly, we all have a dual nature, and secondly, our destiny is predictable but unavoidable. Both, most troubling insights. The oracle at Delphi told Oedipus he would kill his father and marry his mother, a script he performed to perfection soon after. By trying to avoid his destiny and not returning to Corinth, he fulfilled it.

Only days before my near-fatal confrontation with my father, I saw *Oedipus Tyrannus* while at college. It was my warning and the events that followed brought me ever closer to the Oedipus myth.

I've recovered from my scare and decide to stay in Thebes, provided of course I don't run into the crazed woman again. My only question is where to find a hotel. I unzip and stow the flap that covers the straps to my pack, hoist it to my back. *Let's Go* says to stay at the Hotel Niovi. A light complexioned young lady with blond hair in the plateia just up the street understands enough of my Greek to give me directions. After I spot the hotel, I walk into a quiet hall at the end of which is a pizza restaurant, take the winding stairs to the right and end up at the hotel reception desk on the second floor.

George, the hotel clerk, leads me down a dark hall to a room with two single beds. Since I'm the only one in the hotel, he puts me in a room next to the community toilette. "Just like having a private bathroom," he says. George speaks excellent English because he lived in the States for fifteen years, from the time he was twelve, and was educated there. He came back to Greece twenty years ago and has lived in Thebes ever since. For several years George made his living as a sculptor.

I can't see the main street from my room, but I can hear it. I lay my backpack on top of a little rack inside the door and unload some of my clothes. The siesta is over and motorbikes are coming out. My room overlooks a small courtyard with a sagging clothesline, from which swing a woman's bra and panties.

After settling in, I hit the streets to find out what is so familiar about this place. I stop by the desk and ask George about the size of Thebes. "Twenty thousand," he says. I'm surprised. On the way in on the bus, I thought it to be no more than two thousand. George reaches up on a shelf behind him, retrieves a large, foldout map. "Don't let anyone here at the hotel see this," he says. "We don't have many left, and my boss told me not to give anymore away." The map is not for tourists. It's in Greek. On the back, the map contains an artist's conception of the old city center, the Kadmia.

Hunting and gathering tribes, during the Paleolithic age, inhabited the area around Thebes. Nearby, archaeologists have found stone tools dating to 12,000 BC, but permanent settlements in Boeotia Nome started in the Neolithic Age (7000 - 2800 BC) with the introduction of agriculture and cattle breeding.[19] One of the earliest references to Thebes is in the Homeric hymn "To Apollo" where the poet calls it a "forest covered abode,"[20] but this epithet certainly doesn't apply today. To the north lies the Ionian plain where I saw cotton farms on the way in. Further to the west lies the Kopaic Basin where, during the late Bronze age, a swamp was drained and turned into a productive agricultural valley.

According to legend, Kadmos, who was from Tyre in Phoenicia, founded Thebes around 1400 BC. Tyre is only sixty-five kilometers from Nazareth were Jesus spent his childhood 1,400 years later. Kadmos left Tyre in search of his sister, Europa, who had been kidnapped by Zeus. Kadmos couldn't find her, so he went to Delphi to see if Apollo would help him. Apollo told him to forget his sister, and instead to follow a sacred cow to where she first laid down, and on that spot to found a city. Kadmos followed these instructions and founded Thebes. He named the center of the city the Kadmia. Around the Kadmia, he built walls with seven gates.

A serpent that killed many of Kadmos' men inhabited the site. Kadmos slew the "dragon," an offspring of Ares, the god of war, and upon the advice of Athena, buried its teeth (Athena called them "snaky corn"):

...There lay the dragon stretched on the ground, dead, and over the corpse furious Ares shouted in heavy anger. ... Now he Kadmos fathered the fruit of death inside a helmet of bronze, the grim harvest of the creature's jaws. Then he drew upon the land the humped plow of Pallas from her holy place in those parts, and plowed a battle-breeding furrow in the bright earth, and sowed long lines of the poison-casting teeth.[21]

Thebes

Shortly, giants sprouted from the earth, fully armored and primed for battle. They were called "Sparti," sown-men:

One shot up with head high, shaking the top of a mailcoated breast; one with jutting head stretched a horrid shoulder over the opening earth; another bent forward above ground as far as the midnipple, one again rose on the ground half-finished and lifted a soil-grown shield; another shook a nodding plume before him and showed not yet his chest; while still creeping up slowly from his mother's flanks he showed fight against fearless Cadmos, clad in the armour he was born in. O what a great miracle![22]

Kadmos threw rocks at the Sparti, and true to their Ares nature, they started fighting amongst themselves, all but five dying in the ensuing battle. One of Kadmos' daughters married Echion, the leader of the Sparti. Kadmos was Oedipus' great, great grandfather on his father's side, and his great grandfather on his mother's side. Thus Oedipus was a descendent of the serpent and Ares himself.

George was right about the size of Thebes. It's much bigger than I originally thought. The center of Thebes is isolated on a pear-shaped plateau, a kilometer long, half a kilometer wide and sloping downward to the north, the top of the pear. From there, the hill drops rapidly to the residential district. The city sprawls to the north onto the plains and the agricultural valley. Deep ravines bound the center of town on the west and east, the steep banks covered with brown grass.

After locating the museum at the northern edge of the hill, where it slopes sharply downward, I stare off into the distance across the farm-checkered valley, the Aonion plain. The mountains on the far side of it are purple silhouettes in the distance. One of them, a small bald peak glows light tan in the sun, a pyramid-shaped mountain. I pull out my own map to see if I can identify it. Its name is Phicium, obviously from Sfinx or Sphinx. I've just located the "Mountain of the Sphinx."

The Sphinx sat on that mountain awaiting young men entering the city. I imagine Oedipus just after his arrival in Thebes looking across that sunlit plane and seeing a faint object leave the mountaintop, seeing its flat trajectory across the valley, watching it grow into a bird-like object with an eight-foot wingspan, feeling wing gusts and sharp claws dig into the cloth wrapped about his chest, its rear paws plant in his groin. The smell of Sphinx feathers laced with lion's breath.

The sound of cars is everywhere now, mostly teenagers honking and waving at friends. Standing here at the edge of the hill staring across the farm

Thebes

field at Sphinx Mountain with the sound of young voices behind me, I realize what is so familiar about this place and the reason I've fallen in love with Thebes. Thebes is a '50s town, like my hometown during my youth. It's outdoorsy and motor vehicles rule the male social life. Even the farm fields to the north remind me of where I lived as a kid.

I see another tractor parked at the edge of the sidewalk, a Massey Ferguson 399 with a big glass cab on top, something tractors didn't have during my farming days with my father. It's new, body painted bright red and looks as though it's just been washed, maybe even waxed. The huge back tires stand almost to my shoulders. I reach out to feel the firm rubber on a big lip of tread, and suddenly I'm taken back thirty-two years to another set of tractor tires on a hot summer afternoon in California, the day of the confrontation with my father.

My father could never talk to me in words. He used a form of symbolic communication encrypted in action. It's taken decades to decode his actions during our crucial times together. I'm much like a Greek seer trying to divine from the rustle of tree leaves, or perhaps Oedipus answering the Sphinx riddle.

When my mother stopped him short of killing himself, my father walked from the bedroom out of the house and into the backyard where he started rotating the tractor's large rear tires. These tires are formidable objects weighing several hundred pounds and filled with water instead of air. We always used at least three people handling them. But my father was doing it by himself. My mother saw him in this dangerous act and asked me to help him.

Since he couldn't talk to me reasonably, and had been stopped in the act of loading the rifle, he had chosen a symbolic act, one that could have killed both of us. While my father and I dueled with the tires, I remember the sun beating down on us, straining under the weight as we gripped the large lips of black tread protruding from each tire's surface. I was dressed for town, just showered and freshly shaven. My father was sweating profusely, crying painful tears as I had never seen him do. "No son of mine has ever left home mad," he said. He was in such utter agony. I didn't and still don't understand why.

We didn't talk about the situation beyond his few simple words. I said nothing at all. I felt as if I no longer recognized this man, as Oedipus hadn't recognized his father, this man who raised me, clothed and fed me from birth. I was concerned for my own safety around those huge teetering tires but unconcerned for him, though I then knew he was suicidal. I had to watch myself, control my own actions because I had a compulsion to steer him toward catastrophe. There in the heat of the afternoon sun, a profusion of sweat dripped from both of us, sweat which could just as easily have come from the life-and-death tension between us, a part of me was killing my father, passing an unconscious signal: Do it, I don't care, just do it. Like Oedipus, I was standing at the crossroads of my life, and though the blood didn't flow from my father's body and his life didn't cease, I just as assuredly killed everything of him I could.

In the coming days, no one said anything about what had happened. I let it go myself and didn't try to leave home. It wasn't so much that I thought I had won the argument, but that I'd stood my ground. I was a young man coming into my own, and I had passed my first big test. My father's tears had been more of a nuisance than a concern. I thought they were just another ploy in his long train of attempts to control my life.

Not long afterward, I quit college and got married. I had always known the girl I married would have to be acceptable to my mother as we'd always been close. My wife would have to have my mother's values. It didn't take long to find her, a girl from my own hometown whose family was originally from the south, as was mine. Her religious views were the same as my mother's. I remember the first time I kissed that young woman. It was as if I'd struck a tuning fork, the mesmerizing buzz in my head set in perfect pitch by that kiss. After the trouble with my father, I married a woman who was the image of my mother, accomplishing symbolically what Oedipus experienced literally. He lived on in ignorant bliss until learning the truth about himself. My time was also coming.

★

During early evening, I step outside the hotel to experience Thebes' nightlife. George sits with a group of men out in front of the hotel. After talking with him a bit, I stroll the streets around the courthouse plateia, which is thickly populated with milling people. Large groups sit in chairs outside the tavernas, the warm evening air carrying clouds of cigarette smoke toward bright stars overhead. The two main streets are a block apart and one-way, one going south, the other north, and are bumper-to-bumper with creeping cars. Kids are everywhere, adults everywhere. A festive mood predominates.

Thebes has put on a new face and no longer looks like my small California farm-town of the '50s. Tonight it has an unmistakable European flavor, hordes of people clog the sidewalks, making the street the only possible place to walk. The tables out front of the restaurants are packed, and the women have come out. Groups of young men and women sit together, the ratta-tat-tat of Greek flowing freely. The air is full of horns and sirens. The commotion centers on a Communist rally, half a block from the hotel. The Communists blare a continuous stream of taped patriotic music with a religious quality, the irresistible marching spirit of humanity. I could be converted this evening. The national election is this Sunday, day after tomorrow.

A man gets knocked down by a slow moving car then argues heatedly with the driver. Dirtied his pants, but he isn't injured. The military has overrun Thebes. All the young soldiers are from a training base close by. They populate the tavernas and roam the streets in gangs.

Back in the hotel as I lie between the cool sheets, the Communists silence the loudspeaker, and soft night noises loft though my open balcony doors. The voices from the plateia also fade, leaving only the occasional sound of a car or motorbike. I hear a lone siren. The glow of lights above the rooftops slowly dims.

8 Oct, Friday

During the night, I have to use two heavy blankets to keep warm, and wake to pigeon voices, their soft coos and warbles coming through my partially open patio doors. I have a splitting headache but rise early to see the sun come up and get an early start at the museum. For breakfast I have a bunch of grapes in my room, then step out into the coolness of early morning.

As I pass the plateia where the communists held the rally the night before, I notice their banner, red background with the yellow KKE, still up over the bandstand. I've held a security clearance since 1964. Standing before this symbol of the enemy, I feel a little uneasy. Amazing that Greece, staunch ally of the good old US of A, has such a close connection with our cold-war foe.

I grab a greasy goat-cheese pita from the German who runs a little kiosk out front of the museum. The museum is a flat-topped building inside a fenced courtyard at the northern end of the pear-shaped hill. The huge 13th Century AD Frankish Tower looms over the entire complex. I pay just inside the wrought-iron gate and enter the building alone. The museum is vacant except for the attendants and me, all women. When I speak to one of them in English, she confers with the women next to her and answers in a way that tells me she didn't understand. I try a little Greek but that confuses her even more. A woman follows me from room to room, my footsteps echoing among the stone statues and display cases. I hear women whispering about me.

Several artifacts catch my attention. The first is two old fluted columns of solid ivory from a Mycenaean throne, speculated to be legs from the throne of Laios and Oedipus.[23] They are smaller than I would have imagined, cracked and discolored with age, and at one end, terminate in barely visible etchings of papyrus flowers.

Another interesting display is the Oriental cylinder seals made of lapis lazuli, forty-two of which were found in the "Treasure Room" of the old Kadmia.[24] Nowhere in Greece have so many cylinder seals been found in one place. Lapis lazuli is a blue gemstone and contains pyrite flakes, which appear

33

as sparkling stars in the deep-blue firmament. In antiquity cylinder seals were of extraordinary political importance. They were probably sent to the king of Thebes by an Oriental king. This brings to mind that Kadmos was originally from Tyre in Phoenicia. Thebes was a significant commercial and political center during the Bronze Age and may have exceeded Mycenae in importance. Four seal stones were found with the cylinder seals, which were from Minoan Crete where Kadmos' sister, Europa, was taken after Zeus abducted her. The old myth seems at least partially substantiated by the archaeological finds.

Also on display are several ivory plaques blackened by fire. Archaeologists believe ancient Thebes was destroyed by fire around 1225 BC. This evidence is intriguing because the legend of Oedipus and his children also tells of the burning of Thebes. All this is a further verification of Schliemann's hypothesis that ancient legends have a basis in fact. In *The Iliad*, Homer mentioned lower Thebes, not the Kadmia, because the Kadmia had already been burned to the ground.

A religious ritual at Thebes is depicted in a huge fresco that covers an entire wall in the palace, forty-two feet in length, a life-sized procession of women bearing votive offerings of lilies, papyrus and wildflowers. They wear long, flounced skirts, short-sleeved jackets with open bosoms, their large breasts protruding erotically. But I'm most affected by the jewelry. Perhaps it's the young women walking about the museum who have triggered my reaction. Through the jewelry I sense the presence of Oedipus' daughters, Antigone and Ismene. The jewelry consists of many necklaces, bracelets, earrings. They are made of gold, agate and lapis lazuli. Did the jewelry belong to Antigone and Ismene? A curious thought occurs to me. Women leave behind jewelry and art, men leave behind the weapons of war.

I ask a young woman if she knows where the seven gates of ancient Thebes were located. She speaks English in a high-pitched, singsong voice with a shocking nasal quality. She says she'll show me, takes me outside through the museum gate. I rather naively anticipate a guided tour around the exterior of the ancient city, even hope for a little romance. But once we hit the sunlight, she suddenly seems rushed, anxious to get rid of me. "One kilometer. Gates everywhere. Ask anyone." She scurries back indoors.

Right. How do I say "gate" in Greek? I strike out on my own using the map in a guidebook I bought in the museum. I find one gate here at the edge of the hill. It's the Borrhaiai or Northern Gate. The hill area of the central city has been shaded in on the map and labeled, KADMIA. The stone-walled Kadmia lies between Dirce and Strophia torrents, and is isolated from the rest of town by virtue of the lay of the land just as it was 3,300 years ago. The major roads, through which traffic enters and exits Thebes, are at the same locations as the roads of antiquity. This hill, which I've been talking about ever since I got here, is where Kadmos' cow laid down. The ancient city is under my feet.

Thebes is bustling, clean, a little dilapidated in places, but I wouldn't be here if she was born yesterday. The ancient Kadmia is a little wrinkled and squashed, but it's still here: gold, jewelry, weapons, pottery, walls, all buried beneath the mask of the modern city. As I walk toward the center of town, I see a grown man on a motorbike doing a two-block wheelie, the blare of his exhaust shattering the quiet murmur of the wind and chatter of birds. I stop at the corner of Pindarou and Oidipodos Streets to stare through a chain-link fence at the excavated ruins of the House of Kadmos. I spot a hole in the fence and crawl through, hoping no one will catch me.

A half block of archaeological ruins stretches before me. The earth has been dug out six or seven feet below street level, exposing the fire-blackened remains of stone walls, small rooms and corridors of the ancient palace. Deciduous trees grow at the far edge of the site, and volunteer shrubs pock the ancient Mycenaean remains. It's small, fenced-in, intimate. Archaeologists found a palace workshop for manufacturing jewelry, working gold and carving ivory at this site. Some of the jewelry was unfinished, as if work had been stopped suddenly.

We have no description of this palace, but Homer describes another from the same period that could serve just as well. He sees it through the eyes of Odysseus:

> Through all the rooms, as far as he could see,
> tall chairs were placed around the walls and strewn
> with fine embroidered stuff made by the women.
> Here were enthroned the leaders...
> drinking and dining, with abundant fare.
> Here too were boys of gold on pedestals
> holding aloft bright torches of pitch pine
> to light the great rooms and the nighttime feasting.
> And fifty maids-in-waiting of the household
> sat by the round mill grinding yellow corn,
> or wove upon their looms, or twirled their distaffs,
> flickering like the leaves of a poplar tree,
> while drops of oil glistened on linen weft.[25]

Archaeologists also found pottery from Minoan Crete with Linear B[26] inscriptions, and some terra-cotta figurines cast in the characteristic pose (upraised arms) of those found on Crete. Perhaps I'll get to compare them myself if I can get to Crete. The ruins of ancient Thebes are at risk. At the northern edge, a building under construction threatens to intrude on the site.

I have lunch across the street from the ruins of the House of Kadmos at a little fast-food restaurant at the corner of Pindarou and Oidipodos Streets, a burger place popular with the younger set. It's new, modern, very American. I listen to disco music while eating my dish of fried chicken chunks and French fries. This is a nice place to people watch. The hustle-bustle of young Greeks is everywhere. I look at the traffic out the huge windows on the north and east sides of the restaurant. All the vehicles along the gridlocked streets have their horns going at once: cars, buses, tractors. The cars are fairly new: Audi, Peugeot, Hyundai, Ford, Mercedes, Mitsubishi, a Nissan Taxi. I watch a man get a traffic ticket. He argues heatedly with a policeman who writes a while, argues a while. The man shouts continuously. They're both red in the face. Young men sit at the tables outside. No young women sit with them. I see women walking together, women with kids.

I walk back up Epameinondou Street, but just before I get to the hotel, I turn west down Oidipodos Street. It descends sharply into the ravine I saw yesterday, but which today I realize is Dirce torrent. This torrent was famous in antiquity. Pindar (522-438 BC), a native of Thebes, mentioned it frequently in his odes. At the foot of the hill, I turn left along the side of the road and immediately find what I'm looking for.

This is the Krenaiai (Fountain) Gate and the ruins of the Fountain of Dirce, where Kadmos killed the sacred serpent. The serpent lived in a cave that still exists, a shallow hole in the side of the mountain. Oedipus' two sons, Polyneices and Eteocles, also fought in one-on-one combat here at the fountain. Someone has used the site as a garbage dump.

I sit in the grass on the side of the hill west of Dirce torrent, looking back at the Kadmia, Oidipodos Street a black stripe through white buildings. To my right, a dusty dirt road winds west up the hill through a sparsely populated olive orchard. The loose, thirsty earth between the small gray-green trees is full of dead grass, which the setting sun has turned to gold. No rain has fallen in Greece since spring. The sun reflects from the leaves of olive trees like a million flashing mirrors.

Every morning before sunup, George used to run a couple of miles up this dirt road with all his clothes off, even when it snowed, he said. I'd be concerned about snakes, myself. I hear Greece has a lot of adders.

George told me I would find another dig here, part of ancient Thebes that was outside the city walls. The dig is spread over a large area and consists of portions of stone walls and depressions. I see several holes burrowed into the ground, small round openings to large cavernous interiors, seven, eight feet deep, and very dark. This is Lower Thebes, which was mentioned by Homer in his narrative of the Trojan War.

Some fifteen years after Oedipus killed his father and married his mother, a plague ravaged Thebes, and Oedipus learned from the oracle at Delphi that it was caused by a pollution within the city. The murderer of Laios was still among them. Oedipus turned to one of the greatest figures in all Greek myth, the blind Theban seer, Teiresias, to learn the murderer's identity. Though Teiresias was blind, he could see into the human soul and reveal the future. Oedipus, though he could see, was internally blind. But aged Teiresias at first refused to reveal the murderer's identity, touting Oedipus with metaphors of his, Oedipus', blindness. Under threats of physical violence, Teiresias finally told Oedipus pointblank that he was the murderer. Oedipus went into a rage, accusing Teiresias of plotting to overthrow him. Not until two shepherds, one from Thebes who took baby Oedipus from Jocasta and the other who gave him to the king of Corinth, were brought forward was the irrefutable truth revealed. Oedipus had indeed killed his father, Laios, and married his mother. Jocasta then committed suicide, and Oedipus blinded himself and left Thebes to wander as a beggar.

In the search for the murderer, Oedipus had experienced the classic quest for self. Though he could see externally, he was blind within and did not know his own true identity. When Oedipus could see within, see his internal pollution, he blinded himself to prevent seeing the external results, his family and kingdom all built upon the murder of his father.

Oedipus and Jocasta had four children. The two girls, Antigone and Ismene were still very young. The two boys, Polyneices and Eteocles, were the oldest and fought over Oedipus' vacated throne. Initially, they agreed to share the throne, each being king on alternate years, but once Eteocles became king, he refused to step down. Polyneices then went into exile in Argos and formed an alliance to wage war on Thebes and regain the throne. Years later, he made his assault in the famous battle of Seven Against Thebes. Seven armies from Argos, one for each Theban gate, filled the Aonion plane to the north with the blaze of bronze, and they attacked the city. After the initial assault failed, Polyneices and Eteocles agreed to do battle one-on-one to prevent further bloodshed.

Sophocles emphasizes the physical intimacy of Oedipus' children, presenting them as a near unity. He goes so far as to newly coin words especially for the descriptive task.[27] It's as if Sophocles is saying that by having children with his own mother, Oedipus doubled back on his own life to beget himself, four different aspects of the Oedipus personality. The inseparable unity of his sons is then symbolic of Oedipus' own dual nature. Their hatred for each other is Oedipus' hatred of himself.

Polyneices' and Eteocles' battle ended in the only way possible, the only way two halves of a whole can die. They killed each other simultaneously with a "twofold blow."[28] Their struggle to achieve the status of their father, to gain his throne, led to war, and is symbolic of all struggles between men. This is another of the lessons we learn from Oedipus, the great Rosetta Stone. In the first battle we kill our father, and in the second, the search for self, we destroy our lives and wander aimlessly. In the final struggle, we kill ourselves.

The thought sends a chill through me as I realize, I've lost my family and my job and now wander about the Greek countryside, as did old blind Oedipus.

This field, where I sit among golden grass and silver-leaved olive trees, is called "Antigone's Pull."[29] Here she dragged the body of her brother, Polyneices, to the funeral pyre. She tried to carry him, but he was too heavy, so she dragged him alongside Eteocles' burning body and threw him into the pyre.

Creon, Antigone's uncle, had assumed the throne following the death of Antigone's two brothers. He ordered Eteocles' body cremated with full ceremony, but forbade funeral rites for Polyneices because he had tried to destroy Thebes. Creon was motivated by the welfare of the state, "the ship that bears us safe."[30] But Antigone felt allegiance to an even higher authority, that of the great Earth Goddess, Gaia, who demanded all dead be returned to her.

To fully understand any man, it's necessary to understand his feminine side. With Oedipus, it's necessary to understand his daughters. The two sisters also form a subdivision of the central unity of the Oedipus personality. Antigone was high-minded, defiant, passionate in her convictions. Though she had inherited her father's stubbornness and dogged determination, her quest was not of the ego. "'Tis not my nature to join in hating, but in loving,"[31] she told Creon. Antigone paid for her piety with her life. Creon imprisoned her in a cave for the rest of her days, and she committed suicide.

Antigone's younger sister, Ismene, was more practical and recognized her limitations within the patriarchal society and the frailty of her sex. She was passive, even obedient, to Creon's edict. Although Antigone and Ismene clashed over defying Creon, it was not a clash of the ego, and their differences never resulted in violence. Antigone's self-righteous determination was counterbalanced by Ismene's uncertainty and self-doubt. Weak, submissive Ismene was the only one to survive. She didn't have the heroic temper.

I know I'll have to come to terms with this feminine stuff on this journey. And perhaps it can help to explain the change in me resulting from my confrontation with my father. We were big hunters on the farm, and though I never felt comfortable with it, I killed a lot. When I was twenty-one, my father bought a deer rifle for me, and we went into the Sierra Nevada that fall to get a buck. I remember sitting on a huge boulder overlooking a meadow on a mountainside, hearing the frantic animal cascading down through the brush toward me, snorting like a freight train. I leveled my new rifle at where he would enter the clearing and waited. What I didn't count on was my emotional response when the big antlered buck moved into my sights. My heart raced and my breathing was worse than his. I shot, but if I'd hit him it would have been pure accident. I didn't know it until that moment, but I could no longer kill. It was no longer within my nature.

The sun has gone behind the mountain and casts a long shadow past me and halfway up the hill to the edge of the glowing Kadmia. I've been sitting here worrying about snakes for long enough. Time to trudge back up Oidipodos Street.

When I get back to the hotel, I see George sitting behind the desk. He tells me about his days as a sculptor. Ten years ago, he made two copper plates with reliefs of Kadmos and Oedipus. The plates are on display on a wall in the pizzeria downstairs. "Can I see them?" I ask. George is pleased. I'm prepared for some mediocre craftwork, but they're actually done quite well.

The plate of Kadmos shows him with Harmonia, his divine wife, standing beside spray from the Fountain of Dirce. The serpent, which formerly inhabited the site, is in the background lurching toward them. George depicts Oedipus engaged with the Sphinx. He wears a large flat-brimmed hat. George takes the plates off the wall into the sunlight, so I can take a picture of them. He says the plates are becoming famous. He has tried to buy them back, but the owner of the pizzeria won't sell them.

I'm still sweating profusely from the long walk in the sun, and while taking pictures, sweat streams into my eyes and drips on the floor. By the time I get back to my room, my shirt is soaked through.

★

George recommends I eat dinner at a dark little restaurant just down the street from the hotel. The waiter doesn't speak English and motions for me to talk to the cook, but he doesn't speak English either, so I seize the opportunity to polish up on my pointing and grunting. Sometimes I'm too hungry to take a chance on my Greek. I sit alone at a table with chairs for six. I have a plate of chopped pork, a salata and a sliced half-loaf of hard bread. Eight soldiers at a table on the far side of the room have finished their dinner and smoke cigarettes. Their tan uniforms are wrinkled and soiled from a hard day's work.

Thebes

I wake to the restless sounds of pigeons on the adjoining rooftop and a cloud of chatter from sparrows in the trees on Epameinondou Street. Dressing slowly, I breakfast on peaches and grapes. When I first got to Thebes, I bought a kilo each. They sit on the small shelf in the night stand, slowly rotting. I've been thinking about leaving Thebes today but have decided to stay here to watch election returns with George tomorrow evening. I feel comfortable in Thebes, and to be quite honest about it, I'm again apprehensive of moving on. My insecurity is in full bloom.

★

I stand before the hotel staring blankly at the slow-rising sun as it comes between the limbs of trees and over the two story buildings. The only evidence of activity is shopkeepers, stacking boxes of fruit and vegetables. I roam the city east of the Kadmia, walk the dry banks of the Strophia and Ismenos torrents. From time to time I see the haunting silhouette of Mt. Kithaeron off to the south.

I stop to rest at the top of Magalo Kastelli, the hill where legend tells us Polyneices and Eteocles are buried.[32] Thebes is not as clean as I first thought. They dump their trash in vacant lots, on hills, in archeological digs. The torrents are filled with construction debris, chunks of cement and trash. At the edge of every empty lot is a dog toilette.

This hill is crowned with dark pine, the dirt mixed with dry pumice. Ancient inscribed stones lie scattered where archaeologists uncovered Mycenaean chamber tombs, perhaps those of Polyneices and Eteocles. Among the inscribed stones, I see human excrement and discarded male underwear.

My life may have certain parallels with Oedipus, but Oedipus' life was in many ways a parallel of an ancient god's. The lives of the gods were frequently archetypes of mortal existence. Thus, artisans worked in the tradition of Hephaestus. If Oedipus' second mother was Mt. Kithaeron, his second father was the god who roamed tree-laden, mystery-shrouded Mt. Kithaeron: Dionysus.[33] Dionysus, also known as Bacchus, was more than just the patron of theatre, and here in Thebes, as the god of wine, he exhibited his more bizarre nature.

Dionysus was known as the god of frenzy. He traveled in the company of maenads and satyrs, who dressed in flowing garments and held orgiastic rituals where they ripped apart wild animals and ate their raw flesh. Their favorite haunt was Mt. Kithaeron.

Years before Oedipus was born, Laios had been told by Apollo that he was not to have a child by Jocasta or the child would grow up to kill him.

Thebes

But one night, Laios yielded to a wine-induced, Bacchic passion and made love to Jocasta anyway. When Oedipus was born, to avoid the fate imposed by Apollo, Laios and Jocasta gave him to a shepherd to expose on Mt. Kithaeron. Oedipus knew nothing of his own biological parents until a wine-drunk man at a banquet told him he was not his father's son. It was as if the drunk, under the influence of Dionysus the god of wine, could see through Oedipus' persona and into his biological nature.

What is so striking about these two episodes is the role wine played in each of them. Wine was a metaphor for Dionysus. These two episodes in Oedipus' life—his conception and first inkling of his true nature—resulted from the actions of men under the influence of wine.

While Dionysus was a child, the Titans, an ancient race of gods, killed him. With their faces whitened with chalk like spirits of the dead, they surprised Dionysus as he played. They first dismembered his body, then boiled and roasted his limbs over an open fire and ate them. Zeus was attracted by the smell of roasting and chased them back to Tartarus, where he had previously banished them by hurling lightning bolts.[34] He salvaged the heart of Dionysus and swallowed it himself. At the time, Zeus was enamored with unconquerably beautiful Semele, the youngest daughter of Kadmos and Harmonia. After eating Dionysus' heart he re-inseminated Dionysus' spirit into Semele.

But Dionysus' birth travails were not over. During her seventh month of pregnancy, Semele, mislead by jealous Hera, asked Zeus to come to her, a mortal, as he came to Hera, his immortal wife. Zeus was horrified because he knew what would happen, but he had already agreed to do anything she wished when he lay with her to beget Dionysus. Zeus had always come to Hera as a lightning bolt, and when he came to Semele as such, he fried her. Zeus rescued the unborn child from her smoldering carcass, and sewed the premature infant into his own thigh. Thus Dionysus was twice-born and had a dual nature. Oedipus' dual nature can be viewed as a mortal reflection of the god's.

Since to the ancient Greeks, a god's attributes were inherent in his life story, twice-born Dionysus was the god of indestructible life. The ancient Greeks had two words for "life." The first was "bios" from which our word "biography" originates. It refers to a life with attributes, one with a face so to speak. The other word is "zoë," which designates eternal life and is undifferentiated or life without a face. Bios could be interpreted as reincarnations of the same zoë. Bios are spread along a string of zoë like pearls on a necklace.

Dionysus' second birth was here at Thebes, and Thebes became the primary site of his cult. But he wasn't raised here. He was sent away, as was Oedipus, and nursed by Semele's sister, Ino, in Orchomenos, northwest of Thebes on the far side of Kopais Basin. When he got older, Zeus changed Dionysus into a kid and had Hermes take him to Nysa, a mythical mountain, where three Nyssian nymphs raised the goat-child in a cave. He was tutored by an aged, effeminate male figure named Silenos.[35] These nymphs became the maenads who followed him and practiced his frenzied rites.

After recovering from a Hera-induced madness, Dionysus returned to Thebes and stood by the Fountain of Dirce, where yesterday I ruminated over the fate of Oedipus and his sons and daughters. In Euripides play, The Bacchanals, Dionysus himself describes his return to Thebes:

> I to this land of Thebes have come, Zeus' Son
> Dionysus, born erstwhile of Cadmus' child
> Semele, brought by levin-brand to travail.
> My shape from God to mortal semblance changed,
> I stand by Dirce's spring, Ismenus' flood.
> I see my thunder-blasted mother's tomb
> Here nigh the halls: the ruins of her home
> Smoulder with Zeus's flame that liveth yet...[36]

The connection between Oedipus and Dionysus is made even closer by the fate of Pentheus, brother of Oedipus' great grandfather. Pentheus, king of Thebes, didn't accept Dionysus as a god. Enraged by Pentheus' indifference, Dionysus drove the women of Thebes mad, and enlisted them in his orgiastic ritual on Mt. Kithaeron. During their bloodthirsty frenzy with the maenads, they caught and dismembered Pentheus. His own mother returned to Thebes with his blood-dripping head on her thyrsus. Though Oedipus' fate was severe, it wasn't as dramatic as that of his ancient uncle.

Dionysus also got married. Though Oedipus' dual life has strange parallels to Dionysus, Dionysus didn't find it necessary to kill his father. He had other methods of replacing Zeus in his mother's bed. He and his wife took on primordial form. He metamorphosed into a snake; she became his daughter. He visited her in a cave, and "she bore him to himself as his own son."[37] Thus he simultaneously mated with his daughter and his mother. Oedipus' life was markedly like this, doubling back on his own life to mate with his mother and beget four children, each of them, at least in my mind, aspects of his own personality.

The world of Dionysus was forever the world of women, forever the feminine side of man. Coming to terms with him is not a pleasant thought since he was the god of madness. Madness has had its impact on my family. I've had a brush with it myself, though I'd prefer to ignore that on this journey.

I continue my exploration of modern Thebes. Thebes has many new residential areas and many that are old and rundown. Huge red-rose bushes surround a beautiful, white stucco home. Cement factories, farm implement companies, and car parts stores mix among the homes. Many of the businesses are permanently closed. Many construction projects are abandoned, renovations left half finished. I locate another of the ancient gates of Thebes, the Proetides Gate, just north of Antigonis Street next to Strophia torrent.

After a full day on the streets in the hot sun, I reenter the coolness of my room. The flutter and coo of pigeons just off my patio, their deep-throated language, soothes me.

10 Oct, Sunday

I lie in bed recovering from a dream. I usually have visual, movie-like dreams, but this morning I dreamed of a voice lofting up from deep darkness, speaking of murder. The voice reminds me of Teiresias, the blind seer of ancient Thebes, "whose soul grasps all things, the lore that may be told and the unspeakable, the secrets of heaven and the low things of earth…"[38] Teiresias thought it best not to reveal this hidden self-knowledge. He tried to get Oedipus to give up the search for Laios' murderer.

Alas, how dreadful to have wisdom where it profits not the wise! … Let me go home; most easily will you bear your own burden to the end and I mine if you will consent. …for you are all without knowledge.[39]

After Oedipus coerced Teiresias into revealing the murderer's identity, the truth ruined him. That's what Oedipus tells us about self-knowledge. It's useless if not outright dangerous to know your true self. Apollo had already told Oedipus his fate before he killed his father and married his mother. Oedipus could do nothing to avoid it, his every action playing into divine hands.

In my dream the voice was recanting my past and predicting my future. I can only remember the end of a sentence, "…after all, you have killed before." At that point I shut off the dream and I woke. I've had many dreams like this in my life, dreams where I'm wracked with guilt over having killed someone. The knowledge that I'm a murderer comes from a deep-rooted literal guilt. During this morning's dream, I believed the voice. But after waking, like Oedipus hearing the words of Teiresias, I'm not so sure.

On my way out of the hotel, I tell George that in a couple of days I plan to visit the Cleft Way, the place in Phocis Nome on the road from Thebes to

Thebes

Delphi, where Oedipus killed Laios. George doesn't buy it. "Everyone knows where Oedipus killed Laios," he says. "It's the first thing school kids learn about the legend." George drags out a map and shows me where the murder took place in the northeast part of the city. "He killed Laios at Oedipus' Spring, right here in Thebes."

I leave George, walk to an old dilapidated mill marking the location of Oedipus's Spring where Oedipus cleansed himself of his father's blood. Curiously, this is also the burial place of the bones of Hektor, the fiercest Trojan warrior and son of Priam, king of Troy.[40]

The Thebans brought Hektor's bones here because of an oracle saying the bones would provide "innocent wealth." I'll encounter the myth of Hektor again on his home soil where Achilles killed him, provided of course I do make it into Turkey.

According to Sophocles, and with all due respect to George, Oedipus killed Laios in the deserted countryside where the three roads to Delphi, Thebes and Daulis converge, a place called the Cleft Way, or as it has been more recently named, Megas Hill.[41] When I get to Delphi, I'll rent a car and drive there. I'll wait until then because the Cleft Way is much closer to Delphi than Thebes.

After visiting the spring, I come back to the hotel and talk to George some more. George recently married a young woman from Albania, a general's daughter. George and his young wife have a two-month-old daughter themselves. George is forty-eight and, until recently, lived his life as a single man. George is thin, a little taller than me and has gray hair which he combs over his balding head. George still longs for the single life but knows he's married a good woman. In Albania, family life is all-important. She has a job and works very hard to buy things for their home, but she's young and afraid to go anywhere, even with him. He loves to play with his new baby girl in the evenings. "I can't understand what came over me," he tells me. "After forty-seven years, I got married." He looks startled, like he's just realized what he's done. "You fell in love, George," I say. He flashes a puzzled smile.

George is a socialist and not particularly fond of the States. He doesn't like Greece's New Democratic party, which has been in office the last three years. He wants Papandreou back, the seventy-something old man with the young flight-attendant wife. He says Papandreou doesn't take any shit off America and the New Democrats give America everything it wants. Robert Kaplan in his book *Balkan Ghosts*, provides a quote from a Greek politician containing unique insight into the personality of Andreas Papandreou:

"Andreas is like Oedipus... As a boy he was very close to his mother.

Thebes

His revolt against his father continued well into manhood. Revolt against the father often means a general revolt against authority. In my opinion, Andreas was emotionally attracted to radical liberation struggles because of the anarchy they unleashed."[42]

The observation is an interesting one. Like Papandreou, I've always been close to my mother. I was the only breast-fed baby in our family of four boys. As a child, I slept with my mother and father until one night, which I can still remember, when my father told me I was too old to sleep with them anymore and carried me from their bed, my mother's bed, to the room where my older brother slept. I had always slept cuddled against my mother's warm body. I held her silky hair between my fingers and rubbed it until I went to sleep. The ultimate silkiness of my mother's hair lulled me to sleep. I was hooked to and had depended on my mother's body for my life's nourishment and my internal peace. When my father carried me into the other bedroom and broke that bond, I graduated from my mother's bed to my own baby bed, and he gave me my diploma.

My father may not have pinned my ankles and sent me to Mt. Kithaeron to be exposed, but I sure felt abandoned. To replace my mother's hair, he gave me the silk edge of a baby blanket to rub, but true silk was not even in the same league with the softness of my mother's hair. Like Papandreou, I'm still close to my mother, but after my confrontation with my father and the anarchy it released, I've made an uneasy peace with authority, at least on the surface. Sometimes I detect an undercurrent of anger.

★

This evening the results of the Greek national election have been rolling in. The street out front of the hotel is filled with people. The plateia is a mob scene. TV sets out front of the tavernas have hordes of people gathered before them, extending out into the streets. I walk along the sidewalk, snacking on greasy gyros and sticking my nose in front of every TV I see. I'm particularly interested in how the Communists are doing. Cars cram all the parking spaces and move slowly through the crowd. Children chase each other. People eat, drink coffee and ouzo, talk, shout, argue, set off firecrackers.

I watch the cooks in the tavernas making gyros. First they grab a precooked pita, paste it with grease and throw it on the grill. Then they slice three wedges of tomato, cutting them directly on the pita with a long butcher's knife. Then come the precut onions, and a few French fries and pork chunks, which they cut with a long thin knife from the vertical turning spit. They add a little mustard, a splash of tsatsiki, and a sprinkle of exotic spices. They fold the pita in half,

45

closing it at the bottom to form a cone about the contents, and wrap it in paper. That and a 330 ml Sprite is 350 drachmes. I have this at two different tavernas. I also have an ice cream cone from the disco restaurant for 100 dr. So for 800 dr ($3.50), I have dinner. Nothing fancy, and with all the fat, a nutritionist's nightmare, but I can't complain about the taste.

I come back into the hotel and watch returns with George and a couple of his Greek buddies. George is all smiles. Seventy-four year old Papandreou has been returned to office after a three-year absence. He makes a quick TV appearance with his thirty-something wife.

The Communists got four percent of the vote.

★

I lie in bed listening to fast traffic and sirens. Sirens mean nothing in Thebes, only an indication someone wants to make a lot of noise and a horn isn't enough. I'm still apprehensive of being on the road, but I've got to suck it up and move on.

11 Oct, Monday

I'm up long before dawn packing for my bus trip to Delphi. This morning I had a dream about my daughter and son. It must have been triggered by my conversation with George this past evening about his baby daughter. God, I would give my life to see my daughter again. In my dream, I talked to my daughter and told her how much I miss her and my son, sat with my head in my hands crying. I awoke from the dream and cried real tears here in Thebes, missing my son and daughter terribly.

The reason I'm so intent on finding the feelings I never felt the day my father grabbed the deer rifle is that I have a sense something inside me is suffering. Although this morning it was about my kids, frequently I wake crying only for the dream to vanish without a trace, leaving no reason for my tears.

I think of Oedipus and how he never longed to see his sons. Antigone stayed with him in his blind wandering about the countryside and Ismene brought him news of Thebes from time to time, but Oedipus hated his sons. He put a death curse on both of them because he felt they had mistreated him. Oedipus complained Polyneices had once given him a bad cut of meat.

When Eteocles wouldn't honor his agreement with his brother to share the throne, Polyneices went into exile in Argos, married and had a son, Thersander. Thersander avenged the death of his father by returning with an army from Argos called the Epigoni, the After-born. They sacked Thebes and burned it to the ground. The artifacts I saw in the museum during my second day here were found in a layer of ash, confirmation that Thebes was destroyed by fire.

Thebes

Flames blackened many of the ivory plaques I saw. As the Argives sieged the city, Teiresias advised Laodamas (Eteocles' son and king of Thebes) to negotiate and in the meantime to load the women and children into wagons and flee for Apollo's sanctuary at Delphi. Teiresias and his daughter, Manto who helped him walk in old age, planned to leave with the wagons but were captured by the siegeing forces before they could escape. My journey this morning is also to Delphi along the same path used by Teiresias.

The Argives, realizing Thebes was being abandoned, stormed the city. I imagine Thebes falling in the evening, the warriors swarming over the walls and through the gates, the city burning all night and the next morning, the black charcoal still smoldering, pieces of huge wood beams standing stark and black against the morning sky, a midnight blackness the sun could not erase.

All of Thebes' problems were a result of a transgression Laios committed years before. The gods were punishing Oedipus and his descendants because Laios kidnapped and raped a beautiful young boy, Chrysippus, in a fit of homosexual passion. That was the reason Laios was prohibited from sleeping with Jocasta. Oedipus was the personification of Laios' curse. When Oedipus came of age, he was destined to replace the Sphinx, who had been sent to punish Thebes because its citizens had tolerated Laios' rape of Chrysippus.

A few years ago, when I talked to my mother about the day my father almost killed himself, she reminded me, rather heatedly, of the reason he and I had argued in the first place. I had conveniently forgotten, and hearing the reason voiced again was devastating.

47

CHAPTER 3. Delphi

George tells me I can't catch a bus to Λειβαδια (Lavadia) at the bus station in Thebes, so I follow his directions north of the museum and wait at the side of the street. Lavadia is halfway to Delphi in the middle of the Kopais Plain, the agricultural center of Boiotia. I'll have to change buses there. I'm trying to convince myself that busses do travel this street when a young man in a truck pulls over and waves to me. All the guidebooks discourage hitchhiking.

I've hitched only once in my entire life, when our car broke down thirty miles outside of Rawlins, Wyoming, and I hitched back into town, leaving my wife and two kids in the car sitting at the side of the road. The hour and a half I was gone were some of the most agonizing moments of my life, but when I returned with a family in a mobile home, my family was safe.

So here I am suffering from one of the worst bouts of insecurity ever, and a young man asks if I'd like to risk my life for a lift to Delphi. What do I do? I throw my pack in the back of his dirty, white pickup and climb aboard. The pickup is full of paint cans, shovels, plastic tubing, and cardboard boxes. He scrapes some junk off the seat beside him, and we take off down the road. He drinks coffee from a plastic cup. I would like to know his name and take a chance on my Greek. "Τι ειναι το ονομα σου?" I ask. "Διμιτρι (Dimitri)," he answers, and I tell him mine which he repeats several times to get the pronunciation correct. But my memorized sentence has given him a false impression. Dimitri comes out with the most awful mess of Greek I've ever heard. I just throw up my hands. "Δεν καταλαβενο," I say, realizing how little Greek I actually know. Thereafter, we use the point and grunt technique highlighted with single words.

I'm pleased to be on my way to Delphi and should be there in an hour and a half. After we get through town, I see the agricultural plain I've been watching from a distance for the past four days. I'm still struck by how it resembles the San Joaquin Valley in California where I grew up. The two-lane blacktop road through cotton fields is lined with eucalyptus trees. Cotton has blown from the trucks while hauling it to gins, and white locks lace weeds along the shoulder. Cotton pickers roam the fields, their huge baskets bulging with white fluffiness. Small shops and grocery stores drift past. This would look like home except for the Greek signs.

The sun is bright through the rear window, and off to the right, I watch the sunlit Mountain of the Sphinx drift slowly past on the far side of the plain. To the left, Mt. Helicon bathes in its own morning shadow. Mt. Helicon is the location of the "Fountain of the Horse," where the goddess Athena once bathed with the nymph Chariclo, Teiresias' mother. Unfortunate Teiresias chanced upon them and saw Athena naked, her breasts, her bare body:

> Those two were bathing and it was the noontide hour and a great quiet held that hill. Only Teiresias, on whose cheek the down was just darkening, still ranged with his hounds the holy place. And, athirst beyond telling, he came unto the flowing fountain, wretched man! and unwillingly saw that which is not lawful to be seen. And Athena was angered, yet said to him: "What god, O son of Everes, led thee on this grievous way? hence shalt thou never more take back thine eyes!"[43]

The glorious sight of a naked goddess blinded Teiresias. His mother chastised Athena, and she in recompense washed Teiresias' ears with water from the spring, so he could understand the language of birds and, therefore, tell the future. She also gave him a staff of cornel wood, and he walked as well as any man.[44]

The Muses also resided on the slopes of Mt. Helicon where, in the 8th Century BC, they gave Hesiod much of what the world knows of Greek mythology and religion. They also taught him "the mastery of flowing song."[45] From the Muses, he received the story of the origin of the universe and the birth of the gods who rule it. He saw them at night veiled in a glowing mist as they set out for the far reaches of Greece.

Suddenly Dimitri slows, stops at a turnoff going north. He motions for me to get out because he must travel the off-road. We're at the edge of Aliartos, a small town only halfway to Lavadia, one quarter of the way to Delphi. He tells me to catch the bus on down the road. "Το Λεωφορειον," he says, pointing toward Aliartos. I'm in a panic wondering how far I have to walk with my fifty-pound pack. "Στασι. Ειναι μακρια?" I ask. "Οχι, δεν ειναι μακρια απο εδω," he says.

I walk a couple of blocks, feeling suddenly abandoned and looking for something resembling the bus stop he said was here. I see a young couple standing in the shade beside a building. She speaks English and tells me the bus stop is on the other side of the road. Several people are waiting for it here in the shade.

Delphi

Teiresias was buried in Aliartos. He died here after drinking from the Telphusian spring nearby while being brought to Delphi by his captors after the siege of Thebes. He was very old, having lived for seven generations. Manto was taken on to Delphi where she became a priestess of Apollo. The armies of Argos had promised Apollo they would present him with Manto, the fairest of the spoils, if he would allow them to successfully siege Thebes.

While I wait for the bus in the shade of flattop buildings lining the south side of the road, I stand beside the young woman and her boyfriend, feeling a little jealous as she cuddles up against him. In the flat country to the north, farmhouses are scattered among grape vineyards and cotton fields with rolling hills and mountains beyond. Laios and Oedipus both trudged this road 3300 years ago.

Laios' father, King Labdacus of Thebes, died when Laios was a child. Until he was old enough to be king, Laios was sent away to the Peloponnese to be raised. As a young man, Laios became infatuated with his guardian's son, Chrysippus, kidnapped him and took him to Thebes, where Laios then assumed the throne. Chrysippus committed suicide from the shame of being homosexually raped. Laios was credited with inventing homosexuality.[46]

Following Chrysippus' suicide, Laios married Jocasta. As time went by, Laios and Jocasta remained childless, and he came to Delphi to determine the reason. The oracle told him if he had a child by Jocasta, the child would one day kill him. Laios didn't like Apollo's answer and returned twice more to get confirmation. Laios was being punished for the kidnap and homosexual rape of Chrysippus. The curse lasted three generations, thus bringing all the ills on his family that resulted in the ultimately destruction of Thebes.

The part I played in the events leading to my father loading the deer rifle to kill himself is difficult to resurrect through thirty-two years of forgetfulness and memory suppression. I do know that when I mentioned the incident to my mother a couple of years ago, she reminded me, and did so rather heatedly, that my father and I had argued over me bringing a friend home, someone of whom my father strongly disapproved.

I do remember the day. It was warm, perhaps warmer than today here in Aliartos. We had just argued in the kitchen, and I walked out into the living room and turned to look back at him. The sun shone in through the kitchen window on the linoleum floor, and I saw the bright blotch of sunlight behind him. My mother approached through the kitchen doorway, her feet planted in that bright sunlight. It was late July, maybe early August. We were irrigating that day, and through the kitchen window I saw up into the sand patch. There, glistening mirrors of water striped the cotton field between rows of green plants full of red, white and gold blooms. The windows were open, and I heard the whine of a tractor off in the distance as I spoke my words of anger.

Our argument was full of shouting and ill will. I had brought a friend from college home with me, an Englishman, and my father disliked him intensely, wouldn't allow him in our home. This time he was firm, violent in his opposition to this man. My father didn't say why he didn't want this man around. He just tried to bully me. I said, if my friend couldn't stay there, neither would I. "Well, get the hell out," he said. I walked down the hall to my bedroom, fell on the cool sheets and listened to him clicking the bolt action deer rifle in the next room.

I didn't know it at the time, but my father suspected something about my friend soon shown to be true. Something soon to cause more trouble in our household.

Finally, the bus to Lavadia.

★

I sit at the side of the street in Lavadia trying to shade my face from the hot sun, which peeks through the sparse leaves of a small maple tree, waiting for the bus. A woman in the kiosk next to where I sit just provided me with information. "Λεοφοριο, Δελφος. Τι ωρα?" I asked. She wrote the time on her hand with a ballpoint pen. It looked like 72, so I thanked her and walked over here under the maple tree, and now I'm trying to bridge this latest communication gulf.

Europeans write the number 1 with a long line forward at the top so it looks like a 7. After thinking about it, I believe she told me twelve o'clock noon, forty-five minutes from now. Hopefully I'm at the right spot, but nothing indicates that this is a bus stop and no other people are waiting. The traffic on the street is horrendously noisy. Every type of motor vehicle in existence comes through. A two-row, John Deere cotton picker just passed right in front of me, blowing hot air and slinging dirt from its huge tire tread. A backhoe trailed close behind.

Since I have a few minutes, I drag my pack across the street to a restaurant crowded with cheap tables and folding chairs. I buy a greasy cheese pie at a small bakery at the far end of the room, quickly chase it down with a Sprite, and return to street-side to await the bus to Delphi.

In the hills above Lavadia, water from the spring Kryo runs a double stream. One contains the water of Memory and the other, water from the river Lethe. The Lethe runs through the Underworld, where all souls go after death. Lethe means "forgetfulness," and all those who drink from it forget their past.

The water flowing through fields on our farm came from deep within the earth, pulled to the surface by powerful pumps. Many times I've dropped to my stomach, blown foam aside, and drunk a cold draft of flowing ditch water, as if

51

Delphi

drinking from the river Lethe. We, as a family, never talked about bad things that happened between us, and I lost the connection between the events and the way I felt, particularly those of that fatal summer. After my confrontation with my father, we just forgot about it.

Suddenly, a hot-air belching bus stops before me, its loud brakes screeching. A horde of passengers exit, and as the driver unloads luggage, I ask if he's going to Delphi. "Next bus," he says and climbs back inside. But just as it starts to move, it stops again and he gets out, grabs my pack without a word, stows it in the hold and motions for me to board. I hope he's going to Delphi. The bus is almost empty, only one other passenger, an old man.

The bus zips through the agricultural valley of Boiotia and enters another county, Phocis Nome. Off to the right, I see a sign for the road to Daulia. We pass the Cleft Way, where Oedipus killed Laios, at 80 kph. I rise from my seat, my eyes anxiously following the side road as it disappears into a fold between hills. Just a half-kilometer up that country road is where Oedipus and Laios met their destiny. I hope to rent a car in Delphi and return to the Cleft Way. For now I'm excited to have passed this close to such a famous site.

The bus loses steam as it crawls up the southern slope of Mt. Parnassos. To the left, across a rapidly expanding ravine, I see Mt. Cirphis, a green-speckled rock of a mountain standing in thick haze. The town of Arachova swings into view, a small town with beautiful white buildings and orange-tiled roofs pressed against the brown steeps overlooking the ravine. To the right, the giant sandstone cliffs of Mt. Parnassos rise rapidly from the edge of the road to tower above us. The bus slows to a crawl as it snakes through the narrow streets of Arachova, then quickens its pace as we exit.

As the bus negotiates the winding road along the edge of the cliff, I anxiously await my first glimpse of Delphi, the most famous religious site in ancient Greece. I expect a small but sprawling town on the mountainside, a bustling little metropolis inundated with tourists. We enter a tiny village precariously clinging to the steep slope. The bus zips on through and makes a U-turn at a wide spot in the road, stops at the edge of the cliff. The driver exits the bus. I'm confused. Am I supposed to change buses here? The other passenger, the old man, notices my uncertainty. "Δελφος," he says. This wide spot in the road, a few buildings nailed to the side of the cliff, is Delphi.

As the bus driver retrieves my backpack, I look around. Delphi is deserted. I wonder if I've made a mistake by planning to get a hotel here? Delphi only has two streets: the one we came in on and the one the bus will return on. Just beyond where the bus stopped, the road continues on to the Gulf of Itea, which I can see in the distance.

Delphi

I shoulder my pack and walk up the deserted street lined with two-story buildings. On the right, the cliff side of the road, I see Hotel Athena. It appears to be much nicer than I can afford, but I enter anyway. The entry way is quiet, unlit and vacant. I wonder if the hotel is closed, but a woman in an apron appears from a hall off to the right. She doesn't speak English but understands that I want a room, or at least I believe she does, and she's so glad to see me, I wonder if she thinks I'm a long lost friend.

She disappears and returns with another woman who apparently runs the place. She's small, mid-thirties, dusty-brown hair and a light complexion, round figured, very professional. She wears a white button-blouse and brown skirt, which comes just to the top of her knees exposing her fleshy calves. She tells me a single room is 3000 drachmes ($13).

Must not be as nice as it looks.

I follow her down the hall to where she unlocks the door to a sparkling-clean room. I enter and cross the room to the French doors. No one could have prepared me for the view. I take a step back because I immediately sense a little vertigo. The patio is quite small, only enough room for a couple of chairs, and has a wrought-iron railing that is the only barrier to keep me from falling off the cliff. I'm confronted with a vast expanse of nothingness. A kilometer away, across the deep ravine, looms Mt. Cirphis. The sound of a great expanse greets me. The valley to the west ends at the Gulf of Itea, its mirrored surface glistening in the afternoon sun.

The room is so nice and the view so spectacular, I think there must be some misunderstanding about the price. I ask her again. "Three thousand drachmes," she says. I drop my backpack to the floor hoping this isn't the earthquake season.

The religious significance of Delphi predates Apollo's oracle. According to mythology, the site has been revered since primordial times. The stories of Greek heroes like Theseus and Oedipus are not true mythologies but legends occurring in historical times. True mythology is about the gods and comes to us out of primordial time during which the cosmos had its origin.[47]

Zeus, wishing to find the center, the navel, of the world, released two eagles, one at the eastern edge of the earth, the other at the western edge. They flew toward each other and met at Delphi where their descendants circle to this day. An even more familiar myth, that of the flood, has a connection to Delphi. In Greek mythology, Zeus destroyed the world by flood, but the famous shipbuilder was not Noah. He was Deukalion, the primordial man. His ship landed not at Mt. Ararat but here on Mt. Parnassos.[48]

In the beginning, the site was the oracle of the Earth Goddess, Gaia, the mother of all things. The priestess of Apollo at Delphi tells of the matrilineal succession of oracles at the site:

> First of all Gods I worship in this prayer
> Earth Gaia, the primeval prophet; after her
> Themis the Wise, who on her mother's throne—
> So runs the tale—sat second; by those own
> Accepted will, with never strife nor stress,
> Third reigned another earth-born Titaness,
> Phoebe; from whom (for that he bears her name)
> To Phoebus Apollo as a birthtide gift it came.[49]

Themis was Gaia's daughter and her double. Phoebe was another of Gaia's daughters and therefore Apollo's grandmother.

The temple, at the time Apollo acquired it, was guarded by a she-dragon. Apollo, who was still a babe in his mother's arms, slew the dragon and claimed the site for his oracle:

> ...the lord far-shooting Apollon shot her
> with a mighty arrow; rent with insufferable pains,
> she lay panting fiercely and writhing on the ground.
> The din was ineffably awesome, and throughout the forest
> she was rapidly thrusting her coils hither and thither; with a gasp
> she breathed out her gory soul, while Phoibos Apollon boasted:
> "Rot now right here on the man-nourishing earth..."[50]

Apollo was frequently referred to by the masculine form of his grandmother's name, Phoebus meaning "the Bright One." The ancient Greek word "πυθω" (pytho), from which python comes, means "to rot." The priestess who spoke Apollo's words to pilgrims who came to the site was called the "Pythia," Apollo's wish was "to hold dear the lyre and the curved bow and to prophesy for men the unerring will of Zeus."[51] Thus Apollo didn't speak his own thoughts but Zeus' secret counsel, just as did Jesus for His Father in heaven. Apollo was the divine being who brought light, understanding. Belief in Apollo was a belief in clarity, purity, order and harmony.[52] But Mother Earth, Gaia, never lost her influence. She provided a background for all ancient Greek religion,[53] which had its origin in the divine force from which all life flowed.

★

I sit in an ice cream shop at the side of the street, supplementing the cheese

Delphi

pita I had for lunch in Lavadia with a cup of chocolate and vanilla ice cream and contemplating the uneasy equilibrium between my father and me following our confrontation and his near suicide over my friend.

I had known Fred for two years at college. He was an athlete as was I. Even though he was in his mid twenties, he seemed to fit in with our post-adolescent crowd. He talked sports and was a long distance runner. He had come to the States from England along with another athlete, a young man of twenty, whom I roomed with in a professor's home. To cut expenses, the three of us pooled our food money, and though Fred had his own apartment close by, he often came to the professor's home, fixed dinner for the three of us, and we washed the dishes afterward.

After our confrontation, my father backed off about Fred coming to our home. And Fred started coming on his own. Fred had grown quite fond of one of my younger brothers and wanted to take him to Disneyland, a two day trip from my hometown. They would have to stay overnight. My brother was excited about a trip away from home. Fred came to my father and asked for permission. Later, my father said it was like a guy asking if he could take your daughter to a dance. Shortly, my father and I would again stand together in the living room, another life weighing in the balance of my actions. This time it would be Fred's.

★

For dinner, I have a Greek pizza at a little taverna down the street from the hotel. The crust is flaky and delicious, but I could swear the meat is lamb, or possibly goat. I've been afraid of getting a piece of goat meat ever since I got to Greece. I don't much care for the smell of goats. But tonight I rather perversely enjoy the thin slices of meat on my pizza while sitting in the dark on the patio, suspended over nothingness and watching the sparkling lights of the small towns: Itea, Galaxidion and Pendeoria in the Gulf just south of here. Stars circle overhead while a Greek soap opera blares from the taverna kitchen.

★

During the night, I wake and lie in the dark listening to street noises lofting from below my patio. I feel more displaced here in Greece than ever. Even though I'm doing well with the buses now, an uneasiness about the length of my journey has come over me. The creeping insecurity I felt in Athens and Thebes has returned with new force. My dreams are bothering me. When I woke just now, I was crying and I don't know why. I'm afraid.

12 Oct, Tuesday
I wake early as the rosy fingertips of dawn stretch above Mt. Parnassos,

preceded by a pale slice of silvery moon. My dreams have turned violent. Early this morning, I was fighting someone, I don't know whom. He humiliated me, called me "queer." I waded into him pounding my left jab into his face and absorbing his blows with ease. I belted him with lefts and rights until the blood flowed.

★

While having breakfast in the hotel, I meet two Americans: a woman my age, Pat, and her daughter, Marlene, who is a Manhattan playwright. Pat works for a large hospital in Boston. She has a round pixie-like face with curly brown hair. Both are brunettes, thin, forever smiling. I would like to see the site with them but at the last minute, I lose my courage and back out of asking them to accompany me.

★

The ruins of Apollo's temple are two hundred meters up the road back toward Arachova. The site sits on a large, sloping terrace in a recess at the foot of sandstone cliffs. The museum lies to the left of the entrance to the site, and now I know why so few tourists are in the town of Delphi. The site is a hive of buses. Huge tourist buses line the parking lot and zip along the road to and from Athens. None visit the little town.

I enter the site by a paved trail lined with olive trees and pines. Past the entrance, the footpath turns to dirt and doubles back on itself. I enter by the Sacred Way, the same footpath pilgrims have used for 3300 years. The entire site, though sprinkled with olive and pine trees, is a dry, desolate piece of parched earth. In antiquity, both sides of the Sacred Way were lined with monuments from various city-states, of which little now remains.

I pass the ruins of a dedication by the Athenians commemorating their victory at Marathon, followed by two others from Argos. The first are statues representing the generals who led their forces in the futile battle of "Seven Against Thebes," and the second represent the seven generals who returned and succeeded in burning the Kadmia, known as the "Επιγονι," the Afterborn. All the statues once residing in these stone-lined enclaves have either been destroyed or removed to museums. None of this, however, would have been here when Oedipus and Laios visit the temple. They came centuries before.

Where the path curves to the right to ascend the sloping terrace, I pass the remains of stone buildings, which contained treasuries from the Sikyoniands, Siphnians, Megarians, Syracusans, Knidians, Aiolians. The only building now standing is the treasury of the Athenians, a small stone building with a columned portico in recognition of the official incorporation of democracy in Athens in 508 BC.

Delphi

Just beyond this building is the foundation that supported the statue of Oedipus' famous Sphinx, which has been removed to the Delphi museum. The path curves to the left, and before me lay the ruins of the temple of Apollo, the heart of the sanctuary.

I sit in the bright sun on a large hot stone next to the temple that was destroyed many times by war and earthquakes. Now it is all ruins, just stones scattered about the landscape with the large slab foundation of the temple exposed to the sun. In antiquity, a huge building stood here, lined with columns and inscribed with the words, "Know Thyself" and "Nothing in Excess." They were brought here by seven Wise Men, who were assembled from all over Greece.[54] Only six weather-beaten columns remain, rising from the east end of the temple foundation to reach toward the blistering-hot sun. Ivy carpets the side of the foundation. Everything is blanketed with dust that kicks up at every step.

Oedipus came to the Oracle years before Manto became priestess here, and I can well imagine him leaving disillusioned. He'd asked Apollo if the king and queen of Corinth were his real parents, but Apollo ignored his question and instead told him he was destined to kill his father and defile his mother's bed. Oedipus took heed and instead of returning to Corinth, went to Thebes. Apollo was also called Λαξιας, Laxias, the Oblique One.

Laios had been here three times before[55] and was on his way for the fourth try when Oedipus killed him. Laios wanted to know if the son he had exposed on Mt. Kithaeron was still alive, and still sweating his homosexual rape of Chrysippus that had started all his problems. Every time he came, Apollo tightened his grip.

An old goatherd, who received the mantic enthusiasm when he happened upon it, first discovered the oracular character of the site. His goats also received the spirit, skipping playfully about and uttering strange bleats.[56] The temple smelled unusual:

> The building in which they make the consulters of the oracle sit is often, but at no regular intervals, filled with a fragrant smell and breath, which gives off something like the scent of the sweetest and most expensive perfume, which seems to have its source in the inner shrine.[57]

The site has been occupied since the Bronze Age, though those early inhabitants lived under primitive, Neolithic-like conditions.[58]Mycenaean artifacts were found in the eastern part of the sanctuary.[59] The temple has been destroyed and rebuilt many times, and the ruins presently visible are from the 4th

Century BC. No one knows what it was like in the days of Laios and Oedipus.

Delphi was the oracle of Apollo, not his residence. He resided on Mt. Olympus with the rest of the Greek gods. Originally Apollo only came here on his birthday, the 7th of Bysios (February–March) each year, which was called "the day of Many Utterances."[60] But during the golden age of the oracle, it functioned whenever Apollo's attention was detected by pouring water on a sacrificial goat. If the goat shivered, Apollo was listening. If the goat was not consumed in shudders, every limb trembling and the goat emitting quaking noises, the god's attention was assumed to be elsewhere and questioning the Pythia, useless.

Teiresias' daughter, Manto, was a priestess, the Pythia. According to Diodorus Siculus, she was a potent force here:

> This maiden Manto possessed no less knowledge of prophecy than her father, and in the course of her stay at Delphi she developed her skill to a far greater degree; moreover, by virtue of the employment of a marvellous natural gift, she also wrote oracular responses of every sort, excelling in their composition...[61]

She served as the Pythia 1200 years before Christ. Apollo's oracle was the most highly regarded in all antiquity. Barbarian monarchs came from as far as Asia Minor and Egypt. Since the gods appeared in person throughout ancient Greek literature, I always thought the Greeks talked directly to Apollo. Such was hardly the case. His word had to be conjured from the elements just as the word of God does today.

Anyone could receive the mantic enthusiasm, but only a perfectly pure person would be "a well-tuned and resonant instrument"[62] for Apollo to "give her soul light to view the future."[63] The god used the Pythia "in the world of hearing as the sun uses the moon in the world of sight."[64] The Pythia was an old, pious, peasant woman over fifty, a nobody who was thus beyond reproach. According to some, she was dressed in the attire of a young virgin as she mounted the golden tripod of Apollo that spanned a fissure in the mountain. She would breathe fumes from the fissure, chew laurel leaves, become entranced, convulse, and then mumble incoherently. The male priests interpreted her ravings and provided the answer to the pilgrim in hexameter verse.[65]

But others tell a different story. They claim:

> There was no vapor and no chasm: the Pythia experienced no frenzy that caused her to shout wild and unintelligible words; she spoke

quite clearly and directly to the consultant without need of the prophet's mediation.[66]

Whatever the truth,[67] the fanciful stories persist. Christians delighted in telling lies about Delphi, claiming the evil spirit of Apollo created madness in the Pythia by creeping up from below into her genitals. As evidence of the Oracle's stature throughout the Mediterranean, cities as well as individuals consulted it, many seeking advice in times of war.[68] Alexander the Great was among them.

In one true though bizarre episode, when the goat failed to exhibit the mantic enthusiasm after being doused with cold water, the priests continued to soak the goat until it did shiver. The Pythia, having witnessed the artificially induced spirit, mounted Apollo's tripod unwillingly.

> At her very first remarks, it became evident from the roughness of her voice that she was not in control of herself, but like a foundering ship, filled with an inarticulate and evil spirit. Finally, becoming totally hysterical, she raised an unintelligible and fearful shout and rushed for the door...[69]

She suffered a seizure, collapsed short of the exit, and died a few days later.

I leave my seat on the hot stone and walk up a flight of steps to the theatre, a symbol that Dionysus was also worshipped here. Dionysus was Apollo's brother and a welcome presence at his oracle. As a matter of fact, Dionysus was the presiding deity during the winter months. None of the Greek gods or goddesses tried to suppress worship of their compatriots. Apollo was not jealous of his little brother, and this theatre, so close to Apollo's temple, is evidence of their goodwill toward one another.

I climb the steps of the theatre and stand at the top of the seats, staring off into the distance. If the view out my hotel room patio was breathtaking, this is truly awe-inspiring. Beyond the ancient stone ruins of the theatre and temple, the Valley of the Pleistos drops into a dark hazy gorge before rising up as the shadow-shrouded surface of Mt. Cirphis. To the east, the black ribbon of asphalt winds around the mountain toward Thebes.

The wind plays with tourists' voices and light traffic on the road far below, turning them into an amorphous whisper, which seems to come from the far mountain. To the west, the mountain falls away to the valley where Itea sits at the edge of the sea. I watch for the eagles that, according to legend, have circled overhead since Zeus established Delphi as the navel of the Earth, but see nothing.

Dionysus stayed here during the winter months, and his priests sang dithyrambs to awaken Dionysus, in place of the Paeans to Apollo. Apollo, being a sun god, dominated the site during the other nine months. But Dionysus was actually here before Apollo. He sat on the tripod giving oracles in the name of Themis, who occupied the oracle-giving site after Gaia.[70] In the eastern part of the sanctuary, a small temple to Dionysus stood among densely occupied dwellings.[71] The Titans dismembered him here. Apollo was also a healer, and he found the dismembered, suffering and mad Dionysus, and put his pieces in a leather sack. Delphians once believed the dismembered remains of Dionysus were buried here at the temple.[72] Dionysus was not simply tolerated by Apollo. Apollo with his order, logic and stability needed Dionysus, the god of madness whose realm was eternally appearing and vanishing. Together the two gods signified the whole truth.[73]

I'm surprised to see Pat and Marlene enter the theatre. Marlene walks on stage and after a tentative start, sings a beautiful song from a Broadway play, her resonant voice filling the theatre. The tourists are spellbound. After scattered applause, she leaves the stage and another woman with an operatic voice performs.

I leave the theatre to ascend further up Mt. Parnassos, along a set of switchbacks, and sit in the shade of pine trees overlooking the stadium high above the ancient theatre and temple. The stadium was the site of the Pythian Games, which occurred every four years, in the middle of the four year span between games at Olympia.

The sun gets hotter as I ascend the mountain, but the coolness here in the shade is refreshing. I've located a reference to Apollo's' other brother, who was also a significance presence at Delphi: Hermes. Hermes was Zeus' herald, scurrying about from place to place on errands for his divine father. But he was also the protector of athletes, and ruled over games and other duly ordered contests.[74] This stadium is as closely connected with him as the theatre is to Dionysus.

I ascend through dead yellow grass, past many cracks and fissures where the mountain has crumbled away, and sit on the retaining wall of an ancient fortress in shadows a few meters from the base of a sheer rock cliff. A dirt path trails off to my left, leading to a narrows along the face of another cliff, where a small bird sits on a rock chirping. Below, the mountain falls away through tall pine trees to the stadium. I hear voices of tourists but can barely see them for the forest. If I tripped and fell here, I would roll forever.

A swarm of ants and a blowfly keep me company. Ants are eating away the mountainside. A huge bumblebee circles, colored deep black and gold and heavily laden with pollen. Another, then another.

Delphi

I turn my face up to the clear blue sky searching for Zeus' circling eagles. Suddenly a deafening scream comes out of the east as a jet thunders from behind Mt. Parnassos and streaks out into the Gulf of Itea. My solitude, shattered by a 20th Century war machine.

★

I meet Pat and Marlene again on the street out front of the hotel at early evening and congratulate Marlene on her performance at the theatre today. They already have dinner plans, so I eat dinner by myself at an empty restaurant, just me and the old crone who runs the place. I sit thinking about my ex-wife and daughter. My meal, goaty spinach pie and Greek salad, doesn't go down well.

During the evening, I write on my patio sitting in the dark, looking out over the valley at the lights of Itea and the reflection of Galaxidia at the edge of the Gulf. I hear crickets in the grapevine terrace on the level below me, dogs barking down the street, and voices of kids as they bounce a soccer ball on blacktop. The couple on the patio next to mine argue behind the partition, reminding me of my wife and me arguing shortly before we separated. I only hear his side of the argument because her voice is so meek. He's Greek, arrogant and keeps explaining the importance of his heritage, his mission in life, the reason she doesn't fit him.

I'm anxious to leave Delphi. Day after tomorrow, I'll take the bus to Patras on the north of the Peloponnese, take a ferry to Ithaca, the home of Odysseus, the world's most famous traveler, do a swipe across the land mass, ending in Corinth. Then the Aegean islands.

★

During the night, I wake from a strange dream about a TV show, one of the detective dramas. A black man's face fills the screen. He talks to someone not visible, speaks about a suitcase and me losing my job, some matter of life and death. As I watch the screen, a man sneaks up behind me, and I wake with a start.

Hermes was also the bringer of dreams and guide of souls in the Underworld. Today we know him as the guide into the unconscious. The ancient Greeks projected much of their own subconscious motivations onto their gods. This perception allowed them to visualize their own hidden nature and deal with it in ways we of the modern world have lost. When we learn about the Greek gods, we learn about the structure and processes of our own subconscious, how it orders our lives. Hermes is central to that process. He has truly been overactive with my dreams. I wish he would bring something a little less disturbing.

Delphi is too quiet. No sounds enter my room from the outside world. I

61

Delphi

think I hear a cricket, but even that's hypothetical. I feel so lonely.

★

A couple of weeks after my brother went to Disneyland with Fred, Fred came to see us again for the weekend. The house was crowded this time. One of my cousins, a young man just a couple of years older than me, was staying with us, he and his new wife. He had fought a lot during his days working in the potash mines of Carlsbad, New Mexico. We had a shortage of beds, so my parents did what they had always done. They had Fred sleep with me.

We also had another cousin at our home that night. He was the same age as my younger brother. His parents were there too, but they lived only thirty miles away and left for home at bedtime. That evening before I went to bed with Fred and before my youngest cousin and his parents went home, I heard a commotion down the hall. Fred was in my bedroom, and my brother and our young cousin were going in and out laughing and cutting up with him. No one thought much about the ruckus or Fred playing with those two youngsters. Turns out, Fred was passing out blowjobs down there where I was soon to join him.

I stayed up late that night talking to my older cousin's young wife after everyone else had gone to bed. At midnight, she and I took the old pickup down the dark lane to the far side of the cotton field and turned off the pump. When we got back, I tiptoed into my bedroom, pulled off my clothes and slipped between the sheets next to Fred who had been asleep for sometime, or so I thought.

13 Oct, Wednesday

Dawn pushes back the darkness at the foot of Mt. Parnassos and chases away the scattering of stars in the west. Switchbacks of ancient trails zigzag up the slopes across the abyss in front of me. In the bay, Itea lies in heavy shadow. A bulldozer of a bee flies retrograde into the morning sun. The street below, visible through the moist leaves of grape vines, is quiet and crowded with parked cars. That's the last level of land before it takes a precipitous plunge to the valley floor. The sea in the distance is glassy and shrouded in haze.

I sit in a wood chair on my little patio at the cliff's edge, watching the flight of a crow against the background of the looming mountain and listening to his repeated caws as he shoots through the cool air toward the Gulf. Every insect in Delphi knows my room. They come through the French doors like bullets, circle frantically and streak out: hornets, bees, blowflies, horseflies, gnats. I feel crawly things on me and I itch.

Here comes the sun just over my shoulder casting my dark silhouette on the pure-white patio partition before me, a black figure against eye-blinding whiteness. I look young, full haired and brilliant in that bespectacled shadow. As the harsh cries of birds and the pounding of construction workers overtake the softer murmurings of morning, the sun takes Itea.

At breakfast, I talk to Pat and Marlene about writing, publishing, medical insurance, mental illness. A sense of excitement fills the breakfast room. Afterward, I talk Pat and Marlene into coming to my room. We sit on the edge of my bed while I pullout my map and show them where Oedipus killed Laios in Phocis Nome, the place where three roads meet. Then we go out into the street and talk for a while. I'm having trouble letting go of them. Pat invites me to Boston, and Marlene invites me to Manhattan. We say our good-byes, and I take their picture. They are on their way to Patras, where I'll follow the day after tomorrow.

I watch longingly as they walk away, then scurry off to find a rental car. I must be off to the Cleft Way. But while walking the streets, I run into Marlene and Pat again, one at a time, first the daughter then the mother. It's a little embarrassing. "We've been talking about you," Pat says with a smile. "Come with us," she suggests, "let us take you to Patras."

Here it is again. This time it isn't my fantasy. I really have an opportunity to end my loneliness, spend a few hours with these delightful women. I'll turn days of travel by bus into a few hours by car. I feel the purpose of my journey fading into the background. It's as if my whole life, the confrontation with my father, has shrunk to insignificance compared to a few hours with this mother and daughter.

"I would love to," I tell her, "but I'm headed in the opposite direction. I really do have to find the Cleft Way."

We say our good-byes again. As they walk away, I already miss them terribly. I can't believe I've passed up an opportunity to travel with them. It all seems so demoralizing.

I still have difficulty finding a rental car. I finally stop at a grocery store and ask where I can rent one. "Patras," she answers. I'm taken aback. Patras is where Pat and Marlene are going, across the Gulf of Itea. "No Delphi," she says. I've turned down Pat when I could have spent the day with her and Marlene, rented a car in Patras tomorrow morning, crossed the gulf on the ferry and driven to the Cleft Way. Instead, I'm all alone again, wallowing in problems thirty-two years old.

After lunch, I hurry back to my hotel and ask the proprietor, the full-busted woman's husband, about a rental car. He's dark complexioned, well-built and has a tuft of black chest hair sticking out of the top of his shirt. I talk to him

Delphi

in the gift shop just off the entryway. We stand among replicas of ancient vases, their black figures contoured into scenes from Homer's epics. "Lavadia," he says. "Closest car rental." He checks the time. "Too late today. Bus already left. You take bus tomorrow morning. Not long to Lavadia." I know. I came from there. I could have saved two days of my journey if I had rented one when I was in Lavadia two days ago.

*

In Delphi, evening precedes sunset, the rays of light blocked by thick haze. Shadows are deep and diffuse. I sit on the edge of the cliff just east of town overlooking the valley of the Pleistos through which the torrent runs in the winter but is now bone dry. Fifteen young travelers sit with me. They sit perilously close to the edge, a macho disregard for their own safety. I get a frightening feeling when someone passes behind me. We're all writing in our journals, but the bumble bees seem to have taken a special interest in me. They buzz at my feet as if closing the day's business, then dart off into the abyss.

An ocean of haze fills the valley and provides a mystical quality to the far mountain, a looming giant against the setting sun. It looks so close, I could reach out and touch it. I hear echoes from its face. Trees cut stark human-like figures along its ridge, Oedipus trudging the slope, his back bent to the task. The sun's rays stretch long across the landscape, turning brown grass into the burning glow of gold. The green of trees is neon in the sun's fading light. Darkness creeps up the side of the mountain. I watch the moon and evening star, watch planets grind on the axle of the solar system.

All things must pass, decay into ruin, and that is true of the Delphic Oracle also. The last word from Delphi came during the 4th Century AD. The Roman emperor Julian consulted the Pythia and received what was to be the epitaph of the ancient oracle:

> Tell ye the King: the carven hall is fallen into decay;
> Apollo hath no chapel left, no prophesying bay,
> No talking spring. The stream is dry and had so much to say.
> Andronicos, *Delphi*, pg. 9

During the night, I wake again from a dream in which an angry man at work threatens people with an electric handsaw. One man is not intimidated, so the angry man puts the saw to the guy's shoulder. Flesh flies like sawdust and the man writhes in agony. Then in a show of machismo, the angry man turns the saw on himself and then goes into shock, pale and disabled.

My dreams are taking their toll. During the day I'm okay, but in the quietness at night, Delphi seems like the end of the world. I feel like an exile, the problems of my past dictating this journey as punishment. Why am I not off on some sunny island shore skinny-dipping with some gorgeous lady? From Delphi, I've planned to go to Ithaca, home of Odysseus, the world's most famous traveler. But I no longer feel so certain about this whole journey. I still can't believe I turned down Pat's generous offer. Something bad is happening to me. Perhaps in Athens, JoAnn was right. The loneliness is making me crazy.

14 Oct, Thursday

Mid-morning, I leave for Lavadia. The bus negotiates the hairpin turns and squeezes past construction equipment on the shoulder-width streets of Arachova. The bus driver has to stop and honk for someone to move a van, then descends the mountain past the turn off to Daulia, where Oedipus killed Laios, and stops at a little roadside gas station and cafe in what must be Tsoukalades. Everyone but me debuses and has coffee or something to eat. I feel irritable, impatient. I hoped to get to Lavadia early, get a car and make a day of it in Daulia. I'll be lucky to do much of anything if we don't get going.

In Lavadia, I step off the bus looking for a rental car agency. *Let's Go* says nothing about renting a car in Lavadia. I ask at the kiosk by the bus stop again, but the old man buried within the confines of cigarette packs and candy bars doesn't speak English and my Greek just doesn't cut it. Across the street at the restaurant, I get another greasy goat-cheese pastry and ask the young woman who waits on me. She turns to a man in the next room, and I hear him shout, "Οχι! Οχι!" as if he's mad I even asked. She tells me all the agencies are closed. I ask her about Thebes. She turns to the man in the next room again, and I hear more shouting, then the man walks out to see the moron asking all the questions. He's middle-aged, his back hair sprinkled with gray. He's obviously upset. He shouts at the woman again, then turns on me, shouts at me for a few minutes. She relays the bad news, "Athens," she says.

I walk back to the bus stop with my head down, feeling as thought I just took a beating. Another man shouts at me and motions to get off the sidewalk. What is it with these people? Why is everyone mad at me?

Finally the bus back to Delphi. Hordes of people pile off. Just as I put my foot on the first step to board, the bus driver shouts and closes the door in my face. What's wrong this time? But after a few minutes, the driver lets me on.

Once more the bus climbs the rolling hills then descends into the green sun-painted valley before making the climb up Mt. Parnassos. Once more, I zip past where Oedipus killed Laios. I take a snapshot out the bus window. Hope this is isn't all I get. But seeing the Cleft Way is not negotiable. When I get to

Delphi

Corinth I'll try again to rent a car.

In the evening, I lie in bed listening to the mournful warble of dogs. I've never felt so alone as I did on the road today. I was afraid. My dreams must be bleeding into my perceptions of the external world. And the dogs of Delphi bother me. They start moaning in the early morning and continue until late at night. What's most troubling is that they sound so much like a human in agony, tortured.

My uneasiness has escalated the last few days, and my fear while on the road today has completely unnerved me. I have a growing feeling that this trip is ill-conceived and emotionally damaging. I'm not looking forward to two more months of this. I'm considering returning to the States.

I awaken in the middle of the night feeling even more lost. I talk to myself and realize something important. I'm lonely at home too. I have no job, live alone in a small apartment, rarely visit friends. Perhaps that's what JoAnn didn't know about me, what I didn't even realize about myself. I'm alone even at home. How different is it being on the road? I'm buried inside myself so much at home, being on the road alone is simply a normal state. My home is on the road.

This realization has a profound effect on me. I am at home on the road. I even regain a little courage. Perhaps I should leave for Ithaca tomorrow, the kingdom of Odysseus. How can I not visit the kingdom of the most famous traveler of all time? But I've got to quit pushing myself so hard. I have two months left to see Greece. Not seeing the Cleft Way today really upset me. Not everything is going to happen according to plan. And get off this personal mythology business for a while. You'll drive yourself nuts!

15 Oct, Friday

Following a light breakfast at the hotel, I walk to the bus station at the edge of town and ask the man when the next bus leaves for Patras. "Good morning," is his reply, then kindly informs me that the bus comes after lunch. I realize how rude I've become, so preoccupied with myself.

So I have a little time. I walk east along the blacktop past the Castilian Spring where pilgrims coming to Delphi cleansed themselves before visiting the temple. The spring is boarded up with a huge wooden structure enclosing not only the spring but pine trees surrounding it as well.

I drop off the road to a trail leading to the ruins of the gymnasium used by the athletes during the Pythian games, and a little farther east follow the winding path through old gnarled olive trees to the temple of Athena Pronaia (Athena who stands before the temple of Apollo). This was the Bronze Age

Delphi

settlement of Delphi.[75]

The sun approaches the zenith but is still dimmed by haze and not so blistering hot. Before me stand the stacked stones of Athena's temple and beyond it, the dramatic circular foundation and three marble columns of the thalos, which at one time was the temple of the Earth Goddess, Gaia.

Athena was ever a patron of Odysseus, delighting in his many tricks and schemes. I've felt that I had to visit her temple before leaving for Ithaca. In many ways Odysseus was a despicable character. In his dealings with those he perceived to be his enemies, he was a ruthless murderer.

I don't know quite what to think of Athena, championing such a shady character. She would come to Odysseus from time to time, take his hand in hers, talking of bravery and expressing her desire to hear the clash of arms, urging him into battle.

When I was growing up, I tried not to pattern myself after my father's violent nature and assumed my mother didn't approve of him either. But now I realize she has been married to that man for over fifty years. She chose to live her entire life with him. Perhaps it's simply jealousy that has given me such a negative perception.

The spring before the confrontation with my father, I dated a girl I cared for a great deal. Not only was she beautiful, she was intellectual, liked to talk politics and philosophy. After going with her for a couple of months, I learned she was dating another guy at the same time. When I dropped her, she was furious. "Why didn't you fight for me," she screamed. "Why wouldn't you fight for us?" And she meant it. She wanted a fistfight.

I sit across from the bus stop at the edge of the cliff, amongst the sounds of crowing roosters and the mournful quarreling of dogs. The sun has difficulty breaking through the hazy sky, and the distant Aroania Mountains of the Peloponnese to the south are barely visible. Trees in small rowed patches blanket the valley below Delphi.

Hermes was born a precocious child, and his first act, accomplished the first day of his life, was to steal his older brother's cattle, committing a murder in the process.[76] When Apollo questioned Hermes about it, Hermes lied, saying, "...the claim is preposterous! I was born yesterday".[77] Apollo took him to their father, Zeus, but Hermes lied to him also. Zeus laughed aloud because he could see through the divine child's false front and ordered the two to come to an agreement. Hermes didn't give back the cattle but diverted Apollo's attention by offering him the lyre, which he (Hermes) had just invented. Apollo was so taken by the lyre, he offered Hermes an oracle here at Delphi:

Delphi

...there are three awesome sisters,
virgins, delighting in their swift wings.
Their heads are besprinkled with white barley flour,
and they dwell under the fold of Parnassos,
apart from me, as teachers of divination...
From there flying now here, now there,
they feed on honeycomb and bring each thing to pass.
And after they eat yellow honey, they are seized
with mantic frenzy and are eager to speak the truth.
But if they are robbed of the sweet food of the gods,
then they do buzz about in confusion and lie.
These, then, I give you, and do you question them exactly,
and delight your heart; and if you are a mortal man's teacher,
he will often listen to you if good fortune is his.[78]

The three awesome sisters are the divining bees of Mt. Parnassos, the three winged virgins who are the voices of Hermes oracle. The fact that they tell the truth sometimes and lie at others makes them well suited to Hermes, a liar and thief.

Three days ago when I climbed Parnassos above Apollo's temple, I saw three large bumble bees like those mentioned in the Homeric "Hymn to Hermes." Bees have been buzzing my room ever since I got here. Hermes is a noted companion and protector of travelers. As guide of souls in the Underworld, he mustered the ghosts. He is also the bringer of dreams, residing in that frontier between the unconscious and conscious mind, the doorway into the underworld of the soul. On the surface, you wouldn't think Hermes was much of a traveling companion, but in fact, I couldn't be more deserving of him here in Greece on this journey. The talk I had with myself last night about my loneliness and fear has helped considerably. It seems my newfound sense of security and self-confidence come from him. Perhaps all those bees put the right buzz in my ear.

It's time to leave Delphi. The bus has arrived and the young tourists are scrambling to board. I leave the navel of the world with a certain reluctance. When Manto, the daughter of Teiresias, left here, she was a young woman renowned for her prophecies, and probably both saddened and excited by her departure. She had two children while here by Alcmaeon, the leader of the Argos army that abducted her from Thebes, but her children were taken from her and given to the king of Corinth.[79] She spent many years as a priestess before she was directed by Apollo to found a colony at Colophon on the far side of the Aegean in Asia Minor near Ephesus. She was pregnant again, this time by

Delphi

Apollo. Once there, she married and had more children. Perhaps my path will once again cross hers six weeks from now, if I make it into Turkey.

Leaving the land of her father and her childhood would have been traumatic, but to start a colony in a new land must have been exciting to a young woman. During her final hours here, I imagine her standing as I am at the edge of this cliff staring across the valley toward Itea. I envision her departure during the time of the Pythian games, the air full of the roar of the crowd from the stadium and the echoes of voices from the mountain across the valley in front of her, her entourage gathering for the descent to the boats waiting below. She would have spoken a silent prayer to Apollo and bid farewell to the Greek mainland.

The bus negotiates the switchbacks descending into the valley, using both lanes on hairpin turns. The driver honks at other busses and trucks to say hello, and makes the horn yodel as we pass roadside stops. The bus drivers use their horns to say hurry up, get out of the road, watch out, hello, good-bye, shove it, it's a beautiful day. To communicate with a Greek you can either learn their complex language, which descends directly from Homer, or you can learn their more recently developed "horn-ese."

The trees in the valley, that I've been wondering about for four days, are olive trees. They're planted closer together in the valley than on the mountain slopes. The valley is not as dry as the mountains but brown grass still covers the cultivated earth. Tucked within the large olive trees are small orange trees with neon fruit glowing like Christmas tree ornaments.

The ticket agent in Delphi told me the bus would drive onto the ferry in Itea but instead, drops us at dockside, dumps our luggage and leaves. I chase it yelling "Patras! Patras!" The driver shouts back, "Next bus, next bus." So we have a thirty-minute layover in Itea.

Just a few kilometers east of here is Krisa. If I had a few minutes and a car, I could drive along the coast to visit vineyard-rich Krisa, where Apollo forced a Cretan boat ashore and made the sailors his first priests:

> ...here you shall have
> my opulent temple, which is greatly honored by all men,
> and you shall know the will of the immortals, by whose wish
> you shall be honored forever to the end of your days.[80]

The Cretans were concerned about their livelihood since Delphi was perched on the side of Mt. Parnassos with no vineyards or meadows for sheep and cattle to graze. But Apollo told them not to worry. People from all over the world would come to visit his temple, so that they would be slaughtering

Delphi

sacrificial sheep forever.

I hope to be in the first priests' homeland, Crete, early next month.

The sea here at Itea is stagnant, polluted and smells bad, but I see schools of small dark fish swimming in the green water under the cement dock. The air is very humid.

When our new bus arrives, it doesn't drive onto the ferry at Itea either. Instead it travels west along the coast stopping in every town and village along the way. The driver is adept at getting the huge bus around small-town street corners never meant for a bus. Always to our left is the Gulf of Corinth, smooth seawater with hardly a ripple, dotted with tiny clod-like islands.

The bus drops us at the dock in Andirio, the closest approach of the Greek mainland to the Peloponnese, and we board the ferry on foot. Then the bus backs onboard. I stand at the rail enjoying the fresh air, the gentle sway of the boat, my first sea ride in Greece. The weather has cooled, and we have a smooth twenty-minute ride on the ferry.

We make port in Patras, and as I walk off the ferry to re-board my bus, a man asks where I'm going, to make sure he is on the right bus. We discovered my mistake. I thought only one bus was onboard but there were two. The other bus is going to Athens. After a few seconds of panic, I find my bus already full and about to leave. Since my bus has my backpack, getting the wrong bus could have been the end of my journey. This is a neat bit of synchronicity, one sure sign of the presence of Hermes, protector of travelers.

Patras is the largest city in the Peloponnese, the chief seaport and capitol of Achea, a sprawling metropolis but a friendly, bustling city. Boats leave here for all over the Mediterranean. If you're going to Italy, you must leave from here. Its biggest claim to fame is that the Apostle Andrew was crucified here.

The bus leaves the dock, winding along the coastal city streets, and drops us at another dock. After learning that the ferry to Ithaca will leave from this dock tomorrow afternoon, I take a room in the Adonis Hotel just a block off the main street.

During the night, I lie awake listening to street noises. The Apostle Andrew visited Patras in 60 AD. The proconsul Aegeates jailed him because he converted his wife, and she then refused to satisfy him sexually. Aegeates claimed Andrew had done that to all Achea, this northern coastal area of the Peloponnese. He gave orders to have Andrew beaten with seven scourges and crucified. He further ordered they not break his legs so he would live longer and his suffering be greater.[81]

16 Oct, Saturday

Delphi

I rise early and walk through the vacant streets of Patras to the OTE to make another phone call to my brother in California. He tells me everything is still okay at home. I savor the few minutes I have to talk to him, clinging to his every word. I keep telling myself I call so my family won't worry about me, but I feel so good during the few minutes we have to talk. I've worried so much about my family ever since my daughter's disappearance.

After talking to my brother, I walk the street at the edge of the dock for a kilometer or so south to the Church of St. Andrew. Andrew was from Capernaum, "village of comfort," and the brother of Simon Peter. They were two of the original twelve apostles. His name is from the ancient Greek, "Ανδρειος," meaning "manly, valiant, brave." One day Andrew and his brother were casting their nets into the sea when Jesus happened by and said to them:

> "Come ye after me, and I will make
> you to become fishers of men."[82]

Two days before Passover, Andrew and three other disciples sat with Jesus on the Mount of Olives and questioned him about signs of the end of time. Jesus answered them, in part:

> "...the sun shall be darkened, and the moon shall not give her light, and the stars of heaven shall fall, and the powers that are in heaven shall be shaken. And then shall they see the Son of man coming in the clouds with great power and glory."[83]

After Christ was crucified, Andrew came here to Patras. The Proconsul, Aegeates, ordered his executioners to beat Andrew and crucify him. Stratocles, one of Andrew's converts who was prone to violence, attacked the executioners and released him. But Andrew didn't appreciate Stratocles' help and asked him to look beyond this worldly strife, to be above it all. The two of them walked the beach where I now walk, and coming upon the cross intended for him, Andrew addressed it:

> "Hail, O cross; indeed may you rejoice. I know well that you will rest in the future because for a long time you have been weary set up awaiting me. I am come to you whom I recognize as mine own; I am come to you, who long for me. I know the mystery for which you have indeed been set up. For you are set up in the cosmos to establish the unstable. And one part of you stretches up to heaven so that you may

point out the heavenly logos, the head of all things. Another part of you is stretched out to right and left that you may put to flight the fearful and inimical power and draw the cosmos into unity. And another part of you is set on the earth, rooted in the depths, that you may bring what is on earth and under the earth into contact with what is in Heaven. O cross, tool of salvation of the Most High!"[84]

After being reprimanded by Aegeates, the executioners again seized Andrew, and this time tied him to the cross, not nailing him, so dogs would eat him alive. But Andrew preached for a day and a night from the cross. The next day the crowd descended on Aegeates and demand Andrew's release. Aegeates was afraid and went to the beach to see Andrew, but Andrew demanded to remain on the cross. Then in a final Lord-glorifying outburst, he gave up the ghost.

I turn left off the waterfront, thinking about my mother's sacrifice for the sake of her children. She was always quiet, and now that I'm an adult I realize that much of the time she was suffering in silence under a tremendous workload. I walk on through a small parking lot and into a large church, slowing as I come through the huge doors and rather startled by the quietness and solemnity. Greece has been a country of noise, but here in the darkened chamber is an oasis of quietness. I feel like an infidel crashing a secret ceremony. The few people here are old ladies in long dark dress, lighting candles or sitting quietly. One of them looks at me quizzically and nods as I pass. I walk an isle down the side of the church and come to the holiest of holies, a chased, gold and silver reliquary containing the head of St. Andrew. After his crucifixion, Andrew's head was taken to Rome where it remained in exile for four hundred years until 1964 when Pope Paul VI returned it to Patras.

★

By mid-afternoon, I'm on the ferry halfway to Kefalonia, an intermediate stop. One of the crewmen tells me we'll be in Ithaca by eight this evening. The ferry is large with a spacious living room-like area and sofas positioned into conversation areas. The ride is smooth, but the vibration of the engine deep in the hold ripples through the structure. I watch the sea waves through a series of draped windows along each wall.

People are dressed in everything from Levis to suits. The old woman next to me has on penny loafers, brown stockings, a purple dress with small blue flowers, a long sleeve brown sweater with a purple pattern woven through it and a black rag with deep red roses over her head. She's hump shouldered and wrinkled. A family of four sits in front of me: two old men and two old women. One woman knits and talks; the other cuts up an apple and passes it around.

Delphi

Nonstop talking.

I walk out of the room and into the fresh air along the rail to look out through the haze over the water at the mountains of the mainland and the Peloponnese.

Odysseus was gone from Ithaca for twenty years, ten at Troy killing Trojans and ten wandering the Aegean after being driven off course by high winds and a turbulent sea. Before returning, he descended into Hades to determine his fate from the soul of Teiresias, the blind seer of Thebes. To get to Hades, Odysseus sailed out of the Mediterranean in a dark ship without a helmsman to the abyss of Ocean running round the world and to the Land of Death where no sun shines. There he dug a trough, slit the throats of a black ewe and a black ram, and filled it with sacrificial blood as swarms of ghosts hovered round it. In this way, Odysseus lured from the darkness the soul of Teiresias, prince of prophets, to sip the rich black blood. He was the only one to retain an undarkened mind in the Underworld. From Teiresias, Odysseus learned that his wife Penelope was besieged by suitors and that his kingdom was being plundered.

After speaking to Teiresias, Odysseus saw the souls of his comrades who fought with him and died at Troy. He saw Agamemnon who, upon his return, died at the hands of his wife, Klytemnestra. Agamemnon warned Odysseus of his own homecoming. Odysseus also saw beautiful Jocasta, Oedipus' mother and wife, who had hung herself after learning that her husband was also her son.

Odysseus' last stop before returning home was the island of Scherie (now called Corfu) 150 kilometers north of Ithaca where the Phaiakians lived. When they brought him home, he was asleep aboard their boat. They laid him on a beach and when he awoke, they were gone. Odysseus didn't know where he was, no longer recognizing his homeland.

The ferry stops in Kefallonia and rotates 180 degrees to dock. Most of the passengers onboard exit and are replaced by a smaller number from Kefallonia. Shortly, we're on our way again. The sun has been down for some time and darkness hides the waves. A fresh breeze brushes my face as I watch the coast of an island float by. We come perilously close to the rocky cliffs. I'm worried about finding a place to spend the night on Ithaca. It's after eight o'clock. From here the island looks deserted, but as we round the cape and turn toward the deep-set bay, the pinpoint lights of a small town speckle the darkness. A woman's voice comes over the loud speaker telling us to prepare to disembark.

CHAPTER 4: Ithaca

I walk off of the ferry still thinking about Pentheus, the man of suffering, his head being carried on a pole by his murder-frenzied mother, and having visions of the gold-laden box containing the head of St. Andrew who insisted on dying on the cross. I'm looking for the lights of a hotel, when a woman appears out of the darkness at dockside and steps into the dim light emanating from the hold as I step off the gangway. "Δωματια?" she asks, "δωματια?" (thomatia, room). She grabs my arm, pulls me away from the crowd.

After a confusing conversation containing bits of both Greek and English wherein I try to establish what she's going to charge for a room, I follow her up a dark mountain, up several flights of cement stairs, between buildings, beside homes, through alleys. When I falter under the weight of my backpack, she takes my hand in her warm soft hand. "Room very nice," she says, "home very nice." She's right. I am wondering if it'll be worth the climb. In front of a church, the path turns left along the mountainside, through a dark alley, and a man steps out of the darkness toward us. She's brought me up here to an ambush, I think. But the man greets her and walks on past. Finally, at what must be the top of the mountain, we come to her home.

Once inside the room, she throws open the window and pushes out the shutters, so I can admire the lights in the bay far below. She turns on a light, and I finally see who I've allowed to wrestle me up here. She's a little woman with a big smile, must be sixty, in a plain dress and faded sweater. The entire room is new and painted off-white. Two beds, one double, the other single butt up against the right wall. She gives me my choice, and I take the single. A large circular table with two plastic chairs stands in the corner beneath the window. An electrical cord extends from the ceiling with a bare electric light bulb hanging from it. A motorbike below at dockside breaks the outdoor silence.

"Ελλα," she says, "ελλα," and takes me by the hand to their dimly-lit patio under a grape-vined trellis, sets me down and gives me a drink of water which she dips from their well with a rope and pail. In the traditional Greek fashion, she gives me a smidgen of grape preserves she made from her own grapes off the vined trellis above us and proudly holds up a jar of olive oil which she squeezed from trees at the edge of the patio. Between the evening air and drink of cold water, I finally quit sweating. She introduces her daughter, a husky, big-armed girl in a white puffy blouse and a red Spanish-looking skirt. The three of us sit on the patio and talk through my smidgen of Greek and their smidgen of English. When our understanding runs short, we pantomime. Something else I'm not very good at.

Since Odysseus is the most famous traveler of all time, I'm not surprised he has a close relationship to Hermes. Hermes was born of Zeus and Maia, a shy nymph who lived in a cave in the northern Peloponnese just eighty kilometers east of Patras. As a divine child, Hermes was both precocious and resourceful, slipping out to steal his brother Apollo's cattle the night after he was born. An old man named Battus saw him with the cattle but agreed to say nothing in return for one of them. Hermes didn't trust Battus and returned with voice and features changed to test the old man's word. When Battus readily told on him, Hermes mercilessly turned him to stone, the thought and the murder occurring simultaneously. Hermes is nimble of mind but not a deep thinker, not prone to contemplation. For him, thoughts are deeds. When Apollo learned of Hermes theft, he confronted the divine child, but Hermes lied. Apollo then took him to their father, Zeus, but Hermes lied to him also. These actions early in life illustrate Hermes' basic nature as a murderer, thief and liar.

As an adult, Hermes had a mortal son by a girl of fourteen, Chione the snowmaiden. Both Hermes and Apollo were enamored with her, but Apollo planned to wait until night to take her. Impulsive Hermes put her to sleep and violated her immediately in the snowfields of Mt. Parnassos. She gave birth to Autolykos, the "wolf-itself" who, true to his father's nature was a master thief (he could steal anything within his grasp) and a liar.

Autolykos was also a cattle thief, and one of his favorite targets was the prize herd of the primeval king of Corinth, Sisyphus, the rogue who outwitted even Death. Sisyphus suspected Autolykos was stealing his cattle but could never catch him. Sisyphus was cunning with words and one of the first to master the use of letters. He poured lead in the hollow of his cow's hooves so that their tracks left the words "Autolykos has stolen me".[85]

Autolykos had a daughter by Neaera, daughter of Perseus. He named his daughter Anticleia. Autolykos was so taken by the arch-scoundrel Sisyphus that he befriended him and offered Anticleia to Sisyphus so she might give birth to the cleverest of all men. Anticleia became pregnant, Autolykos wasn't interested in having Sisyphus raise the child, so he gave his daughter as wife to Laertes, king of Ithaka. Laertes gladly accepted the pregnant girl and became the child's foster father. Homer describes the naming of this child by his grandfather. The baby's nurse set him on Autolykos' knee and told him to name him. Homer tells the story:

> Well, Autolykos, on a trip to Ithaka
> arrived just after his daughter's boy was born.
> In fact, he had no sooner finished supper
> than Nurse Eurykleia put the baby down
> in his own lap and said: "It is for you, now,
> to choose a name for him, your child's dear baby,
> the answer to her prayers."
> Autolykos replied:
> "My son-in-law, my daughter, call the boy
> by the name I tell you. Well you know, my hand
> has been against the world of men and women;
> odium and distrust I've won. Odysseus
> should be his given name.[86]

Autolykos invented the name on the spot using the ancient Greek word, οδυσσομαι, (odyssomai), to be wroth against, to hate.[87] Odysseus lived up to his heritage as the great grandson of Hermes, god of swift murder, theft and lies; grandson of Autolykos the master thief; and son of Sisyphus the arch-rogue. Odysseus was known as the man of many wiles.

Hunger has attacked me like a disease. I haven't eaten since early morning. By the time I get to bed, all I can think about is breakfast. My bedroom window is open, the fresh air entering in great breaths along with small night noises from the cove far below. I lie in bed with sleep overtaking me, listening to the rustle of wind in the olive trees.

17 Oct, Sunday

Roosters speak the same language the world over. I wake to the sound of their voices cracking through the morning quiet over the bay. One rooster is close to my room and another is off in the distance with a third farther yet. I hear a fourth and now a fifth farther around the bay as light invades my room.

Ithaca is one of the Ionian Islands, a small group spread thinly along the western coast of Greece in the Ionian Sea, only 350 kilometers from Brindisi, Italy. Vathi is the name of the town where I'm staying. It's located at the end of a deep cove (Vathi means "deep") recessed in the southeast side of Molou Bay which almost cuts Ithaca in half from the northeast. Vathi is a port town with a population of 2,000. The population of Ιθακη (Greeks pronounce it Ith.a'.ki) is less than 4,000. The island is formed of two mountains joined by an isthmus only 700 meters across. Its appearance on the map is that of an elongated amoeba about to regenerate by splitting at its middle. Its length is twenty-five kilometers from tip to tip and its width is nine kilometers.

Outside my window, I see Vathi through the leaves of olive trees off the terrace. The buildings spread around the horseshoe cove are all white stucco, some one-story, some two, with orange tile roofs. Small fishing boats line the edge of the water at dockside. On the opposite side of the bay, the rocky hillside is pocked with a scattering of white stones and a layer of thinly spread brush. The hillside appears desert-like, a touch of Arizona.

A bell clangs rapidly down in the plateia. The hum of a ferry motor mixes with the sounds of roosters, which were stark earlier, but now recede into the background noise of town. I hear a dog bark and a cow in the distance. And now the perennial motorbike. The Sunday morning air is cool and fresh, although I get a whiff of ferry exhaust from far below. A horn blast lofts like a motorbike's mating call, and a flat-sounding bell is struck rapidly, an endless trail of tones lofting out over the cove followed by silence and then two slow strokes at the end, short periods on a long train of peals. A chorus of men's voices.

A ferry drops anchor in the cove. I hear the loud rattle of its chain uncoiling against the housing as the weight descends into the sea. After a few minutes, the ferry leaves port, blaring its horn and raising me from my chair to get another peek. Its blue hull slips through the sea leaving eddies in its wake.

What a glorious morning to be in Ithaca.

For breakfast, I decide on a little waterfront cafe furnished with dark glass tables and black metal chairs. Large mirrors decorate the black walls. In the kitchen to the right of the bar, I hear the clang and bang of pans by the young Greek woman fixing my breakfast, an omelet and bacon. I hear it sizzle. She and I are the only ones in the restaurant.

The woman walks back through the dining room, past me and out the front door, then returns from checking on her son who plays beside the street as cars whiz past. He follows her in and stands by me while she delivers my eggs, bacon and toast, a glass of orange juice. His head is just level with the tabletop. The omelet she and I discussed comes as two eggs sunny-side up. But the bacon is cooked just to my taste, not too crisp and a little chewy. I've learned not to trust myself concerning when my next meal will come, so I eat everything on the table, every pad of butter spread on every slice of bread, thick jelly on top. I've developed a rather perverse pleasure in tricking myself into skipping meals to lose weight and save money.

Today is a busy day, a time for taking care of my affairs. I find a supermarket, where I pickup some bananas and apples, and a laundry where I drop off some underclothes and my only short-sleeved shirt. I'm a little apprehensive about leaving them at a Greek laundry, but the man who takes them is friendly, professional and speaks a little English.

After a walk around the horseshoe cove, staring out at a tiny islet in the smooth-watered bay, I ask about a bus to Stavros, the town in the northern part of the island where Odysseus' castle stood in antiquity, and learn that the bus leaves at eleven.

By mid afternoon and after several hours of waiting, I've been told three conflicting times for the bus to Stavros, 11:00 AM, noon and 1:30 PM. All are wrong. The only bus on the island is now used for school children and no longer available for touristas. Most of today is already gone. I've thought it over and decided tomorrow I'll rent a motorbike and have a day racing around the island creating a little noise myself.

In the meantime, I check my guidebook and trek to the Cave of the Nymphs, where Odysseus first reentered Ithaca after twenty years of being away at Troy and wandering the Greek isles. The cave is four kilometers from the Vathi. The trail starts at the dock in the cove and follows the west coast for two kilometers, then turns south up the mountain.

I walk past a silo-like building that could be a large beautiful home or church off to itself nestled on a hillside among green shrubs and trees. The blacktop road becomes gravel. I hear the clang of bells and soon a herd of goats appears. I climb a mound of earth at the side of the road and motion to the young dark-haired goatherd that I would like to take a picture. The goats rustle past in a close cluster, the dull clank of their bells reflecting their increased pace as they pass. The dank, skunk-like smell of goat.

Houses at the side of the gravel road become more frequent as the scattered trees become a forest. Homes with chickens, barking dogs, piles of used lumber, garbage, tractors, barns, sheep that baaaa as I pass. I see a house on the hill almost hidden by trees with a yard full of chickens, several brown hens and a red rooster. I come upon another house in a hollow so deep the roof is barely visible. I hear dogs in the backyard. These aren't the ordinary "woofs" of civilized dogs.

These are descendants of the Kerberus, hound of the Underworld. According to Hesiod, he was an

> ...unspeakable creature,
> Kerberos, the fifty-headed dog of Hades,
> that mighty and shameless eater of raw flesh,
> whose bark resounds like bronze.[88]

Ithaca

I've read that if you bend down to pickup a rock, the dogs of Greece will turn tail and run. This is to be the supreme test of that hypothesis, so I grab a nice throwing-size rock knowing I can never get all of them. Just as my heart hits maximum rate, those dogs hit the end of their chains, and thus my life is spared for another day when the dogs may have more freedom. The "turning tail" hypothesis is yet to be tested by me. What's perhaps of more concern, the story goes on to say that Kerberus will let you into Hades but won't let you out. I'll encounter these dogs again on the way back.

The world of Hermes is not all theft, murder and lies. When Hermes became an adult god, Zeus made him herald of the gods and patron deity of travelers. He had a special relationship with the Underworld. He was the guide of souls. This transitory nature, moving so easily between life and death, gives his world a sense of suspended animation. He hovers between worlds, brings sleep and dreams.

This was the world Odysseus wandered for ten years, his unwanted journey forced upon him by the sea god Poseidon in his wrath over Odysseus blinding his son, the one-eyed Cyclops, Polyphemus. He encountered strange creatures, the sirens who lure sailors to their death with their song, and was held in love bondage for seven years by the sea nymph Calypso on the island of Ogygia. He eventually even descended to the Underworld. He encountered Hermes from time to time, but Hermes, in his role as protector of travelers, is not persistent in or conscientious about this responsibility. Odysseus' voyage hovered between life and death, sometimes without a helmsman, sometimes at the whim of the wind, sometimes being thrown overboard and swept about by arbitrary sea currents. But his return home was most telling. While in the care of the Phaiakians just north of Ithaca, he fell asleep after boarding the boat that was to bring him home. He slept the entire voyage in a state of exhaustion, as if his dream world finally became literal as he approached his homeland.

When the Phaiakians reached Ithaca, they left Odysseus asleep on the beach. They also left a great treasure bestowed on him by their king. When he woke, Odysseus no longer recognized his homeland and was filled with despair. But gray-eyed Athena, who was always with him in times of trial, came to him disguised as a young shepherd. She wore a cloak off her shoulders and carried a hunting lance. She lifted the mist from Odysseus' eyes so he could see that the land about him was indeed Ithaca. Then Athena helped him hide his treasure in the Cave of the Nymphs just up the mountainside in front of me.

I walk through coves covered with olive trees, old gnarled trunks with fat knuckle-like knots, twisted but strong, green, healthy. The earth is moist, the vegetation lusty. Switchbacks finally bring me to a sign pointing up a stone walkway and promising that the Cave of the Nymphs is further up the mountainside. I'm the only visitor on the road and wonder why others are not at such a famous landmark. The cave and a little green shack are at the top of the walkway. I see why Odysseus needed her help. The cave is two kilometers from the sea.

I see no touristas and no guard at the gate. The place is in fact closed. Standing there with sweat dripping from my brow, my shirt soaked through, I'm terribly disappointed. I'll have to repeat the climb tomorrow. Yet I'm alone with the Cave of the Nymphs. I remember Homer's description of this setting as seen through the eyes of the goddess Athena:

> Here is the cove the sea lord Phorkys owns,
> there is the olive spreading out her leaves
> over the inner bay, and there the cavern
> dusky and lovely, hallowed by the feet
> of those immortal girls, the Naiades--
> the same wide cave under whose vault you came
> to honor them with hekatombs--and there
> Mount Neion, with his forest on his back.[89]

The entrance to the cave is a vertical slit the height of a man, a locked iron gate across it. The opening is lined with large white rocks and gradually closes toward the top. I peer inside, see the floor of the cave dropping into blackness. I take a couple of shots with my camera and come back down the hill considerably disappointed.

As with Oedipus, Odysseus' life becomes another piece of the Rosetta Stone whereby we can again go beyond the limits of firsthand self-knowledge. His journey around the Greek isles occurred at mid-life, a time when many of us wander aimlessly, encountering a bizarre world we no longer understand, blown about our own lives by renegade winds without a helmsman to guide us. When we do finally return home, it's as though we are awakening from a dream. We've been given a great gift that will sustain us for the rest of our days if we accept it. But the return is painful. The world we return to has changed, plundered by those we trusted, and those we love, lured away from us.

I haven't been as lucky as Odysseus. I lost my wife, lost my home, lost my job, lost everything. I can't find my way home, not the one I had before I started drifting.

As I pass the three vicious dogs, I pick up another rock, not caring if they are chained. A man comes up the hill toward me. As we draw closer, I speak my Greek greeting, "Γαια σας," and he asks if I speak English. I tell him that I speak American English and he smiles, says he's German. He's headed to the Cave of the Nymphs. He has on gray shorts, tennis shoes and a short sleeve white shirt. He knows the cave is locked but believes we can get in anyway. I turn around, and we climb the hill together.

He's a doctor and at one time worked for several years in Saudi Arabia where he learned English. He's seventy-two but looks much younger, slim and fit. Though it's not late, the light is fading as the sun falls behind the mountain. The iron gate has a pad lock on the left side which intimidated me, but the right side is totally free. One has but to swing the gate open, which the good doctor does. He crawls through the opening while I attached my camera flash.

> The goddess turned and entered the dim cave,
> exploring it for crannies, while Odysseus
> carried up all the gold, the fire-hard bronze,
> and well-made clothing the Phaiakians gave him.[90]

I follow him in, hunching through the small opening, and hold the cold iron rail as I descend to the first landing. I retrieve my flashlight from my camera pack and flash the walls, dark earth drinking the light. At this landing, the cave is still small but perhaps half again the height of a man and the far wall, five strides into the mountain. To the left, green metal stairs descend steeply.

We allow our eyes to adjust to the darkness, and with me in the lead we descend the stairs. Or at least, I think the doctor is behind me, but when I step from the metal stairs onto the soft earth, he's still at the top peering down. The flashlight worked fine on the stairs and now works better on the dark sides of the cave as my eyes continue to adjust. The ceiling, twenty feet above, has a dim hole through to the outside. I take a few cautious steps further into the room, notice a hole where the floor of the cave falls through, and decide to stay put.

The doctor finally joins me, so I shine the light on the green stairs as he descends. I shine the light around the walls of the room, into recesses that, if explored, might lead to other passageways and other rooms, rooms even darker than this, which my flashlight can barely light. He and I talk of how neither of us would have descended the stairs if we had come alone. We stand for a while watching the beam of light, neither of us willing to proceed along the thin planks that provide a walkway over the hole in the floor, both of us using the courage we find in the presence of another to remain within the cave.

When we leave, he ascends further up the hill, and I descend through dark olive trees with large gnarled trunks, past the vicious but chained dogs, past chickens, sheep and stacks of used lumber, past a flock of black turkeys with huge oval bodies, black feathers and small red heads, turkeys that stand their ground in the middle of the road. They gobble but don't acknowledge my presence there in the deepening shadows of evening. The turkeys and I are on the hillside where Odysseus and the goddess Athena hid his treasure in the Cave of the Nymphs before he went home disguised as a beggar with mass murder on his mind.

As I descend the gravel road down the dark mountain, I think about the German doctor. He would have been twenty-four when World War II ended. He could have fought for six years, fought Americans, killed Americans. Yet we had stood next to each other, used each other's presence to ward off the fear of darkness and the Underworld.

I have dinner at a grill in the plateia, pork slices, a Greek salata and a Sprite. More than I should eat when you consider the mound of French fries and bread. I leave a slice. This is my first food since breakfast. I eat inside watching the fat man cook, spits of chicken turning, lamb and pork sizzling in the background, kids running in and out, women coming to get the family dinner. While the man cooks at the grill, his teenage daughter runs in and sticks two red roses in the top of his T-shirt, throws her arms around his neck. He looks down into her smiling face, his expression never changing. His wife enters and busies herself waiting tables.

A man has moved into the other bedroom just across the entryway. He's from Italy. I hear Verdi blasting from his room. He's short, plump, full of laughter, and has the worst breath I've ever smelled on a human being, saturated with wine and garlic.

I sit at the table in my room writing in my journal. The landlady's daughter stops by on the walkway out front, puts her elbows on the windowsill and says a few words to me. I look out through a pitch-dark evening at lights that line the cove, listen to the rumble of a ferry in the bay, a motorbike up the street and a dog barking in the distance. The window is simply open, the two halves rotated in, the shutters pushed out, no screen. The sky hangs like a black sheet. The air, cool, refreshing. The bay glistens with vertical streaks of bright city lights dancing in its ripples.

Hesiod personified night and placed Night's gloomy home in Hades, the Underworld:

> ...the harmful Night, veiled in dusky fog,
> carries in her arms Sleep, Death's own brother.

Ithaca

There, too, dwell the children of black Night,
Sleep and Death, the awesome gods who are never seen
by the rays of the blazing sun when it rises
on the sky, or moves on its downward path.
Of these, the one wanders over land and broad-backed sea,
ever at peace and ever gentle to mortals,
but the other, a ghoul even the gods detest,
has a heart of iron and feelings hard as bronze,
and no man gripped by him can free himself again.[91]

The night I went to bed with Fred, shortly after I drifted off to sleep, I woke suddenly. Fred had hold of me, hands tight on my hips. His head was at my bellybutton, his face working down into private territory, his breath hot and rapid under the covers. I remember the frightening strength of his hands. I spoke his name with a tone of irritation, and he released me and turned quickly away. I laid there with a strange feeling creeping over me. Had I been dreaming? Was Fred really doing something sexual? I finally dismissed his conduct as some sort of sleep aberration and went back to sleep myself. That was the only incident during the night, although now it seems he may have made another attempt. I was asleep, and thirty-two years is a long time.

Early the next morning, our young cousin's father called my father complaining about the "after dinner snacks," as my uncle put it, that Fred had been soliciting down the hall the night before. What followed is the most bizarre episode of my life. My father called my brother into the living room and asked if what our young cousin had said was true, if blowjobs had been on Fred's desert menu. My brother confirmed it with a sinking look in his eyes like the life had just drained out of him. The word "blowjob" lay on the floor like a writhing snake.

For the second time in two months, my father and I stood in the living room confronting a life and death situation. I was facing the hall in the direction of my brother, who was facing me, his eyes vacant but water filled. My older cousin, the fighter, was standing to my right, finger tips in the tops of his Levis. My father had just come from talking on the telephone in the kitchen and was standing to my left with my mother standing in the kitchen doorway behind him. No words can describe the emotional state of my father. As for me, I had just passed into a strange surrealistic world from which a part of me has never returned. The realization that my father had been right about not allowing Fred in our home fell on me like a deathblow.

Fred was down the hall still in my bedroom. My father turned to me and made the strangest request I've ever had made of me. The look in his eyes was that of a rabid dog. "Let's kill him," he said, already leaning toward the hall. I felt a surge of emotion go through my body, powerful enough to dim the light in my eyes. I almost fainted. I had but to make a move forward, and he and I would rush down the hall and kill a man I had known for two full years and until that instant had considered my friend. My response was immediate, impulsive and I've regretted it ever since.

"No, Dad, let's not kill him."

I've never understood why my words stopped my father. He looked confused, disoriented. "What should we do with him then?" he asked, as if since we weren't going to kill him, he had no idea what to do. I felt our roles switch, me the father, he the son. "Get him out of here," I said. Then my older cousin, standing to my right, took a step forward. "I'll get rid of him" he said. "And if he won't go, I'll beat the shit out of him." My father agreed to this. "Okay," he said, you two get rid of him. If I go in there, I'll kill him."

We did. My cousin and I walked to the back bedroom where Fred and I had slept together, and we told Fred in no uncertain terms he was no longer welcome in our home. Fred didn't seem concerned at all. He nonchalantly started packing his suitcase, folding his clothes like maybe that afternoon sometime he'd leave. "You don't understand, you dumb cocksucker," my cousin told him. "Your life is in danger. Get the hell out of here." Still he packed in what seemed like slow motion. After he got his clothes in his suitcase, he was going to walk out through the living room, but we shoved him out the back door.

I was in the living room, living the reality of the disaster I'd created, when my father went to the window and in a quivering voice, told Fred as he opened his car door that he could just as easily be leaving with a bullet in him, and if he ever came back again, he would personally put one in him. My father was like a lion with his fresh kill resurrected and still on the hoof in front of him.

If he'd known the full truth, he would have killed Fred and no words from me could have stopped him. But if I had known the full truth, I would have too, or at least when I did find out I thought so.

★

The wind howls tonight. I hear it in the olive trees, brushing and twisting them. I hear singing, faint voices from the church. They're carried by the wind, or is it just the sound of the wind? They're louder now. Yes, they're voices. The many voices of the wind.

18 Oct, Tuesday

I wake early, well before dawn, dreaming of a woman with a hard life in a traveling circus. I try to help her. Perhaps it's the four-day stands in each Greek town that reminds me of a circus. I'm not sleeping well, but I feel well if a little confused. The roosters are confused too. They've been at it all night.

I feel safe here in Greece, and I've found a new courage in traveling alone. I accept rides from strangers, take buses and ferries to places I've never been and where I don't even speak the language. The doors and windows to my room remain unlocked at night. I leave all my valuables on the tabletop. But I'm concerned that my landlady might put another person in here with me since the room has two beds. I don't want to share a room with a man.

I rise early, make a breakfast of fruit, and eagerly descend the mountain to rent a motorbike. At the rental agency, a weasel of a man who speaks no English interrogates me by holding up a cardboard sign containing several questions in English, the last of which is, "Have you ever operated a motorbike?" He motions with his hands to show that the road is steep and has sharp turns. I answer the questions, assuring him I will go slow, but I've never operated a motorbike. He backs off like I'm a leper. "Οχι!" he shouts, turns his back and walks away leaving me standing among shiny new motorcycles, dirt bikes and a row of dilapidated motor scooters. I wonder what he is so pissed about? You'd think I was trying to steal one instead of rent it. I don't need his protection.

I've retrieved my underclothes and shirt from the cleaners and everything is very professionally cleaned. At least something has gone right today, but to get to the site of the ancient city of Odysseus, I decide to try a taxi. I negotiate with a huge dark Greek who worked as a cook in New York City for several years and speaks excellent English. He won't budge and wants to charge me 2500 dr ($10.80) one-way. After trying to talk to another taxi driver who doesn't even have the time to mess with me, I accept the first taxi driver's offer. I'll have to find my own ride back. "Won't be a problem," he says.

Being in an automobile again is a treat in itself. I feel as though I'm in a hang glider hovering above the skinny spine of the isthmus with the ocean far below on each side of the car. We arrive in Stavros, a sleepy little village on a hill overlooking a bay. After I pay him, my driver walks toward an outdoor restaurant to visit with a small group of locals sitting in the shade.

I walk across the street to a small park with a slide for kids and shaded by huge trees. A whitewashed pedestal with a larger-than-life bust of Odysseus stands in the center of the park. The figure is older than the pedestal, chiseled from brown stone. Bearded Odysseus stares sternly out to sea as if he regrets his return. An inscription is imbedded in the pedestal: ΕΥΧΗΝ ΟΔΥΧΧΕΙ, Bless Odysseus.

In Homer's *Iliad*, Priam the king of Troy asks Helen about one of the Greek generals as he views their army from within the walls of Troy:

> "Tell me, dear child,
> who is that officer? The son of Atreus Agamemnon
> stands a head taller, but this man appears
> to have a deeper chest and broader shoulders.
> His gear lies on the ground, but still he goes
> like a bellwether up and down the ranks.
> A ram I'd call him, burly, thick with fleece,
> keeping a flock of silvery sheep in line.
> Helen shaped by heaven answered him:
> "That is Laertes' son, the great tactician
> Odysseus. He was bred on Ithaka,
> a bare and stony island, but he knows
> all manner of stratagems and moves in war."[92]

Antenor, a respected Trojan elder of conservative temperament standing with Priam and Helen, then told them of meeting Odysseus years before when he came to Troy with Menelaus seeking the return of Helen. Antenor describes the encounter:

> "Once long ago he came here, great Odysseus,
> with Menelaos—came to treat of you.
> They were my guests, and I made friends of both
> and learned their stratagems and characters.
> Among us Trojans, in our gatherings, Menelaos,
> broad in the shoulders likewise, overtopped him;
> seated, Odysseus looked the kinglier man.
> When each of them stood up to make his plea,
> his argument before us all, then Menelaos
> said a few words in a rather headlong way,
> but clearly, not long-winded and not vague;
> and indeed he was the younger of the two.
> Then in his turn the great tactician rose
> and stood and looked at the ground,
> moving the staff before him not at all
> forward or backward; obstinate and slow
> of wit he seemed, gripping the staff; you'd say
> some surly fellow, with an empty head.

But when he launched the strong voice from his chest,
and words came driving on the air as thick
and fast as winter snowflakes, then Odysseus
could have no mortal rival as an orator!
The look of him no longer made us wonder."[93]

I hear a clip-clop behind me, a donkey coming up a trail from the east with a man riding sidesaddle. The man dwarfs the donkey, but the donkey looks stout, unstressed by his oversized burden. The man wears a dark shirt and pants, has a shiny gold wristwatch. He has a black mustache and gray hair underneath a black fisherman's cap. He looks at me as the donkey walks past, the man's expression grave, unchanging.

After Athena and Odysseus stored his treasure in the cave of the Nymphs, she disguised him in the manners and dress of a beggar, so he might return to his kingdom incognito. He entered his fields surreptitiously to regain the confidence of his goatherd and son, and to have them help him slay his wife's suitors. He left the cove, took a stony trail, and walked to the high hills where his trustworthy swineherd lived. From him, Odysseus learned of his wife's fidelity and also met his son, who had grown into a young man during the twenty years Odysseus was away. Telemachus was wide-eyed, awed at the sight of his father. Penelope had resisted the suitors for three years by saying she would choose another husband when she finished weaving a shroud for her would-be father-in-law. She wove the shroud during the day and unwove it at night.

After looking around Stavros, I trek down the road to the southwest of the village, where I've heard the remains of the ancient Mycenaean port city sit in a cove called Κολπος Πολι, which translates literally as Bay City. The road winds down several switchbacks. I find the beach, windswept and deserted except for a lone man in a red swimsuit coming out of the water alongside a wood dock. He has black hair and a deep tan. I speak to him in Greek. "I'm sorry," he says. "I only speak English."

He's young, early twenties, and from South Africa. He's staying in Ithaca with his grandmother, who has lived on the island for twenty years. I ask him if he knows where I can find the ruins of the ancient city, and he tells me it was visible until 1953 when it submerged during a tremendous earthquake. He points out into the water. "It's out there," he says, "fifty feet down." He's been swimming in the bay but discourages me from doing so because of the trash blown in by the stiff breeze. "The water's filthy," he says.

He wants to walk with me back to Stavros, so I look around the cove while he changes clothes on the dock. Beyond the small beach, the land is covered with hay and slopes gradually up toward Stavros.

When we get to Stavros, he introduces me to one of the restaurant owners who also drives the town's taxi. I make an appointment to meet him at the restaurant at five o'clock, shake hands with the young man from South Africa, and walk up a side street to the town's small museum which sits on the site where archeologists believe Odysseus' castle stood.

Odysseus and his son plotted the murder of his wife's suitors, then left for his palace, entering separately so as not to draw attention. Outside the gates, Odysseus saw the dog he had trained as a puppy twenty years before. The old dog lay on a dung pile full of flies. Upon seeing his master after twenty years, he wagged his tail once and died. Odysseus entered his castle:

> ...Odysseus came
> through his own doorway as a mendicant,
> humped like a bundle of rags over his stick.
> He settled on the inner ashwood sill,
> leaning against the doorjamb—cypress timber
> the skilled carpenter planed years ago
> and set up with a plumbline.[94]

The museum is a converted wood house, and as I open the screen door, I hear a flood of Greek coming from two women sitting at a table inside. One of them, the large pretty one, is the museum's curator and also from South Africa, although she doesn't know the grandmother of the young man I just met down in the cove. She immigrated to Ithaca several years ago, but is not as thrilled with the island as she thought she would be after the new wore off. A Greek woman is visiting with her. The museum has no patrons other than me and I'm the only one today. She is, in fact, about to close for the day and for the year.

She tells me to take a seat, the only other chair in the room, and pumps me for information about myself. She's thrilled I can speak a little Greek and has me say a few words of hello to the Greek woman who smiles sheepishly. "She's embarrassed because she speaks no English," the fat lady says. The Greek woman then leaves and the curator talks to me before showing me around the small museum. "It's seldom I get a tourist who knows something about Greek mythology," she says. "I usually have to tell them the story of Odysseus and they never understand the significance of the artifacts. Tell me about yourself. What's your profession?"

She gives me a guided tour of the museum, explaining where the artifacts were found, pausing longer on those from the Mycenaean period, the age of

Odysseus. She stops at one shard, saying, "This is the only evidence connecting Odysseus with the island." She points to a small gray piece of pottery with the faint words "Bless Odysseus" in ancient Greek. "This is the most important artifact ever found on the island." She apologizes several times for not allowing me to take pictures. "It's forbidden," she says begging forgiveness with sad cocker spaniel eyes.

As I pick up my daypack and camera case, she follows me to the door. "Wait for me to lock up," she says. "I'll drive you back to Stavros." She has trouble setting the alarm. "It's new but more trouble than it's worth. The wind sets it off." As she drives back to town, she wants to know more of my work as an aerospace engineer, so I tell her of the NASA earth-imaging radar that I coordinated with the Germans and the Italians for three years and that is supposed to go into orbit with the Space Shuttle next April. When she reaches the center of Stavros, she stops her VW beetle in the shade of a large olive tree. "You're a man of some importance," she says, "aren't you?" "Not really," I reply. "I'm unemployed." We shake hands, but she won't turn mine loose. "You've had a long career in aerospace, worked on very important programs. You are a man of considerable importance."

When she finally lets go, I walk off wondering why she needed me to be so important but reveling in the praise she heaped on me. It's nice to go from a man who can't even rent a motorbike to one "of considerable importance," all in a matter of hours.

★

I sit outside a little restaurant in Stavros sipping a 7 Up, sitting under a canopy that protects me from the bright sun of Ithaca. A 330 ml 7 Up here cost 250 dr ($1.09) and the two pieces of Greek cake, called ροβανι (rovani), were 700 dr. Sitting in the warm shade watching the sun bake the brushwood on the hillsides, I realize I am very tired. I put my head down on the table and nap right where I sit.

After sizing up the threat from his wife's suitors and even testing her faithfulness, Odysseus strung his bow, nodded to his son and put an arrow through the leader's throat, thus starting the blood bath. Homer describes the first suitor's death:

> Backward and down he went, letting the wine cup fall
> from his shocked hand. Like pipes his nostrils jetted
> crimson runnels, a river of mortal red,
> and one last kick upset his table
> knocking the bread and meat to soak in dusty blood.[95]

Ithaca

Following the slaughter of the suitors, on the steps of the palace, he hanged twelve of Penelope's female servants, the fair maids who had slept with them on the quiet:

He tied one end of a hawser to a pillar
and passed the other about the roundhouse top,
taking the slack up, so that no one's toes
could touch the ground. They would be hung like doves
or larks in springes triggered in a thicket,
where the birds think to rest—a cruel nesting.
So now in turn each woman thrust her head
into a noose and swung, yanked high in air,
to perish there most piteously.
Their feet danced for a little, but not long.[96]

Thus was justice served by Odysseus 3200 years ago near what is today Stavros, island of Ithaca. Odysseus took their lives as easily as Hermes turned the old man to stone. Penelope, Helen's cousin, had proven herself the most faithful of women, and her name is synonymous with fidelity to this day.

★

In the late afternoon with the sun casting long shadows, I wait for my taxi back to Vathi. I fight the flies for my dinner at the little restaurant across the street. A very good cheese omelet (a real omelet this time) with German sausage, two slices of tomato, several wedges of cucumber and toast. A big black and white tomcat glares at me from under a nearby table.

Finally the taxi driver comes. On the drive back, he says you have to milk the goats, and chickens too, to make ends meet in Ithaca. His son is in the Greek army and his daughter works. He says that Ithaca is overrun by tourists in the summer. The patio in front of his restaurant has fifty chairs. He says it's packed in the summer. I was the only customer today.

Ithaca is a beautiful island. Before I came, I had heard it was all rocks, but it's covered with trees and bushes. In places, it's absolutely lush. We travel the spine of the island. At its narrowest, it's just 700 meters across with 300 meters of steep-sloping hillside to the water below on each side of the road, frightening with a Greek at the wheel. Before I left Colorado my Greek tutor told me what to expect. "They're all first generation drivers," she said.

In early evening with a light wind rustling leaves along the dark cement stairs, I return to my room. The stairs start one block off the main road along the dock. They come in sets of four with a gentle slope of cement path in between. Twenty-two sets of these steps and slopes make two forty-five degree turns. I'm huffing and puffing. Then comes a steep cement walkway, laterally grooved for traction. This slope is ninety-six strides with no turns. Next, a turn to the left, twenty-five more stair steps to the front of the church, another left turn under the shade of tall oak trees and a very gentle slope of gravel that levels off to twenty meters of shaded alley behind homes. I've broken a good sweat. Then back into the sunlight and a sharp right turn up four steps through a green metal gate beside the home where I stay, another set of eight steps, a 180 degree turn and up another set of four steps to the balcony. One more right turn and I'm there, high above the sea and town which are both visible through olive trees. Purple and yellow snapdragons line the walkway, and pink and blue periwinkles border the steps. Through my window, I see a bush of pure-white roses winding up from below.

I stand on the dark balcony, looking out at the lights of the cove far below us. The daughter joins me. We share a few words through my halting Greek. After standing with me for a while, she walks around the corner of the house, down a short flight of steps to the patio, and the mother comes up to replace her. She takes my hand in both hers, holds it to her bosom like it's something precious. I'm not sure even my own mother has ever displayed such warm affection toward me. "Τι κανετε?" she asks. "Καλα, εσεις?" I respond.

She invites me down to the patio to sit in the dark and look out over the lights of the plateia. She shoves a bowl of grapes in front of me, fresh off the vines above our heads, while telling me of her new boarder, the Italian with the bad breath.

I plan to leave Ithaca early in the morning, so I pay my bill. My room is more expensive than I thought. They charge me 8,500 dr ($36.95) for three nights. The room was 2,500 per night instead of 2,000 as I had been told. What the extra 1,000 is for I don't know, and I don't speak enough Greek to find out. They must be charging me for the grapes and the cocoa, possibly even the dab of preserves they served the night I first arrived, maybe even the well water. The daughter takes care of the finances, but she doesn't have correct change. She owes me 500 dr. She tells me she will give me change after dinner. I think about her words for a while and wonder if she's telling me to bring change after I eat dinner. But I've already eaten. I won't have the time to solve this problem in the morning because the ferry back to Patras is at 7:00 AM. The mother gets a plastic bottle of well water for me, says "καλινιχτα" and they retire for the evening, leaving me alone on the patio.

★

Ithaca

The afternoon following Fred's sudden and forced departure, my cousin's young wife got the rest of the story out of my brother. During his trip to Disneyland, Fred had repeatedly raped him. Fred had threatened my brother, said if he told anyone what he was doing to him, he would kill him. The threat and the demand for sex had been repeated down the hall the previous night. Fred told my brother, "I know you think you could hide from me, but if you ever tell anyone, I'll kill you even if it's twenty years from now." What had happened down the hall the night before was not as I perceived it. Fred wasn't cutting up with those two kids.

After the full story came out, my father was angry that I had stopped him from killing Fred, but he didn't hold a grudge. We decided my cousin and I would go to Bakersfield, find Fred and "beat the living shit out of him." This would be my chance to redeem myself. My mother was against us going and kept saying, "Don't kill him. He's not worth ruining your lives over."

On the way to Bakersfield, I suffered from the highest anxiety of my life. I was the embodiment of a scream that couldn't come out. I didn't want to beat up Fred. I didn't feel angry. I was terrified. But we couldn't find Fred, and finally, at my urging, we went to the police. They picked him up the next day. They couldn't prosecute him for molesting my brother because he was fifteen and beyond the age where molestation laws applied. Homosexual rape didn't exist then. The crucial factor was his threat on my brother's life. But they could get the son of a bitch deported. And they did. It just took a little longer than I expected.

★

I go to sleep early, but shortly a commotion outside awakens me. I hear kids' voices and people moving about inside the house. People shouting. A motorbike buzzes the neighborhood.

I've been dreaming of Romania. The friends I met in Athens wanted me to visit them in Bucharest. I'm afraid of my dreams and what they might mean for me in the future, what kind of trouble my newfound courage might get me into. I turn on the light to write in my journal.

Hermes is the god who brings sleep, opens the world of dreams and wakes us in the morning. A close association exists between the world of sleep and the Underworld, and Hermes is comfortable in both. In his role as guide of souls, Hermes took responsibility for Penelope's suitors after they departed earth and led them along the misty path to their new home:

> ...the suitors' ghosts were called away
> by Hermes of Kyllene, bearing the golden wand

92

with which he charms the eyes of men or wakens
who he wills.
            He waved them on, all squeaking
as bats will in a cavern's underworld,
all flitting, flitting crisscross in the dark
if one falls and the rock-hung chain is broken.
So with faint cries the shades trailed after Hermes,
pure Deliverer.
            He led them down dank ways,
over gray Ocean tides, the Snowy Rock,
past shores of Dream and narrows of the sunset,
in swift flight to where the dead inhabit
wastes of asphodel at the world's end.[97]

Homer doesn't mention what happened to the souls of the fair maids.

Roosters start crowing. I hear at least six at varying distances from me, including one just outside. Perhaps it's the light from my window confusing them. The one closest to me started it all.

Slowly, they give it up.

                                                    19 Oct, Wednesday
My wristwatch alarm goes off at 6 AM, and as I surface from the sea of sleep, I realize someday I will be dead, this consciousness I call myself will be nonexistent. The realization is profound and comes as a stroke of enlightenment. This is not a normal intellectual awareness that someday I will die, but some deep primordial, perhaps cosmic, understanding. I've had it before, but this morning it seems to have a special relation to my journey, as if I've already experienced a death of sorts, and now I'm unattached, drifting in space. My journey is simply an earthly manifestation of what has already occurred internally. Though I'm not frightened, I have a consuming sense of loss.

But I'm up a little late for my leisurely pace, and suddenly I'm frantic to finish packing. After zipping my backpack, I sit on the edge of the bed, hurriedly slipping on my socks and hiking boots and realizing I'd better get a move on or I'll miss the ferry.

The sun is not quite up, and lights from inside the ferry hold glow through the darkness as I walk the gangway. I stand in the cavernous hold, breathing fumes from cars, trucks and motorbikes while the ticket agent takes my money and issues my slip of paper so I can board. I already miss Ithaca. It's much different than I'd been told. It's so green, not Ireland mind you, but green by

Greek standards.

When Helen of Sparta, the world's most beautiful woman, became of marriageable age, suitors besieged her. Her father was afraid his daughter's choice would cause a fight among those she had rejected. The suitors were full of murderous feelings toward one another. Odysseus was one of Helen's suitors, but realizing she would undoubtedly pick Agamemnon's wealthy brother Menelaus, he struck a bargain with her father. Odysseus, the man of many wiles, suggested he make all the suitors vow to defend Helen's chosen husband against any harm, which would come to him because of his marriage. Her father took Odysseus' advice and in return saw to it Odysseus received Penelope, Helen's cousin, as his own bride. Penelope was the epitome of loyalty and fidelity. Not so Helen.

The vow binding Helen's suitors soon became the active force that would unite the Greek kingdoms in war against Troy. Paris, a prince of Troy, came to Sparta on a visit, and stole Helen. Even though she went willingly, Menelaus held the suitors to their vow. Odysseus wasn't interested in leaving Ithaca to fight a war, so he feigned insanity. When the herald came to Ithaca to get him, they found him wearing the headgear of a madman and sewing salt with a horse and an ox yoked to his plow.[98] They took him anyway.

My path will cross Odysseus' again when I get to Troy, but now I'm headed to Olympia, where the Olympic games originated almost three thousand years ago. Oedipus' father, Laios, was raised there, and there he kidnapped Pelop's illegitimate son, Chrysippus.

The winds I heard last night out my window work the sea today. The ferry rocks from side to side, and I hear waves breaking on the bow. I go out on deck and talk to a man from Holland who's traveling with his wife.

I thought they were Americans because of their blond hair and flashy clothes, hi-tech running shoes. They both have huge backpacks. This is the second time they've been to Greece. They've been here two weeks and are leaving for Holland Thursday. He tells me some experts believe Kefallonia is the Ithaca of antiquity, not the island I just visited. We stand at the rail with the brisk breeze blowing our hair, watching Ithaca float past and Kefallonia drift into view. The sea calms as we come closer to port. They exit the ferry.

The ferry is full of dark-haired, olive-skinned Greeks. Most Greeks do not lose their hair, it simply turns gray and even that, late in life. The many families onboard are a mixture of old people and younger family members. They travel as a group. Rarely do I see a lone Greek. The Lone Ranger, whom I grew up listening to on the radio, was not Greek. Before I left Colorado I was told by some Greek friends that Greeks are very affectionate with each other, that they hug, kiss and shake hands a lot, and that they argue constantly. I've not seen it.

Ithaca

Men sit around a small open bar in the middle of the enclosed passenger area, sipping Greek coffee from tiny plastic cups. Every time the waiter makes a coffee, the machine sounds like a man clearing his throat, but louder, more drawn out. I sit close to the front of the ferry, this time in the no smoking section. I didn't realize it had one.

After a short noontime nap I walk out on deck again, and the waves have grown considerably. I eat a ham and cheese sandwich standing at the rail. The air is cool. I see white caps on sea waves and the mountains of the Peloponnese in the distance. My next trial will be to catch the train in Patras for Pirgos. From there, the train will take me to Olympia, where I'll spend two days before going on to Sparta, the home of Helen and Menelaus. After Sparta, I'll visit Mycenae, the home of Agamemnon, the man who sacrificed his daughter for favorable winds so the Greeks could sail to Troy.

Perhaps by nightfall I'll be within the modern city of Olympia.

A fine sea spray hits my face. A young woman in shorts suns herself. She pulls her blouse down her large breasts to the top of her nipples. She has an eight-inch surgery scar on the inside of her right knee. This is my first taste of rough water and only a premonition of what the weather can do in the Aegean during the months of November and December. I have Dramamine in my first aid kit, but no medication can cure my perception of the sea. It reminds me of death.

The recognition of my own death I had this morning doesn't connect with what was going on inside me when I had the confrontation with my father. I still don't know what I felt then. And here I want to draw a clear distinction between thoughts and feelings. I do not mean what I was thinking at the time; I mean feeling: fear, anger, hurt, whatever I was feeling at the instant I heard him click that deer rifle.

Not long after the events of that summer, I got married, joined the Air Force. Two kids followed shortly thereafter. I was a happily married man for eighteen years, until six months before I turned forty, my wife suddenly left me. From her departure onward, I've been adrift. During the last twelve years, I've been like Oedipus, an old blind man wandering about the countryside. I've also been like Odysseus, unattached, floating free on a bewildering internal odyssey, but unlike Odysseus, I haven't found my way home. I learned something important when I was back in Delphi. My home is on the road. Is this the home I've been searching for these last twelve years? This is a true task for Hermes. Gently, he comes with his golden staff gleaming, the swift ghostherd leading the newly dead along the misty path home to the Underworld.

I leave the large-breasted girl and watch the crew in their deep-blue uniforms manning the helm. My eyes are attracted to the compass, the boat's sense of direction. They always know where they're going, but I'm like Odysseus on his way to the Underworld without a helmsman and blown about wherever the north wind carries me.

The white buildings of Patras come up fast, with the mountains of the Peloponnese looming behind them. The ferry gives a blast from its horn as we enter port. Shortly we'll be at dockside.

CHAPTER 5: Olympia.

I planned to take the train from Patras to Olympia but will have to wait three hours, so I take the bus instead. This time we have assigned seats, and guess who isn't in the right one and causes all the commotion? After they get me straightened out, everything goes smoothly although the intolerable heat inside the bus causes me to drip in sweat. The bus travels south among the small villages of the western coast, narrow streets, winding roads, olive orchards, orange orchards, mountains, horns, horns, horns.

At Pirgos, the capitol of Elis Nome, I change buses. The bus stations I've seen in Greece have been old, dingy, dirty, colorless. This is no exception. I grab a pack of peanuts and a soft drink and stand among crowds of cigarette-smoking, coffee-drinking men with suffering, country faces sitting at tables sandwiched into the room. I spot a young couple, tall, thin, good-looking kids in their late twenties, speaking English with a Greek. Their blond hair stands out like a beacon in deep darkness. I can't keep my eyes off them.

As we enter the shaky old local bus, I pick a seat beside them and strike up a conversation. Hans and Margo are from Holland, just south of Amsterdam. They speak excellent but heavily accented English. I spend the few minutes it takes to traverse the seventeen kilometers to Olympia telling them about my two-day visit to their hometown six years ago. I had a woman with me then, my last real relationship, and talking with this couple from Holland brings back that trip and increases my sense of loneliness on this one. What I wouldn't give to have a woman sharing this journey with me.

The Greek at the bus station had good words about the Pension Poseidon in Olympia, so when the bus drops us at the side of the street, we exit together and walk along main street looking for it.

Olympia is a one street town, a two-lane highway with cross streets, full of pensions and small gift shops. The Pension Poseidon is at the end of one of these small cross streets, two blocks from the highway. How these world-famous towns can be so small still amazes me. I could walk the entire length of Olympia in five minutes.

According to myth, Zeus wrestled his father, old Kronos, here at Olympia to become the god of both immortals and men. He instituted the Olympic games to honor the event. The gods then held the first games, during which Apollo beat Hermes in the footrace and Ares at boxing.[99]

The ancient Greeks were fond of festivals, and of all the ones held throughout the country, few attained Pan-Hellenic scope, but the grandest of all was here at Olympia: the Olympic Festival, which included sacrifices, feasting and the athletic contests from which we derive our modern Olympic Games. Ancient Olympia was both a religious and sports complex. Sacrifices were made to the "Twelve Gods," who constituted a corporate body ruling earth. They were Zeus, Hera, Poseidon, Demeter, Apollo, Artemis, Ares, Aphrodite, Hermes, Athena, Hephaestus, and Hestia.[100] Other gods and goddesses were loosely grouped to one of the twelve.[101]

After a quick shower and change of clothes, I exit the pension hearing Hans and Margo in the shower together talking and laughing, the sounds of splashing water warbling their words. I walk past the door feeling jealous and thinking how long it's been since I took a shower with a woman.

I take a quick walk across a bridge over the quiet Alphaios River, which flows like a mighty torrent in the spring, to the ruins of the ancient city. The countryside around Olympia is low, wooded hills covered with deciduous trees and farms. The ruins are just closing and will reopen at seven-thirty tomorrow morning, but I didn't plan to visit them this afternoon anyway. I've come to see a hill close by.

The Hill of Kronos overlooks the archaeological site, and was occupied in prehistoric times, as early as 1900 BC.[102] Kronos was the son of Gaia and Uranus, Earth and Heaven, from whom all the other gods descended. As at Delphi, Olympia was originally the site of Gaia's sanctuary here on the southern slope of the hill. Both her daughter Rhea and her granddaughter Hera were also worshipped here, a hill dedicated to goddesses.

I climb the slope through thick dark pines, my feet crunching on cones in the soft earth. The trees are so thick, it's as if darkness has fallen. I stop at a small clearing and gaze over the ruins of ancient Olympia in the plain below, the silence broken by the flutter and tweet of finches bedding down in the pines. I've climbed this hill to look over the site I'll see tomorrow, and to pay tribute to Gaia at the place where her sanctuary stood thousands of years ago. I'm becoming increasingly aware of the role goddesses played in the advancement of civilization and wondering about their replacement by male deities. Was this a trend all over ancient Greece?

Olympia

On the way back, I meet Hans and Margo, window-shopping and arguing over some gold jewelry she wanted. They look rejuvenated beyond what a simple shower could accomplish, and invite me to join them for dinner. We decide on a large outdoor restaurant sparsely populated with patrons. Before our food is served, the wind comes up, forcing us to don our sweaters.

Being around these two reinforces how isolated I am from world events. It's only been three weeks, yet I've dropped off into a strange internal world of mythology and personal history. They've just entered Greece and are full of information. I immediately question them about the turmoil in Russia that I heard about while in Athens. They tell me Yeltzen stormed the Russian White House and imprisoned his Communist and extreme nationalist foes. The crisis is over for the present. They have unsettling information about the US. A dozen US troops have been killed in Somalia and scores wounded. The humanitarian effort is in jeopardy and the public demanding withdrawal. Clinton is also considering invading Haiti because the military has refused to allow deposed president Aristide reentry into Haiti to restore the civilian democracy. The Justice Minister has been assassinated and violence is spreading.

The waiter interrupts to set our dinner on the table, and during the lull in the conversation, I reflect on how far from home I am. I feel a little guilty being in Greece with all the trouble at home. All this news of war is unsettling. The darkness around our outdoor restaurant in Olympia pulls in about me.

For dinner they both have mousaka, a baked lasagna-like dish with eggplant and a custard topping. I've ordered a skimpy dinner of fruit, bread and coffee. I look greedily at their meal while trying to understand why I should feel guilty about being in Greece. My father used to call me when he was having problems on the farm. Even though I had a wife and two kids and a good job in aerospace, he thought I should drop everything and run home to keep him from losing the farm, something he thought impending every summer.

While we eat, they continue to bombard me with current events. The Nobel Peace Prize has gone to Mandela and De Klerk in South Africa and that for literature to Toni Morrison of the US. I feel as though I've been living in a Black Hole.

★

At midnight I lie in bed in the Pension Poseidon with music drifting into my room from the disco across the street, hoping it closes soon so I can sleep. The music stops suddenly, and a rooster crows. His hoarse voice rattles like the bus I came in on, lofts a little, cracks and stops. A rooster with a broken larynx.

20 Oct, Wednesday

Olympia

I sit on the edge of a huge shaped stone in the middle of the temple of Zeus, among the ruins of ancient Olympia. The site lies to the north of the Alphios River, where it comes together with its tributary the Kaladeos. Both rivers have frequently overflowed their banks and changed direction through the centuries, destroying and covering the ruins with silt.

I came here early this morning, before eight o'clock, and had the site to myself. The sun had mounted the surrounding peaks, night's darkness just lifting from among the trees. The sky was the clearest of any morning I've been in Greece. Yesterday's wind cleaned the cool air and left a dewy gloss on the grass.

But already the sun is hot on my face, and its glare is blinding me. I wish I had a hat. To the south, the blue silhouette of a mountain range defines the horizon. To the west, a mountain rises up out of the plain, white homes dotting its ridge. Olive trees, oak trees, evergreens populate the ruin-strewn landscape. The earth is parched and dusty. Dead wildflowers occupy the space between stones, their thin stalks supporting barren shells of seedless pods.

Behind me, ruins butt up against the foot of dome-shaped Kronos Hill. I feel dwarfed sitting among the monoliths. Before me, a huge circular stone stands on edge, flat as a table and one third of it buried in earth. For one hundred yards in any direction I see the same thing, huge clumps of stones in the disarray caused by earthquakes and plundering.

Tourists begin to infiltrate the site. A teacher lectures a group of two-dozen French school children as they pass before me. Behind them, another group and yet another, all speaking French, all carrying backpacks and notebooks.

The religious center was known as Altis, the sacred grove of Zeus. Altis contained temples to many gods and goddesses, the most significant of which were dedicated to Hera and Zeus. Though Zeus' temple, where I now sit, came to be the religious center, Hera's temple was here first, being built around 600 BC. In her temple, Hera sat on the throne and Zeus stood beside her as a supplicant in beard and helmet.[103] Clearly Zeus, as Hera's husband, was a latecomer to Altis, as Kronos had been to what we know now as the Hill of Kronos.

Hera, the granddaughter of Gaia, was by far the most gloriously beautiful of all the goddesses.[104] She was the goddess of monogamous marriage, who raged over her husband's infidelities. Hera was older than Zeus and chose him, her youngest brother, as her husband as soon as he was born.[105] They were married on Mt. Kithaeron[106] where Oedipus would later be exposed by his parents. Zeus seduced Hera by transforming himself into a cuckoo, a bird who lays its eggs in other birds' nests.[107] He performed a similar act here at Olympia by replacing Hera as the primary deity at the site. The two children of Hera and Zeus were Hephaestus, the physically deformed god of arts and crafts, and Ares, the gigantic god of war. The rest of Zeus' children were illegitimate and the cause of Hera's rage.

Other than the famous statues, the primary object inside Hera's temple was a cedar chest. Pausanias describes it:

> There is a cedar-wood chest with figure on it in ivory and gold, and carvings in the cedar-wood itself. ...the figures on the chest have inscriptions in ancient lettering, ...the chest has the following decorative scheme. Oinomaos is chasing Pelops who has Hippodameia...Those daring to box are Admetos and Mopsos Manto's son... Menelaos in a breast-plate with a sword is coming at Helen to murder her, obviously at the fall of Troy. ... There are the sons of Oedipus: Polyneikes has fallen on one knee and Eteokles is coming at him. Behind Eteokles stands a woman with ferocious teeth like a wild beast and curved nails on her fingers; the inscription calls her Doom, as Polyneikes is being carried off by destiny, and Eteocles is dying as he deserves.[108]

These inscriptions depicting legends of places I've visited are only a small part of the cedar chest's decorations. Cedar chests always remind me of my mother's. It's a large object, but contains no such inscriptions or designs. My mother keeps it in her bedroom and fills it with valuables as well as things she wants to hide, like Christmas presents. She keeps birth certificates, old family photographs, baby shoes and spoons, report cards, school pictures, and letters from her family. My father also keeps a few things there; his two pistols are what I remember most, occasionally a rifle. I always welcomed the sharp smell of cedar when the lid swung open.

Pausanias doesn't mention what was inside Hera's cedar chest.

Zeus' temple replaced Hera's in importance. The most significant work of art in his temple was a statue of a forty-foot Zeus seated on his throne made of ivory and gold (long since stolen from the site), sculpted by the Athenian, Phidias.

> The god is sitting on a throne; he is made of gold and ivory. There is a wreath on his head like twigs and leaves of olive; in his right hand he is holding a Victory of gold and ivory with a ribbon and a wreath on her head; in the god's left hand is a staff in blossom with every kind of precious metal, and the bird perching on this staff is Zeus' eagle. The god's sandals are gold and so is his cloak, and the cloak is inlaid with animals and flowering lilies. The throne is finely worked with gold and gems, and with

ebony and with ivory.[109]

The statue, one of the seven wonders of the ancient world, was confiscated and taken to Constantinople, where it burned in a palace fire in the 5th Century AD.

I sit on the grassy slopes at the side of the stadium as did spectators at the first Olympic games held in 776 BC, 2769 years ago, watching the French school kids race the length of the track in street clothes, their street shoes clopping loudly against the hard dirt. The teacher stands at the end of the stadium calling times from a stopwatch as the students cross the finish line. Even from twenty meters, I can smell their strong body odor.

Pelops, for whom the Peloponnese is named (Pelops Island), held the games in celebration of his defeat of Oenomaus, king of Pisa, a nearby city. Pelops was in love with Hippodameia, Oenomaus' beautiful daughter. But an oracle had warned Oenomaus that his daughter's husband would kill him, and he would only give her to the man who could beat him in a chariot race from Olympia to the Isthmus of Corinth. Oenomaus would relinquish, not only his daughter, but also the kingdom of Pisa as her dowry.

Oenomaus had the fastest team of horses in the land and, even though he handicapped himself by sacrificing a goat after his competitor had already left for Corinth with Hippodameia at his side, Oenomaus always caught the suitor, decapitated him and mounted the head above the entrance to his palace. But Pelops, realizing Oenomaus' charioteer Myrtilus was also in love with Hippodameia, promised him half the kingdom and a night in bed with her if he would help him win the race. Myrtilus, who was a son of ruthless and conniving Hermes, couldn't refuse a night in bed with Hippodameia, so he failed to put the locking pins in one of the wheels of Oenomaus' chariot. During the race, the wheel came off and Oenomaus was dragged to death by his own horses.

But Myrtilus had met his match in Pelops. Pelops had no intention of living up to the bargain and drowned Myrtilus in the sea. As he fell into the pounding surf, Myrtilus pronounced a curse against the descendants of Pelops. Pelops was the father of Atreus and the grandfather of Mycenae's Agamemnon, general of the Greek forces in the Trojan War. Myrtilus' curse was to haunt the house of Atreus for the next three generations, filling the halls of Mycenae with blood. Pelops was the first to build a temple of Hermes, Myrtilus' divine father, to ward off the curse imposed.[110]

I'll pickup the bloody trail of this legend in Mycenae, where Agamemnon ruled and where I'll be in a few days.

But all this mythology belies the fact that the men's sporting events were not the first games in Olympia. Just as the religious site originally belonged to Hera, the first games at Olympia were also dedicated to her. Hippodameia started them to give thanks to Hera for her marriage to Pelops. Hera's games started with the weaving of a robe for the goddess by sixteen women who also organized and conducted the games. The events consisted of races for virgin girls, who ran with their tunics above their knees, their hair flowing free and right shoulder and breast exposed.[111] They raced here at the stadium, but the most important event was the race to the top of the Hill of Kronos.[112] The winners received a crown of olive branches and shared in an ox sacrificed to Hera.

Another legend concerning those who conducted Hera's games tells us even more about the politics of Olympia at the time. Pausanias tells the story of an ancient dictator who performed dreadful acts against neighboring townships. But since his people did not participate in the acts, after the dictator died, the people of both townships wished to make peace. To do this they:

> ...chose a woman of the most venerable age and the most distinguished position and reputation from each of the inhabited cities of Eleia at that time to settle their quarrels for them. ...afterwards they were put in charge of holding Hera's games and weaving Hera's robe.[113]

The women defined the course of peacemaking between warring factions of men. Hera's games were in honor of marriage, coming together. Zeus' games were born of strife, of one god's victory over another. After Zeus defeated Kronos, he exiled him and the rest of the Titans of his generation to Tartarus in Hades, the Underworld.

Hermes ruled over the men's games here at Olympia and duly ordered contests[114] throughout Greece. At the entrance to the racetrack were two altars, one for "Opportunity" and the other for "Hermes of the Games."[115] Hermes himself first visited Olympia when he rustled Apollo's cattle. He sacrificed two of them here and divided the meat into two portions for the Twelve Gods.[116]

Hermes was also the giver of oaths.[117] During the opening ceremonies of the games, athletes and officials took a solemn oath of honesty and sportsmanship.[118] No cheating occurred until the ninety-eighth Olympiad when six boxers were fined for accepting bribes.[119] Even in antiquity, the games were not about money or big prizes. The winners won only an olive wreath, but the games were of such great importance that time was measured relative to the four-year interval between them, the first official Olympiad being held in 776 BC. In times of war, all hostilities were suspended in a Sacred Truce. No one in armor was allowed

Olympia

to enter the city.

The male Athletes trained for ten months before competing and came to Olympia for the final two months. The games were held consistently for over one-thousand years. The festival occurred during the full moon following the summer solstice, another legacy of Hera who was a moon goddess, and the full moon signifying her fulfillment. As many as 200,000 spectators attended. Only one of them was a woman, the priestess of Demeter of the Ground,[120] an homage paid because the ground for the stadium had been taken from her.[121] Although women were barred from watching the games under the penalty of death, virgin girls were not.[122] The stadium did not have seats, the view areas made of huge mounds of dirt, which now are rather small due to erosion through the thousands of years.

> ...the crowd which assembled at Olympia was drawn by various motives. Some came simply to enjoy the spectacle, some to compete in the games, and others to buy and sell. Baths and tents were set up, not only traders and cooks, but also since the panegyris national festal assembly lasted several days, as temporary lodgings for the assembled multitude.[123]

During the large-scale sacrifice, hundreds of animals were slaughtered, roasted and distributed to the people. The ancient Olympics were a five-day event. The opening ceremonies occurred on the first day followed by chariot and horse racing on the second. The morning of the third day included a procession to the temple of Zeus and the sacrifice of a herd of oxen. This was the day of the full moon. Only the fat and bones were burned before the altar, the meat being saved for a huge feast on the fifth day. The boy's wrestling, boxing and footraces were held the afternoon of the third day. On the fourth day, the sprints and distance races were held in the morning followed by men's wrestling, boxing and pancration. Pancration was one-on-one combat with no holds or atrocities barred. Mutilation was the result. Closing ceremonies were held on the fifth day, followed by the feast of the herd of oxen at which singing, eating and drinking by the light of a thousand campfires continued until dawn.[124]

I walk back through the stone arch at the entrance to the stadium and sit cross-legged on the ground among a dense population of sandstones and columns at Hera's temple. Nothing is left of her statue or the throne on which she sat, although a limestone head believed to be hers has been found. It seems even statues' heads roam the Greek countryside. My shadow lies before me, eclipsing a rock shaped by human hands twenty-five hundred years ago, a shadow cast by a sun born five billion years ago.

Olympia

I return from my visit to the ruins of the ancient city, walk through the museum and come back to my room for a nap.

Afterward, I walk groggily around town and meet my two friends from Holland. They buy me a beer at a deserted restaurant at the edge of town not far from the train station, an Amstel, a Dutch beer. Hans tells me rather sheepishly he calls Margo "the barbarian," almost as if he's ashamed of her. She was raised on a farm. He talks about her father's herd of cows and Margo being the milkmaid. She doesn't seem particularly fond of him divulging her background. I tell her of my own upbringing, of the years my father had a dairy, my day of slopping through dung-filled corrals and milking cows. Hans was raised in the city and is obviously proud of it. Margo has an earthiness about her I really appreciate. She reflects purity in her smooth fleshiness, her peaches-and-cream complexion and blue eyes.

I ask their opinion of the Berlin Wall coming down, the reunification of German. A nervous glance passes between them, and at first I think they won't answer. But gradually they express pleasure that the barrier between the east and west has been eliminated but concern about the reunification. The neo-Nazi movement in Germany is very strong and Germans are still culturally arrogant. When Germans come to Holland, they insist the Dutch speak German.

I say that, while I was in Holland, I noticed a strong resemblance between Dutch and German. My comment offends them, and they assure me the two languages are very different. They also tell me the war has resumed in Bosnia, just to the north of Greece. The Serbs have broken the shaky truce and are once again shelling Sarajevo. More refugees are fleeing into Greece.

★

I have dinner alone at a little fast food place on the main street, a gyro and a piece of the sweet cake pastry heavy with honey. My visit to the ruins of ancient Olympia have brought back my two years at Bakersfield College. I too was an athlete, not Olympic caliber, but I did make the college track and cross-country teams. My older brother was a world-class athlete, and I had followed in his footsteps all my life, which had been a little fast and far apart for me. Through him, I met Fred. During my second year, my brother had gone on to a university on an athletic scholarship, and I was left to discover what to do with myself without his guiding light. I gravitated away from athletics toward writing poetry, developed an interest in literature, physics and philosophy. For the first time in my life, I was choosing my own path. I even found the courage to stand up to my father, but it all went up in smoke with the single click of a deer rifle.

The legend of Pelops is intermixed with that of Laios and Oedipus. Laios' father died when he was a child, and because of the danger to him by those who assumed the throne of Thebes in his place, he was sent to Pelops to be raised. When he became a young man here in Olympia, Laios became fond of Pelops illegitimate son, Chrysippus, while teaching him to drive a chariot. I imagine them to be practicing for some ancient form of the Olympic Games. Laios kidnapped Chrysippus and returned to Thebes to assume the throne. Chrysippus was humiliated at being homosexually raped and committed suicide. Laios had betrayed the trust of his guardian and benefactor.

Fred's rape of my brother was also a betrayal of my trust when I brought him home to meet my family. I had taken his side against my father. I had also saved Fred's life even though he had raped my brother. I saw Fred once more before he was deported. This final incident has always seemed contrived to me, part of the grand contrivance of life.

I was in Berkeley going to summer school, renting a room in the Acacia fraternity during the waning days of summer. I walked out the front door one afternoon going to my car, and there coming toward me was Fred, walking up the steps with his head down. I had thought if I ever saw him again I would beat him beyond recognition. Instead, I spoke to him and walked on. He was sullen and didn't reply. I've never told anyone of that chance meeting. I had my opportunity to get him and I didn't take it. At the time, I thought it was cowardice. Perhaps it was, perhaps it wasn't.

Fred was coming to see my other English friend, the athlete with whom I still roomed. Fred told him he wasn't homosexual, that nothing had happened between him and my brother, that we were mean people who just wanted to see him deported. He was, in fact, on his way out of the country. My roommate had trouble believing Fred was homosexual. He had known Fred for several years in England, although they had not been friends until they came to the States. But I knew firsthand of Fred's sexual orientation. We had slept in the same bed together.

Ever since that last encounter with Fred, I've wished that, when my father turned to me and said, "Let's kill him," I had made that move down the hall. I can see us now flinging the bedroom door open and Fred standing there in his white undershirt and striped boxer shorts, startled by our sudden move toward him. I would hit him first and my father would join in. I'd pound his head until he spit blood and teeth, shove him up against the wall and my father and I'd beat the life out of every living ounce of flesh in his body, beat and stomp and cuss until the light faded from his eyes. Everyday since I said no, I wish I'd said yes. Like Odysseus and his son, Telemachus, my father and I would go on a blood-driven rampage.

What stopped me is a mystery, because it is as if I couldn't kill him more than I believed it wasn't the right thing to do. But a few years ago, I told a wise old man about my guilt for stopping my father from killing Fred, my cowardice. He looked at me straight and said, "So what you're confessing to is not killing a man, to acting civilized in an extraordinarily difficult time. You're not confessing to committing murder, you're confessing to not committing murder."

"That's right," I said. "I can hardly live with myself."

I've tried to take his supportive words to heart and appreciate the maturity of my actions, but still lapse into thoughts of cowardice and wishes that I had bowed to my father's will. I feel a lot of guilt over what happened. After all, I was the one who brought Fred into our home, didn't listen to my father when he protested. I didn't back off even when he loaded the deer rifle. Fred remaining alive is a problem for my younger brother. He didn't commit suicide, but a marriage of sorts still exists between them. Fred's death threats will remain active for as long as they both shall live.

*

I lie in bed listening to a cricket's cheerful chirp and thinking of the fifth and final day of the ancient Olympics, thinking of the evening feast with the smell of roast beast filling the night air, smoke from a thousand fires rising to the stars circling overhead, and voices of the multitude raised in praise of Zeus.

21 Oct, Thursday

Roosters wake me shortly before sunrise, and I pack for my day of travel to Sparta. The roosters in Olympia have the worst voices I've ever heard on a chicken. It's not just that rusty-bucket sucker outside my window. All their cock-a-doodle-doos have something wrong. Some never get going well, can't hit that high pitch at the beginning and though they hold their notes, they have no heart. Others are truncated, and stop in mid-sentence as though they don't believe what they're saying. The one with the broken voice has contaminated them all. The rooster is the sun's sacred bird[125] and the symbol of resurrection. The message may come garbled here, but they still get it across.

While I pack, my thoughts take another detour through the land of Oedipus. When I was in Thebes, I made the observation that Oedipus had the intelligence, as demonstrated by answering the Sphinx's riddle of life, to solve the riddle of his own. Oedipus had not only the intelligence but also more than enough information. He had been told in Corinth that he was adopted and the rumor had spread throughout the land. Subsequently the oracle at Delphi told him he was to kill his father and marry his mother. Just before he met the Sphinx, he had killed four men. After he answered the riddle of the Sphinx, he was made king and given the hand of an older woman in marriage. You

107

might argue that Oedipus didn't take the rumors about his parentage or the oracle seriously, but his actions don't support this. He went to Delphi because of his concern over the rumors and he wouldn't return to Corinth because of the oracle's answer. These two sets of information were active in his mind at the same time, and he couldn't, I will say wouldn't, resolve the paradox. His answering the riddle of the Sphinx proves to me that he knew the answer to the riddle of his own life but refused to act on it. Or more correctly, he did act on it. He just took the road less traveled.

I imagine Oedipus standing before the bridal chamber, the smell of sweet Jocasta wafting up from the silk sheets, goose bumps running up the back of his neck as he contemplated the oracle's declaration and realized that the next foot was about to fall. At this point, I feel less of a sense of frustration at being jacked around by the oracle and more his sense of fascination with life, a fascination with the paradox of Fate governing our lives and even though we have freewill. When he looked across the bed at Jocasta as she threw back the covers for him to slip in beside her, I think he at least suspected he was courting Fate, but he smiled and slipped off his sandals, dropped his robe to the floor and slipped into bed beside the queen of Thebes.

In the same way each grain of sand contains the history of the universe, Fred's every move contained the revelation of his sexual orientation, never mind my other English friend not knowing and not believing he was homosexual. In my own way, I had an encounter with the Sphinx. Only a matter of weeks before my confrontation with my father, I had read Sophocles' three Theban plays in one of my college classes. We had seen performances of them, had long discussions and wrote papers about them in class. I remember sitting in an outdoor theatre on a spring afternoon shading my eyes from the bright sunlight as we discussed the merits of the case for and against Oedipus. I remember arguing that he must be guilty because he had all the information in front of him, that life would be meaningless if in the hands of the Fates we are only a machine grinding to the music of some god's angry tune.

When I stood with my father in the living room the first time, the two of us shouting hot volcanic words at each other, at some level I must have known what my father was concerned about. Even his aborted assault on his own life was not enough for me to back off and tell Fred he wasn't welcome in our home. I wonder if the confrontation wasn't what I wanted, after all. What may be crucial is that we were arguing in the presence of my mother. When my father went to the closet and shoved shells into the chamber of that deer rifle, did he do so in self-defense?

I have the uneasy feeling that my ignorance was only a surface ignorance and, at a deeper level, an elaborately disguised assault on my father, an attempt to attain my father's stature in my mother's eyes. And my father, why did he let me sleep with Fred if he knew he was homosexual? Did he think I was homosexual also? Or was he letting me find out for myself? I'm convinced the entire incident had little to do with Fred. Those surrealistic summer days were purely between my father and me.

And as for Fred, that night, when I came back from turning off the pump with my cousin's young wife, kicked off my shoes, dropped my pants and slipped between the sheets Fred had been warming for a couple of hours, was I really so naive as to not know he was homosexual? What the hell was I thinking anyway? The answer is I was thinking about my cousin's young wife. She was a couple of years younger than me and quite attractive. Our little excursion to the far side of the field at midnight was loaded with eroticism. Looking back on it through the perspective of thirty-two years, I find it somewhat amusing: the naive twenty-year-old, heavy adulterous thoughts of a young woman floating like lollypops in his head, crawling into bed with a gay man.

After Fred's deportation, I assumed it was all over. I'd made a bad mistake for which my younger brother paid a terrible price, sort of a sacrifice of the innocent, and I had harvested a terrible guilt. But this was history, and life would go on as planned. Little did I realize that for me this was only the fall of the first few dominoes.

The roosters are quiet again, my room lit by the morning sun. I zip my backpack, hoist it and make the short trek to the bus stop on the main street where I meet Hans and Margo at the tourist information office. They look fresh in their bright shorts and T-shirts and are eager to get going. We'll take the bus to Tripoli together and then split up, they to Nafplion in Argos and I south to Sparta. A burglar alarm has been going off at one of the local businesses for the last hour, and it's driving everyone crazy. The loud screech is like a hacksaw in my head. Here's the bus to Tripoli.

One last story of Olympia as I leave it. It's about a famous statue of a mare that induced "horse-madness" in stallions. Pausanias tells the story:

...what happens to this mare is in fact obviously the work of some skillful magician. It is not nearly the biggest or the most beautiful of the Altis horses, and its tail has been docked which makes it look even worse; yet stallions go wild for it, not only in spring but every day in the year. They break their halters and escape from their grooms and come galloping into Altis and leap up on it much more madly than they would on the finest living mare that was used to being mounted. Their hooves slip on it, but they go on and on whinnying all the more and leaping up on it more and more strongly until you manage to drag them away with whips and main force: until you do so nothing can release them from that bronze.[126]

This ancient story says a great deal about the male's infatuation with the feminine image, and how little he understands of her true nature.

As we leave Elis Nome and enter Arkadia, the mountains become huge, the ravines deep, the cliffs precipitous, the turns sharp. The lush countryside in the heart of the Peloponnese is something I've not read about. The depth of the canyons, I can only compare to the Grand Canyon. And, of course, they don't stand up to the Grand Canyon, but I like the comparison anyway because they are so spectacular.

Herds of goats and sheep roam the thick undergrowth. The precipitous mountainsides are covered with huge oak trees, fir, pine, orange trees, fig trees, huge maples, cypress, cedar. The bus encounters lots of road construction and creeps through narrow passages overlooking cliffs, passing perilously close to the crumbling dirt edge. We crane our necks at the windows to watch the edge of the mountain disappear beneath us.

When we get off at the station in Tripoli, the capitol of Arkadia, I wait for a few minutes with Hans and Margo, reluctant to leave them. They're having trouble finding a bus. All the schedule postings say nothing about Nafplion. The station is a dark, hangar-like building and drab as I've seen. The exhaust from the buses is simply asphyxiating. Buses drive in, idle in stasis and drive out belching exhaust. Horn blasts reverberate off the walls, which look as if they've been painted with motor oil.

I go to the window and get my ticket to Sparta. My bus is about to leave. I say good-bye to Hans and Margo, hoist my pack and walk to the bus. As we drive out, I look anxiously for them, but they are gone.

★

I watch the countryside grow darker as we dip deeper into the Arkadian Mountains. This is Pan country, the shepherd god's abode. Pan was born with the feet and head of a goat. His appearance frightened his mother so badly that she fled from him. But the gods all loved this bearded, goat-footed god and named him, Pan, which in ancient Greek meant "all." Our word for "panic" comes from the feeling Pan induces, his mother being the first to experience it. Pan was born here in Arkadia, and I must pass through his old stomping grounds to get to Sparta. He's a dark, terror-awakening god who reminds me of an old hobo uncle.

The gods came to earth in human form. Gaia had no single form, but being a great multiple goddess, had many forms depicting her different aspects. These forms included the goddesses Hera, Athena, Artemis, Demeter and Aphrodite, among many, many lesser goddesses. When we view her in whole, we see the world's entire feminine spirit. Hera, as one aspect of Gaia, was the spirit of womanhood, marriage and the lives of women in ancient Greece, a spirit that resided in all women. Athena was the warrior goddess, who thrilled at the battle cry and the clash of arms, the protectress of cities. Artemis was the virgin goddess, mistress of childbirth and of all things wild. Demeter was goddess of cultivation, the spirit of all things springing directly from the earth. Aphrodite was the goddess of erotic love. Gaia was the way women of ancient Greece experienced the world. In Sparta, we'll get another look at Artemis, and this time we'll see an aspect of her that might be a little surprising.

CHAPTER 6: Sparta

The bus traverses the Arkadian plain, and we ascend through mountains as a series of upland plateaus, tall pines shadowing dense underbrush. I lean back in my seat and contemplate Hermes, who was born in a cave on Mt. Kyllene, just a short distance north of Tripoli. Hermes was also a phallic god, and this aspect of his character showed up in his children. Hermes had two sons: Pan the goat-footed god of shepherds, and Priapos a phallic god of fertility. Priapos was a small, little-heard-of god with a huge perpetually erect phallus, a deformed freak used by some as a scarecrow. But Pan was widely know and much loved. Pan's mother was Dryope, the fair-tressed daughter of the Arkadian shepherd Dryops, the "oak-man."[127] Hermes was pasturing sheep for Dryops when he fell in love with Dryope. True to his nature, Hermes swiftly mated with her and a divine child was soon born. Pan's appearance terrified his mother:

> ...she bore
> to Hermes a dear son, from birth monstrous to behold,
> with goat's feet and two horns, boisterous and sweet-laughing.
> His mother sprang up and fled; the nurse in turn left
> the child behind because she was afraid
> when she saw his wild and well-bearded visage.[128]

But swift Hermes came to the rescue and carried his son to Olympus for the other gods to see, proud that he was of him:

> Helpful Hermes quickly received him Pan into his arms,
> and in his divine heart the joy overflowed.
> He wrapped the child in snug skins of mountain hares
> and swiftly went to the abodes of the immortals.
> He then set him down beside Zeus and the other gods
> and showed them his boy: all of them were delighted
> in their hearts and Bacchic Dionysos above all others.
> They called him Pan because he cheered the hearts of all.[129]

Though bearded, sweet-laughing Pan was the archetypal abandoned child.[130]He spread panic not only in his mother and nurse but also in the hearts of mortals. Pan was "dark, terror-awakening, phallic,"[131] the goat-god, a hot, hairy, animal-smelling god with an erection.[132] His favorite companion was Dionysus, god of madness; where one appeared, the other was sure to be close by. Pan saved Dionysus from being eaten by the Titans after they had dismembered and roasted him and were feasting on his limbs. The sound of Pan's conch horn filled them with panic.[133]

Pan danced mountainsides, through clouds of valley-clinging mists and waterfalls inhabited by nymphs. The inhabitants of Arkadia heard haunting Pan piping in the Arkadian crags.[134] He had an oracle here in Arkadia, and his prophetess was Erato,[135] the muse of dance and "awakener of desire."[136] The most striking image of sharp-eyed Pan is of him on a mountaintop, hand shading his eyes, peering into the distance as he watched over his goatherd.

Like Apollo, Pan was unlucky in love. Though he cavorted with nymphs, his true loves were elusive. From one such encounter, with the woodland nymph Syrinx, he invented the flute. Syrinx was a follower of Artemis, the virgin goddess of wild animals. Pan chased Syrinx, but as he drew close she resisted him by changing shape:

> ...when Pan had caught her
> And thought he held a nymph, it was only reeds
> That yielded in his arms, and while he sighed,
> The soft air stirring in the reeds made also
> The echo of a sigh. Touched by this marvel,
> Charmed by the sweetness of the tone, he murmured
> This much I have! and took the reeds, and bound them
> With wax, a tall and shorter one together,
> And called them Syrinx, still.[137]

My parents' first son they named for my mother's older brother, and before I was born, my father's older brother demanded they name me for him. Uncle Jud was the family black sheep, an alcoholic hobo who hopped freight trains along the Pacific Coast to pick fruit. In stature, he was tall and lean, a little stooped due to an animal-like ungainliness. His heavily tattooed skin had leathered from the sun. He drank cheap wine and lived in lean-tos in sloughs among the tulles and cattails. If he was around, you knew a bottle of wine was close by, Pan and Dionysus ever close companions. After months on the road, he'd come home drunk, beat up, another tooth missing, crazy from bad wine. He liked to get drunk and invade my grandmother's kitchen, fry onion-potatoes and catfish, chase her screaming round the house with a butcher's knife. He'd hum an old country tune while dancing a foot-stomping jig, chewing on a stick of salami and eating garlic by the clove, shouting lewd remarks to anyone within hearing distance. He was a whoremonger, a champion of loose women and a good time. He never hurt anyone, just loved the bloodcurdling scream, the terror-filled home, the smell of flesh sizzling on the stove.

When I was six months old, my parents were traveling from Carlsbad, New Mexico to California, and as they passed through El Paso, they saw a hitchhiker standing at the opposite side of the road. As they whizzed past, they thought they recognized him, thought it couldn't possibly be, then turned back to make sure. It was my Uncle Jud, AWOL from Fort Bliss and trying to get back to Carlsbad. He wasn't particular which way he went and continued on to California with them. He turned on the radio to verify a news story he'd heard at a coffee shop. The date was December 7, 1941, the day Japan bombed Pearl Harbor. America was at war, and this was the first time I saw my namesake.

Of course, I don't remember my reaction to him that day because I was only six months old, but I was afraid of Uncle Jud and ran from him as Pan's mother and nurse had run from him. I'd slink away into the corners or hide behind my mother, his course voice growling after me. He was abrasive, belligerent toward adults, and perpetually teased us kids. He used the most offensive language. When I was a teenager, he was fond of asking me, with my parents close by, if I was getting any pussy from my high school sweetheart. But in the summertime, he'd take us kids into the potholes of Snelling at the edge of the Sierra Nevada, gold country, where at night we'd put out a trot line and listen to the rubber-throated bullfrogs, leaning back on our sleeping bags to watch the constellations of stars cut arcs across the black sky. He told mysterious stories of the creation of the universe and questioned the meaning of life. Everyone in our hometown loved him. Whenever I'd meet someone on the street, they'd always ask, "How's ol' Jud doing?" When he was sober, he was quiet, gentle, reverent in his respect for my father and his family. Uncle Jud died of prostate cancer a few years ago, his body swelled badly from a liver ailment.

I didn't go to Uncle Jud's funeral. I always disavowed him, even using my middle name to avoid the association. But during the few years since his death I've received an unwanted inheritance. I've been forced to realize I have a little of his nature, and since I've suppressed it, I've been blindsided by it at the most vulnerable times.

The bus rounds the final ridge and descends into a large valley. We've left

Arkadia and are now in Lakonia Nome. Before us to the southwest, stand the majestic jagged-peaked Taygetos Mountains, the wildest range in Greece.[138] A touch of snow lingers there even in late October. To the southeast lie the less impressive Parnonas Mountains. Both ranges converge in decreasing cascades forty kilometers to the south at the edge of the sea. The Eurotas River winds along the floor of the valley southward between the mountain ranges. On the west bank of the river sprawls modern Sparta, an undistinguished metropolis at the head of the Eurotas alluvial plain. The entire valley is a monument to the Earth goddess, Gaia, her rich soil there still among the most fertile in Greece.

The legends of Sparta go far back into antiquity. According to Pausanias, the river received its name from Eurotas, the son of Gaia.

> ...Eurotas channelled away the marsh-water from the plains by cutting through to the sea, and when the land was drained he called the river which was left running there the Eurotas. As he had no male children he left the crown to Lakedaimon, whose mother was Taygete after whom the mountain was named and whose father is supposed to have been Zeus; Lakedaimon had married Sparta, the daughter of Eurotas. Once he was in power, he first of all renamed the country and the people after himself, and then founded a city and named it after his wife: the city is called Sparta to this day.[139]

The bus takes a road west off the main road and soon I feel as though I've reentered Athens; the roar of motorbikes comes at us from all sides as we snake though the city streets, and the bus drops us at the station. I retrieve my pack and walk south a couple of blocks to Lykourgou Street where I turn west toward Mt. Taygetos in the distance, past shops and tavernas, past a large plateia and the town hall to Hotel Cyprus. I soon have a cramped room with a balcony and clothesline. The clothesline makes the place worthwhile because I've got to do laundry.

After slumping my backpack against the wall, I hit the street again, walk north from the plateia to the Akropolis Lakedaimonia. The low-lying hill is the site of a 1st Century BC theatre, half-hidden in an olive grove, and on past it, the foundation of the temple of Athena. At the very top of the acropolis, shadowed by eucalyptus and pine trees, is an old Byzantine monastery. During Byzantine times the theatre was raided for building materials for use in nearby Mysra.

Although Sparta was a powerful military state, and in 404 BC conquered even Athens, Sparta's reputation as a highly disciplined, war-obsessed state where children were introduced to the rigors of military discipline from birth has been grossly exaggerated. Evidence has surfaced rather recently to paint a different picture.[140] Through the arts, another side of Sparta has emerged and is particularly displayed in the poetry of Alcman, who wrote during the 7th Century BC. He had a sharp eye for a pretty girl and was fond of good food and the easy life. He is now known for his gay and lively maiden songs, of which many fragments have been recovered. The lightness and gaiety of his compositions certainly belie the traditional image of Sparta. Here's one that demonstrates his use of the language of love, which he wrote for maidens to sing while dancing:

> Olympian Muses, fill my heart with longing for a new song: I am eager to hear the maiden voice of girls singing a beautiful melody to the heavens... it will scatter sweet sleep from my eyes and leads me to go to the assembly of Antheia Hera of the flowers, where I shall rapidly shake my yellow hair...[141]

Sparta's agricultural valley produced better food and had a better climate than most localities throughout Greece and resulted in a rather laid-back lifestyle. The image of an extremist, military Sparta was generated for internal political consumption and for export as propaganda to the rest of Greece.[142]

I stay long enough among the eucalyptus trees to watch the sun prematurely disappear in a blinding flash behind Mt. Taygetos. I have one more quick stop before I can try to find something to eat. To the west of here is perhaps the most famous temple in Sparta, the temple of Artemis where, according to legend, many evil deeds were imposed upon children. This is the site that will give us a different view of the goddess than we've seen before.

I leave the acropolis and walk west, the late afternoon traffic frantically seeking its destination. On the outskirts of town, I enter the ruins of the temple of Artemis Ortiz, "upright Artemis," so called because her statue was found standing. During classical times, Sparta was known as a fierce military power. Our word "Spartan," meaning simple, frugal but also marked by strict self-discipline and denial, comes from the characteristics of this Sparta. Both sexes were subjected to intense physical training. According to legend, boys were flogged here as a public spectacle. The victims maintained a cheerful outward appearance even unto death.

The temple is on the bank of the Eurotas River, among oleanders and rushes. The river used to run though the temple but has now been diverted a little east. Archaeologists uncovered carved bone and ivory objects here that show close connection with Ephesus, a major city on the western coast of Turkey also devoted to Artemis worship during antiquity. Sparta had its connections throughout the Mediterranean.

The shadows have deepened considerably, and I feel a chill. I make the kilometer walk back to the hotel and shower, change clothes. I spend an hour washing my underclothes in the sink with what's left of the small white bar of soap. The clothesline sags under the weight of wet cotton.

I step out into the night air, whiffs of exhaust blasted about by motorbikes. I make the short walk to the plateia, where it seems the entire town has congregated, a much larger scene than that on election night in Thebes. I stop at an outdoor taverna and take a seat at a metal table. Shortly, I'm gorging myself on tasty baked chicken and potatoes. Afterward, I have a Greek coffee and watch the young girls walking to the plateia in the company of their mothers.

After eating I walk to the center of the large plateia, where a tremendous volta is taking place. The entire city must be here, promenading back and forth along the courtyard in front of the courthouse. Young girls stop to fuss over each other, and the men—all dressed to the nines, suits, high heels—greet one another as if they haven't seen each other for years: much handshaking and backslapping.

★

The coffee keeps me awake in spite of my weariness after a long day. I lie in bed with the image of Mt. Taygetos, which looms over this city in the background of my thoughts, imagining what it would be like up there now. I've spent many nights in a tent in Colorado's mountains. Perhaps it's my homesickness for Colorado that won't turn loose of that mountain image. The 6th Century Spartan poet, Alcman, described the night scene on Mt. Taygetos:

> And the mountain-peaks are asleep and the ravines, the headlands and torrent-beds, all the creeping tribes that the black earth nourishes, the wild animals of the mountains, the race of bees and the monsters in the depths of the surging sea; and the tribes of long-winged birds are asleep.[143]

Eleven kilometers south of here, along the south-flowing Eurotas, are the ruins of ancient Amyclae. Amyclae was the home of Hyacinthus, a beautiful youth with whom Apollo fell in love. One day while throwing the discus together, Apollo accidentally killed the lad. The crimson flower, which sprang up from his blood was named the Hyacinth.

Greek mythology contains many stories of men's love for boys. Zeus' favorite was Ganymede, a royal Trojan, whom Zeus kidnapped and made his lover and cupbearer. So Fred's sexual orientation is not without precedent, perhaps even archetypal in heritage. But so is the damage done to the youth involved. Laios' male lover committed suicide. Even classical Greece was very much a bisexual society, and the kidnapping and rape of boys institutionalized. According to Ephorus, a 4th Century BC ethnographer, in some Greek societies, as a youth's initiation to manhood, an older man kidnaps him with only feigned family opposition, and takes him into the mountains for two months of feasting and hunting together. During this time, the youth is homosexually ravished. Afterward, the youth is given presents, including a military uniform, and sent home.

This is just another of the many mythic parallels that have popped up in and around my life. All these atrocities would appear to occur within the realm of Dionysus, the madness he brings. In the ancient Greek world, it seems even this practice was viewed as a necessary mechanism for the youth to become fully adult.

For the life of me, I can't understand how that could possibly be true. All it caused in my family is pain, emotional scars, and difficulty in later life.

22 Oct, Friday

I'm up early this morning and on the run to get to the Menelaion and back to catch the bus to Mycenae. After a quick breakfast of fruit and bread, I exit the hotel into the cool morning air with the sun just breaking the mountaintops. I walk Geraki road across the Eurotas River and turn south on my way to the Menelaion, where speculation tells us Menelaus castle stood. Helen and Menelaus lived in the 13th Century BC, long before Sparta got its reputation as a military power.

During the Bronze Age, Helen was Sparta's most famous citizen, and her birth was as bizarre as any in Greek mythology. Zeus was infatuated with and pursued Nemesis, goddess of retribution, who ran frantically from him. She changed herself into a goose, but Zeus changed himself into a swan and raped her anyway. Nemesis then laid a hyacinth-colored egg[144] in a Spartan grove, where shepherds found it and gave it to Leda, the wife of king Tyndareus. Helen hatched from the blue egg. Though some say she was born of immortals, Helen was mortal and others said her parents were Leda and Tyndareus.

Helen had a traumatic childhood and narrowly escaped death during a human sacrifice to save the city during time of plague:

> When a Plague had overspread Sparta, the god gave an oracle that it would cease if they sacrificed a noble maiden each year. Once when Helen had been chosen by lot and had been led forward adorned for the sacrifice, an eagle swooped down, snatched up the sword, carried it to the herds of

cattle, and let it fall on a heifer; wherefore the Spartans refrained from the slaying of maidens.[145]

Even Helen's beauty was to cause her pain. When Theseus the king of Athens was fifty, he and his friend Pirithous came to Sparta. They didn't come on a friendly visit but to kidnap Helen, who, while only twelve, had a reputation as great beauty. Theseus and Pirithous attended a maiden dance at the temple of Artemis Orthia. Such a maiden dance is described in Aristophanes' play *Lysistrata*. The play was written in 411 BC, some 800 years after Helen was kidnapped:

> Now the dance begin:
> Dance, making swirl your fringe o' wooly skin,
>> While we join voices
> To hymn dear Sparta that rejoices
>> I' a beautifu' sang,
>> An' loves to see
> Dancers tangled beautifully,
> For the girls i' tumbled ranks
>> Alang Eurotas' banks
>> Like wanton fillies thrang,
>> Frolicking there
> An' like Bacchantes shaking the wild air
>> To comb a giddy laughter through the hair,
> Bacchantes that clench thyrsi as they sweep
>> To the ecstatic leap.
>> An' Helen, Child o' Leda, come
> Thou holy, nimble, gracefu' Queen,
> Lead thou the dance, gather thy joyous tresses up i' bands
> An' play like a fawn. To madden them, clap thy hands,
>> And sing praise to the warrior goddess Athena
>> templed i' our lands,
> Her o' the House o' Brass.[146]

During one such ceremony, Theseus snatched up Helen and took her to Aphidnae just north of Athens, the small town I passed two weeks ago during my bus ride to Thebes. Helen's brothers, Castor and Polyduces, retrieved Helen. The ensuing war with Athens resulted in Theseus being exiled to the island of Skyrus where he was murdered.

When Helen became of marriageable age, Tyndareus invited all those interested in vying for her hand. Odysseus was among the suitors, but realizing his lowly status as king of a small island, he knew he could never win the vain woman's heart. Noblemen from all of Greece came to plead their cause for the ravishing beauty, and when hostilities broke out between the suitors, Odysseus, the man of many wiles, was quick to offer Tyndareus a solution in exchange for his support in gaining the hand of Penelope, Helen's cousin. He advised Tyndareus to make the suitors swear to protect the winner against any harm caused by his marriage to Helen. Helen chose the wealthy Menelaus, brother of Agamemnon the powerful king of Mycenae.

Menelaus didn't have a kingdom, so when Tyndareus' two sons, Castor and Polyduces, were killed in a battle with their cousins, Tendareus gave the throne to his daughter's husband. Thus, the line of descent of Sparta in Mycenaean times was matrilineal as it was at Thebes, Oedipus gaining the throne there by virtue of his marriage to Jocasta.

Shortly thereafter, Odysseus came to Sparta seeking the hand of Penelope. Tendareus paid his debt by speaking for Odysseus in his desire for Helen's cousin. But Odysseus didn't get by so easily when he came to pickup Penelope. He still had to win her in a footrace.[147]

Though the Trojan War was caused by events here at Sparta, the events were put into motion by problems in Greek heaven. All the gods and goddesses assembled up north in Thessaly for the marriage of Peleus and Thetis, the parents-to-be of Achilles, the greatest warrior of all time. Peleus, a mortal, was marrying Thetis, a beautiful sea nymph on Mt. Pelion. All the gods and goddesses were invited with one exception. The goddess Eris, "Strife," wasn't invited but crashed the party anyway. When she was barred entry, she threw a golden apple into the crowd. Inscribed on the apple were the words, "To the Fairest." The vain goddesses squabbled over it, Hera, Athena and Aphrodite, all claiming the apple was for them. To settle the dispute, Zeus told Hermes to take the three goddesses to Mt. Ida in the land of Troy where Paris, the world's most handsome man, lived. All three goddesses tried to bribe Paris, but Aphrodite offered him the hand of the world's most beautiful woman. Tales of Helen's beauty had spanned the Aegean to Phrygeia, the land of Troy. Aphrodite, in offering Helen to Paris, ignored the fact that Helen was already married.

After four and a half kilometers walking the road south along the bank of the Eurotas River, I turn east onto a footpath past a chapel and ascend a hill to the remains of Menelaus' castle. When the site was excavated in 1973, it was underneath the ruins of a 5th Century BC building that archaeologists found the much older ruins of a Mycenaean complex, which they assumed to be the home of Helen and Menelaus.

The hill, known as Mt. Therapne, is arid and scrub covered, not an impressive sight until I turn to look back west from where I've come. From my vantage point, I overlook the entire Eurotas plain, and in the background, the morning sun has unmasked the looming presence of Mt. Taygetos. The peaks glow brilliantly, their height forming a wall of impenetrability to protect Sparta. Though the site seems sparse compared to the legends that form its infamy, the breeze whispers its greatness, birdcalls breaking the near silence.

I mount one ancient wall's foundation to rest my weary feet. Two bees buzz me aggressively and ants make for me like I may be their last chance for a meal.

Paris, knowing he could win the heart of Helen, built a ship and sailed to Sparta on a princely visit. As fate would have it, Menelaus was called away to Crete, where his grandfather had died, and while he was gone, Paris stole Menelaus' treasure and stole Helen. The code of conduct governing hospitality to strangers was strong in ancient Greece, and Paris' violation of Menelaus' trust demanded severe retribution. Even Menelaus' reason for being gone from Sparta, his grandfather's funeral, added to the outrage. Paris may have been handsome, but he was indeed a lowlife.

The archaeological remains from the Bronze Age, the age of Helen and Menelaus, indicates that it was well populated and prosperous. But the Bronze Age settlement came to a mysterious end just after 1200 BC, perishing by fire,[148]after which it disappeared as a city-state, only a few stragglers living in poverty among the ruins of old homes.[149] Menelaus and Helen were buried at the Menelaion.[150]

After spending an hour on the hilltop, I suddenly realize the time and gather up my pack and camera and start back down the hill, the hot sun sporadically blocked by drifting puffs of clouds.

As I turn north along the Eurotas River, I reflect on the last great legend of the Bronze Age here at Sparta. This legend fits in well with Mycenae, where I'm headed. Agamemnon, the king of Mycenae who led the Greek forces at Troy, was murdered when he returned home. His son avenged his father's death. The son's name was Orestes. After the deaths of Agamemnon and Klytemnestra, Menelaus and Helen, Orestes who'd married Hermione, the daughter of Menelaus and Helen, became not only king of Mycenae but also of Argos and Sparta. He died in Tegea, an ancient city just south of Tripoli, from a snakebite. Centuries later, Sparta tried to conquer Tegea without success, and the generals finally went to the oracle at Delphi to see what it would take. The Pythia told them to bring the bones of Orestes back to Sparta. His bones were surreptitiously located in Tegea, and in 550 BC, the city finally fell to Sparta's forces.

I quickly check out of the hotel and lumber under my pack to the bus station. My pack feels twice as heavy after my long morning walk, and I'm sweating profusely. The bus station is dark and crowded, smoke-filled. I buy my ticket and stand for a half hour in the shade outside, trying to dry my sweat-soaked shirt.

During the bus ride back into Arkadia, Pan country, thoughts of my Uncle Jud return. Pan was often in the presence of the Earth goddess, or as she's also called, the Great Mother, who played such a prominent role in the prosperity of Sparta. Pindar spoke of the two of them in his maiden songs:

O Pan, that rulest over Arcadia,
and art the warder of holy shrines ...
thou companion of the Great Mother,
thou dear delight of the holy Graces![151]

Pan's flirtation with her is understandable when you consider that he was also the frequent companion of Dionysus, the god of madness. The Earth goddess also had her influence on madness as evidenced by Agamemnon's son Orestes. When Agamemnon returned home after the Trojan War, his wife Klytemnestra killed him, and Orestes avenged his father's death by killing his mother. This act ran counter to everything the Earth goddess stood for and she sent her Furies after him. The Furies were the avenging fiends of the Great goddess, and they punished wrongs against parents committed by their children. They drove Orestes mad. He wandered throughout the Aegean but was cured at a sanctuary just to the west of here, which has a small tumulus with a finger of stone. During his madness, Orestes bit off his finger there. Close by the finger stone, another sanctuary was dedicated to the Furies. The place is called the Cure, because Orestes was cured of his madness there when he saw the Furies turned from black to white.[152]

★

The drab bus station in Tripoli seems an old acquaintance after being here with Hans and Margo yesterday, though it still doesn't seem friendly. No bus goes from Tripoli to Mycenae, so I have to catch the train though I don't know the location of the station. I finally find a man who's directing passengers about and ask him if he speaks English. He says no, so I try my Greek. "Τρανο σταθμος. Που ειναι?" I ask. He understands me immediately, repeats my question to make sure, and points in the direction of the train station. "Ειναι κοντα?" I ask, wanting to know if it's close. He takes out an ink pen and writes 200 on his hand, 200 meters. "Ευχαριστω," I say. I hoist my pack and hit the fresh air for my walk to the train station.

Without thinking about it, I've adopted a way of communicating with Greeks who do not understand English. When I ask if they speak English and they answer no, I speak to them in Greek. Invariably, they answer in English. Most of them know a little. They continue speaking their pidgin English and I speak my pidgin Greek. We are confined to a very limited vocabulary in each other's language, a demilitarized zone of communication, but it works wonderfully. This business of straddling boundaries is another Hermes phenomenon. He is ever the gateway between worlds.

I walk straight to the train station, asking one person to confirm that I'm going in the right direction, and soon I'm inside a large red brick building, standing in line to get a ticket. I ask the man behind the window if he speaks English and again get "No," for an answer, a very emphatic "Οχι!" this time. He turns his head as if I should get away from the window, but when I say "Εσιτιρια, Αργος, Μικηναι," he immediately turns back, grabs a ticket and starts writing on it. The change in him when he realized I speak a little Greek was amazing. He motions for me to give him a 1000 dr bill from which he returns 350 dr in change. I asked him "Τι ωρα?" and he shows me where he has already written the train's departure time on my ticket. Just as I get my pack straps zipped inside their pouch, the train pulls up. I climb onboard, asking frantically if it's the train to Argos and Mycenae (my insecurity knows no bounds), and I'm assured that it is by two Greeks. I navigate my big bag through the crowded car toward the front and take a seat by a huge young man who looks as if he would rather have both seats for himself. If Hermes hadn't been with me, I would have had to wait two hours for the next train.

On to Mycenae.

CHAPTER 7: Mycenae

I lean back in my seat and relax as the train lurches forward. Finally, I'm on my way to Mycenae, or actually Μυκηναι (Mykinai), the small town on the outskirts of the ancient city. I hoist my pack to the overhead racks, realizing I'm handling the weight better than when I first started my journey. I'm in the front car and get a quick look inside the cockpit-sized engineer's station, which is definitely not hi-tech, more like a 1950's automobile interior.

The loud non-ceasing clickety-clack along the rails is accompanied by a physical jarring. The car rocks from side to side, making it difficult not to bump into the guy next to me. It also lurches sideways and snakes, a dance-like slithering. I get out of my seat and walk down the aisle to look at the route posted over the door (which interestingly has nothing to do with where we're going), and find standing much more difficult than in a bus. All this and we're not doing fifty kilometers per hour.

We stop at several stations, and at one, a man a couple of seats over buys σουωλακι (a small shish kebab on a wood stick) for himself and his wife from a vendor on the sidewalk. My light two-banana breakfast isn't standing up very well, and it's after two o'clock. My mouth floods at the smell of roast pork. After his meal, he demonstrates the Greek attitude toward the environment. He lowers his window a little, stands up, and drops the aluminum soft-drink can to the fast-moving ground below. No one in the crowded train protests this flamboyant gesture to the countryside.

I feel someone tap my knee and look up to see the motherly woman sitting across from me open a package of cookies and hand three to me. She must be forty-five, dark hair, a gray long-sleeved, full-length dress and black shoes, a pleasant smiling face. I thank her and accept the cookies gratefully. Several times I've watched traveling Greeks share food among family members, and I realize what a friendly gesture this is. I wish I could talk to her.

We're traveling Argolid Nome, which contains the ancient kingdoms of Argos, Tiryns, Nauphlia, Epidaurus and also my destination, Mycenae. The Argolid is a fertile agricultural plain by the sea, separated from Corinthia Nome by mountain ranges to the north and Arcadia Nome to the west. From the

Mycenae

time of Agamemnon, its most famous and powerful ruler, it has been known as "horse-rearing." Though it's ringed with mountains, passes provide easy access to Corinth, the coast at Nauphlia and Epidaurus. The Argolid plain is formed of limestone hills covered with citrus and olive orchards, pine woods, green fields of tomatoes, artichokes, melons, an occasional patch of tilled earth.

The woman taps my knee again and hands a napkin full of dried fruit and nuts to me, which I also greatly appreciate. She doesn't try to talk to me, but when the train stops at one of the intermediate stations, I ask if we're in Mykinai. She says, "Οχι," and points in the direction we're going. When the conductor comes by, she asks him something, and he tells me in English that Mykinai is the next stop. I get my pack from the overhead rack.

As the train slows, a commotion erupts among the passengers, and they strain to get a look outside. The woman across from me rises from her seat and exclaims "Τοριστας!" Touristas! As I pull my backpack from the overhead rack, I crane my neck also and see a gang of twelve young people in shorts and T-shirts, all looking very American, scrambling for their packs. I didn't realize we travelers were such a curiosity to the locals. As I exit the train, I nod to the woman who shared her food with me, and she smiles farewell.

The young Americans board, and I'm the only person to get off. When the train pulls out, I stand alone outside the closed train station in the middle of nowhere. Then I spot a tall thin young man walking toward me who doesn't look Greek. I ask him if he speaks English. "I am English," he says. He has just come from the Mycenaean ruins, just got off the bus a block away. I quickly determine that he's from London, not far from where my own son spent six months a few years ago. "Do you know how I can get to Olympia?" he asks, a little impatient to get on his way. He's shy, reserved, the unfriendliest traveler I've met in a while. I tell him I've come from there and explain that he should take the train to Tripoli and there change to the bus. He gives me directions to a hotel where I can spend the night here in Mykinai. I shoulder my pack and walk away, feeling as though I'm deserting him as he stands before the closed train station with no way to get a ticket or schedule. He seems lost and as lonely as me. Too bad we're traveling in opposite directions.

I walk to a tourist shop nearby and learn that I'm actually in Fychtia, still two kilometers from Mykinai. The Englishman was wrong about finding a hotel here, but a stunningly beautiful Greek woman (well-drawn features and captivating dark eyes) tells me I can find one in Mykinai. I stand outside the shop looking back inside at that beautiful girl, unable to walk away from her. I've never felt so drawn to a woman because of her looks. Finally, I trudge toward town all hunched over under the weight of my pack, wishing I had brought my

Mycenae

Samsonite suitcase with wheels. I keep stopping to look back at the tourist shop, can't get the girl out of my head. She's the most beautiful woman I've ever seen. The Greeks have had 3200 years to improve on Helen, and I don't think they've wasted any time.

I stop halfway to Mykinai at an isolated restaurant with two tour buses full of formally-dressed Japanese parked out front, catch my breath and cool myself in the afternoon breeze. Alongside the road cornstalks, plowed fields, a grape vineyard glow in sunlight. With a sigh and a glance back in the direction of the beautiful woman, I trudge on.

On the outskirts of Mykinai, the road starts a slow uphill grade that progressively steepens through the small nearly deserted town. With my heavy pack, even the slightest incline means work. At the Klytemnestra Hotel on the far side of town, a man sitting at a table on the second floor notices me mounting the steps and comes to take my pack, addresses me in English.

At dusk, I walk down the street to a restaurant, the Electra, named for Agamemnon's vengeance-minded daughter. It's turning a little cool. I order mousaka, a large Greek salata and a Sprite. The evening in Olympia when I had dinner with Hans and Margo, both had mousaka. I've been wanting some ever since, even though they both said it gave them diarrhea. Eating the mousaka is work, an ever-replenishing meal with layers of pasta, a ground-lamb sauce, eggplant and a layer of baked custard on top that distinguishes it from anything I've eaten before. I'll find out what new adventure my dinner has in store for me.

Agamemnon and Klytemnestra had four children, three daughters and a son. The eldest daughter and the most beautiful was Iphigenia, whom Agamemnon sacrificed at the temple of Artemis in Aulis when she was eleven. Electra was several years her junior and Crysothemis a couple of years younger yet. Orestes, their only boy, was just a baby when Iphigenia was sacrificed.

Ten years later, when Agamemnon returned from Troy, Klytemnestra was still fuming over Iphigenia's sacrifice and had taken a lover, Aegisthus, Agamemnon's hated cousin. Klytemnestra killed Agamemnon with an ax as soon as he arrived home from Troy. She describes her act:

> An endless web, as by some fisher strung,
> A deadly plenteousness of robe, I flung
> All round him, and struck twice; and with two cries
> His limbs turned water and broke; and as he lies
> I cast my third stroke in, a prayer well-sped
> To Zeus of hell, who guardeth safe his dead!

Mycenae

So there he gasped his life out as he lay;
And, gasping, the blood splashed me. ... Like dark spray
It splashed into my face, a dew of death,
Sweet as the rain–drops blown by God's dear breath...[153]

Electra sorely missed her father and raged for years over his murder. She sent little Orestes away to be raised by Agamemnon's brother-in-law, Strophius the king of Phocis, so that one day he might return and avenge their father's murder. When Orestes came of age, he returned to Mycenae after conferring with Apollo at Delphi and, with Electra's encouragement, killed both his mother and Aegisthus.

Following the murder of his mother, the Furies hounded Orestes insane. He fled from them throughout the Greek isles, finally returning to Delphi, where Apollo sent him to Athena's temple on the Areopagos in Athens. There Athena tried him for the murder of his mother. Apollo defended Orestes and the Furies prosecuted. Once Orestes had been acquitted, he returned to Mycenae and married his cousin Hermione, Helen's and Menelaus' daughter. He ruled as king, also succeeding to the throne of Sparta following Menelaus' death. Thus Orestes became the most powerful king in the Peloponnese, worthy of his name, which means "man of the mountain," a reference to the hill on which Mycenae rests. Orestes was the last major figure of Greek mythology.

I'm the only guest in the Hotel Klytemnestra, which is dead silent except for the repair work going on down the hall. The banging of hammers echoes through these thin walls like hand grenades. I hope they quit before bedtime. The entire town is deserted except for dogs. I hear their hollow voices from all over town. Occasionally, a motorbike screams through town without slowing. Greece is shutting down for the season. I've taken a chance by coming to the mainland before traveling to the islands. I could have problems with ferry schedules, weather and accommodations. I must start my trek through the islands soon.

A mosquito wakes me just at midnight, and after battling for two hours, I finally kill him with a thundering handclap at the edge of the bed. I've scratched two bites on my chest, and when I pull off my undershirt, pale spots of blood dot the inside. I've started picking up some miniature hitchhikers. I have something growing on my left ear. It's crusty and flaking, feels leathery. The side of my face stings, and I've been drawing flies.

A man moved into the room next to mine late this evening. His snores come through the wall as I chase mosquitoes. I hear his every move through the thin wall. He just went to the bathroom. I hear his bed squeak and all the bathroom stuff. Now, it's very quiet. I haven't heard a rooster since this

Mycenae

afternoon.

When Orestes returned to Mycenae after being raised by his uncle in Phocis, he had been to the oracle at Delphi and received Apollo's order to avenge his father's murder by killing his mother. Electra was champing at the bit for him to do their mother in, but his resolve weakened with his mother's plea:

> Hold, O my son! My child, dost thou not fear
> To strike this breast? Hast thou not slumbered here,
> Thy gums draining the milk that I did give?[154]

Orestes was caught between the old and new order of Greek gods: Apollo who represented the new Zeus religion, and the Furies who were three daughters of Earth, serpent-haired, black-skinned crones who dressed in gray raiment and had voices like baying dogs. They directed their wrath against the minds of those who wronged their parents. Orestes described his own murder of his mother as a "victory that sears me like a brand," and immediately afterward sensed his mind going:

> ...methinks I steer
> Unseeing, like some broken charioteer,
> By curbless visions borne. And at my heart
> A thing of terror knocketh, that will start
> Sudden a-song, and she must dance to hear.[155]

Orestes' "thing of terror" was the Furies.

The fall following the fateful encounter with my father, I enrolled at the University of California at Berkeley to study physics and philosophy. I was interested in Plato, Aristotle, quantum mechanics, astronomy. I bought a copy of the Iliad. For the first time, I was living in the center of my life. But one evening a college buddy from Bakersfield came to visit. We went out to one of the local student-cramped coffee houses and discussed Dostoevsky for hours among the din of raised voices, the clatter of dishes and the lofting wisps of cigarette smoke in the darkened room. I went back to my apartment that night, slipped between the sheets of my bunk bed and dropped off to sleep. Or almost dropped off. As I dozed, something came into my mind, the magnitude of which I can only compare to visions of Hell itself. I saw grotesque images, animated faces, so vivid they had the undeniable mark of reality.

I sat up for a second to clear my head, looked around in the dark room. Another man slept in a bunk bed off in the corner, and I heard the soft steps of his rhythmic breathing. But as soon as my head hit the pillow again and my eyes closed, the terrifying shapes returned.

Dionysus is the god of the mask, and behind the mask lurks the world of madness. His epiphany is sudden and terrifying. I was not in some sleep-filled dream world but fully awake. I would rise up in bed and the faces would disappear, but when I closed my eyes, there they were again. My body shook. I dressed, went into the living room and tried to study. My mind started working on its own, a runaway freight train. I can't adequately describe the terror that filled me knowing I could no longer control my though processes.

Dionysus was "the spirit of a wild being. His coming brings madness."[156] Otto describes his epiphany:

> The eternal depths gape open and out of them a monstrous creature raises its head before which all the limits that the normal day has set must disappear. There man stands on the threshold of madness--in fact, he is already part of it even if his wildness which wishes to pass on into destructiveness still remains mercifully hidden. He has already been thrust out of everything secure, everything settled, out of every haven of thought and feeling, and has been flung into the primeval cosmic turmoil in which life, surrounded and intoxicated with death, undergoes eternal change and renewal.[157]

But the god himself is not merely touched and seized by the ghostly spirit of the abyss. He, himself, is the monstrous creature that lives in the depths.

I have no doubt that I could have given myself up to madness and gone completely insane. Looking back through thirty-two years, I see it as having all the characteristics of Dionysus' world, full of terror, murder, madness, ecstasy. The ancient Greeks spoke of Dionysus as coming to the person. We don't have to seek him out. Perhaps I was experiencing panic, a panic attack as a psychiatrist would say, but this was much more than a feeling. I had no thoughts of impending death. I was being visited by something from which no escape was possible. The epiphany was occurring within my consciousness. Dionysus was frequently seen in the company of Pan, from whom our word "panic" derives. That night I felt the presence of both gods. Uncle Jud, my namesake, was evidence I could travel that path as an inheritance.

Pan was also frequently seen in the presence of the Earth goddess and her defenders, the Furies. I knew well what Orestes had experienced. In Orestes words:

Mycenae

Ah! Ah!
Ye bondmaids! They are here: like Gorgons, gowned
In darkness, all bewreathed and interwound
With serpents! ... I shall never rest again.
...
You cannot see them. I alone can see.
I am hunted... I shall never rest again.[158]

Orestes was twenty,[159] my age at the time of my problems. I had to get out of my apartment, go somewhere, but I knew I needed help, couldn't take care of myself. I was going crazy. I ran.

I had an uncle (a man who died just recently) to whom I had been close since childhood. He was paranoid schizophrenic and had been hospitalized several times, always against his will, and given shock treatments. At times, he claimed to be God. Schizophrenia manifests in early adulthood, and I had always wondered if I would develop his illness. Until that night, my wondering had been an intellectual exercise. My uncle lived close by on the outskirts of Oakland, only a half hour away in a small one-room shack in a Mexican camp. When I ran that night, I ran to him.

23 Oct, Saturday

Up a little late this morning. I sit in the hotel restaurant, the only customer waiting to be served a breakfast of bread, jelly, butter and milk. The proprietor had to go to the store to get it. The front of the restaurant is all glass, and I see out over the street in front to the light traffic. The sky is covered with clouds, and I can barely see the mountains in the distance. A pickup with fruit and vegetables in the back passes slowly. A song by the rock group "Tears for Fears" blares through the pickup loudspeaker. The proprietor returns from the store with my breakfast, and shortly I'm shoveling it down. An English woman comes down the stairs and asks him for a roll of toilet paper. She says good morning to me, and I speak back but she keeps staring at me. I hope its not because I look so scruffy. I wonder if she is the "man," I heard snoring last night?

Despite the proprietor's forecast of a sunny day, which he pronounces as I leave the hotel, intermittent rain follows me to the ruins of Mycenae. The walk is all uphill, two kilometers of gentle slope along a blacktop road, with towering Mt. Zara to the right, where the sun peeks through the clouds as it starts to sprinkle again. Mycenae was the most powerful kingdom in the late Bronze Age and gave its name to the entire Aegean civilization of the time. The ruins of Mycenae are beyond the winding road in front of me, covering

130

a hilltop and looking camouflaged, their tan coloring blending into the rolling hills. Triangular-shaped Mt. Ayios Elias looms behind Mycenae to the north.

The legend of Mycenae is intimately connected with that of Pelops at Olympia. The founder of Mycenae was Perseus. Perseus, like Theseus, was of uncertain parentage. His mother, Danae, told her father that Zeus had impregnated her, taking the form of liquid gold and flowing into her womb.[160] Perseus was the famous mythological character who traveled to Libya and decapitated the Gorgon, Medea. He subdued his enemies by holding up her snake-haired head, which was so ugly it turned men to stone. Perseus became king of Tiryns, south of here, and later founded Mycenae, having the giant one-eyed manlike Cyclopes erect the walls of the palace from huge stones.

Several kings of Mycenae descended from Perseus, but his grandson, Eurystheus, died without leaving a son to succeed him. The Mycenaeans chose Atreus, the son of Pelops, therefore, as their king. Atreus was a powerful king, and the influence of Mycenae steadily grew. He married Aerope, the granddaughter of Minos, king of Crete. Atreus had two sons, Agamemnon and Menelaus. But the curse on Pelops' family, a result of his murderer of Myrtilus, was still active and led to the infamy of the "House of Atreus."

The Argolid was inhabited during the Stone Age, as far back as 20,000 BC,[161] and Mycenae's natural citadel between two ravines was first inhabited in the Neolithic Age.[162] The city was named after Mycene, the daughter of the ancient river god, Inachos.[163] Perseus simply walled the citadel of an existing city. Agamemnon was Mycenae's most famous king.

I sit just inside the tourist entrance to Mycenae, at the edge of an asphalt walkway proceeding on past through the famous "Lion Gate." Four huge stones frame the entrance, over which stand the triangular limestone slab containing the relief of the lions. The lions have been decapitated, the soapstone heads not surviving the 3200 years since Agamemnon was king. In his time, Mycenae was surrounded by 900 meters of huge stone Cyclopean walls six meters thick, much of which remain today. The first fortifications were built about 1350 BC.

I enter the ruins of the ancient city and walk through the huge stone gate with the headless lions towering above me. Inside the walls stand the remains of the guard's sanctuary, and beyond it, the primary attraction at Mycenae: the famous Mycenaean Grave Circle A. When the amateur archaeologist Schliemann came here in August of 1876, he came looking for gold, and it didn't take him long to find it. He butchered the site, slicing large trenches through the earth to expose the stone slabs of the Grave Circle.

The Grave Circle is composed of vertical-standing sandstone slabs forming two concentric circles a meter apart. The space between the concentric circles was originally covered with similar slabs, but now stands open as a narrow circular walkway around the graveyard. Six rectangular pits inside the stone circles descend for several feet to royal graves. Each burial was followed by a feast with the remains of the meal left covered with soil.[164]

The ancient Greeks believed that we are all the children of the great Earth goddess and burial of the body was the return of the deceased to her. Here, in part, is the Homeric Hymn to Earth:

I shall sing of well-formed Earth, mother of all
and oldest of all, who nourishes all things living on land.
Her beauty nurtures all creatures that walk upon the land,
and all that move in the deep or fly in the air.
O Mighty one, you are the source of fair children and goodly fruit,
and on you it depends to give life to, or take it away from,
mortal men.

I think back to the picture of Schliemann, his wife and crew that I saw in the Athens museum. They stood among loose piles of rubble, looking unbearably hot in their long-sleeved, baggy, 19th Century clothing and hats. But now, a group of well-dressed tourists spreads around the circle, a guide lecturing them from within the stone circle. Several umbrellas are poised over their heads to ward off rain splats. The tourists are quiet, attentive, the men in suits and the women in long dark skirts. The voice of the guide rings within the circle of stones. The connection is unmistakable, a funeral service here at the ancient Mycenaean gravesite.

In the royal graves, Schliemann uncovered the remains of ancient Mycenaean kings, queens and their families. Gold masks (those I saw in the National Archaeological Museum in Athens) were placed over some of their faces. Nineteen members of the royal families were buried here, eight men, nine women and two children, along with "gold vessels and jewels, ...bronze swords with gold and ivory hilts... daggers decorated with gold and silver inlaid blades...." In all, Schliemann uncovered fifteen kilograms of gold.[165] Later, a more detailed analysis of his finds revealed that the remains were all from the 16th Century BC, much earlier than that envisioned by Schliemann. He had not found the bones of Agamemnon and Klytemnestra as he thought, but those of a royal family who lived some four hundred years earlier.

I leave the grave circle, ascend stone stairs up a gentle slope strewn with boulders to the ruins of Agamemnon's ancient palace. All that remains are short stone walls, paved floors and courtyards.

Mycenae

I sit at the very top of the ruins at the temple of Athena, which was built at a later date on top of old palace ruins. From here I overlook hills and valleys, patches of brown grass, squares of orchards and vineyards that stripe the hills with golds and greens. Heavy clouds cover the tops of mountain ranges in the distance.

As Vincent Scully points out in his book, *The Earth, the Temple, and the Gods*, all the problems of the House of Atreus may also be attributed to an unparalleled arrogance. The ancient Greeks didn't take the setting of their citadels lightly, and with Mycenae they were unusually particular. Most ancient Greek cities lay below the temples of their gods, but Mycenae was placed on a hill between two peaks. The ancient Greeks view this as a representation of a prone woman, Mother Earth, with her knees raised, legs wide-spread with Mycenae sitting on her privates, the entrance to the womb. When the king mounted his throne, he was pronouncing his dominion over the earth, and in particular, his authority over Mother Earth. Thus the most powerful kingdom in the Bronze Age was founded on a profound demonstration of mortal arrogance. One can well imagine Agamemnon's uneasiness as he mounted his terrible throne, which sat over the womb of the World. This crime against Mother Earth was echoed when Orestes murdered his mother. Interestingly enough, that was also Oedipus' transgression, to lie with the mother.

Two artifacts from late 13th Century Mycenae, the time of Agamemnon, are of particular interest. One is a large bowl-shaped jar used for mixing wine. The paintings on the sides of the bowl depict six warriors with shields and spears leaving for the Trojan War with a woman waving good-bye. The other artifact is a fresco of a beautiful large-busted woman. Her head tilts slightly, peering down at something in the missing portion of the fresco. She's smiling and has just a hint of a double chin. Her delicate well-formed hands are drawn in detail. Could the beautiful woman be Klytemnestra, sister of Helen and wife of Agamemnon? Do we have an actual snapshot of the queen?

Wisps of wind bring more cold drops of rain, and I break out my small black umbrella. When Agamemnon returned home from sacking Troy, Klytemnestra rolled out crimson tapestries for him to enter the palace. He protested the red carpet, claiming such honor should be only for a god, but at Klytemnestra's insistence, he gave in.

If you are so determined--
Let someone help me off with these his shoes at least.
Old slaves, they've stood me well.

Hurry,

and while I tread his splendors dyed red in the sea,
may no god watch and strike me down with envy
from on high. I feel such shame—
to tread the life of the house, a kingdom's worth
of silver in the weaving.[166]

Shortly after Agamemnon entered the palace, Klytemnestra killed him in the bathroom with an ax. From where I sit, I can see the marble-paved floor. Electra, Iphigenia's sister, brooded here day after day, year after year waiting for her brother, Orestes, to grow into manhood so he might return and avenge their father's murder.

Orestes did return and plunged a hot knife through his mother's heart. Because of her years of brooding and her hatred for her mother, Electra is considered by many to be the Rosetta stone for the relationship between mother and daughter. But in this instance, unlike Oedipus where he unknowingly killed his father, Electra's hatred is specifically and knowingly for her mother. And another curious fact: Electra is impotent against her and relies on her brother to commit the murder. Plus, unlike Oedipus, she has a valid reason for hating her mother, the murder of her father. All of Oedipus' problems came from his own unknown nature, but those of Electra were a part of her conscious everyday life, and therefore would seemingly be of little interest in revealing her hidden nature. I'm skeptical that the story of Electra reveals anything significant about the relationship between a mother and daughter. I had hoped it might reveal something about my own feminine side and its relationship to my mother, but now I doubt it.

The sun comes out again, and it turns warm. As I exit the archeological site through the Lion Gate, I meet my two friends from Holland again, Hans and Margo. We smile and shake hands as if we're family. Traveling has brought me unreasonably close to these strangers. They've rented a car in Nafplion, driven up to Mycenae and have just entered the site. Ah, to have a car myself! I'm glad to see their smiling faces, all that blond hair. We part again, they to the ruins of Mycenae and I to the Treasury of Atreus, or as Schliemann called it, the "Tomb of Agamemnon," which is in a hill across the road to the west. The Treasury, built in 1250 BC, was definitely here when Agamemnon was king and may have been his resting place.

I walk from the site across the blacktop road to a dead, grass-covered hill. A mound of earth covering the tomb has been partially removed to reveal a ramp way and arch. The place is cluttered with tourists. I mill about for a while, and eventually they leave. Once inside the massive stone archway cut from the hillside, I'm overwhelmed by the size of the interior (15 meters in diameter and 14 meters high), the architecture and the craftsmanship of the stonecutters. The inside is beehive shaped, thirty-three concentric circles of fitted stone that come together at the apex.

A small adjoining chamber to the north, hewn out of rock, is not nearly as impressive. I have to use my flashlight inside it since it has no entrance to the outside. Just as in Odysseus' Cave of the Nymphs, the walls of this chamber drink the light. The comparison with the Cave of the Nymphs reinforces another aspect of ancient Greek burial practice. Caves were sacred to the ancients, and here in this large mound of earth, the entrance to this cave certainly brings to mind the privates, the womb, of Earth. Agamemnon's tomb is then an entrance to Earth's womb, and instead of being a place of death is one of rebirth.

Back in the large stone-lined beehive chamber, I walk along the base of the walls inspecting the workmanship, look in disbelief at the 180-ton stone slab over the archway. No wonder the ancient Greeks believed Cyclopes built these large structures. As the last straggling tourists leave, I suddenly find myself alone in Agamemnon's tomb, and then notice a loud clicking noise. When I stop walking, the sound stops. I walk to the center of the chamber just beneath the apex. My footsteps are amplified and come back as tremendous echoes. I stomp my foot and hear thunder. It's a sound like that from a deep well, as if the chamber is acoustically much larger than is visible. The room is acoustically tuned to its center. I can find no mention of the effect in guidebooks. When others come into the room, the effect disappears.

I walk back outside and up the small hill created by dirt piled over the site by ancient grave makers. I stand on top and look back at Mycenae. Agamemnon himself must have seen this sight many times. Perhaps he chose it himself for his own grave. The view of the ancient city is indeed magnificent. But this was also the home of Iphigenia, and I can well imagine she also stood here. I have a feeling that before my journey is over, I may have to come to terms with their troubled relationship, as well as that between my own daughter and me.

By the time I finish visiting Agamemnon's tomb, the clouds have disappeared and the sun is hot on my head.

★

In the evening I go downstairs and follow the sound of voices to the lounge, where a young man sits alone watching TV. He nods at me and motions to take a seat on one of the two couches. He turns off the TV, starts talking to me as if we've known each other for years. All around us is darkness, the hollow building echoing sounds of the night.

He's the son of the owner, mid-twenties, single, startlingly handsome. He would be a good match for the young lady I saw just up the road at the tourist shop when I first got off the train yesterday. Her Paris. He has the archetypal Greek bushy-black hair, dark-olive skin. His family is originally from Greece but immigrated to Australia where they lived for nineteen years, returning three years ago.

I ask him how he likes living in Greece compared to Australia. Most people I've met on the road take a day or so to size you up before they speak without skirting questions. He only pauses long enough to ensure his answer is precise. "Summers here are hectic with all the tourists," he says, "and the rest of the year is boring. I have a small circle of friends, but we have nothing to do."

I tell him I feel safe in Greece, much safer than in America.

"It is safe," he tells me. "In three years, I've never seen a fight, no violence."

"But Greeks argue a lot," I say.

Big smile. "They argue all the time, but it's good-natured. Nothing they like better than arguing. But Greeks are a petty people, most will stab you in the back if given the chance."

"Why is it so much safer in Greece than America?"

"American television," he says without hesitation. "That and Hollywood. All the violence. In Greece, everything is the family. That's the reason I'm having difficulty returning to Australia."

"Your mother and father want you to stay?"

"Especially my father. It will kill him if I leave."

The more I talk to this guy, the more I realize he will tell me anything, everything about himself.

"My parents, they have no education," he states without animosity. "They are hardworking and own land here, could retire if they wished. But years ago, my father used to come home drunk, and my mother would argue with him about it. I've always had a strong sense of who I am, had strong moral convictions. I held our family together while he did his drinking. When I was eight, I talked with him about his drinking, that he should quit. He finally did, but it was a struggle. My parents used to keep all their money in jars in the house, and already as a kid I knew that wasn't right. I told them they should put it in a bank, so it would draw interest. It took me two years to convince them. My friends have always been older than me. I've always been grown up. My friends tell me I should be a psychiatrist, but I have no idea what that would be like. I want to be an architect because I once worked in construction."

He reminds me of my father who also held his family together, took care of his alcoholic father. His brother and sisters looked to him as a stabilizing

Mycenae

influence in their lives even after they were married and on their own. He once told me that when he was thirteen, he suddenly realized he was grown. Quite a load for a kid to be carrying around.

Next he starts on Australia. "Australians love to hunt kangaroos," he says. "The country is overrun with them. Even though killing kangaroos is necessary to control the population, I wouldn't do it. A lot of my friends here in Greece hunt, but I don't."

"You don't like violence," I say.

"Not always," he says. "But I like boxing, probably the most violent of all sports. I don't fight but I like to watch fighting." I'm surprised at his insights into himself.

If one characteristic distinguished me from my father, it's my distaste for hunting, killing. But I also like boxing, an interest I share with my father.

"My parents," he says, "they do not understand about boredom. I'm bored to death here. I only intended to stay two years when we came from Australia. I'm an only child. In Greece, a man must have a son. My father's adamant about me staying. If I'm going to be an architect, I must return to Australia to attend college."

"You seem to have made up your mind," I tell him.

He smiles. "Yes, but I don't know how to tell my father even though we're very close. It'll break his heart."

I've never been close to my father. Hate is a very strong word for a son to use about his feelings for his father. Of all the world's literature on love, precious little has been written about hate. No one feels just one way about anyone, particularly about their father. No one wants to deal with their own hatred. This is the first time I've recognized the hostility I have for my father. As I write these words, they come to me as a revelation sending a chill up my spine. I can also say I love him and say it with more conviction, more certainty than ever, as if my hostility no longer contaminates my other feelings. Perhaps this is a remnant of that night he lifted me from between my mother's sheets and laid me in my own baby bed. My anger at him has stood between me and my own good judgment at crucial times. It's an undercurrent I've never been able to get beyond.

24 Oct, Sunday

A lone rooster crows. He has no followers, just a single voice raised against the darkness of early morning. My dreams have gone into a strange, alien land where I visit cities as a child. I learn to direct and control the flow of glass-encased rivers. I see weird bridges and dams. Strangers take care of me in dark unfamiliar homes. I work jobs unfamiliar to me, dream of women. In one, a

Mycenae

pregnant woman comes to stay with a female friend who is ecstatic to have her in her home and covers her with kisses. I'm neither in the dream nor am I viewing it. I don't exist. Some dreams are dark, happy, others full of fear and strange longings, denial and crude excess. Strange, prebirth dreams set in a dark land in an primordial time. I've melted, dissolved into the landscape.

This morning early, I'll leave for Corinth, the home of young belligerent Oedipus. I see him there, tall, broad-shouldered. A man who would provoke a drunk into lashing out with the only tool, only weapon, he could use against him: his suspicion concerning Oedipus' parentage. I see Oedipus as a man of arrogance, privilege. Perhaps he even wore his limp with a certain grace, a man of strong conviction who provoked jealousy, envy. I'll go to Corinth to find this young man, hopefully find him among the stones and dust, see him standing at the Acrocorinth staring out to sea.

I stand at the window awaiting sunrise, looking out at the surrounding hills. Snores come from the next room. Morning comes to Greece not as a bolt of sunlight, but as a lifting of haze that uncovers first a village, then the countryside, a hill, a mountain, a mountain range. Sunrise in Greece is not a revelation but a slow discovery from within the mists of morning.

It's time to move on.

I decide to walk the two kilometers to Fychtia rather than wait for a bus from Mykinai that was recommended by the proprietor of the hotel. I'm not sure he can forecast the buses any better than he can the weather, and I can't afford to take the chance. The walk is mostly downhill, but I still have to stop a couple of times to rest from the weight of my pack.

Once in Fychtia, I buy a ticket for 550 dr at the roadside coffee shop across the street from the bus stop. I have forty-five minutes to dry my sweat while I await the bus to Corinth. I'm already drawing flies, sitting here in the morning sun with my bus ticket in my pocket. Four men sit at a table not far from me, drinking Greek coffee and water. They always serve water with Greek coffee.

Thinking back on the frank conversation with the young man last night, I realize I've developed a new openness myself on this journey. I talked to Pat and Marlene in Delphi about things I won't tell my own friends. I felt the same comfortableness and urge to talk about myself with Hans and Margo in Olympia. I'm beginning to understand what a liberating experience traveling can be. It's like watching a sped up movie of the walls of Mycenae crumble through the millennia, the walls I've built around myself.

Flies swarm my backpack, my Levis, my arms. A taxi pulls up and stops in front of the cafe. An old man in one of those blue fisherman's caps (which I want very badly) gets out. Flies swarm the old man. His features converge at

Mycenae

a focal point just in front of his face. His eyes, his nose, his chin all point at the same imaginary spot. He drives a Mercedes. No flies on the Mercedes.

I've not been tempted to undergo Orestes' treatment for his madness. Pausanias tells of his cure:

> When the goddesses were going to drive Orestes mad they are said to have appeared to him all black, and when he bit off his finger they suddenly seemed to turn white, and the sight of them sobered him and he consumed offerings in fire to turn away their wrath, and performed divine sacrifice to the white goddesses. ... Orestes cut his hair... when he came to his senses.[167]

But then I was only sitting on insanity's doorstep, hadn't yet gone off the deep end. I ran as Orestes did, right into the jaws of a life I never intended to live.

I feel better with my ticket to Corinth in hand, and while waiting for the bus, I read my guidebook. Hera's most important temple in all Greece is not far from here. But I can't get there by bus. The air is cool, even as I sit in the hot morning sun. The four men have split up now, one to his pickup; two have moved their chairs into the shade behind me and are still talking; one stays put with his elbows on the table, his hand at his mouth, eyes staring off into the flatland with the mountains of Mycenae in the distance just below the burning sun.

CHAPTER 8: Corinth, Epidaurus, Argos

The bus from Fychtia to Corinth takes forty-five minutes and the driver puts me out three blocks from the plateia at the edge of the sea. Corinth lies at the headland of the Peloponnese, on the isthmus to the mainland.

The cry of gulls breaks the quiet. The cool, humid air has dampened the shadowed streets on this early Sunday morning in new Corinth. The ancient city, where Oedipus was raised, is a little south of here, but this place has been around a while, too. From dockside, I look up the street south and in the distance see a mountain, the Acrocorinth, the acropolis of the ancient city. I'm anxious to get a room and catch a bus to the ruins. A man straightening tables at an outdoor restaurant looking out over the sea tells me that Hotel Byron, which is recommended by *Let's Go*, has been closed for five years. He motions toward the Hotel Acti across from the dock-side plateia.

The young man behind the desk speaks English with a thick Greek accent. He's congenial and helpful, mid-twenties, tall, big around the middle with a protruding face and widely-spaced buck teeth. He has on sloppy dress pants and shirt. I follow him up the creaking stairs and along the echoing hall of the second floor. The double doors to my room are narrow, very tall. As I step in with my pack, the floor gives and creaks as if it might not hold my weight. All is wood except the crinkled linoleum floor and white porcelain sink. The linoleum is buckled in several places and the gray baseboard is rotting. Green-and-blue–flowered wallpaper covers not only the walls but also stretches over electrical cords and plumbing. The towel rack is pulled from the wall and hangs by a bent screw. My balcony overlooks the main street. It comes with plenty of noise, motorbikes and horns, no extra charge.

I dump my backpack on the floor and walk uptown to catch the bus to the ruins. At the station, I meet a young woman from Italy, a tall gorgeous girl, short brown hair, fat face, dressed in a white sweat suit and toting a black daypack. She sits with me on the bus to Corinth. She's just come from ten days in Crete. "Crete is great," she tells me, through a thick Italian accent. "Lots of Minoan ruins, great buses. You must see it." Her name is Letizia. "It means happiness," she says.

Odysseus' biological father, Sisyphus, founded the ancient city of Corinth. Sisyphus was the cleverest man alive, having outwitted Autolycos, "the wolf itself," who was Odysseus' grandfather. Sisyphus even outwitted death and remained on Earth long beyond his time. When he did die, Sisyphus was punished by spending eternity at the futile task of rolling a boulder up a mountain only to have its weight overcome him and roll back just as he reached the top.

Letizia and I exit the bus and follow her guidebook's instructions to the archeological site's entrance. After circumnavigating the ancient city in the hot sun, we realize the entrance has been moved.

We visit the museum first to get out of the sun, luxuriating within its cool but small rooms that echo with the voices of touristas. In the courtyard we discover a row of ten standing statues of women, all headless. Letizia has me take a picture with her standing among them, she the only one with a head on her shoulders. Very stern, no smile.

The sun is a real scorcher today, and it's brought out a snake. He's small and brown, quick as a lizard. We see him in the weeds just past the museum at the entrance to the ruins. A security man comes running. "It's the children I'm concerned about," he says. He believes it's an adder, poisonous. It flits out of sight between rocks.

Corinth was one of the most important commercial and military cities in antiquity because all overland traffic from northern Greece and Attica had to pass through the Isthmus nearby to get to the Peloponnese. Sea-lanes radiated in all directions by virtue of its two harbors, one on the Gulf of Corinth to the northwest that gave access to the Ionian Sea, and the other on the Saronic Gulf to the southeast providing access to the Aegean. Oedipus grew up in Corinth.

The Apostle Paul came here in 52 AD after visiting the agora in Athens. While here, he preached the gospel in a synagogue at first, and later in a private home. He was more successful here than he had been in Athens. In the agora, Paul defended himself against accusations by Corinthian Jews that, "This fellow persuadeth men to worship God contrary to the law."[168] Apollo, Poseidon and especially Aphrodite (the goddess of erotic love) were still worshipped here at the time. Paul stayed with Aquila and Priscilla, a Jewish couple recently expelled from Italy, and wrote Romans and Thessalonians I and II while here. After he left Corinth, he also wrote two epistles, Corinthians I and II, to calm the waters between the bickering Greek Christians here.

The 6th Century BC Temple of Apollo, with its chubby monolithic columns, dominates the ruins. Only seven of the original forty-two columns still stand. As with most ancient cities, Corinth was surrounded by stonewalls. The earliest inhabitants made their homes at the foot of the Acrocorinth during the Neolithic period, about 4000 BC. When I arrived, I saw the Acrocorinth, the magnificent mountain overlooking the ancient city. It has a commanding presence over the landscape.

Next to Apollo's temple is the agora, or marketplace, its ruins now dominated by the remains of an arch alongside the ancient walkway. To the sides of the path are the shops, which illustrate the flourishing commerce of the town's ancient past. The rostrum where St. Paul defended himself before the Roman Proconsul in 52 AD is in the middle of the shops. Running beside the agora was the paved Lechaeum Road that connected the city with the Gulf of Corinth. The port was situated a little west of the city of modern Corinth.

We exit the site, and I sit in the shade. I listen to birds tweet in the trees while I wait for Letizia, who's reentered the museum. A cool breeze blows. Corinth is also where Diogenes died, the 4th Century BC philosopher who was the original Cynic. He's said to have gone out in broad daylight with a lantern in search of an honest man. The word "cynic" means "dogish"[169] which is a pretty accurate description of Diogenes. He lived in a storage pot, carried a stick and wore a cloak that he used as a blanket. He slept in the open or in public buildings, the original street-person. He pronounced vicious criticisms of humanity and masturbated in public.[170] He was the first to claim to be a citizen of the world. Most of his writings have been suppressed and lost because of their shocking support of cannibalism and incest.[171] They buried him here, by the gate to the ancient city. My own Uncle Jud doesn't seem so bad after contemplating Diogenes, although certain embarrassing behavioral parallelisms are evident.

Here comes my Italian girlfriend out of the museum, approaching me with long proud strides and a smile. "Walk with me to the top of the Acrocorinth," she commands.

I hadn't thought of hiking up there today. As a matter of fact, I'd imagined taking a taxi since the walk is supposed to be strenuous. "We'll have plenty of time to make it back before the last bus," she tells me. I'm eager to get to the top myself, want to know if Oedipus could see Delphi from there.

We walk the side of the asphalt road, and though I'm energetic at first, the heat and steep slope eventually get to me. I didn't bring a water bottle, and when we make a rest stop, Letizia is good enough to let me have a sip of her water. My shirt is soaked through with perspiration, but she looks as cool as when we started. At the entrance to the fortress, I slip inside a cafe just outside the gate, sweating like a pig in castration. I down a Sprite on the spot and buy a 1.5 liter bottle of cold water.

The Acrocorinth was the domain of Aphrodite, goddess of erotic love. She was born off the coast of Cypress. When her father, Kronos, overthrew his father, Ouranos god of the sky, Kronos lopped off Ouranos' testicles.

> As soon as Kronos had lopped off the genitals with the sickle he tossed them from the land into the stormy sea. And as they were carried by the sea a long time, all around them white foam rose from the god's flesh, and in this foam a maiden was nurtured. First she came close to god-haunted Kythera and from there she went on to reach sea-girt Cyprus. There this majestic and fair goddess came out, and soft grass grew all around her soft feet. Both gods and men call her Aphrodite, foam-born goddess, and fair-wreathed Kythereia; Aphrodite because she grew out of Aphros, foam that is, and Kythereia because she touched land at Kythera. She is called Kyprogenes, because she was born in sea-girt Cypress, and Philommedes, fond of a man's genitals, because of them she owed her birth.[172]

Since she was so fond of man's genitals, she was the goddess of sexual love and beauty and was worshipped in brothels.

A medieval castle sits astride the Acrocorinth, its rock walls snaking around the summit, a crown on the sacred mountain. We enter through shaded stone arches and continue to climb, passing through the inner stone gate. Before us is a rolling stone-and-weed-covered mountaintop. We follow the wall along the west face of the mountain to the remains of stone houses and rest at the edge of a cliff overlooking what seems the entire earth. The sun casts long shadows and misty mountains rise up in the steamy ocean of air, the gods' stepping stones that vanish in the distant haze.

Letizia is ready to return, but I coax her on up the mountain to the northeast. I've busted my butt to get here, and I'm going to see what I came to see. Finally, we sit on the very top of the Acrocorinth looking north over the ruins of the ancient city far below and beyond to the Gulf of Corinth. I'm well into my water bottle and feeling better.

I stare off into the distance with the cool breeze whipping about me and the earth falling away just beyond my feet to the ground 300 meters below. I take another long swing with Letizia chiding me not to drink so much. She's sitting just a few feet from me, her arms folded about her knees, still protesting the climb up here.

"This was the site of Aphrodite's most important temple," I tell her. She's not impressed.

Sitting suspended in air on this precipice overlooking the countryside, I see past both the ancient and new towns of Corinth to the water of the Gulf and on its opposite bank, the small town of Itea masked by haze. I'm seeing it from the southeast now as I had from the northeast while in Delphi. I make out the valley north of Itea and just to the east, a glimmer of white against the distant mountainside, Delphi. I imagine young Oedipus standing here 3300 years ago, looking over this same landscape. The view must have been clear in his day without all the motorbikes and cars pumping exhaust into the air.

I imagine him sitting here brooding the morning after the banquet during which the drunk raised the question of his parentage. Perhaps he came to the Acrocorinth after talking to his father, the king, but was still convinced there was some truth in the drunk's wild accusation that he was not the biological son of his mother and father. He must have seen Delphi off in the distance, as I can now. Perhaps he had an inspiration: he would go to Delphi and get the final word concerning his parentage from the Oracle. Apollo would surely tell him the truth.

What interests me about this stage of Oedipus' life is the uncertainty the words of the drunk unleashed. You'd think he would have brushed the cheap shot about his parentage aside or perhaps gone into a rage and beat the man. Oedipus was certainly prone to violence. But he didn't. Since Oedipus is our Rosetta Stone for unlocking our own inner secrets, here is the birth of uncertainty leading us on our quest for self-knowledge and eventual self-destruction.

From here at Corinth Oedipus went to Delphi, which, taken metaphorically, tells us that the ancient gods hold the key to self-knowledge. Sigmund Freud took his psychoanalytic technique from the Oedipus myth, the quest for self. But his student, colleague, and later, professional enemy, Carl Jung, went a step further and proclaimed that all mythology, and in particular the gods and goddesses of the ancient Greeks, was the key to understanding human nature. He envisioned them as archetypes of human behavior, postulating that they exist within all of us.

The world's great religions tell us that, to find God, we must look within. But what the ancient Greeks, and even the major religions of today, would have recognized as a divine presence within themselves, the psychological community recognizes as our own emotional makeup. Whether or not it is then possible to separate religion from psychology has become one of the more interesting questions facing us as we enter the 21st Century. Because of this, many psychologists have proclaimed god dead. With the birth of psychology, we have the rise of atheism.

That night in Berkeley, when I came home from the coffeehouse and tried to fall asleep, I interpreted my near-hallucinatory experience as imminent insanity. That was all I had to explain it. If I had been an ancient Greek, I would have recognized the experience as the epiphany of a god, perhaps of several: Pan, Dionysus, the Furies. They all hang out together. During my uncle's bouts with schizophrenia, when he lost his mind completely, he proclaimed he was God. We might well ask the question: Does the ancient Greek religion lead us only to the discovery of ourselves and say nothing about spirituality? At this point in my journey, I don't have the answer.

I still have my eyes fixed on that white speck on Mt. Parnassos, which I suspect to be Delphi. Getting to Delphi from Corinth overland would be an arduous journey. I don't believe Oedipus went over land but walked to the Isthmus, just a few kilometers from here and, as the prince of Corinth, commandeered one of the boats being pulled across on wheeled platforms. My theory is that he sailed the waters of the gulf to Itea, where he started the journey by foot up the slope to Delphi. He was probably with friends who helped him chat away the miles.

Whatever the case, after visiting Delphi, Apollo having ignored his question and telling him he was to kill his father and marry his mother, Oedipus decided not to return to Corinth. He said good-bye to his friends and his old life and sought a new one in another land. He was alone when he had the dispute with Laios over the right of way and killed him and three of his four companions.

I must see the site where Oedipus committed the four murders. Tomorrow I'll try again to rent a car and drive to the Cleft Way. I cannot possibly leave Greece without seeing it. Letizia says she's going back down the mountain. She's slipped on her black daypack and stands looking at me defiantly. Off in the distance I hear the yelling and sawing of a mule.

On the bus back to new Corinth, I ask her to have dinner with me, but she smiles bashfully, turns her head away. "We'll see," she says.

After a cool shower and change of clothes, I hobble down to dinner at a large outdoor restaurant on the waterfront, my knees aching after today's strenuous hike. I'm the only customer among rows and rows of tables and chairs sheltered by a plastic partition from the breeze that blows in from the Gulf. Nearby, a group of Greek men watch a basketball game on TV. Shortly after the waiter seats me, Letizia arrives. Her hair is still a little wet, but her face radiates youth and energy, drawing a stark contrast to my flushed face, exhaustion and pain-pulsing knees.

Corinth's main street is at the edge of our table, and the sound of traffic is consuming: motorbikes, cars, trucks, the exhaust. The restaurant is across the street, next to Letizia's hotel, so the waiter has to bring our food through the traffic. In addition to the olive oil on our salatas, they have an extra topping of motor oil. A gray cat slinks close to our table, eyeing my kalamari. Our waiter crosses the street to shoo her away, but soon she's back, surveying my plate and crying mournfully.

"Tomorrow I'm renting a car and driving into Boeotia," I tell her. "Why don't you come with me? I'll show you where Oedipus killed his father. We can see the canal cut across the Isthmus on the way."

She swallows a big bite of bread. "I saw the canal when I came into Corinth by train. I'm going to the temple of Hera tomorrow."

The cool sea breeze flaps the clear plastic partition. A car horn starts two blocks away, stops for a second, starts again. The occupants are dressed in suits, a large bouquet of flowers tied to the antenna. Letizia's gaze follows the car down the street. "A wedding," she says. The cat hops into one of the extra chairs and sticks her head above the tabletop. Letizia shoves her away.

My Greek salata is very good, the usual large wedges of tomatoes, olives, sliced onions, cucumber wedges, and a large block of tart feta cheese. The eight oval kalamari of various sizes are lightly breaded and fried, still a little slick, but absolutely delicious and served with a lemon wedge. They remind me of small boiled eggs but are a little tough to chew. Letizia stuffs bread into her mouth.

After dinner we stroll the dock, browsing the boats. I hobble around after her. "Go for a walk around the city with me," she says.

"I can't," I admit. "You walked me into the ground today. My left knee is killing me." My condition is severe or I'd certainly not pass up this invitation. She smiles and walks off down the street.

As I enter the hotel, loud music from the bar attracts my attention, and I maneuver through the crowded doorway to the bar, order an ouzo, my first. It tastes strongly of licorice. I expected a disco from the blaring bouzouki music and laughter, and I guess it is a sort of disco. A sleek Greek in dark pants and white shirt dances by himself in the middle of the crowded room. Where are the girls? I've heard Greece called the world's largest men's club, and this bar is certainly a testament to that sentiment. But they are singing. No doubt this is one happy group. They're singing to each other.

★

I wake at midnight. Sleep in the Hotel Acti never progresses beyond a doze. The music from the taverna beneath my room comes to me unattenuated. Cigarette smoke seeps up the walls. Motorbikes stop at the traffic light just below my window, and when they take off, fairly blow the walls out of this hotel room. The lights in Corinth dim every couple of minutes. Occasionally they go out completely.

My leathery ear feels better now that I'm using my athlete's foot medicine on it. If I have to go to the pharmacy for more, how will I say "athlete's foot" in Greek? Αθλητικος ποδι (athlitikos pothi) is as close as I can come using my dictionary. The gender of the words may not match, but maybe they'll do the job. I hope I don't catch anything from the bed I'm sleeping in here.

I'm so sleepy, I believe I can shut out the noise and smoke for a few more minutes and doze again.

25 Oct, Monday

I've rented a Subaru, and I'm off to the Cleft Way with a detour by Mt. Kithaeron where three-day-old Oedipus was exposed on the mountainside. First I stop at the Isthmus, which separates the Gulf of Corinth from the Saronic Gulf. Except for the Isthmus, the Peloponnese would be a large maple leaf-shaped island.

A canal across the Isthmus had been envisioned as far back as the 7th Century BC.[173] At that time, sailors who wished to avoid the sudden violent storms at the southern tip of the Peloponnese, unloaded their boats onto a tram and dragged them across the six kilometer Isthmus on a paved road called the diolkos. The diolkos were a set of deep grooves cut into stone roadway.[174] Nero started a canal in AD 67 using Hebrew slaves, but work was abandoned when he died. A French company took up the challenge in 1882 but ran out of money in 1889. It took determined Greek engineers to finally finish the job in 1893, one hundred years ago, officially making the Peloponnese an island.

I stand on the bridge spanning the canal, looking down into the water one hundred meters below. The canal is only thirty meters wide at the waterline and is a thin blue stripe at the bottom of the tan cliffs cut through the earth. The bridge is a metal truss structure, a gigantic erector set, which rattles and shakes when cars and trucks cross.

I eat a chocolate pie and a ham-and-cheese croissant, watching crumbs fall into the water below. I look south, trying to see the small town of Kenchreai where the Apostle Paul caught a ship bound for Ephesus on the western coast of Asia Minor (Turkey), but Kenchreai isn't visible from here. Nor is the Temple of Poseidon, where the Ismithian Games were held. So little time, so many tough choices.

Oedipus may have stood here where I now stand and commandeered a boat for the short trip to Itea. Undoubtedly, he would have envied my trip by car. I should be at the Cleft Way by late afternoon. First I'll take a drive up the mystery-shadowed mountain where he was left to die as a child of three days, Mt. Kithaeron.

To get there, I drive the freeway along the south side of the Isthmus, past Megara, to a turnoff just before Eleusis. Megara is where the seer Calchas lived.

Corinth, Epidaurus, Argos

Agamemnon respected him enough to go to his home to convince him to go to Troy with the Greek fleet. But Agamemnon grew to hate Calchas because it was he who divined that Agamemnon must sacrifice Iphigenia to get favorable winds to sail to Troy. Eleusis at the edge of the sea is where Theseus buried the Argos generals who died in the battle of Seven Against Thebes. After the turnoff just before Eleusis, I head north to Mt. Kithaeron.

A sign, "Κιθαιρωνας" (Kithaeronas), points to a paved side road. On the switchbacks up the side of the mountain, I see the strangest goats: large, dark-brown creatures with black, flat horns. When seen on edge, the horns give the goats a Spanish look, as if they've donned sombreros. Could be they donned hats to go out this afternoon to visit dance-loving Pan, the goat god. An old male chases a young female, and I imagine the fun he'll have with her. According to Greek tradition the goat "is the most efficient in copulation."[175] Just the animal I'd expect Pan to hang out with.

I pull off the side of the road halfway up the mountain to snap a picture but have to get back in my car quickly because of the smell. Just off the edge of the road where it falls away down the mountainside, people have dumped trash and animal remains. The smell of the dead is simply unbearable.

The top of Kithaeron is not as picturesque as I'd hoped. It's not a peak really, just a large knoll with a government facility standing nearby, a bland cement building with big dish antennas. Could be a military installation, but it's deserted, my Subaru the only car on the mountain. I look northeast at small cities and villages spread around Boeotia. Far in the distance, Thebes is a flat scattering of white specks.

Of the many atrocities committed on this mountain, none is more infamous than those that occurred during the women's rites in worship of Dionysus. During these orgiastic rites, they ripped apart wild animals and ate their flesh raw. They carried fire in their hair and remained unscorched.[176] During one such ceremony, Pentheus, Oedipus' great grandfather, also a king of Thebes, was killed and dismembered by the maenads, the same fate experienced by Dionysus at the hands of the Titans. Pentheus' own mother, who had lost her senses during the ceremony, returned to Thebes with her son's blood-dripping head on her thyrsus. She became hysterical when her reason returned.

Kithaeron also played a part in relaying news of the Greek victory at Troy. The night Troy fell, the Greeks sent a signal to Mycenae. A series of fires on mountaintops, starting with Mt. Ida in Troy and ending with Mt. Aigiplanctos in the Argolis, told of their triumph. One of those fires was right here high atop Kithaeron, an echo of the fire ravaging Troy as the Greeks murdered, raped and looted. Aeschylus' play *Agamemnon* opens at night with a watchman trying to stay awake, staring out into the darkness for a glimmer of firelight as he had been all year. Finally the flame in the distance appeared, and he woke the entire city to celebrate the victory. Mt. Kithaeron got its signal from Mt. Messapion and relayed it to Mt. Aigiplanctos where it was visible to the Mycenaean watchman standing in the city's tower called the Spider's Crag. Klytemnestra describes the sequence of fires and tells of that on Kithaeron:

> And onward still, not failing nor aswoon,
> across the Asopus like a beaming moon
> The great word leapt, and on Kithairon's height
> Uproused a new relay of racing light.
> His watchers knew the wandering flame, nor hid
> Their welcome, burning higher than was bid.
> Out over Lake Gorgopis then it floats,
> To Aigiplanctos, waking the wild goats,
> Crying for "Fire, more fire!"[177]

On the brighter side, Zeus and Hera were married on this peak. He carried her here from Euboea, the long thin island to the east of Attica, which was Hera's and known as "the good cow country."[178] Hera was a little girl and Zeus' sister. She struggled against his advances until he promised to marry her. This type of incestuous behavior was reserved for the immortals, and incestuous mortals were punished unmercifully, as Oedipus found out.

The top of Kithaeron is above the smog and layer of pollution that extends from ground level to the clouds. But still, it's an impressive site in all directions, 1409 meters above sea level. The Gulf of Corinth, to the southwest, lies like a blue mirror with its face to the sky. To the north lies the valley of Boeotia with its network of roads and towns, Plataea at the base of the mountain just underneath me, Erithrai further out, and Thebes in the distance.

Baby Oedipus would have met his death on this mountain if it hadn't been for the kind-heartedness of two shepherds. Jocasta gave her three-day-old child to a trusted shepherd (an act which she denied) with instructions to expose him on Mt. Kithaeron. The baby's ankles had been pierced and pinned together by Laios. Kithaeron is a good day's journey by foot from Thebes, so I imagine the shepherd received the baby in the morning and traveled all day with the baby in his arms until he reached the slopes of Kithaeron. But he didn't have the heart to set the baby out to die, and perhaps met the shepherd from Corinth that first night. I imagine them sitting around the campfire soothing the baby's swollen ankles and discussing his fate. The other shepherd, a trusted member of the

Corinthian royal household, knew his king and queen could have no children, and, since the baby was of royal lineage, decided he would make them a present of the child.

I leave Kithaeron sooner than I would like in a terrible rush to reach the site where Oedipus killed Laios before nightfall. According to Pausanias, after Oedipus killed Laios and his companions, Damesistratos, the king of Plataea, found the bodies and buried them at the Cleft Way.[179] I will be at the gravesite shortly. Perhaps by the time I return to Corinth this evening I'll have seen the Cleft Way that I've passed three times but was unable to see by bus.

On the road again, I go up the grade toward Thebes, past the ruins of Eleutherai where the common soldiers of Argos, killed in the battle of Seven Against Thebes, are buried. Theseus retrieved the Argive dead by force from Thebes, stopping short of sacking the city. He cremated them in the shadow of Eleutherai's cliff on the dry-grassed hillside just off to the right of the road. I pass through the quiet outskirts of Thebes along the road next to the Fountain of Dirce, where I stood a little more than two weeks ago, and then travel on the road through Levadia.

By the time I approach the stony crack of Mt. Parnassos a few kilometers in the distance, the sun hangs close to the crest of Kithaeron. I see a sign pointing to Daulia off to the right, and slowly pull off the road onto the dirt.

I exit the car, and finally stand on a dirt path at the Cleft Way. In front of me is a small ravine, and on the other side, up the opposite slope, is a small square patch of golden grass, alfalfa with a lone olive tree growing in its middle as a quiet simple symbol of peace. The field is on fire with dying sunlight. The dirt road, a trail really, winds around the mountain close to the bottom of the ravine, the very path where Oedipus and Laios approached each other. The trail is cluttered with tracks and droppings of sheep and goats.

To the north, the hill rises and is lush with brush. I see the white speckles of sheep on a far slope. The sight of sheep calls to mind the words of Hesiod concerning the many races of men, and in particular the fourth that died in a war over Oedipus' flocks:

> Zeus, son of Kronos, made upon the nourishing land
> yet another race—the fourth one—better and more just.
> They were the divine race of heroes, who are called
> demigods; they preceded us on this boundless earth.
> Evil war and dreadful battle wiped them all out,
> some fighting over the flocks of Oidipous...[180]

Corinth, Epidaurus, Argos

At this narrow gap between hills, Oedipus would not give way to the chariot, so Laios struck him with a two-headed goad. Oedipus flew into a murderous rage, killing not only Laios but three of his four companions as well. The fourth escaped back to Thebes and years later was the missing link in Oedipus' quest for the identity of the murderer. Red-haired Oedipus was so enraged even after killing Laios that he bit him and spat out the blood.[181] I see no sign of the graves dug by King Damesistratos.

I imagine Oedipus wandering down the Sacred Way from Delphi, disgusted with his life, the uncertainty in it since receiving the words of Apollo, maybe kicking dust as he went, when he came to this narrow ravine where a horse-drawn carriage suddenly sprang up before him. As issues go, this should not have been a major one, and who can deny that at a tight place in the road the right-of-way would go to the horse and carriage instead of a lone man on foot. One can well imagine a reasonable man tipping his hat and stepping aside as the carriage sped past. But not irritable Oedipus. He would not yield nor would Laios, two men made of the same stubborn stuff. Euripides describes the action, putting words in Jocasta's mouth:

> Then Laius' charioteer commanded him Oedipus—
> "Stand clear, man, from the pathway of a prince."
> Proudly he strode on, answering not. The steeds
> Spurned with their hoofs his ankles, drawing blood.
> Then—why tell aught beyond the sad event?—
> Son slayeth father...[182]

In my own case, who would deny I should have yielded to the older, more experienced man in his own home concerning who he would welcome as a guest? Was I spoiling for a fight? Oedipus didn't know his own identity when he encountered Laios on the road, didn't know the man was his father. The lesson we learn from Oedipus, the great paradigm, is that we never know who we really are and the man we struggle with on the road is always our father.

At this fateful junction, three roads meet: one east to Thebes, another west to Delphi and the third to Daulia, a small town north on a sacred road not so frequently traveled. In Sophocles' *Oedipus Tyrannus*, both Jocasta and Oedipus describe this crossroads. Jocasta's description is translated as "the place where three roads meet." Oedipus' words are more variously translated, but I'm fond of the translation that calls it, "this triple parting of the ways."[183] These words describe metaphorically what happened to me the fateful day I stood my ground against my father. Oedipus doesn't say which road he was planning to take, that to Daulia or Thebes. I imagine him on his way to Daulia, the road less traveled but, following the confrontation with Laios, changing his mind and deciding to go to Thebes, and there to meet his fate head on.

I wasn't Oedipus. My life didn't literally parallel his, although the inclinations are close enough to suggest something more than accident. The experiences of the human race down through the millennia have frequently paralleled this theme. The essential difference between Oedipus and me is that I didn't kill my father, although a few days later I toyed with a situation where it could have happened. Obviously, that has made all the difference.

My triple parting of the ways occurred when I heard my father clicking the deer rifle. My life disintegrated, fragmented. I proceeded a ways down the road I was on, driven by the momentum of my life, but I found the road blocked that night in Berkeley when the monsters within turned me back. Like Dionysus being ripped apart by the hands of the Titans, I was fragmented, and in a sense, even died, since I no longer knew who I was. After being reborn, Dionysus was driven mad by Hera and wandered throughout the world. I also wandered, lost within myself, half-crazed.

I was living close to all the myths then, and I chose the road also chosen by Oedipus, the conventional road symbolically represented by that to Thebes, one that ends in marriage, kids. I receded into the comfort of family and profession. But something had awakened within me that could never again be put to sleep. Eventually it caught up with me.

I don't want to make too much of my short stay with my uncle after I abandoned my studies in Berkeley. I simply used him as a gateway into a new life. What is important is the simple fact that I chose to run to my uncle, who, at times, had bouts of insanity. He was a kind, considerate man and deeply religious. I thought that possibly he would understand what others would not. He was experienced in the wilds of the mind.

My uncle lived in a Mexican camp on the outskirts of Oakland, and when I arrived at two in the morning, it was dark and desolate, small rundown cottages bordering a dirt courtyard crowded with cars and littered with kids' toys. My older cousin, the fighting cousin, and his new wife had come from my parents' and were staying with my uncle in his one-room shack. Though crowded already, they were glad to see me and made a place for me to sleep on a pile of freshly washed laundry. My uncle slept in an easy chair pushed up against the front of his refrigerator, and my cousin and his young wife slept in the only bed, pushed against the wall. I remember books stacked everywhere, on the floor, nightstand, kitchen table, in corners, the middle of the floor. Much the way my apartment is now. When I told my uncle I was losing my mind, he smiled, put his hand on my shoulder and spoke with complete confidence. "Absolutely not possible," he said. The sight of his baldhead and white mustache was such a comfort.

When my uncle was in his mid-twenties, he had his first bout with schizophrenia. He was institutionalized and underwent a series of shock treatments. Not long after, his wife left him for an older man and deprived him of contact with his two kids, thus precipitating his further mental deterioration. From then on, he was committed periodically but always escaped. He used to tell me stories of wandering in the desert living in abandoned buildings, drinking from mud puddles left by rain. Once he kidnapped his daughter and ran off to east Texas, where he took a room in a motel and left his three-year-old daughter with a babysitter while he worked. He couldn't bear to be without her, couldn't stand to think of another man being the role model for his son. The authorities caught him, took his daughter away, returned him to the insane asylum. More shock treatments. He drifted for the rest of his life, coming to see us now and then when he wasn't working. I came to know him as the most sane man in my family, humble, honest, caring, easy to talk to, willing to discuss the hidden-side personality.

The morning after I arrived at his place, he drove me to my parents' home, where I spent the following year, met a girl, and married. I realized I couldn't face the world without a woman at my side. It all makes so much sense now. Before I left home, I had to have a woman to replace my mother. Oedipus had done the same thing, only, in his case, his mother was his wife. My wife had a timeless quality, sort of a mythic manifestation of all women. Just as Orestes had fled from the Furies and eventually ended up at the temple of Athena on the Areopagos in Athens, so had I fled into the arms of a woman. Eighteen years of marriage, two kids and a divorce followed. My wife satisfied a longing I'd had from the time my father took me from my mother's bed and put me in my own baby bed. I used to wake in the middle of the night, astonished I could love her so much. Her silky hair and warm body were like a tonic to an illness.

During this time of marriage, all seemed well with me. I spent eight years in the Air Force, during which I underwent and passed human reliability testing, became a member of a Titan II ICBM launch crew, pulled alerts in missile silos. We mothered the missiles that could have destroyed the world. I got a master's degree in astronautical engineering from Stanford University and dealt with all the normal problems juggling professional and family responsibilities. But my wife's departure years later unleashed something I had suppressed all those years. I was spring-loaded toward something wild and violent, which her presence had counter-balanced. Without the steady, guiding influence of a woman, I drifted toward those deep uncharted waters I had dipped into that night in Berkeley.

Corinth, Epidaurus, Argos

Here at the Cleft Way, the sun is set, the golden grass turned to shadow. The breeze feels cold on my bare arms. I hear the dull clank of goat bells in the distance.

The drive back to Corinth is endless. Just before I re-cross the feet of Kithaeron, traffic on the crowded two-lane road comes to a stop. An accident blocks the road ahead, and soon a white ambulance wails past with red lights flashing. A kilometer further, I come upon a single-vehicle accident, an overturned truck pulling a cotton trailer, partially protruding into the road from the shoulder. I drive on through the dark with the trail of red taillights before me snaking into the distance. Along the freeway next to the Gulf of Corinth, city lights on shore reflect out into the bay. Traffic is fast and reckless. Cars come up behind going 110 kph, get so close their headlights disappear behind my rear bumper before swerving around and cutting back in front, almost clipping my fender.

After I return my rental car (it costs 30,000 dr or $125.00 including mileage and gas), I walk the dock looking at the boats, the small ones, the very old, well-used, the yachts. I meet Letizia there. She has just returned from climbing a mountain in Argos, the Acroargos, forty kilometers south of here. She liked the area so much, she's moving to Nafplion tomorrow. "We just keep running into each other," she says joyfully. She's such a pleasure, her easy laugh.

"How was Hera's temple."

"Oh, David, you wouldn't believe the setting. It's on a hill beneath a mountain. Nothing left but foundations, but the view of the surrounding countryside is worth the trip. And all of it was for Hera, no mention of Zeus, her unfaithful husband. She bathed there every year to regain her virginity. Can you imagine that?" She blushes a little, turns from me.

"I would like to see it. Maybe that's where I'll go tomorrow."

"Oh no!" she says. "Go with me to Epidaurus. The best preserved theatre in Greece is there."

She's convincing. I need to leave for the islands, but perhaps they can wait a couple more days. My first island will be Mykonos from which I'll make a day trip to Delos, where Apollo and his twin sister Artemis were born, then Santorini and Crete. "I'm really anxious to see Crete," I tell her.

"I know," she says, "and you'll love it. But first you must see Epidaurus."

★

I wake shortly after midnight, kill two mosquitoes I've been battling for two nights. My blood splatters in two ragged blotches on the wallpaper's blue-and-green flowers. The music from the taverna downstairs dies out and so does the sound of traffic outside. Last night I gave serious consideration to changing hotels. I guess it was the helpfulness of the young man downstairs that changed my mind. Early yesterday morning, I found him asleep on the couch in the entryway, still in his clothes. When I left for the Cleft Way, he was at the top of the stairs standing guard while the maid cleaned the rooms. His eyes were bloodshot, and he looked like the living dead. I wonder if he ever leaves the hotel?

26 Oct, Tuesday

I'm up early for the bus to Epidaurus. First it goes to Nafplion, where I change buses and meet Letizia. She's glad to see me but seems preoccupied. "My room is not clean here in Nafplion," she says. "The shower is so bad I had to bathe with my shoes on." From the bus we see the ancient theatre sitting in a shallow, dream-like valley within a sacred grove surrounded by shrub-covered hills. It was built into the side of Mt. Kynortion in the 3rd Century BC and has a seating capacity of 12,000.

We exit the bus and walk the short distance to the theatre. Letizia goes her own way. I watch her from the top of the stadium and look out at the rolling hills basking in the sun. A man comes to the center of the stage, asks for quiet and drops several coins onto the circular stone surface. I hear a metallic ring as each coin hits the stone stage, demonstrating the stadium's perfect acoustics. This theatre is one more tribute to Dionysus, but the big attraction for the ancients was not the theatre. Epidaurus was the largest healing center in Greece and dates from the 6th Century BC.[184] After a quick walk around the top row of stone seats, Letizia and I leave the theatre and walk to the ruins of this ancient medical facility.

Apollo was the god of light and order, a healing god, but he also had a dark side. He brought plague. The plague at Thebes that devastated the countryside and drove Oedipus to search for Laios' murderer came from Apollo. Death from plague was seen as caused by his sharp arrows. But he was also a healing god, though he turned over this attribute to his son Asklepios.

Asklepios' mother was the mortal Coronis, the "Crow Maiden." While Coronis was pregnant with Apollo's child, she married a mortal and so angered Apollo that he had his sister Artemis kill her. While her body was on the funeral pyre, Apollo became frantic over the pending death of his unborn child and pulled him from the flames. Thus Asklepios had a fire birth, as did Dionysus. Apollo took Asklepios north to Mt. Pelion where the half-horse, half-man Centaur, Cheiron, raised him. Cheiron was the wisest and learned of all earthly beings and taught Asklepios the healing arts. Zeus was ever protective of his own powers and particularly vengeful toward mortals who stepped on his toes.

Corinth, Epidaurus, Argos

Asklepios became a great healer, eventually learning to resurrect the dead. This so angered Zeus that he killed Asklepios. Apollo again rescued his son by making him immortal. Worshipers of Asklepios built his healing center here at Epidaurus.

The patients who came to the health center were first ritually cleansed and then ingested therapeutic herbs. They spent the night in the sanctuary, sleeping in a special building set aside for them, the Abaton. Asklepios appeared as a serpent in their dreams and touched them or otherwise provided for their cure. Inscriptions testifying to the effectiveness of this primitive form of psychotherapy were chiseled into tablets on view here for the patients to read.

The Abaton is currently being excavated. I stand before the roped-off dig, staring into the uncovered ruins beneath the red scaffolding of the archaeologists. One of the more interesting buildings excavated is a circular stone structure, only the foundation of which now stands. But beneath the foundation is a labyrinth of rock slabs and steps leading to a lower level. No one knows the purpose of this building, but speculation tells us that it is the tomb of Asklepios. Since Asklepios was a chthonian god but also at one time a mortal, his two aspects are represented here: the below-ground portion signifying his immortal Underworld aspect, and the above ground portion, his life as a man.

So psychotherapy was invented here at Epidaurus, and 2600 years later, I submitted myself to the modern form of psychotherapy a few years after my wife left. The art of healing is illusive, particularly when it comes to diseases of the emotions and mind, sometimes making the patient worse before he gets better. I certainly didn't understand what I was getting myself into. Something like this trip to Greece, which I'm using to precipitate reactions to my past. Too bad I don't have Asklepios to chase down my long-buried feelings. Now that I think about it, the dreams I've been having while on this trip are precipitating something, although I question their therapeutic value.

Letizia and I take the bus back to Nafplion, where she's staying. She's learning Greek, and I teach her a little while we wait for the bus back to Nafplion in the shade of fir trees. She tells me that her friends think she's strange for traveling like this. They don't understand her interest in foreign countries. When we get to Nafplion, she waits with me for my bus to Argos. We sit on an elaborate wooden seat in the bus station, the only one I've seen so far that isn't drab. "You must see the Acroargos," she says. "It's better than the Acrocorinth." She looks at me seriously. "When you leave me, please go there." We exchange addresses and telephone numbers. I take her request to heart, but still I'm more saddened by leaving her. She's been such a joy to be with my short time here at Corinth.

Among Nafplion's claims to fame is the legend that it is named for Nauplius, the father of Palamedes, who exposed Odysseus' attempt to fake insanity when asked to join the Greece forces going to Troy. While there, Odysseus got even by having Palamedes stoned.

It's mid-afternoon, and I'd like to get back to Corinth, but Letizia's insistence has convinced me to stop in Argos. Oedipus' son Polyneices went into exile in Argos when his brother, Eteocles, wouldn't share the throne of Thebes. While there, Polyneices married and formed an alliance of seven armies, which he then used to try to regain the throne in the battle of Seven Against Thebes.

★

Late afternoon the bus arrives in Argos. In the middle of a large plateia, I run into a small group of American men (one from Colorado) who give me directions to the ancient city, but I have difficulty finding the ruins anyway. Shortly I'm lost within a city where I wanted to spend no more than a couple of hours. The sun seems to be sinking faster than normal. Finally I spot some ruins at the foot of Larissa Hill (the Acroargos) within a dilapidated barbed-wire fence grown over with weeds. I can find no tourist entrance, no place to pay. The wire gate is locked, so I climb over the fence and have the ancient city to myself. Few Mycenaean ruins remain. The stone walls and dirt street are Roman. The most impressive of the ruins are the Roman baths built in the 2nd Century AD.

Another not-so-well-preserved theatre is just above the ruins of Argos at the foot of the Acroargos. It was built in the 4th Century BC. It overlooks both the ancient city and the modern town. Its stone seats and steps are worn slick with age. I'm the only one in the ruins and I climb the slick stone steps, uneasy at the steep slope and slick rocks, to sit at the top. Below me are the ruins of ancient Argos and the modern town, apartments and businesses bordered in the distance by a range of hills.

Before Polyneices came here to spend his days of exile, he stayed with Theseus in Athens to earn his respect, then came to Argos and formed an alliance with Adrastus, the king of Argos, by marrying his daughter Argeia. Sitting here against the mountain where Polyneices must have come many times, I recall another of the many versions of the Oedipus myth, one in which Jocasta does not commit suicide after learning that her husband is her son. She's still alive during the battle of Seven Against Thebes and talks to Polyneices when he comes into Thebes to make one last attempt to get his younger brother to share the throne. He has already mustered the Argos forces outside the city gates. Jocasta asks her son about being an exile living in Argos:

Jocasta: Well then, first I ask thee what I long to have answered.
What means exile from one's country? is it a great evil?

Corinth, Epidaurus, Argos

Polyneices: The greatest; harder to bear than tell.
Jocasta: What is it like? what is it galls the exile?
Polyneices: One thing most of all; he cannot speak his mind.
Jocasta: This is a slave's lot thou describest, to refrain from uttering what one thinks.[185]

The one problem between my father and me that galled me most was that he never let me speak my mind. I spent most of my childhood days out in the fields alone, staring off into the distance toward the small town nearby and longing to be with friends, anyone I could speak to honestly. I was an exile in my father's land. The day I stood my ground against him, I was trying to establish myself, my own identity, something he would never permit.

I leave the ruins of ancient Argos and walk toward the top of the Acroargos, the fortress, following a footpath shortcutting the asphalt road. I walk the edge of an olive grove, city and countryside dropping ever farther below, another tough climb. Undoubtedly, Letizia also negotiated this mountain more easily than I will. Argos is beautiful from above and silent, the white buildings with orange-tile roofs spread out in one giant oval.

Polyneices led the Argives in a futile attempt to siege Thebes. All the Argive leaders were killed, including Polyneices, but Thebes wouldn't give up the bodies. At the request of Adrastus, Polyneices' father-in-law, Theseus retrieved the bodies of the Argive dead by force.

Eteocles was also killed, but Oedipus' line did not stop with the death of his two sons. Polyneices and Argeia had a son they named Thersander who also lived here in Argos. Thersander was among the Sons of the Seven, the Epigoni, who avenged the Argos defeat by destroying Thebes. Thersander was also with the Greek forces when they left for Troy.

The ancient stone wall completely encircles the mountaintop. Someone has spray-painted METALLICA on one of the vertical members. My only companion here within the fortress walls is a flock of grouse. Their round gray bodies scurry ahead of me through the dead grass, waddling like runaway children, stopping occasionally to feeding on grass seeds.

★

I have dinner at the same restaurant where I ate two nights ago. I couldn't resist the kalamari. The waiter brings a small Greek salata and I make him take it back because I ordered a large one. I'm being an ugly American this evening. I came into the restaurant like I owned the place, didn't even ask the waiter if he spoke English. Turns out he can't, and I should have used my Greek. But I feel so at home here. The clear plastic windbreaker has been raised tonight, and

Corinth, Epidaurus, Argos

I enjoy the light breeze off the sea. I have a Greek coffee. The cat has returned to stroll by under my table. I miss Letizia.

Following dinner, I walk around the pier toward the sea from Hotel Acti across Dimaskinou Street, along the waterfront past the restaurant, across a cement plateia with benches scattered about under palm trees. From there, the dock extends out into the sea with two branches off to the right, one for smaller boats, the other for larger ones. The small outboards sport such exotic motor names as Johnson and Evinrude. The fishing boats, called Καικι (caique), are old and well-used, with peeling paint and basket-like spindles for hauling in fishing nets. Some nets are left to dry in stacks on the dock. These boats have tiny compartments extending above deck, little houses for motors. Yachts are in the second docking area, some with masts standing high above deck and sleeping compartments. In one, soft glowing light comes from two small windows. I hear muffled voices. The speedboats at the end of the dock have that swept-back look, open deck with a windshield.

A multitude of large granite stones lines the dock on which sea waves break during stormy weather. I sit on a jagged rock under a big streetlight. The weather is calm tonight with an occasional sprinkle. Small ripples wiggle in the vertical stripes of city lights reflected off black water. The slight breeze is cool, fresh. The weather has gradually changed since I came to Greece. Almost every day now we have clouds. I see a three-quarters moon high above, a wisp of mist fuzzing its pale edges. Across the Gulf, a line of lights dances at the water's edge and gradually disappears into the sea's darkness. Two Greek men talk their machine-gun language on a rock not far from me, one sucking a cigarette that glows brilliant red.

At the end of the dock, a greenish-blue light sits atop a tall pole. A sign next to me says, "ΘΕΣΕΙΣ ΞΕΝΟΝ ΕΚΑΦΟΝ (FOREIGN CRAFT ANCHORAGE)." I hear a woman's voice and the murmur of the sea licking rocks. Something suggestive about the combination. I miss Letizia.

★

I wake in the middle of the night on the verge of vomiting. I had only two pastries to eat all day followed by that large Greek salata and greasy kalamari. I hope the rich food is my only problem. Could I have gotten something from the squid? I keep burping salata. The waiter was right, I should have had the small one. Cigarette smoke coming through the floor from the taverna below isn't helping either.

I slip on my clothes, race down the stairs and outside to the local twenty-four-hour kiosk. Darkness pervades the city, and the streets are barren of traffic, the lonely kiosk light at the edge of the plateia the only sign of life. I can't decide which my stomach needs, a carton of Μιλκο or a can of Sprite. My stomach feels like a ball of vomit. I buy both.

I sit on the edge of my bed wondering which to try first. Maybe the Sprite. At least I'll get to burp. And I was sleeping so well tonight. Not a mosquito in sight. Last night, I finally gave up trying to kill all the mosquitoes in Corinth and put on repellent. I didn't hear a buzz after the Cutters. Think I'll pass on the kalamari next time. Now for the Μιλκο. The carton says, "ΓΑΛΑ ΜΕ ΚΑΚΑΟ (milk with cocoa)."

I plan to leave Corinth in the morning, spend a night in Piraeus before continuing my trip by ferry to Mykonos.

Will I ever see you again, Letizia?

27 Oct, Wednesday

I wake late and tired, decide to spend one more day in Corinth. I walk to the waterfront, look out at the haze covering the Gulf. It's so thick I can barely see the town of Loutrakion and Gerania Ori, a mountain range, looming ominously in the distance. A bank of clouds sits on the western horizon. A man stands in large jagged rocks dipping water in a wide-mouth bucket that he lowers into the sea by a small rope. He drops to his knees, bends over two dead octopuses and washes them in seawater. The octopuses are pale gray and look like thick strings of soft slippery rubber. He flushes them, then puts them in a plastic bag. Two men stand with him laughing good-naturedly. Off to my left, a quarter of a mile away, three shipping boats unload huge cargo boxes with tall cranes that pivot about a steel tripod.

Let's Go was wrong again. I've been looking for a Laundromat. The young man in the hotel has assured me that Corinth has no place I can get my underclothes cleaned, so I've washed them myself and now my room looks like the great surrender, white flags flying on every sharp corner. I've given a dry cleaners four shirts and one pair of pants. I hope this will discourage the fun that flies have been having with me. My clothes are due out at 1:00 PM, just before the place closes. Today is not a day to lose track of time.

What form of pestilence is this? Until a few days ago, I'd been eating at least four pieces of fruit each day, peaches, pears, bananas, but I quit when I ate the mousaka in Mycenae for fear of diarrhea like that experienced by Hans and Margo. Now I'm in a panic to find a Φαρμακειον, a pharmacy, drugstore. Tomorrow, I'm traveling all day on buses and ferries, not a day to be bathroom happy. Today, my Greek dictionary has taught me two new words: δυσκοιλιος (constipation) and κλυσμα (enema). Every traveler's worst nightmare, plumbing problems.

Corinth, Epidaurus, Argos

By early afternoon I've found a drugstore and the man is very understanding, if a little suspicious. Hope he doesn't think I'm doing this for fun. I tell him in both Greek and English, try to get across the severity of my condition. He's deliberate with his words, providing all the options: the several-day solution, the tomorrow-morning solution, the today solution. "Κλυσμα σημερα," I say. "Φερρυβοατ αυριο." (Enema today. Ferryboat tomorrow.)

Before I return to the hotel, I retrieve my laundry from the dry cleaners, although I don't open the large paper-wrapped package tied very neatly with brown string to see if it's all there. I have more pressing business. I read the instructions, administer to myself, and lie on my side on the floor, on the grungy crinkled linoleum, waiting for thunder to strike. Here comes an ant to check on my condition.

*

I'm out on the rocks at the end of the pier. Clouds completely cover the sky and blend with haze on the horizon. Can't tell if the sun is down. I feel a drop of rain. In the east, large clouds form, but the wind is out of the west, so maybe I'll be able to sit here at dockside again tonight. The little blue-green light at the top of the pole is to my left, a red one on top of a pole at the end of the other dock. Just in front of me is a white sailboat with lots of rigging but no sail, a red life preserver tied to the forward end. Tonight the water is not just lapping at the rocks, it's scrubbing them with splashes and pops. I see a white cap now and then, and foam at the edge of the rocks. The lights of homes and businesses break the darkness across the bay.

I've solved my bathroom problem and verified I have all my clothes. Cost me 5000 dr ($21.75) to dry-clean four shirts and a pair of pants. Can't afford much more of that. I've also talked to the travel agent about a ferry. The young woman behind the desk assured me one leaves for Mykonos from Piraeus, on the coast just south of Athens, at eight o'clock tomorrow morning. I'll have to catch the bus from Corinth to Athens at 5:30 AM. It'll get me into Athens by 6:30. In Athens I'll have to switch buses to get to Piraeus, but I won't have to spend a night there after all.

When the Apostle Paul left Corinth for Ephesus, he left from Kenchreai, a small community to the south where he had his head shorn because he'd taken a vow.[186] He must have looked like a modern day skinhead, but that is all they would have had in common. The couple with whom he had stayed here in Corinth, Priscilla and Aquila, sailed with him to Ephesus. Ephesus will be my first destination in Turkey. Paul was also here a second time to raise money for the poor Christians of Jerusalem. He was here for ninety days, then left for Jerusalem, the start of an ill-fated journey that would cost him his life.

Corinth, Epidaurus, Argos

I see a familiar face coming up the dock toward me. As she gets closer, I recognize her chubby, smiling face. It's Letizia.

I rise earlier than expected because of the mosquitoes and pack for the bus to Piraeus. I've killed three mosquitoes in the last few minutes. In my dreams, I've been chasing gurus through India all night. And something has been bothering me, the scene with me lying on the bed and my father clicking the deer rifle in the next room. It's eating at me more than usual.

This morning I'll be traveling the same path Theseus traveled 3400 years ago, when he went to Athens to meet his father for the first time. After Athens, I'll travel the Aegean as far south as Crete, where Theseus also went a short time later. Due to Theseus' thoughtlessness, his trip to Crete would cost his father his life.

★

I've fallen asleep on the bus and have to ask the driver where we are as we pull into the Athens station just at daybreak. I hurry outside and across the street to catch the rickety local bus. The wind is ferocious and cold. I put on my black sweater. The bus to Piraeus is worse than a paint shaker, vibrating, rattling, seemingly on the verge of disintegrating in the street. I harass the driver with constant questions about the ferry to Mykonos, if we'll be at the dock in time. The driver is patient, reassuring.

The wind and cold are worse in Piraeus. I make the dock in plenty of time to buy a ticket and board a gigantic ferry with a stream of other passengers. Inside, I look out through the windows and see derricks and towers of hoisting equipment at the dock. Ships and ferries float past. We leave the dock ourselves, and I look out to open sea as the ferry maneuvers to clear boats in the harbor, the silhouette of boats along the horizon. This ferry, a huge liner, is larger than that I took to and from Ithaca, and glides smoothly through the sea in spite of the wind. The deep-blue seats are arranged like a jumbo jet, and it's hot inside. A couple of smokers don't care that this is the nonsmoking section.

A young American woman, Anna, dressed in a suit, white blouse, sits near me. She's been in Greece only two days, all in Athens, and had to escape the noise, pollution. She'll spend a couple of days in Mykonos. She's a paralegal from Washington DC. I borrow her International Herald Tribune. Nice to know the rest of the world still exists.

By mid morning, the rough sea collects whitecaps and foam. The ferry rocks like a slow motion bronco, spray streaking the windows. I have difficulty standing, feel nauseous. I go out on deck and stand back from the rail to protect myself from the cold wind bringing clouds of seawater. I have on my black sweater underneath my waterproof hiking jacket with the hood drawn over my head. Still, I shiver.

When my father stood in his bedroom clicking the deer rifle with me face down on my bed across the hall, a question clicked back and forth in my head. Him or me? Him or me? A few minutes afterward my mother told me that he was preparing to commit suicide. Now I think she hid the truth from me, or perhaps he hid it from her. My father's choice of weapon is the defining detail. He had two pistols in a cedar chest in that same room, yet he chose a rifle, the weapon of a hunter. The hunted had walked into his bedroom across the hall and flung himself on the unmade bed. My father saw him lying prone, defenseless.

Sea spray streaks my glasses, producing a sort of blindness. I realize for the first time the correct answer to my question, and it isn't the one my mother gave me thirty-two years ago. Perhaps I've known the truth all along but suppressed it. Before she interrupted him, my father had no intention of killing himself and every intention of killing me.

We're out at sea now, running southeast into the middle of the rough Aegean. A vast expanse of cold water lies before the ferry, and a coldness runs through me, one running much deeper than that from the wind.

PART II: Greek Islands

CHAPTER 9: Mykonos, Delos

The sea is full of white caps and foam, and the boat bucks and pitches from side to side. A shudder travels from the front of the boat to the back, as we lunge into a large wave.

After Zeus whipped his father, Kronos, and gained power over the world, the three brothers, Zeus, Hades and Poseidon, divided the world among themselves. Zeus took the sky, Hades the Underworld, and Poseidon became god of sea and land. Poseidon was known as "Lord of the Brine" and "Earthshaker," or god of earthquakes. He was a grudge-holder, perpetually irritable, volatile and violent, the god who churned the sea to foam. He kept Odysseus from finding his way home. Poseidon was a bearded, gigantic god with tangled, seaweed-like hair, and he hurled a trident. He was the god who made the Aegean islands:

> ...at the very first the mighty god Poseidon smote the mountains with the three-forked sword which the Telchines mythical artificers fashioned for him, and wrought the islands in the sea, and from their lowest foundations lifted them all as with a lever and rolled them into the sea... And them in the depths he rooted from their foundations that they might forget the mainland.[187]

More recently, Poseidon has come to represent the deep sea of the collective unconscious, that hidden knowledge shared by all human beings and the storehouse of mythology.

Poseidon was the father of Theseus. When Theseus and Minos left Athens for Crete, as a part of the nine-year tribute to the Minotaur, the two argued and fell to telling tall tails of their parentage. To test Theseus' claim of being the son of Poseidon, Minos threw his own signet ring into the sea and told Theseus to ask Poseidon to help him retrieve it, if he was the god's son. Theseus dove into the sea, without hesitation, and with the help of dolphins and sea nymphs, returned not only with the ring, but also with a jeweled crown given to him by the sea goddess, Thetis.

Mykonos, Delos

Today, Poseidon is showing us his old irritable self, the ferry loping through a rough sea. The heat in the ferry is stifling. We make a quick stop at Syros, and I step out on deck to shoot a couple of pictures of the island. Wind still blows, but it's warmed some. The rain has stopped. The buildings in Syros are tan and climb the slopes of mountains. The island looks sun-baked, desolate.

I feel different, now that I'm among the islands. The lands I've traveled felt warm and mothering, but being in the Aegean feels unfriendly, threatening. No matter which direction I look, I see the pale-purple outlines of naked islands protruding above the rough sea. I feel unbalanced, as if I'm stone-stepping, but yet excited at this new adventure. The ferry is homey with the Greeks' chitchat.

Of the 2000 Greek islands, only 166 are inhabited.[188] We are in the Cyclades, so named from the Greek κυκλος (kyklos), meaning circle or cycle, which the islands form around the ancient religious center at the small island of Delos. Delos, the birthplace of Apollo and his twin sister Artemis, is the most important religious center in the Aegean. Delos is uninhabited, and to get there, I must stay in Mykonos and take a day trip. Mostly though, I'm looking past these two islands to the southern extreme of the Cyclades and Santorini, still an active volcano. South of Santorini, the large island of Crete, with its elongated, east-west profile, defines the southern edge of the Aegean. I'll spend perhaps a week there. Letizia said Crete was wonderful.

The direction of my journey after Crete is a question mark. The Athens travel agent told me that, from Crete, I could not reach the Dodecanese, in the eastern Aegean, and must return to Athens first to catch the ferry to Rhodes, which is just off the western coast of Turkey. The word Dodecanese comes from the Greek word for twelve, δωδεκα (dodeka), meaning twelve islands. If possible, I'll go from Crete to Rhodes, the southern-most of the Dodecanese. From there, I'll go to Patmos, the northern-most island in that group. I'm still in a hurry to get to visit the cave where St. John wrote Revelations. After visiting Patmos, my three-part journey among the Aegean islands will be complete, and I'll try to enter mainland Turkey to visit Troy, site of the Trojan War.

We make another quick stop, this time at Tinos. More beautiful buildings, white with orange roofs, and at dockside, a row of Greek flags, the blue and white stripes flapping frantically in the brisk breeze. I go back inside and sit next to Anna, talk to her about DC and her work as a paralegal, try to get my mind off my father. She seems distant, formal, hints she's not interested in talking to another American.

Never before have I wondered what went through my father's head during the fifteen seconds it took him to walk the hall and open the closet, grab the deer rifle. At some point, between the time we argued and him opening the closet door, he made a decision. Did it really take no more time than that to decide to kill me? No long hours of anguish, contemplating the consequences what he was about to do, thinking of his feelings for me, before he decided? His action was spontaneous, impulsive. Was this the first time he'd contemplated killing me, or had it been a touch-and-go issue with him for some time? Was our argument simply the last straw? Had my father been actively planning my murder for days, months, years? Since he already knew Fred was homosexual, did he believe I was too? Was that what made his decision easy? Or had he hated me my entire life?

In Carl Jung's essay, *On the Relation of Analytical Psychology to Poetry*, he speaks of the collective unconscious as an image within the individual handed down from primordial times:

> The primordial image, or archetype, is a figure... that constantly recurs in the course of history... therefore, it is a mythological figure... When we examine these images more closely, we find that they give form to countless typical experiences of our ancestors. They are, so to speak, the psychic residua of innumerable experiences of the same type. They present a picture of psychic life in the average, divided up and projected into the manifold figures of the mythological pantheon. ... In each of these images there is a little piece of human psychology and human fate, a remnant of the joys and sorrows that have been repeated countless times in our ancestral history, and on the average follow ever the same course. It is like a deeply graven river-bed in the psyche, in which the waters of life, instead of flowing along as before in a broad but shallow stream, suddenly swell into a mighty river. This happens whenever that particular set of circumstances is encountered which over long periods of time has helped to lay down the primordial image.
>
> The moment when this mythological situation reappears is always characterized by a peculiar emotional intensity; it is as though chords in us were struck that had never resounded before, or as though forces whose existence we never suspected were unloosed... At such moments we are no longer individuals, but the race; the voice of all mankind resounds in us.[189]

No doubt, my father and I experienced a "mythological situation." Perhaps, he had not been actively plotting my murder, but had been swept up in the "peculiar emotional intensity" of the moment. My discovery of my own hostility toward him, when I was in Mykinai, is not something I'd consciously noticed either, but now, I'm aware it has always been there. It was active during our argument in front of my mother and while dueling with the tractor tires. I felt nothing when he was loading the deer rifle, but a little later, when we dueled with the tires, I filled with emotion, a curious blend of pleasure that he had finally taken me seriously, and pain at seeing him so disturbed. And condescension, outright arrogance.

Searching out Jung's "deeply graven river-beds" of emotional content in my life has produced results. I've found parallels to the ancient myths. Our lives seem a sort of artwork. In the same way a novelist pieces together a story, I have been piecing together my personal myth. In this way, I'm beginning to decode the underlying meaning inherent in my own life.

My family has a secret history. Skeletons hang back in the shadows of our closets, dancing the delicate dance of family inheritance. Our failure to air these troubling stories is reminiscent of Thebes' failure to hunt down the murderer of Laios. My own problems are like the plague that eventually forced Oedipus to delve into his own past. When the shepherd returned to Thebes after witnessing Oedipus murder Laios, he found Oedipus ruling the city and married to the queen. Instead of exposing Oedipus, he asked to be sent to the far fields to herd sheep. He suppressed the truth. Even the officials of Thebes, including Jocasta's brother Creon who was ruling Thebes as regent, made no attempt to bring the murderer to justice.

My family is marked by hardworking, socially responsible, self-sufficient citizenship (with a certain notable exception). We get along well at family get-togethers, anniversaries, weddings, Thanksgiving, Christmas. But an explosiveness beneath the surface erupts from time to time and redirects our lives. No one wants those events exposed to public scrutiny. We talk around events like those surrounding my paternal grandfather's move from Magazine, Arkansas to Tishomingo, Oklahoma. I had heard about his relocation all my life, heard my father and grandfather talk about it many times, but what they never said was that my great grandfather forced him to leave. He got my grandfather out of Magazine because he was planning to kill a man.

This story slipped out one afternoon just a few years ago when we were sitting at my aunt's kitchen table. We had all gathered there for my uncle's funeral. My father told the story quietly, in almost a whisper. My grandfather was going to kill a man, who, along with some other men, had disgraced his father, my great grandfather, by tying him up and pulling out all his pubic hair. This group of men humiliated my great grandfather because they'd heard he was illegitimate. Like the mothers of both Theseus and Perseus, his mother was unsure of the father, although she did give the surname of the man she thought might be the father to him. If she had lived in the time of the ancient Greeks, I could well imagine that she would have stated quite emphatically, "Zeus did it. He took the form of liquid gold and flowed through my womb." But with no such explanation readily available, my great grandfather almost went crazy with uncertainty. The word "bastard" has floated down through the generations with a particularly weighty meaning. My family still seems to be cursed by these events. The ancient Greeks knew about inherited curses. Sophocles wrote of them and their impact on Oedipus' family in his play *Antigone*:

> Blest are they whose days have not tasted of evil. For when a house hath once been shaken from heaven, there the curse fails nevermore, passing from life to life of the race; even as, when the surge is driven over the darkness of the deep by the fierce breath of Thracian sea-winds, it rolls up the black sand from the depths, and there is a sullen roar from wind-vexed headlands that front the blows of the storm.
>
> I see that from olden time the sorrows in the house of the Labdacidae Oedipus' grandfather are heaped upon the sorrows of the dead; and generation is not freed by generation, but some god strikes them down, and the race hath no deliverance.[190]

Since learning this family secret, I've wondered if it is the reason my paternal grandfather was an alcoholic and abused his family. He once held my grandmother to the floor, with a butcher's knife to her throat, shouting that he was going to kill her. Their kids—my aunts, uncles and father—cowered in the corners of their home. This may explain, in some twisted fashion, why Uncle Jud used to chase my grandmother around the house, threatening her with a butcher's knife.

This tendency toward emotional explosions is part of my entire family's emotional backdrop. It's a contagion, a disease passed from generation to generation. Perhaps this is a part of the "remnant of the joys and sorrows that have been repeated countless times in our ancestral history." It's like the inherited curse that both Laios and Atreus left to succeeding generations of their families.

I also know some interesting stories from my mother's side of the family. My maternal great grandmother was borne of a surrogate mother. My great great grandmother could not have children, so they talked their neighbor's wife into having a baby by my great great grandfather and giving it to them. When my mother told me, she said that her mother had told her, and only one child

Mykonos, Delos

in each generation was to know.

What was not passed along by my mother, and probably left unsaid at the time, was how my great great grandfather felt the night he crawled into bed with this woman and slipped between her legs. They don't tell how many times he had to go to bed with her before she conceived, her husband's voluntary celibacy, possibly months, to ensure he wouldn't be the father. These were religious people living righteous lives. The stories are antiseptic, sterile, but the actual events were messy, full of erections, vaginas, bodily fluids and heavy breathing. They don't tell about the mother's anguish when she gave up the baby to my great great grandmother.

This is how the story stood for the last couple of decades. But now, to illustrate the really mythical quality of these stories, I'll slip in a little variation. My mother recently told me that my great great grandfather on my father's side was not a bastard, but definitely legitimate, and now I've even started questioning the details of my grandfather's reasons for leaving Arkansas. She also told me that he never terrorized my grandmother with a butcher's knife. And later, she told me that the surrogate mother, who gave birth to my great grandmother, was a widow. So much of the intrigue, the husband's anguish, of that situation vanishes. Myth is like that. Memory is like that. The facts, and the memory of them, drift. Many ancient Greeks accused Homer of lying in his epic poetry. Some of the details are changed, some events covered up, and others added, to increase the emotional impact, or provide a more compelling storyline. All of it is affected by the magnetism of what Jung termed the "mythical situation." I'm no longer even so sure that emotional abuse is what causes the emotional inheritance to be passed from generation to generation. We may impulsively pull mythic material out of our subconscious and into the story of our lives, and, in so doing, contaminate our memories. We human beings are really complex, mythical creatures.

★

Arriving at Mykonos is like a homecoming, a welcoming crowd at the dock anxiously awaiting our arrival. I stand at the railing as we enter the quiet seaport, the ferry towering over the dock, seemingly dwarfing the entire island.

The afternoon sun is bright, the air warm; and the small crowd waits patiently while the ferry rotates 180 degrees to dock, aft end first. I take a deep breath and head for the gangway. The place seems so delightful, I can't wait to see what kind of room I can commandeer.

Mykonos was of scant importance to the ancient Greeks, but is famous today for its beauty and nightlife. It looks so tiny, friendly. So many smiling faces. Some have come to meet relatives, but most have come for other travelers like me, who need a place for the night. A woman with golden hair and a pretty face tries to commandeer me for an apartment she has available. After looking at her three-ring binder with snapshots of the luxurious interior, I'm suspicious of their authenticity because of the low price.

I walk away from her to the Tourist Information Office. They quote prices I can't afford but are uncommonly helpful, saying that I may do better working my own deal directly. So I go back to the blond woman. She throws my backpack in the trunk of her car, and we make the short drive to the center of town. She's German and has lived on Mykonos for the past seven years. She says that I've come to Mykonos during a tourist's no-man's-land, past even the end of the off-season, and accommodations are very cheap. I'm still wondering about the room. Can't be that nice, I think. She parks in a plateia at the edge of the sea, then leads me through a maze of whitewashed buildings and tiny streets.

We enter the newly renovated apartment through the kitchen, which has a white refrigerator to the right and cabinets and sink directly before me. Immediately I know: I'm taking this apartment. The place is beyond her glowing photos and words. A large hot plate sits on the counter top. A sofa sits to the left against the wall, and at the end of it, just before I go into the hall, a rectangular table and three chairs is pushed against the wall. Through the hall, the bathroom is to the right with the bedroom straight ahead. It has two single beds separated by a nightstand, a closet, a window, and a ladder that ascends to a loft, which contains another bed. The apartment is two toned, with pure-white walls and varnished, natural-pine doors, cabinets, and baseboards. Quite a change from the dirty old hotel in Corinth. The place is clean, positively antiseptic, and has no mosquitoes. Only one fly.

So why do I suddenly miss my hotel room in Corinth? I tell you, Greece has a way of working on the mind. In spite of all the offenses each place has perpetrated on my senses, they are all jewels. I'd hate to think I'll never get to visit them again.

The beautiful German woman scribbles her name and telephone number on a business card and is out the door quickly. "Call if you need anything," she says.

I go for a walk and run into Anna, the young lady from DC. She's replaced her gray skirt and business jacket with Levis and a T-shirt and looks much younger, almost childlike; her manner is tentative, guarded.

We walk the streets together for a while, the warm neon-glow of lights relfects off the stunning white-stucco buildings with deep-blue shutters and a labyrinth of narrow streets and tourist shops giving Mykonos a magical feel. The town is almost deserted: no trucks, no motorbikes. Huge cartoon-like pelicans, with long beaks, stand outside the shops like beggars, wisdom emanating from their sad eyes. They stand tall as my shoulder and attract crowds as if they are celebrities.

The wind has picked up again, and it's cold.

Anna still has little to say, still guarded, and defensively justifies her choice of a room after I tell her about my apartment. We go our separate ways.

★

I wake in the middle of the night and hear the wind rattling the shutters. That is the only sound on this isolated island. For the first time, I strain to hear a motorbike. I lie awake thinking of my father and hoping this new insight into his motive for loading the deer rifle will not open the door to the madness I experienced that fall, when I tried to resume college. I remember the extraordinary loneliness I felt that night when the grotesque faces came out of my mental darkness, like horrible Dionysus begging me into his world. They sent me running to my insane uncle. Again I question my decision to get into this emotional material while alone in a foreign country. But it all seems irresistible while visiting these ancient sites and mulling over the mythology.

The wind, which raked the shallow slopes of this island, has stopped. Not even the rattle of the shutters do I hear. Mykonos seems such a desolate part of the world tonight, out here in the middle of the Aegean.

29 Oct, Friday

I go to the waterfront for breakfast, have an apple pie and a carton of Milko at the local bakery. Waves pound the shore, rakes the shops and streets. I hurry to the tourist office to see about a ferry to Delos. The man tells me that no ferry will leave for Delos today. "Tomorrow?" I ask. He throws up both hands. "The only ferry from Mykonos is going to Santorini tomorrow morning." I'm shocked and stand before him, sorting through a mass of inappropriate responses, trying to find a reasonable one not laden with the anger welling up within me. "What do you mean 'the only ferry?' When will there be another to Santorini?" He throws up his hands again. "A week, two weeks. Who knows? The weather, it is not good for the ferryboats."

I had my heart set on seeing Delos, and spending all of today on Mykonos instead is really depressing. To see Delos, I'll have to miss the ferry today and stay here for a week afterward with nothing to do. Maybe coming to Greece in the off season was a mistake. With the kind of problem I now have, I can also imagine what I'll be up against trying to get into Turkey.

I walk to the old pier, where boats to Delos depart, and find an American couple trying to coerce a skipper into taking them across the short strait to Delos in his small boat. Realizing that this is my battle also, I join their negotiations and offer to help make it worth the man's while. Finally, he relents, and soon we're being tossed about on the rough sea, and I'm wondering what I've gotten myself into. Sea spray drives me to look for cover against the side of the cabin. I'm instantly seasick. I don't quite make it to the rail for my first episode of vomiting and hear a tirade of unappreciative Greek when the skipper sees what I've done to his deck. I could really give a shit.

The half hour it takes to get to Delos is an eternity in sick-time, and I feel my stomach quiet as the water smoothes, and we dock at the most desolate looking countryside in the world. Delos is a barren island, although the ancient Greeks knew it as "the far-seen star of the dark-blue earth."[191] Callimachus described the island in one of his hymns, written in the 3rd Century BC, this way:

> Wind-swept and stern is she set in the sea, and, wave-beaten as she is, is fitter haunt for gulls than course for horses. The sea, rolling greatly round her, casts off on her much spindrift of the Icarian water the Icarian sea. Wherefore also sea-roaming fishermen have made her their home.[192]

The setting is the same today, although no one is allowed to live on Delos, except archaeologists. Delos was the hub of the Cyclades and the birthplace of Apollo and Artemis. On his way to the Trojan War, Odysseus came to Delos to sacrifice to the two gods. He saw the tree Leto used as an aid in giving birth and described it:

> ...when I saw that palm, my wonder
> was piercing, lasting, for no trunk has ever
> grown from the earth to match that tree...[193]

Theseus also came to Delos when he returned from Crete after killing the Minotaur. Minos' beautiful daughter Ariadne, who was madly in love with him, had assisted Theseus in the murder. She returned with him on his journey back to Athens, but died in childbirth on the island of Naxos near Delos. In his grief, Theseus:

> ...put in at Delos, and having sacrificed to the god of the island, dedicated to the temple the image of Venus Aphrodite which Ariadne had given him, and danced with the young Athenians a dance... consisting in certain measured turnings and returnings, imitative of the windings and twisting of

the labyrinth. And this dance... is called among the Delians the Crane.[194]

Theseus was still in mourning for Ariadne when he returned to Athens. He forgot to switch the color of his flag from black to white, and his father, thinking Theseus was dead, threw himself from the Akropolis and died.

Zeus and Leto (not his wife Hera) were the father and mother of the twins, Apollo and Artemis. Leto was one of the most-liked goddesses. "She was swathed in dark raiment, but was always gracious, mild as honey, and the most pleasant divinity on Olympus."[195] According to Hesiod, the twins were "comelier than all the other sky-dwellers."[196] Leto gave birth

...as she leaned against Mount Kynthos, on the rocky and sea-girt island of Delos, while on either side a dark wave swept landwards impelled by shrill winds...[197]

First-born Artemis assisted in delivering Apollo, to whom Leto could not give birth for nine days and nights. Zeus was continuously unfaithful, and Hera took her jealousy out even on good-natured Leto, doing everything within her power to cause Leto trouble during delivery. The goddesses were all present except except for two: Eileithyia, goddess of labor pains, and Hera, who restrained Eileithyia from going to Delos to assist Leto. The goddesses sent Iris to steal Eileithyia away from Hera:

And when Eileithyia... set foot on Delos, the pains of labor seized Leto, and she yearned to give birth. She threw her two arms round the palm tree, and propped her knees on the soft meadow while the earth beneath her was all smiles. Apollon sprang forth to the light, and all the goddesses screamed.[198]

Of all the events of my life, my greatest joy has been the birth of my children, and the sound of children's voices around the house. My son was born first, and my daughter three years later. The morning my son was born, I fell asleep in the hospital waiting room. Hospitals didn't allow fathers in the delivery room then, and I remember feeling left out as my wife walked away with the nurse. I saw my new-born son in the incubation chamber, and that evening, saw my wife during visiting hours. I never expected my son to be so sourly disposed toward me when I tried to attract his attention as he nursed. He grew up willful and creative, with a definite fondness for beating things, and loved to destroy what he'd created with his building blocks. My son and I didn't repeat the confrontation I had with my father. Before he became a young man, my wife left me.

All most three years later, I saw my daughter for the first time when I walked down the hall toward the delivery room. The doctor was walking toward me with a bundle in his arms. She was wrapped in a blanket. When I first held her, she was still waxy, had a sunk-in forehead and blood on the side of her face. Ultrasound did not exist then, but I had had a premonition that our second child would be a girl, so I wasn't at all surprised. In the same way that the islands of the Cyclades form a circle or wheel spinning around the small island of Delos, so does the second part of my life spin around a single event, my daughter's disappearance.

I walk onto the island and through the largest site of ruins I've seen so far, still trying to shake some equilibrium into my swirling head. The island is an absolute desert, a lizard-infested, granite-covered piece of dirt, plopped down in the middle of a nest of islands that I see off in the distance. It's very small, only five square kilometers. In spite of its wind-blown, sea-pounded, desert terrain, Delos has been inhabited since the 3rd Millennium BC. I walk away from the dock, and instead of turning left to the Terrace of the Lions, I walk to the right to climb to the top of Mt. Kynthos where Artemis and Apollo were born.

I ascend a flight of steps to the 113 meter summit. From here, I can see Mykonos in the east, Rheneia just to the west, Paros and Noxos to the south, and Tinos to the north. Quite a cluster of islands, jutting up out of the raging sea. But I can't concentrate on these ruins, knowing I have another trial ahead of me, the trip back to Mykonos.

★

Sure enough, the boat ride back is just as sick-logged as that to the island. The other two Americans also throw up their socks. When we hit dock, I don't waste any time disembarking, desperately seeking firm ground again. Our skipper doesn't seem very impressed with our seafaring performance. As I shell out the extra cash he demanded for the trip, he mutters something about it being a lot of money for a little misery.

I have a late lunch with the American couple at an outdoor restaurant at the edge of the sea. They are from San Antonio and have been on the road for two weeks. They will leave for Crete tomorrow. I ask if they are going to see Santorini, the island volcano. They don't have time, they say. They only have two days left and plan to fly back to Athens from Crete day after tomorrow.

Emptying my stomach on the boat has left me ravenous, and after the kalamari, I have a little piece of honey-dripping dessert. The tables have two tablecloths again, one red, the other white. The wood chairs are baby blue. What

174

is so appealing about this restaurant is its closeness to the sea, the bright sunlight reflecting off the choppy water. An occasional cloud of cold spray, from the waves crashing on shore, washes over me as I sip a Greek coffee.

After lunch, I walk farther around the bay to where windmills sit at the edge of the sea. The windmills are brilliant white, thick circular structures with dark thatched roofs and fan blades that almost reach the ground. A short, rock fence, with a gap for an entrance, circles each. I look past them, out over the vast open sea pocked with white-capped waves with heavy clouds sitting over the pale cliffs of Delos in the distance.

I walk away from the sea to the far side of town, where the whitewash-soaked streets and buildings gradually become ordinary asphalt and stucco. They lose their magic as they climb the rocky hillside. This little town has been set up as a showpiece for tourists. The rest of the island, where the Greeks evidently go about their lives, is rather common. I wonder if I should take another day and explore what is undoubtedly the more interesting part of the island?

In the evening, I sit at a table in the plateia in the center of town, listening to waves breaking and thinking about my predicament. It's decision time. The ferry to Santorini comes bright and early tomorrow morning. The next arrival may be another week away. I fight the wind to keep the pages of my journal open, as I write in the pale light of the plateia. From the beginning of my journey, I've been afraid I would have problems with ferry schedules this late in the year, and here I am in trouble on my first Aegean island.

Finally, I make the decision. I would like to see more of Mykonos, but I'll be on the ferry when it leaves tomorrow morning for Santorini.

Two rows of cars are parked end-to-end in the center of the dark plateia. They are pointed out to sea, and the wind rakes a fine sea mist across them. Several people stand around a pickup parked in the dark at the edge of the pier. I stick my journal in my daypack and walk into the small crowd, where a man is selling fruit and vegetables out of the bed of the pickup. The rush of sea waves, breaking on the retaining wall, fogs my glasses, and I shudder from the cold. The customers jostle for position and argue with the man about the selection of fruit, as it disappeas quickly, particularly the bananas. Everything is expensive. I shove my way in, point at the bananas and grapes saying, "κιλο, κιλο," then try to discourage him from selecting rotten fruit. The condition of the grapes isn't apparent in the dark. The sea spray is bitter cold. The wind whips at my hair, coat, and pant legs.

I leave the plateia to get out of the wind and move to the white, shoulder-width street in front of my apartment. All the buildings in Mykonos are whitewashed, as are the seams between the large cement blocks paving the alleys. Everything not white is trimmed in white. Only porch lights light the streets. The light flickers just above me on the second story apartment. I have trouble seeing the steps that ascend to it. The glow from the lights against all the white surfaces is like snow, a whiteout. Even the shadows have a strange glow to them. The deep blue of the dark sky is visible in the stripe the street carves out between buildings. At the end of the street, puffs of clouds reflect the whiteness of Mykonos. I eat one of the bananas. It's the sweetest banana I've ever tasted.

The quietness of last night has been shattered by a local "pump & hump shop," a gymnasium, where one woman and several dark men with huge arms lift weights. The disco music echoes down the alleyway. A television blares a Greek news broadcast.

I was never mad at the man who took my wife away from me. I was very civilized about the whole thing. He wouldn't come into my home because he was afraid of me. When my ex-wife told me this, I thought it was funny. But something not so funny came of it. Seven years ago, I had a run-in with a business associate while on a business trip in Europe. There were four of us traveling together: my son, my boss, and Harry, who had been a good friend for several years. We were in Munich during Oktoberfest and had each just drunk a liter of dunkel weissen at the English Garten in the center of Munich, then walked through a park littered with nude sunbathers, and entered a pub close to our hotel. We were having another beer when a girl came by selling flowers. Harry bought one and told her to give it to a blond woman at the bar. He told the flower-girl to tell her it was from me. When the blond found out where the flowers came from, she asked the four of us to join her and a female friend at the bar. A few minutes later, I became someone I had never been before.

All is quiet again. The music has stopped, as has the metallic clang of weights and the blare of television. But the wind continues to whine through the streets and rattle shutters. Down the alleyway, I hear a dog bark.

30 Oct, Saturday

Up early, but the ferry to Santorini leaves at eight-thirty, so I take my time packing. My backpack gets heavier at every departure. I now have quite a collection of guidebooks. I'm writing so much that I bought another journal here in Mykonos, a blue one with a hard cloth binding, internally stapled instead of sewn, and definitely not from the States. I lumber back to the dock and then along the street where the German woman drove me two days ago. The weather is clear, but the wind gusts tug at me as I stand at the dock talking to a young American couple on their way to Crete. The ferry is late, but by nine o'clock we see it off in the distance, a thin sliver of white against blue sea.

Mykonos, Delos

We enter the ferry and walk up the gangway into the hold. The motor is so loud that we have to shout to be heard. We turn to the right, walk through a metal door, and climb metal stairs. This time, we're not allowed inside the passenger compartment, the one with the cushioned seats. Guards are posted at all the doors. I feel like a convict as they force us farther up the stairs to the top deck, where we sit outside in rows of cold, plastic seats. I throw my pack across two of them and stand at the back of the boat by the rail alongside a group of tourists watching the long stripe of bubbles in our wake as we leave dock. The cool air in my hair feels refreshing, but the sea gets progressively choppy the farther we get from the island. We're headed south, and off to the right, less than a kilometer away, I see the pale blue coast of Delos.

CHAPTER 10: Santorini

By early afternoon, I've been freezing for what seems an eternity. I've turned irritable again, wondering why they've forced us to stay on the top deck in the cold where we can find no safe place from the wind. I finally take a seat in front of the open door where warm air rises up the stairs from below. Still I shake.

The water smoothes a bit, and passengers mill forward. A tip of the volcanic island drifts into view from where it has been hidden by the front of the ferry. I grab my camera and run to the bow. A crowd has formed at the rail. I hear shouts, laughter. The click of camera shutters is like popcorn popping. The sea has calmed considerably, and even the breeze feels warm.

My first impression is that Santorini is smaller than I expected, the group of five islands closer together, but the cliffs much higher. This is a small group of vertical islands. It's as if we've entered a towering stage set for a Sophoclean tragedy.

To our left, the large, quarter-moon-shaped island of Thera forms the largest part of the caldera, which protrudes above the surface of the sea. Its dark cliff faces us, with white stucco buildings crowded in at the water's edge. The brilliant white of cities crests the top of the cliff, like frosting on cake. To the right of the ferry is Therasia, a smaller part of the caldera above water. A black volcanic island is directly in front of the boat, growing larger as we enter the caldera. It is called Nea Kameni and is the very center of the volcano.

Santorini owes its existence to plate tectonics. The grinding of the African and Aegean plates has produced this volcanic island.[199] The cliffs of the caldera are striped with layers of lava: black, tan, rust, white, purple, deposited during the volcano's eruptions. The top layer, which is forty meters thick in places, came from the 1628 BC eruption that blew the large island into these remaining fragments.

The name "Santorini" is a corruption of St. Irene and was given to the group of five islands after the 4th Crusade in 1400 AD. The island has had several names, the most ancient going back to a time before the eruption when it was called Strongyle, meaning Round One. It was one large island then and was inhabited, as evidenced by the ruins of one of its towns, Akrotiri, which is being unearthed by archeologists on the southern extremity. Following the eruption, most of the island sank into the sea. Then, only Thera, Therasia and Aspronisi protruded above the water's surface. The civilization that lived here was destroyed, and only many centuries later did the island once again become inhabited.

Following the explosion of the volcano and the fragmentation of the island, it was called Kalliste, the Fairest One.[200] Many eruptions have occurred since, all smaller, but one in 197 BC resulted in Palaea Kameni (Old Burned) rising up out of the sea, followed by Mikra Kameni (Small Burned) in 1570, and Nea Kameni (New Burned) in 1707-11 AD. Nea Kameni and Mikra Kameini merged in 1925-26 to form one island.[201] In the center of Nea Kameni, the temperature is 180 degrees Fahrenheit. The name Thera, which applies to the largest of the five islands forming Santorini, comes from an ancient Greek king, Theras, who came to rule the island around 900 BC. Theras was a direct descendent of Oedipus.

On the mainland at Thebes, I encountered the legend of Kadmos, who wandered from his home in Phoenicia looking for his sister, Europa. Zeus had abducted her. Kadmos searched in vain, for Zeus had taken her to Crete, and Kadmos never found her. But in his wanderings, Kadmos spent a short time on Kalliste, founded a colony, and left it in charge of a man named Membliarus. Kadmos continued to wander Greece and founded Thebes. The direct line of descent from Kadmos includes Laios, Oedipus, Polyneices, Thersander and three generations later, Theras.

Theras lived in Sparta and was acting regent for his two young nephews. He left when they were old enough to assume the throne. But his short time ruling Sparta had instilled in him a taste for power, and he thought of Kalliste. Since he was a direct descendent of Kadmos, founder of the colony there, he decided to go to the island and see if they would let him rule. He set sail from the Peloponnese in three thirty-oared galleys.[202] The people of Kalliste were pleased to be ruled by a direct descendent of Kadmos. After becoming king, Theras named the island for himself. But the hereditary curse on the family, brought about by Laios and Oedipus, had followed him here.

We dock at the small white village at the base of the towering cliff. It's a little like seeing New York City skyscrapers for the first time, everyone's neck craned to see the top of the cliff. A Greek man, dressed in a short-sleeved shirt and slacks, who hasn't shaved in three days and smells like that billygoat I encountered on Ithaka, picks me up at the dock, along with a young Australian man and a woman from Albuquerque, New Mexico. He's promised all of us rooms in the center of town. His van slowly climbs the switchbacks up the 250-meter cliff. After entering Fira, the largest town on the island, he continues along the lip of the caldera. Contrary to his word, his pension is in a new housing development a kilometer north of Fira.

The place is sparkling new, and the price is most reasonable, three nights for 8000 dr ($33.33). "See," he says, "center of town." I look at him and shake my head.

Late in the afternoon, I walk to a restaurant just off the cliff that overlooks the volcano. As the waiter takes me to my cliffside seat, I feel a growing uneasiness. The view of the vertical drop from the patio is dizzying. I back away a little, but still take the table, right at the edge with the sea and islands spread out far below. I still feel the fright, and it's worse than it was at Delphi. The sun peeks through the only cloud in the sky and glistens toward me in a broad stripe across the Aegean. Only the large island in the middle of the caldera and a tiny islet on the other side interrupt the glare of water-rippled sunlight. The thin haze blends sky into sea, a sunset without a horizon.

When the waitress comes, I order an American coffee (instant Nescafe, turns out) and a piece of layered, chocolate cake to match the brown earth on the rim of this volcano. The scene here is absolutely surrealistic, a dream landscape, not of this world.

I've had curious, marvelous dreams concerning both my paternal grandparents. The night before my grandmother died, she came to me in a dream. We walked in the backyard of my grandparents' home where I had played in the dirt as a kid. She and I talked of our short time together here on Earth, and she said good-bye. I didn't know she was close to death since she lived in California, and I lived in Colorado, but I got the news the next day by phone.

A few months ago, seventeen years after my grandfather died, he appeared to me in a dream. I'd just been laid off and was struggling with rejection and loss of identity. He unzipped the cocoon of death he inhabited and appeared to me in person. That old farmer was dressed in a new suit and tie, had a fresh haircut. In spite of his worldly shortcomings, he was doing well in the Afterlife. He'd come to tell me not to worry. Before I gave him the boot back to the Underworld, I asked him to hug me. I wasn't going to pass up that one last chance.

Sometimes it seems as though I experience a form of dream therapy similar to that practiced at Epidaurus.

To my left, the brilliant white and blue buildings of Fira glow within the deep chocolate-brown earth, which plunges to the edge of the dark-blue sea. This quarter-moon-shaped island extends both arms, bringing the rest of the islands, the rest of the caldera, within its reach. I feel like the man in the moon. A strange bird high above the white buildings flutters in stasis, then dives at the bay making stark, piercing shrieks. The cold wind blows the pages of my journal. If I had the skill of Teiresias, I could certainly read something of portent in that bird's flight. After ordering a second coffee, I slip on my black sweater.

The sun descends toward a dark bank of clouds painted in pastel yellows and pinks. Gradually, it disappears, and only a glow of pastel pink reflects from wisps above the silhouette of a thin cloudbank. The islands present dark sculptured faces to the sky, and the cliff's features fade. The brilliant white of buildings turns dull gray. Evening comes to Santorini.

On the way back to my room, I spot a motorcycle rental shop. Tomorrow morning, I'll make another try at renting a motorbike. I'm prepared to lie about my previous experience.

As I climb the steps to my room, I hear a horse whinny and look over a short stone wall to the west. I see a tall cliff made of black volcanic rock. Recessed in the cliff are six caves, three of them occupied. The left one has a fenced garden in front with tomatoes, carrots and potatoes. The middle cave has a wood doorframe over the opening but no door. The third is occupied by a pale white horse that tosses his head and whinnies as I watch. A lone fig tree stands in the field in the front of the caves. I have followed the trail of Oedipus' family to its end here where Theras ruled, and I sleep before the mouth of a cave inside of which resides a pale horse.

In the southern tip of this island, archeologists are hard at work uncovering the ruins of an ancient city, Akrotiri, which was buried in volcanic ash by the explosion in 1628 BC. The city is remarkably well preserved, but no bodies have been found, so the speculation is that the people knew the volcano was about to erupt and escaped before the city was decimated. The explosion was large enough to create a 250-meter tsunami that caused massive damage on Crete and the northern coast of Africa. Since 198 BC, thirteen eruptions have occurred, plus an earthquake in 1956 that flattened most of the towns on the island. Tomorrow, I'll visit Akrotiri. Perhaps, I'll get away unscathed during my short visit.

The nature of this island before the explosion is the subject of much speculation. Many people, both lay and professional, have thought that Strongyle may have been the lost isle of Atlantis. The writings of Plato, the two dialogues *Timaeus* and *Critias*, are the only sources for the Atlantis myth. Critias tells the legend as he received it when a child from the writings of Solon, who heard it from an old Egyptian priest. During the gods' distribution of the Earth, Poseidon was given a large island. He had ten children by a mortal inhabitant woman named Cleito, five sets of twins. Poseidon distributed the island among them. He made the oldest, Atlas, king. The people were known as the Atlantic and the island was called Atlantis. Critias describes it:

> It has mineral resources from which were mined both solid materials and metals... There was a plentiful supply of timber for structural purposes, and every kind of animal domesticated and wild, among them numerous elephants. For there was plenty of grazing for this largest and most voracious of beasts, as well as for all creatures whose habitat is marsh, swamp and river, mountain or plain. Besides all this, the earth bore freely all the aromatic substances it bears today, roots, herbs, bushes and gums exuded by flowers or fruit. There were cultivated crops, cereals which provide our staple diet, and pulse (to use its generic name) which we need in addition to feed us; there were the fruits of trees... --all these were produced by that sacred island, then still beneath the sun, in wonderful quantity and profusion.[203]

During Atlas' reign, a great civilization that ruled far and wide emerged on Atlantis:

> On this island of Atlantis had arisen a powerful and remarkable dynasty of kings, who ruled the whole island, and many other islands as well and part of the continent; in addition it controlled, within the strait, Libya up to the borders of Egypt and Europe as far a Tyrrhenia. This dynasty, gathering its whole power together, attempted to enslave, at a single stroke, your country Athens and ours Egypt and all the territory within the strait.[204]

After Athens defeated Atlantis in this war, the catastrophe occurred. Plato, through the words of Critias, describes the destruction of Atlantis:

> ...there were earthquakes and floods of extraordinary violence, and in a single dreadful day and night... the island of Atlantis... was swallowed up by the sea and vanished.[205]

The parallels between the devastation of Atlantis and the destruction of Strongyle are unmistakable. First, a severe earthquake destroyed Akrotiri, causing its inhabitants to evacuate the city. Some time lapsed between the earthquake and the eruption because the inhabitants came back to Akrotiri and started repairing some of the buildings. But then Strongyle exploded, and the center of the island did in fact sink into the sea, where it now sits at a depth of 400 meters.[206]

Santorini

The excavations of Akrotiri have produced the wall paintings I saw at the National Archaeological Museum in Athens. Those paintings have given us a unique insight into daily life on the island. If Santorini is Atlantis—and it is the only place on Earth with a legitimate claim—we have a wonderful window into its ancient world.

According to the legend, however, Atlantis was not in the Mediterranean as is Santorini. Critias placed it in the Atlantic Ocean beyond the Pillars of Heracles (the Strait of Gibraltar). Critias also says that the time of the sinking of Atlantis was 9500 BC, not 1628 BC, which is the time frame of the eruption. But Critias learned all the information he relays when he was a child of ten. Perhaps the time of the explosion and location of the island became distorted through the years as the story was told and retold. Plus, geologists say that it is impossible for Atlantis to have been in the Atlantic. Thus, Santorini is the only credible source for the Atlantis myth.

My room overlooks the east side of the island, the outer side of the caldera where the mountain slops gradually to the sea, and the lights of houses sprinkle the darkness. All is quiet, barren, desolate. I look out the open French doors into the darkness and farther at the slow rise of a full Halloween moon. I still feel the effects of my boat ride; the ground still floats.

★

In the middle of the night, I dream of losing my job, of being alone. I'm in a dark town of winding antiseptic streets. Another man and I kill two guards and rob a bank. I cast a spell on the vault to open it, take the contents, and we walk along vertical walls of buildings to cover our tracks. We leave no fingerprints. No one even knows a robbery has taken place. The police are to believe that the guards died of accidental asphyxiation. There is no chase, no pursuit. All that remains is my guilt. The man, who masterminded this episode of robbery and murder, tells me to lie flat on the floor because we are about to be caught. I know there is no pursuit, so I realize that he is going to kill me, too. I do as he says until he leaves, then I escape. He and the rest of the world think I'm dead. I roam the Earth as a perfect nomad and exist only in my own thoughts.

The silence is broken only by the sound of wind against the eaves and a strange, almost musical noise. At first, I think the music comes from downstairs, perhaps a gigantic wind chime or slow, lingering musical chord from the strings of a giant harp, but then it seems to be the wind lingering wispily along the side of the building. It's an accompaniment to my loneliness and guilt. Perhaps this haunting music from nowhere is being played by ancient musicians of Atlantis, their ghost-music.

Following the confrontation with my father, I became congenial, easy to get along with. I was a master at resolving conflict, a pillar of stability, a shrine to tolerance. But something monstrous lurked inside me following my wife's departure, and I uncovered it that evening in Munich shortly after my friend gave the girl the flowers and said they were from me.

The German girls asked us to join them, and my son and I sat with the blond between us. We were a friendly group. I liked the woman, who spoke excellent if accented English. The two of us were getting friendly when she lit a cigarette and sparks flew. She screamed that her purse was on fire. Impulsively, I tipped my beer into it. My overreaction brought curses from the girl and laughter and condemnation from my friends. The mood turned serious, disapproving. I was overwhelmed with embarrassment and sat quietly for a few minutes shrinking down on my stool. I got up to go to the bathroom, realized I was drunk, and when I returned, Harry was talking to "my girl." I went into a rage. Perhaps it was the overwhelming symbolism of the situation: a man, his son, a woman, and another man trying to take her. I looked across at that asshole and made a decision. I decided to have it out with him right there in Munich.

31 Oct, Sunday

I skip breakfast and hurry down to get a motorbike. A couple of young Americans run the rental agency, and they could care less if I'd ridden one before. I'm giddy with the feel of speed and drunk with revenge, blasting the rim of the caldera with exhaust and noise. I feel liberated, but the wind is howling and forces me to drive a swerving path along the asphalt. To my right, the island drops away precipitously to the sea. The exposure is frightening. On the way to Akrotiri, I stop at a bakery and pick up two small pizzas and an oversized, honey-dipped donut.

The ruins of Akrotiri are on the gentle slope of a hill one kilometer from the sea. To the south, I see a small harbor and enter through the door of a large flat building with a corrugated metal roof. The ceiling is low, with gaps that let sunshine cast a pale light over the ruins. Before me are the re-erected 3600-year-old stone buildings with wood cross members that provide structural support and frame windows and doorways. Tall clay storage jars stand in front of them. The jars have large swirling designs, and some are as high as my shoulders. The ruins are so accessible that the entire setting has an unmistakable intimacy about it. Everything is blanketed with volcanic pumice, which is fine, like brown talcum powder. To the right, scaffolding and shovels litter an excavation in progress. Fragments of walls and urns protrude above the surface of volcanic ash.

I walk an ancient street called Telchines' Road, and up a makeshift ramp with a wood rail. I remember the wall paintings from Akrotiri that I saw in the

Santorini

National Archeological Museum in Athens: the paintings of boxing children, the playful movement of antelopes, and the lady with the large lolling breasts. I walk the board bridge over the ruins toward Mill Square, so named because of a nearby granary. The two- and three-story structures with stone walls were originally plastered both inside and out. The plaster was of fine limestone colored pink, yellow and white. The wall paintings in the upper stories, where light splashed in from large windows, were painted on fine white plaster. The lower levels, where the temperature was coolest, were used for food storage. The floors were paved with stone slabs, broken seashells and pebbles. Stone and wood staircases led to upper stories.

Nothing of any value, other than archaeological, has been found in Akrotiri, and no bodies were among the rubble. Akrotiri evidently had been evacuated before the volcano erupted. Earthquakes had already rocked the city many times before they destroyed it. I keep wondering if this was a great city on the island of Atlantis.

I make a pass through the ruins, taking pictures. The security man at the exit talks to Japanese tourists. I watch, bathed in sunlight shining through the open exit, as he kids one young Japanese woman. As she exits, he says good-bye to her, then grabs her and kisses her on the cheek. She blushes deep crimson. He spots me, through the crowd of people gathered about him, and asks where I'm from. "Αμερικι," (America) I say.

He asks if I speak Greek. I answer, "Μιλαο λιο Ελλινικα" (I speak a little Greek). The Japanese laugh. He wonders if I'm a scientist. He has noticed me taking a lot of pictures. After talking to him for a few minutes, I leave the crowd and reverse my steps through the ancient city, the three-story buildings and the huge clay bowls and pots. The city even had a sewer system.

The tourists are all gone now, and I have the ancient city to myself, except for an occasional security guard. I go through one more time, starting at the entrance. I feel sad, sorry for the people of ancient Akrotiri, disrupted from living what seems to be a peaceful life, if one can draw an accurate picture from their wall paintings and the pastoral beauty of the island they depict. It is indeed an irony that the richness of the soil on Thera comes from the volcano that ultimately destroyed the island and will in all probability destroy it again.

*

Back at my motorbike, I sit on the ground eating one of the small pizzas I picked up earlier at the bakery. I spend the rest of the day on the motorbike making noise. The wind blows me all over the road. I see several caves like the one next to my pension, in which the pale horse lives. Some of the front surfaces of these caves are smoothed and rocked along the entrance. Others are

Santorini

cemented and whitewashed. These Hobbit-like dwellings shine brilliant white in the morning sun.

Finally, rattled from the wind and noise of my motorbike, I park at the side of the street in Fira and have two gyros and an order of fries at a small, touristy, fast-food place in the middle of town, just across the street from where I rented my motorbike. I eat standing at a little bar, sandwiched between the wall and the serving line, the only place to eat out of the wind. The place is crowded with Americans. A young lady in dreadlocks smiles at me a few times, and I ask where she's from. "Boulder, Colorado," she says. "I start college there in the fall." This is truly amazing. We're neighbors," I say. "You're my next door neighbor." I look at her longlingly, thinking that if I were thirty years younger, this serendipity might amount to something.

★

I spend the evening in my room, staring out at the full moon rising over the Aegean, listening to evening sounds punctuated by whinnies from the pale horse.

The night in Munich, after I embarrassed myself so badly in front of the German girl, I went to the bathroom and returned to find my friend Harry actively pursuing her, the girl he had set me up with. Harry was married, and I was divorced. He had a cavalier attitude toward marriage, an institution I valued even after my wife of eighteen years left me, maybe especially valued after she left. I had never experienced such a strong feeling of hatred until the evening I saw Harry making up to that German girl.

I decided to have it out with him and walked outside looking for a club, a knife. I wondered what kind of weapon I could buy there in Munich? Through the few years since this episode, I've lost the handle on the rage I felt that night. It has metamorphosed into a benign, even humorous view of the events, making it impossible to convey the depth of my hatred and the precarious, knife-edge of violence on which I trod.

I assessed the situation for a while, walking the streets of Munich alone, but when I went back inside the bar, my companions were arguing with the two women and a couple of German men, something about them just not liking Americans. "Superficial" was the word I kept hearing. I sat down again and tried to resume my conversation with the blond, but we rapidly started arguing also. She had a bad impression of Americans, and me dumping my beer in her purse had convinced her it was worth talking about.

As I came to my senses, I knew I had better leave, and walked most of the way back to the hotel before remembering my son. I couldn't leave him. He was twenty-three years old, but still, I couldn't walk off like an idiot without telling him where I was going. I went back to the bar and ignored my two business associates, who were standing outside, and who asked me what I was up to, as they shook their heads in disbelief.

I sat at the bar again, with my son and the two women. They seemed more agreeable. I paid their bar bill, and they left. But my anger didn't leave. I was still in an absolute rage. My son and I walked back to the hotel, and when I entered our room, I picked up my open suitcase from the foot of my bed, and threw it to the floor, dumping its contents. I fell into bed, embarrassed at what a sorry father I was, and full of self-hatred.

The next morning, I didn't want to face my traveling companions, but had no choice. I wanted to check out of my life as well as the hotel. How would I explain my bizarre behavior? My biggest embarrassment was that I had done this in front of my son. The episode did help me realize how close to the edge I always tread. I felt as though I should see an exorcist. But this still wasn't the end of it.

Two years following the Munich incident, I had another episode similar to that many years before in Berkeley, a second encounter with the Furies. I was in the Alps hiking hut-to-hut with two business associates. We were one day out of Brand, Austria, sleeping in a pitch-dark hut high on a mountaintop, when I woke during the night terror-stricken.

★

The full moon has risen high enough that it no longer casts bright rays through my French doors. And now the slow, almost silent music of the wind plays this building like a mystical instrument. My curiosity gets the best of me this time, and I slip outside and up spiraling metal stairs to the roof. I stand on the flat white-stucco roof, where backpacking tourists sleep in the summer, and listen for the source of the sound. The west wind is as strong as gravity. I look to the east at the moonlit landscape dotted with the yellow points of light from homes, and in the distance, I notice the white light of a ship at sea. To the west I see the cave and, standing in its dark entrance, the pale horse. He shakes his head at me and whinnies. I cup my ear into the wind. The mysterious music has come again, and this time I'm sure it's the wind's song.

1 Nov, Monday

I rise late, have a breakfast of fruit and donuts, and work off a little of it trying to start my motorbike. Finally, all my kicking pays off, and I follow the wind and road signs to the ancient city of Thera. The road first leads through the small town of Kamari, then along a black-sand beach, and finally curves inland and up the switchbacks of a cobblestone road. My old motorbike vibrates until

Santorini

I believe I'm going to lose body parts. It barely has the power to make the grade at the hairpin turns. Slowly, I ascend the mountain with the sea falling away behind me to the east. The wind is strong, whipping at my clothes, and several times almost blowing me off the road.

Finally, I stop in a large, circular, unpaved parking area just below the top of the mountain. Up a few stone steps, I see the edge of ruins protruding from an outcropping of rocks. I park my motorbike nose-to-the-wind to keep it from blowing over. I see no cars and only a couple of other bikes parked here.

I start up the steep trail and think I have found ancient Thera at a small stone church, the inside of which has barely enough headroom to stand. At first I think this is the extent of the ruins, but I notice a path continuing around the north side of the mountain. Again, I ascend a set of switchbacks, crossing isolated monuments to various Greek gods. Spread all along the top of the mountain, overlooking the sea far below, are the vast ruins of ancient Thera. The ruins run along the narrow mountaintop with a precipituous drop-off to the northeast. I can see the town of Kamari with its black-sand beach, where I started my ascent up the mountain. To the southwest is the town of Perissa, a single blue church dome at its center.

The ruins of ancient Thera consist of an agora; sanctuaries for Apollo, Dionysus and several other Greek gods; public buildings, including a gym, private homes, and an ancient theatre, which is by the cliff overlooking the sea. Membliarus founded the ancient city under the orders of Kadmos, as he wandered about Greece looking for Europa. It is also the city of Theras, the descendent of Oedipus who, generations later, came seeking to be king.

The wind howls, rakes the mountainside. The sparse trees are bent, and their limbs are combed in the direction of the wind. I reach the end of the peninsula and start back on the west side of the mountain, and pass even more ruins. I find a place shielded from the wind beside a group of college kids, Americans in shorts sitting on a ledge, eating and talking. I eat my chewy honey-dipped donut, laced with sugar granules and pull off my jacket. Even my black sweater feels too warm. The sun is blistering.

The coming of Theras brought trouble to the island, for the curse on the descendants of Oedipus was still active. All of Theras' children died.[207] He journeyed to the oracle at Delphi and learned that, to rid his family of the curse, he would have to erect shrines to Laios and Oedipus. This Theras did, and henceforth his children lived. Today, I have looked in vain for that sanctuary.

This business of curses that affect innocent children is disturbing. I'm sure that, if there was any heart within Theras at all, he felt more than a little anguish over his own children dying. To feel that you are responsible for the death of a child is a terrible burden, but to know that you are the cause and not know the actual events that resulted in it, seems unbearable. I have never been able to get over knowing that I was the cause of my daughter's disappearance.

On the trail down the mountain, the wind is fierce, and I have to remove my clip-on sunglasses, and eventually, even my glasses as the wind threatens to pull them from my face. It blows sand and pebbles off the mountain and into my eyes. I have my jacket on over my sweater again and wish for the down parka I left in Colorado. At the parking area, I'm glad to see my motorbike still standing, although another has been blown over and lays flat in the dirt, dripping gasoline.

I follow the cobblestone road back down the mountain, my idling motorbike taking the switchbacks easily, only the wind driving it off course. Back on the main road to Fira, the wind pressing against my face and driving my hair back, I see to my left the vast bay below the cliffs of the volcano on which I ride.

★

I sit in a restaurant at cliff-side, having a piece of dark chocolate cake and a cup of high-octane Greek coffee. I look out to sea, the sun gradually setting through rapidly moving clouds. Beams of sunlight break through, spotlighting the surface like some mighty flashlight of the gods searching the caldera for something lost.

The cold iron cables, along which the cable cars travel, glisten like silver threads that dip and bow to the edge of the sea. I hear a clatter below me and peer over the edge to see a donkey-train, hooves scraping the stone walkway. It's still cold, although the pension owner has told me that ten days of good weather is coming. This is my last evening in Santorini. I can use the warm weather of Crete.

2 Nov, Tuesday

I rise early and talk to the owner of the pension, whom today has bathed, shaved, and looks like a prosperous businessman. He wears a crisp white shirt and slacks. He complains about a meeting with his attorney, how the attorney keeps him in trouble. He tells me that I can catch the bus that will take me to the ferry at one o'clock in the center of town. As I leave the pension, I hear the pale horse and take one more glance in his direction. For some strange reason, I feel that he has been watching me and sending back information on my actions to some unknown personage.

I return my motorbike to the rental agency maintenance building, where it's inspected for damage. A middle-aged American, who looks like a retired surfer, long blond hair and weathered skin, gives my motorbike a clean bill of

Santorini

health.

On the way to the bus, lumbering under my heavy pack again, I pass fishermen at the side of the road selling their catch in cardboard boxes: large silvery fish, squid, an octopus. Some sit cleaning nets and arguing with their neighbors. They're a tall, thin people with grizzly, unshaven faces. The fishy smell of their catch fills the air. I'm reminded of Jesus' words to the brothers, Peter and Andrew, "Follow me, and I will make you fishers of men."

The boundary between Greek mythology and their ancient religion was not as clean as are modern-day life and religion. Upon death, many of the ancient Mycenaeans ascended to become gods themselves. Some were whisked away to Greek heaven. Oedipus was one of these. He ascended (or perhaps descended) to the land if the Furies.

My maternal grandparents were extremely religious and toward the end of their lives, we heard rumors that they would not die, but be taken directly into heaven and simply vanish from the surface of the earth, as did Oedipus. I attended both their funerals, and if they ascended, it was spiritually rater than bodily. There are also, however, reports of Oedipus' funeral, a pyre, and his gravesite at the Areopagos in Athens.

I sit at the pier awaiting the ferry to Crete. The wind has calmed, although the gentle breeze feels cool in the shade. This place sure runs hot and cold. When the ferry arrives, I board but have to wait a half hour before we depart. I look out at two small islets in the middle of the caldera visible from the ferry. Both islets are made of black volcanic rock, and the largest, Nea Kameni is flat across its surface, its straight sides dropping into the sea.

The ferry leaves dock and drifts toward Nea Kameni, then turns south toward Crete. Thera moves along the left side of us. Soon, we pass its southern tip, and Aspro drifts by on the right. It's a wonderful sight. As Nea Kameni passes, I see light brown spots on its sides where earth shows through the black rocks like sunlight, but Palea Kameni is solid black. Aspro comes up on the right. The top half is light-colored, obviously the original soil before the eruption that destroyed the island. We pass over the underwater part of the caldera. to my left, I see the southern tip of Thera, the sun ahead of us, and the bright light rippling on the water. To my right, drifting slowly past, is Aspro. I may be leaving, but what is going on inside this volcano is not over yet.

★

We're several miles out to sea. Santorini is just a faint brown mist with white cities on the mountaintops, like vanilla frosting on chocolate cake. I look over the side of the boat, and swear I have never seen water so blue, deep navy blue.

Santorini

When the people of Akrotiri fled the island, it was under much more dramatic circumstances than mine. The city had been destroyed by a tremendous earthquake, and the volcano was spewing fumes and lava. I imagine the rumble of the volcano coming from the bowels of the earth and the landscape trembling as they loaded the boats, smoke billowing from the volcano. They must have felt a fine, dry mist of ash falling, and heard the cries of their children, the screams of women, and frantic, panic-stricken shouts of men.

CHAPTER 11: Crete

I'm startled by lively bouzouki music (Zorba the Greek) from the loudspeaker, accompanied by a woman's voice welcoming us to Crete. I grab my pack and run up on deck in time to see the tiny island of Dia drift by followed by an outcropping of Crete itself. Straight ahead are the dark faces of the buildings of Iraklion, deep in shadow. We dock just at sunset, but the waterfront is deserted except for taxis and those coming to pickup passengers. Iraklion is a large city, over 70,000, but the entire island has a population of only 500,000.

I consider taking a taxi but decide to walk to the center of town, which looks to be only a hundred meters or so up a gentle incline. Darkness descends on the city as I enter, stooped like an old hunchback under the weight of my pack. In the center of town people are everywhere, and the small one-way streets are crowded with cars. But I sense a friendliness here I've not felt anywhere else. A couple of people actually make eye contact and return my smile. It's a hustling-bustling city without a sign of a tourist. I try to follow the city map in my guidebook, but the maze of dark unmarked streets and alleys makes it impossible.

I look for a hotel or pension while standing among the rapidly moving pedestrians, feeling out of place with my huge pack. I've seen no one with a backpack since I left dock. Finally, I see a sign for the Hotel Mediterranean. A room is twice what I can afford, but my pack feels like it weighs a ton. I take the elevator to the second floor. The elevator doors in Greece don't move back and forth laterally but swing in and out like a normal door. The elevator cannot move with the door open or it will be crushed. My room is the first carpeted one in which I've stayed. It's a large room with dim lights, a bathroom with a curtain for the shower (another first), two single beds pushed close together, white sheets and pillowcases, bright green blankets.

I have a quick dinner, mousaka again, in a little restaurant one block from the hotel, just off a huge crowded market. I also order French fries and watch horrified as the cook lowers the basket of already-cooked potatoes into the grease to warm them and pours them onto my plate. My food floats in grease.

Crete

After the indigestion I experienced at Corinth I'm in no mood for the grease-plate and have to pick over my food.

I crawl into bed early as a French horn blows from far off, accompanied by an occasional firecracker. I hear several people practicing musical instruments. My hotel must be next to a school. After an hour of badly played bits of music by several soloists, the entire orchestra plays one long song, then quits. The French horn continues its lament, a stark presence superimposed on a background of street noise.

This evening when I walked the tight, labyrinthine streets, I saw evidence in the tourist shops and markets of the primary symbol of ancient Minoan society, the bull. This aspect of Greek mythology, which I've always disliked, may have more to say about me than I've cared to admit. It's the seductiveness of this friendly city that suddenly makes the bull seem palatable. The myth of the Cretan bull goes all the way back to Europa.

In Thebes, I encountered the myth of Kadmos, Europa's brother, who left home in Phoenicia to search for his sister but was told by Apollo to found a city instead. She had been kidnapped by Zeus from her home in Tyre and brought to Crete. When Zeus appeared to Europa, who was playing in wildflowers at the edge of the Mediterranean, he came as a beautiful white bull. Ovid describes Zeus' seduction of her:

> And the king's daughter looked at him in wonder,
> So calm so beautiful, and feared to touch him,
> At first, however mild, and little by little
> Got over her fear, and soon was bringing flowers
> To hold toward that white face, and he, the lover,
> Gave kisses to the hands held out, rejoicing
> In hope of later, more exciting kisses.
> Is it time? Not quite. He leaps, a little playful,
> On the green grass, or lays the snowy body
> On the yellow sand, and gradually the princess
> Loses all fear, and he lets her pat his shoulder,
> Twine garlands in his horns, and she grows bolder,
> Climbs on his back, of course all unsuspecting.[208]

The next thing Europa knew, she was in Crete and pregnant with a child, a child who would one day rule the island as king. She named him Minos. These two branches of the Agenor line, Kadmos and Europa, unite the mythology of Crete with that of the Greek mainland. Europa's line of descent would lead directly to that of Agamemnon and Menelaus. A single visit to Crete by Menelaus would setup the circumstances that led to the Trojan War.

Many of my earliest childhood memories are of heifers and bulls. My father was a dairyman and an artificial inseminator. Many times I saw him in the barn with a single cow in the stanchions. He would have one arm up her rear end and with the other, slip a long glass tube into her vagina. He inserted the tube so far I wondered if it would poke out her mouth. The tube had a little rubber ball on the aft end that he squeezed to spurt semen into her.

I remember a bright sunshiny day in the middle of summer when I was eleven. I looked out over the corral into the neighbor's pasture where his herd of heifers and a lone bull ran free. I was afraid of that bull, but sometimes I stood back from the fence and threw clods at him. He would glare back at me, aloof and unimpressed. I remember the huge bulk of him, the rippling muscles in his neck and shoulders, and his snorting as he kicked dirt over his back, the dust billowing and fogging. He was the epitome of arrogance, aggression, anger.

The bull approached a heifer, put his nose to her rear end and as she moved away, he took a few fast steps and mounted her. His front hooves hung limp at the sides of her shoulders, pawing uselessly at the air. His huge bulk engulfed her. Then I saw his blood-red shaft, long thin and pointed, emerge from the tuft of hide and hair at the bottom of his stomach. It was longer than I could have ever imagined, at least three feet it seemed and already dripping. It flashed along her side, probed her rear end, searching seemingly with a mind of its own, then entered her. As his hind quarters churned to keep up with her slow trot, I wondered how hot she must be inside, how slick and pulsating. His nostrils opened, turned outward in tremendous snorts, his hips churning. He was a locomotive, a steam engine of sexual energy, thrusting deeper and deeper. He mounted her many times. It was like a mystery, his throbbing shaft solving the mystery inside that womanly presence. His huge pink testicles swung from side to side like a bell clapper, their ring tolling for my own awakening sexuality.

After Zeus kidnapped Europa and brought her to Crete, she had a child she named Minos. Since Minos was a mortal with a divine father, he claimed divine right to the throne of Knossos, the kingship that ruled all kingdoms of Crete. To illustrate his divine right, he bragged that Poseidon would do anything he requested. He prayed for the god to send him a bull, which he promised to sacrifice. Immediately, a beautiful bull appeared from the sea. Some say it was the same bull that brought Europa from Tyre to Crete. But Minos thought the bull was so beautiful that he couldn't sacrifice it and substituted another. As revenge, Poseidon made Minos' wife Pasiphae fall in love with the bull. To satisfy her passion, she had Daedalus, the consummate Cretan artisan and follower of divine Hephaestus, build a model of a cow covered with hides, and she hid inside. Minos' bull was attracted by the artificial heifer and mounted her, thus satisfying Pasiphae's passion. Subsequently, Pasiphae gave birth to the Minotaur (Minos' Taurus), which had the body of a man and the head of a bull. As for the bull who had fathered this monstrosity, Minos gladly got rid of him when Herakles was ordered to bring the bull to the Peloponnese as the seventh of his ten labors.[209]

As far back as I can remember, my father had me help him milk the cows. For a cow, being milked can be an unsettling experience. First she is forced to stick her head in a stanchion, which is clamped tight to keep her from moving. Then her udder is washed with a warm rag and the milking machine, that pulsating, throbbing suction machine, is attached to her four teats. Some cows are nervous, the hide on their back twitching and shimmering. My father taught me how to soothe them, to rub them on the flanks and speak softly. He also beat them with 2x4's and shovels, but not as a part of his intended instruction. My father never got along with the cows, but when he left the barn they always calmed under my kind attention and care. They liked to be touched, and their hides were particularly soft and sensitive in their flanks. Their teats were hard and puckered at first, but became soft and pliable after washing. Heifers are warm creatures. I've always seen them as mothers. I fed their calves with a bucket of their mother's milk. So I can understand Pasiphae's affection for the bull if not her literal sexual passion.

Heracles took the bull off Minos' hands, but that wasn't the end of Minos' troubles with him. Minos had a son, Androgeus, who grew up at Athens. Though Heracles originally took the bull to the Peloponnese, the bull wandered across the Isthmus of Corinth into Attica, where he plundered and killed. Aegeus the king of Athens sent Minos' son to Marathon to kill the wild bull. But the bull got the best of Androgeus, killing him instead. When Minos heard of his son's death, he declared war on Athens. Crete could not subdue Athens but would not quit waging perpetual war. Aegeus wanted the war ended and asked Minos to state his demands for peace. Minos demanded a tribute of seven young men and seven virgins every nine years to feed the Minotaur.

In the meantime, young Theseus came from Troezen in the Peloponnese to Athens searching for his father, Aegeus, the king of Athens. Aegeus didn't recognize Theseus and fearing him, sent him to kill the wild bull of Marathon, expecting Theseus to be killed also. But Theseus killed the bull. Aegeus then recognized Theseus' sword as the one he left with Theseus' mother and realized that Theseus was his son. Two tributes had been paid to Minos for the Minotaur, but when it came time to pay the third, Theseus asked his father to let him be among the seven young men as he believed he could kill the Minotaur. After all, he had killed the Minotaur's father, the wild bull of Marathon, and now he would get his chance at the son.

Theseus had already cast himself as a traditional Greek hero by following in Heracles' footsteps. Theseus had killed beasts, monsters and outlaws as he sought his father on the way from Troezen to Athens. But killing the Minotaur would not be easy. Minos had been so ashamed that his wife gave birth to the monstrous Minotaur, he had Daedalus build a Labyrinth to hide and imprison it. No one who entered the Labyrinth ever came out.

When Theseus came to Crete, he must have docked close to where we docked this evening because he was on his way to Knossos, just as I am. That center of the ancient Minoan civilization is just a few kilometers from here. I'll see Knossos tomorrow. The Minoans were a peace-loving people known for sophisticated art and embellished architecture. A Greek merchant, appropriately named Minos Kalokairinos discovered the ruins of the Minoan civilization. He interested Schliemann in his find, and although Schliemann tried in 1890 to buy the land for excavation, he never could consummate a deal. Sir Arthur Evans, the keeper of the Ashmolean Museum at Oxford, England finally bought the land and started excavating in 1900,[210] immediately uncovering the ruins of Knossos.

Until Kalokairinos' and Evans' discoveries, no one knew that the Minoan civilization actually existed. References in ancient Greek literature to Knossos, thought fictional, were once again shown to have a basis in fact. The Minoan civilization was even more ancient than the Mycenaean and may have had a paternal relationship with it. It lasted for 1500 years, from 2600-1100 BC.[211]

★

I wake at midnight with the French horn still blowing, but alternating with male voices, tenors raised for only one note. Another horn blast, a firecracker. A chant. The mousaka weighs on my stomach like a ball of sulfuric acid and each horn blast turns the heat up a notch. Another noise, close by, a sound like that of a giant washing machine scrubbing a giant's clothes.

Finally, the scrubbing noise stops and so do the horns, male voices and firecrackers. I only hear the low rumble of sparse, late-night city traffic and the creaks and thumps of the man in the room above moving about. Silence in a Greek city.

3 Nov, Wednesday

I wake at daybreak, after dreaming of my older cousin who helped get rid of Fred before my father could kill him. I was arguing with my cousin about his smoking. He died at the age of forty-two from cardiac arrest. Also present in this dream of dead people was my aunt (my mother's younger sister), who died at the age of forty-five from an enlarged heart, and my uncle who had several stays in an insane asylum. My uncle also died recently. The last time I saw him, he was crawling around on all fours like a dog because of arthritic knees. My mother, who is still alive, was also in the dream, quarreling about me with my uncle. They were sitting around a table on the lawn of my great-great-grandfather's plantation in the South. I was sitting nearby picking fish from nets as the fishermen had done yesterday in Fira, arguing with my cousin, and somewhat bemused at all this negative attention.

Many of the ancient heroes descended to the Underworld: Orpheus, Odysseus, Theseus, Herakles. Orpheus went to retrieve his wife, whom he couldn't live without. He was unsuccessful. Odysseus went to consult blind Teiresias, who was the only mortal in the Afterlife with an unclouded mind, to find out how to get home. Theseus went to help a buddy steal Persephone from Hades. Herakles went to save Theseus. What I was doing there, I'm at a loss to say. Was I fishing for souls during this journey into my own mythology? They weren't openly hostile, but I can't say they were too pleased with me either. Since this was my great-great-grandfather's home, maybe they were just letting me know that they were saving a place for me.

★

I catch the bus to Knossos and enter the site through a long tree-shrouded walkway, a statue of Sir Arthur Evans standing in the shadows. Evans used some artistic license resurrecting the ancient ruins; consequently, they are gorgeous if unrealistic. The ruins are a maze of partially reconstructed stone buildings, walls and stone-paved courtyards, surrounded by fir trees and rolling hills.

King Minos' palace was a huge structure built on several levels with flat roofs and bright-red columns, stone walls. "Sacred horns," large two-pronged sculptures representing a bull's horns, lined the roofs of many buildings. Only one of these sacred structures has been re-erected and stands at the edge of the courtyard. Many of the sculptures found here depicting Minoans are with arms upraised in salute or welcome, a rather startling resemblance to the horns. I remember the terra-cotta sculptures I saw in the museum in Thebes. The resemblance indicates a connection between ancient Thebes and Knossos, as one might expect from mythology.

The myth of the bull here on Crete carries special, if not so evident, significance. First, the bull is Zeus the kidnapper, then one sacred to Poseidon, and finally one in human form, a half-man half-beast monstrosity born of a woman's base passion for an animal. And another god of the island looms in the background rather unnoticed. It's Dionysus, with his ability to transcend the boundary separating mankind and nature. Jealous Hera at one time transformed Dionysus into a bull. He was also at one time human, thus transcending the boundary separating mankind from the divine.

All of Dionysus' characteristics are prevalent here on Crete, but one other aspect is even more important: his connection with the goddess Earth. This aspect brought him to the forefront of Greek religion. The Minoan civilization was not focused on war, as were the mainland Mycenaeans, but instead upon the love of nature and its spiritual reflection in the human soul. As Kerenyi put it, here on Crete, "A hymn to Nature as a Goddess seems to be heard from everywhere, a hymn to joy and life."

The principal Minoan god was female:

The main deity is always the Mother Goddess, who is portrayed in her different forms. She is the chthonic goddess with the snakes, the "Ministress of Animals" with lions and chamois, and the goddess of the heavens, with birds and stars.[212]

Two figurines of the Snake Goddess were found here at Knossos. Both depict her with bare bosom, open bodice pulled together at the top and bottom pushing her breasts together in a globular cluster, prominent nipples protruding from the two masses of flesh. In the smaller of the figurines, the goddess has a snake in each of her upheld hands, and in the larger one, the snakes are coiled about her outstretched arms. Her face is wide-eyed, severe. Minoan society was noted for its perpetual peace, and one wonders about this society that was older than the Mycenaean and retained its reliance on female goddesses rather than male gods.

On the Greek mainland, I encountered ancient religious sites that were wrestled from the Mother Earth goddess, Gaia. At Delphi Apollo killed the Python guarding her temple; and in Olympia, Mt. Kronion originally housed the sanctuary of Gaia and later Hera before the temple of Zeus was built. Minoan society didn't have a heritage of war like that of the great one against the Trojans to spur an oral tradition. But the peace was shattered by the Minoans' connection with the Mycenaeans. Only through Crete's external conflict with the Mycenaeans, the war between Athens and Knossos, do we retain any of its mythology. But who was this snake goddess? And did she have a mortal manifestation? What do the ancient myths tell us about this woman with the bare breasts?

Many of the rooms in the palace have been reconstructed with frescoes decorating the interior and exterior walls. I stand before the "Toreador Fresco" of a reddish-brown bull with long sharp curving horns. The fresco depicts:

> ...a contest or game involving young men and girls and a bull. It required exceptional dexterity and daring (they grasped the horns of the bull, executed a double somersault on its back and lept to the ground on the other side) and frequently became dangerous.[213]

The games occurred in conjunction with Cretan religious festivals, but the bull was not sacrificed. Remembering my own experience with bulls, I can't imagine having the courage to grab a bull's horns and propel myself up on its back. But the association of Dionysus with the bull here on Crete might have made all the difference.

Farther on, I see the throne room of King Minos. What is most striking is the throne's modest size, that of a kitchen chair. The small armless alabaster throne is against the east wall, which sports a large fresco of griffins lying among reeds. Stone benches line the walls. At the other end of the room, or antechamber, a lustral basin rests in the center of the floor. Minos established law in Crete through a system given him by Zeus at about the same time God gave Moses the Ten Commandments. Minos was known as the most just ruler in the ancient world. Among the archaeological finds here at Knossos is a beautiful black sculpture of a bull's head with gilded gold horns, eyes of crystal and a muzzle of mother-of-pearl. But I see no sign of the intricate Labyrinth made by Daedalus to hide the Minotaur.

As I sit at the edge of the stone-paved central court, a group of highly agitated people enters, hurrying toward the exit. They separate a little, and I see someone on a stretcher. I ask a small Englishman sporting a gray mustache and pipe what's going on, and he tells me the old lady collapsed from the heat. It is warm today, the sun glaring from above and reflecting hotly off the courtyards.

By the time Theseus came to Knossos, in approximately 1270 BC by my reckoning, the place had a heavy Mycenaean connection. Many of the old palaces had been destroyed. Before Theseus entered the Labyrinth to kill the Minotaur, he knew he must have a foolproof method of finding his way out. In this, he was helped by one of Minos' daughters, Ariadne. Ariadne had fallen in love with Theseus. She solicited the help of Daedalus, the architect of the Labyrinth, who devised a large ball of thread that she was to give to Theseus, telling him to tie it to the entrance and unroll it along the twisting and turning pathway. This Theseus did, and started his descent. At the very deepest part of the Labyrinth, he found the Minotaur.

Crete

From what I've seen of Minoan architecture, I imagine the Labyrinth to be a formidable structure with huge stone doorways, and dark as pitch. Since it hasn't been found, we can only speculate about its location. I suppose Daedalus constructed it underground, the entrance in the foot of a mountain. Possibly it has been concealed by centuries of rockslides caused by earthquakes. Perhaps it still lies unfound in the side of Mt. Ida.

My own perception of the Labyrinth has been forever corrupted by my first visit, at the age of six, to Carlsbad Caverns in New Mexico near my grandparent's home. My grandmother, the daughter of the woman born of a surrogate mother, a woman who was forever gardening, sort of an earth-mother, took my hand and led me through the maze of tunnels, with stalactites and stalagmites filling the echoing halls and vast stone rooms. Through almost half a century, I still feel my hand wrapped in the warmth of hers. At the bottom in the King's Room, I had a strange, uncomfortable feeling that made me want to get out of there. Little did I realize that this was simply my grandmother's guided tour of territory that would become all too familiar. Many years later, I would experience it again, but with ever-increasing intensity, in the underground missile silos, and in the Alps. Finally, it would come to get me even in my own living room.

I imagine Theseus entering the Labyrinth with a torch, descending through the windings and twisting of the tunnel, walking through dung that increased in depth as he descended. As he grew close to the Minotaur, he'd heard him snorting. The Minotaur had been in the Labyrinth at least eighteen years, and though he couldn't find his way out, he still must have known the far end of his prison very well. He would have known all the sounds of the darkness, and the footsteps of Theseus would have been distinctive, startling and perhaps frightening. In the ensuing battle, Theseus beat the Minotaur to death with his fists. Then Theseus followed Ariadne's thread back to the entrance.

As a result of my embarrassing episode in Munich, I recognized something strange going on inside me, something not me. During the coming months with the assistance of a psychiatrist, I made a conscious effort to notice more of this hidden part of myself. I, like Theseus, had started my first few tentative steps past the entrance of my own Labyrinth.

As I exit the site, I stop for a few minutes to watch archaeologists working in a deep trench bounded by ancient stone walls. Three men and a woman work with shovels, picks and rakes, one writing in a notebook. The trees surrounding the edge of the trench are dead and lean threateningly toward the excavation.

*

I sit beside the street outside Knossos awaiting the bus back to Iraklion while soaking up the beautiful day: bright sunlight, wisps of clouds, a cool refreshing breeze. I wonder about Minos' and Pasiphae's reactions to the appearance of the Minotaur when he was first born. If he was so grotesque, why didn't they simply slit his throat and throw him in the trash? Is it possible the Minotaur wasn't the grotesque beast he has been made out to be? Did Pasiphae, when she first saw him, fall in love with him? Perhaps even Minos had a sheepish grin of pride. If you've ever seen a curly-headed little bull just after being born, and I've never seen one that wasn't curly headed, you'd realize that they're difficult not to love, and belligerently playful. I suspect he had little horn buds even then. But Minos was ashamed of the Minotaur, so he had him confined in the Labyrinth. In another version of the myth, Minos is the father, thus the name, Minos' Taurus, Minos' bull. This makes sense because Minos was born of Zeus, who had taken the form of a bull when he seduced Europa. Thus, the Minotaur constituted that part of Minos' own animal nature of which he was ashamed.

A friend of mine once brought to my attention the precarious bond between a father and son who are both second sons. They have suffered the same remoteness from their father, the indignation at the hands of an older brother. My father and I were both second sons. Did he, had he always, equated me with himself? His base self? I'm the only one who came within seconds of being murdered by him.

Here's the bus back to Iraklion.

★

Early afternoon, I sit at the entrance to the market near my hotel on a bench in the middle of the Plateia watching traffic and Greek girls, listening to city noise, cars, motorbikes, busses, trucks. Behind me, a compact-disk store plays music in accompaniment to the hustle-bustle of the street. A lot of women ride motorbikes, mostly young women. A beautiful woman glides by on one now: tight skirt (nice legs), white blouse and dark brown hair. Olive skin. Straight across the square staring down at me is a gigantic Pepsi sign. The gaudy tasteless ones are always American.

I walk through the market, a pedestrian street jammed with shops, jammed with shoppers. A store at the entrance to the market has vegetables and fruit in boxes, all tilted forward for the consumer to get a better look. He has boxes of lettuce, broccoli, onions, tomatoes, eggplant, green beans, cucumbers, bananas, green apples, red apples, pitiful looking oranges, lemons, passion fruit, packages of dried figs, nuts, spices, bread, herbs. This is just his outdoor display. Inside, he has carrots, turnips, potatoes... Further on, the best leather goods in Greece hang on the walls of shops: bags, travel packs, women's purses, men's purses, wallets, attaché cases. The rich chocolate-brown leather, the sharp acid smell.

Huge nets filled with sponges and baskets are suspended on crossbeams above the walkway.

I turn right down a side street and follow a particularly ripe smell to find open boxes of gray fish, black fish, blue fish, big, small, round, flat fish, octopus, squid, shrimp, all fresh, all out in the open air and sunshine. In the front window of a butcher shop, I see the full head of a hog from the shoulders forward with all the hair removed, its skin rough and leathery. The slit of a mouth looks particularly thoughtful. And pigs' feet, from their hooves all the way to their knees. Skinned rabbits hang by the fur on their feet. They still have their heads. I see the skinned head of a bull hanging vertically by the neck, a little tuft of black hide and hair on his chin, bulging screaming eyes. Its jaw muscles and the top of its head are blood red; its fat is lard white. This could be the head of a Minotaur.

★

Late afternoon, I walk to the bus station and stare up at the schedule on the wall for the bus to Phaestos. It leaves at eight in the morning. I'll have to be up early. The air feels cool and fresh, with a slight breeze. The sky is overcast and I feel a few drops of rain. The voice of the athletes from a nearby stadium mixes with traffic noise. On the way back to my hotel, I stop to get a spinach pie, a cream pie, four bananas and a kilo of apples. Breakfast, and perhaps lunch. I enter the hotel and take the elevator to the second floor.

When I first started this journey, I was concerned about traveling in a foreign country alone, and my concern had its origin in an experience, which occurred only a few years ago during a hike in the Austrian Alps. I hiked for six days, stopping in the evenings at huts, or hüttes as Austrians call them, strategically placed throughout rugged mountains. At the beginning of the trek, a friend of mine from Texas and I stored our street clothes and suitcases at the airport in Zurich and took the train to the station in Bludenz, Austria. We were joined there by a German colleague, who drove us to the trailhead in Brand. Late that afternoon, the three of us started our trek into the Silvretta Mountains in southwestern Austria on the Swiss border. We spent the first night in Douglass Hütte beside an ice-blue mountain lake. My first night's sleep was uneventful.

The next day was filled with strenuous hiking, the trail going either straight up or straight down. We climbed a snow-covered peak, the Schesaplana, in sparkling sunlight. I felt an unusually strong fear of heights walking the switchbacks up cliffs. I spoke German, emptying my mind of English. And I developed an attitude. I was ill-tempered, disrespectful. That night I was exhausted and thought I would sleep like a stone.

The hüttes of the Austrian Alps are huge two-story buildings with a kitchen and dining room on the first floor, a place close to the heater to dry wet hiking boots, and barn-like sleeping quarters upstairs, just wood rafters and a roof. I crawled inside my own sleeping-bag liner and spread two wool blankets over me.

At eleven-thirty I woke so suddenly and from such a deep sleep that I thought someone had shaken me. But the hütte was perfectly quiet and pitch black, and my companions were asleep. I put my head back on my folded-Levis pillow and tried to sleep, but sensed again that something was wrong. At first I thought someone was in the room, someone evil. I listened closely but could hear nothing. I strained to see, but the ink-black darkness was impenetrable. I convinced myself no one could commit a crime in pitch darkness and settled back to sleep again, realizing quite suddenly that the problem was inside me.

I felt claustrophobic. My sleeping-bag liner felt like a coffin. I had retained a sense of falling from looking down the side of so many mountains. When I closed my eyes, I fell through space. Since I had purposely tried to purge my mind of English, I felt remote from my own language. Even my two companions, one from a different state, the other from a different country, seemed like strangers. I was far from family, country. I heard snoring. It sounded unnatural, inhuman, monstrous.

The six hours remaining before morning were an eternity. I remembered the experience in Berkeley years before when I ran to my uncle realizing that this time I was trapped. Nowhere to run. I also realized that visual images were a distraction from what was going on inside me, the grotesque faces, skulls, wide-eyed screaming faces. If I could only fill my mind with an image, they would disappear, but I couldn't because of the absolute darkness. I flipped on my flashlight. The mental effort of forming an image brought me out of my own personal horror show. I shined the light along the wood beams, ran my hand along them for the rough tactile sensation. All was well until I flipped off the light. As I descended into sleep, I woke with a jolt. It wasn't until five o'clock in the morning, when a pale light infiltrated the room and I heard some restless kids whispering to their mother, that my panic disappeared and I slept.

The writings of Carl Jung talk of the ego and the interfaces that allow it to cushion itself from the external and internal worlds. The persona protects the ego from the outside world and allows the individual to present an acceptable face outward. But internally, we face the unknown, the unconscious and its many mythological connections. A female presence stands before the unconscious, a female presence for men and a male presence for women. These are called the anima and the animus. That night, somehow, it was as if I had been stripped of my anima, or at least she'd turned her head, and I viewed directly into the collective unconscious.

The next morning I had a new attitude, and at breakfast I cautiously told my companions of my problem. They were understanding but couldn't relate to the magnitude of the situation. I told them I might have to return to the States, but they smiled and brushed off the comment. As we stood outside Lindauer Hütte adjusting our packs for a hard day of hiking, it started to rain. I donned my bright orange poncho, stood waiting like a Halloween goblin to start the trek, believing I was having an emotional breakdown. And there I was, eight-thousand miles from home.

I'd felt trapped in the Alps, trapped in that barn-like structure, trapped in the mountains, trapped in Europe. It would take an eternity in panic-time to get out. When I was at home milking cows with my father, I was trapped in the barn, a real barn, trapped at the far end where the gate closed it off, trapped in that room where he would go into a rage and beat those cows with shovels and 2x4's, cows who were trapped with their heads in the stanchions, jerking against the restraining timbers until I'd think maybe their heads would pop off. He would shout and beat and push, curse the cows, shout orders at me. I didn't know but what, at any second, he'd turn on me, kill me on the spot.

But it wasn't just in the barn. Though my father was a big man, his presence was even larger. He diminished everything around him in my eyes. At home the chairs and sofas shrunk in his presence. We had a fifty-acre farm, and his persona reached into the corner of the farthest field. Nowhere, even within myself, could I find a place to hide from him. He filled me up.

Never before, not even the night in Berkeley, had I felt so trapped. In Berkeley I was vulnerable but not trapped. That day as we hiked up the sides of mountains, down the sides of mountains, crossed back and forth over the Austrian-Swiss border, inside I was crossing that boundary between sanity and madness. Dionysus, the deity who has the ability to bring insanity into the sane world, was hot on my trail. I felt as though I inhabited the body of another person. I was descending into my own Labyrinth, only unlike Theseus, I didn't have Ariadne and her golden thread to help find my way out. I had four more days and three nights in the Alps, and was already a beaten man.

I've felt a little of that terror on this journey, particularly when I was in Delphi where I had the talk with myself. The nagging possibility that the problem could return is always there. Every night as I fall asleep, I wonder if I'll survive, if I'll find my way back from the terror of the Labyrinth of my dream. But at Delphi I also noticed a sense of centeredness, perhaps of home, that my journal provided. It has become more than that. My journal is my traveling companion. I feel strongly that I'm writing to someone, and if anyone ever reads this mess of a narrative, they'll have played a part in my retaining sanity on this voyage.

4 Nov, Thursday

I wake early, checkout of my hotel and trudge the dark deserted streets to catch the bus to Phaestos. I'll spend tonight in a small town called Agios Ioannis, just down the hill from there. I hope to get a room in a home as I did in Ithaca. Tomorrow night I'll spend in Matala on the southern Mediterranean coast. Crete is a long thin, east-west island, and my trip to Matala will cut it in half.

★

On the bus to Phaestos, I sit next to the window, and a man with a black hair net over his head sits next to me. He's constantly moving, and I wonder if there's something wrong with him. But I notice his movements aren't random. He's crossing himself. Sometimes he stops, and I think he's going to be all right, but he starts again as if he's in a hurry, two, three times he crosses himself. I notice a woman a few seats toward the front doing the same thing. Their motions are synchronized. I try to make some sense of this religious urgency. Something must be wrong. It's as if every few seconds a life-and-death situation occurs. Finally, I realize my two fellow passengers have religious spasms whenever we pass a church. I lean back in my seat and tell myself to relax.

The countryside becomes rougher, large mountains loom to the sides of the bus and we follow a ravine between. The earth is chalky white and covered with cultivated plots, mostly vineyards and vegetable patches.

After an hour on the road during which the bus empties, it climbs some switchbacks, then drops me off on a mountaintop overlooking a valley. I ask the bus driver if he goes on to Matala, but he says that's another bus. He's on his way back to Iraklion. I expected a small town around Phaestos, but see none, just a parking lot outside the ruins. The setting of Phaestos is more spectacular than Knossos. To the north, the mountain plunges to the valley floor. Beyond the valley is Mt. Ida where, according to some, Zeus was born in a cave. Although Mt. Ida is many kilometers away, it looms over Phaestos. I shoulder my pack and walk through the gate and up the asphalt ramp, where I find a visitor's center with a coffee shop.

The man behind the counter lets me stow my pack in an adjacent room but declines any responsibility for its security. I walk outside and down a ramp, where the ruins of the ancient city of Phaestos are spread out in front of me, and in the distance lie the rolling hills covered with grape vineyards and olive trees.

Minos had a brother. His name was Rhadamanthos and he was king of Phaestos, the second most important Minoan settlement in Crete. Phaestos had two palaces. The first existed from 1900-1700 BC and was destroyed by an earthquake a few years before the volcano on Santorini erupted. The second, built to an even grander scale, existed from 1650-1400 BC.[214]

I descend ancient stone steps, wide enough to serve as theatre seats, overlooking a courtyard used for ceremonies. I walk through a series of stone walls to a second palace with another, larger stone-paved ceremonial courtyard. Off to one side is a corridor with towering walls and doorways. These were the magazines and workshops central to the commerce of the ancient city, which subsisted on agriculture.

One artifact found in these ruins from the early palatial period is most interesting. It's a clay disk imbedded with hieroglyphic characters arranged in a spiral. The characters were impressed in the wet clay with a punch. This is the earliest form of writing developed in Greece and is called Linear A. Although Linear A has never been deciphered, some believe the disk to be an ancient hymn.[215]Many of the symbols are recognizable as geometric figures: a profile of a man's head with a Mohawk haircut, a circle surrounding seven dots, a Gumby-like human figure, a walking man, a sunflower, a fish and a duck, among others.

The other form of writing found in ancient Greece, called Linear B, was deciphered in 1953 by a young Englishman, Michael Ventris, who was an architect, but more importantly, a cryptographer during World War II. He used statistical analysis to show that Linear B is a hieroglyphic form of ancient Greek.[216] But neither of these pictographic forms of writing was used by the Greeks to record their ancient myths. According to legend, when Kadmos came from Tyre to Thebes, he brought with him the Phoenician alphabet that, centuries later, was phonetically adapted to ancient Greek to record the words of Hesiod and Homer. It's the same alphabet used today for Modern Greek.

At midday I sit at the bus stop outside the ruins at Phaestos, trying to catch a bus to Matala. I've talked to a German man who has been staying in the area for the past two weeks, and he says Agios Ioannis has no rooms to rent, so I've given up on spending the night close to Phaestos. I've decided to go on to Matala on the southern coast, and while I wait for the bus, I enjoy the spectacular view. In front of me the road takes a sharp left turn and descends steeply along the side of the mountain. In the distance, clouds sit on Mt. Ida's top and puff their white thunderheads into the deep-blue sky, their shadows lying dark over the side of the mountain. I sit on a stone fence in the shade of a fir tree. A gentle breeze blows.

With the view of Mt. Ida before me, I can't suppress thoughts of my trek through the Alps. After my miserable second night in the hütte, we hiked all day and late that afternoon arrived at the Tilizuna Hütte where we were to spend the night. I made my bed next to a window, hoping to get a little light. And it did help somewhat although I woke frequently. When I looked out the window at stars circling overhead and the rocky landscape with dark patches of pines, I experienced a tremendous loneliness, a sense of abandonment. But I managed to avoid the abject terror of the previous night.

The next night we spent in the small mountain town of Gargellen, a beautiful sparkling-clean village nestled between heavily wooded mountain peaks, a loud river rushing through town. I had my own room in a bed-and-breakfast that night, and strangely, even though I was alone, I finally got a good night's sleep. The next day we followed muddy cow trails, stopping now and then at a dairy where a family would offer us fresh warm milk. The day was filled with the dull clank of cowbells, herds of sheep sleeping on the green mountainsides like large white wildflowers.

That night the problem returned. Even in daylight, as I entered the upstairs sleeping quarters of the hütte, I felt the panic well up inside me. We stayed in a cramped room with a small window at the far end where I slept against the wall. The tiny room increased my claustrophobia, as did sleeping so far from the door. I felt buried. During the night, we opened the window, which swung inward pinning me to my bed. I spent another night struggling with myself.

I woke the next morning knowing I wasn't physically well. After breakfast, we stood outside the hütte in the cold morning air with bright sunlight reflecting off snow, talking to the proprietor and watching a group of mountaineers repel into a crack in a nearby glacier. It was my birthday. I told my friends and they shook my hand and patted me on the back, and we took off for the long hike to the Silvretta Sea where we would catch the bus back to Bludenz. As the day progressed, I felt physically strong but my body seemed to glow. I wasn't feverish. I simply felt like a neon sign, like there was an out-of-control light source within me. The fanciful reports I'd read of the spontaneous combustion of the human body no longer seemed so laughable. We hiked alongside a fast moving river, the milk-colored water from the glacier dumping into a chalk-white lake. Silt from the glacier that was grinding away the mountain colored the water. By the time we got to Bludenz, I had developed dysentery. But my trek through the Alps was over, and I breathed a sigh of relief. Little did I realize that the monster that woke while I was in the Alps wasn't going back to sleep. I was now just as vulnerable at home.

By mid-afternoon, I'm concerned that there will not be a bus to Matala. I've been talking to the thin, dark-haired German from Berlin and two other Germans who've joined us. They're trying to get a bus south also. All the times on the bus schedule have come and gone and no bus. Gradually we realize there will be no bus from Phaestos to the southern coast of Crete this late in the tourist season. After talking it over, we decide to hitchhike.

I vowed before I left on this journey not to hitchhike. All the guidebooks discourage it. The young man in the truck who picked me up outside Thebes caught me by surprise, and accepting his offer was an impulse that I did not intend to repeat. But here I am with a choice between a ten-kilometer walk in the hot sun or accepting a ride.

After trying to flag down several cars, one finally stops. The driver is a German woman, and the man from Berlin talks to her for us. I know a little German, maybe more German than Greek, but not from a cold start and definitely not up to engaging in conversation. I stand off to the side, waiting to see if she wants to give us a ride. Finally, the three Germans load their packs into the small car. Obviously I haven't been invited. I think of catching the bus back to Iraklion. Phaestos could be the end of my visit to Crete. But suddenly the guy from Berlin says something to the woman and motions toward me. She gets out of her car and frowns at me. I'll hold my pack in my lap, I tell him. Finally, she motions for me to get in, but she's not pleased.

After five kilometers, the road splits, and since I'm the only one going to Matala, she drops me off, telling me it'll be easy to catch another ride. "Danke schön," I say, but she's already pulling out.

The road to Matala has little traffic, and after waiting patiently for several minutes, I reluctantly shoulder my pack and start the uphill trek. I have five kilometers remaining, two hours of hard, hot, uphill hiking with the sun in my face. I hear a car coming up behind, so I stick out my thumb, but it whizzes on past. I trudge on. Several cars pass without even slowing at my upraised thumb. I think that the road must start downhill soon because the sea must be very close, but it doesn't. Then I wonder: What the hell's my hurry anyway? Why am I killing myself? From the shoulders up, I'm drenched in sweat.

I stop and look around, finally realize what a treat it is to be in the absolutely gorgeous Greek countryside. Here I've been clumping along with my head down, feeling sorry for myself. Though my load is heavy, I have several hours to make it to Matala. This is my first country hike in Greece. Why not enjoy it? The sun is low on the horizon, but it's not yet four o'clock. I throw my pack to the ground and sit on it, stare across a small meadow banked by golden rolling hills. I have to laugh at myself. Off to the west between two hills, just below a bank of clouds, I see the Mediterranean, just a slice of seawater. I'm close to my destination after all.

The meadow is decorated with sparse trees and brush. Light brown grass and patches of volunteer grapevines cover the hillsides, their yellow leaves glowing in sunlight. To the right, up the other side of the meadow, small patches of olive trees stand in the white plowed earth. Mt. Ida, with clouds resting at its top, looms over us. In front of me is a small herd of sheep. A black-eyed ewe stands watching me, her two white lambs nursing on each side of her with their back ends pointed toward me, their tails twirling furiously like little propellers as they suck and butt her flanks. I no longer bother to stick out my thumb as the occasional car whizzes past. I'm content to remain here soaking up the view while I write in my journal.

Two thousand years ago, St. Paul passed Matala on his way to Rome, where he would eventually be executed. The Alexandrian grain ship on which he sailed would not ordinarily take a route south of Crete, but sailing after the middle of September was dangerous, and it was already well into October.[217] Hoping for better weather, they sailed along the southern coast of Crete and put ashore at the harbor of Fair Havens to the east of here. This turned out not to be a good place to winter, and they set sail again, trying for another port farther west on the Cretan coast. But when they rounded the tip of Cape Matala, sailing the same black water that is in front of me now, a fierce wind blew them out to sea, and they didn't reach land until they ran aground at a small island south of Sicily. Prior to this ill-fated voyage to Rome, Paul had visited many of the islands that are on my itinerary: Rhodes, Samos, Chios. He also spent considerable time in Ephesus and Troas, where the ancient city of Troy is located. Even though Paul knew he was sailing to his execution, he provided the strength the crew relied upon when they panicked at the bad weather. Perhaps tonight I'll spend my time in Matala, that safe haven that eluded Paul.

I do want to get to Matala before dark, so I reluctantly shoulder my pack and resume my uphill hike. By the time I round the top of the last hill, I'm again sweating profusely. The small town of Matala lies before me at the edge of the sea. Matala is built around a horseshoe cove with chalky-tan cliffs on the left and right. I follow a shaded street off the main road to a pension. After negotiating unsuccessfully with the woman running the place, I take the room anyway and throw my pack to the floor. Then I walk outside and across the street to get a bottle of cold water.

★

I'm alone on the dark beach at the edge of the Mediterranean, sitting with my legs folded on coarse sand listening to the relentless surge of waves. Before me, the cove is dressed in darkness. I've brought my journal and flashlight, so I can write in the dark. This is the cove where Zeus came ashore, still in the guise of a bull and having swum with Europa on his back all the way from Tyre in the east. I imagine him rising up from the black sea in front of me, first the sharp tips of horns, then the massive curly head and shoulders, a look of hatred on his face to see me sitting here when he had wanted to be alone on the beach with Europa.

A wave washes across the sand every five seconds. On each side of the cove, pale-white cliffs, dimly lit by a nearby Taverna, bound the sea. The cliff on my right is pocked with dark caves, which were inhabited and used as tombs five thousand years ago. Above, the Milky Way spreads across the heavens. I trace the tail of the Little Dipper to the North Star. Behind me, Sirius burns bright, and that fuzzy patch of stars called the Pleiades, the Seven Sisters, rises above the horizon. Only six stars in the tiny constellation are visible, the seventh, Merope, has paled because she blushes from the shame of marrying a mortal.

Thirty-two hundred years ago, while the Greek fleet was stalled out at Aulis on the mainland awaiting favorable winds to sail to Troy, Agamemnon watched Sirius traverse the heavens as he dealt with insomnia caused by his decision to sacrifice his daughter Iphigenia. Agamemnon was no astronomer, and it was an old attendant who enlightened him:

AGAMEMNON: What star can that be, steering his course yonder?
ATTENDANT: Sirius, still shooting o'er the zenith on his way near the Pleiads' sevenfold track. [218]

Just as Sirius and the Pleiades have stalked the heavens for the last three millennia, always circling overhead, so my daughter's disappearance, and the part I played in it, ever stalks me. I hear it now in the sound of waves, like death lapping at the shore of life. Sophocles used a similar metaphor to describe Oedipus' misery after learning he had killed his father and married his mother:

Concussive waves make stream
This way and that in the gales of winter:
It is like that with him:
The wild wrack breaking over him
From head to foot, and coming on forever...[219]

I look out to sea where the world disappears in darkness and listen to the Mediterranean swashing at the shore, watch the ancient caves in the nearby cliffs and the spread of sprinkled stars overhead. I sit here alone on the beach, the pale beam of my little flashlight on the page. In a nearby grove of trees, a group of young people gathers about a campfire. Their shiny faces reflect firelight, and I smell the smoke, hear the murmur of their voices, the occasional burst of laughter. I would like to join them, but instead sit here in the coarse sand not a meter from where the waves whoosh against the shore, looking out into the blackness beyond the cove. Why do I not join them?

I spend so much time alone, so preoccupied. Following the episode in the Alps, I was afraid of what was going on inside me. Like Theseus descending into the Labyrinth, I was descending within myself and what I found was frightening. A couple of years ago, as I sat in my own living room on a sunshiny Saturday morning minding my own business, so-to-speak, I quite suddenly became frightened. At first I thought the stereo was too loud, but when I shut it off, the silence was even worse. My palms were dripping sweat. I was emotionally out of control again. I started to call my psychiatrist, who had become a father figure to me and with whom I had been sharing these extraordinary experiences. Then I remembered he was out of town and would not be back for three days. I started to go to the next-door neighbors, but thought that if I told them they might have me committed. I felt more than lonely. I felt abandoned, incapable of taking care of myself. I thought that maybe I should be hospitalized. That night I dreamed I had gone to see my psychiatrist but that I got lost and couldn't find his home. I wandered aimlessly. Finally, I found his home, but he had company, and I couldn't barge in. Later when I returned, he was gone. I was lost as a child gets lost, unable to find his way home. Never in my life have I felt so alone as in that dream. In the coming days even though every tick of the clock, every second was an eternity, I somehow survived until Tuesday when he returned.

For several weeks afterward, I had the feeling I was experiencing my life for the first time, as if I had been absent for years while my life had gone on without me. Walking through my home was a discovery, working as an engineer, a revelation. I was astonished at how I could simulate missile trajectories, present analysis results to a room packed with people, and assign work to subordinate engineers. I was discovering myself as if I were another person.

At the same time, my dreams were regressing. Through them, I relived childhood experiences. One of the most profound was of a hospital scene with newborn babies all in small beds lined against a glass wall. I was one of them. The series of dreams culminated in one where I was suspended in fluid being sucked through a small hole in a slick membrane into a dark cave. I was overwhelmed with claustrophobia and screaming. Like Theseus I had descended into a Labyrinth. In my dream, at the very end of my descent, I discovered myself in the womb. My umbilical cord was Ariadne's, the mother goddess' thread leading back to my mother.

My terrifying experiences continued in daylight hours. At times I no longer seemed to be in control of my limbs, my arms worked on their own.

Crete

I remembered my uncle describing his insanity, how he seemed possessed by another being who controlled his actions. I was afraid of the knives in the kitchen, what my hands might do with them. I became hostile at work, irritable, dissatisfied, conniving, resentful, explosive.

I experienced my descent in two ways. The first was like Theseus, a hero's descent into the Labyrinth, but in the second, my reference shifted. I was the Minotaur hearing Theseus coming. My terror was hearing the echoing footsteps of Theseus, the murderer, descending the Labyrinth to kill me. Can this be the metaphorical truth behind the myth of the Minotaur? Do we descend into our own Labyrinth, Jung's unconscious, and there find our own base selves? Is the murder we commit, the animal we beat to death with our fists, our own?

When I look back on life, I see that my descent has occurred many times. The first was when my father and I descended the hall when he was to load the deer rifle to kill me; the second, when he asked me to go with him down that same hall to beat the dark beast of homosexuality to death with our fists; and another occurred during the slow descent that started in the Alps, and continued until that Saturday morning at home alone. And now, I've been on another as I've descended to the southern tip of Crete to stare into the darkness beyond the cove at Matala. My descents into the Labyrinth keep occurring, recurring like the ever repeating waves breaking on the sands here at Matala.

When I started this journey, all this was of concern to me. What if I should re-experience what happened in the Alps or on that Saturday morning at home? I barely made it out of the Alps without collapsing, and I was with friends. Would I survive a similar experience alone in Greece?

So who was the Minotaur, really? Coins found here at Knossos show four joined meander patterns reminiscent of the labyrinth and embracing a sickle moon. The Minotaur of the older myth was both bull and star at the same time. Again I return to Kerenyi:

> ...astronomical signs were added beside the four meander patterns: one or two sickle moons—one waxing and one waning—and in the middle, inside the labyrinth, a star. "Minotauros," "the bull of Minos," was not a true name. For the inhabitant of the labyrinth the names "Asterios" and Asterion" have come down to us, both synonymous with *aster*, "star." They also became names of the first Cretan king, who received Europa, the beloved of the bull-formed Zeus.[220]

The Minotaur was the "star," the light, of the Labyrinth. The mistress of the Underworld had a son who was the light of the Underworld.

Crete

I look up from the brightly lit pages of my journal, turn off the flashlight, and stare into the darkness of the sea beyond the cove.

I rise early and sit at the edge of my bed, staring through the French doors and out over my balcony at the morning sunlight dappling maple leaves. Today is the start of the second half of my journey. I've been on the road thirty-five days. I'm tired. I still haven't recovered from the five kilometer hike into Matala yesterday. But mostly I'm concerned about the buses here on Crete. Will I have to walk back to Phaestos to catch a bus to Iraklion? I want to visit the Minoan ruins in the eastern part of Crete, but I'm having second thoughts. My journey could stall out here on Crete. Since seeing the two Greeks who crossed themselves repeatedly on the bus to Phaestos yesterday morning, I've been thinking about Patmos where St. John wrote the Apocalypse. I still don't know if I'll be able to catch a ferry from here to Rhodes. Even if I get to Rhodes, I don't know if I can get from there to Patmos. The earlier I try, the better my chances.

I put off checking out of my room until I find out about the buses and walk to the clay caves in the side of the cliff at the edge of the cove. The caves are fenced. But a fair-haired young man from Alberta, Canada who camped on the beach last night, one of the group with the campfire, shows me an open gate. The caves are carved into the mountainside and have low-roofed rooms with recesses in the walls for chairs. Some have faded wall paintings. Most are trashy and have been used as latrines. The stench is gag-inducing.

I stand on the beach staring out at the tiny island just past the entrance to this cove. Farther out yet, another sixty kilometers, is the legendary island of Ogygia where Odysseus was stranded for seven years with the nymph Kalypso. She held him captive until his pining for Ithaca convinced her to let him go. I hope my luck will be better than that of Odysseus, and my stay so close to this famous island will not be prolonged by the scarcity of buses. But, if it was a nymph who imprisoned me here...

★

Mid-morning I wait at another bus stop (if it is a bus stop) by a small kiosk and coffee shop in the center of Matala. I've checked out of my room after talking to several people who gave me several different times for today's bus. Two things they agreed upon: this is the only bus going to Iraklion, and it will be the last until Monday.

Another gorgeous day in Matala: a light breeze, sunshine and a scattering of clouds. At eleven o'clock, the bus pulls in. The bus driver tells me he'll leave at eleven-thirty. The horse's mouth is all that counts in Greece in the off-season. Still, I won't leave the side of the bus, negating the off-chance that he might leave early without me.

On the bus back to Iraklion, I meet a young man from Los Angeles who has been biking through Europe with his sister for the last six months. His sister has gone to Germany, and he is in Greece alone. He is tall, thin, has on a white T-shirt, white warm-up pants, spectacles, and wears his long hair thrown back. He reminds me of a young Jeff Bridges. He worked a few years for Hughes Aircraft and UPS. He's going from here to Athens where he plans to spend a couple of weeks with a Kenyan girl he met, a black girl. Then he's off to Florence, Paris, and back to the States. He camped on the beach last night with the group from Canada. He has a small pack, couldn't have more than a change of clothes and toilet articles, and here I'm carrying fifty pounds.

The two of us spend the afternoon in Iraklion in the cafeteria at the dock, with me trying to find out something about ferry schedules to Rhodes. The guy from LA buys a ticket to Athens with no trouble, but when I ask about Rhodes, the ticket agent tells me to try next door. But the other agency is closed, and the guy won't even talk to me anymore, just closes the window and turns his back on me. Even my smidgen of Greek doesn't change his disposition. I sit remembering that, when I was in Athens, a travel agent told me I could not get to the Dodecanese without returning to Athens. Could be he was right.

I wait all afternoon for the agency to open their office, but they never do. The guy from LA will leave for Athens at seven this evening. After a sandwich and a carton of Milko, I ask him to watch my pack, and I walk along the dock to the Port Authority. As I walk away from him, I experience a sudden stab of distrust and wonder if he'll be there when I return. I would trust a Greek, but is my pack safe with an American I've known for only two hours?

Port Authority looks closed. It's unoccupied, no papers on the desk, very sterile. No cigarette butts in the ashtray. But the windows are open. Outside, I see a man in a dark-blue uniform and ask if he speaks English. He doesn't. What I want to talk about is too complex for my Greek. Besides, he's trying to start an old van and doesn't look as though he has anything to do with Port Authority.

While trying to decide what to do next, a Mercedes pulls up and five little men get out, all dressed in dark expensive suits and white shirts, all freshly groomed. The smell of after-shave fills the air. None of them are taller than five-five. Their faces are flushed and the whine and groan of their inflected voices shows great emotion, great affection. One of the little men is evidently leaving and the others are filled with sorrow over it. Their hands are all over him, and as he starts to walk away they start kissing him. Each in turn takes his face in their hands and plants big puckered kisses on his flushed cheeks. I've heard that Greek men are affectionate with each other, but this is my first confirmation. Startling. Absolutely startling.

A woman drives up in a new car, gets out, looks through the window into Port Authority, then talks to the uniformed man trying to start the van. He walks into the Port Authority office, pulls out a three-ring binder that he thumbs through to answer her questions. I ask her to ask him about a ferry to Rhodes. She speaks English very well and answers my question herself. A ferry leaves tomorrow at 5:00 AM for Rhodes and another Wednesday. She's most pleasant, smiling continuously as she answers my questions with great attention.

Now that I know I can get to Rhodes from Crete, I'm confronted with another decision. Either I take the ferry to Rhodes tomorrow or wait five days. I would like to see the Minoan ruins in the eastern part of the island. Letizia said they were great, that I shouldn't miss them. But I'm tired of fighting bus schedules. I could get stranded here. Finally, I decide to go on to Rhodes. The deciding factor is my obsession with getting to Patmos.

I say good-bye to the guy from LA, who faithfully watched my backpack, and follow the hotel signs away from the dock, up a very steep hill with my fifty-pound pack. I must be getting in shape because I make the climb with ease, but I'm sweating profusely when I get to the top. The hotel is closed and so are two others down the street. Darkness is falling fast, so I stop at a grocery store to see if someone knows where I can find a room. None of the six people inside speaks English. I ask in Greek where I can find a hotel and that produces a flurry of conversation and arguments. They look so worried about me, but won't answer, won't even talk to me. They look at me as though I'm something escaped from the Labyrinth.

Finally, one young man decides that if I can speak Greek (as poorly as I do), he can speak English. He takes me by the arm and leads me out of the store, tells me to walk to the center of town or catch a taxi down by the church. I was in the center of town when I first came to Crete and know the problems of finding a hotel there with the winding, unnamed streets. So I go to the church. I flag the first taxi I see and tell the driver I want a hotel close to the dock for no more than 3,000 dr. He just shakes his head no. He takes me to one of the nicer hotels, maybe the only open hotel at dockside, and waits for me to talk to the girl behind the desk about a room. The taxi driver doesn't have change for my 1,000 dr bill. A likely story, I think, he's just trying to scam me for a big tip. The woman behind the desk doesn't have change either, but both of them scramble to find change, and she finally comes up with some. The hotel room costs 6,000 dr. ($25.00). Pretty stiff for a guy on a 7000 dr per day budget. I'm simply a river of sweat and very tired.

I shower even though I have to put on dirty clothes. I've been recycling my underwear the last few days. I'll be up at three-thirty to catch the ferry to Rhodes.

6 Nov, Saturday

When the alarm sounds, I wake painfully, struggling through a sleep that seems more like rigor mortis. My eyelids are like sandpaper. The woman behind the desk looks as tired as I, her eyelids hanging like inverted half-moons. As I push apart the hotel doors and step out into the cold street, I see the dock at the bottom of the hill, dark and deserted. I approach the pier, humped from my pack, and see a lone light in the travel agency but no one inside. No evidence of a ferry coming this morning. A cold breeze blows and the black sea slaps the cement dock. The coffee shop where the guy from LA and I talked all yesterday afternoon is dark and foreboding. I drop my pack to the cement and sit on it, walking once in a while to peer inside the travel agency, where pictures of a huge luxurious ferry named the Daliana line the walls. A car pulls up and turns off its lights, sits silently in the dark. A young couple, travelers with large backpacks, come out of the night to sit on a bench nearby. I say good morning and learn they're also going to Rhodes, the confirmation I need so badly.

Sitting here in the dark, I think of Theseus leaving Crete. He took Ariadne with him, but she died in childbirth on Naxos. Word has it that Dionysus convinced Artemis to kill Ariadne for him. After her death, Dionysus took Ariadne to heaven and she became his wife. So who was this Ariadne? Mistress of the Labyrinth and queen of Crete? And how did she, as a mortal, rate so highly as to be worthy of a god with the stature of Dionysus?

She was a priestess of Aphrodite, a goddess who was one of the manifestations of Earth, Gaia herself. And if we remember that Dionysus was Zoë, god of indestructible life, we might begin to see a connection between Ariadne and Persephone, the first mother of Dionysus. Dionysus had metamorphosed into a snake so that he could double back on his own life and beget himself upon his own mother. And all these bulls running around Crete, Zeus's bull, Poseidon's bull, and Dionysus himself transformed into one, start to look like the same god. Also, Persephone was married to Hades, so maybe he's the same god also. One might well wonder: Is ancient Greek religion polytheistic at its heart, or monotheistic with a mask of polytheism?

After Ariadne's death, Theseus went on to Delos, made a sacrifice for her, and danced the Crane with the Delians. Years later, Theseus was the first to marry Helen. He kidnapped, raped and married her when she was eleven years old and left her in Aphidnae just north of Athens in the care of his mother, Aethra. Because of his treatment of Helen, Theseus was banished from Athens and fled to Scyrius, where he was murdered. So much for the hero who killed the Minotaur. Helen's brothers raided Aphidnae, retrieved Helen, and took Theseus' mother with them as Helen's slave. Years later when Helen left for Troy with Paris, she took Theseus' mother with her. Later, Aethra's grandsons went to Troy with the Greek army to retrieve her.

I also think of Minos as he left Crete in search of Daedalus, never to return. When Minos found out Daedalus had helped Theseus find his way out of the Labyrinth, he confined Daedalus within the Labyrinth. However, since Daedalus had built the Labyrinth, he escaped and went to Sicily. Minos followed him but was himself murdered by Cocalus, the king of Sicily.[221] Odysseus saw Minos in Hades when he went to talk to the ghost of Teiresias in the land where no sun shines at the cold home of Death. His account of Minos in Hades is the last recorded of the law-giving king:

And now there came before my eyes Minos,
the son of Zeus, enthroned, holding a golden staff,
dealing out justice among ghostly pleaders
arrayed about the broad doors of Death.[222]

Although known by the Athenians as cruel, to others Minos was the most just king in the civilized world and in the afterlife had been called upon to pass sentence upon the dead.

Yet another fateful connection exists between Minos and the Mycenaeans. A unity, or interconnectedness, exists between all these myths. The two children of Agenor king of Tyre, Kadmos and Europa, branched out, one to Thebes, the other to Crete, and their descendants came together at the Trojan War. Catreus, a son of Minos and Pasiphae, sent his daughter (Minos' granddaughter), Aerope, to the king of Nafplion in the Peloponnese, who married her off to Aetreus, king of Mycenae. She bore Aetreus two sons, Agamemnon and Menelaus, great grandsons of Minos, who were the driving force behind the Trojan War. And Minos' descendants, who still ruled Crete, also supplied soldiers for the war against Troy. Idomeneus, Minos' grandson led them. And Menelaus also came to Crete. He came to officiate over the funeral of Catreus, his grandfather, and while he was gone from Sparta, Paris seduced Menelaus' wife, Helen, and took her off to Troy along with Menelaus' treasure. This event caused the Trojan War.

By the time the huge white ferry Daliana comes steaming out of the black sea, the bellow of its horn echoing off the sleepy city hillsides, the dock is crowded with port police and dockworkers. Where only a few minutes ago nothing broke the silence and darkness, now I hear hurried voices and shouts, see the piercing white beams of port police flashlights as they direct traffic. The roar and spew of dark rushing water fills the air as the ferry comes about to dock aft end first. When the gangway lowers, the loud whine, clank and bang of machinery is frightening. Whistles come from the sailors as they throw mooring ropes to the dock workers, who wrap them around the large metal lugs protruding from the cement dock. All the activity before daylight seems rude, violent. But the ferry has come for me as much as anyone, and I walk out of the darkness, up the metal gangway into the bright neon light of the hold. I feel relieved to get out of Crete, not because I didn't like the island, but because of the difficulty getting around in the off-season.

The Daliana is large and warm. It has airliner-type seats but everything is skewed. The luggage racks at the front of the room are not parallel with the ceiling and the seats aren't square with the rest of the interior. But the place is comfortable, at least to a tired traveler. Sleeping passengers are scattered throughout the room, some on the floor, others stretched out on seats, squeezed under armrests, wrapped in sleeping bags, blankets, clothes.

Just as I stretch out to take a nap, listening to the clatter and pop of this old tin bucket, a large group of Greeks enters the room, raising a ruckus. One woman stands over me shouting, her motor mouth blaring in a constant stream. Everywhere they go, Greeks make noise.

After a nap, I no longer feel so irritable. We approach the island of Karpathos, which lies between Crete and Rhodes. All these islands are along the ancient trade route: Athens, Cyclades, Crete, Karpathos, and Rhodes. The Daliana, which looked so luxurious in photographs on the agency walls, has been shaking and rattling ever since we left port. I feel blue today.

Sitting in the ferry trying to kill the twelve hours to Rhodes, I miss the people back home. I miss my family. I miss my apartment, getting up in the morning and drinking a pot of coffee, staring out at the Rocky Mountains. I miss America. America is my home regardless of all its faults, its violence, its conceit, its excesses. I listen to my tape of the American composer Samuel Barber's violin concerto with soloist Nadja Solerno-Sonnenberg. She's Italian, mounds of dark flowing hair, piercing eyes. She plays just for me, the sharp singing strings of her violin knifing into me. I sense a consuming sadness, a loneliness to the second movement, a gentleness which enters like a whisper of sad love, the sadness of a lost love. I have another month on the road. I watch the waters of the southern Aegean float by, my eyes misty with loneliness.

CHAPTER 12: Rhodes

We steam into Rhodes with light fading from the sky, leaving a surrealistic glow. Rhodes is an almond-shaped island twenty kilometers off the southwest coast of Turkey. The island is only fifty kilometers from tip to tip but still the largest of the Dodecanese, which spread in a swipe of small land masses along the coast. I'm at the edge of Greece, its southeastern extremity. As we enter the harbor, I get my first look at the dark, foreboding landscape of Turkey off to the north. Turkey is Muslim country and an enigma to me. I'm afraid of the place, and now that I'm so close, I wonder if I'll have the courage to go there alone. I've heard frightening stories of the violent nature of Turks, and I speak none of their language. Plus the two countries are still at odds with each other. Greece was under the subjugation of the Ottoman Turks for almost 400 years from 1456 AD until it was liberated in 1830.

The silhouetted skyline of Rhodes is intriguing because of the medieval fortress wall surrounding Old Town. It's more massive than I expected. The city of Rhodes, the island's largest, is on the island's northern tip. It covers the entire peninsula, which extends northeast toward the coast of Turkey. We dock on the east side of the peninsula, where three harbors are separated from each other by protruding cement docks. The northern harbor, Mandraki, has a small shallow entrance and is for local traffic. The Commercial Harbor, used by large ferries, such as ours, and international traffic, is just to the south. Acandia Harbor, also just south, is for smaller commercial traffic. The city is separated into New Rhodes, which covers most of the peninsula, and Old Rhodes, a walled fortress close to the dock. Old Rhodes has changed little in five hundred years. The Crusader Knights of St. John of Jerusalem built these walls after they took over the island in 1309 AD.

I exit the ferry struck by the rapidly fading glow of the sky that silhouettes the huge turrets strategically placed along the ancient city walls. I walk along the cement dock with the sound of sea waves lapping. Across the road along the end of the dock, light spills from an open doorway. It's a travel agency with signs out front telling of ferries to Israel, Cypress, Turkey, Patmos. Even though I'm anxious to find a room, I step into the flood of light.

An atmosphere of excitement fills the place. Perhaps it's the sparkling eyes of the Greek girl who greets me; perhaps it's the knowledge that the Holy Land is so close and accessible from Rhodes that has caught me within its spell. I could just as easily abandon the rest of my journey through Greece and visit Bethlehem, Jerusalem, Nazareth. While I'm talking to this bright-eyed girl about the ferry schedule to Patmos, I overhear a conversation between another agent and a traveler on his way to Egypt. The Sphinx, with a pyramid in the background, glares down at me from a wall poster. I've stepped into a smorgasbord of world traveling and have access to every place I've ever wanted to visit. I feel like Paul on his way to Tyre, or Kadmos who also put in here, on his way from Tyre, 1400 years before Paul.

The girl puts my concern to rest. Ferries leave Rhodes for Patmos daily at noon. I'll accomplish with ease what the travel agent in Athens told me was impossible. I once again shoulder my pack and walk around the building and through the huge medieval wall of the old city. The rock wall, which is in excellent condition, is fourteen meters thick, and must stand three times my height. Rhodes is the first place I've been in which the bronze-age Mycenaean world and Christian history come together with such impact. Only an hour south of here, along the eastern coast of Rhodes, is the ancient town of Lindos where Menelaus and Helen stopped on their voyage home from the Trojan War. That's where Menelaus had to come to terms with what he would do with the recently retrieved, adulterous Helen.

I enter the city through a huge stone archway with no sidewalk, cars zipping within arm's reach. I stand in a sparsely lit courtyard waiting for my eyes to adjust to the dark. I see trees, a fountain with splashing water, park benches. Pigeons warble on a dark rooftop nearby. After asking several people, who all tell me the hotels are closed for the winter, I finally get directions to a pension off the central plateia, along a deserted cobblestone alleyway between dark stone buildings. It appears to be a residential district, not a place for a pension, but I notice a small dimly lit sign over a doorway in an old building, Fantasia Pension.

I walk through a small, unroofed entryway with large plants lining the walls. A woman comes to the door, looks me over, then calls her husband. I smell dinner cooking, the unmistakable odor of garlic. The pension is actually a home. To get to my room, I walk through two small work areas in which the family congregates. A barefoot old man sits in his undershirt with his pant legs rolled to his knees. He works his toes like fingers. The family interrupts its conversation to greet me, and the hallway is so narrow that they all stand for me to pass.

Rhodes

My room is spacious and has two single, widely spaced beds with natural-pine frames and a nightstand beside each. I have a private bathroom. Two small shuttered windows on the far wall are recessed in thick stone. I have three wrought-iron patio chairs with plastic cushions and a table with a green-and-white plaid tablecloth. A small dresser and a circular mirror stand against the right wall.

I drop my pack to the floor and go back out into the dark in search of a fast-food restaurant. I need a gyro fix. I haven't had one since I left Santorini. I'm tired and anxious to get to bed early.

The occupation of Rhodes dates to Neolithic times, and according to Greek mythology, the island belongs to Helios, the sun god. After Zeus defeated his father, Kronos, at Olympia, he gained power over gods and men and divided the world between himself and the rest of his brothers and sisters. According to Pindar:

> ...the tale is told in ancient story that, when Zeus and the immortals were dividing the earth among them, the isle of Rhodes was not yet to be seen in the open main, but was hidden in the briny depths of the sea; and that, as the Sun-god was absent, no one put forth a lot on his behalf, and so they left him without any allotment of land, though the god himself was pure from blame. But when that god made mention of it, Zeus was about to order a new casting of the lot, but the Sun-god would not suffer it. For, as he said, he could see a plot of land rising from the bottom of the foaming main, a plot that was destined to prove rich in substance for men, and kindly to pasture...[223]

Helios named the island after the nymph of the island, Rhode, whom he took as his mistress and who bore him seven children. One of these was Pasiphae, the wife of Minos, who gave birth to the Minotaur.

The island has always had a close connection with Crete because the Minoans were the first Greeks to settle here. Catreus, the son of Minos and Pasiphae, had a son named Althaemenes, who exiled himself in Rhodes because of an oracle saying he was to kill his father, a story similar to that of Oedipus. In his old age, Catreus came to Rhodes to get his son to return to Crete so that he, Catreus, might bequeath his kingdom to him. But Althaemenes mistook his father for a pirate and killed him with the thrust of a spear, thus fulfilling the oracle. Menelaus, king of Sparta and the grandson of Catreus, came to Crete to preside over his funeral. While he was gone from Sparta, his wife Helen ran off with Paris of Troy, thus releasing the forces that resulted in the Trojan War.

Rhodes

★

After a couple hours sleep, I wake from a dream about my ex-wife. She and I were still married and my son and daughter were small kids. My wife was getting in the car to leave to spend Christmas with her family, taking our son and daughter with her, leaving me behind. She explained matter-of-factly the necessity of visiting her family at Christmas and gave more reasons why she would not return until after the first of the year. She acted as if taking the kids and leaving was no concern of mine. I overheard women wondering among themselves why she married me anyway. They said I should learn to be a man. My son was crying and being led off by another man. I was powerless, only an observer to the pillaging of my home.

I hear voices from the other room, a child crying.

7 Nov, Sunday

I rise early and hurry to catch the bus. I'm worn out from Crete, but this morning I feel compelled to get to Lindos. Perhaps it's the dream of my wife deserting me that has me on the move so early. I'm still reeling from a sense of inadequacy and wondering if this is how Menelaus felt when he heard Helen had run off with Paris.

Several times during our marriage, my wife tried to get me to move out, to get an apartment and live separate from her and the kids. They were bizarre, unprovoked requests, as heartless as her words in my dream last night. I never thought anything would come of her fits of dissatisfaction, but in 1980 on the day after Thanksgiving, she made her own attempt to leave. That morning she packed her clothes and left to stay with a friend, but after being gone only six hours, she returned. I was in the kitchen drying the last of the Thanksgiving dishes, when I heard a noise and turned to see her standing before me, crying. She asked if she could come back home.

Five weeks later on New Year's Eve, we stayed home and argued heatedly instead of going to a party at the neighbors. I ended the war of words by throwing the ottoman into the sofa and standing over her shouting. The next morning we decided to divorce.

The bus negotiates the turns along the eastern coast with the sun easing into the sky above the sea. After passing several small coastal towns, the boxy, window-pocked, whitewashed buildings of Lindos come into view on a peninsula beyond a sandy beach with another giant fortress cresting the landscape. To my dismay, the bus lets us off outside Lindos. I've had my share of walking lately, but the town is only open to pedestrians and donkeys. No vehicles allowed. The sparkling-white buildings below the overpowering presence of the dark medieval

222

fortress make me regret that I left my camera in my room. I'm absolutely sick of having that albatross around my neck. I don't have just a camera. I have two camera bodies and three lenses in a case that hangs by a strap around my neck. I also have forty rolls of film. I left it all.

I feel a chill as I walk the narrow streets even though the sun sparkles brightly off the sides of buildings. I had wanted to zip through Lindos, but I'm caught up in the atmosphere of the place: vined trellises, blooming flowers and stone mosaics in courtyards. My chill is short-lived. The town is small, and on the other side of it, the grade increases to the fortress that was also built by the Knights of St. John, a tougher walk than it looks. The fortress is not my destination either. Inside is the acropolis containing the ruins of the temple of Athena Lindia. Artifacts from the Neolithic age indicate that the site has been inhabited since 5000 BC, and a temple has been here since 1510 BC. According to an ancient inscription, both Helen and Menelaus came to the temple. One of my guidebooks suggests their visit followed the Greek siege of Troy.

As I round the top of the enormous open-air stairs, the world unveils before me. I'm facing east, the sun just overhead at its fall-time zenith. The Aegean spreads in the distance to the pale faceless coast of Turkey, the water glittering with the sun's rays on its rippling surface. I walk to the edge of the ruins, past the temple of Athena Lindia, the stark columns standing like skeletal remains of some petrified beast, and look down the cliff to the Aegean far below where waves break on rocks leaving swirls of foam. The world seems ancient this morning, like it aged three thousand years during the night. That boat I see drifting away from shore could belong to Helen and Menelaus returning from Troy.

Even though the island belongs to Helios, Athena claims it also because she was born here, high in the sky above Lindos. Athena's mother was Metis, Zeus' first wife. Metis was "wiser than all gods and mortal men."[224] But it was foretold that she would have two children, first gray-eyed Athena who would be her father's match, "and then a male child, high mettled and destined to rule over gods and men."[225] Zeus swallowed Metis to prevent the son from being born and also to ensure that he would have access to her wisdom. Since Metis was pregnant with Athena when Zeus swallowed her, she did not have a conventional birth. Zeus' head was split with an ax. Pindar tells of the birth, midwifed by Hephaestus the god of fire, high in the emerald-blue sky above Rhodes:

> ...in olden time, the great King of the gods Zeus shed on a city a snow-shower of gold, what time, by the cunning craft of Hephaestus,

at the stroke of the brazen hatchet, Athene leapt forth from the crest of her father's head, and cried aloud with a mighty shout, while Heaven and Mother Earth trembled before her.[226]

Pindar also describes how the temple of Athena Lindia came to be:

Then it was that the god that bringeth light unto men, even Hyperion father of Helios, enjoined his dear children to give heed to the rite that was soon to be due, how that they should be the first to build for the goddess an altar in sight of all men, and, by founding a holy sacrifice, gladden the heart of the Father, and of the Daughter with the sounding spear.[227]

Athena was not a goddess of peace, though she was the bringer of civilization. In ancient art she was depicted with crested helmet, spear and shield. She was the "… weariless leader of armies, dreaded and mighty goddess, who stirs men to battle and is thrilled by the clash of arms."[228] Athena sided with the Greeks in the Trojan War. After Menelaus retrieved Helen, this would have been the perfect place for him to sacrifice her to Athena.

Menelaus initially planned to kill Helen, but when his eyes once again beheld her beauty, he decided to wait until the siege was over. Later, he made further excuses, saying he would kill her when they arrived home. I wonder, when they entered the bay far below this promontory, if Helen feared he would sacrifice her to Athena, rip her throat with a dull-edged knife and let her warm blood spill forth on the cold stones of the temple.

Menelaus, like Odysseus, wandered seven years with Helen at his side before returning home. They had been blown off course by winds from Zeus and Poseidon's mountainous seas. After wandering from Kypros to Phoinikia, Egypt, Sidon, Arabia and Libya,[229] they returned home. Fair-haired Helen was in Sparta living with redheaded Menelaus when Telemachus visited them seeking news of his long-overdue father, Odysseus. Homer describes Helen in The Odyssey as "a moving grace like Artemis, straight as a shaft of gold."[230] Menelaus had put aside his jealousy and anger and forgiven her for running away to Troy with Paris. At home in Sparta, they were congenial, close, even affectionate. Menelaus addressed her as "my dear."

Helen had lost her desire to stay with Paris in Troy sometime before the city fell, or perhaps she saw the handwriting on the wall and switched allegiance before doom struck. Helen tells of her change of heart and her regret about going to Troy in the first place:

Rhodes

...I had come round, long before,
to dreams of sailing home, and I repented
the mad day Aphrodite
drew me away from my dear fatherland,
forsaking all--child, bridal bed, and husband...[231]

After my own wife moved out, she pushed relentlessly for a divorce during a stormy six-month relationship with a doctor. Then several months after it was final, she called expressing the desire for reconciliation. Our two kids had spent the intervening months with me. She thought she would have but to enter the front door as she had done at Thanksgiving to resume her place as mother and wife. I said no. The next Thanksgiving, just after a young lady I had grown affectionate toward moved in with us, I received a screaming-and-crying telephone call from my ex-wife demanding I get that bitch out of her home, out of her bed. But I didn't have the forgiving soul of Menelaus.

I leave the temple of Athena Lindia and walk to a spot on the promontory to view a small bay to the south. Almost two-thousand years ago, an Alexandrian grain ship docked there on its way to Rome. The Apostle Paul was aboard. He was on the final leg of his third missionary journey to Greece and on his way back to Jerusalem. When he paused briefly here at Lindos, he had money donated by Greek Christians for those less fortunate in Jerusalem. He had made the decision to return there when he left the port of Kenchreai on the Isthmus of Corinth. When I was in Corinth at the canal across the Isthmus, I remember reflecting on Kenchreai and regretting I didn't have time to visit the port.

From Kenchreai, Paul sailed north to Thessalonica and Philippi, gathering the donations for the Jerusalem Christians. He spent a week in Troas, near where the Trojan War had been fought 1300 years before. From Troas, he sailed to Mytilene on the island of Lesvos, then to Chios, Miletus on the coast of Turkey, on to Kos, and finally to Rhodes. He docked here at Lindos, then traveled to the city of Rhodes. From there, he transferred to another ship bound for Tyre on the Phoenician coast and eventually to Caesarea where he went by horseback into Jerusalem. Jerusalem at the time was in turmoil and anti-Christian. Paul was imprisoned and after two years sent to Rome for trial and beheaded.

The bay spread out below me, where Paul came ashore 1,945 years ago, is the most gorgeous I've seen in Greece, a deep circular lake nestled among black twisted volcanic rock with only a small outlet to the sea where fishing boats exit and enter. It's past noon, but I have no desire to eat here in Lindos. I'm tired, and though the expanse of sea before me certainly merits a lengthier visit, I'm anxious to get back to Old Rhodes.

Rhodes

★

Mid-afternoon, I sit inside the National Archaeological Museum at the top of the stairs overlooking a courtyard. The sun casts a shadow over the north side of the courtyard. It's warm and no breeze blows. I hear fussy sparrows in a tree top. This building was at one time a hospital run by the Knights of St. John. The second floor of the museum, where I sit, is a mezzanine-like corridor all the way around the square. Centuries ago, the rooms behind each pillar of arches were filled with doctors' offices and hospital beds but now contain artifacts: statues, vases, jewelry, headstones, some dating from Minoan times. The Knights built all these buildings in Old Rhodes when they arrived in 1309 AD, after being expelled from Jerusalem. Their exodus from Jerusalem ended their influence in the Holy Land and effectively ending the Crusades.

Pope Urban II initiated the 1st Crusade in 1095 AD with a call to arms to fight the Seljuk Turks who were expanding into Asia Minor. The church had been frustrated for years by the Turks' interference with European pilgrims traveling through Asia Minor on their way to worship at the Holy Sepulcher in Jerusalem. The knights took Jerusalem in 1099 following a massacre of the Muslims and Jews who held it. The crusaders lost Jerusalem in 1187 during the 2nd Crusade. Six more crusades followed, but Jerusalem was never regained. Christians were ejected from the Holy Land in 1291.

The Muslims who occupied and controlled the Holy Land before the Crusades were tolerant of Christians. Two-hundred years of slaughter by the crusaders not only turned the Muslims against the Christians but also destroyed much of Muslim intellectual heritage. The Muslim pre-Crusade tolerance of Christians never returned.

After leaving the museum, I walk to the pier outside the walls of the old city, walk the dock watching fishermen, young men with girlfriends, an old man. One guy scrubs a pale-pink octopus against a large rock. He has it by the dome and scrubs the eight-legged apex, the octopus' mouth, against the rock. What this does for the octopus, I'm not sure, but I don't believe it enjoys it. The rock is white with octopus residue. He slaps it against the cement deck, throws it with a splat. The octopus is limp, jelly-like.

Another young man catches a long thin fish. Skinniest fish I've ever seen, and stiff as a stick. It has more of a beak than a mouth, long and pointed. He has trouble getting the hook out. I notice a dark blob at the water's edge. At first I think it's seaweed. Then I notice another, and another. I step out on a large rock to get a closer look and discover jellyfish with pale-violet pulsating domes. Several limp tentacles hang from their aft ends. The longer I look, the more I see: five, eight, ten of them, fifteen. And out of nowhere comes a dark streaking object, long, black and thin. A water snake? An eel?

Nereus was the ancient sea god, the Old Man of the Sea. He had the power of prophecy and the ability to change shape. The fifty Nereids, the sea nymphs, were his daughters. All that feminine energy must have been quite a show. Proteus was another form of the Old Man of the Sea, Poseidon's sealherd. When Menelaus and Helen grew tired of their wanderings after the Trojan War, Menelaus captured the shape-changing Proteus to learn why the gods wouldn't allow them to return home. Menelaus and three of his best fighters disguised themselves as seals and waited in ambush on a sandy island off the coast of Egypt for the kind and just, if elusive, Proteus. A goddess dabbed their noses with ambrosia to drown "the stench of those damned seals."[232]After they captured him, Menelaus described Proteus' shape-shifting:

> First he took on a whiskered lion's shape,
> a serpent then, a leopard, a great boar,
> then sousing water, then a tall green tree.[233]

Seeing no way to escape, Proteus asked Menelaus why he had captured him. Menelaus replied that he wanted to know why the gods wouldn't let him go home. Proteus replied:

> You should have paid
> honor to Zeus and the other gods, performing
> a proper sacrifice before embarking from Troy:
> that was your short way home on the wine-dark sea.
> You may not see your friends, your own fine house,
> or enter your own land again,
> unless you first remount the Nile in flood
> and pay your hekatomb to the gods of heaven.[234]

Since my wife left me, as I've said many times before, I've also been drifting. Perhaps that's another reason I'm in Greece. I'm trying to find my way home. I've quit going from woman to woman and now live alone. I can't get back what I lost. When I was married, at times I would wake at night, cuddle against her warm body, and she would roll over into my arms. I'd drop into a mesmerizing glow of love. This, like the feeling of panic and also the feeling about my own death, was a profound feeling, shocking in its depth, as though the experience was sacred. When she left, my life unraveled, as if it was an intricately woven fabric, with the sound of her receding footsteps. I wonder if I must perform some sacrifice before I can go home, or if my home will always be on the road?

I walk down to the beach where, in the distance, I can barely make out the slim silhouette of the Turkish coast. I look back at the skyline of the old city and watch the sun set behind the walls, tall white spire, and red church domes. Off to the right, boats come into harbor from the open sea. The end of another day and the start of another evening in Rhodes.

★

I sit on my bed listening to my Walkman radio, bouzouki music and the machine-gun chatter of Greek. Occasionally, I come across a station with the wail of Muslim music from Turkey and wonder if I'll be in that country next week, if I'll find the courage to cross the border. I'm suffering from loneliness again this evening and continue turning the small dial listening for a familiar voice. Quite suddenly, I hear English and wonder if I've pulled in London. Then I hear something I haven't heard in perhaps forty years. "This is the Voice of America ...." A chill ripples through me. I haven't heard the Voice of America since childhood. It's such a pleasure to hear good old American radio, and particularly this voice from the past.

I slip between the covers but feel restless, and shortly after falling asleep, I wake from a dream of the old farm where I grew up. The cotton has opened, all the stalks full of white fluffy bolls. The entire dream is steeped in the uncertainty of what my father might do. He frequently exploded over nothing. Chris, the missionary I met in Athens, is also in the dream, saying a prayer. The combination of the two, the explosiveness of my father and Chris' words are like voodoo, generating an immense anxiety. I'm starting to feel like I did in the Alps, only this time, the source of my anxiety is driven by a dream of my father and religion.

I turn on the light and grab my journal. I can't afford an experience like I had in the Alps, not alone. The mythical quality of my journey has been swept away by the seriousness of my problem. Writing in my journal slowly brings me out of my anxiety.

My dream's connection with religion is also troublesome because the next island on my itinerary is Patmos where St. John wrote the Apocalypse. This process I'm using to understand what happened to me when I heard my father clicking the deer rifle once again seems artificial and inwardly abusive, as I realized while in Delphi.

Several years ago, I was in another situation that cut even deeper into the facade of my life, exposing the naked essence of my superficiality, like slicing through flesh to reach bone. The event was the disappearance of my daughter. I found a shameful artificiality to myself I never expected. Saying a prayer for her safety seemed a trivial act, even an insult to the seriousness of the situation. My concern for her life went beyond my beliefs, convictions, into a shocking reality. Her disappearance tried my faith in God. And to put it quite bluntly, I found I had none.

8 Nov, Monday

I slowly surface through a dream that the heavyweight champion of the world holds me hostage. Now and then he breaks one of my fingers just to let me know he means business. My hands are mangled masses of pain. I find a .22 rifle and one bullet. Other hostages try to talk me out of killing him, but I'm very determined. Though it takes a while to find a good finger with which to pull the trigger, I shoot him. I aim at his head but only graze his skull. That changes his tune, and he backs off. But his change of attitude doesn't change my desire to kill him. And as daylight infiltrates the room, the images of me stalking him slowly fade into morning sunshine.

★

At noon I sit in the crowded square on Sokratous Street (mostly British here in Rhodes), enjoying the cloudy weather, a light breeze and motorbikes burping by. An old dog sleeps on his back at my feet. I splurge by having a cup of coffee to celebrate my three accomplishments of the morning. First I went to the Laundromat that has promised clean underclothes by one-thirty for a nominal fee of 1500 drachmes ($6.30), 1000 to wash and 500 dr to dry. I don't want to start drawing flies again. On the way back, I stepped outside the fortress gate and bought some fruit, apples and oranges. Then I reentered the fortress and exchanged two-hundred dollars for drachmes. The exchange rate is 238 dr/$ minus a 1.5% commission. These achievements aren't monumental, but for a traveler they can be gratifying, something to celebrate with a cup of coffee.

During the afternoon, I walk to Mandraki Harbor just north of where we docked yesterday, where the Colossus of Rhodes stood in antiquity. The Colossus was a 32 meter bronze Helios erected in 290 BC. It was toppled by an earthquake 65 years later. In its place, on each side of the harbor, small statues of deer stand atop cement columns. Not a very impressive replacement. I wonder if Helios isn't a little disillusioned over the treatment of his statue. St. Paul saw its pieces in the harbor while he was here.

Just outside the city walls is a dry mote occupied by real deer, who are direct descendants of those imported more than eight hundred years ago to rid the city of a snake infestation. The deer killed the snakes with their antlers. Their life here seems a pleasant one, a leisurely existence with no fear of predators. I see a doe with two fawns.

Rhodes

I keep eyeing the coast of Turkey in the distance. My next stop will be Patmos, and then I'll go to Samos to see if I can get a ferry to Turkey. If I can find none this late in the season, I'll travel north to Lesbos and return to Athens. The coward in me secretly pulls for the border being closed. Through a window in the stone wall, I see a ferry at dock.

★

I plan the rest of my journey till midnight and still have trouble getting to sleep. During the night I wake to the deathly stillness that has fallen over the Fantasia Pension. I just dreamed that I'm in a deserted building reenacting an old western movie with another outlaw. This is the same character with whom I committed the two murders and robbed the bank within the dream I had on Santorini. My companion reminds me of Hermes, the Greek god who was the protector of travelers. Hermes was also a thief and the guide of souls in the Underworld. In tonight's dream, we are actors playing prisoners incarcerated for robbery. We shoot our way out of jail and get to the rooftop where we jump from building to building and finally onto a fast moving stagecoach to make our getaway. The most peculiar aspect of the dream is the mechanical movement of the props, the stagecoach, and how guilty I feel while playing a robber.

Every time I leave one island for another, I have a strong sense of guilt, as though I'm an escaped convict on the loose in Greece, running from the law. It's a hidden perception lying just below the surface and an ulterior motive for all my moves. I plan all my escapes much like storyboarding a movie. I plan which island I'll visit next, my mode of transportation, how long I'll stay, which clothes I'll wear, where I'll go when I get there. I rehearse the questions I'll ask, what I'll say if they speak English, what I'll say in Greek if they don't. I choreograph every move. I always find a place to stay, a place to eat, a street to walk, a ruin to visit. It's as if Hermes, that outlaw I'm running around with, is going ahead scouting out the countryside. It's like planning a robbery, and although it's amusing on the surface, my sense of guilt is real and a continuous problem.

At three o'clock in the morning, I'm still wide awake. Maybe I'll sleep on the ferry to Patmos.

9 Nov, Tuesday

At noon, I stand at the rail on the top deck of the good ferryboat ΡΟΔΟΣ (RHODES), staring across the harbor at a large fishing boat coming to dock. The weather is clear, the sun blinding. Looking out across the Aegean, I see quite plainly the coast of Turkey with a thin cloudbank lying above it. The water is calm, only ripples caused by a light breeze break its mirror surface. I feel comfortable in my short-sleeved shirt. Just in front of me, a small one-man boat

Rhodes

maneuvers slowly in the water while the man aboard retrieves a trotline, dumps four moderate-size fish on deck.

At the end of the ferry where it meets the long cement dock, people, cars, trucks, vans, motorbikes, buses, come aboard. On the other side of Old Town, New Rhodes, with its glistening-white, box-shaped buildings, sits on top of a hill. We won't be in Patmos until 10:00 PM. I'm concerned about finding a room so late at night.

As I leave this island where Helen and Menelaus made a brief stop on their way home from the Trojan War, I also think of Helen's last visit to the island. Many years after their return to Sparta, Menelaus died, and Helen was no longer welcome in her own home. Her stepsons forced her to leave. She came to Rhodes and stayed with Polyxo, the wife of Tlepolemus who had been exiled from Argos because he had accidentally killed his uncle. Tlepolemus came to Rhodes and became king. He died fighting in the Trojan War, helping Menelaus retrieve Helen. The Rhodian's tell of Helen's return to Rhodes to stay with his widow:

> ...when Menelaos died and while Orestes was still wandering, Helen was exiled by Nikostratos and Megapenthes Menelaus' illegitimate sons, and came to Rhodes as a friend of Tlepolemos's wife Polyxo, who was an Argive by birth and blood, but being married to Tlepolemos shared his exile to Rhodes, and now Polyxo was queen of the island; she was a widow with an orphan son. Now that Polyxo had Helen in her power, the story goes that she wanted to take vengeance on Helen for Tlepolemos's death; while Helen was washing Polyxo sent slavewomen dressed like the Furies who took her and hanged her on a tree...[235]

Thus, this island is where Helen died, where Polyxo got revenge for Helen causing the Trojan War and the death of her husband. When Helen arrived on Rhodes, I wonder if she realized Polyxo's hospitality was laced with animosity? Was she afraid? Did she go kicking and screaming to the hangman's noose, or did she go quietly, preparing her final words?

I walk back inside the ferry and sit in a soft padded chair next to my backpack that I've thrown on the floor. This is the nicest ferry I have been on: deep carpet, mirror-lined walls, well-dressed crew, and overnight cabins for those traveling to Athens. I feel a slight lunge as the ferry leaves dock. The city slowly recedes behind us.

Ten hours to Patmos.

★

Rhodes

Just before nightfall, we arrive at Kos and execute the 180-degree dipsy-doodle to dockside. Kos is the rockiest island I've seen so far, no sign of foliage. The cove is surrounded by black mountains, the city of Kos resting on their flanks. Town lights speckle the blackness. A little cocoon of glowing neon surrounds the shops. High above, the pastel-blue sky softens to pink just above the silhouetted hills. The ferry rumbles in stasis.

Hippocrates, who was born around 460 BC, was from Kos. He was the father of medicine and gave us the Hippocratic Oath by which physicians swear their ethical conduct. A large temple of Asklepios was on Kos, and that is where Hippocrates practiced and taught the budding science of medicine. He was one of the Asklepiadae, the sons of Asklepios. Asklepios was said to have been taught the healing arts by Cheiron, the immortal centaur, who was also the teacher of Achilles and Jason. This island, which I'm reluctantly not going to visit, is one of the many jewels of the Aegean. So many islands, so little time.

The docking process has become a fascination of mine. The ferry comes up to dock nose-first, stops short and executes a 180-degree maneuver, which I call the dipsy-doodle, to get the rear of the boat toward the dock. The rotation then stops, the boat goes into reverse, backs up close to the dock while lowering its gangway to seventy degrees. The crew throws the weighted ends of two coiled ropes on dock; they are immediately picked up and pulled ashore. Attached to these ropes—one on each side of the ferry—are the huge docking ropes that the dock crew pulls ashore and slips over large, lipped lugs. The gangway is then lowered the final twenty degrees and the ropes winched tight. The mad rush of people follows: bicycles, cars, buses, motorbikes, trucks. A crowd gets off, a crowd gets on. We're at dockside for no more than thirty minutes.

The gangway comes up now, the docking ropes thrown back onboard. Time to leave Kos.

St. John came to Patmos from the northeast, from Ephesus, by boat, but I'll be coming in from the south. Sailing in the Aegean can be dangerous during winter. In antiquity, sailing was cut back in September and boats rarely sailed after the 11th of November.[236] Then, few boats would attempt the sea this late in the season, the 9th of November. On John's trip here, a tempest came up and swept a man overboard. While the others panicked, John remained calm and called upon God to quiet the waters. The sea gave up the man alive.

St. John came to Patmos during the winter of 95 AD. He was living in Ephesus, just a short way from here on the coast of Asia Minor. Unlike Paul, John was one of the original twelve apostles, the first apostle to join Jesus. John was also a second son; his brother James, also an apostle, was the older of the two. James, John and Peter were the closest to Jesus. John was among those to whom Jesus spoke the words, "Follow me, and I will make you fishers of men." John was at Golgotha, witnessed the Crucifixion, and saw the risen Christ. The Christians were later expelled from Jerusalem, sometime between 37-42 AD, and went to Ephesus. The Virgin Mary was with them.[237] After Paul's decapitation in Rome, sometime after 67 AD, John settled permanently in Ephesus and became the leader of the church. While in Ephesus, the Roman emperor Domitian had John taken to Rome, tortured, and then exiled to Patmos.

It's dark when we make a half-hour stop in Leros, and after another hour, at 8:25 PM, we get word over the loudspeaker that we're coming into Patmos. Time to disembark. I put my journal away and hoist my backpack. We've docked at the town of Skala in the center of the island on its eastern coast. We're one and one-half hours early.

CHAPTER 13. Patmos.

As we enter the harbor, deep-cut from the east into the long island of Patmos, I see stringed arcs of sparkling lights stretched along the dark pier. We dock at the town of Σκαλα (Ska'la, harbor, port). Patmos, only thirteen kilometers long, is shaped like a sea horse facing the coast of Turkey. The belt round its middle is cinched tight and the deepest indentation is Port Skalas, the isthmus only 300 meters across. Few people get off the ferry with me. The town is right on the water, and I'm hopeful that finding a room won't be difficult. Two dogs come to meet me: one black, sturdy, the other white, feisty. I ignore them, but they follow along behind. I walk toward an equally dark plateia with a couple of closed hotels. The town has shutdown for the night. I walk along the edge of the plateia but can find no pension. Perhaps I've made a mistake coming to Patmos this late in the season, this late at night.

One thing I've learned since I've been in Greece is to have confidence that something will occur to solve any problem, to have patience. I walk past the first row of buildings and turn down a dark alley. For the first time, I see people, a few men milling about. I wonder if I'll get mugged. As I walk past a man trying to start a motorbike, he shouts at me, asks if I'm looking for a room. I tell him yes, and he says he knows of one up the hill. "Not far," he says. "Four thousand drachmes."

"Too much," I say and walk on, amazed at my audacity.

"Three thousand five hundred," he says. I walk on. But he won't let me go. "How much you pay?"

"Three thousand, no more."

"Three thousand. Up the hill. Three thousand drachmes."

Secretly, I'm smiling at myself for negotiating so well in spite of being desperate. He pats the seat on the back of his motorbike, but I tell him my pack is too heavy, too unstable for the motorbike. "It is not far," he says. But negotiating with him seemed too easy. Skala is very dark. I feel like I did on Ithaca when the little old lady commandeered me up the mountain to her home, only this time it's a man. Am I really going to follow him up the mountain in the dark?

Patmos

But a woman with a little girl walks out of the darkness from down the alleyway. The man speaks to her in Greek and tells me to follow her. She's his wife and the girl is their daughter. The two of them walk with me up a gentle slope away from the dock and through an alleyway to Hotel Effie. The woman's name is also Effie.

Hotel Effie is a large white structure and stands out brilliantly in the darkness, lit by a streetlight. The small lobby is empty, but the hotel is brand-new. She flips a light switch. When she shows the room to me, she says the price is four thousand. "No," I tell her. "The man said three thousand." "Three thousand five hundred," she says, obviously irritated. "Room very nice." And she's right. The room is nice. But I heard her husband tell her we agreed on three thousand. "Tria," he said to her, "tria."

I stoop to hoist my backpack that I've thrown on the floor, but she stops me. I can tell she's really concerned I might leave. "Three thousand," she says, patting my arm. "But please, don't tell other guests. They pay four thousand. Room very nice, three thousand." I'm still pissed but feel fortunate because the room is very nice, white walls with light pine trim, a private bath.

Before unpacking, I step out on my patio. Dark buildings block my view of the bay, but I see the distant hillside speckled with lights. I bask in a certain sense of completeness. I've reached a milestone on my journey. I told myself from the beginning, if I made Patmos, my journey would be a success. It's a little strange that I've hinged my success on fulfilling my mother's wish. She wants a picture of the cave where St. John wrote Revelations.

I go back out into the dark to get a better look at Patmos, but this episode with Effie still bothers me. I can't get over the fact that she knew her husband told me three thousand and still tried to charge four. I walk the dock wanting to punch her in the mouth. It wasn't really much of a confrontation. The argument gradually evolves, and an argument with my mother emerges from behind it. And perhaps this is the reason my confrontation with Effie bothers me so much. My mother and I had the worst argument of my life just before I came to Greece. It was over a novel I'm writing. She read part of it and threw a fit over the bad language, called me from California to tell me. I blew my stack at her. The next morning, I called to apologize. We both cried. And we said something we've never said before, not in my entire life. We said we love each other. And now it's the first issue I have to deal with on this island.

I lie in bed thinking of Hermes, the Greek god who brings sleep and dreams, he who hovers between being and non-being. He is also the god of revelation. Even though it's only ten o'clock, I hear a cock-a-doodle-do as I drop off, the first in many days.

Patmos

Up at daybreak to get pictures of sunrise on Patmos. My excitement builds as I dress. The religious significance of this island is overpowering this morning. I still feel fortunate to have such a marvelous room at a reasonable price. It's cool out, but I feel comfortable in my short-sleeved shirt. I stand in front of the Hotel Effie, amazed at how great it looks. The white-stucco building with orange trim is glorious in the bright morning sunlight.

I walk along a path from the hotel toward the center of town. The sky is clear, only an isolated cloud that I use to hide the sun for a dramatic shot of the nearby islands beyond the cove's glistening ripples. Skala is a small seaport town, and this morning, two commercial ships unload cargo. A crane on one of them off-loads crates of water bottles to a truck backed up against the dock. The air is perfectly still, and shouts of dock workers pierce the quiet. Close by is Passenger Transit where we docked last night, and on the east side of it, Port Authority. After rehearsing a couple of Greek phrases, I walk in to see about the schedule for ferries to Samos.

A man in a blue uniform tells me a boat will be here Sunday morning and to see the DRM travel agency, across the plateia, for a ticket. The DRM agency is a small white building with a glass front just past the end of the dock, where several small boats are roped to the bank. But DRM is closed. A chalkboard sign out front says they have ferries to Samos every Sunday and Wednesday at 10:00 AM. I'll have four days to explore Patmos.

Skala is an old town of white buildings, lying on the flat part of the island forming Patmos' midsection. The island is mountainous both north and south of Skala. Across the harbor is a gray cactus-strewn hill. I stand by a lighthouse looking south of Skala, up the pine-covered hill to the small town of Chora (Χω'ρα, the Greek word for chief town or region), which is a stark whiteness below the Monastery of St. John that crests the mountain. The monastery is a majestic, inaccessible-looking structure, a fortification with massive brown walls and a jagged tooth-like upper edge. In ancient times, the town wasn't down here by the bay because the island was easy prey for pirates. The population lived at the top of the mountain. The monastery will be my first destination this morning. The Cave of the Apocalypse is also somewhere on the mountain, but so far, I haven't seen it.

★

I stand at the bus stop in the plateia accompanied by the two dogs who met me when I stepped off the ferry. They act as if I'm a long lost friend. Eventually, the bus to Chora arrives. After following the switchbacks to the edge of town, it drops us off, and I walk past blazing white buildings to the entrance of the monastery. Through the huge rust-iron door with an imbedded cross at the top, I enter a large cobblestone courtyard with a two-story portico constructed of ancient caramel-colored stones. A rope hangs from a bell on the roof. I'm the lone visitor to the monastery and only hear an echoing voice in some remote room. The courtyard is a maze of stone-lined arches leading to other parts of the monastery.

I spot an open door through an archway to the southwest and leave the courtyard, ascend several flights of stairs onto the roof, and step into bright sunlight. A light wind buffets me. It's an absolutely glorious sight: sparkling-white walls, a wealth of deep-red roses, deep-blue sky, and in the distance the even deeper-blue, almost purple, sea with brown islands dotting its surface. An open freestanding bell tower at the edge of the roof has five bells, three encased in a bottom row with two above.

In 1088 AD, the Byzantine emperor, Alerios Comnenos, issued the crysobull establishing the Monastery of St. John the Theologian on Patmos. In that same year, a papal bull was issued to build the Monastery of Cluny in France from which, in 1095, the first Crusade was proclaimed by Pope Urban II. According to Athanasios Kominis, Professor of Byzantine Literature at Athens University, this date marks the:

> ...common reference to the evolution of the two, now rival Christian worlds. Cluny represents the vigour and aggression of the Latins, Patmos the resistance and struggle for survival of Byzantine Orthodoxy.[238]

Through religious life at the Monastery of St. John, Patmos became not a center for spreading war, but instead the most influential religious and intellectual center in the Aegean.

The monastery was built on the ruins of the temple of Artemis erected by Orestes around 1200 BC. When I was in Mycenae, I visited the home of Agamemnon, where his wife killed him, and where Orestes avenged his father's murder by killing his mother and her lover. But his mother's Furies, those avenging goddesses of the Underworld, hounded Orestes as he fled throughout the Greek isles. Patmos is one of the many places he sought refuge. Here he erected a temple to Artemis, the goddess who raised Patmos from the sea. Ruins of Artemis' temple were still visible when construction on the monastery began in 1088 AD but none are visible today. The monastery has been renovated and expanded many times during the 905 years of its existence and today is in marvelous condition.

Patmos

I walk back downstairs and find a gift shop tucked away in a corner at the foot of the stairs. The man inside tells me that if I come back tomorrow at one o'clock, the monastery museum will open for a group of touristas. I buy two small books, one titled *The Revelation of Jesus Christ* and the other, *"I was in the isle of Patmos..."* about the life of St. John.

I exit the monastery by the way I came and stand outside viewing the many purple islands visible in the distance. The sky is so clear. A stone donkey trail winds down the mountain to the sparkling-white buildings of Skala at the edge of the harbor. Beside the trail lies a small ravine with rocks and brown bushes, and below it, a cultivated field bounded by a stone fence. I hear the caw of crows and the chug of a fishing boat in the harbor. The breeze is cool, a little too cool for my short-sleeved shirt, but the sun is still hot on my back. The loud boasting of a rooster.

With such a beautiful day, I decide to walk back instead of taking the bus. I walk a little farther down the mountain and find the Cave of the Apocalypse on the road halfway back to Skala. The cave is inside a church made of a series of square, box-like buildings stacked together to form one structure that stair-steps the mountainside. A lone dark door stands tall in front of the whitewashed building. A sign to the left of the entrance indicates that the Cave of the Apocalypse will open at eight tomorrow morning. I put my daypack on the ground and sit, leaning against a stucco retaining wall in front of the church. The sun warms me while I read the little books I bought at the monastery.

I sit among eucalyptus trees, listening to the wind rustle leaves. During his exile here, John brought a message of which the ancient Greeks knew little—brotherly and divine love—but it didn't take long to corrupt it. Shortly after John came to Patmos, he had a fight with Cynops, a local priest of Apollo. John was soundly beaten and left for dead, but was discovered to be alive by his scribe Prochorus. The next day, John and Cynops had another confrontation. This one resulted in the death of Cynops. The previous day Cynops had dived into the sea and retrieved images of some local deceased citizens of Patmos, and when he did it again on this day:

> John raised his hands, made the sign of the Cross, and prayed in these words: "Thou who dist give to Moses through this sign to cast down Amalek, Lord Jesus Christ, cast down Cynops into the depths of the earth, that he should no longer see this sun, and no more be numbered among living men."

While the pagans waited in vain, fasting, for three days for Cynops to rise from the waves, as the priests of Baal waited for fire to descend from heaven to consume their burnt-offerings, Cynops was turned to stone in the depths of the sea.[239]

The stone is still in the harbor. What strikes me afresh, glancing through the book about the teachings of Jesus, is the emphasis He placed on love and forgiveness. And how different that is from the Greek gods. The Greek gods contained much of the internal makeup of mankind, including many of our weaknesses, and they had some crucial deficiencies:

> Greek gods... were moved by considerations of personal honour, and anything which might be construed as an affront to it, excited their anger and called for violent vengeance. Forgiveness was not in their nature, and once a man had offended them, he had no excuse and could expect no mercy.[240]

Not until their civilization began to collapse did the Greeks form their first glimmerings of the brotherhood of men, and even then, it was more of an abstract ideal than a purposeful conviction. What we miss in Greek religion is love. "...there is nothing that can strictly be called a love of God..."[241] The gods represented forces at work in the world, most likely forces in the human psyche, and the ancient Greeks honored them whether they were admirably motivated or not.

The only time I remember the word "love" being mentioned around our home occurred while I was a kid. It was late one night when my father and older brother came in from the field. My brother passed through my bedroom to get to his. Shortly afterward, my father came through the dark, stuck his head in my brother's room and told him he was sorry for what he had said to him. "I still love you," he said. Hearing my father express "love" for my brother stung into me. What did "love" have to do with it? I wondered. Through the thin wall, I heard my father tell my mother, "If a man makes a mistake, he should be man enough to admit it."

I never heard the word before that night or after. It was a single event in my childhood and followed an act of emotional violence. At the time, my father's statement bothered me. Now, what seems most strange is my reaction to what my father said. I was horrified. "Love" was a word we just didn't use. Admitting guilt and making amends was something entirely new. It was as if all the ground rules had changed.

Prometheus is the only Greek god who comes close to expressing divine love for mankind. Not only did Zeus not love mortals, but after he overthrew his father Kronos, he planned to annihilate wretched mankind. But Prometheus thwarted this plan. He describes how he circumvented Zeus:

> I hunted out and stored in a fennel stalk the stolen source of fire that hath proved to mortals a teacher in every art and a means to mighty ends.[242]

Prometheus had bolstered mankind by giving them fire. To punish him, Zeus ordered Hephaestus, the god of fire, accompanied by the daemons Kratos (Might) and Bia (Force), to chain Prometheus to a mountainside for thirty thousand years. The scene is set by Kratos as they lead the captive Prometheus to the desolate crag to bound him:

> To earth's remotest confines we are come, to the Scythian[243]tract, an untrodden solitude. And now, Hephaestus, thine is the charge to observe the mandates laid upon thee by the Father—to clamp this miscreant upon the high-beetling crags in shackles of binding adamant that cannot be broken.[244]

While chained to the mountainside, an eagle ate out Prometheus' liver in the blinding heat of day, and it grew back during the freezing night. The image of Prometheus spread against the mountain with his side gushing blood is the ancient Greek harbinger of Christ on the cross. Prometheus had defied Zeus for the sake of mankind but was forcefully taken to the mountainside. Christ went willingly to the cross.

It's turned cold. Great swells of wind bow the eucalyptus trees. The sun has gone behind the mountain, and a large shadow extends to the harbor. Skala is still bathed in sunlight. Out at sea, a fine speckled cloud of white gulls follows in the wake of a fishing boat. I must go. I've been all alone here at the site where St. John wrote the Apocalypse. I shall return tomorrow morning to visit the cave.

★

I lie in bed but sleep eludes me. I keep hearing all the bad things I've said about my father and worry that I've portrayed him unfairly. My father was a most kind and generous man, a principled family man. Since he had four boys and no girls, he always ensured one of us stayed home to help our mother. His father was an alcoholic, and as a young adult my father had held their family together. He never allowed liquor in our home. He was a peace maker. Even in heated arguments with my mother, never once did he raise a hand to hit her. His brothers and sisters looked to him to solve their own family disputes. I remember one sister calling him to stop her husband from beating their kids.

On Saturday afternoons, we'd come in from working in the field, and he'd take us to the movies, sit with us to watch Roy Rogers, Hopalong Cassidy, and the continuing Zorro serial. He coached my little league team for two years. He never once raised his voice in anger at any of the kids. With his farming, the number of people he has clothed and fed would number in the thousands. His most formidable enemy, the man he feared the most and loaded a deer rifle to eliminate, was me.

11 Nov, Thursday

I wake early and dress, eager to see the Cave of the Apocalypse. I'm fidgety and nervous. I visit the local bakery for breakfast, standing before the glass display case pointing and grunting to a young woman about a chocolate pudding-filled croissant. Outside, I stand in the bright morning sunshine trying to eat the thing. The dark filling gushes on my face, hands, and finally, on my shirt. It's like eating a live snake wrapped in piecrust.

I walk up the hill along the old donkey trail, then cut across to the sanctuary on a footpath through pine trees. When I enter the building that encloses the cave, no one is present. The room is like a small greenhouse with huge arched windows from which fans of sunlight fall on large flat stones paving the floor. African fern trees and a large-leafed rubber plant arch the ceiling. A long table stacked with potted ferns sits against the right wall.

I sit on a bench and load my camera with fast film, mount my flash, a wide-angle lens. A man comes out of an adjoining room, and I greet him, but he passes on. Then a priest dressed in a smock, a rather large stout man with white full beard, comes out of the same side room, and I ask him in Greek if he speaks English. He says "Οχι." I point to my camera and ask, "Εννταkoη?" (All right?). He nods. Another man, tall and very thin, comes into the room from a side door. He's dressed in a green jacket with high collar and rolled sleeves, Levi's, brown shoes, and white socks. The two of them share some words about me, this old tourista, and then the tall thin man taps me on the shoulder, motions for me to follow him.

This I do, out the side door into the bright sunlit corridor overlooking a dramatic view of islands spread along the distant Aegean, down stone steps through a brilliant white passageway lined with deep-red bougainvilleas and roses, and past several landings to a door he unlocks. We enter the small, vaulted room called the Chapel of St. Anne. To the right, just under a rock overhang, are two pedestals, one of rosewood with a flat gold circular surface on top, the other entirely of silver.

Patmos

Through another stone arch, lies the cave sanctuary, a row of stained-glass windows on the left through which colored sunlight filters. The rooms are deathly silent and still. To the right, this larger room is shrouded in darkness. My guide takes a lighter from his pocket and puts flame to several candles in the darkened chamber, illuminating the inside of the cave, a low overhang, a looming thundercloud of rock, and below it, two long benches before the apse. When he finishes lighting candles, we stand face-to-face. I point to my camera again. "Ναι," he says, yes. Still, I don't feel right taking pictures in such a sacred place. He sits in a small chair beneath the stained-glass windows to wait for me, continuously crossing himself and praying.

I lower my camera and sit on a bench before the apse, staring at the dark wall decorated with four paintings of deep red and luminescent gold. One is of Jesus standing and speaking to St. John, who sleeps below him, receiving his words. In the center of the wall is a red and gold tapestry with a blazing cross.

Though I haven't planed to, I bow my head and pray, feeling the cold air off the cave's rock walls. I remember the words John dictated to Prochorus, his scribe, in this same cave:

> I John, who also am your brother, and companion in tribulation, and in the kingdom and patience of Jesus Christ, was in the isle that is called Patmos, for the word of God, and for the testimony of Jesus Christ. I was in the Spirit on the Lord's day, and heard behind me a great voice, as of a trumpet, Saying, I am Alpha and Omega, the first and the last: and, What thou seest, write in a book...[245]

My prayer is for my own writings, that I don't write something to further inflict pain on those whom I've hurt so much in the past.

When John heard the trumpeted words, he turned to see who was speaking:

> ...I saw seven golden candlesticks, and in the midst of the seven candlesticks one like unto the Son of man, clothed with a garment down to the foot, and girt about the paps with a golden girdle. His head and his hairs were white like wool, as white as snow; and his eyes were as a flame of fire; and his feet like unto fine brass, as if they burned in a furnace; and his voice as the sound of many waters. And he had in his right hand seven stars: and out of his mouth went a sharp two-edged sword: and his countenance was as the sun shineth in his strength.[246]

Patmos

My guide's prayer murmurings are the only sound in the cave besides my rustlings and the snap of my camera shutter. He rises, says something to me of which I can understand not a single word. I realize he's telling me it's time to go, but I'm not ready to leave. I feel a sadness hovering over me as I stand between the two chapels, inspecting the stone ceiling and walls, trying to fix the image of this most beautiful setting. Something is building inside me, but he speaks again, and I have to give it up. Outside, we ascend the stone steps to the waiting room. Before my guide departs from me, he smiles broadly, a deep friendly smile, pats me on the shoulder. I exit the building into the bright morning sun and cold breeze that has blown since yesterday. I walk a few steps from the building and lean against the retaining wall.

Standing here with the sun beating down on my head, I start to cry, feeling a great sadness. Something is wrong, and I don't know what. It has something to do with what I did to my brother, what I did to my father. I remember my encounter with the missionaries from Romania while I was in Athens, the young man, Justin, and his question concerning my religion. "Are you a Christian?" he had asked. I remember my mother when I was eight reading the story of Abraham and Isaac, of me questioning why God would ask a man to kill his son and why the man would do it. I remember her anger.

Standing at the edge of the Aegean so close to the coast of Asia Minor, indeed I see its pale shape in the haze off in the distance, I sense a connection between the Biblical story and my father loading the deer rifle to kill me. Were my father and I reenacting an event that has echoed through the ages?

As I descend the hill and enter the town of Skala by the steep stone donkey trail, I see an old, awkward woman walking toward me, a plastic grocery sack in each hand. I wonder if I should help her with the bags but notice that, in spite of her withered appearance, she seems to be doing quite well. As she comes closer, I greet her, "Γεια σας," I say. She doesn't reply, but looks as if she recognizes me, as if she's shocked to see me. She turns toward me, arms out a little, her mouth gaping in an exclamation of surprise. I turn toward her, nod and continue on. She turns to watch as I descend the stone walkway, some strange astonishment chiseled into her face.

★

At one o'clock I catch the bus by the dock to the Monastery of St. John. It's me, the bus driver, and three monks in their gray habits. The bus drops us off at the edge of Chora, and I walk ahead of them along the stone path. Once inside, I'm told the Monastery will officially open at two o'clock, and the museum will open just before the touristas arrive. I sit waiting for them in the courtyard with the extraordinary blue sky overhead.

Patmos

A monk comes to me, one of the monks on the bus, and to my surprise, gives me a large loaf of dark-brown bread, says something I understand to be a blessing. I take it with pleasure. It's a sesame-seed bun with no wrapper. I quickly put it in my black daypack, so it won't dry out. This act, the simple sharing of bread, seems so symbolic in light of where I just came from that I'm overwhelmed. The Last Supper comes to me with new meaning. Every human act now seems symbolically important.

A monk comes into the courtyard, takes a long, thin board from the wall, and pounds it rhythmically with a wooden mallet. Several monks hurry into the courtyard, then enter an adjacent room. I hear voices raised in prayer, followed by singing. A monk comes out carrying a long string of bells he shakes loudly. A few minutes later the rest come out and enter another room down a hall, the refectory, which has two long, stone tables end-to-end. The wind is most forceful on the walls of the monastery, cold gusts tear at the sanctuary walls. I have on my long-sleeved shirt and black sweater, but still I shiver.

At three o'clock, still no touristas. I ask the man who runs the souvenir shop if he knows the weather forecast. He says a cold front is coming down from the Alps. It will be very cold for a few days. I'm sorry I left my down parka in Colorado. The Alps, my old nemesis. Nemesis is the goddess of retribution for undeserved good fortune and a harbinger of things to come. She is closely connected with the Fates.

Suddenly I hear loud voices at the entrance. Three well-dressed women enter, one black, one Mexican, the other Japanese. Two of them are dressed in slacks, an oddity on Patmos, lots of colors, bracelets, rings. They go into the chamber where the monks prayed, and I follow as I hear a crowd of touristas at the entrance. We've entered a small cathedral made of deep dark wood, with tall vertical-backed seats built into the wall, a domed ceiling with stained-glass windows.

A giant chandelier with lit candles hangs in the center of the small room. All so very old and so very beautiful. It's called the Katholikon and is the monastery church, built shortly after its founding in 1088 AD. I trail along behind the girls. First chance I get, I ask where they're from, and learn that all three are from Los Angeles, the City of Angels. They have light-chocolate skin, flashing ebony eyes, and are delightful to talk to. They are passengers on the cruise boat, but not a part of the tour. Before coming to Patmos, they visited many of the islands I've been on, plus they've been to Turkey. They tell me that the ruins of Ephesus are unbelievable, the most impressive they've seen. Their enthusiasm is contagious. I'm so excited about going to Turkey, and absolutely giddy about being with these three women.

Patmos

After leaving the church, we walk to the museum together, view several walls of old paintings, most dating back to the 15th and 16th centuries. Inside a glass case, we see glorious parchment texts with multicolored ancient Greek lettering, some with illustrations, one from the 6th Century. The bindings of the scriptures are most impressive, the silver-relieved covers fold back on hinges and close with metal lever clasps. Small intricately detailed icons, some of molded silver, some carved from wood, sit on dark wood tables. Cloth robes, inlayed and woven with gold, line the walls.

But none of it compares to the beauty of these three women, exotic, Oriental, African. We pause at the robes, and they talk about their own clothes that they made themselves. They want me to feel the fabric, and when I do they show me how to feel it, take my fingers in theirs and mince the fine woven threads, mince the flesh of my hands. They start laughing, and soon, we have all our fingers mixed together massaging until all I see are visions of dark pools of eyes spinning about me. Their words melt into a comforting murmur, and I find myself overcome with a sort of strange insanity that these women are my sisters and that together we're massaging the Cloth of Life woven on the Loom of Time.

I try to concoct a scheme to hang on to them, but they're out the door in a flurry, and I hear the echo of their footsteps in the courtyard, then the silence of their absence. I'm alone again.

I descend the mountain, this time with the cold wind tearing at my clothes and mussing my hair, feeling lonelier than I've felt since I left Letizia in Corinth. The weather is still clear, only a renegade cloud here and there. When I get back to Skala, after buying the largest chocolate bar I can find, I decide to see if the sunset is visible from the west shore of Patmos.

The isthmus in the center of Patmos is very narrow, and the walk from one side of the island to the other is a short one, along a narrow street, over absolutely flat terrain. As I get close to the cove, the street widens, houses end, and I quite suddenly feel despondent, as if I've walked into a setting I've witnessed before during a time of great tribulation. The wind howls, and the sea is in a rage. Two geese are the lone inhabitants of the cove, and they're not pleased with me being here. They scold and snap at my pant legs as I pass, guardians of the gate, so-to-speak.

It's as though I've walked into a war zone, the roar of waves crashing on shore, pounding black volcanic rock, sending geysers of sea spray spewing skyward. In the distance, along the point of a small peninsula, sea waves pound the silhouetted coastline sending towering sprays up from black rocks. The deep-orange sun sinks into a dark cloudbank, creating glowing silver linings and

245

sending out shooting beams of light. I watch the ragged, bloody, circular surface plunge into the sea.

Many years ago, I had a dream that the world had been destroyed, and my wife and I with our two children were standing on a foreign shore, where someone in a ship was to pick us up, staring out to sea at a sunset. We were the only earthly survivors. It was a powerful dream set in a cove such as this. As we stared out into the orange glow of sunset that turned the sea to gold, the ruins of our civilization lay behind us, just as the ruins of the Minoan and Mycenaean civilizations I've seen all over Greece lie today. Just now, as I entered this cove, I had the eerie feeling that dream was set on this same shore thirty-two hundred years ago.

In my dream, we were being taken to a place where we would have a new beginning. I'm reminded of John's description in Revelations of the second coming of Christ:

> And I saw a new heaven and a
> new earth: for the first heaven
> and the first earth were passed away...[247]

I didn't see a new civilization in my dream. I just knew we were being taken to a new world. What bothers me about all of this now are the recent experiences I've had concerning my death. They've only occurred since my divorce. John tells us who will be let into the new world:

> And there shall in no wise enter
> into it any thing that defileth,
> neither whatsoever worketh abomination,
> or maketh a lie: but they
> which are written in the Lamb's
> book of life.[248]

I've always felt guilty over getting divorced, I had made a promise to God, but never so much as I do now. I sense a new consequence of it as foretold by my premonition of my own death. It's as if my name has been stricken from the Book of Life.

As sunlight fades and shadows take the features from the faces of the large boulders lining the cove, I make the short walk back, past the scolding geese, past the Sunset Taverna, back to the quiet, protected harbor of Skala. It's very cold now that the sun has set. I buy a plastic container of Ρωσικι Σαλατα (some kind of salad) and go to my room to eat, taking the loaf of bread the monk gave me from my daypack. The salata (macaroni and small chunks of potato) tastes rancid even though the date on it is December 15th. It's bound together with pure mayonnaise and could use some salt. The bread is slightly sweet and delicious. The loaf is round, flat on the bottom and dark brown, sprinkled heavily with sesame seeds.

★

I wake in the middle of the night to the many angry voices of dogs. I've been dreaming of trying to escape from a war-ravaged country with closed borders. I was with several people in a car. They didn't understand the urgency of our situation and were dilly-dallying. This was my first war dream since I've been on this journey, but only one of many during my life.

Later, I wake again, this time crying. I don't know why.

12 Nov, Friday

Morning comes with a chorus of roosters. None are very close, and they don't go in sequence. They crowd their voices together like a flock of gobbling turkeys. The sky through my window is emerald blue. The wind brushes the bright-red nose of a rose bush back and forth against a glowing white-stucco building. The intermittent sound of a buzz saw shatters the morning quiet. I hear the voices of men, the pounding of hammers mixed with birds chirping in the trees, a dog bark, and the whine of a begging cat, a motorbike down by the harbor.

★

I'm in the northern part of the island, sitting on a rock under the shade of a eucalyptus tree overlooking Agriolivadiou Bay. It's been a cold, windy walk. I count seven, eight islands, starting in the bay and going out into the Aegean to the southeast, where they merge into the coast of Turkey, just a fine blue line along the horizon.

Every step of the way up here, I was thinking of the three women I met at the monastery yesterday. When I was eight, my family moved into a new home, a very old plantation-like home. It had an ivy-trellised courtyard with a large dinner bell suspended from a crossbeam. Not long after we moved into the old decaying home, it burned. But two things have stayed with me all these years since: someone I found, and something I lost when the house burned.

I remember a warm afternoon the day before. I was sitting at a patio table in the courtyard with my mother nearby folding clothes as she took them from the clothesline. The sun shone through vine leaves, casting a dappled shadow across the tabletop. Just that morning in the mail I had received a small golden ring I had ordered from a cereal box. The ring had a tiny catapult on its flat top, and within it sat a tiny gold rocket that it launched. As I sat at the table, the partially filtered rays of the sun casting both shadow and brilliant speckles of light through leaves, I repeatedly launched my rocket off the edge of the table into the void. The afternoon was leisurely. Seemingly hour after hour, I launched my rocket with my mother close by, the two of us exchanging words about some fantasy of mine.

That night when I went to bed, I put my gum on one bedpost and on the other, the small golden ring with the tiny golden rocket. I remember distinctly what I fantasized as a means of hurrying sleep. I conjured a girlfriend, a companion for my fantasy travels and adventures. We could fly through space, Hermes-like companions, as equals. I remember stealing shameful kisses.

Early the next morning, our new, old home burned to the ground and along with it, the vine-covered trellis, the table in the courtyard, the dinner bell, and my little golden ring. I've never lost my imaginary friend.

In the months following the confrontation with my father and after I dropped out of college, I went out consciously looking for a wife. I knew I could not face the world alone. Perhaps I had become dependent on the fantasy girlfriend I conjured years before, on the night our home burned, someone who had a strong connection with my mother. My wife became that companion. Years later when she left me, I sought out my daughter for companionship to movies, amusement parks, concerts, much as Oedipus clung to his daughters following the suicide of Jocasta, his mother and wife. In Greek mythology, the Great Mother goddess was a trinity. These three women form a trinity: mother, wife, daughter. Relative to Zeus, Rhea (his mother), Demeter (his wife), and Persephone (his daughter) are three representations of the Great Mother goddess. Zeus plus the three women form a quaternion.[249]

As an aerospace engineer, I worked with satellites in space. A satellite's orientation, its reference, can be mathematically described by a quaternion formed of one real and three imaginary quantities. My own orientation within my internal universe, my space, is defined by three women and myself. Even though I no longer live in the presence of my mother, my wife or my daughter, they still and always have had an internal presence.

In Greek mythology, the Fates were the most powerful forces in existence. They came in the form of three ill-tempered old women. Even Zeus was subject to the Fates. The three Fates, also among the most ancient of goddesses, were Clotho, who spun the wool of life, Lachesis who measured it, and Atropos who cut it. For the first half of my life, I felt as though my thread of life was still being spun. But with my recent sense of my own death, I believe Atropos has cut it back considerably.

The wind howls through the leaves of the two rows of eucalyptus trees that line the blacktop road. The hills above this northern port are covered with loose rocks and small thorny bushes. Patmos is ruggedly beautiful and desolate. Finally I turn back from Agriolivadiou Bay and return in the gorgeous midday sunshine.

In Skala, I go again to Port Authority to see about a ferry to Samos. The man confirms what he told me the other day. A ferryboat will be here Sunday morning at ten-thirty, "Δεκα μιση," he says. He also confirms that the ferry belongs to DRM travel agency. So I'm all set. Samos on Sunday. I walk to DRM for further confirmation, but it's still closed.

Two of the dogs in the plateia always welcome me as if I'm an old friend. One is small, a mama dog with her teats and small udders showing, and the other a larger male dog, very slim, both young and active. The male likes to spar with the female in front of me. First they come to me wagging their tails and licking my hands, then they chase each other, biting and pawing, rolling on the ground.

At the dock just at dusk, I pause to watch two kids slap octopi against the cement. I think this activity is catching on. They have four, maybe five octopi, small ones they're busy pounding into jelly. This cannot be a fun thing for the octopi. They leave dark greasy spots on the cement.

I walk to the clothing store just off the plateia. I've been wanting a fisherman's cap ever since I first got to Greece. The one I buy is all blue except for a black, braided band just above the short bill around the front, and has a circular flat top that is high in the front and slopes down in the back. I slip it on after I pay the man, and he smiles his approval.

★

I hear the man in the next room snoring. The halls of Hotel Effie are like echo chambers. Every step down the hall is an announcement, every click of a lock an invitation. I'm seeing fewer and fewer touristas. I haven't had a friend to pal around with since Letizia in Corinth.

I'm lazy after all that walking today and a bad night's sleep last night. In the evenings for the last few days, I've been listening to Barber's violin concerto on my walkman. It's the only music I have heard since I left Colorado a month and a half ago, except for little snippets of Greek music from tavernas and passing cars. As I went in and out of dreams last night, the melody, that sad haunting melody, went through my head like a musical thread holding my dreams together. I've woken from dreams crying the last three nights, but surfaced so rapidly I couldn't remember what they were about. I have a problem, but I don't know what it is.

And I still have lewd fantasies about the three women I met in the monastery yesterday.

★

During the night, I wake from the worst dream I've had since I've been in Greece. I dreamed of something too painful to remember, and I'm consumed by a devastating sadness. I try to slip back into the sleep state, try to retrieve the dream. Gradually it comes to me. I sit in the Cave of the Apocalypse talking to God about something I've done. God listens, but nothing can change my mistake, the terrible unspoken consequence. Why have I dreamed of God in this form? He was not a forgiving God, not like Jesus. He was much more like the ancient Greek gods, like iron-willed Zeus. While chained to the mountainside, Prometheus prophesied that Zeus would not rule forever:

> Yea, verily, the day will come when Zeus, howbeit stubborn of soul, shall be humbled, seeing that he purposeth a marriage that shall hurl him into oblivion from his sovereignty and throne; and then shall straightway be fulfilled to the uttermost the malison his father Cronus imprecated as he fell from his ancient throne... Such an adversary is he Zeus now preparing in his own despite, a prodigy irresistible, even one that shall discover a flame mightier than the levin and a deafening crash to out-roar the thunder...[250]

Prometheus' prophecy is that Zeus' own son, who will have a much different countenance, will overthrow him. Perhaps Jesus represented the crumbling of the kingdom of Zeus foreseen by Prometheus, and represented by the struggle between John and Cynops, the priest of Apollo, here on Patmos.

Maybe now I'm in a position to answer the question Justin, the young missionary I met in Athens, posed to me. He asked, "Are you a Christian." The answer that has come from my dream, the God I conjured from within me, was not a loving, forgiving God, not like Jesus. In the years and centuries following John's exile here, Christianity replaced the Greek gods of antiquity as both Cronus and Prometheus prophesied. But evidently not for me.

13 Nov, Saturday

Today has started as a lazy day. I'm still in bed, even though the roosters have tried to raise me since dawn. I see sunshine on the windowpane and deep-blue sky through the thin drape. A gentle breeze lifts the long arms of the delicately decorated bush of red roses to stroke the white sides of a Byzantine church. I hear sparrows in the trees and a motorbike on the street out front. I want to keep this, my last full day on Patmos, a lazy day. The ever-present call of the chanticleers down the lane welcomes a quiet day of contemplation on the isle where St. John wrote the Apocalypse.

★

I sit at dockside in the midmorning sunshine with my two canine buddies, the male stretched out in the sun at my feet licking his privates, the female up close beside me curled into a ball. I've just realized she's pregnant. That's the reason for her prominent teats. It's still cold today, very cold, and I have on a long-sleeved shirt, my black sweater and hiking jacket. I'm also wearing my blue fisherman's cap, feeling a little foolish in it, maybe wearing it because I feel foolish in it. The wind brings the cold in very close. I like the shadow the visor of my cap casts across my face. I like cold, sunny days.

I walk out to the end of the pier and sit on the cement foundation of the small lighthouse. I enjoy watching the moored fishing boats bobbing in and out of sync. As I watch the small boat closest to me, a man enters it. It rocks robustly in the water. He starts its chugging motor. At first, the chugs are far apart but come together as the motor warms, a low comfortable chugging as the man pulls in the anchor. The two young dogs have followed me to the lighthouse, and the male, black all over with a white belly, is at my feet. The mama dog, white with brown spots, has been gone for a while, but now comes back to lick my hand and resume her place warming my side. White clouds come in from the west, a thin layer of quilted clouds, threatening the sunshine.

As I walk through the village on my way to my room, a man with a three-day beard stops me, big toothy smile. He pulls off his black baseball cap with scrambled eggs and CAPTAIN across the front, and through his mess of Greek, indicates that he wants me to trade caps with him. Mine is a lowly fisher's cap, and I should be wearing a CAPTAIN's cap, is what he's pantomimed. Well, I really don't want to trade, but he's so pleased with what he's doing, I think maybe it's a cultural thing, and I would hate to offend him. So he takes my really-nice-new-blue fisherman's cap and just walks off, leaves me with this disgusting baseball cap, and it's okay, I guess, but I do so wish I had my new fisherman's cap back. This is disappointing, but then if it's a cultural thing, maybe it's kind of nice, or is it? His cap is made in China; mine was made in Greece. I just got ripped off. If he'd asked me for my shirt and pants I bet I'd have given them to him too. Damn!

During the evening, I have the night-before-traveling blues again. I've become attached to Patmos. I worry about the mama dog and papa dog. She's close to delivering her puppies. They're the first mated pair of dogs I've known. They don't belong to anyone and roam the dock and alleyways. Though I have little food to give them, they still like me. They play around me, bite on each other's ears. She likes to cuddle up to me, and he likes to stretch out at my feet licking his privates. But these two dogs, left on their own, aren't wild or vicious. They're playful, loving, devoted to each other.

Before bed, I wash underclothes, one pair of shorts, socks and a shirt, and hang them out to dry on the little clothesline on the patio. Every evening I scan the radio for the Voice of America I heard on Rhodes, but get only static.

★

Rain splashes wake me from a dream of my childhood, and I realize my clothes will not, shall not, cannot dry in rain. I rush outside to bring them in. They're at the wringing-wet stage again. While wringing them out in the sink and placing them on the corners of the bed, I remember bits of the dream that has projected me back into my childhood. When I was a little boy, my mother read the story of King David of the Bible to me. I retained a vivid impression of David, the little shepherd boy, tending his sheep on the mountainside, killing a lion and a bear to protect his flock. At the time David went up against Goliath, he was "...but a youth, and ruddy, and of a fair countenance."[251] And my mother told me, David means "beloved." The little boy I was, David Sheppard, felt a kinship to that David, the little shepherd boy, the coincidence of name a little overpowering and misleading.

I remember fantasizing that someday when I became a man, I too would slay my Goliath, I would be the righteous underdog against the most feared and evil of enemies. In this context, it's easy to understand the dramatic impact of the confrontation I had with my father. When I came to my own bout, my Goliath was my father, and instead of being the righteous underdog, mine was the unjust cause. I had delivered up my own brother into the hands of a pedophile. I had betrayed the heritage of my own namesake.

14 Nov, Sunday

The rain ceased some time ago. We have a windy, cloudy day. The balcony is dry, and my underclothes are out on the line again. I must watch them closely, for the possibility of rain is ever-present. My solitude has produced a giddy euphoria. I catch myself talking aloud to the walls, the wind in the trees, the clouds. I'm glad I'm moving on today. To be quite honest about it, I'm not doing so well. The effect of loneliness, this strange smile on my face, is disturbing.

I've had a banana (rather sticky and chewy) and an apple (rather grainy) for breakfast, and I'm looking forward to a warm shower. The roosters are having a slow time of it this morning. Several just got started. Perhaps it's the rustle and tweet of sprightly sparrows that's shamed them into it. The clouds are low, heavy, and traveling fast. The sun comes out for a second but is immediately snuffed by a black cloud. Blue sky to the north.

I check out of my room, pay the bill, and walk with my increasingly heavy backpack to sit at dockside, awaiting the ferry after first buying a "Patmos Special" cheese pie from the bakery. Papa dog sits at my feet, but mama dog is off scrounging food. I saw her trotting at the edge of the dock a couple of minutes ago. I give the male a piece of crust from my cheese pie, but he sets it on the ground, walks off. He treats food differently than she. Even though he's hungry, he's not desperate. I've also been talking to the dogs but manage to shut up when anyone is around. I believe I'm still sane, at least the dogs think so.

We'll see who's right about the ferry schedule. Port Authority says 10:30. The fresh chalk sign in front of DRM says 10:45, but the DRM agent last night said 11:00. It's warmed some today, but still cool. Here comes a dark ominous cloud. Hurry up, ferryboat!

By noon, I'm concerned enough to return to Port Authority. They have bad news. No ferryboat today. Next ferryboat Tuesday, day after tomorrow, maybe. A ferry will come tonight at eight o'clock but will go directly to Athens, and even it may be canceled because of weather. It's sunny now, but the constant wind blows in ominous clouds. Even if I wait until Tuesday, there's no guarantee I can get to Samos. Even if I get to Samos, I may not be able to get into Turkey. Everything depends on the weather. Zeus! What are you doing to me?

I check back into the hotel. Effie is glad to see me.

Ever since I came to Patmos, I've been curious about a black man who walks the same road as I, back and forth to Hotel Effie. He sits on the old stone fence staring out to sea, never smiles, never speaks. He's there again as I make the rounds to the travel agencies. I speak to him, and he responds with "Good afternoon." Realizing he speaks English, I stop to talk. He's an American national from Jamaica and has lived for a while in New York City. He's well-dressed, dark pants and shirt, a brown sports jacket, but is unusually thin. His manner is smooth, easy-going, with a definite sense of anger underneath.

We chat at the edge of the sea, with geese honking in the background, as he readily reveals his woes. He's in trouble with the American government and in exile on Patmos, a situation he's trying to rectify. He's told the government the truth about himself, given them all the information as honestly as possible, and now waits to hear if he can return to America. His dealings with the government are classified, he says. He loves America and wants to go home. Hum, I think, a man without a country.

Then he gets serious, tells me what happened to him before he came to Greece. He spent some time in Germany. "Uniformed police robbers slit my bag and took all my money." His bag is at his side and he shows me the gash. "They tied me up, took my blood. The German authorities said the police robbers were from another country. They took my health. I came here because Greece was the only country willing to take me. I entered at Athens and came to Patmos, but I'm starving to death."

Once I get him started, I have trouble shutting him off.

After thinking about the black man while walking the dock scrutinizing a new group of touristas, I enter the shop where I bought my little blue fisherman's cap a few days ago, the one I was tricked out of. I've noticed most of the men wear black ones, and I've developed a fondness for them. Shortly I'm the proud owner of a black fisherman's cap with a felt top, a felt brim, the inside lined with red silk. It's a STAMION, made in Greece. Very distinctive.

Back at the dock, I meet two Americans from Wisconsin who've also had an encounter with the Jamaican. They have a perverse attitude toward him, laughing and shaking their heads about what they call his "dementia." But they are much more concerned that they haven't located the Cave of the Apocalypse. I take a hike up the hill with them to show the way, but the sign at the entrance has been removed. The Cave is closed for the season.

As a consolation, I invite them to my favorite beach where I witnessed the sunset yesterday. We walk past the deserted taverna and the cranky geese guarding the cove. I experience none of the surrealistic otherworldliness of my previous visit until we reach the water, where we see two old men at the water's edge laboring to dry-dock a small fishing boat. The motion of the man's hand for us to help seems slowed, and the spray from the waves crashing into the rocks behind him levitates skyward. The pastel-gray boat with a rusty-red keel glows in the muted sunlight.

They've attached a winch to a large spindle mounted to the prow and have laid boards across the rocky beach for the boat to skid along, but they can't budge it. I grab hold of the rope and pull with all my strength while the old man in front of me strains to his limit. He cuts a striking figure superimposed on the waves crashing against the rocky shore, geysers spewing skyward, golden clouds in the distance, and all set within the blood-red disk of setting sun. Though he pulls hard, he seems weak, fragile. The other old man of the sea struggles as he pushes the boat toward us. I feel as though I've walked into a dream.

Prometheus was the god who gave mankind the art of sailing. As he says, "'Twas I and no one else that contrived the mariner's flaxen-winged car to roam the sea."[252] Perhaps this volcanic cove is one of Prometheus' workshops, these two old men, his first mariners.

Prometheus was forever working for the benefit of mankind. After saving us from extinction with the gift of fire, Prometheus set upon improving our lot.

> ...though they mankind had eyes to see, they saw to no avail; they had ears, but understood not; but, like to shapes in dreams, throughout their length of days, without purpose they wrought all things in confusion. Knowledge had they neither of houses built of bricks and turned to face the sun, nor yet of work in wood; but dwelt beneath the ground like swarming ants, in sunless caves. They had no sign either of winter or of flowery spring or of fruitful summer, whereon they could depend, but in everything they wrought without judgment, until such time as I taught them to discern the risings of the stars and their settings, ere this ill distinguishable.

> Aye, and numbers, too, chiefest of sciences, I invented for them, and the combining of letters, creative mother of the Muses' arts, wherewith to hold all things in memory. I, too, first brought brute beasts beneath the yoke to be subject to the collar and the pack-saddle, that they might bear in men's stead their heaviest burdens; and to the chariot I harnessed horses and made them obedient to the rein, to be an adornment of wealth and luxury.[253]

This description of Prometheus' gifts is symbolically the same as Adam and Eve being ejected from the Garden of Eden after they had eaten fruit from the Tree of Knowledge. Just as the two of them were then on their own, Prometheus gave us self-sufficiency. And just as God punished man for eating the apple, so Zeus punished mankind for Prometheus' gifts. Zeus' reaction was a little unorthodox:

> ...the father of gods and men Zeus roared with laughter. Then he ordered widely acclaimed Hephaistos to mix earth with water with all haste and place in them human voice and strength. His orders were to make a face such as goddesses have and the shape of a lovely maiden; Athena was to teach her skills and intricate weaving, and golden Aphrodite should pour grace round the maiden's head, and stinging desire and limb-gnawing passion. Then he ordered Hermes the path-breaker and slayer of Argos to put in her the mind of a bitch and a thievish nature.[254]

The first woman was Pandora, who had a jar from which she removed the lid and turned loose all the ills of mankind, keeping only hope within.

After we finish dry-docking the boat for the old men, my companions and

Patmos

I walk along the water's edge, watching the final sliver of orange sun sink into the sea. They are wide-eyed at the sunset and ask me the name of the bay. I tell them it's called Χοχλακα Κολπος, Seething Bay, Boiling Bay, which is as close as I can come to a translation. I tell them I call it "End of the World Cove."

As the sun's rays fade from the sky, we walk back to the plateia and enter a busy, bustling taverna adjoining Port Authority. We drink ouzo and play backgammon, trying to bang the chips as loud as the Greeks. They invite me to dinner, and I suggest a restaurant I've heard about called "Grill," just up the bay from where I turn off to go to my hotel. We walk north along the waterfront, through the cold wind, along the stone fence, past dark houses, closed businesses, an open field where a donkey stays and several cats eat scraps during the day, to a lone lit sign, "Grill," a beacon in the night.

The Grill is dimly lit and filled with square tables with plastic tablecloths. As we enter, a small gray-haired man shouts us into the kitchen, asks us to select our dinner. The kitchen is dark metallic with stainless-steel sinks and cabinets. The man works as we scrutinize the assortment of fresh sea creatures. His daughter cuts up boiled eggs for a potato salad she says won't be ready until tomorrow. My two companions decide on roast beef. I select octopus and avoid looking at the one I'll eat. I've developed sympathy for their plight in the evening dockside ritual.

Four other people are in the dining room, two Greeks talking over dinner and two young newlyweds from Montana who are also staying at Hotel Effie. They're very quiet and just acknowledge my presence. I let them be. After all, they are here on their honeymoon. When I point them out to the couple from Wisconsin, they tell me rather sheepishly they've also been married for only two weeks. Patmos, the island of love. Both of these newlywed couples are leaving tonight on the ferry to Athens.

They ask if the Jamaican told me about his wife and kids, but just then the waitress brings our food, and I don't respond. I ogle my octopus. All the plate has on it are two shriveled lemon halves and two tentacles with rows of suckers down their sides. They are gray with a purple-pinkish tinge, large at one end, where they were severed from the octopus, tapering to nothing at the other as they curl. I cut them crosswise into cylindrical pieces. The meat is tough, a little like eating a fishy gum eraser with a bitter aftertaste.

On the way back from the Grill, we see a cruise ship floating in the dark bay, decorated with arced lines of lights swooping like Christmas tree ornaments. They remind me that shortly after I return from Greece, I'll travel to California for Christmas to visit my parents, brothers and son. I'll be glad to see them all. My heart will ache with pains of loneliness and grief for my daughter.

Patmos

★

During the night I have the first Space Shuttle dream since the Challenger disaster. I've spent fifteen years working on the Shuttle and Shuttle-related programs. Before Challenger blew up on January 28, 1986, I had a string of Shuttle disaster dreams stretching back ten years. When the catastrophe occurred that clear, cold morning and Challenger fell back into the Atlantic Ocean, I was inroute to Cape Kennedy. I first heard about it when changing flights in Dallas. I had just stepped off the ramp onto the concourse, when I overheard part of a sentence, a fragment of words about an explosion. Immediately I knew it was the Space Shuttle.

Tonight I dreamed of a fireball on the launch pad, the telltale sign of SRM smoke weaving corkscrew paths. I saw two jet liners in flames, a midair collision. A huge two-prop military helicopter went out of control, entered the fireball and broke up. My dream was like the Apocalypse, the world in flames.

Though Prometheus' gifts to mankind were an awakening, he also gave us blindness. "I caused mortals no longer to foresee their doom" and "caused blind hopes to dwell within their breasts."[255] The most powerful manifestation I know of Prometheus' fire and our blind hope followed by doom, occurred that cold day in January with the explosion of Challenger, when the spaceship, turned fireball, fell into the sea. It was a time of reckoning in my life. The Challenger explosion brought a recognition of mistakes I'd made concerning my daughter. It was a time of my own judgment.

15 Nov, Monday

Morning at the dock is cold and windy, with a bright sun and hardly a cloud. The water is choppy and gurgles at the dock's edge. I go to DRM travel for news of tomorrow's ferry to Samos. I'm in luck. I see the agent enter the small white building and return with an eraser and a piece of white chalk. Out front, leaning against the building, is a green chalkboard with a schedule for all DRM ferries to and from Patmos. He dips an old washrag into a bucket of water, washes away the date and time of yesterday's ferry that didn't come, and writes a new date for the next ferry to Samos, 21 Nov. Not tomorrow as promised, but six days from now. My situation is getting serious.

I talk to him for a moment about the ferry, and just before I leave, as an afterthought, he tells me of a hydrofoil to Samos at ten o'clock tomorrow morning. Hydrofoils are more expensive, he says. This one will cost 2365 drachmes ($11.00): a small price to pay if I can actually get to Samos. Hydrofoils are twice as fast as ferries, but even more susceptible to rough seas. I wonder why he thinks the hydrofoil might make it when the ferry can't?

Patmos

Mid-afternoon, I walk past the Sunset Taverna, cross the path of the two geese, the Guardians of the Gate that scold and honk and make a run at me, to the End of the World Cove. I walk past the fishing boat we dry-docked last night to where the road ends at water's edge, walk along the base of the cliff through volcanic rocks to where a huge chunk of it has given way, forming a small recess with a ledge. Inside, I sit beside my shadow, sheltered from the wind and basking in warm sunshine. The rock's porous, foamy texture is bubbly and sharp, black lava now cold and jagged. To the left and right, the cliff sends forth arms to envelope me. At my feet, waves swish at shore like breaths, in and out, sift through rocks, grinding rock against rock. A wave hits a boulder, geysers, then trickles back between rocks ground round as a woman's breasts.

A fishing boat with two men aboard—one young, one old—bobs in the cove. The older man rows the boat backward into the wind, toward the open sea. The younger man casts a net into deep water, an arced flare to his movement. His actions remind me of my fishing dreams, when I cast into dark water expecting a small catch and instead retrieve something formidable, terrifying. I remember fishing with my father. The young man throws a large wood float into the sea, takes the oars from the older man, turns the prow toward shore, and rows with the wind. They moor among the rocks.

As I write in my journal, a small cloudbank forms overhead, and rain comes. I scoot further into the recess and listen to the rhythmic splat of large drops against the cliff. A downpour ensues, and as the time passes, I wonder if I'll have to walk back in the rain. But after a while, it quits as quickly as it began, and a full rainbow arches the sky. Its outer edge is deep red and metamorphoses through the spectrum: orange, brilliant yellow, pale green, blue, purple and violet at the inner edge. Its arc bounds all I see.

I vacate my hideaway and scramble through the rocks to the Sunset Taverna, where I'm met joyously by papa dog and mama dog. Their hand-licking ritual leaves my hands sticky. I stand with them, watching the sunset. The wind has picked up. The sky to the west has a thin covering of clouds that gradually absorb the sun's rays as it falls through them, spreading its glow. The disk that was so well-defined a few nights ago is this evening a large orange glob within silhouettes of clouds from which rain streaks to the sea.

I raise my hood over my fisherman's cap and fasten the Velcro flaps about my chin for protection against the wind. The dogs have gotten into something rotten, and their breaths are thick with death. The smell of my hands gags me. I shoo them away and turn to leave, with the brilliant glow of sunset slowly fading to the pastels of evening, when I notice the little fishing boat back in the cove. The same old man leans into the oars; the younger man pulls at the net, bringing in the catch. The boat dips and rolls in the rough water, turns into the waves. The young man stands at the prow, pulling the net across the spindle, stopping now and then to remove a fish.

I remember an evening such as this, years ago on a lake in California. I was with two other fishermen, my father and my wife. We'd been at it all day without much luck and were on our way in as the sun set beyond the golden hills of the Diablo Range. We saw a strange streak of dark-blue water in the center of the lake that started at the dam and ran for at least a mile along the surface. As we grew closer, we saw that the stripe teemed with fish, so we pulled alongside and cast into it. With every cast, we retrieved a two-to-three pound striped bass. Fish were coming into the boat so fast, I quit fishing and simply unhooked the fish for my father and wife, releasing most of them. I'd never seen the two of them interact before, and as they fished together, my father laughing and my wife squealing and shouting, I simply enjoyed them enjoying each other as the sunlight faded. To me, my father was the consummate archetypal man. Watching my wife enjoy herself with him was a joyous experience. The boat rode low in the water, which seemed to rise up and envelope us like a flood of happiness.

As the sunlight fades from the horizon, the boat in the cove dips and rolls, dips and rolls while the young man pulls the net, hand over hand. I walk past the Sunset Taverna, past the scolding geese, back to the security of the plateia.

I have dinner at a large but sparsely visited restaurant. The couple from Wisconsin ate here two nights ago and said it was now closed. Tonight, it's open but with a limited menu. The two of them talked excitedly about witnessing a wedding, the party and music afterward. I'm disappointed I missed it. Tonight the restaurant is mostly empty, two men drinking at one table, and two women and a man at another having dinner. A TV blares in a corner. Above the TV stands a huge, stuffed peacock in full bloom. A long fishing net stretches across the front wall above the door, held down by huge nautilus shells. I have a pork cutlet, french-fries, bread.

After dinner, I have a cup of coffee, instant Nescafe, and lean back in my chair. The image of King David has haunted me all day. Another incident with my mother occurred during the year following the confrontation with my father. I had quit college and was farming with him. My father was gone that day and would be gone for several more. It was just the two of us, my mother and me, home alone. I was accustomed to going into town in the evenings, drinking and roaming the streets until the small hours of morning. On this particular night, I left my mother alone, and when I returned that morning, I saw a light on in the house. The curtain was pulled back, and I saw into the living room, saw her walking the floor. I immediately thought something had happened to my father.

When I opened the front door and stepped into the living room, she lit into me. "Where have you been?" she scolded. "I've been worried sick about you. I wanted to call the police but was afraid they'd tell me they found you dead beside the road." Then she burst into tears, hard sobbing tears that broke my heart. I realized how alone she had been all night in that large, creaky, poorly-lit home in the country, not far from a highway that frequently brought bums and thieves into our community. How could I have been so inconsiderate? This was the first time I realized I was a man, and that, by God, I had better start acting like one. My mother was depending on me. I had let her down.

For years, I had anticipated the day I would become a man. I thought when that time came, I would always know the right thing to do, be accepted unconditionally by other adults, looked up to, respected. My mother's reaction let me know I had become a man. But inside, I still felt like a child. Somewhere along the line, I had failed my rite of passage.

But the image of the man I thought I would one day become was that of King David, a godlike image I could never live up to. I also had an image of my mother, a goddess-like image of a woman who would never be afraid. It also burst that night. My godlike perception of my father had also crumbled with the click of a deer rifle. My perception of all three of us had forever changed, the stalwarts of my childhood crumbling like the ancient statues of gods and goddesses littering the Greek landscape.

But even King David had his problems. Although initially he was the righteous hero, he also couldn't live up to his own image. He fell in love with a beautiful, married woman, Bathsheba, and committed adultery. Her husband, Uriah, was a Hittite under David's command fighting the Ammonites on the front-line. David had him murdered, then married Bathsheba. As punishment, God raised up an evil against David that caused his child born of Bathsheba to die.

I walk along the dark foreboding sea. On the opposite side of the bay, a large cross of lights appears suspended in mid air on the black mountainside, and I visualize two figures superimposed on it: Prometheus and Jesus. I hear the bitter complaints of Prometheus:

> Behold, with what shameful woes I am racked and must wrestle throughout the countless years of time apportioned me. Such is the ignominious bondage the new Commander Zeus of the Blessed hath contrived against me. Woe! Woe! For misery present and misery to come

Patmos

I groan...[256]

And even the questioning of Jesus, "My God, my God, why hast thou forsaken me?"[257]

In the plateia, a man spreads freshly cut laurel branches through the streets and between buildings, the sacred smell of laurel leaves. I've heard that today's touristas will be the last to visit Patmos this year. More businesses in Skala have closed for the winter.

★

My room is freezing cold, and I quickly slip between the covers. My feet are like fresh fish from the End of the World Cove. I still smell on me the dead thing the dogs ate. The image on the mountainside of that brilliant cross of lights submerged in darkness reminds me that Jesus was the only son of God. I wonder if God asking Abraham to sacrifice Isaac could be connected with the Crucifixion. Perhaps God was stewing over whether He would allow His own Son to be crucified. I wonder how many fathers He asked before finding Abraham, a man with faith in God equal to that of God's in mankind? Abraham gave God his answer, but it was another 1400 years before God sent His Son to the cross.

16 Nov, Tuesday

Rather optimistically, I check out of Hotel Effie and pay my bill, again. I tell Effie I might be back before nightfall. She smiles, says she'll be glad to have me. While I wait for the hydrofoil, I drop my backpack on the dock and take a walk. Everywhere I go, my pack of dogs follows, but now it's not just two. This morning I have six. I go to the bakery for a couple of sausage pies, and the swarm of dogs follows me through the streets like bloodhounds on the trail of an escaped criminal. I shoo them away. And the mama dog and papa dog, who were with me at the End of the World Cove yesterday, still smell bad from getting into that dead thing. I've spot-washed my clothes, but still can't get the smell of death off me.

No hydrofoil. I could catch the ferry back to Athens tonight but want to give Samos one more try. I keep telling myself I have lots of time, three weeks yet to see Samos and Turkey. My flight back to the States is not until the 8th of December, but I've got to be realistic. Just as I feared at the beginning of my journey, I'm stranded.

I walk back and forth between the four agencies, and end up talking to the Olympic Travel agent, a rather light-complexioned Greek with thinning scraggly hair and stubble beard. We're standing outside his office when I hear the solemn Jamaican across the plateia talking loudly to a policeman. They shout angrily at each other.

But it doesn't stop there. The Jamaican crosses the plateia, and much to my surprise and concern, comes up to me anxiously requesting that I to talk to the policeman on his behalf. He explains that the policeman is stupid and violent. "Talk to the policeman," he implores. "Have him call the immigration authorities in Athens to come pick me up and ship me out of the country." Yesterday when we talked, he seemed solemn, resigned. Now he's animated, agitated, inflamed. "Help me," he demands. "I'm dying! You can speak Greek. Make the police understand."

I've been proud of my little bit of Greek until this moment. "No, no! I don't speak Greek," I tell him, "just a few words."

Disillusionment consumes him. To convince me of his desperation, he reviews what happened to his family. "My wife and four kids were murdered in Jamaica. I just want them to send me back there so I can live out my life, or kill me here if they have to. Instead, they want me to leave on the ferry tonight. They'll give me a ticket, but I'll be lost in Athens."

He has me backed up against the building. The travel agent smiles, evidently getting a kick out of my situation. The Jamaican is a young man of about thirty. He talks very loudly. "The policemen are stupid and violent. They won't do a simple thing like call the immigration authorities in Athens so they'll stamp the papers, come and get me and escort me to Jamaica where I was born. They are starving me to death. Someone on the island wants to kill me. The world is trying to kill me."

When I suggest he accept the offer from the local police to send him to Athens on the ferry tonight, he puts his hands to the sides of his head and shouts, "Didn't you just hear me? The police must call the authorities in Athens! They must come get me with the proper papers to deport me! They must send me to Jamaica where I was born! The police want me to starve to death! I've been robbed, beaten..."

The travel agent and I talk over the man's problem. I tell the agent that the black man is a man without a country. He hears me say this and throws a fit. "No! No!" he yells. "I have a country! I'm a citizen of Jamaica where I was born!" I'm afraid he's going to hit me and quickly retract my statement. The travel agent then calls the Patmos police and talks to them for several minutes. When he returns, he tells the Jamaican to accept the ticket and go back to Athens where he can solve his problem. But the man says, "No! No! They must call the authorities in Athens, and they must come get me with the proper papers. The police are trying to kill me. I'm illegal here on Patmos. The police are stupid and violent. I'm not supposed to be here. I have no visa. They have to deport me."

He calms some, tells me about the woman, Effie, who runs our hotel. She has been most helpful to him, providing a room at no charge. I suggest he ask Effie to call the authorities in Athens; she can speak Greek, she is Greek. All at once, he's a new man. He'd never thought of that. Much to my pleasure, he leaves for the hotel with quick, decided strides.

Rain has come again to Patmos. Outside my window, I hear the wind tugging at the building, the splash of drops from the overhang above my French doors. I hear voices, American voices. I walk to the lobby and meet an older couple from Washington State. They're talking to a Greek couple whom the woman knew when she was eighteen, when she lived here on Patmos. I detect an uneasiness between the two couples. The American woman is bubbling over with enthusiasm about seeing her Greek friend after thirty years, the woman who was her best friend. But the Greek woman is cold, unsmiling. The American couple did not tell them they were coming to Patmos and called only a few minutes ago. "You should have told us you were coming," the Greek woman repeats.

While I'm talking with these two couples, the Jamaican comes in and sits in the small leather sofa at the hotel entrance. He has his knife-slit bag at his side and sits purposefully erect, full of expectation. I can't resist finding out what's happened. Against my own better judgment, I walk over to him. Effie has talked to the Patmos police on his behalf, and they've fixed papers for him to take to Athens. He's leaving on tonight's ferry, if it comes (the weather is very bad), and the authorities in Athens will get him back to Jamaica. After telling me of his good fortune, he turns to the couple from Washington. "I was robbed in Germany," he tells them. "The German robber police took my money and my blood, ruined my heath. My wife and children have been murdered in Jamaica. The Patmos police have been trying to starve me to death. The American government..."

I go back to my room and later walk to the Grill. As I enter, I see the older couple from Washington. They motion for me to join them. They want to talk about the Jamaican. For dinner, they have fish and wine, and he offers to buy enough wine for me. I order a Greek salata and roast beef with patates. My companions utter a string of superlatives about the fish, the lemoned olive oil in which it bathes. They're still marveling over the man from Jamaica. She shakes her head. "He means trouble, big trouble."

I think about her statement for a second. "But if everything he says has in fact happened to him," I say, "his wife and kids murdered, being robbed in

Germany, his mental condition is understandable."

"You believe him?"

"His bag has been slit. He showed it to me. A foot long gash down the side."

She shakes her head. "But no one took his blood, and no one on Patmos is trying to kill him."

We walk back through the rain to the hotel. I open my umbrella, breaking a stay in the process. One side of the black umbrella looks like a broken bat wing. I offer it to him, but he refuses. She and I huddle under it. She takes my arm, and he walks beside us. It's dark and the cars whizzing past us from behind are scary, but it feels so very good to have a woman on my arm.

At the hotel, I talk to her while he retrieves their luggage from their room and loads it into the taxi that will take them to the dock. At eight-thirty tonight, they'll catch the ferry to Athens with the Jamaican.

I'm all alone here in the hotel, the only patron and the only tourist on the island. Even the crazies have departed. I slip into bed to warm my feet. I can't get the Jamaican off my mind. I don't know that he and I are so different. The cataclysmic events of my own life have distorted my perception. It's as if my dreams, nightmares really, bleed into the daytime world. On this journey, leaving each island is like an escape. My inability to get off Patmos has left me feel as though I'm held prisoner. It's as if even during my waking hours, my consciousness sits on a fence, the boundary between the conscious and unconscious. Like Hermes, the guide of souls and bringer of dreams, my consciousness dips into the blackness beyond the edge, into the river Lethe, forgetfulness, and activates whatever drifts by.

During the night, I wake from the worst nightmare of my life. My neck and shoulders are dripping sweat. I was in a foreign country under political suppression. A friend of mine, a native of that nameless country, had just been taken away by military guard. Perhaps he was the same shady character with whom I dreamed of robbing banks and killing guards. I was concerned for my own life, and had just crawled out of bed in an old barracks, slipped on my clothes, and was about to leave when the military returned and took me prisoner. My son was gone but was to return soon, and I was concerned for his safety as well. They questioned me, then put a rifle to my head to execute me. I suddenly remembered that my daughter, my beautiful, lovely, golden-haired daughter was dead. I remembered her death had not been a grievous one, but one she had accepted with resignation and courage. I went into a fit of grief, banged my fists on the floor. I screamed, "No, no, no! Not my daughter! Not my daughter." I woke to find myself back on Patmos, back in the little room in the

Patmos

Hotel Effie, crying streams of real tears, a knot of unbearable grief within me.

Sunshine. No wind. A scattering of clouds. It's quiet outside my window without the wind and the splash of rain. I hear a lone sparrow and the distant call of roosters. Today marks three weeks left in my journey. With the break in the weather, my optimism runs high. I want to see Samos, the home of Pythagoras. Everything depends on the weather.

Another day at the dock in Skala, port town of Patmos. Another rumor of a hydrofoil to Samos, squelched immediately by the man at Apollon Travel, who makes a call to Kos and learns it'll stay there because of weather. I'm told Kalimnos has a ferry to Samos today at eleven, but Kalimnos told me two days ago, "No ferryboat until 21 Nov." His chalkboard sign still says the same.

I talk to Port Authority for an update. They tell me to check with a shop just off the plateia. They sell tickets for a ferry that should be here tomorrow. I check with a woman at the shop, and sure enough, a ferry to Samos should be here tomorrow evening. Time will tell.

I walk back to the pier to pass the time, sit in the sun. Not far from me, two fishermen cast their lines, one dressed in a white shirt, pullover gray sweater and black slacks. He fishes with a large plastic wheel, the line wrapped around its rim. His tackle is simple, a hook inserted into the mouth of a small fish. He slings it out into the sea and manually rewinds the line around the wheel.

I give the mama dog a pastry. First she licks the white powdered sugar on the outside then breaks through the sweet bready crust to the inside, which is filled with honey, brown sugar and walnuts. She licks and smacks, then pulls chunks of crust off, holding the pastry to the cement with her paws. She gobbles the remaining chunk, swallowing hard to force down the dry sweetness, licks the cement. I had one myself earlier and now feel guilty that I didn't give her both. She crawls up on the yellow tarp-covered fish nets to soak up the warm rays of sun, shielded from the wind.

A woman with brown hair, wearing a black sweater and long red dress, paces the dock. She holds a baby close to her breast singing lullaby's in its ear. She's the wife of the fisherman. The wind has picked up again. My new black fisherman's cap keeps my head warm and shields my eyes from the bright morning sun.

The dogs' breaths are not so bad this morning, although I still smell a little of the old dead thing on the black male. A flock of geese stays farther up the harbor where fishing boats dock at small wooden piers extending out into the water. Up there, most of the fishing boats are dry-docked, pulled ashore over

Patmos

parallel wooden slides. The black male goes up there to scatter geese, to hear their squawks and frantic squeals as they flap their wings for deep water. He won't catch them. I've seen him stop when he's had the chance. He's the same with the cats. He'll scatter a bunch of them to hear their screeches, but when he corners one, even a kitten, and it turns to defend itself with a pfffttt, he backs off. He's not a killer, just has a mean streak. When the cold wind blows, he shivers.

Out at sea, no boats are in sight, no ferryboats, no fishing boats, only islands hopscotching to the horizon. As the day wears on, the clouds change, become fat, and balloon into the blue sky. They have dark bottoms, large fluffy tops, and congregate in a conspiracy against ferryboats. The wind picks up again from the northwest, a cold, persistent wind. I watch a man heavy into the "Ritual of the Octopi." He has a large one by the dome, scrubbing it on the cement, forming a frothy residue of pinkish-white gunk.

Hermes, in addition to assisting travelers (Where is the sucker when you need him?), is the guide of souls in the Underworld. The ancient Greek Underworld is not the same as Christian Hell, but is the place where all souls go when they die. To the ancient Greek, souls were shadows, shades or phantoms of what they had been during life. When Odysseus went into the Underworld, he visited Teiresias, the Theban seer who was the only mortal to retain an unclouded mind after death. The god who rules the Underworld is Hades, Zeus' brother. The name "Hades" stands for both the god and the Underworld. The river running through Hades is the Lethe (forgetfulness). When the dead drink from its waters, they forget their previous lives. The boundary of Hades is the river Styx, which runs round it six times. The aged and grumpy ferryman, Charon, takes those who enter across a dark lake. All souls come to Hades as their last stop, except for the few who are deified and go to live with the gods. Oedipus was one of those. King Minos of Crete judges the souls. Only a select few are punished.

I stand before the gate of the Skala cemetery, just a few meters from the sea. An old woman slowly, hesitatingly walks the aisle between gravestones. A large marble box, trimmed in blue, sits over each grave. The boxes are wider than a casket and have a large white cross at the head. Every grave has flowers and plants, except those where the covering has been removed. Evergreen trees grow randomly throughout the cemetery along with one large fern. Plenty space for more graves.

The mistress of the Underworld is the maiden goddess Persephone, the daughter of Demeter. She was but a girl when she was taken there. Hades wanted a wife, and Zeus agreed he could have Persephone, his daughter. So Hades kidnapped and ravished her, brought her to live with him as mistress of the Underworld. At the time of the kidnapping, she was playing in a field, "gathering flowers, roses, crocuses, and beautiful violets all over a soft meadow: irises, too, and hyacinths she picked."[258] Hades lured her close to the entrance of the Underworld with a beautifully bloomed narcissus. When she came close, the earth gaped and out sprang Hades with his immortal horses, snatched her screaming, and took her into the Underworld. Demeter hadn't been consulted and didn't know what had happened to her daughter. She searched for Persephone, roaming the Greek countryside, much as I did looking for my own daughter when she vanished.

I enter the cemetery, remove my black fisherman's cap to show respect, and walk the rows of graves. Small marble boxes with glass fronts stand before some. Inside one such box is a picture of the deceased, a beautiful young woman snatched into the Underworld before her time.

More and more, I find that I don't get to pick and choose what I deal with on this journey. I can't get last night's dream of my daughter's death out of my thoughts. That dream of another Space Shuttle disaster also contributes to my distress. Two years after my wife left me, I had an opportunity to move to San Diego for a position on the most challenging program in the aerospace industry. General Dynamics was building the most dangerous payload ever to fly on the Space Shuttle. It was a booster rocket for sending spacecraft to the outer planets. The first two spacecraft to use the new booster rocket would be Galileo and Ulysses.[259] Galileo would go into orbit about the planet Jupiter,[260] and Ulysses would use Jupiter's enormous gravity-well as a slingshot to put it in a polar orbit on an odyssey about the sun.

The booster rocket would be propelled by liquid hydrogen and liquid oxygen, cryogens, in violation of an original ground rule adopted when the Space Shuttle was first built. No cryogenic payloads were to ever fly on the Space Shuttle because of hazards involved in having onboard propellants that were close to absolute zero. But NASA changed its mind under the pressure of needing more and more kick to get heavier payloads to the outer planets. General Dynamics was the only company with the technology that could do it. It was a suicide mission, but most of the Shuttle program had been run that way. Russian roulette was becoming a way of life on the Shuttle program. The name of this new rocket was the Shuttle Centaur.

I had been working at a do-nothing job in Phoenix for four years and desperately needed a change in my professional life. My son had graduated from high school and was on his way to college. The only obstacle in my path was my daughter. She had two years of high school left. I felt a little like Agamemnon must have when he got the news that he would have to sacrifice his daughter if the Greek armada was to get favorable winds to sail for Troy.

I received a reasonable offer from General Dynamics, and though I would not lead the troops into battle as Agamemnon had, as a lead engineer I would be in charge of several million dollars of engineering and have several engineers working directly for me. My hardware would be mission critical, and at times I would work directly with astronauts to develop emergency EVA procedures.

I wanted my daughter to go with me to San Diego. She and my son had lived with me after their mother left. She thought it over for a while and decided she would prefer to finish high school in Phoenix with her friends. My ex-wife and I decided that our daughter would stay with her mother and continue her schooling in Phoenix. On a blistering day in August 1983, I made the trip alone across southern California's Mojave Desert to San Diego on the Pacific Ocean.

If my wife had been a mythical presence in my life, my daughter was even more so. Perhaps it had to do with that mysterious companion I conjured the night before our home burned and my little golden ring with it. Being with my daughter was an important part of my life, and now she was growing into a young woman, but just at this crucial phase, I threw it all to the wind and moved to San Diego. I wanted to prevent a Shuttle disaster. My intent was serious and calculated. I had been having Shuttle disaster dreams for seven years.

I started paying for my mistake immediately. It took me a long time to get out the front door of my deserted home. I fell to my knees on the carpet in my daughter's empty bedroom and cried it full of tears. I hurt so badly that I didn't know if I could stand it. Little did I know that this was only the beginning. I had no idea what real pain was all about.

★

I've been reading the Athens News,[261] an English independent daily published in Athens. The world news headlines: "Croats prepare for offensive against Bosnian Muslim forces." The war in the former Yugoslavian republic continues as I attempt to get out of Greece and into Turkey to see the battlefield of the most famous war in all history, the 13th Century BC siege of Troy. Not a lot has changed in 3200 years. The paper also has a picture of Prime Minister Papandreau, the man who was elected that Sunday evening when I was in Thebes. He was sworn in last month and is meeting with the former prime minister to discuss "domestic and foreign issues." I also read an article on the Kurds' war against Turkey, where I hope to be soon. But the war is isolated to Turkey's eastern border with Iraq, not the western coast where I'm headed. The Kurdistan Workers Party says that, in October, it killed more than 1300 Turkish soldiers and "agents" and captured 186 soldiers and 3 foreign tourists. It's the three tourists who concern me. I'm no war correspondent.

Patmos

Before going back to my room, I drop by the store, which sells tickets for the ferry to Samos tomorrow, buy a chocolate bar, and ask the young woman about the ferry. I don't understand her answer, and when I question her, she gets surly with me, hurts my feelings. What it really amounts to is that, because of the winds, she doesn't know when the ferry will be here. I'll just have to wait until tomorrow. But I've made the decision to leave on the ferry to Athens tomorrow night if I can't leave for Samos, terminate the rest of my journey. I could get stranded on Patmos and miss my flight back to the States.

I eat dinner at the Grill again, the only place open for dinner now. I'm the first customer, and the owner tells me to take a seat. Shortly, he calls me into the kitchen, asks what I want. He has fish, roast beef, stew. "Ψαρι," I say (Psari, fish). So he shows me my choices. I can have either a bunch of tiny ones (about three inches long) for 600 dr, or three medium-sized ones (about six inches long) also for 600 dr. The big ones are more expensive. I choose the three medium-sized fish and watch him scale them as he asks how I want them cooked: grilled or fried? I have them grilled. I also have the potato salata I saw his daughter making last night while here with the couple from Washington. The three fish, when they arrive, are swimming in olive oil splashed with lemon juice. The daughter brings them. She's a gorgeous, trim young woman with a fat face and hair pulled back severely in a bun, wears wire-rimmed glasses. The shiny silver fish still have their heads and dull eyeballs.

The fish are delicious and the potato salata superb. I rake the black skin back with my fork and raise the white flakes of meat from the large spine bones, extract the small ribs with my fingers. The lemoned olive oil adds a flavor I've never had with fish. It removes the fishy taste but adds a healthy robustness. I wonder if these fish are from the End of the World Cove?

The Grill is a half step off the main road along the waterfront. I have to watch it when exiting, or I might step into the path of a screaming car or motorbike. All these places are dives and the service poor compared to American standards, but somehow I prefer them. You don't get a nice padded booth where you can kick back and relax. You don't get a well-lit room. You don't get a smiling waiter. You don't get a heated restaurant. You don't get a glass of ice water, a nonsmoking section, everything on the menu. You don't get asked if your meal is okay, if you want desert. You don't get a check or asked to come again. What do you get? Food, a chair to sit in, a table to eat on. Someone to serve you, sometimes. But tell me where in the States you're expected to walk into the kitchen, inspect the food before it's prepared and make your selection, tell them how to cook it. And you get a sense of welcome, almost a sense of family, totally unmatched by the artificial, antiseptic restaurants in the States.

Patmos

★

During the night, I wake from another powerful dream. I agree to set up an encounter between a notorious criminal and the authorities. To do so successfully, my impartiality is crucial. But while placing plate-sized gold coins on checkered squares in the sidewalk outside the bank, I make a mistake. I get in a hurry because I'm running short of time. The criminal seizes this opportunity to turn on me, says I've lied to him, that I'm not impartial. I try to defend myself, but he persists in proclaiming my guilt. He says I delayed because I hate him. I admit, he's right. I'm guilty. I can't be impartial toward a criminal. My admission further infuriates him. He pounces on me, enters my body where he tears apart my insides, inflicts infinite pain. He keeps me from dying while making me spout fountains of blood. He's Satan.

In St. John's conflict with the priest of Apollo, he used hatred and violence, which ultimately led, not to the conversion of Cynops, but to his death. Why did St. John, the Minister of Love, not use love instead of anger? Was he not responding the same as did the ancient Greeks gods, to a thirst for power? In my dream, I recognize the pitifulness of Satan, feel sympathy for him, love. I'm no longer afraid. He runs, terrified of me. When I catch him, Satan takes a female form. I kiss her. She's my wife, my ex-wife.

18 Nov, Thursday

I wake to gorgeous rays of sunshine on my patio. It's cold, a breeze blows, and wisps of cloud streak the emerald-blue sky. I do so hope this is my day of escape. Last night, I washed underclothes again and hung them out to dry on the patio. How hopeful I am this morning.

The surly woman at the tourist shop tells me my ferryboat will leave Rhodes at ten this morning and should be here by six or seven this evening. But, she adds, they don't know for sure.

Whatever the time, I'll be here.

I buy a ham and cheese pastry and feel guilty for stuffing myself while somewhere out there, mama dog huddles in a corner protecting herself and the puppies inside her from the cold wind. I haven't seen her all morning. While I was inside the bakery, Papa dog huddled against the building waiting for me to come out, trying to protect himself from the cold. He looks particularly thin this morning, his eyes sad and questioning.

A ferry enters the harbor. I watch it do the dipsy-doodle in the afternoon sun. It's not going to Samos, not a ferryboat for me. It's long and white, with a blue belly, and belches smoke as it stands proudly above waterline. After only a few minutes at dock, it pulls away. Quick in, quick out. I give papa dog half of

270

my sausage pastry. He has the shivers, huddling against the cement wall. I watch the ferry power into the distance, and then sit watching dockhands unload more water bottles. Nearby fishermen clean their nets.

Of all the dogs I've known, the wild dogs of Patmos are the best. They civilize themselves while subjected to adversity. They're loving toward each other and are the least aggressive toward strangers that I've ever seen. They never fight. They beg food but stand their distance when asked. Wild dogs of Patmos, my heart goes out to you.

★

Mid-afternoon the female comes running to me, flirting, her cute continuous inventory of movements, mama-dog twists and wiggles, but looking lanky and desperate. I know immediately, she's had her pups. I take her for a walk, let her lead the way. When we pass a small clump of bushes and shoulder-high palm trees, she makes a run at a cat lurking close by, and this time she means business. She chases the cat across the street and up into a tree. If she had caught the cat, she would have killed it. Definitely out of character. I walk into the bushes to a small red pump house and can hear them before my eyes adjust to the dim light. I see two white puppies with brown spots like mama dog and three black with white spots like papa dog. I don't want to see anymore, don't want to get anymore attached to them than I am already. Five newborn puppies, with eyes still closed tight as zippers, yelping and squirming on the cold pump-house floor. No wonder she's so desperate.

I walk back to the steps of Port Authority, where I've been sitting in the sun awaiting tonight's ferry. I'm just about in tears, maybe shedding a few, feeling lost, forlorn and desperate myself. I hoist my backpack to my shoulders, buckle the big belt, pick up my camera case and walk to the plateia. Most of the stores are closed this time of day. After checking several, the supermarket I frequent and a couple of mini markets, all closed, I find a small grocery store open. Three Greeks are inside, two men and a woman, laughing and talking. I go in with my pack on looking like a huge Neanderthal stalking about. Mama dog is a carnivore, but no meat in sight. Even the refrigerator has nothing substantial: chips, soft drinks, potato salata. Then at the end of the empty meat counter I spot what I'm looking for, a lone package of wieners.

When I get back to Port Authority, I creep into the bushes realizing I must keep from being seen and also keep other dogs from invading the pump house. Papa dog is always around, even though I've kept him at a distance since he got into the dead thing at the End of the World Cove. I have to shoo him away now. I open the plastic wrapper on the wieners with my pocket knife and quickly enter the pump house, mama dog going through hysterics from the smell. I throw the open package in the corner behind the puppies but she can't find it, so I pull them out for her. She eats them in chunks. I back out to keep other dogs away.

The package had six large wieners. She couldn't possibly eat them all at once. I bet she's never seen that much meat in one meal in her life. Maybe her milk will give the puppies a start, but Patmos can't support five more dogs. What is so heartbreaking is her look of pride, what she has accomplished. Bringing five wonderful little puppies into the world will soon turn sour and may cost her own life. I just want to give them one night together with full stomachs. Maybe just this one night they will lie together, feel the comfort of each other's bodies, and experience the togetherness that makes life on this planet so wonderful. For just one night I want to forestall the pain, suffering to come.

★

Late in the afternoon, I buy my ticket to Samos. The surly lady is very pleased, most helpful. My enthusiasm soars even though she tells me the ferryboat will not be here by six this evening as she said earlier. She's talking more like one o'clock in the morning. She'll know more by seven this evening.

I wait outside the tourist shop in the cold dark, trying to protect myself from the wind by leaning against a tree. Pandemonium breaks out as a large pack of dogs enters the plateia. I can't figure out what's the matter, when suddenly a huge red dog strides into the pack. It's frightening the way he bounds into the plateia, but he's not interested in me or any other human being. His red coat glistens a phosphorescent bronze in the pale light from the shops. All the dogs surround him licking his lips, sniffing and kissing him. They can't contain their excitement in his presence. He's a dignitary in the world of dogs, perhaps the messiah who has come among them.

★

Joy! Oh joy! I'm lightheaded and giddy over my good fortune. The ferryboat left Rhodes at five-thirty this evening and will dock in Patmos at one-thirty tonight. This is from the horse's mouth. The ferryboat is on its way!

★

It's dark, and I sit in Passenger Transit, the taverna frequented by local Greeks. The building also contains Port Authority and is next to the old red pump house where mama dog and her pups are right now, hopefully with their stomachs full. The coffee shop is in a large room with eight square pillars. Between them are three-sided booths with padded seats and coffee tables. Greek men have congregated to play cards and backgammon. They really slap the chips, and the place sounds like a pool hall. Not a woman in sight. The men range in age from late teens to sixty, seventy. I count over thirty. I watch a man

272

with a mobile phone up to his ear, the short antenna sticking up above his head. He has gray hair, gray beard, and wears a gray coat with hood, grungy slacks and sneakers. The bar and kitchen, where they mix drinks, brew coffee and make simple sandwiches, is in the corner of the room next to the door. Seven electronic computer games, one of which is Pac-man, line two walls. The younger set crowds around the machines. They look as though they could be from any decade of the century.

Mid-evening, the nightly ferry to Athens arrives and cleans out the coffee shop. Only two small groups of men and a couple of stragglers like myself remain. The lighting is bad and darkness hangs like a depression in the windows. The ferries are so large, they remind me of cities. They dwarf the little town of Skala. I've been cold all day, but this evening I'm absolutely frozen. It's like the North Pole outside, and yet they keep the front door open. If I don't get sick over this, it'll be a miracle. I ask a man if he speaks English. "Οχι," he replies. I try speaking a little Greek, but my Greek is so bad that the guy thinks I'm still speaking English. "Δεν καταλαβαινο Αγγλικα," I don't speak English, he repeats with irritation and looks away. The dock is quiet, the restaurant quiet, and it's a long time until one-thirty. But I'm used to getting rid of the hours.

Eighteen months after John was exiled here, the Roman emperor Domitian was assassinated, and John was permitted to return to Ephesus. I don't know if the Virgin Mary was still there or if she had died, Assumed as the Catholics believe. As I leave the island of Patmos, what impresses me is that John witnessed the crucifixion of Christ at Golgotha with the Virgin Mary and was on Patmos for eighteen months, walking the same ground I've walked for nine days. From the cross, Jesus told Mary, "Woman behold thy son," and He told John, "Behold thy mother."[262] From that time forth, John was in charge of Mary and took her with him when he went to Ephesus, where I hope to be in a few days.

Something strange has happened. A woman with a baby has come among us. Men fog around her to see the child, and she takes a seat away from the drafty door.

At one-thirty, I step out into the cold wind, hear the horn and see the bright lights of the ferry to Samos steam into port, then go back inside quickly to get out of the light rain. Ten of us are waiting. That doesn't include the papa dog that keeps coming into the coffee shop to see me off. He sneaks past the owner and sleeps curled close to me. The owner has chased him out several times.

I give the old papa dog one last pat, take his face in my hands. He has such sad eyes. I would like to kiss him, but the smell of the dead is still on him. The rush for the door starts, but I wait until last before boarding and go out behind the dark-haired woman with the child in her arms wrapped in blankets. I hold the door for her, and she pauses for a second, takes her eyes from the child nestled against her breast to thank me. She smiles like an angel.

In that instant of hesitation, the story of Abraham and Isaac passes before me one more time as I stare into the bright eyes of the child. This time the story comes with my father, deer rifle in hand, as Abraham, me as Isaac. Once again, I hear the footsteps of my mother down the hall and into the bedroom, see her standing over my father's shoulder, my mother the angel, holding fast my father's hand. All these years, I've been misinterpreting my mother's message when she first read the story to me. When the time came, when my father and I performed the ritual of death, she appeared to stay the arm drawn to sacrifice me. I realize for the first time that, thirty-two years ago, my mother saved my life.

Rain hides my tears as I follow the woman through the dark to walk the gangway, and beyond, into the warm glow of the ferry hold.

PART III: Turkey

CHAPTER 14: Turkey: Ephesus I

19 Nov, Friday

After nine days and five hours on Patmos, I'm finally on a ferry again. We mill around the rumbling hold for an eternity, breathing exhaust from cars, trucks and motorbikes, before the crew finally lets us into the passenger compartment. The warmth of the ferry feels good, but I've not been on one this dirty. The carpet looks as though it hasn't been vacuumed since October. The shabby crew drifts around with their chest hair sticking out their open shirts and their pants wrinkled. Dirty dishes decorate the tables in the dining room, and the trashcans are full. I try to find a quiet place to unload my backpack where I can sleep, but small groups of shouting Greeks are everywhere.

I sit next to the dark windows, trying to see the coast of Turkey through the darkness. Gradually, as we enter the strait between Samos and the mainland, pinpoint lights speckle the darkness. We should be at dockside by five-thirty, a little early to look for a hotel. I'm sick and tired of being out in the cold.

The announcement over the loudspeaker startles me, even though I've been unable to sleep with the loud voices and smoke. We're coming into Samos Town. I wait impatiently down in the hold with a handful of people, listening to the whistling wind and rush of water pumps maneuvering the ferry, while the docking crew tries to straighten out the mooring ropes. The wind blows the ferry laterally, stretching the ropes across the exit as the metal gangway scrapes and pops against the cement dock. The clang and scream of the ferry's motors, coupled with the frantic shouts of men, are frightening. The cars and trucks can't move with a rope across the exit, but it doesn't stop the passengers from crawling under and over the rope, adding to the chaos and interfering with the crew. I hurry off myself, bending low under the rope, which sings under the high tension. I feel a tingle ripple through me, realizing I could be dragged to death.

I step off the gangway into the cold, driving wind and stinging rain. I use the pink glow of a neon sign, Hotel Samos, as my homing beacon though the dark. I push through two sets of glass doors, thinking I surely can't afford a room in this place. The man behind the desk and another manning the coffee and pastry shop are the only people around. The carpeted dining room with a cathedral ceiling is dark and empty. I drop my backpack to the floor next to a group of sofas in the foyer, wondering if they'll run me out if I don't take a room. I'm so tired. But perhaps they won't mind. Samos used to have a Hermes festival during which everyone had a license to seal.[263] I'll steal a little warmth and comfort.

After pulling off my coat and gloves, I talk to the man behind the desk and find that a single in this magnificent hotel goes for only 3900 dr ($16.00). No singles are available at the moment and won't be until nine o'clock. I ask where I can find a travel agent to see about a ferry to Turkey. "Right next door," he says.

While waiting for the agency to open, I walk to the OTE to call my son in San Francisco. The weather outside is still cold and windy and the sky overcast. Today is his birthday, but it's 8:00 PM yesterday there. His voice sounds so fresh, young and familiar. It's nice to be reassured he's well. He's a freelance illustrator. When I tell him I'll be going to Turkey sometime during the next few days, he's thrilled. He's painting a Turkish mural on the wall of a woman's clothing store. Just a little synchronicity, Hermes on the prowl again.

Let's Go says I must leave my passport overnight before entering Turkey. At least I'll have the rest of today and this evening to discover Samos. With the weather, it may be a week before I get a ferry.

Nine o'clock comes and goes, and still no room. In the meantime, I walk next door to the travel agency, which has just opened. The agent hasn't even pulled off his coat. I step into the small room, which is still dark and cold, ask when I can get a ferry to Turkey.

"Today, three o'clock," he says.

I stand there for a second, my dull mind trying to absorb my good fortune. I feel a rush of fear. I'm not prepared for Turkey, not today. "That won't leave enough time for me to get through passport control," I tell him.

"No problem," he says.

I'm dumbfounded, find myself searching for another excuse. But this is no time for petty bickering with my own cowardice. "What's the price?" I ask, pulling my security pouch from inside my shirt.

As I go out the door, he tells me, "Be at the dock by two-thirty."

I walk down the street away from the hotel, looking for a taverna, a sense of doom hanging over me. The war with the Kurds in eastern Turkey looms

Turkey: Ephesus I

larger.

I find a dark greasy taverna, and order two gyros and French fries. The entrance is small and the room long, with a dark greasy kitchen in the back. I chomp on the gyros and stare out at the sea and a ferry in the distance. A lone dog hobbles in and stands three-legged at the entrance, her nostrils elevated and twitching at the smell of my food. Her fourth leg, the left front, is broken just above the first joint and flops like a rag. She shows no pain, the leg evidently broken some time ago. The proprietor comes to shoo her away.

I reenter the hotel and take a single room until two o'clock at a half-day rate. I take the elevator to the third floor. After a shower, I climb into bed for a nap, hoping the alarm on my wristwatch will make enough noise to wake me. Three hours won't be much, but I can't face Turkey with no sleep.

A quick check of *Let's Go* reveals that ferries from Samos dock on the Turkish coast at the port town of Kusadasi. Troy is my primary destination, and it's north of Kusadasi about 350 kilometers, but I also want to see Ephesus. Ephesus is just a few miles inland from Kusadasi, so I'll spend the night in Kusadasi and catch the bus to Ephesus the following morning. All these logistics are worrisome in a country totally unknown to me. Now for a little sleep.

Just as I doze, the telephone rings, raises me straight out of bed with my arms and legs flailing. It takes a few seconds to realize I'm not at home in Boulder, Colorado, that I'm in Greece, on the island of Samos. The voice must be the man at the front desk, I think, but it's not. It's the travel agent. He says the schedule has changed. The ferry leaves for Turkey at one o'clock instead of three; he suggests I be at dockside by a quarter to one. I'll have to go to the dock immediately.

After I hang up the phone, I'm rattled and still trying to surface through drowsiness. How did the travel agent know to call me at Hotel Samos? I didn't even have a room when I bought my ticket. Was the call real or was I dreaming? My first chance to get a little sleep, and that damn Hermes, god of synchronicity and guide to travelers, takes it away.

I lumber to the dock, but no ferry is in sight, just a fishing boat moored sidewise at the pier, a few men milling about onboard. No one is available to ask about my passport, so I enter the coffee shop, wondering if the spooky telephone call was really meant for me.

A large group of young people surrounds a couple of tables watching MTV on a television suspended from the ceiling. As I slide my backpack off into one of the plastic chairs beside a vacant table, a brunette with an infectious smile and captivating gray eyes speaks to me. Her name is Sarah. She and her female traveling companion are both Australians, as are several others. One of the girls is from New Zealand, a Kiwi. "What state you from, mate?" asks a big Aussie with a black beard sitting beside a dark-haired heavyset woman. Their names are Tim and Jane. "Colorado," I say, and get a chorus of cheers. I'm a little dumbfounded at the commotion I've created. "Here's two of your neighbors," the Aussie adds, slapping a young man on the back. The embarrassed couple are newlyweds from Denver. The entire group has been waiting several days for the ferry to Kusadasi.

The agent finally shows, followed by scooting chairs and rustling backpacks as we scurry for the door. The agent stands at the dock calling names and returning passports, but mine hasn't been processed. I wait outside Port Authority, feeling uneasy. The ferry also concerns me. When I first came to the dock, I saw it, but thought it was a small fishing boat. I don't know how they'll get us all aboard.

I strike up a conversation with an English couple, two very thin, rustic people, both with golden hair. They live on a yacht at the marina in Kusadasi and are in Greece only to get their Turkish visas renewed. They're the friendliest people I've ever met, bubbling over with conversation and laughter. I'm captivated by their English accents and easy manner. They think the Turks are wonderful and disapprove of the fussy Greeks. He says the change in our departure time, one o'clock instead of the three, is because the Greeks are forcing the Turkish ferry to leave the dock early. The Greeks are simply being difficult.

I ask about getting my two cameras, three lenses and forty rolls of film into Turkey. *Let's Go* tells me I can't get into the country with more than one camera and five rolls of film. They scoff at the question. "I could believe it about Greeks. They're a picky, antagonistic people," they say, "but not the Turks. They're thrilled to have you in their country." I wonder if the relationship between the Greeks and Turks isn't due to the 400 years Greece was a part of the Ottoman Empire. From 1456 to 1830 the Greeks lived under Turkish suppression.

The woman says that I should be careful of what I eat and drink in Turkey. "Don't drink the water, and don't eat any fruit that you can't peel. I contracted hepatitus a while back. The Turks use human waste for fertilizer."

Finally, our passports arrive, and we board, not by walking over a large metal gangway, but by stepping from the dock directly onto the side of the boat. I feel it give a little under my weight. A car sits expectantly on deck, and I wonder how it got there, if the boat will sink under the weight. We stack our luggage on deck and walk down a short flight of stairs to the covered passenger compartment. The English couple finds seats and motions me over. We're packed in like sardines. I don't know if I can handle all this attention. My loneliness and depression have been replaced with a giddy euphoria. With the rough water we'll likely encounter, I'm concerned about seasickness.

Turkey: Ephesus I

The ferry slips away from dock, and soon we're lunging through the white-capped sea, loping along with the chattering voices and shouts of approval, when we break a large wave. I want to keep the horizon in sight but keep losing it watching Sarah. She has an easy intimacy about her that disarms me at a glance.

We survive the rocky boat ride although a couple of women are a little pale around the mouth. When I step from the side of the boat onto the dock, a Turk takes my hand to make sure the rocking boat doesn't dump me into the sea. They throw our packs from the boat into a big stack, and we scramble for them. The English couple disappear quite suddenly, and I'm disappointed because they asked me have a drink with them on their boat.

As we exit customs, two young Turks approach us. "Ephesus?" they ask. "New Zealand Pension? Seljuk?" Seljuk is the small town just outside Ephesus. Sarah says she's heard of the New Zealand Pension, and it's supposed to be great. Ten of us pile in the van, me against my better judgment. I'm afraid of becoming a tourist and forgetting my purpose for being on this journey, but I go with them anyway, quite honestly, because I can't take my eyes off Sarah.

First they take us to a bank where we exchange traveler's checks for Turkish lira, and then we're off to Seljuk. I sit at the back of the van against the window, and Sarah sits in the seat facing me, telling me about her home in Australia.

In Seljuk, the van pulls up at a nondescript building with a cinder-block fence and a wrought-iron gate that would look at home in any neighborhood in the States. Just inside the front door, we climb stairs to the second floor. I've thought about dumping this group of tourists in Seljuk, but Sarah has changed my mind. Besides, they've solved all my logistics problems. I've made up a full day of the five I lost stranded on Patmos.

Arhman, the young Turk, who drove the van, unlocks the door of one of the community bedrooms, pushes it open. As I enter, I see that it's new, white walls and ceiling, spotless linoleum floor. Three single beds butt up to the wall on the right. A fourth single bed is sidewise, flush against the left wall. The beds all have tan box springs on short-legged frames, firm mattresses with tucked-in white sheets and green blankets, the covers folded back military style, a fluffy white pillow. I can have one of these beds for 50,000 lira ($3.67) or a single room to myself for 200,000 lira ($14.68).

An Aussie walks past and throws his pack on the bed against the far wall, below the window overlooking the street. Realizing I've already lost the best bed in the room, I take the bed by the door. The two other beds are vacant. After my isolation on Patmos, I have a warm feeling about being with people.

After unpacking, I walk downstairs to the living room where the rest of the group has gathered and is being served Turkish tea in tiny glasses that look like miniature flower vases. My glass sits in a tiny circular metal saucer and comes with a miniature spoon. I ask Sarah if she thinks the water in the tea might make us sick, but she just smiles and lifts her cup to her lips.

We talk to a youngish blond woman from England named Alison, who owns the Pension with her Turkish husband, Turgay. Alison bounces her infant son on her knee. Turgay owns the New Zealand Carpet Shop just down the street. I'm stuck in the middle of the Turkish carpet industry, something I'd hoped to avoid.

After tea, Arhman asks if we'd like to go to dinner. It seems a little early, but the light wanes as we pile into the van again. Not surprisingly, Arhman stops by the carpet shop first. The carpet shop is one large room, running from alley to street. We enter through a lounge just off the kitchen where we sit around a table, and they pass out tiny cups of tea again. Beyond, down a slight incline, exotic Turkish carpets cover both the floor and walls of a larger room. Turgay, Alison's husband, introduces himself. "Don't worry about the carpets," he says. "We won't pressure you if you're not interested." He takes several people into the carpet area, turns on an overhead spotlight, and spreads carpets of fine-woven wool and silk. The golds, reds and blues sparkle in the overhead light. He quietly explains how they're woven by children.

I don't like the way they've railroaded us into the carpet shop under the pretext of taking us to dinner, but it only takes a glance from Sarah for me to join her. She's out in the middle of the floor on her hands and knees. "What do you think?" she asks, sliding her hand along the furry surface. "Aren't they luxurious?" It's as if my ex-wife just spoke to me.

Turgay explains the design, an Islamic double-prayer pattern based on the Muslim family who wove it. The large crosses in the middle tell the number and sex of their children, light outside for a girl, dark outside for a boy. The camel heads tell the family's wealth. Flowers mean good luck. The goat horn, camel feet, and scorpion are the symbols of nomads. The alternating pattern of the outside border provides religious instruction: pray five times a day, fast, once in life go to Mecca, believe in God and Mohammed as our prophet, look after poor people.

After the carpet show, Arhman leads us through dark streets to a crowded restaurant where they push three long tables together for us. We order plates of spicy-hot meatballs, stuffed tomatoes, spinach, white beans, tsatsiki, rice, tons of bread, French fries, potato salad, eggplant, a sour-cream dish that looks like mashed potatoes, a clear licorice-tasting liquor called raki (pronounced "rocky").

Turkey: Ephesus I

Before we finish eating, Arhman leaves to dress for his cousin's wedding. "I'll be right back," he says. "If you like, you can go with me." When he returns, he has changed into a dark suit and tie, looks very dashing, tall and thin, dark hair and dark skin, very European. The girls create a fuss over him. He blushes.

After dinner, Arhman walks us through the spacious but crowded streets of Seljuk with monuments and ruins lit by spotlights, glistening water spouting from fountains. We enter a huge theatre with well-dressed Turks coming and going, some with turbans, but most looking European in white shirts and dark slacks.

We go up two flights of stairs onto a balcony overlooking the stage. We've missed the ceremony, but the newly married couple is just cutting a multi-layered cake. They cut it together, four hands on a long knife, one long slice, a symbolic cut down each layer. He's dressed in a dark business suit and tie, overly long baggy pants. She's dressed in a pure-white, low-cut wedding dress offsetting her dark skin and black hair.

A live quartet blares eastern music and a vocalist warbles in Turkish. A tall gray-haired man comes out with a microphone, calls on members of the two families to dance. The two fathers come out first, perform an eastern dance where they elevate their arms from their sides, fingers snapping, and move their feet while wiggling their hips. They're followed by the two mothers and other adults, women dancing with women, men with women, kids with other kids and adults, locking arms across their partners' shoulders. Men come on stage to shower the dancers with paper money, sending kids scrambling. Others pin money on the mothers and fathers or stick it down the top of a dress or in a shirt pockets while the band plays and the man sings the same song over and over.

Sarah leans on my shoulder to shout something in my ear. Her warmth is startling, mesmerizing, a quiet hint of perfume. Slices of cake pass through the crowd and eventually reach us, a white two-layered cake with creamy frosting. I've come to believe what the English couple told me this morning. The Turks are genuinely glad we're here.

Arhman goes to pay his respects, and when he returns, asks if we'd like to leave. He wants to get out himself. He's not particularly impressed with the whole affair. He drives us back to the pension, the music ringing in our ears. I sit by Sarah, as I have all evening, but a sort of dreariness has come over me, realizing I already like her more than any woman I've met in years.

Back at the pension, Arhman builds a fire in the wood stove, and Sarah sits with me for a while before excusing herself off to bed.

20 Nov, Saturday

Turkey: Ephesus I

Early in the morning, the long warbled wail of the Muslim call to prayer seems far off and otherworldly. I fall back to sleep but finally manage to rouse myself and have breakfast downstairs. Alison serves me a boiled egg, sliced tomatoes, sliced cucumbers, jelly, butter and all the bread I can eat, plus a mandarin orange, all the time trying to pacify her fussy eighteen-month-old son, who sits in a highchair banging a spoon on his tray. When I finish breakfast, I ask Alison if she's seen Sarah and Wendy. "They've already left to see Ephesus," she says. I had hoped to see Ephesus with Sarah.

Three Aussies return from the farmer's market close by and encourage me to see it. From the pension, I walk a couple of blocks to the intersection of the main road from Kusadasi and the road north to Izmir and Troy. A hazy fog hangs in the distance. To the east, the road is blocked off and swarming with people. Seljuk is a small town, but it doesn't look it from the size of the market.

The merchants are still setting up long wood tables and arranging fruits and vegetables: onions, garlic, leeks, eggplant, artichokes, tomatoes, cabbage, lettuce, cucumbers, large sacks of carrots, turnips, hazelnuts, walnuts, almonds, peanuts, olives in huge jars, mandarin oranges, bananas, haricot, broad beans, lentils and chickpeas, potatoes. North of the crowded street, the entire block is filled with rows of sheds containing tons of fish and meat, and beyond the sheds, acres of fabric, ties, scarves, shirts, pants, dresses.

Remembering the English woman's warnings of hepatitis, I select only fruit I can peel, mandarin oranges and bananas. I would like some olives but don't trust the water they come in. Negotiating isn't possible. All the prices are marked. A kilogram (2.2 lbs) of bananas is 20,000 lira or about $1.50, more expensive than at home. The man with the bananas is dipped in wrinkles, old as Kronos, Father Time himself. He weighs the bananas on an old balance scale, juggling bronze weights and swapping bananas to get the pivot stable.

I return to my room, grab my daypack, throw in some oranges and bananas. I'm in a hurry to catch Sarah. As I go out the door, I hear a woman's voice call my name. It's Bronwyn, the Kiwi. She has her black hair pulled back in a ponytail and has on a black sweat suit. "Mind if I tag along?" she asks.

Arhman volunteers to take us to the ruins in the van. After a short ride, he drops us off outside the gate at a small tourist shop selling handmade statues and ancient coins. We each buy a guidebook and enter the site. "He's dropped us off at the exit," she says. She reads a little in her guidebook, then turns to me again. "Starting here will actually work better. This used to be the main entrance to the city, the Magnesia Gate. If we'd entered at the main tourist entrance, we would have been in the middle of the ruins."

In ancient times, the entire western coast of Turkey was not Turkish but

Turkey: Ephesus I

Greek. Even though Ephesus was founded in Mycenaean times, the Ephesus at this site has nothing to do with the Mycenaeans. Originally, Ephesus was closer to Seljuk and was moved here in 299 BC by the Roman emperor Lysimachus, a successor of Alexander the Great. The residents of the original Ephesus didn't want to move, so Lysimachus cutoff the water supply into the old city. This new Ephesus was coastal, built along an east-west road running between two mountains. The ruins look chiseled into the crease between the hillsides. The sea eclipsed the western edge of the city.

I remember thinking the night before I left Corinth, back on the 27th of October, almost a month ago, about Paul's voyage to Ephesus from Corinth. He had his head shorn and had taken a vow. He came with Aquila and Priscilla, his two friends from Corinth. He left them here to start a Christian church and then traveled on to Antioch. They came in 51 AD, and this was the end of the first of Paul's three missionary journeys to Asia Minor and Greece. Christianity wasn't spread among the Jews. Paul, Andrew and John spread it among the Greeks, and just as the ancient Greeks gave us democracy, so Greece became the gateway through which Christianity came to western civilization. I would imagine the Greeks were easily taken with his words of a loving, forgiving God after centuries of the war-loving gods of Homer, their bickering interference in human affairs.

Paul also had been in Ephesus earlier, before 51 AD. Five years after Jesus was crucified, around 35 AD, the Christians were expelled from Jerusalem, and Paul, John, the Virgin Mary, and Mary Magdalene came to Ephesus to live. At that time, Ephesus was a growing metropolis of marble and stone. They may have entered the city here, at Magnesia Gate.

Bronwyn and I enter the ruins from the east, along what was, centuries ago, the Sacred Way. The two mountains, Mt. Pion to our left and Mt. Koressos to the right, are covered with rocks, brown grass and bushes. They look damp under the heavy cloud cover and drizzle. When Lysimachus founded the city, he built a stone wall around it. Many of the huge stones still stand. The Magnesia Gate was an arched ceremonial one with three entrances and a tall rectangular tower on each side. Beside the gate are the ruins of the Eastern Gymnasium, which was an education and sports complex. To our left, on the flat between the mountains, is the State Agora, not a marketplace but a semi-sacred area for political and religious meetings, which is now only a flat field pocked with marble blocks. It's much larger than a football field, 160 meters by 65 meters. The Varius Baths are to our right, dug into the side of Mt. Koressos. They were divided into rooms named for the temperature of the water, the frigidarium (the cold room), the tepidarium (the warm room), and the caldarium (the hot room).

Turkey: Ephesus I

Ephesus was a plumbed city with several fountains, wells and cisterns. Water came from the four directions. Springs near Kusadasi provided water from the west through stone-block ducts; a spring to the north on the road to Smyrna (now Izmir) brought water by open canal; from the east, the source was a spring in Sirince, a small village in the mountains; and from the south, the Marnas Spring on the road to Aydin.

Just beyond the baths is the Odeon, an indoor theatre made of stone that seated 1,400, carved into the side of Mt. Koressos. All the seats are now exposed to the elements. The Odeon was originally used for state concerts and meetings of the assembly of the three hundred Bouleutes, the legislative council. Remnants of the exterior walls and the huge stone entryways are all that remain of the exterior.

Next to the Odeon is the Prytaneion, where a distinguished group of citizens kept the city's eternal flame. It burned night and day for centuries in what was known as Hestia's Sacred Hearth. Hestia is the Greek goddess of the hearth, the guardian of its fire, and the patroness of household activities, the home, family, and community. At the entrance to the Prytaneion stands the nude image of Hermes, carved into the face of a marble slab, his hand holding the horns of a ram. Hermes is always depicted with winged feet and winged cap. In this relief, his cap and face have been chipped and his penis and testicles chiseled away. Christians have disfigured many of the ancient sculptures throughout Greece.

We've now reached the far side of the agora, standing at the temple of Domitian, but we're still not halfway through the site. Domitian was the Roman emperor who was in power when St. John lived in Ephesus. Domitian was hell on Christians. He was the one who had St. John brought to Rome, tortured and exiled to Patmos. He was hell on a lot of people. One of his own servants assassinated him. The pediment of his temple depicted a scene from *The Odyssey* in which Odysseus and his men poked out the eye of the Cyclops Polyphemus.

The marble columns and granite stones strewn about are so thick they hardly leave a path to walk. The two remaining columns tower above, forming the entrance of the temple. Tall figures carved into the top of each column peer down upon us.

Bronwyn has run into Sarah and Wendy. They've been seeing Ephesus from the opposite direction. I've been wondering all day how I'd feel about Sarah when I saw her again. The four of us sit at the parapet in front of the temple built into the foot of Mt. Pion. All agree this is the most impressive archaeological site we've seen, much larger than anything in Greece. Sarah and Wendy have

Turkey: Ephesus I

decided to go to Istanbul and are debating when to leave.

"Are you interested in going to Istanbul, David?" Sarah asks.

I'm startled by the question. And the strangest thought occurs to me. Perhaps my reaction is because I've just been thinking about Odysseys, but it's as if I've just heard the voice of a Siren. She's calling me away from the purpose of my journey. So far, I've not let anything take me from my planned course. Even Pat and Marlene, the mother and daughter I met at Delphi, couldn't sway me. And now this. I ask if they'll be going to Troy. "We won't have time," Sarah says. I remember the words of Homer about Odysseus' trial at hearing the Siren's song:

> On the way, they passed the shores of the Siren's island. But Circe had warned him of their powers of persuasion and told him if he wished to listen to them sing, his crew must seal their ears with beeswax and lash him to the mast of his ship. This they did, and when they sailed past their green clover-sweet shore, white with the bleached bones of their victims, he heard the Siren's song and begged his crew to release him, but they only cinched him tighter. Thus Odysseus escaped the lure of the Sirens.

I can't speak at first, then swallow, look away from her. "I can't," I say. "I've got an itinerary and a problem I'm trying to solve. Istanbul isn't on my agenda." The words come with great difficulty.

We leave the two of them, me still reeling at the unimaginable mistake I've just made, the four of us agreeing to have dinner together this evening. I keep looking back at Sarah, reluctant to let her go. Bronwyn and I continue down Curetes Street, which is paved with large flat slabs of marble, stopping now and then to take pictures.

Just past the Trajan Fountain, we leave the ancient road and walk between the remains of walls leading up the side of the mountain. "What's this?" I ask. Bronwyn has been reading to me all the time we've been seeing ruins. She has such a soft voice and easy manner.

"Is this your first visit to a brothel," she asks with a smile.

"This was a brothel?" I ask, a little wide-eyed.

"Yes. All these rooms," she says. "Aphrodite did have her followers."

We exit the brothel into the adjoining Scholastikia Baths and the lavatory. The baths are made to the same configuration as the Varius Baths we saw earlier, a frigidarium, tepidarium, caldarium. The toilet is marble, walls lined with benches, holes cut in the top like gigantic key slots for human waste to fall through.

Bronwyn asks, "Who was Priapos?" Priapos is a Phrygian god of fertility and the son of Aphrodite. I look over Bronwyn's shoulder at her guidebook. She's wondering about the picture of his statue. His protruding erect phallus is as long as he is tall. "Looks like a tribute to wishful thinking," I say. She laughs and walks away.

We step out of the lavatory onto a wide north-south road, paved with marble, and appropriately named Marble Road. At the south end, where the street we were on and Marble Road intersect, stands the tallest structure at Ephesus, the Celsus Library. Since the library was built from 114-117 AD, it was not here when John, Paul and Mary were here. Twelve thousand scrolls were kept inside.[264] It is now a standing tribute to the literary interests of the Ephesians in the 2nd Century AD. All that remains of the library is the intricately carved facade, which is two stories high and sixty feet wide.

Bronwyn and I eat lunch on a big group of stones on a hill lining the courtyard outside the library. Tourists mill about below us. I open my daypack and pull out a banana. She sits next to me, eating a sandwich. I watch as she loads a new roll of film, then reads to me from her guidebook, wisps of hair falling about her face. Her hands are smooth and nimble. She's a sculptor and a weaver.

After lunch, we walk north from the library along Marble Road. We locate the walkway that in antiquity led to the brothel. Only one footprint remains of the series that was chiseled into the marble. Then we walk on, to a large theatre off to the right at the western foot of Mt. Koressos. This is the most famous of all the ruins at Ephesus. St. Paul preached in Ephesus and almost lost his life because of it. Ephesus was the city of Artemis, and the powerful and influential jeweler, Demetrius, manufactured her statue, which he sold all over the city. He saw Paul as a threat to his income. This theatre was used for gatherings of the citizens, as well as theatrical performances. During one such large meeting of the citizens, Demetrius worked the crowd up against Paul, the crowd shouting, "Great is Artemis Ephesia," obviously hurt and angry over his attacks on her. The city security official rescued Paul, admonishing the crowd to file their complaints against him through official channels. Artemis was the heart and soul of Ephesus. Paul's view that Artemis was a devil goddess would not have gone over well.

By the stadium, Bronwyn and I turn west off Marble Road onto Harbor Street, which runs west toward Kusadasi. Two thousand years ago, the sea came right to the very edge of Ephesus, at the end of Harbor Street. Dignitaries docked and entered the city there. Harbor Street was a marble walkway lined with towering columns, covered porticos and fifty oil-fueled lamps. Ephesus, along with Rome and Antioch, was one of the few lit cities of antiquity.[265] Most of the columns along Harbor Street are gone now, the marble block pavement vanishing into tall weeds.

Bronwyn and I turn north off Harbor Street to the ruins of the Church of the Virgin Mary. This is the original site of the home where Paul, John, Mary, and Mary Magdalene stayed when they first came to Ephesus. The Ecumenical Council of 431 AD met here to argue whether Mary was the mother of Jesus, the Son of God, or Jesus, a mortal man.[266]But the authorities have blocked the road north, and we can only see it off in the distance. Little remains of the Church today, only a portion of a stone circular wall and several tall marble columns with nothing to support.

We walk out the main entrance, along the asphalt road lined with tourist shops, and start the three-kilometer walk back to Seljuk. Before we come to the highway, off to the right we see the depression of an ancient stadium. During Roman times, Christians were killed by wild animals inside this stadium to the roar of the crowd. In one such episode, Paul was fed to the lions but escaped when the lion recognized Paul from a previous encounter. Paul had baptized the lion.[267]

Past the stadium at an unpopulated intersection, a gray Mercedes stops and the man inside asks if we want a ride back to Seljuk. We tell him no several times, but he shuts off the motor and gets out, leaving the car in the middle of the intersection as he walks toward us. He's a prosperous-looking Turk wearing slacks and a sports jacket. He's anxious to know where we're from. But we still won't accept a ride from him. He's a businessman and has an office just beside the Tourist Information Office at the edge of Seljuk. He asks us to stop in for a visit when we get back to town if we would like to know about Turkish culture.

Bronwyn and I take the road east, paralleling the highway toward Seljuk, and walk to the Cave of the Seven Sleepers. According to a local legend, sometime around 250 AD, seven young Christians sought refuge in the cave. They fell into an eternal sleep. An earthquake woke them, to their astonishment, two hundred years later. When they finally died, they were buried here. A church was built over the site.[268] The ruins of the church are still visible, imbedded into the northern side of Mt. Koressos.

This is also the site where Mary Magdalene was buried. According to many biblical scholars, Mary Magdalene was the closest to Jesus of any of the disciples. She was at the crucifixion, and the first to witness the empty cave and see Jesus following his resurrection. In 1896 in Cairo, a 1st Century manuscript surfaced containing *The Gospel of Mary* (Magdalene), which is included as a part of *The Nag Hamada Library*.[269] In her gospel, Mary Magdalene was taught by Jesus to understand the nature of his resurrection. *The Library* also contains the *Gospel of Philip,* which alludes to Jesus kissing Mary Magdalene on the mouth. Jesus' affection for her offended the other disciples and provoked jealousy.[270] Mary Magdalene has been wrongly painted by the church as a prostitute and has been the victim of a smear campaign lasting two millennia.

Bronwyn pokes me in the ribs, motions for me to follow. We have a long walk back to Seljuk.

When we reenter the outskirts of town, the man in the Mercedes is waiting at the side of the street. He still wants to visit with us. I'm resistant, but Bronwyn wants to go. Sure enough, he owns a small carpet shop, a narrow affair with no exit at the rear, sort of a rectangular cave lined with carpets. We sit on benches covered with carpets, rolls of carpets standing around us. No pressure here.

An ultra-thin young man enters with a tray of tea. Our host lights a cigarette. He's college-educated, a teacher. "There is no money in teaching in Turkey," he says, "so I run a carpet shop." His family is from eastern Turkey, where the war with the Kurds currently rages. They live where Noah's Ark came aground. "Explorers recently found it in a glacier but lost it again when the snows came," he says. He then goes on to tell us about the traditional way of building homes in Turkey. They are made with two floors, the family living on the top floor with the bottom floor for the animals: goats, sheep, chickens, pigs, etc. Heat from the animals rises and keeps the home warm. He draws a picture for us as he talks. We talk about the Soviet Union disintegrating, the high unemployment rate in Turkey, me losing my job in aerospace. Three things he doesn't like, he says: fundamentalism, nationalism and egotism.

And I don't like salesmen.

As we leave, he tells us that if we want to know more about Turkish culture, we should visit him again. He will tell us how the carpets are made, the dyes, the weaves. He asks where we're staying, and I lie to him, say that I'm not sure of the name of the pension. Then he lectures me, says that Turks are straightforward and that I'm not being straight with him.

Just at dusk, Bronwyn and I go out to dinner. Another man joins us, a redheaded guy named Richard from Cincinnati. We haven't seen Sarah and Wendy since we talked to them at Ephesus even though they promised to have dinner with us. During dinner, Richard raises a fuss over his dinner, calls the waiter over. He doesn't like his Turkish pizza.

Just as we arrive back at the pension, Sarah and Wendy come down the stairs with their backpacks. To my dismay, they're on their way to the otogar (bus station) to catch the night bus to Istanbul. As they walk away into the dark, I call after her. "Sarah, I didn't know you were leaving so soon. I had hoped to talk to you again." She takes a few steps toward me. "I know," she says. "I'd hoped to also. But maybe we'll meet again. We should be back in Seljuk in a few days. Get my address from Tim and Jane. Write to me." I wonder how much the airfare is to Australia.

21 Nov, Saturday

I wake late and have breakfast downstairs again with Alison serving me while playing with her little boy. She changes his wet diaper. The kitchen and living room are together in one large area, and several people have congregated after eating. Two young men I've not noticed before have joined our group. They've taken the single room with the big bed. One of them is sullen and sits quietly in the corner of the sofa. The other is flighty, floating about the room like a butterfly, talking about the English rock star, Cyndi Lauper. I make a comment about her because she was one of my daughter's favorites, and the guy cruises over in front of me to talk, stands before me to monopolize my attention. His buddy scowls, glares at me. It finally hits me. These two men are homosexuals.

★

I walk north from the pension to the intersection of the main roads that run west toward the coast and north to Izmir. I walk west past the edge of town to a little-used side road beside the freeway. On the left and right, rows of tall eucalyptus trees run far into the distance blocking the midday sun and creating an infinitely long tunnel of shadow.

Just beyond the last few buildings, I come to the ruins of the temple of Artemis, the goddess who raised Patmos from the sea and who was the heart and soul of Ephesus. The ruins are off to the right of the road in a flat field. Only a scattering of stones remain. The temple was one of the seven wonders of the ancient world. It stood at the edge of the sea, but since then, the entire seaport from here all the way to Kusadasi has filled with alluvial deposits from the Kucuk Menderes River, which runs just north of Seljuk. The coast has receded eight kilometers west in the last two thousand years.

According to mythology, in Mycenaean times, three Greek migrations to this part of the western coast of Asia Minor occurred. The first came from Crete around 1400 BC when Miletus fled from king Minos. He settled just south of here where he took over a Carian city and renamed it for himself.[271] The city of Miletus is still there today, where the Maeander River (now called the Menderes) empties into the Aegean. The most ancient relics found here at the temple of Artemis come from the hill overlooking this site, a Mycenaean grave that has been dated to the 14th Century BC.[272] The name "Ephesus" comes from the time of Heracles and Theseus. The sanctuary of Ephesian Artemis is said to have been named for Ephesos, the son of the river Kayster.[273]

The second wave of Mycenaeans came around 1220 BC with Manto, the daughter of the Theban seer Teiresias. Here's where I once again pick up her trail. I remember, when I left Delphi back on December 15th, thinking of Manto's departure for Asia Minor and that our departures were separated by 3200 years. This is the original site of Ephesus before Lysimachus moved it to the location I visited yesterday. Since Ephesus already existed at the time, Manto might have docked here first, then moved a few kilometers to the northwest and founded Colophon.

St. John spent some time here at the temple even though he didn't care much for Artemis. He called her a "demon" and a "deceiver of this great multitude."[274] The Artemis of Asia Minor is skewed somewhat from the one born on Delos, who is the daughter of Zeus and sister of Apollo, a virgin huntress. On Asia Minor, Artemis is a merger of that Greek goddess and the great Mother Goddess, Cybele, the virgin mother of all life, who was worshipped from Scandinavia throughout Asia Minor and even into Egypt and Arabia. She dates back to 7000 BC. This Neolithic Artemis was worshipped by some as a meteorite that fell to earth in the shape of a woman. The meteorite is mentioned in the New Testament.[275]

The temple of Artemis was the largest structure ever built of marble. It was the size of a football field and six stories high, a forest of columns, 127 in all, and built over a foundation of leather-covered coal. It was destroyed and rebuilt seven times.[276] St. John was one of the destroyers. During his first visit to Ephesus, coming here by way of Miletus, John decided to visit the temple "... for perhaps if we are seen there, the servants of the Lord will be found there also." Once inside the temple, he called upon God to destroy it:

> ...the alter of Artemis split into many pieces, and all the offerings laid up in the temple suddenly fell to the floor and its goodness was broken, and so were more than seven images: and half the temple fell down, so that the priest was killed at one stroke as the roof came down.[277]

Later, John resurrected the priest as another show of God's power, showing a good deal more mercy than he had with Cynops on Patmos. The priest was converted and remained with John thereafter.

Little of the temple remains today. The lone semblance of a column has been pieced together from misfit sections, and re-erected among scattered stones at a pond's edge, where ducks float on the dark mirror surface. The remains of the temple were scavenged to build the Basilica of St. John, which sits on the side of Ayasulk Tepesi, the hill overlooking the temple. I can see part of the basilica from where I stand and above it, the Seljuk Castle. This Byzantine citadel, on the top of the hill, casts a medieval, ghostly, presence over the entire landscape.

★

Mid afternoon, I walk north past the main intersection in Seljuk along the road toward Troy, past the carpet shop, along a side street, and up Ayasoluk Hill. Shortly, I'm at the ruins of the Basilica of St. John. Before I get to the site, I encounter some unprotected ruins swarming with kids. I take one picture with the kids and would like another without them, but they scurry to reappear in front of me anyway, posed with gigantic smiles.

An ancient story tells of St. John not dying but being taken directly into heaven, reminiscent of the death of Oedipus and what my family anticipated for my own grandparents. The other eleven apostles were murdered. Out of the twelve apostles, John alone lived over one hundred years.[278] But some believe John died a natural death and was buried here at the Basilica. According to this story, John had a premonition of his own death. He left Ephesus at dawn, walked past the cave where Mary Magdalene was or would soon be buried, past the temple of Artemis, which he had destroyed, and came to this hillside.

> Having looked for the last time on his beloved city of Ephesus, relieved now of all care, he told his disciples to dig a grave in the shape of a cross, and laid his cloak in it. Then, entering it, he lay down and told his disciples to cover him with soil up to the knees. They, weeping, embraced their master for the last time. John then gave them his blessing and told them to cover him up to the chest, first with a white shroud and then with earth. As the sun rose, John commended his sanctified soul into the hands of his beloved Lord.[279]

Since the death of John, his gravesite has prompted several structures to be built here. In the 4th Century, a basilica with a wood roof was built over his grave, followed by a church in the 6th Century, and fortification walls after attacks by Arabs in the 7th and 8th centuries. Dust from his grave was thought to have medicinal powers, and the sick and injured traveled from far away to be healed.

I enter the site through the towering Pursuit Gate, an arched doorway in the fortification wall, and walk along a marble path that opens into a courtyard. What strikes me immediately is the forest of reconstructed doorways, some square, some arched, some with red-slab brick walls standing about them, some standing alone. In the center of the site, around the burial place, bright marble columns, now reduced to purposelessness, jut up from ground level and stand stark against the blue sky. At the far side of the ruins, I walk among large chunks of marble populating a grassy slope leading to the top of the mountain and the Seljuk castle and look back over the top of the basilica, stare down into the roofless rooms.

The sun is low on the horizon now and casts a glow over all the ruins, as if the entire landscape has been dipped in gold. The town of Seljuk lies to the east below me, the whitewashed buildings turning orange in the muted light. The few visitors mill about; two men in black suits talk softly at the edge of the steep slope. A hushed sacredness comes to the site.

Something is bothering me. I say a quiet prayer, walk back toward the entrance, and sit on a marble slab to try to understand what's going on with me. Fir trees, thick with the chatter of finches, cast a shadow across the ruins. A stone walkway winds off to the left and right. The empty rectangular door frames standing alone seem to be saying something. I felt something symbolic every time I passed through one, as if it was an open invitation. But to what? Memories of my daughter as a child flood to the surface.

Every spring my daughter used to come to me, take my hand in her little hand, lead me into the living room in front of the TV. "Sit!" she'd command, as if I were the old canine pet. She'd climb into my lap, my chin behind her head, her ponytail swishing back and forth across my nose. Year after year, spring after spring, we performed the ritual, watching the "Wizard of Oz" together, my arms around that beautiful little golden-haired goddess. Perhaps I'm finally beginning to understand what those times were all about. In the movie, Dorothy also disappeared. Dorothy and her friends form a quaternion: Dorothy the real girl, and the Tin Man, Cowardly Lion, and Scarecrow her imaginary friends. My daughter and I formed a quaternion. She was Dorothy, and I represented the three imaginary companions. That movie was like those doorways, an open invitation to disappear, an invitation she accepted a few years later.

I'm reminded of Artemis as a child of nine:

>...sitting on her father's [Zeus] knees—still a little maid—she spake these words to her sire: "Give me to keep my maidenhood, Father, for ever: and give me to be of many names... And give me arrows and a bow... give me to be the Bringer of Light and give me to gird me in a tunic with embroidered border reaching to the knee... And give me sixty daughters of Oceanus for my choir... and give me for handmaidens twenty nymphs of Amnisus who shall tend well my buskins... give to me all mountains...[280]

Turkey: Ephesus I

Give me, give me... What did my daughter want? I've never understood.

On the other side of the stone walkway is a patch of ice plant and beyond, a marble walkway, rose bushes, two small pine trees, and the ruins of the church itself, the fortress standing menacingly at the top of the hill. High in the air above the fortress, a large flock of dark birds flies in a swarming circle. Their sharp screeches pierce the quiet whisper of city noise as the wraiths storm the skies in some rude-sounding flock ritual. The scattered, individual cries coalesce into a chorus emanating from the heavens. Above the fortress walls, a lone red flag with the yellow crescent and single star, the flag of Turkey, flaps in a light breeze.

The sun is set, its last full rays glowing off the ruins, casting tree shadows across my shoulders.

★

During the evening, I have dinner again with Bronwyn and Richard. She's bubbling over about her fourteen-kilometer hike up the mountain to the east to the small town of Sirince. I'm lost in thoughts of Sarah and planning tomorrow's visit to the Home of the Virgin Mary. The day after tomorrow, I'll take the bus to Troy. I really cannot delay my travel plans for the possibility of Sarah returning.

22 Nov, Monday

Mid-morning, I walk Bronwyn to the otogar. She's going south to Miletus, and I'm jealous for two reasons. First, I'll not get to see Miletus because tomorrow I'm going north. But my worst jealousy is that she's leaving with Richard, the dork from Cincinnati.

When we get to the otogar, a man approaches them to try to get Richard to use his company's bus. The man is followed by six other young Turks from competing bus companies. An argument ensues between Richard and one of the hawkers, who's very aggressive. Richard stands provocatively in front of the man, throws out his chest and tells him how obnoxious he is, not realizing his own foolishness. The hawkers argue among themselves for several minutes, Richard purposely pumping them up.

Eventually, he and Bronwyn walk away from all of them to the main intersection and buy tickets for the first bus south, which costs more than any of the hawkers' buses. Bronwyn looks disillusioned. Richard seems a little shocked himself. They don't even know for sure where the bus is going. I give Bronwyn a hug and watch the two of them step aboard. I've spent more time with her than anyone since Letizia in Corinth, and I hate to see her leave with Richard.

★

Turkey: Ephesus I

In the early afternoon, I walk to the town square to get a taxi. I negotiate with a likable young man, and shortly we're on our way, past the gate where Bronwyn and I entered the ruins of Ephesus, up Mt. Pion on a winding road, and through pine-covered hills overlooking the farm-checkered valley created when the Kucuk Menderes River filled the bay with alluvial deposits. I see the Aegean in the distance. We enter a thick forest and, shortly, the site of the home of the Virgin Mary.

He stops at the entrance and tells me I have thirty minutes, then walks over to a group of men sitting at a picnic table under the shade of a tree. I walk along a tree-shrouded path, past the ruins of a cistern. At the side of the walkway stands a full-size bronze statue of Mary, a beautiful young woman with a hooded cape draped about her shoulders. Her long-flowing skirt covers all but her toes. She wears a crown, arms at her sides, with palms forward in welcome, head tilted slightly downward, as if in submission. Her expression is solemn, contemplative.

The biggest difference between Greek Orthodox Christianity and the Catholics is the perception of Mary, the mother of Jesus. Greek Orthodox believe she was a normal woman and mother; however, Catholics believe she was immaculately conceived, and a perpetual virgin. Prior to her birth, her parents, Joachim and Anna, were distressed that they had no children.[281] Joachim was upset and went into the desert to fast for forty days. Anna stayed home and sang dirges of woe. But an angel came to her, saying:

> "Anna, Anna, the Lord God heard your prayer, and you will conceive and give birth, and your offspring shall be spoken of in the whole inhabited world." Anna said, "As the Lord my God lives, if I give birth, whether male or female, I will present it as a gift to the Lord my God, and it shall be a ministering servant to him all the days of its life."[282]

When Mary was three, Anna kept her promise to God and gave up her child to the temple. Mary was raised there until the age of twelve, when an angel let it be known that Joseph had been chosen by God, and that Mary was to be his ward. Joseph protested, "I have sons, and I am an old man, but she is a young maiden—lest I be a laughing stock to the children of Israel."[283]

Sometime between the age of twelve and seventeen,[284] Mary conceived while Joseph was away building houses. When he returned and found her six months pregnant, he was afraid for his own safety because he had received her as a virgin, and yet he hadn't protected her. And he was concerned for her safety because, if he told the priests of her pregnancy, they might kill her. But an angel

294

of God appeared to him in a dream and told him that the baby was conceived of the Holy Spirit. He took her to the priests and told them about his dream and that she was pregnant. But they were not convinced and tested them both, making them drink "water of the Lord's testing"[285] and sent them into the desert, from which they returned whole, and thus, redeemed.

Muslims also revere Mary and consider Jesus a prophet. The Koran has an interesting description of Mary's delivery:

> And the pangs of childbirth drove her unto the trunk of the palm-tree. She said: Oh, would that I had died ere this and had become a thing of naught, forgotten! The (one) cried unto her from below her, saying: Grieve not! Thy Lord hath placed a rivulet beneath thee, and shake the trunk of the palm-tree toward thee, thou wilt cause ripe dates to fall upon thee.[286]

This description of the birth of Jesus, with Mary's arms wrapped around a palm tree, is reminiscent of the birth of Apollo, the son of Zeus, on the island of Delos.[287]

I walk past the dark bronze statue, through the shade of tall oak trees, and into the bright sunlight in front of a small brick home with a flat roof. Sunlight through fall leaves casts a golden glow about the building. A tall, arched doorway stands empty and dark before me.

Thirty-three years following his birth, Jesus was crucified by the Romans at the request of the Jews, and Jesus put His mother in the care of John. John brought her with him to Ephesus, and years later, during her dotage, she lived somewhere on Mt. Pion. No one knew exactly where she lived, until it was revealed in a dream to a German nun named Catherine Emmerich. She had received the stigmata, the wounds of Christ on the cross. Although she had never left her hometown in Germany, during her dream, specific directions to Mary's home were revealed to her. The dream was taken seriously and the search on Mt. Pion began in 1891. Archeologists finally located the foundation and parts of the walls. Coal found during excavations has been dated to the 1st Century.[288] The controversy over whether this was in fact the Virgin's home was put to rest in 1961 when Pope John XXIII designated it a place of pilgrimage. Pope Paul VI visited the site in 1967 and Pope John Paul II in 1979.

I step through the doorway, into a small room, the darkness broken by the light of many candles on wood tables against the walls. I walk through another arch leading to a vaulted vestibule with a stone apse on the far wall. A one-hundred-year old statue of the Virgin, surrounded by red roses, is inset within the apse. At her feet stands a small statue of Jesus on the cross, its size a rather blatant reminder that this chapel is for His mother. A red and gold carpet covers a kneeling platform before the apse.

A connection exists between Mary of Catholicism and the quaternions of both mathematics and Greek mythology. Mary is the "real" or earthly element of the quarternion, and the three "imaginary," heavenly, components are the Father, the Son, and the Holy Ghost.[289]

Through the centuries following the Crucifixion, many of the devout have seen apparitions of various Christian figures, but since the 11th Century, around the time the Monastery of St. John was built on Patmos, apparitions of the Virgin have predominated. In the last two centuries, the sightings became public, and in some cases continued over months or even years.[290]The apparitions that appeared at Medjugorje, Yugoslavia promised retribution for the ills of mankind, and presaged the war that has wracked that country since the fall of the Iron Curtain. A recurring theme of these sightings is that "an individual's sins are bound up with, and are symptomatic of, the sins of the community."[291]This also was true of the plight of Oedipus at Thebes on the day of his downfall, when the priests, elders and children came to him because the city was being consumed by a plague. An old priest describes the plague of Thebes:

> For the city, as you yourself see, is now too sorely vexed and can no more lift her head from beneath the angry waves of death. A blight is on her in the fruitful blossoms of the land, in the herds among the pastures, in the barren pangs of women.[292]

The "blight" of which the priest spoke was the plague caused by Oedipus himself, because he had unknowingly killed his father years before.

In many of the apparitions, Mary offers a solution to the problems of the community. One such solution is the request for the establishment of a shrine,[293] such as the chapel built at the grotto in Lourdes, France, where the Holy Virgin made the request of Bernadette Soubirous.[294] In Greek mythology, Delphi made several similar requests, such as that in response to Theras of the island of Thera (Santorini), when all of his children were dying. Similarly, Orestes erected the temple of Artemis on Patmos to rid himself of the madness caused by the Furies during the years following the murder of his mother.

I leave the apse, walk though another arched doorway to the right, and into a small room known as "The Bedroom," which contains an apsidal niche where Muslims pray.[295] The niche contains a beautiful painting of Mary, her creamy complexion accented by black hair, black eyebrows and red lips. Her face is full and unwrinkled, but mature, eyes cast downward. Before the painting are two vases, one with purple asters, the other with yellow and pink carnations.

I exit the building into bright sunlight.

Mary is not always perceived as a loving, problem-solving mother. On a personal level, Mary is seen as a tender and concerned mother, who calls her children away from the brink of disaster and offers safety and comfort under her sheltering mantle. On a social level, however, Mary is presented as the leader of a mighty army of spiritual warriors ready to do battle with the forces of evil. These two images of Mary, set in the context of the last times the Apocalypse, have very frequently led to a militant Marian ideology united with conservative political forces.[296]

This image of Mary reminds me of "gray-eyed Athena, weariless leader of armies, dreaded and mighty goddess, who stirs men to battle and is delighted by the clash of arms."[297] In several instances, the apparitions and seers of the Virgin have been exploited for political gain,[298] just as has Jesus in the visions of John. In Revelations, Jesus is portrayed as a warrior draped in blood-soaked raiment, leading the troops in a rout of the forces of evil. While he was here on earth, Jesus had no interest in war-loving, power-driven causes. It's as if this image of a war-loving mother and father is imbedded within us and becomes superimposed on all our religious images.

★

In the evening I have dinner with Tim and Jane, the Aussie couple, and a young man from Kenya named Alan. Alan has been traveling for fifteen years. He's smallish, fit, looks young but must be at least thirty-five, friendly, but a little unorthodox. I'm not sure why, but he scares me. Perhaps it's because I see some of myself in him, something dark, hidden. The thought of staying on the road for fifteen years is terrifying. I'm afraid I might end up doing that. This voyage I'm on has been the most invigorating time of my life.

During the fifteen years he's been on the road, he has called his mother every two weeks to get updated on world news, which countries are safe to enter, which are not, where the conflicts are. He sends her all his journals. He's written everyday for fifteen years. He also pastes his snapshots into his journal.

At dinner, I mention that I'm a big coward while traveling, that I experience a lot of fear every time I change locations. He laughs. At first I think he's making fun of me, but then realize I've touched on his experience as well. "I've never gotten over it," he says, smiling at me. "I'm always afraid, but I don't let that stop me. You develop a sixth sense, learn what real trouble is about when you're on the road alone."

He's financed all his trips by working illegally. He goes into a country with no money, takes a menial job, and gets a second job as a professional. He lives on the money from the menial job and banks the money from the professional job. After he has accumulated enough money to see the country, he quits both jobs and travels. When he's broke, he moves on. He's been in many countries, some of which no longer exist. He brings nothing into the country and takes nothing from it. He's an English teacher and a banker by avocation, a traveler by profession. He doesn't like working illegally and wants all countries to recognize traveling as a profession, to legalize travelers working in foreign countries.

★

I have a new roommate tonight. Her name is Janice. She's Canadian, but this fall she'll attend the University of Houston to work on her PhD. She has blond hair and delicate hands, baby-blue eyes. Very attractive, soft-spoken.

I hear a roll of thunder. I've wondered when Zeus would rear his ugly head again. I'm concerned about traveling tomorrow, and this evening, when I asked Alison about the weather forecast, she told me, "Don't worry. The weather is always bad at Troy."

CHAPTER 15: Turkey: Troy.

I leave my backpack at the pension with Arhman and take only my daypack with toilet articles, a change of underclothes, my black sweater and hiking jacket, mandarin oranges, and my camera. Catching the bus to Izmir is a breeze. A large statue of Artemis, which is at least three times my height, stands at the side of the highway. Large globular nodules cover Artemis' midriff. The nodules have caused a controversy argued through the centuries. Some claim they are breasts, others, myself among them, that they are bulls' testicles, a symbol of fertility. The shape is a dead giveaway. I stand at the edge of the road under this statue of Artemis until a bus comes by. I flag it down.

Halfway to Izmir, the rain starts. A dismal, overcast day. Water stands in the streets and glistens on cars. Out my bus window, I see a herd of goats wandering a field of brown cotton stalks. Little tufts of cotton linger in the open bolls. The Turkish buses are even nicer than those in Greece, but they permit smoking. When someone next to me lights up, I suffocate.

The city of Izmir spreads along the shore of the deeply indented gulf, crisscrossed by freeways, more modern than any city I've seen on my journey. St. Paul and St. John were both here. It was called Smyrna then, and they started one of the seven Christian churches of Asia here. Not far inside the city, the bus exits the freeway, and, at a roundabout outside the otogar, we're immediately caught in a traffic jam of major proportions. After an interminable trial with clogged traffic, we break free and are on our way to the terminal.

I mill among the acres of buses, trying to figure out which one goes to Canakkale, the small town north of Troy where I hope to spend the night. A young man walks up to me. I say "Canakkale," and he motions for me to follow him, takes me to a shed covering rows of huge buses, where another man makes a telephone call, and shortly a third man arrives to walk me through the hordes of people to the ticket counter. The ticket agent tells me 70,000 lira, and I try to negotiate with him as my guidebook says I should, but he won't budge. Instead, he's offended, and after I purchase my ticket, he will no longer talk to me. The man next to him takes pity on me, tells me my bus number and where to catch it, that it will leave at 12:30.

I stand with a crowd, loud-talking Turks, many in suits, some in leather jackets, women in head rags and long dresses. I'm still shaken from the ticket agent's reaction. When I try to get on the bus, the other passengers stop me. A man checks my ticket and says, "Change bus." "No," I tell him, "I paid for a ride on this bus and I'm getting on." After witnessing Bronwyn and Richard's difficulties yesterday, I'm certain these people are simply trying to get me to use another bus line. I try to get on again, but a woman grabs my shirt and pulls me off. Finally, a man shows me with arm motions that this bus will pull out and another will take its place. The new bus will go to Canakkale. They're all trying to help, and of course I'm like Richard from Cincinnati yesterday, arrogant, antagonistic, and determined to have things my way, the wrong way.

When the new bus pulls into the space, it has a big sign on the front "Truva" (Troy) and below it "Canakkale." No one tries to stop me from getting on the new bus, but I have difficulty finding my seat. A young Turkish woman notices my confusion and speaks to me in broken English. I thank her, and she smiles like I've never been smiled at before. It's an exotic smile, beautiful, dark, mysterious. She sits a couple of seats away. Romantic fantasies combust but drift gradually from dreams of love to confrontation with a Turkish man. I imagine him to be full of hatred over my love for the Turkish woman. I fantasize a physical struggle, violence. I kill him with a barrage of lefts and rights.

A woman paws at my arm, and my murderous fantasy evaporates. I don't understand her question, so she speaks German. "Schreiben," she says. She wants to borrow my pen. But my thoughts drift back to the girl and my imagined confrontation. Recently, undercurrents of anger have surfaced as fantasies of violence.

Back on the freeway, the bus turns north at the waterfront, and we're one lane from the Aegean. At the dock, ghost-like cranes off-loading cargo gawk about in dense fog. We zip past dilapidated houses, yellow walls, red crumbling tile, more sea, more rain. The wet swish of cars. Another dock, more cranes, land, trees, light poles, power lines, apartment buildings, billboard after billboard, clotheslines, laundry. Inside the bus, the wail of Turkish music. More apartments, spiked spires standing tall and religious, old trucks, a garbage dump, a Shell service station, an intersection with stoplight.

The bus stops at the intersection, and I watch the pedestrians crossing the street, in and out of shops. The bus starts again, and I see a Kosem Kiraat Hanesi, more shops. We stop at another stoplight, rain. The bus windows fog, the quiet murmur of Turkish voices. Three lanes of clogged traffic. We start to move again. Trucks with tarps line the roadside. Sea again, eucalyptus trees, four lanes now separated by a median, a lumberyard, a mountain of used tires, a vacant field of wet brown grass, the Aegean through dilapidated buildings. All this on the way out of Izmir, Smyrna, where the giant of Greek literature, Homer, was born.

The steward walks through the bus with a bottle of cologne and dumps a large splash into each person's hands. I don't get my hands up in time and get a couple of drops on my clothes. The bus smells like a beauty parlor. He passes through the bus again, passes out small cellophane packets of raisin bread, ETi kek Uzumlu.

The rain has stopped and the windows are dry, but streaks of mud remain. I see blue sky to the west but an ominous cloudbank to the north, where we're headed. The young woman who smiled at me gets up from her seat and closes two circular vents in the ceiling of the bus. She's even more beautiful than I thought. It's turned cold. I haven't been cold since I left Patmos. A road to Kozak cuts through a green field to the right. Olive orchards line the road and cover the rolling hills as far as I can see.

We pass a turnoff west to Ayvalik, where the warm-weather ferry goes to Lesbos, the isle where the great Greek poetess, Sappho, lived. The mountains of Lesbos are silhouettes in the distance, twenty kilometers away. I hope to be in Lesbos in less than a week.

We round the top of a hill and descend into the small town outside Bergama. The bus pulls into a roadside stop. In antiquity, this region of the coast was called Mysia. The Greeks' first attempt to siege Troy went awry here. They attacked Mysia by mistake and were driven back by Telephos, the grandson of Heracles.[299] Thersander, son of Polyneices and grandson of Oedipus, who had recently destroyed Thebes, was the only one to stand his ground against Telephos, and even though he died as a result, he was known as the bravest of the Greek warriors. Achilles wounded Telephos as the Greeks retreated, and the thigh wound would not heal. Telephos went to Delphi seeking a cure, and the oracle told him the wound could only be healed by rust from the wounding sword. Telephos sought out Achilles, and after being healed, agreed to guide the Greeks to Troy.

The bus leaves the roadside stop. Haze shrouds the horizon, but the copper-coin sun is still too bright to look at as it dives toward the blue-gray Aegean, where silver-edged waves rush the sandy shore. Olive trees come between the sea and us. Glistening olive orchards climb rolling hills. Wind has shaped the trees here, bowed them inland.

Mt. Ida looms to the right, where Zeus, father of gods and men, watched

Paris duel Menelaus for Helen, until Paris showed his cowardice and ran to the security of the walls of Troy. The rumble and shimmy of the bus, the wail of Turkish music, the murmur of obscure voices. We turn inland, the bus struggling with the grade, up a boulder-filled ravine covered with olive trees, a switchback, a momentary view of the white-capped sea far below, and suddenly, huge firs looming between us and the cliff. Bushes line the side of the road, yellow, orange, red. Heavy clouds sit on the rocky peak just above us. A naked pine trunk topped with a bonnet of green needles. Maple trees dressed in bright orange. Window dirt set aglow by sunlight.

The bus turns left into the setting sun, past farms and into the middle of a forest and the small town of Ayvalik. The windows fog again. A short stop, and we're on our way back to the main road. The time on the big red LED clock above the driver's head reads 16:47. A road sign points off to the left, Truva. We whiz on past toward Canakkale.

The dawn of the Bronze Age brought a demand for metals to the Aegean world. Asia, and in particular the Black Sea region, was a primary source for copper and iron. Ancient Troy, located at the mouth of the strait of the Dardanelles, prospered as a result of the traffic in metals.[300] Troy sat on a hill overlooking the mouth of the strait, which flows with water from all over Eastern Europe and the former Soviet Union, coming by way of the Black Sea.[301]

The Don River[302] originates in the central Russian upland, cuts a lazy path through the Ukraine, the bread basket of the former Soviet Union where the famous Don Cossacks lived, eventually emptying into the Sea of Azov at the port town of Rostov. The Sea of Azov is shallow, fourteen meters deep at its maximum, and separated from the Black Sea by a large peninsula, the Crimea, known to the ancients as the Tauric Chersonese, which was visited by Orestes. He came to the temple of Artemis where his older sister, Iphigenia, following her narrow escape from being sacrificed by her father at Aulis, was priestess. Water from the Sea of Azov flows through the Kerch strait into the Black Sea.

The Dniester River[303] drains the north slope of the Carpathian Mountains and the southwestern Ukraine, meandering for 1,400 kilometers before dumping into the Black Sea. The Black Sea's other primary source is the Danube,[304] the most important river in southeastern Europe. It originates in the Black Forest of Germany and flows for 3,000 kilometers through Austria, the Czech Republic, along the Slovakian boarder, through Hungary, across the northeastern edge of Serbia, and along the Romanian-Bulgarian border, where it dumps into the Black Sea.

Many famous stories of Greek mythology are set at the mouth of the Phasis River on the far eastern coast of the Black Sea. Jason and the Argonauts retrieved the Golden Fleece from Colchis, a city on the southeastern coast of the Black Sea. This, to the ancient Greeks, was the edge of the world. The fleece was nailed to a giant oak in the sacred grove of Ares, the Greek god of war, and guarded by an unsleeping dragon. Among Jason's crew on the good ship Argo were Theseus, who later became the king of Athens, Mopsus, the son of Manto and grandson of Teiresias, and Orpheus, Homer's direct ancestor,[305] who possessed superhuman gifts in music and song. In Colchis, Jason fell in league with the evil sorceress and murderess, Medea. Also, in the Caucasus Mountains on the untrodden Scythian tract north of the Black Sea, Prometheus was chained upon a "high-beetling crag" and suffered for thirty thousand years the torment of having his liver devoured by an eagle during the day and freezing temperatures at night.

All this water from the Black Sea either evaporates or dumps westward through the Bosporus Strait and into the Sea of Marmara[306] at Istanbul, which the Greeks still call Constantinople. In turn, the Sea of Marmara dumps into the Aegean through the sixty-kilometer strait of the Dardanelles. The strait was named for Dardanus, the first ancestor of the Trojans. His city, Dardania, was just south of Canakkale. His grandson, Tros, named the entire region after himself when he became king. Homer knew the Dardanelles as the fish-filled strong-stream of Hellespont.

Water through the Dardanelles, strangely enough, flows in both directions simultaneously. The top sixty-four meters of rapid surface current flows from the Aegean into the Sea of Marmara, but below, the water is colder, heavier, and more saline and flows into the Aegean. The narrows of the Dardanelles is one kilometer across at Canakkale. The name Canakkale comes from the Turkish word "canak" which means "pot," but pottery is no longer the city's central industry. The Dardanelles is rich in fish because of migration from the Aegean to the Sea of Marmara and the Black Sea. The strait is full of red mullet, salmon, bream, sturgeon, herring. Canakkale is the center of the fish canning industry in northwestern Turkey.

The ruins of Troy are just south of Canakkale, strategically located on the southern coast of the Dardanelles on a hill called Hisarlik (Turkish for "place of fortress"[307] but known by some as "Hill of Doom"[308]), overlooking its Aegean entrance. Historians have speculated that the Trojan War was not actually fought over a woman, but for control of the Dardanelles.

Even though Hellespont was of considerable commercial and strategic importance, according to Homer the Greeks laid siege to Troy for a woman, Helen. And even though Hellespont was teeming with fish, it was the feminine commodity that occupied the Greeks, for they not only sieged Troy but many of her allies as well, slowly destroying all Troy's support over a ten year period. Achilles spoke Homer's lines that tell us the most about Greek motivations:

> Many a sleepless night I've spent afield
> and many a day in bloodshed, hand to hand
> in battle for the wives of other men.
> In sea raids I plundered a dozen towns,
> eleven in expeditions overland
> through Trojan country...[309]

It was a harvest of women, the Greek warriors casting nets of war and retrieving the wives of other men.

Canakkale is dark and cold. I break open *Let's Go* to get directions to a hotel before exiting the packed bus. Darkness hangs on this place like a disease. Canakkale is a bustling metropolis, lit only by shop windows, neon signs, and car lights. People scurry in all directions and cars streak off to everywhere. I walk through the doors into the otogar, through the waiting room, and out the front door into the wet street. A few blocks later, I'm staring across the dark, rapidly moving current of the Dardanelles at the sprinkle of lights of Kilibahir on the opposite bank.

I walk a few meters down the street, past a restaurant with the smells of dinner escaping through the door. I'm so hungry that it's difficult to walk past. I spot the Hotel Amzek only a few meters farther. The man behind the desk says the rooms are heated, so I take one with a private bath. My room has a heater on the far wall and is almost warm.

I flop my daypack on the bed, go back outside, and walk the few meters to the restaurant in the bitter cold. Everything on their menu is displayed in the restaurant window. A young, formally dressed couple are the only ones in the place. They look to be about fifteen, possibly brother and sister, but professional and strikingly handsome. The young, thin, dark-haired man sets the table for me. I have spicy-hot meatballs, beef stew, rice, bread, and bottled water. Price 53,000 lira ($3.75). A green pepper in the beef stew scalds my insides.

★

In the middle of the night, I wake from a long nightmarish dream about work. My coworkers laughed at me for quitting my job over something trivial. After thinking it over, I went back to the program manager and asked for my job back.

The first word in Homer's *Iliad*, is Μηνιν, anger, wrath, and it's the wrath of Achilles of which the muse sings. If the ten-year siege of Troy and her allies is the tale of Helen, *The Iliad*, which concerns only fifty days[310] in the ninth year, is the tale of two women, Chryseis and Briseis. Chryseis was from the tiny island of Chryse, just off the Trojan coast. This island no longer exists, and according to Pausanias, sank into the sea sometime in the 1st Century BC.[311] Briseis was from Lyrnessus, an inland city in Mysia. Achilles plundered both cities and took all the women. Agamemnon had taken Chryseis as his concubine, and he valued her above his own wife, Klytemnestra. But her father, who was himself a priest of Apollo, wanted his daughter returned. Apollo sent a hail of arrows, which had their worldly manifestation as plague, to decimate the Greek forces, but Agamemnon refused to release the girl. Achilles chided him until finally Agamemnon relented, but he demanded recompense and took Achilles concubine, Briseis, to replace her. Thus the wrath, Mηνιν, of Achilles, who then returned to his ship and refused to fight.

The Iliad opens, not with murderous demonstrations by the greatest warrior of all time on the battlefield, but with him retiring to his boat to sulk like a spoiled child. His sulk would cost many Greek lives. Only when his best friend was killed on the battlefield did Achilles return to the fighting. Agamemnon finally returned Briseis and sweetened the pot for Achilles by throwing in seven of the world's most beautiful women from Lesbos. Such was the commerce determining the flow of events in the Trojan War. But Achilles' sulk was destructive to both himself and his fellow warriors.

I too recently ruined my career to sulk, although not over a woman. I was working on the Earth resources experiment that will fly on the Space Shuttle this next April. I had been promised a position, to become Technical Manager over our entire project, second in command to the Program Manager, but instead, I was called in one morning and told that the position had been given to another man. I didn't fly into a rage as I had that evening in Munich two years earlier. I simply announced that I would leave the project, much as Achilles left the war. I had them in a bind. The project was pushed to the wall with technical, budgetary and schedule problems. My experience working NASA programs was critical, and when I left to sulk, NASA took what we had completed, pulled the rest of the program in-house, and canceled our contract.

The earth resources radar will still fly aboard the Space Shuttle this coming April, and much of the hardware will be ours. Some would say I over estimate my value to the project, but my quitting was a big factor in NASA's decision to cancel our contract. I did it because of Mηνιν, anger, wrath. I went to work on a Star Wars contract that was later canceled when we got a new president in Washington. I got laid off, which enabled me to come to Greece on this extended journey of a lifetime.

Turkey: Troy

24 Nov, Wednesday

Up very early. It's still dark out, but the sound of rain floods my room here in Canakkale, water gushing from the eaves of the hotel, lights from shops glistening in puddles. The wind comes in great swells, rattling shutters and slinging great waves of rain.

At seven-thirty, I go downstairs to have breakfast, but the dining room is dark and empty, the help still setting tables. I go back to my room and sit on the bed, looking out into the drenched darkness. Tomorrow is Thanksgiving. I wanted to be back in Seljuk, so I could celebrate with another American or two, but now wonder if I might have to stay here another day for my visit to Troy. Sarah was supposed to return to Seljuk late yesterday from Istanbul. The possibility of seeing her again weighs heavy.

After breakfast, I bundle up in every piece of warm clothing I brought in my daypack, long-sleeved undershirt, long-sleeved button shirt, thick black sweater, all under my hiking jacket, the hood pulled over my head. The rain has let up, but the wind still comes in great waves. I walk away from the coast to the main street we came in on last night, spot a small square with several minibuses, and look for one to Truva. None in sight. A taxi driver approaches me. "Truva?" he asks. "No thanks," I say. I certainly don't want a taxi when I can get a bus for a fraction of the fare. "Truva bus, two blocks," he says, pointing on down the street. I've misread another person who is only trying to help.

The shabby otogar sits on a street corner in a field of mud. I enter uneasily. It's besieged with dark, severe-looking Turks, and not a tourist in sight. I've never felt so conspicuous. My dark-purple hiking jacket stands out like a neon sign. Why they're all huddled in the otogar is a mystery. No one leaves on a bus. They're all crowded about the tables as if with friends, but no one smiles. I feel out of place, vulnerable, and finally, can't take it anymore. I go back outside to huddle against the building, get beaten by wind and a fine rain, watch the line of minibuses parked alongside the street. Finally, a driver shows, and I board a minibus with the sign "Truva" on the front. Other Turks board with me, but it won't start, so they pile out to push.

A few kilometers back toward Izmir, the minibus turns west, off the main road. After a ride through desolate, grass-covered fields with the windshield wipers flapping and the Turks chattering comfortably, the driver stops at a closed tourist shop. A long paved driveway with conspicuous, unnecessary sidewalks leads into the distance, seemingly to nowhere. No other human beings in sight.

I step outside and stand, reluctant to close the sliding door. "Truva?" I ask pointing down the lane. "Truva," he confirms. "Next bus?" I ask. He answers,

"Three hours, return Canakkale." Resistantly, I close the door and start my one-kilometer walk through light rain. I see the outline of a dark horse standing above the trees at the site.

After the Greeks first attempt to find Troy, and the aborted, disastrous landing in Mysia, their ships were scattered by bad weather, and they returned to Argos. They reassembled at Aulis, off the eastern coast of Attica, and this time Telephos, who had been healed of his thigh wound by Achilles, led them to Troy. Homer provides a list of those participating in the war. From just the areas of Greece I've visited, here is the number of ships and the names of the commanders who fought under Agamemnon. Athens, Athena's city, fifty ships, Menestheus commanding. The Boeotians, including Lower Thebes (the Kadmia had just been burned to the ground by the "Sons of the Seven") and Haliartos, one hundred twenty ships, Peneleos, Leitos, Arkesilaos, Prothoenor, and Klonios captains. The Phokians, including Delphi, Apollo's oracle, forty black ships, led by Skhedios and Epistrophos. Ithaka and Samos, twelve good ships, led by Odysseus. Argos, including Epidauros, eighty black ships, commanded by Diomedes. Mycenae and Corinth, one hundred ships, commanded by Agamemnon. Sparta, home of Helen, sixty ships, led by Menelaus. Crete, including Knossos and Phaestos, eighty black ships, commanded by Idomeneus. Rhodes, nine ships, commanded by Tlepolemos. The total ships from all over Greece was said to be a thousand.[312]

Just inside the entrance, beside the museum, stands the gigantic Trojan horse made of dark wood and standing ten meters into the dreary sky. The reconstruction of the horse followed the inscriptions on ancient Greek vases and descriptions found in ancient writings.[313] It still seems overdone, Hollywoodish, its house with windows sitting astride it like a saddle. I leave the horse and walk up a slight incline, up a set of shallow steps. Before me stands the hill called Hisarlik and the ruins of Troy, besieged by a driving wind. It's cold, but not bitter cold or I'd have to turn back. Only two other people are here at the site, a young woman with long brown hair dressed in black jeans and purple sweater. With her is a young man with bushy-brown hair and full beard, Paul Bunyan-like, hunkered under a large backpack.

Instead of descending the steps into the ruins, I walk to the right where archaeologists have piled their dirt, forming a mound above the ruins. Off to the left and below me stand the stone walls of Troy. A flat plain lies before me, quilted with brown, plowed fields and deep-green squares roamed by cattle. Beyond this plain, a small patch of water glistens blue, the mouth of the Dardanelles.

In antiquity, just inside the southern lip of the strait, the Greeks grounded their boats in a small, quiet harbor. But in the 3200 years since the Trojan War, the sea has receded five kilometers from where the Greeks beached. Similar to Ephesus, the harbor has filled with alluvial deposits from the Scamander River, which runs to the west of Hisarlik, and the Simoin River, which runs to the east, the two now meeting in the plain before dumping into the Dardanelles. Their traces are barely visible. The sea's retreat has reduced the bay to a fertile, cultivated plain, some fields covered with brown cotton stalks, a rather startling reminder of the farm on which I was raised, where my father, brothers and I labored daily in the cotton fields.

After Achilles left the battlefield to sulk, Agamemnon had to rally the demoralized troops to fight the Trojans without their most fearsome warrior. Agamemnon cut a striking presence:

> Agamemnon's lordly mien
> was like the mien of Zeus whose joy is lightning;
> oaken-waisted as Ares, god of war,
> he seemed, and deep-chested as Lord Poseidon;
> and, as a great bull in his majesty
> towers supreme amid a grazing herd...[314]

Although Agamemnon may have resembled Ares on the battlefield, his help from above did not come from the god of war. Ares was on the side of the Trojans. Besides, Ares was no good at war even when accompanied by his two offspring by his mistress Aphrodite, Phobos and Deimos, "Fear" and "Panic," who drove their father's chariot. Athena kicked Ares' butt at every encounter. Even his father, Zeus, didn't care for him. After Athena hit him in the belly and a mortal wounded him, Ares ran from the battlefield to Zeus who had this response:

> Do not come whining here, you two-faced brute,
> most hateful to me of all the Olympians.
> Combat and brawling are your element.[315]

Like the vision of the Virgin Mary leading the troops, Athena was Agamemnon's ally, and as he mustered the warriors for another assault on the walls of Troy, she provided the inspiration:

> And Agamemnon,
> marshal of the army, turned at once,
> telling his criers to send out shrill and clear

to all Akhaian troops the call to battle.
The cry went out, the men came crowding, officers
from their commander's side went swiftly down
to form each unit—and the gray-eyed goddess
Athena kept the pace behind them, bearing
her shield of storm, immortal and august,
whose hundred golden-plaited tassels, worth
a hekatomb each one, floated in air.
So down the ranks that dazzling goddess went
to stir the attack, and each man in his heart
grew strong to fight and never quit the melee,
for at her passage war itself became
lovelier than return, lovelier than sailing
in the decked ships to their own native land.[316]

Here, Athena is the very essence of the Virgin Mary as seen socially, the leader of a mighty army of spiritual warriors ready to do battle with the forces of evil.

I crowd to the edge of the hill, look down the uneven slope, and try to imagine Achilles chasing Hektor three times around the walls of Troy before he finally stopped to fight. Hektor, eldest son of King Priam and the Trojan's fearless leader in battle, knew he had no chance against Achilles. The most touching scene in Homer's narrative of the war occurs when Hektor left the battlefield and entered the city walls to get his cowardly brother, Paris, to rejoin the fighting. Paris, who caused the war in the first place, was in bed, entwined in the arms and legs of Helen. After Paris agreed to return to the foray, Hektor returned himself but was stopped by his warmhearted wife, Andromache, and a nurse carrying his baby boy. Andromache called to him just before he left the fortress through the Skaian Gate to the south. The interaction between Hektor, his infant son, and his wife is what I find so touching:

... Hektor held out his arms
to take his baby. But the child squirmed round
on the nurse's bosom and began to wail,
terrified of his father's great war helm--
the flashing bronze, the crest with horsehair plume
tossed like a living thing at every nod.
His father began laughing, and his mother
laughed as well. Then from his handsome head
Hektor lifted off his helm and bent

to place it, bright with sunlight, on the ground.
When he had kissed his child and swung him high
to dandle him...
into his dear wife's arms he gave his baby,
whom on her fragrant breast
she held and cherished, laughing through her tears.
Hektor pitied her now. Caressing her,
he said: "Unquiet soul, do not be too distressed
by thoughts of me. You know no man dispatches me
into the undergloom against my fate..."
He stooped now to recover his plumed helm
as she, his dear wife, drew away, her head
turned and her eyes upon him, brimming tears.[317]

Hektor rejoined the battle, and the confrontation with Achilles. Three times around the walls Achilles chased him, Hektor thinking of his wife and child, before he stopped and Achilles killed him.

When I was a child of eight, a violent event occurred, which almost deprived me of my father. It happened in our front yard. It was just before we moved into the old home that burned to the ground. My aunt's husband came over one dark evening to kill my father. He was the uncle who beat his kids, and the man my father had gone to see to stop the abuse. The evening he came to our home, my father must have anticipated something because, as my uncle stood in the driveway and called him out, he told my mother to stay inside. My father didn't run three times around the house to avoid him.

As my father approached, my uncle told him, "I've been waiting a long time for this." The story was, my uncle had once whipped four sailors at once. My father grabbed him by the tie with his left hand and with his right fist beat him senseless. When they tried to put him in the backseat of his car to drive him home, piss ran out his boots, and as my father stooped to pull them off to empty them, he noticed a wetness around his own midsection, and discovered that my uncle had stabbed him in the abdomen. He really had come to kill my father. What followed was a frantic chase to the hospital, emergency surgery and a long wait. The doctor came to my mother and told her the knife had penetrated to my father's stomach. "To, but not through," he said. And thus, my father lived.

But Achilles didn't live to see the siege of Troy either. He was killed by an Apollo-assisted arrow from the mighty bow of cowardly Paris, who let loose his evil-plumed missile from within the safety of Troy's walls. Achilles, son of the mortal Peleus, was born to the goddess Thetis, a Nereid. Achilles was mortal, so

Thetis took him to the Underworld and dipped him in the river Styx to make him invulnerable to injury. But she held him by the heel which left him weak in that single spot, thus the infamous "Achilles Heel." Paris' arrow hit him in the heel, and he died from the unhealing wound. Achilles' son, Neoptolemus, was then enlisted to take his place. Neoptolemus was among the forces that succeeded in siegeing Troy.

After ten years, the Greeks routed the Trojans on the battlefield but still couldn't penetrate the walls of the fortress. In one last desperate enterprise, Odysseus, the man of many wiles, inspired by Athena, came up with the Trojan-horse scheme. They built a gigantic horse of pine from trees taken from Mt. Ida. Outside the city walls, they left the horse with an inscription dedicating it to Athena, in hopes she would provide a safe trip home. Then they burned their tents and vacated the coast, sailing to the nearby island of Tenedos. They left behind a single warrior, Sinon, with the story that the Greeks had been intent on using him as a human sacrifice. He told the Trojans he had escaped and lingered by the horse to join them. They tortured him to learn the truth but could not break him, though they cut off his ears and nose and burned him with fire. The Trojans came to believe him, and even though Priam's daughter, Cassandra, prophesied their doom, they brought the horse inside the city walls. Cassandra was a seer also, one who titillated Apollo, but refused his advances, and was thus given the fate feared most by a seer, never to be believed.

During the night, Helen suspected what was afoot and lingered by the horse, disguising her voice in the manner of the wives of the Greeks, chiding those inside. But she didn't give them away, and at midnight, the Greek warriors came out of the horse, killed the guards, and opened the gate, signaling their fellow warriors with torches to come help them take the city.

I look beyond the battlefield, searching for a pale mountain in the distance. Poseidon watched the War from Fengari, a granite peak that is the highest in the Aegean, 1611 meters above sea level and seventy-eight kilometers away, on the island of Samothrace. Homer describes Poseidon as

> Enthralled, watching the battle,
> he sat on woody Samos' highest ridge
> off Thrace, whence Ida could be seen entire
> and Priam's town and the Akhaian ships.
> He had climbed up from the salt sea...[318]

The cloud cover prevents me from making out anything that far in the distance.

Turkey: Troy

I leave the archeological mound, walk down the stone steps to the site, the crumbled foundation of the east tower and the sloping stone wall of the ancient city to my left, and the Dardanian Gate in front of me. This is the main gate to the ancient city. I'd imagined a magnificent entry, huge doors swinging on great hinges, but this is hardly wider than the span of a man's arms. And obviously doorless. Still, such a narrow entryway must have been easily defensible. The stone walls, which stand only four and one half meters high today, stood thirteen in antiquity.[319] Now they still serve a purpose, shielding me from the wind. Sure enough, the walls are sloped just as depicted by Homer.

The two young people, the guy with the Paul Bunyan beard and the girl with dark-brown hair, are loading their cameras with film while leaning against the sloping stone wall. I stop to inspect a crack in the wall that was caused by an earthquake around the time Troy fell. I talk to them for a minute, thankful that the rain is no longer falling. We talk across a large puddle spanning the width of the dirt path. He's an American, and she's from Australia. They met a few days ago and are hitchhiking through Turkey together. I caution them, saying all guidebooks talk against hitching, but he scoffs at me. "It's as safe as being in a bus," he says, while sighting through his camera at me like he's pointing a gun. She says they're on their way to Ephesus after Troy, so I tell her I met several of her countrymen at the New Zealand pension in Seljuk. He shuts me up, saying they already know where they're staying in Seljuk. He keeps standing in front of her as if he's trying to protect her from me. I hope she's not in danger. I wish them good day and move on.

I tiptoe through the mud at the edge of the puddle in front of the Dardanian Gate. The stone ruins to my left are old and gray, moss-covered portions of walls, now sparsely populated with wind-swept oak trees. The hillside is covered with loose earth and brown grass, new green grass showing through. The primary entrance to the city was formed by the overlap of a leaning rock wall to the left and the lip of a second wall to the right. The gap between the two is the Dardanian Gate, now undoored.

I go through it, turn to the left and up a set of steps, gravel crunching under my hiking boots, and suddenly, the ruins of the entire city of Troy lie before me. Today, Troy is a partially reconstructed mountain of rubble 200 meters by 150 meters. Troy (or Ilium as it was also called, Iliad means poem of Ilium) was founded by Ilus, who participated in the games of Phrygia,[320] winning at wrestling. As a prize, Ilus was given fifty boys, fifty girls, a spotted cow, and told by the oracle at Delphi to found a city where the cow laid down, similar to the story of Kadmos founding Thebes. Ilus followed the cow to a hill, where she laid down, and Ilus founded a city, and named it for himself.[321]

Turkey: Troy

I look along a dead, shrub-covered ravine cut into the slope of the hill to the Plane of Simois, now a water-logged field. I walk a second flight of steps, and off to the left, see the stone remains of houses, which in antiquity had wood columns supporting roof beams covered with mud, covered with branches. I imagine all this burning in a ferocious fire. A horse skeleton was found here, somewhat of a verification of Homer's epithet, "horse-taming Trojans." Troy prospered because of its metallurgy and the transport of metals westward from the lower Danube, through the Black Sea, the Sea of Marmara, and the Dardanelles into the Aegean.[322]

The siege of Troy by Agamemnon and his forces was not the first. Schliemann's excavations uncovered nine cities dating back to the first Bronze Age city, which prospered from 3000-2500 BC. It was built on bedrock thirty-two meters above the plain. Debris from the nine successive cities, some destroyed by earthquake, others by fire, raised the tumulus another sixteen meters by the time Schliemann excavated it.[323] Homer's Troy is believed to be either Troy VI (1800-1275 BC) or VII (1275-1100 BC). Schliemann excavated this site in 1870 during his mad search for King Priam's treasure.

As I saw in Mycenae, Schliemann's approach was to cut large trenches through the earth. He had caught gold fever in the hills of California during the gold rush, not far from my own hometown. And here, he found treasure in abundance. He assumed that he had found Homer's Troy, but in fact, he had destroyed the remains of that city and found another, even more ancient city, Troy II, which had been destroyed in 2200 BC. Schliemann destroyed much of Priam's Troy in his frantic search for gold.

Alexander the Great came here in 334 BC to ruminate over Achilles, his ancestor.[324] Aeneas, a Trojan, was a descendant of Dardanus and Tros (the brother of Ilus). Virgil would write of Aeneas in *The Aeneid*. He was one of the few Trojans who escaped death during the burning of Ilios. Aeneas resettled in Italy, and his descendants founded Rome. Caesar came to Troy in 48 BC, walked the ground I'm now walking, and claimed to be a descendant of Aeneas. Perhaps blood from those fighting on both sides of this great war flows in all our veins.

For years, Menelaus had promised to kill his wife when he got his hands on her, but when he finally found her, his tune changed. Somewhere within all this rubble is where he finally found Helen:

Menelaus mid the inner chambers found
At last his wife, there cowering from the wrath
Of her bold-hearted lord. He glared on her,
Hungering to slay her in his jealous rage.

But... powerless all
Was he to lift the sword against her neck,
Seeing her splendour of beauty...
All his great strength
Was broken, as he looked upon his wife.[325]

To save face, Menelaus promised to kill Helen when they returned home to Sparta. With the city of Troy at last firmly in hand, the Greeks burned it:

The fire-glow upward mounted to the sky,
The red glare o're the firmament spread its wings,
And all the tribes of folk that dwelt around
Beheld it, far as Ida's mountain-crests,
And sea-girt Tenedos, and Thracian Samos.
And men that voyaged on the deep sea cried:
"The Argives have achieved their mighty task
After long toil for star-eyed Helen's sake.
All Troy, the once queen-city, burns in fire...[326]

The Greeks slaughtered the men and took the women and children as slaves, but one great injustice was righted. Demophoon and Acamas, the sons of Theseus who had joined the forces against Troy, retrieved Aethra, Theseus' mother. Years before, when Helen had been kidnapped and raped by Theseus, Helen's brothers had retrieved her, and kidnapped Aethra in the process. Aethra had been enslaved by Helen and brought to Troy when Helen ran off with Paris. Aethra's grandsons narrowly avoided killing this aged and enslaved noble woman because they mistook her for Priam's queen, Hekuba. Andromache, Hektor's comely wife, was allotted to Achilles' son, Neoptolemus. Her small son, Astyanax, whom Hektor loved so much, was jerked from his screaming mother's arms and thrown to his death from a high rampart.

At the crown of the hill are the scattered remains of the temple of Athena, where, in the bedlam of the siege of Troy, Aias of Locris raped Cassandra, the virgin daughter of King Priam. Athena could not bear to look upon the act:

Yea, she would not look
Upon the infamy, but clad herself
With shame and wrath as with a cloak: she turned
Her stern eyes to the temple-roof, and groaned
The holy image, and the hallowed floor

Turkey: Troy

Quaked mightily.[327]

But archaeologists have found no remains of Athena's Mycenaean temple. The few marble blocks of ceiling coffers and fluted column bases and capitals are from Troy VIII and IX.[328]

On this high promontory, the wind is so strong I turn my back to it, lean into the gale-force wind, tighten my hood about my head.

Athena, enraged at the desecration of her temple and the failure of the Greek generals to do anything about it, elicited the help of Poseidon. By the end of the war, Poseidon had aligned himself with the Trojans. The two of them then joined forces with Athena's father, Zeus, to scatter the Greek ships as they tried to return home. They destroyed the treasure-laden Greek fleet:

> Thousands perished; corpses thronged
> The great sea-highways: all the beaches were
> Too strait for them: the surf belched multitudes
> Forth on the land. The heavy-blooming sea
> With weltering beams of ships was wholly paced...[329]

Those who didn't die were sent wandering about the Mediterranean. Menelaus and Helen took seven years to return home, Odysseus ten. Athena let Agamemnon reach home knowing that his wife, Klytemnestra, would murder him immediately for his sacrifice of Iphigenia at Aulis.

I wander back out of the ruins toward the entrance, stop at the museum to take a look around. They have a model of the ancient city as archaeologists say it must have appeared at the time of the Trojan War. A much less formidable-looking construction than I'd imagined, the power of myth. The Trojan horse looms darkly over me as I exit the site.

★

Early afternoon. I sit in the minibus at the end of the long driveway leading to the ruins of Troy, waiting for the driver to come back so I can get to Canakkale and catch a bus south. Out the minibus window I see the sun, pale as a moon, trying to break through a crack in the clouds. Shortly, the driver comes back with five other Turks, but the minibus won't start so they try to jump it. Something is wrong with the ignition system. They have to push it again.

I sit here after seeing the most famous battlefield of all time, and I remember the one chance I had to go to war. The year was 1971. I had been in the Air Force for eight years, and at the time, was performing a stateside assignment supporting B-52's that were being used to bomb the North Vietnamese. One morning, I came to work and on my desk found a postcard with orders stating that I was being sent to Vietnam.

The orders came at a bad time. My wife was sick, had been for several months with a life-threatening illness, and I asked for a six-month deferment. We had two small kids. I could have just gone on to Vietnam in true military tradition, but my family meant a great deal to me, and I didn't feel I could leave just then. I was shocked when word came back that I should apply for an "early-out." I still had a six-year commitment and was planning to retire in the Air Force.

Since making the decision to leave the military, I have had a lot of guilt over not going to Vietnam. Particularly when I talk to those veterans who fought there. I've never been to war, but dreams of war have plagued my sleep. I've wondered how much of my motivation came from my family situation, and how much from cowardice. It was my chance to see war firsthand. I would have been stationed in Da Nang, which at the time was a safe place. But during my projected tour, the city would have come under heavy fire from the Vietcong.

The minibus travels a narrow dirt road through grass-covered rolling hills lined with fences made of piled brush. We come to a small village, honking to let people know the minibus is here. By mid afternoon, I'm back in Canakkale, waiting at the otogar for the bus south. I have a long split-pita sandwich filled with goat meat carved from a turning spit, lettuce, red sauce, and spices. I board the bus, and shortly hear the chatter of a man behind the bus shouting directions to the bus driver as he backs up. The Turks are not too shabby when it comes to buses. This one is a Mercedes.

The scattering of my family has been devastating. First my wife left me for a doctor, and I left for San Diego. My son went off to college, and my daughter, Cyndi, went to live with her mother. Actually, I've not been willing to tell the full story of the break between Cyndi and me. When I was in Rhodes, I mentioned that, after my ex-wife moved out on her own, a young lady had moved in with my kids and me. My ex-wife called one day, a screaming and crying telephone call, telling me to get that bitch out of the house. Well, the "bitch" didn't leave. She stayed, and we got married.

After deciding to move to California and while interviewing for the job with General Dynamics, a problem arose between my second wife and me concerning Cyndi going with us to look over San Diego while I interviewed. Cyndi wanted to see if she would like to go to high school there before she decide whether or not to go with us. Cyndi liked her stepmother, but my new wife was jealous of her, and talked about her behind her back. The day before we were all three to leave for my interview, my new wife and I had a screaming and shouting argument about Cyndi going with us. I've always felt that the argument was the big reason that Cyndi stayed in Phoenix. I never forgave my new wife for this outburst. I sold my home in Phoenix, and just before leaving, I walked into my daughter's deserted bedroom and cried it full of tears. Then I drove to San Diego, alone.

The events leading up to Cyndi's disappearance occurred over the next two years. Cyndi said she was staying in Phoenix with her mother so that she could be with her friends, but shortly thereafter, her mother moved to another area of Phoenix and Cyndi had to change schools anyway. She became lonely and withdrawn. My calls to her revealed a growing sadness and isolation, relieved only when her mother moved back, and Cyndi was able to return to her old high school. But it wasn't long before ominous stories of Cyndi's activities came from Phoenix, and I became more and more concerned about her.

The most telling of these incidents occurred when Cyndi's best friend tried to burn down her parents' apartment. Her father was beating her, and one night, she poured a stripe of gasoline down the hall and set fire to it. The smoke woke her parents, thus, the building and the lives of many people were saved. Cyndi had been with her friend during the plotting stage of this act and would have helped kill her parents if she had asked. Cyndi told me so, rather heatedly. The police took her girlfriend into custody, and Cyndi was also taken to the police station, but released later that evening. The next day, my ex-wife called from Phoenix to relay the bizarre events, and I talked to my defiant daughter. I should have gone to Phoenix to assess the situation myself, but my job on the Shuttle Centaur program demanded every second of my attention, and my ex-wife said everything was under control. I used her confidence as my excuse for not going.

A couple of months later, Cyndi's girlfriend, who had been put in a juvenile detention center, ran away. My daughter seemingly accepted her friend's disappearance with a certain philosophic resignation, but another event occurred, a few months, later when Cyndi came to San Diego for Christmas. This event should have told me all was not well.

We're nearing a wide spot in the road marking the junction east to Bergama, the ancient city of Pergamon. It's turned dark, the night settling on the gentle Turkish coast like a soft carpet pricked by the bright jewels of car lights. I'm about to take a chance. I've been thinking about it ever since I left Canakkale. I would like to get back to Seljuk tonight, Sarah has been in my thoughts a lot the last couple of hours, but I have several reasons for wanting to stop in Bergama. This coastal area is where the Greeks first attempt to siege Troy went awry, mistaking Mysia and the town of Teuthrania for Troy. Telephos, the king of Teuthrania, repulsed the attack, killing Thersander in the process, but was wounded in the thigh by Achilles. Then, at the advice of the Delphic oracle, Telephos sought out Achilles. After Achilles healed him with rust scraped from his sword, Telephos led the Greeks to Troy. A most un-neighborly act.

Hektor's wife also spent the end of her life here. Following the siege of Troy, she was enslaved to Neoptolemus, the son of Achilles. She became his concubine, and bore him three sons, one of whom she named Pergamus. When Agamemnon's son, Orestes, killed Neoptolemus at Delphi over Menelaus' and Helen's daughter, Hermione, Andromache returned to the coast of Asia Minor, and her son Pergamus captured Teuthrania and renamed it Pergamon. Pergamon is now named Bergama.

The bus parks face-first into the roadside stop. I step tentatively off the bus, into the dark, wondering if I'm putting my life into the hands of some mad Turk. I'm eight kilometers from Bergama, and as the bus belches exhaust off south to Izmir, I feel lost and alone. I don't see a ride in sight. The only car is a '60 Desoto parked with its tail to me, window light reflecting from the chrome bumper. An old man comes out of the building, waddles toward me, thick gray mustache, wrinkled black shirt open down the front, shirttail flapping in the breeze. His baggy pants could have used a washing two months ago.

"Bergama," I say, and he motions toward the Desoto shaking his head that he already knows where I'm going. As I get in, I see the big black word "DOLMUS" written in black letters across the top of the car. Ordinarily, I would get to share this ride and fare with several other travelers, but tonight it's just me.

CHAPTER 16: Turkey: Pergamon.

The ride to Bergama is eight kilometers of panic as the driver sideswipes each bar ditch, his oscillation synchronized by some psychic radar with oncoming car lights. I sit in the front seat with him, my daypack and camera case at my feet, the glow of his cigarette in the corner of my eye, wishing desperately for a seat belt. Shapes appear out of darkness then flash out of existence behind us. Just before we get into Bergama, I'm at the point of hoping he is a mugger. I will gladly let him take my money and camera, if he will only leave me at the side of the road. He slows as we enter the city, and a marked civility comes over his driving. I tell him I need a pension, and he drops me off along the side of the street.

The pension is an old, Greek-styled mansion. I enter a quiet courtyard, where I'm met by quiet amorphous sounds and the clack of shoes against stone, a hollow emptiness. The rooms have high ceilings and private baths, and are centered on an open courtyard. I leave my daypack and camera case in my room, and go out into the dark in search of dinner, thankful to have survived the ride.

Cyndi came to see me during the Christmas holidays, following the spring her girlfriend disappeared. I had been in San Diego a year and a half. She seemed better adjusted than I had anticipated. We talked, went to movies, shopping. Then, late one evening as we watched videos on MTV, we heard a knock at the door. I opened it to find a young man staring at me. "Is your daughter at home, sir?" he asked. I figured he had the wrong apartment, but Cyndi was right behind me claiming she knew the guy. The two of them talked for a while in the hall, and she came to me. "Dad," she asked, "can I go out with him for a few minutes?"

It was almost ten o'clock. "No," I said, annoyed that she would ask at that hour. "Tell him to call tomorrow." She looked at me straight, a look I'd never seen from her before. "I know this guy, Dad. I'm not a little girl and I'm going," she told me. "I only asked as a matter of courtesy. I'll be back by midnight."

I was so taken aback by the transformation in her, I wouldn't have questioned it if she had told me she was going to rob a bank. But she didn't return by midnight, not by one o'clock, not by two. By three, I had my hand on the telephone, rehearsing my speech to the police. And a miserable speech it would have been. I had no idea who she was out with, no name, address, license plate number.

A little after three, she strolled in as though nothing was wrong. I lit into her, and we had a knockdown, drag-out verbal battle. She ripped into me as if she were the parent, deeply offended I should question her judgment. I was overmatched.

I didn't realize that the guy Cyndi was out with wasn't from San Diego, and she had never seen him before that night. She wasn't even interested in him. She had, in fact, anticipated that knock at the door. During the hours between ten and three in the morning, she had visited with an old friend, and they laid the groundwork for what was to come four months later. I was so naive as to believe our confrontation had been simply a teenage daughter rebelling against her father.

25 Nov, Thursday

I'm up later than I would have liked, grab all my bathroom articles, and scurry down the hall to the community toilet. Just when I get my clothes off, I realize I forgot my soap. I wrap a towel around me and hurry back to my room. When I return, the door is locked. I pound on the door and shout, and finally an angry voice shouts back that, if I'll just let him pee, he'll let me have it. Shortly, a gray-haired American emerges murmuring to himself and staring daggers at me.

Today is Thanksgiving, for those of us who are Americans. For the rest of the world, it's just another day. I have breakfast off the courtyard, with sparrows on the windowsill and a couple from Germany who speak little English. My German is only enough to create embarrassing silences, but just as I abandon the conversation, in comes the man I confronted over the bathroom. He's with his wife and seems to have calmed some, although he's still stiff-faced. They sit at the long table across from me, and I feel guilty about being so pushy with him. She has the brightest, shiniest face I've seen since I've been on the road, and immediately wants to know who I am, where I'm from. They're from Long Island, New York, and I mention that I used to travel there frequently during my days in San Diego, before the Challenger disaster. I was overseeing a subcontract that Grumman Aerospace had with us. Finally, her pokerfaced husband gives me a glance. He's an aerospace engineer also and works at Grumman. We compare notes, and learn that I know his boss quite well. When we break company, we're on much better terms than when we met with the bathroom door between us. It was like meeting myself on the road.

I worked with Grumman on that subcontract for a couple of years. Part of the time, someone else was also living in Flushing, not far from Shea Stadium. I passed within a mile of where she was staying several times. I would have given anything to know she was there and alive.

Bergama is warmer and dryer than Canakkale yesterday, and more than I bargained for, certainly more picturesque, with the akropolis at the northeastern edge of the city. Although the road from the coast to Bergama is east–west, just before entering the city, the road turns northward. The town sprawls along the akropolis' western edge. The huge mountain stands over this city like some amorphous dark-faced earth goddess. The sun pokes through fast-moving thunderheads as I cross the busy street in old town, in search of Kazil Avlu, Red Basilica. I find it at the foot of the mountain. The structure is a huge, crumbling monolith formed of the flat red brick from which it takes its name.

In Revelations, St. John mentioned the seven Christian churches of Asia, and one of them was here in the ancient city of Pergamon. In John's vision, the Son of Man told him that this is "where Satan dwelleth,"[330] and that the people here held the doctrine "to cast a stumbling block before the children of Israel, to eat things sacrificed unto idols, and to commit fornication."[331]

What galls me about this passage from Revelations is that the ancient Greeks did not worship idols. Can these truly be the words of Christ, or are they a corruption of a more accurate thought? An idol is a man-made object. The gods of ancient Greece were viewed as divine spirits that were given physical representation by the great sculptors of the time, much the same as Christ is depicted on the cross today throughout the world.

The redbrick Basilica sits astride two vaulted tunnels through which the water of the ancient Selinus River, now called Bergama Cayi, passes underneath the ruins. The structure was originally built as a temple to the Egyptian gods, Isis and Serapis.[332] Only small remnants of the wall of the Christian church remain. It's a stark presence, rising into the morning sky and casting long shadows across the flowing water. The remains of pale brick walls tower above me like the bleached red bones of some prehistoric creature.

At the end of the Trojan War, Hektor's wife Andromache was awarded to Neoptolemus, son of Achilles. She accompanied him back to Thessaly on the Greek mainland, where he was king. Neoptolemus married Hermione, the daughter of Menelaus and Helen, but she bore him no children. Andromache, as Neoptolemus' slave and concubine, however, bore him three male children. Hermione accused Andromache of casting a secret spell to make her barren, and with help from her ruthless father, Menelaus, planned to kill Andromache and her children. But Achilles' father, aged Peleus, who was also Andromache's children's great grandfather, protected her until word came that Agamemnon's son Orestes had killed Neoptolemus at Delphi. The throne again returned to Peleus, who then helped Andromache and her children escape. Eventually, she returned to the western coast of Asia Minor with her son Pergamus.

At the time, a king named Areios ruled the town, called Teuthrania.[333] Pergamus engaged Areios in one-to-one combat and killed him. Pergamus renamed Teuthrania, calling it Pergamos, after himself. This would have been shortly after 1200 BC. Andromache lived out her life here at Pergamus. The remains of the ancient city of Teuthrania have never been found. Some believe it was closer to the coast, although it could have been here at the akropolis.

I leave the ruins of the basilica and cross the bridge over the Selinus River, taking a footpath at the southern foot of the akropolis at the site of the Lower Agora. I walk among the huge stone blocks, beside reconstructed columns of ancient two-story shops. Shortly, I'm high above the city, looking down on flattop buildings and bright-white spires. Along the southern flank of the mountain, past the ruins of a small temple dedicated to Hera and another to Cybele, I come to a naturally formed terrace, where the ruins of the temple of Demeter, which date from the 3rd Century BC, lie scattered about.

This site is the major reason I've come to Pergamon.

Demeter was the sister of Zeus and lived on Mt. Olympus with the rest of the Olympian gods, but she was concerned with the Earth rather than the shenanigans of the more social and political gods and goddesses. She was the goddess of vegetation, and in particular, farm crops, with the exception of the bean, which she considered impure. She caused all green things to grow. The line by the English poet Dylan Thomas, "The force that through the green fuse drives the flower..."[334] is a marvelous depiction of her influence.

Cultivation of the soil was a holy act presided over by Demeter.[335] She's frequently associated with corn, but not the corn we know in America. Corn was developed by Native Americans, and not taken to Europe until Columbus returned from America in 1492 AD. "Corn" meant either wheat or barley to the ancient Greeks.

Demeter's worshipers practiced her ancient Mysteries. They were the best-kept secret of all antiquity. The Mysteries were unveiled in an elaborate ceremony that was so secret, it continued uninterrupted two thousand years.[336] The ancients didn't leave enough clues for archeologists and scholars to decode it. The ancient Greeks believed the Mysteries made existence possible, and held the entire human race together.[337]

Turkey: Pergamon

Demeter's temple, as with the rest of this site, has been destroyed. The only remains are architectural fragments, portions of walls, and a few remaining columns standing vertical, but now supporting nothing but blue sky. I enter the temple through the propylon, and walk down a flight of ten stone steps between two tall marble columns. The ruins lying before me are the size of a football field, and sparsely covered with tender green grass beneath the tall coarse shafts of last year's crop. To my left, at the edge of the site, the mountain falls precipitously away to the vast open expanse above the city, giving me a touch of vertigo.

I'm here a little later in the year than I would like because the Mysteries were celebrated during the month of Boedromion 12-23. This would have been in the late summer or early autumn of August-September, the time of desolate fields, and prior to renewal, the sprouting of all things green.

The Mysteries were practiced in several locations throughout ancient Greece: here at Pergamon, on the nearby island of Samothrace, where Poseidon watched the Trojan War, and in Crete, where some believe they originated.[338] When Jason and the Argonauts sailed the northern edge of the Aegean to the far side of the Black Sea to retrieve the Golden Fleece, Orpheus had them stop off at Samothrace to be initiated into the Mysteries before entering the Dardanelles. That way, if they died in the attempt, they would have the consolation of eternal life. During the Mysteries here in Pergamon, the initiates sung Orphic Hymns.

Orpheus was the earliest of all religious figures, and labeled "famous Orpheus," even when his name first appears in writings of the 6th Century BC.[339] He was the mortal son of Apollo and the muse Kalliope. Apollo taught him to play the lyre. He was the earthly prophet of Dionysus, serving to moderate the ritual madness of his cult and make it more civilized. Orphism had a code of conduct, and was ultimately moral in its belief. Orpheus was a gentle shepherd and minstrel who played a golden lyre, and whose music made rocks move, trees congregate and wild beasts lie together at his feet.

Dionysus also played a major role in the Mysteries. The Orphic Hymns are prayers directed to eighty-seven different deities. The hymn "To Dionysus" recognized his wild side, but called upon his softer nature:

I call upon loud-roaring and reveling Dionysos,
primeval, two-natured, thrice-born, Bacchic lord,
savage, ineffable, secretive, two-horned and two-shaped.
Ivy-covered, bull-faced, warlike, howling, pure,
you take raw flesh, you have triennial feasts, wrapt in foliage,
   decked with grape clusters.
Resourceful Eubouleus, immortal god sired by Zeus

323

when he mated with Persephone in unspeakable union.
Hearken to my voice, O blessed one, and with your fair-girdled nurses
breathe on me in a spirit of perfect kindness.[340]

The Mysteries were based upon the disappearance of Demeter's daughter, Persephone, and Demeter's search for her, as well as Demeter's wandering and grieving. The story was ritualized, as was the death of Jesus by Christians: the Last Supper, his Crucifixion and Resurrection. Persephone was abducted as she played in a field of flowers, snatched as she reached for a narcissus blossom. Mother Earth and Zeus participated in the abduction. Zeus okayed his daughter's abduction, and Mother Earth caused the narcissus to bloom as a snare to attract Persephone so that her abductor could spring from the Underworld to grab her.

Everyone, except for Persephone and her mother, understood what was happening. Even those who heard and saw the abduction did nothing to prevent it, and the story takes on a lighthearted sense of tragic necessity, even though they were concerned about the grief of Demeter and her unnecessary pain. From her cave, Hekate, a torch-bearing goddess of the Underworld, heard Persephone's scream. Helios, the sun god, saw and heard the abduction from his brilliant orbit high in the heavens. Too late, her mother heard her shrill cry. Neither of them helped Demeter find her daughter, "... none of the gods or mortal men wanted to tell her the truth and none of the birds of omen came to her as truthful messenger."[341]Hades, Lord of the Underworld, had abducted Persephone. Afterward, Persephone herself became Mistress of the Underworld, and was so feared that no one was permitted to speak her name in public.

The most famous site for initiation into the Mysteries of Eleusis is on the coast just west of Athens, where people came from all over the known world in search of life after death. I hope to see Eleusis in a few days.

I leave the temple of Demeter and struggle up the slope, past more ruins of a gymnasium and magazines imbedded in the side of the mountain, walk the stone-paved road to the temple of Dionysus. Here, Dionysus' position as god of wine comes into full focus. The people of ancient Pergamon came here to eat food and drink wine left on the marble podium. The worshipers lay down and got drunk, thus opening the door to Dionysus, his joy, his madness.

From the temple of Dionysus, I wind along the western slope, the walkway formed of huge, flat stones buried in earth, with green sprigs of grass growing between them. I come to an ancient theatre carved out of the mountain, overlooking the modern city, a view to strike awe in anyone. Along the lower edge of the theatre are the ruins of a long promontory lined with ancient shops.

Turkey: Pergamon

At the far end of the 250-meter promontory is another temple of Dionysus, patron deity of theatre and god of the mask, gateway into madness. The priests of Dionysus conducted bloody sacrifices here prior to each performance.

The theatre, which seated 10,000, is more dramatic than that at Ephesus due to its commanding height on the mountainside. The steep-sloping seats fan outward from the stage, the first cupped funnel ending at a terrace, only to resume climbing the mountain to another terrace, and above it, the largest fan of seats dominating the entire expanse of city and countryside. The two upper sections are partial fans, lying flatter on the decreasing slope of the mountain. The acoustics were poor, and walls were built along the edges to hold in the sound.

I walk around the theatre, up the slope to the remains of the temple of Zeus, its ruins dominated by two large oak trees. The oak was sacred to Zeus, the rustle of its leaves being read by seers as the voice of Zeus. I walk above it to the temple of Athena, and look down on the theatre. The view is even more dramatic, the entire countryside now visible. Four tumului, ancient gravesites, pock the plane. The city is an amorphous sprawl of white and red speckles.

Next to the temple of Athena are the ruins of the famous Pergamon Library, home to 200,000 books. The term "book" originally applied to clay tablets and papyrus rolls. The ancient Greeks wrote on papyrus manufactured in Alexandria, Egypt. But the library here in Pergamon came to rival that in Alexandria, so Egypt placed an embargo on papyrus in about 190 BC. This forced Pergamon to switch to parchment made from animal skins. The word parchment evolved from the name "Pergamon." Parchment was used in the form of a codex, with both sides used for writing. Consequently, the modern form of the "book" was invented here at Pergamon.

Above the temple of Athena are the remains of the Royal Palace and beyond it, at the top of the akropolis, the arsenal where food, weapons and ammunition were stored. Much of the ammunition was stone-size shots hurled from the city walls by catapults.

I stand at the summit of the akropolis and survey the landscape. The region is more mountainous than I had thought from the plain below. To the north, the Bergama Cayi flows through a ravine cut sharply into the mountains. To the south, rolling hills are now turning a faint green. To the west, the plane, along which runs the road to the coast, lies between rolling hills. Perhaps I'm kidding myself, but I believe I can see the island of Lesbos in the distance. Lesbos has a rather bizarre connection with Orpheus. I hope to be there in a few days.

I grab a bite to eat at a dive off the main drag, give up looking for something exotic and have pide, a small, elongated Turkish pizza, tourist food. Afterward,

Turkey: Pergamon

I make the long trek to the western part of town and the other significant archaeological site in Bergama, the Asklepion. This huge site is tucked into the fold of rolling hills. The earliest remains date from the 4th Century BC.

The entrance to the site is adjacent to a car park. I walk an ancient Sacred Way, which is paved with large, uneven blocks of andesite and lined with tall-standing portions of columns. The propylon, or entryway, contains a few pieces of large marble monuments. The Asklepion is a huge rectangle. The entry side was reserved for buildings, and the other three sides were colonnades; many of the slender columns with Ionic capitals still stand. They enclosed galleries. At the far side of the site, to the northwest, a small theatre is recessed in the hillside. In the middle of the site is a Sacred Fountain.

When I was in the Peloponnese, Letizia and I visited Epidaurus, the most famous of all sites devoted to Asklepios, the god of healing. Asklepios was the divine healer, the physician, who had been educated by the centaur Cheiron. Asklepios' two mortal sons, Machaeon and Podaleirius, were among the Greek forces at Troy. Eurypylus, the son of Telephos, killed Machaeon in the war, but Eurypylus himself was killed by Neoptolemus. Machaeon was the first surgeon. He had been coerced into fighting in the Trojan War because he was one of Helen's suitors.

Hypocrites, the father of ancient and modern medicine, was a member of Asklepios' cult, the Asklepiadae, sons of Asklepios, as I related when we docked at Kos on our way to Patmos. Hypocrites gave us the Hippocratic Oath, which some physicians still take before starting practice. Galen (130-200 AD), Greek founder of experimental physiology and the most famous physician of the Roman Empire, was born and received his training here at Pergamon. Thus the tradition that began with the centaur Cheiron was passed on to Galen and disseminated to the Romans. I suspect more than a coincidental connection between Achilles' cure of Telephos using rust from the sword that caused his wound, to a modern treatment technique for diseases, inoculation.

Asklepios' downfall as a mortal was due to his extraordinary healing powers. He was not content to heal the living sick and injured, and started resurrecting the dead. Zeus was afraid he would let the race of men live forever, and killed him with a lightening bolt. But Apollo rescued him and made him immortal.

Asklepios is closely related to Demeter by his snake aspect, which the ancients believed to be connected with healing. Snakes live both above and below ground, as do herbs with their healing powers.[342] During the Mysteries, the following hymn was sung to Asklepios:

Asklepios, lord Paian, healer of all,

you charm away the suffering of men in pain.
Come, mighty and soothing, bring health,
and put an end to sickness and the harsh fate of death.
Helper, blessed spirit of growth and blossoming, you ward evil off,
honored and mighty scion of Phoibos Apollon.
Enemy of disease, whose blameless consort is Hygieia,
come, O blessed one, as savior and bring life to a good end.[343]

Asklepios, like Dionysus, was born of a mortal mother who died from a lightning bolt thrown by Zeus. Both of their births occurred during their mothers' deaths. Asklepios was originally mortal, whereas Dionysus was always a god. But Asklepios was the god who healed the human psyche through dream therapy. A belief held in Pergamon was that Hades, Lord of the Underworld, could not enter the Asklepion; therefore, no one ever died here.

I walk through the site to the north corner, where a small theatre sits recessed into the hillside. The theatre was used for concerts and plays connected with the treatment of patients. It seated 3,500. The grandeur of the theatre on the akropolis is not present here. This small theatre projects an intimate, quiet atmosphere, as a part of the rolling hills.

I walk diagonally across the quadrangle to its center, where I hear the gentle gurgle of healing water flowing from the Sacred Fountain. The water is slightly radioactive, which is supposed to give it healing qualities. Just beyond the sacred spring is the cryptoportico, a stone-enclosed walkway eighty meters long and built below ground, a man-built cavern. Water from the sacred spring ran down the center of the cryptoportico causing small waterfalls, and playing musically with the damp, dark atmosphere. It leads to the south corner of the quadrangle and the temple of Telesphorus. Telesphorus was a dwarf-like, nocturnal companion of Asklepios, a child-god in a hooded cloak,[344] and known as the Bringer of Fulfillment.[345] Telesphorus, being nocturnal, was complementary to Asklepios, whose epiphany came with sunrise. The proper sacrifice to Asklepios was a rooster.[346]

The round building dedicated to Telesphorus is known as the Therapy Building. Next to it is another round building, the temple of Asklepios. Patients slept in both buildings, praying until they fell asleep. The next morning, attending physicians interpreted their dreams. Treatments also consisted of "faith healing, self-suggestion, psychology, sports, mud baths, and baths in the water from the sacred spring."[347] The round building and adjacent structures are a maze of large stacked stones forming arches, walls, stairs. Large, amorphous, crumbling sections of walls made of small rocks and dirt rise up into the afternoon air.

Turkey: Pergamon

Asklepios' daughter was Hygieia, who frequently accompanied him and was his feminine counterpart, the archetype of the modern nurse.

★

I'm back on the main road, sitting on the bus to Izmir and Seljuk. We're a few kilometers from Bergama and moving rapidly. On the trip back from Pergamon, I avoided a dolmus by taking the bus. I changed buses at the roadside stop, and now I'm on a high-riding Mercedes. A baby crying a few seats from me, a snoring Turk up front, and the murmur of a few random voices only faintly penetrate the silence. The sun is set, but the glow of twilight has turned the landscape surreal. I should get to Seljuk by nine o'clock tonight.

After the Trojan War, a great upheaval came to the Mycenaean world, and sometime around 1190 BC, the civilization progressively declined and gradually collapsed, thus ending the Bronze Age. In the years following the Trojan War, a strange Sea People, many of whom were aligned with the ancient Greeks, plundered throughout the Mediterranean. Once Ares, god of war, had been awakened, he couldn't be put to sleep again. All over Greece, kingdoms were sieged and burned to the ground. A great migration occurred in the 11th Century BC, and a "Dark Age" fell on Greece, during which they lost the ability to write. The pictographic scripts of Linear A, which was used on Crete, and Linear B, which was used on mainland Greece, had been used primarily for official documents and inventories. They were preserved on clay tablets that were baked in the conflagrations of the cities during siege.

Many Mycenaeans, particularly those from Athens, resettled in Asia Minor, and the entire western coast of Asia Minor became Greek. They called the central coastal area Ionia, along with the two islands Samos and Chios. Androclus founded Greek Ephesus a hundred years later. Androclus was the grandson of Melanthus, a legendary king of Athens. To become king, Melanthus had killed Thymoites, the last descendant of Theseus.[348] Melanthus was succeeded by his son, Codrus, and Codrus' son was Androclus, who led the expedition to Ionia and founded Greek Ephesus in 1087 BC.

King David of the Bible, circa 1000 BC, fought against the Philistines, an evil enemy in the eyes of ancient Hebrews. But now we can put a face on that enemy, one more objective than that provided 3000 years ago by the Hebrews. The face is that of an ancient Greek. Goliath, calling out a Hebrew to fight him one-on-one, is similar to the time-honored custom of the ancient Greeks.[349] As examples, consider Polyneices versus Eteocles during Seven Against Thebes, Menelaus versus Paris, and Achilles versus Hektor during the Trojan War. Goliath's armor was also similar to that of Achilles:[350]

And he had an helmet of brass upon his head, and he was armed with a coat of mail; and the weight of the coat was five thousand shekels of brass. And he had greaves of brass upon his legs, and a target of brass between his shoulders. And the staff of his spear was like a weaver's beam; and his spear's head weighed six hundred shekels of iron; and one bearing a shield went before him.[351]

Goliath may have been a rather recent descendant of the Mycenaeans.

The Dark Age lasted four hundred years. Pergamon and Ephesus were but two of many new Greek colonies. From archeological excavations, we know that many Greeks also resettled in Phoenicia, the homeland of Kadmos and Europa, and what was at the time called Canaan by the Hebrews. For the descendants of Kadmos and Europa, it must have been like a homecoming of sorts.

The Mycenaeans gradually merged into the cultural landscape. During the Dark Age, which was marked by poverty and social chaos, stories of the Greek gods and the Mycenaean kings, Oedipus, Theseus, Achilles, Agamemnon, Odysseus, Menelaus, were sung in the ruins of ancient palaces, and about the campfires during the long night of Greek civilization. Stories passed from generation to generation through this oral tradition gradually consolidated, and around 750 BC, the works of Homer and Hesiod were written on tablets, perhaps a century after their verbal composition. A new civilization emerged from the Dark Age, one no longer based on palace-centered bureaucratic states,[352] but on the polis or city-state.[353]

As the Mycenaean Greeks merged with the local communities on the coast of Asia Minor, Cypress and Phoenicia, so the Greek gods merged with the eastern religions, and thus, Artemis merged with the Great Mother goddess of the East, Cybele. Ephesian Artemis became the heart and soul of that city. This was the situation when St. Paul came here in 53 AD, hot on the trail of all idolaters.

When Manto, the daughter of the Theban seer Teiresias, who came here from Delphi, first reached the coast of Asia Minor, she encountered a colony of Cretans, possibly those who came with Miletus. She married one of them, Rakios, and had a son. She named him Mopsus. Manto founded Colophon, just a few kilometers from Ephesus, several years before the Trojan War. In addition to being a seer, Manto was famous for her poetry. Diodorus Siculus says she wrote some of Homer's best lines:

This maiden possessed no less knowledge of prophecy than her father Teiresias, and in the course of her stay at Delphi she developed her skill to a far greater degree; moreover, by virtue of the employment of a marvellous natural gift, she also wrote oracular responses of every sort, excelling in their composition; and indeed it was from her poetry, they say, that the poet Homer took many verses which he appropriated as his own and with them adorned his own poesy.[354]

Homer was also from this area, lived in Smyrna (Izmir), where I'm now headed, around 750 BC, almost 600 years after Manto. Manto's son, Mopsus, followed in his mother's and his grandfather's footsteps and became a gifted seer himself.

Calchas, the seer who went to Troy with Agamemnon, saw into the future. He realized the problems the Greeks would have returning home, because of the rape of Cassandra at Athena's temple during the siege of Troy. So after the war, he, along with some of his followers, wandered down the coast of Asia Minor and also settled at Colophon, where he met Manto's son. Calchas was jealous of Mopsus' powers of prophecy, and challenged him to a duel, a duel of seers. Calchas asked Mopsus:

> ...how many figs were growing on a wild fig tree nearby, Mopsus answered, "Ten thousand and a bushel and one fig over," and the answer turned out to be correct. Mopsus then asked Calchas how many pigs a pregnant sow was carrying in her womb and when was she due to give birth to them. When Calchas answered eight, Mopsus smiled and said, "Calchas, you fall short of true prophecy but I, who am the son of Apollo and Manto, have a wealth of keen vision. I say that there are not eight, as Calchas says, but nine in the womb, all males, and that they will be born tomorrow exactly at the sixth hour." When it turned out to be so, Calchas died of a broken heart...[355]

Thus brought to an end one of the most notorious seers of Mycenaean Greece.

Mopsus' story doesn't end there. He drifted along the southern coast of Asia Minor, and eventually, into Phoenicia. According to the ancient Lydian historian Xanthus, he went to the Philistine city of Ashkelon, and quarreled with the priests of the local goddess. In an event reminiscent of St. John's encounter with Cynops on Patmos, Mopsus threw her into the city pond, thus destroying her power.[356]

The legend of Mopsus has striking parallels to that of Samson from the Bible.[357] Samson's tribe, the Dan, was much like the Danaans, and apparently, not always one of the tribes of Israel.[358] Samson's physical strength and sexual exploits are characteristics of the ancient Greeks, not the Hebrews. Eventually, he was betrayed by the Philistine, Delilah, which led to his death. Samson was fond of riddles, which reminds us of the myth of Oedipus. Since the time period for both Mopsus and Samson overlap, some believe they may be the same person.[359]

The bus is very quiet, everyone lost in their own thoughts. Darkness has consumed the landscape, and all that's visible is car headlights whizzing past us on the left and bright-red taillights in front.

★

I sit on the bus in Izmir. We leave for Seljuk in just a few minutes, at eight-thirty. A Turkish game show shouts from a TV up front. Game shows have taken over the world. The bus from Bergama had aisles so narrow, I had to turn sidewise to walk through. This bus is the most plush I have been on, a Mercedes as before, but this time brand new. The seats are gray felt, with a stripe of geometric design down the middle, purple, blue and red. The interior of the bus is gray. The paneling on the sides below the windows is dark violet, as are the drapes that are pulled open and belted to the posts. I should be at the New Zealand Pension by 10:00 PM. We've started to move, only ten minutes late.

★

We should be in Seljuk by now, but we've stopped at a gas station that is also a market, fast food restaurant and fruit stand, just up the road from Seljuk. I'm impatient and irritable, sitting on the bus alone in the dark. I've got to get a bed at the New Zealand pension before they all go to sleep. The passengers are now re-boarding the bus. The bus starts and begins to move. Off to Seljuk.

The young man sitting next to me opens his pack, takes out a candy bar and offers me two squares of chocolate. After refusing once, I accept, because they look so delicious, and I'm so hungry. After putting the creamy milk chocolate in my mouth, I chide myself for accepting candy from a stranger. He asks in French if I speak French, and I tell him no in English. We sit quietly for a while, and I keep checking my condition to ensure I've not been drugged.

When I see buildings in the dark at the side of the road, I ask him if we're in Seljuk. "Seljuk?" I ask. He says something that I interpret as yes. Evidently he's getting off also, because he closes his pack, puts on his coat. He says a few words to the bus steward, and the bus slows, stops. "Seljuk," he says to me as he gets out of his seat. I look out the window at the buildings in the dark, and nothing looks familiar. I shake my head no. "This isn't Seljuk," I say, knowing my words are useless. Then the bus steward steps forward, "Seljuk," he says and motions me off the bus.

331

Turkey: Pergamon

Both of them are insistent I should get off, but I'm really at a loss. I know this isn't the main intersection in Seljuk, where the road from Izmir crosses that from Kusadasi, but then I think maybe they only make one stop in Seljuk, and perhaps the intersection is a short walk away. I grab my coat and daypack and exit the bus behind the young man who shared his chocolate with me.

As the bus roars off in a cloud of smoke, I realize I've done the wrong thing. I'm nowhere near the New Zealand pension or carpet shop. The darkness about me fills with all the bad stories I've heard of the violent, murderous Turks. The young man walks away from me, and I'm glad, as I was beginning to believe he was in cahoots with the steward to get me off the bus so he could mug me.

But the young man looks back, sees me standing at the side of the road befuddled, and walks back. "Monsieur, pension?" he asks. "New Zealand pension," I answer. "Ah," he says, and motions for me to follow. "Taxi," he says, "taxi."

I'm relieved that he understands my predicament, but I see no taxi, and assume he's taking me to a phone booth so I can call one. I follow, with him emitting a stream of French, all comforting sounds, but totally lost on me, except for an occasional "Monsieur." But he doesn't take me to a phone booth or a taxi. He takes me to his car.

All of this is happening rapidly, and with my misgivings mounting exponentially. Here is a man who has insisted I get off the bus at the wrong place, insisted I follow him under the pretext of getting a taxi for me, and now expects me to get into a car with him. He unlocks the passenger door, throws it open and walks to the other side, unlocks his door, and crawls inside.

I'm now at the decision point, and I realize most emphatically I could be putting myself in danger. I'm losing control of the situation. But the young man is nicely dressed, dark suit and tie, and his car, although not a Mercedes, is almost new and looks expensive, well kept.

What the heck. I slip in the passenger seat and put my daypack on the floorboard in front of me, buckle my seat belt, still with considerable misgivings. He turns the ignition key, the motor roars to life, and the tape deck immediately starts playing a Mozart piano concerto. I convince myself muggers don't listen to Mozart on their car stereos.

He drives in what I believe is the direction of Seljuk although I'm no longer certain of anything. I could have stayed on the bus too long and passed the intersection I'm looking for. As we come into the downtown area, a welcome sight appears, the New Zealand carpet shop. I now know where I am, but when I motion for him to turn left to the New Zealand Pension, he turns right, out to what I know is open country, dark open country toward the ruins of Ephesus.

Turkey: Pergamon

Then he makes another right up a dark alley, all the time a stream of what to me is unintelligible French coming from him, makes another right up an even darker alley and stops the car.

All my uncertainty has evaporated. I brace myself knowing this is where he mugs me. I look to see if he has a gun or a knife. Is mugging all he has on his mind? Does he just want my wallet, or does he also want my life?

But he says "New Zealand Pension, okay?" I say "No," the word coming out in a little frightened squeak, and then he sees a sign, "Australian-New Zealand Pension," and realizes this is the wrong pension.

He drives back to the center of town, me pointing and shouting to show the way. I tell him to stop, shake his hand, thank him very, very much, and walk through the dark to the New Zealand Pension, thrilled I'm still alive.

CHAPTER 17: Turkey: Ephesus II.

Inside the pension, I run into Tim and Jane, the Aussie couple, and learn that Sarah never returned from Istanbul. This is, indeed, bad news, but not unexpected. They also say that anyone who could rent a room to me is partying at the carpet shop. I take a stroll through the dark, back along the highway where a few minutes ago I thought I was going to get mugged. I also have to get my backpack from Arhman. All the time I've been gone, I've worried about the first volume of my journal and my film.

They're watching a soccer match on TV, Turkey against Barcelona, all about half looped and very glad to see me. First, I talk to Turgay about a ferry to Samos. He keeps up with them, because it's good business to know when potential customers for the carpet shop enter the country. He tells me to come see him at the carpet shop tomorrow afternoon, and he will call a travel agent.

Arhman gives me a glass of raki cut with bottled water, and quickly drags it out of me that I haven't eaten. He runs into the kitchen, fixes a big plate of baked chicken, potatoes and eggplant. A wonderful meal, the Thanksgiving dinner I've been wishing for all day. It's good to be home, and "home" is how I feel about the New Zealand pension.

I sit at the kitchen table eating, while talking to two young women from South Africa, Susan and Deborah. When I mention I've followed in Oedipus' footsteps in Greece, Susan comes to life. In college, she's studied the classics as well as psychology, knows all about Freud and the Oedipus complex. She's studied Homer and wants to see the setting of *The Iliad* firsthand. The two of them are leaving for Canakkale tomorrow. I tell her about seeing the Cleft Way, where Oedipus killed his father. After talking to Susan for a few minutes, I'm so excited I tremble. What's happening to me? Why am I so emotional?

Suddenly a ruckus breaks out by the TV, much shouting and obvious disappointment. The soccer game between Turkey and Barcelona has ended in a tie. Two Turks shout at each other, and I see the unmistakable flash of rage. Chairs are thrown back from the table, and people scatter as Turgay steps between the two hot-heads. One is a tall older man, well-built and commanding. The other

Turkey: Ephesus II

is young, even better built, his face flushed with rage. The rest of us stop talking, and I reluctantly keep my chair. The Turks push the older man out the door and down the street, he resists all the way, while four restrain the young man, arms interlocked with his to contain the raging bull he has become. He calms and they release him, but suddenly, he's out the door with another man following close behind. Four more men hurriedly exit through the back door.

★

Sometime after midnight, I sneak into the same room I was in before I left for Troy. The bed by the door where I slept is occupied, and Janice with the golden hair and delicate hands is still in the one beneath the window. The center bed is vacant. I take the fourth bed against the left wall, just a step from Janice, slipping my clothes off in the dark.

26 Nov, Friday

I wake when Janice stirs. She winks, slips out of bed already dressed in psychedelic stretch pants and takes off for a shower. The young man in the bed by the door slowly rouses, and we strike up a conversation from opposite sides of the room. He gets dressed, while I tell him of my adventure coming back from Pergamon, the man I thought was going to mug me. Michael was in Troy yesterday himself, coming from Istanbul. He had a bad experience that wasn't so benign, but he sheepishly declines to elaborate. "Perhaps when I know you better," he says. But he can't shut up, keeps telling on himself, and the story gradually unfolds.

In Istanbul, Michael got hooked up with a seemingly nice man who showed him the sites, fed him dinner, carried his pack for him, and ripped off his passport. Michael was into what he had thought was an "ethnic experience." His only hint of the coming disaster occurred while they were having dinner. One of the man's friends came to their table and talked with him briefly. The other man was frightening, an evil-looking, angry man.

I hear a commotion on the street outside our window, so I dress and stand before it while Michael talks and dresses. Outside, the school kids, must be high school, are on their way to their classes. They are all dressed in uniforms, girls in white blouses, blue sweaters and plaid skirts; the guys in blue suits, white shirts and ties. Amazing how European the next generation looks.

Michael's story sounds scary after my experience last night on the outskirts of Seljuk. It was a sobering experience, he says. Looking back on it, he realizes he was dealing with a professional. He believes that once the man hooked up with him, he would have gotten his passport one way or another. The part Michael didn't want to tell me was that his passport was in his backpack instead of his security pouch on a string around his neck, as it should have been. He had to get a new passport at the American consulate. Now he may have trouble getting out of Turkey because he doesn't have an entry stamp.

Michael also had a bad experience on the bus coming from Troy to Seljuk. He was traveling with a young lady, another traveler he met on the road. The steward asked if the two of them were married, and Michael made the mistake of saying no. Since Michael wears an earring, the bus steward assumed he was homosexual and separated them, forcefully. He then made several advances at the girl, assuming she was a prostitute. He tweaked Michael under the chin and flipped his ear, made derogatory comments.

Just as Michael finishes his story, the young man from Denver, one of the newlyweds I was with when I first entered Turkey, bursts into the room with the Seljuk newspaper. Seems they've published a picture of a snowstorm in Denver, Colorado. Back home, they have a foot of snow, and traffic has been brought to a standstill on I 25. Seven-thousand miles away and still getting news of home.

Michael and Janice walk to Ephesus together, and I spend the morning in the living room of the pension, listening to the light chatter of travelers and writing in my journal. Alan, the fifteen-year traveler from Kenya, is still here. He's leaving tomorrow, on his way to southern Turkey to photograph the giant sea turtles before they become extinct. Their only breeding ground has been sold to private companies, and is being destroyed.

Alan is an enigma. I ask him the purpose of all these years traveling. I've struck a chord. "I'm looking for the cause of war," he says. "I want to know why countries can't resolve their conflicts peacefully."

"Sounds a lot like the reason I'm traveling," I say.

"Have you found an answer?" he asks.

"Oedipus," I say. "Sophocles had all the answers."

In the afternoon, I walk to the carpet shop to see Turgay about a ferry to Samos. He knows all the travel agents. I'm anxious to get back to Samos and travel on to Lesbos. Outside the shop, I encounter the most gorgeous camel I've ever seen. He has huge feet, a large head, mouth foaming from a long journey. His owner stands beside him, engaged in conversation with another man.

I go inside the shop and talk to Turgay about a ferry, and he calls a travel agent. The ferry to Samos left yesterday, and another won't sail until Thursday, six days from now. My other option is to leave Turkey by plane. A flight leaves Izmir for Athens on Tuesday, four days from now. The price is $112, American. I must find a dependable way to get back into Greece, or I'll miss my flight back to the States. But I'm not ready to put out that much money or pass up Lesbos yet.

Turkey: Ephesus II

When I come out of the shop, I see the camel again, and hurry to the pension to get my camera before he walks off. I mention to Jane that I want to take a picture of a gorgeous camel, and she says, "You mean that big stuffed one out front of the carpet shop?"

I've been disoriented all morning. I feel sick: headaches and stomach feels strange. I don't feel comfortable in Turkey, regardless of how nice the people have been. I feel comfortable in the pension, but not out in public. I'm suspicious of people, and Michael is not the only one who has had bad experiences. One of the women staying here with her husband had a frightening experience in Izmir while showering. A masturbating man took his pleasure watching her silhouette through the glass door. And not being able to tell the difference between a real and a stuffed camel has set me to wondering if I could take care of myself in a hazardous situation, if I, like Michael, would mistake it for an ethnic experience.

Michael and Janice have been out together all day, and I'm jealous that he's had her to himself. The three of us go to dinner together. Janice still has two weeks before going back to Houston. "I'm going to Egypt before returning," she says, as if she's trying to convince herself. She confesses to being a little apprehensive, and wishes she had a companion. She looks me in the eye. "I'll marry you for a month if you go with me," she says. I know she's kidding, but her statement still has an emotional impact.

When we get back from dinner, I stay downstairs with Susan, talking about Oedipus, before she catches the night bus to Canakkale, and Michael and Janice go upstairs to our bedroom, saying they'll be right back. But I can hardly talk to Susan for thinking about the two of them in our bedroom. A flood of fantasies clouds my thoughts about the two of them engaged in sex. Suddenly, I'm enraged, unreasonably sensing a violation of trust. I force myself to remain in the living room talking to Susan, talking about Oedipus killing Laios. I'm certain it would be okay for me to go upstairs, but would prefer to remain down here basking in a jealous rage. No sense destroying this emotional windfall by confronting it with reality.

Janice and Michael eventually come down after Susan leaves for the otogar. The three of us talk again, mostly Michael yakking, Janice and me listening, until Michael and I get into a heated argument over California history. I feel the anger rising again, see his hostility escalate to match mine. He defends his position by saying he was educated in the California school system, and I respond that I was raised in California too, spent twenty years there.

When I get mad, I'm not good at arguing. My thought processes shutdown. I leave the argument, wallowing in thoughts of killing him in his sleep. Janice

337

notices none of this. She's simply mesmerized by his monologue. Michael continues talking until bedtime, me losing myself in Janice's dreamy blue eyes.

We all go upstairs to bed.

★

I wake from a dream set in a land at war. We plot strategy, then carry rifles while walking dark barren streets and over brush-covered hillsides. It's a desolate dream, born of hopelessness and an unbearable sense of predestination. I lie awake thinking of war, and drift into thoughts of Agamemnon's daughter, how she gave her life for the sake of the Trojan War. I have the feeling the parallel between Iphigenia and my daughter is even closer than I've realized.

During the months following my daughter's Christmas visit, she became distant, wasn't communicative during my telephone calls. I realized that kids push away from their parents at her age, but this seemed different. She had always looked forward to college, but now would no longer discuss it. She became more involved in rock music. I bought her a keyboard to augment her lessons on the guitar. She was serious, dedicated. She devoted herself to choir at school. But instead of growing up, she appeared to be reverting, or at least hanging on to adolescent inclinations. Though she was a senior, most of her friends were freshmen. She put ads in a small weekly newspaper called New Times, corresponded with kids about rock stars. On the surface, all this seemed harmless enough, but she was a recluse and uncommunicative. At least, this was the way it appeared to her mother and me.

I was involved at work and eager to believe all was well. I was supervising several engineers and overseeing the procurement of critical flight hardware. I frequently flew to Los Angeles on the company plane. At other times, I traveled to Long Island, New York to coordinate a subcontract with Grumman Corporation. I was a manager, responsible for several million dollars worth of engineering and very much enjoying my new responsibilities.

27 Nov, Saturday

I wake early, but remain in bed, soaking in drowsiness. Michael talks to me from across the room about going with him to Aphrodesia today. Our conversation wakes Janice, but she also seems too tired to rise. Michael sees me writing in my journal and admits to being a poet. After we're dressed, he shows me some of the poems he's written on his journey. Michael is young and excitable. I expect his poetry to be trite, but that's just my residual anger about last night. His poetry is well-constructed, lyrical and dramatic, full of rhyme. Reminds me of Shelly. The voice of his poems jumps out at me, shouts as it rumbles about in images of the ancient ruins, the gods and heroes coming to

338

Turkey: Ephesus II

life. My words of encouragement are well received.

He tries again to get me to go with him to Aphrodesia, but I've decided to stay here and buy a plane ticket from Izmir to Athens. The plane will leave at noon on Tuesday. I can't afford to wait for a ferry that might not actually sail for several weeks. I've been thinking a lot about Aulis on the coast of Attica, where Agamemnon sacrificed Iphigenia.

After Michael leaves, I grab my sweater and head for the market. The place doesn't seem as intimidating as it did a week ago. Still hordes of people. I'm particularly interested in the mandarin oranges. I've become addicted to them.

★

Mid-afternoon, I go back to the market for a goat-meat sandwich. Tim and Jane have just come in with one each, and I'm starved. The one I had at Troy has changed my taste buds, I guess. This time I walk back into the sheds, where they have the clothing laid out on tabletops. Every article of clothing on the planet must have migrated here for this single day. The tables are so crowded, I can't get close enough to shop.

After I return to the pension, I sit in the living room chatting with Tim and Jane, when Janice comes to say good-bye. She has her large backpack and a folded carpet. "Would you like some help?" I ask. She gives me a rather severe look. "I've made it this far without you," she says. I sit back down. "I just wanted to see you off," I say. She squints a little through those dreamy eyes, a faint smile. "You could carry my carpet if you like." She's also on her way to Canakkale to see Troy. I walk beside her while she tells me of her plans to first go north to Troy, then south, possibly to Rhodes, and eventually, to Egypt. I suggest she catch the bus at the side of the road, as I did when I went to Troy, instead of going to the otogar. She flags down a big bus with an "Izmir" sign on the front, and I wrap my arms around her for second. The shampoo smell of bushy-blond hair. She disappears inside.

I watch her bus belch smoke into the distance, then walk across the street to the travel agency to get a plane ticket. A carpet salesman accosts me on the sidewalk. He's wild-eyed and desperate. "Best carpets, straight from Istanbul, one hundred dollars. Come look, please, come look. Good carpets, very good carpets." I'm afraid of him, taking to the road to get around him as he shouts after me.

At the travel agency, I learn the price previously quoted, $112 for the flight, was for a student fare. The price for me is $180. When I shake my head, tell him I can't afford it, he sits silent for a second, then tells me he received a call yesterday about a ferry to Samos, leaves Monday at eight-thirty in the morning. I buy a ticket for the ferry. It's the same small ferry I came to Turkey on. After I have my

339

Turkey: Ephesus II

ticket in my hand, he tells me they are ninety-nine percent sure the ferry will sail, and the one percent uncertainty is weather. Have I heard this story before? Check-in time is seven-thirty. Tight schedule but workable," he says. I don't trust his judgment on this, and plan to talk to Arhman at the pension.

I already feel the loneliness of leaving.

★

I wake in the middle of the night feeling very bad. I've been dreaming of descending into a cave-like labyrinth where people lived years before, an ancient cave with a rusty-hinged door. I squeeze through constricted places between ancient rocks, the walls growing tighter and tighter.

Several people are sick here at the New Zealand pension. Alex from Australia has had a fever and general weakness for several days and is staying here to recover, and Tim was coming down with a cold this evening. Michael has had a cold for a month. I can't stop thinking of arguing with Michael, and my restlessness is like something trying to get out of me, something frightening rebelling against me. Sometimes I believe I am a murderer, that I've acted on my murderous impulses sometime in the past. Having three other people in this room bothers me: the sounds of sleep, of people snoring, mumbling, and wrestling around are frightening.

28 Nov, Sunday

I'm still in bed, but the other two men I'm now rooming with are getting dressed after an aborted attempt to shower. No hot water. Alison, the owner, is frantically searching for the repairman. The girl in the center bed, who came in in the middle of the night, is still asleep, and I can see the bottom of her chubby foot sticking out from under the pink-flowered duvet. She talked in her sleep last night, lots of mumbles and erotic sighs. I bet her dreams are more interesting than mine.

A man from Washington DC now has the the bed where Janice of the golden hair and delicate hands slept. While he slips on his clothes, we talk. He's tall, stout-looking, hairy and dark-complexioned. He's half-Turkish on his father's side, and here looking for distant relatives. His grandfather fled Turkey to avoid fighting in the 2nd World War.

I've been undecided as to what to do today and considering going back to Ephesus. Although I enjoyed seeing the ruins with Bronwyn a few days ago, not having the solitude to write in my journal during my visit there has left me with a sense of incompleteness about the experience. I'll go back this afternoon.

At breakfast I meet my new roommate, the girl who uttered the erotic sighs all night. She came in with a man and another young woman. They're traveling in a van they bought in London. They've traveled through the Czech Republic, Slovakia, Romania, and Bulgaria. They say you can't get diesel in Romania, and the queues at the gas pumps are miles long.

Michael comes in to have breakfast with me. He's just finished packing and excited because he's leaving for Israel this morning. He's full of historical facts about Jerusalem, the Jordan River, the Dead Sea, and looking forward to walking in the footsteps of Jesus.

★

Early afternoon, I walk east along the side road paralleling the main road to Ephes. On the way, I'm accosted by a man on a motorcycle who wants to give me a ride. I decline, saying I'm enjoying the walk. So he drags out a plastic bag of old coins. He says in broken English that they were found at Efes. I don't want to offend him, so I smile and say they are nice, but then, of course, he wants me to buy them. I feel a little uneasy out here all alone, but eventually, the guy takes no for an answer and roars on.

★

I sit in the bright sun in the ruins at Ephesus, beside the Hydreion Fountain with flies buzzing and the dull clank of goat bells in the distance. I hear the chatter of tourists to my left at the Pollio Fountain and the temple of Domitian, where last week, I talked with three women, Sarah, Wendy and Bronwyn. To my right, farther down the Marble Road, stands the Celsus Library. A black dog, agile and thin, trots up the road in front of me. In the field in the distance, past the library, are more ruins. Beyond the church, cars whiz along the road to Kusadasi, where I'll catch the ferry tomorrow morning. North of the road, which is lined with evergreens and deciduous trees, I see more cultivated fields, and beyond them, the gentle slope of mountains rising out of haze.

I move on down to Celsus Library. The sun casts long shadows even at midday, but I sit in bright sunlight, warm enough to shed my hiking jacket. Tim and Jane pass by on their way up the slope to find a quiet place to have lunch. The sun goes behind the mountain, and cold follows fast. The birds in the trees come to life, their sharp, crisp cries punctuate the soft flutter of wings.

I jump at a gunshot echoing off the mountains in the distance, then settle back on the rock. It was just a car backfire, but I reacted as if it was a gunshot. I hear another. I've always had a problem mistaking loud noises for gunshots, but I never thought of the reason until now. My reaction is possibly a result of my father standing across the hall in his bedroom, loading the deer rifle. My father will always be in that bedroom; I'll always be face down on my bed, fingers clutching at the cold, white sheets, waiting for the gunshot. Every time a car backfires, every time a hammer drives a nail into wood, my father fires the deer rifle.

I move down the marble road in front of the theatre to catch a few more rays of the fast-sinking sun. A tour group of Turks walks past, up the Marble Road. The theatre is closed for repairs due to damage caused during a recent Sting concert. I'm not much on crashing gates in foreign countries, but I scramble over some rocks, climb an embankment, and shortly, I'm inside the theatre. I stand on the top row, looking over the vast expanse of seats and northwest to the ruins of the Church of the Virgin Mary, where the Third Ecumenical Council met in 431 AD. A capacity crowd of 24,000 must have been a tremendous sight in this ancient theatre, and quite a frightening sight to St. Paul, when his preaching here caused a near riot.

I see the road to Kusadasi in the distance. I'll be on that road tomorrow morning, on my way to Samos. Perhaps this time, I'll get to visit the temple of Hera on the island's southern coast. Hera was the goddess of marriage and family life. It's very quiet, just the tweet of small birds and the cough of a child from far below. I see Tim and Jane wandering about in front of the theatre.

St. Paul may have been initiated into Demeter's Mysteries.[360] He was an educated man, raised in the Greek city of Tarsus on Turkey's southern Mediterranean coast. Tarsus was an old Ionian city settled a thousand years before, during the wave of migrating Greeks following the Trojan War. It had a university where Greek philosophy was taught. His knowledge of the Mysteries is reflected in the language of his letters to the Corinthians, "... we speak the wisdom of God in a mystery, even the hidden wisdom which God ordained before the world..."[361] He even uses the metaphors of Demeter, goddess of cultivation:

> And that which thou sowest, thou sowest not that body that shall be, but are grain, it may chance of wheat, or of some other grain: But God giveth it a body as it hath pleased him, and to every seed his own body. It is sown a natural body; it is raised a spiritual body. There is a natural body, and there is a spiritual body.[362]

The sewing of grain is the central metaphor of Demeter's Mysteries.

The sun has gone behind the hill for a second time, shadows creeping along Marble road as it sets, and I leave the stadium to meet Tim and Jane below. Another couple from the pension walks back with us. We walk through the main gate into the sunlight, past the ruins of the temple of Artemis, on along the road to Seljuk, where St. John the Divine is buried. I feel all alone walking between these two couples, one couple in front talking quietly, Tim and Jane just a few steps behind, chuckling quietly, walking arm in arm.

Before we reach Seljuk, I break off from them, slow my pace so they move on ahead. The sun casts two rows of tree shadows across the field. As I reach the ruins of the temple of Artemis beneath the Basilica of St. John and the medieval fortress on the hilltop, an old lady and a young boy out in the field to the north catch a white horse and bring it out toward the road. They step out of the eucalyptus trees lining both sides of the road. Suddenly, the horse breaks loose from them. He's saddled and runs in my direction, a wild look in his eyes. My first inclination is to step aside and let him pass, but then I step forward to see if I might turn him.

He's a big, beautiful horse, dirty white in color from rolling on the ground. When I was a kid, I had a horse on the farm. I used to ride him bareback, until I took a bad spill when I was twelve. My father saw me take the fall, and forced me back on the horse immediately, even though my pride and confidence were badly shaken. My daughter was also a horse lover. She and I have been horseback riding together.

The horse rears on his hind legs, pawing at the air, and remarkably, stops in front of me. I take the dangling rein, pat him on the neck where his skin trembles, and on impulse, grab the saddle horn and mount him. I haven't been on a horse in years. He starts to gallop away from Seljuk, and I let him go, lean forward close to his neck and listen to the pounding hooves, feeling wild and exhilarated. As he slows, I turn him, dismount and walk him back to the old lady, a grand smile lighting her face.

★

I have dinner with the same two couples I walked back from Ephesus with, minus Tim. Tim is sick this evening, and stayed at the pension. We eat at the same restaurant where we ate our first night in Seljuk. I like Tim, but this evening it's kind of nice without him. It's Jane and me, and the other couple, two couples having dinner together.

★

I go to bed earlier than usual. I'm the only one in my room tonight. Michael is on his way to Israel, and the guy from DC left for parts unknown. The young lady in the center bed, little miss mumble and sigh, has gone on to south Turkey. Tomorrow morning, I'll rise at six, and a Turk from the carpet shop will take me to the ferry in Kusadasi.

While thinking of my departure, I wonder what went through my daughter's mind the evening before she disappeared. In April 1985, I was a busy man. I had astronauts calling me, was heavily involved in developing emergency EVA[363] procedures. I made several trips to Johnson Space Center, where a full-

343

scale mockup of our payload was being built inside the astronaut Water Test Facility, where astronauts test EVA procedures. I went regularly to Kennedy Space Center, where I received console training for the ground team to monitor flight hardware status during the Shuttle mission.

And the fact was, the Shuttle Centaur project was in trouble. All our hardware was behind schedule, and the managers at NASA wondered if we could make our launch date. We had a two-week window in May 1986 to get two Shuttle missions off. No schedule slips were possible, because both spacecrafts were going to Jupiter, and the Space Shuttle had to be launched when Jupiter was at the right spot in the heavens. It looked as if we would have to fly unqualified hardware, if we were going to launch at all. Some of us on the project talked openly of frying astronauts. All this excitement lured me further away from my daughter.

Four months after I saw Cyndi at Christmas, on Thursday April 19, 1985, I got a telephone call at three in the morning from my ex-wife. I remember my heart pounding from being shocked awake. I tried to shake a dream. She asked if I knew where Cyndi was. But Cyndi lived with her. Why would she call to ask me where she was? She told me Cyndi was missing.

My ex-wife had thought it unusual when Cyndi didn't come home the previous evening, but reasoned she was probably at the local pizza place, where she had a part time job. Around midnight, she started to worry, called the pizza place, and learned Cyndi hadn't been there at all. Then, my ex-wife looked in Cyndi's bedroom. All her music equipment was missing, her keyboard, amplifier, guitar. She wondered if Cyndi had been kidnapped during a robbery. She had called the police, but they told her to call back after eight in the morning when Detective Sim, who was in charge of the juvenile runaway cases, would be in.

I stayed awake the rest of the night, walked the floor thinking of all the bad things that could happen to a young girl out in the world. She had disappeared without warning, as if the earth had opened and swallowed her.

I went to work that morning in a daze, and called my ex-wife to get an update. She'd talked with many of Cyndi's classmates, but they knew nothing. She'd found more things missing, two hundred dollars from her own purse, clothes, Cyndi's jewelry. She'd talked to Detective Sim, but he said that, with no evidence of foul play, no sign of a struggle, no blood, they wouldn't look for her. The search was up to us.

I hung up and immediately called the airlines, made reservations on the next flight to Phoenix, and reserved a rental car. I then called my son, who attended college at Arizona State, but lived off-campus, and asked if he could put me up for a couple of nights. That afternoon, I caught a plane to Phoenix.

Turkey: Ephesus II

The call to prayer, a loud warble, comes through the quiet morning air, as my wristwatch alarm wakes me for the journey back to Greece. It's still dark outside. I must hurry to shower and finish packing. A Turk will be here in one hour to take me to Kusadasi. By eight-thirty, I'll be out of Turkey.

My ride is on time, but they have sent the violent young man who wanted to fight over the soccer match. His car is low on gas, the gauge first blinking red, then burning steadily the rest of the way. But I make it in plenty of time, arrive early, and wait for the travel agent to collect my passport. I'm soon aboard the good ferryboat Diana, the same small ferry I came to Turkey on. Last time, we were packed in like sardines, but today, only a handful make the trip. The Aegean is calmer, the boat a lazy duck in the water, rocking 'n rolling to the lethargic sea. I remember Sara walking about the boat last time. Her ghost will be with me for a while.

After seeing a little of Samos, I'll go on to Lesbos, the island to the north of Samos, just off the coast of Turkey. I have several reasons for visiting the island. First, Achilles raided the island during the Trojan War. Second, the ancient poetess Sappho was born there. Lesbos was the island of the world's most beautiful women.

While the boat chugs through the sea, I talk to a young Canadian who's been traveling for three months in Europe and Turkey, and now returning to London. He has a couple weeks to get there. He wants to see as much of Greece as possible on the way. He'll travel from Samos to Mykonos, Santorini, Crete, then Athens and Patras, where he'll catch the ferry to Brindisi, Italy. He's traveling with a young couple, but plans to split from them in Samos.

In the distance, I see the dock and another familiar sight, Hotel Samos. Now, for my reentry into Greece, Ελλαδα.

PART IV: Greek Islands and Attica

CHAPTER 18: Samos.

As soon as we dock, I head for the travel agency to see when the next ferry leaves for Lesbos. I want to see Samos, but I'm also concerned about getting stranded and missing my flight to the States. I learn that a ferry will leave for Chios tonight at eight. Good news, but still sooner than I hoped. I'll miss seeing Samos. Besides, the ferry gets into Chios at one-thirty in the morning, and the ferry to Lesbos won't arrive until three-thirty, a two-hour layover at an ungodly hour. I ask the travel agent when the next ferry goes to Lesbos, but he says this one may be the last for a while. He tells me to stop by the agency later in the day. They'll get a weather check and an updated ferry arrival time this afternoon.

I'm uncertain what to do. I want to see Samos before I leave, and don't want to get stranded on Chios tonight, spend several hours out in the cold rain. Back at the hotel, I take a room for a full day. The perpetually smiling woman at the front desk is English, but has lived in Greece for twenty years. I tell her about my predicament, wanting to see some of Samos, but also wanting to get to Lesbos, and about the middle-of-the-night layover in Chios. She says I still have time to see the temple of Hera. "And you must see it," she says. "It's magnificent. Take a taxi. You can get there and back in a couple of hours." She also tells me the layover in Chios may not be as bad as it sounds, because the ferry to Chios is always late. I may not get there until morning. Chios is a major center for ferries to Lesbos and Peiraias. She believes I'll have no trouble finding a place to hold up in Chios, regardless of the time.

Sounds like I'll spend the night traveling.

I walk through a light sprinkle to the National Bank of Greece. I need to change my Turkish liras and an American traveler's check to Greek drachmes. The exchange rate has gone to 240.58 dr/$, up 12 dr/$ since I came to Greece back on the third of October. I also stop by the OTE to call my brother in California. When I tell him I made it out of Turkey okay, he asks if it was really that dangerous. I'm bewildered. "What do you mean?" He's emphatic. "You sound terrified," he says. I didn't realize my uneasiness was so transparent.

Before catching a taxi, I stop off at the fast-food restaurant and have two gyropitas, while thinking of my brother's remark. I walk back to the hotel through a light rain. Shortly, I'm whizzing along eleven kilometers of mountain road in the rain, to the southwest. We dip down to the coast to Pythagorion, where ruins of the ancient city are located, and then on west.

Samos is a fertile island, its most important crops historically, tobacco and grapes. Habitation dates back to the early Bronze Age. Pythagorion, built on a hill above a natural cove, was the ancient capitol. The prosperity of the island is also due to its commercial connection with Egypt and the Near East. Samos was, at one time, known as Parthenia, island of the virgin, in honor of Hera.[364] Here, she came closest to being viewed as virgin goddess instead of only as Zeus' wife.

The taxi goes on west another eight kilometers to the Ireon, the ruins of the temple of Hera. In antiquity, civil engineers built a stone-paved footpath, called the Sacred Way, to connect the site with Pythagoria. They diverted a branch of the Imbrasos River.[365] The Sacred Way stretched for six kilometers, and was lined with two thousand statues.

By the time we reach the site, the light sprinkle has become a downpour. Rain falls in sheets of glistening wetness. We're at the edge of the sea. In the distance, a few kilometers off the coast, lying faceless under a shelf of heavy clouds, is a protruding peninsula of the Turkish coast. I don't relish walking about the ruins in the deluge, but finally I pop the taxi door open, spread my umbrella, and step out into the watery world.

The cult of Hera on Samos was transported from Argos during the great migration at the turn of the 1st millennium BC,[366] although it flourished most in the seventh and sixth centuries. The sanctuary was not panhellenic, and the rise and decline of the sanctuary was closely tied to the prosperity of the island.[367]

According to Samos tradition, white-armed Hera, mother of gods and men, who walked in golden sandals, was born here under a lygos (willow) tree in a thicket at the mouth of the Imbrasos River. The tree was imprinted on Roman coins. When Pausanias was here in the 2nd Century AD, he saw it, and pronounced it the oldest living tree.[368] Archeologists uncovered a tree stump in 1985 that was thought to be the tree; subsequent tests have shown it wasn't a lygos but a juniper. Carbon 14 dating revealed that the tree died sometime between 750-450 BC, and had lived only eighty years.[369]

Hera, the most beautiful of all goddesses, was married on Samos. She was the sole wife of Zeus. To mortals, she was the goddess of marriage and the life of women. All marriage ceremonies occurred during the winter month of Gamelion, our January.[370] Earthly couples viewed marriage as a sacred act owed Hera, and performed in her honor.[371] Marriage was a three day affair:[372] the offering and sacrifice on the day before, the feast and procession on the day of the wedding, and the songs and presentation of gifts on the day following. The offerings were most frequently locks of hair left at the temple of Artemis, enlisting the protection of the goddess during the bride's transition from a maiden to a woman. Sacrifices to Artemis were also made for the bride giving up her virginity.

The day of the marriage started with the nuptial bath in a river or spring, followed by the feast provided for by the bride's father. Homer describes the feast during the marriage of Menelaus' and Helen's daughter, Hermione, to Achilles' son Neoptolemus, after their return from Troy:

> Down the great hall in happiness they feasted,
> neighbors of Menelaos and his kin
> for whom a holy minstrel harped and sang;
> and two lithe tumblers moved out on the song
> with spins and handsprings through the company.[373]

During the evening, as the feast wound down, the parents of the bride presented her to the groom. The groom clasped her, not by the hand, but by the wrist, a symbolic act of taking possession. The songs sung during this time were of ritual lament, reflecting the close association between marriage and death. The wedding procession followed, which is also described by Homer, but this time as depicted on the shield of Achilles, forged by the great god and artisan Hephaestus:

> ...wedding feasts and brides
> led out through town by torchlight from their chambers
> amid chorales, amid the young men turning
> round and round in dances: flutes and harps
> among them, keeping up a tune, and women
> coming outdoors to stare as they went by.[374]

During the procession, the bride's mother carried torches to protect the bride from evil spirits. When they reached the bridal chamber, the groom's mother met them at the doorway, also carrying torches. The door to the bridal chamber was closed and guarded by a friend of the groom. Friends of the couple stood outside the door singing songs, pounding on the door and cracking obscene jokes. The morning after the wedding, the newlywed's friends sang to awaken them, and presented them with gifts.

Zeus and Hera were brother and sister, born to Kronos and Rhea. Hera married her own brother even though, in ancient Greek society, marriage between brother and sister was strictly forbidden and considered the only true incest. By marrying Zeus, Hera was given a husband, who was her equal, a unique honor among Greek goddesses. The two of them lived happily together for three hundred years, but eventually quarreled. Zeus was forever unfaithful, and Hera dealt out her jealousy against both other goddesses and mortal women pursued by Zeus.

An old man with a cane and a young woman dressed in black exit the site as I enter. The huge site is spread over several acres of swamp, at the edge of the sea. Hera's temple was the largest of its day, and the envy of the citizens of Ephesus. The temple of Artemis at Ephesus that I visited a few days ago was patterned after this temple. The site was used as a stone quarry for hundreds of years, the buildings being dismantled, leaving only the foundations. The lone, standing column, one of the original 155, may have been left standing so that those coming to pillage the site could more easily spot it as their ships approached the island.[375] Today, the ruins have been reclaimed by swamp. Ancient stones, tufts of marsh grass and reeds, break the surface of the water.

The marshy landscape was an archaeologist's dream. The permanently waterlogged earth preserved wood artifacts that vanished at other ancient sites, due to natural decay. The wood artifacts came in a range of types and artistry, from more practical utensils and well-crafted furniture, to sculptured masterpieces. Hera's sacred animal was the cow, "cow-eyed" was one of her epithets, and the bones of sacrificial cows predominate the site.

After a few minutes sloshing about, my hiking boots are soaked through, and I return to the taxi. The driver is glad for my return, and we make the drive back to Samos Town, while lightning bolts streak to earth and thunder shakes the car.

What strikes me about the ancient Greek marriage ritual is the emphasis on satisfying the spiritual and emotional needs of the couple getting married, the focus on the transitional nature of the act. They saw it as a sacred and psychological experience, both of which were treated with ritual. Today, we see marriage as a literal, external change: cohabitation, mingling of finances, shared sex.

During the ride back, I think of my own marriage, both because of minor similarities and major differences. My wife and I were married in Reno, Nevada, in January 1963, the proper month according to Hera's cult. It was a modern marriage, a sudden decision following several months of being engaged, and followed immediately by a long drive from California to Reno where my older brother lived. A friend of ours went with us, a guy she had dated before me. My buddy and I sat in the front seat, and my fiancée in the back.

We bought the license in Reno, and got married at some indiscriminate Christian chapel the next day. My brother was my best man. After we all went to dinner, my new wife and I spent the night in a fancy gambling hotel, the name of which I can no longer remember. The next morning, we spent the day with my brother's family, and my brother took me to his friend's home, saying we would return shortly, but we spent the entire afternoon there. I didn't have the courage to tell him I had to get back. My wife was not pleased. The following day, we made the long drive back to California. We didn't have a honeymoon. My wife-to-be didn't say anything but later told me that she regretted making the decision to marry me all the way up there and back.

After a few days of her continued prodding, I realized what a debacle I had made of our marriage, and can still feel the embarrassment. I regretted the hell out of what I had done, but was still more than pleased to have that young woman with me for what I thought then would be the rest of my life. Perhaps I had already sown the seeds of dissatisfaction that grew inside her and finally yielded the fruits of divorce eighteen years later.

My marriage followed the confrontation with my father by about a year and half. During the intervening months I dropped out of college, took a job as a teller in a bank just south of San Francisco, quit the job after a few months, and returned to the farm to work with my father. I still had an identity problem. The impact of my father loading the deer rifle, and learning that I had set up my brother to be raped by a homosexual, cost me all sense of whom I was. But my marriage, although not an elaborate ceremony compared to that of the ancient Greeks, accomplished that transition from the kid I was to the young man who joined the Air Force, educated himself at both Arizona State and Stanford University, fathered two children, worked in the space program to put two robots on the surface of Mars, and worked on several satellites that flew on the space shuttle.

I guess, what I'm questioning now is whether all the problems I had were a sign of dysfunction. Were they possibly the cornerstone my life was successfully built upon? Even my marriage ritual was not a happy experience, but the marriage lasted eighteen years, the most wonderful years of my life. In spite of the fact that it ended in divorce, I consider my marriage my most successful venture. At no time was I ever loved so much, or did I love so much. I wonder if divorce, for me, wasn't necessary during my mid-life transition, if continued personal growth was to follow? Odysseus was "divorced" from Penelope during his years of wandering.

But one problem remains: what was going on inside me when my father loaded the deer rifle? If the process was ultimately healthy, does what I felt matter? The answer is, yes, and the reason is that, even though we get along, a gulf exists between us. Every time he tries to come closer, I turn my back on him.

As soon as I arrive at the hotel, I walk to the travel agency with my hiking jacket hood pulled up over my fisherman's cap. The ferry will arrive at eight this evening, and that is a ninety percent certainty. I sit in my room, looking out over a courtyard of palm trees and red chrysanthemums surrounded by blue-shuttered patio doors and wrought-iron balconies, three floors of them, all in brilliant white stucco. Is that holly I see, or do I have Christmas fever?

Gradually, the light fades, leaving a dull, lonely darkness. I still can't quit thinking about my daughter. Against Hera's marriage ceremony of a young woman's happy public attainment of life's most precious gift, an ancient cult practice was posed, depicting the emotional transition of the maiden who was marrying for the first time. What happened to her internally was closely associated with the sacrifice of Iphigenia at Aulis. Iphigenia came to Aulis under the pretext of being married to Achilles, but instead was sacrificed by her father to Artemis. This constituted a rite of passage from the maidenly, virginal state to that of the married woman, the bride participating in the betrayal and sacrifice of her own maiden self. The maiden comes assuming she will be married, only to discover that she, as a maiden, is to be sacrificed, die, and be reborn as a woman. This cult practice is also closely connected to the disappearance of my daughter.

At the time my daughter disappeared, I hadn't seen my ex-wife for a couple of years. The afternoon following her telephone call, I caught a flight to Phoenix, arriving just at sundown, with sunlight casting a golden flow over the cactus-strewn landscape. My first stop after getting a rental car was my ex-wife's townhome. My daughter's dog, Brandi, was the first to greet me, my ex-wife, standing behind him with puddles of tears in her eyes. She was glad to see me, but introduced me to her live-in boyfriend, who was in the kitchen doing dishes.

My ex-wife no longer thought our daughter might have been kidnapped. She had found a note from Cyndi's girlfriend Danielle saying, "Guess who's back in town?" She was concerned that Vicki, the girl who had tried to burn down her parents' home and ran away the year before, was back in town. She believed Cyndi had run off with her. After getting the names and addresses of

Samos

Cyndi's closest friends, most of whom my ex-wife wasn't very complementary about, I left for my son's apartment, where I was to spend the night, feeling somewhat relieved.

It was late when I arrived, but he fed me, and we talked for awhile before he made a bed for me on the sofa in the living room. He said something that evening I should have taken to heart, but it seemed insignificant at the time. He said that his sister had changed during the last two years, that he had seen Cyndi at rock concerts with a crowd of kids fogging around her like she had a following. I understood him to mean she was popular and thought, Sure, she's bright, beautiful. Why wouldn't she be popular?

The next morning, I rose early and started the search for some of the derelicts she ran around with. The most promising was Danielle, a sixteen year old who had been pronounced *sui juris* by the courts because she wouldn't stay in school. Her mother had given her up for adoption when she was in elementary school, and her foster parents had also given up on her as a teenager. Danielle worked at a laundry, but when I questioned the manager of the place, she told me Danielle hadn't been at work for two days.

I finally tracked down Danielle's stepsister, but she couldn't tell me much either. She did say she knew of two other girls who were also missing. One of them worked at the same pizza place where my daughter worked. The girl's name was Bear. I mentioned that if they worked at the same place and disappeared at the same time, it would be easy to infer they ran off together. "If she did," Danielle's stepsister said, "she's running in good company, because Bear is a responsible young lady. Everyone likes her. She's more mature than most girls, and will take care of your daughter." I wondered why, if she was so responsible, didn't she just stay home instead of running away.

Danielle's sister also mentioned another girl, Mary, originally from California, who hated Phoenix and wanted to get back to the beach. She was also missing. She speculated that Bear and Mary had run off to California, probably Huntington Beach in Los Angeles. But Danielle's stepsister had never heard of my daughter.

When I hung up the phone, I realized suddenly that maybe my daughter was in trouble, possibly pregnant, and that just possibly she had run to me. If I had stayed in San Diego, she might have shown up on my doorstep. I had a growing feeling that I had made a mistake by coming to Phoenix. It looked as though five girls had run off together. Bear, Vicki, Mary, Danielle and my daughter. Perhaps she wasn't as vulnerable as I thought. At least she wasn't on her own.

I made one last stop before returning to San Diego. My ex-wife had given me the address of Troy, Danielle's boyfriend. Perhaps he could help. Troy was in his mid-twenties and the leader of a New Age church, a group of young adults who's only connection with religion seemed to be the ritual use of drugs. Troy owned a home in north Phoenix, but when I arrived at the rundown, fairly new home, which had no landscaping and a large tractor tire covered with plywood for furniture, no one was home. Somehow, I just knew my daughter was waiting for me in San Diego. She was probably sitting on my front step right then. I called the airlines and caught the next flight back to San Diego.

During that day of searching, I reached a degree of despondency I had never experienced, not even during my divorce. I had difficulty talking. The words stuck somewhere behind my tongue. Remembering names was impossible, so I used a notebook. I could barely write. I had roamed through north Phoenix for an hour before finding Troy's home, even though I was familiar with the neighborhood. A sort of debilitating grief set in even though, as yet, I had no evidence she was even in danger. I felt that, by leaving her in Phoenix and moving to San Diego, I had cost my daughter her life. I had sacrificed her for the sake of a job. The lingering effect of that grief is the reason I now know I must visit Aulis, the site where Agamemnon sacrificed his daughter.

★

A little before eight, I leave the hotel and walk out into the dark rain, toward Port Authority. A pack of dogs waits patiently at the hotel door for anyone who will give them a scrap. They anxiously whine after me. The large red female with the broken, flapping front leg is among them. She hobbles around on three legs, begging food and fighting off the male dogs who want to play with her. The ancient philosopher Pythagoras, who believed in the transmigration of souls, once told a man who was beating a puppy, "Stop, do not beat him; for it is the soul of a dear friend -- I recognized it when I heard the voice."[376]

Pythagoras was born here on Samos in the 6th Century BC, and lived here until driven out by the tyrant Polycrates. He was the founder of a brotherhood called the Pythagoreans. They believed in a "wheel of life" into which we are all born and reincarnated until we perfect ourselves. Once we lead a pure life, our soul is released into the starry heavens, the body being a prison of the soul. The connection between the Pythagoreans and Orphism was a close one, and both would later have an influence on Christianity. Pythagoras had also been initiated into the Eleusinian Mysteries,[377] and believed the human race to be eternal.[378]

I see a small ferry in the darkness at the edge of the dock, no bigger than the one I came back from Turkey on. Not good news, the weather being what it is. I start to board, but the agent calls me over and tells me I must buy my ticket from him instead of onboard. We stand in the rain and dark together by

Samos

Port Authority while he writes out the ticket. I pay my money and walk off into the night, up the small gangway onto the good ferryboat Καπεταν Σταματις, Captain Stamatis. For bad weather, this is definitely not the ferry to be on, not a very big boat. The biggest problem is that I'm traveling in the dark, and will not have a reference point on which to fix my eyes to prevent seasickness.

I stand at the railing, the lights of Samos scattered around the harbor. The wind has stopped, for now. The streaks of multicolored lights on the smooth water's surface are absolutely gorgeous. Christmas comes to mind again. It's the home of the Virgin Mary I visited in Ephesus that triggered the feeling. In the true spirit of leaving, I'm sad again. For the first time, I feel the closeness of the end of my journey, and realize I'll never see these places again.

Back inside the cabin, the dim lights flicker and go out for a few seconds. A little frightening. The rumble of the motor shakes the boat, as I watch the dock lights through the windows slipping rearward. The bay is smooth and glassy. Maybe the open sea will not be so bad after all.

The ferry lopes, a slow long-distance breaststroke, and gently rocks from side to side. By one-thirty, my ride will be over, whatever the condition of my stomach between now and then. Only three passengers are onboard, a Greek couple sitting in a row farther back and me. They brought their dinner, bread, sliced meat and cheese, fruit and nuts. Smells good. They roar with laughter, then snicker to themselves, quiet whispers.

As the boat moves out of the bay, the sea gets rougher. The gentle to-and-fro rocking of the ferry reminds me of a whale moving through the ocean. I lean back, close my eyes, and relax, think how it would feel to be a whale swimming the sea at night. My problem in the rocking boat is similar to the one I had in Delphi, my first really frightening feeling of traveling alone. It's a problem of reference. My solution in Delphi was to realize I was at home on the road. Instead of watching the shoreline as a reference, I now realize I can switch to the reference of the boat, or perhaps even closer, to myself. I close my eyes and imagine I'm a whale lumbering through waves as they break over me.

After a short voyage, we drop anchor at Καρλοβασι (Karlovasi). This is a stop I didn't anticipate, and explains the relatively smooth water we've experienced so far. We've navigated close to the northern shore of Samos, and have yet to test the water of the open sea.

I step out on deck for a couple of minutes to get a glimpse of the churning sea here close to dock. Karlovasi is draped in darkness except for the cocoon of glowing light around the coffee shop. Just as the ferry quivers and is on its way again, I see a Christmas tree in a window. Yes, I have Christmas fever.

I reach my seat, and shortly, the waves grow larger, frightening. I remember that in St. Paul's day, boats didn't normally sail the Aegean later in the year than November 11th. We're seventeen days past the cutoff. I feel the perspiration pop out on my forehead, and I settle back in my seat, close my eyes, and resume my shift in reference to that of a whale swimming the Aegean. The sea throws waves like mountain cliffs, the boat moans. I'm no longer so concerned about my stomach as I am about my life. We're completely at the mercy of Poseidon, god of the sea. I remember what he did to the Greeks returning from Troy, how he scattered their ships, and how their bodies blossomed on the beaches.

The crew is deathly silent. I concentrate, desperately now, on the sea, and imagine stroking, breaking into the huge crests. Crash, lunge, crash, lunge. Again and again the ferry plunges into the waves. I feel them against the prow, feel the waves lapping my sides, rocking 'n rolling, splitting waves, slicing into the night.

The two people behind me are restless, and their laughter has stopped. Shortly, I hear the rustle of a paper bag followed by gagging as they throw up their just-eaten dinner. I lean back further into my soft seat and force intense visions of the sea, while hearing the couple's gagging breaths bringing up chunks that plop against the floor. The sour smell of vomit.

30 Nov, Tuesday

At two in the morning, we make dock in Chios, and I walk off the ferry into the light rain, looking for shelter. The other passengers, the two Greeks, are pale green, won't look at me, and don't speak to each other. Usually, we dock at a deep-set bay, but not here in Chios. The dark dock extends north-south along the waterfront, on the east side of the island facing Turkey. A taxi driver shouts at me, jumps out to put my pack in his trunk, but all I want is directions to a cafe. He points to the far end of the dock, perhaps a kilometer away. I see an oasis of light in the darkness, glistening in the puddles all the way to me. "How much?" I ask. "Five hundred drachmes," he says. Two dollars seems a small price to keep dry.

"You stay in Chios?" he asks as I get in the front seat beside him. "No," I tell him, "Lesbos." "No," he says. "Must stay in Chios. I show you," and damn if he doesn't make a left turn off the dock and up a dark alley. "No extra charge," he says. "Still five hundred, no extra charge."

Here I go again. This is where I get mugged for sure. It's two o'clock in the morning, and the guy wants to give me a tour of a dark town. I can feel it coming.

"Please stay in Chios," he says. "A beautiful island." A few blocks into the darkness, he stops, rolls down his window. I look past him at some amorphous sculpture in front of what could be town hall. He goes on and on about the statue, none of which I can understand. "Very nice," I tell him. "Very nice."

After a couple more memorable stops, he navigates back to the dock and drops me off at the coffee shop. "Think about it," he says. "Chios is a beautiful island. Many nice pensions." As I pay him, he looks resigned to me not staying. "Ferryboat to Lesbos, right here, three-thirty," he says, pointing to the dock in front of the coffee shop. "Good coffee shop," he adds, as he gets back in his taxi.

I wish I did have time to spend a couple of days here. This is another possible birthplace of Homer. In the Homeric hymn to Apollo, the poet makes reference to the island and himself when speaking to the Delian maidens who are followers of Apollo:

> I ask you to call me to mind
> in time to come whenever some man on this earth,
> a stranger whose suffering never ends, comes here and asks:
> "Maidens, which of the singers, a man wont to come here,
> is to you the sweetest, and in whom do you most delight?"
> Do tell him in unison that I am he,
> a blind man, dwelling on the rocky island of Chios,
> whose songs shall all be the best in time to come.[379]

Even though most scholars would agree the hymn was not written by Homer,[380] the idea that Homer was a blind poet living on Chios persists.

Sophocles was also once here, on his way to Lesbos to fight a war. The poet Ion wrote of meeting him.[381] He describes Sophocles as agreeable over wine, and witty. Sophocles related Pericles' opinion that he, Sophocles, was a great poet, but not much of a general.

I squeeze through the door of the coffee shop, expecting to be confronted by the proprietor, but he's busy arguing with another man who's eating and doesn't even acknowledge me. The open kitchen is to the left, and a row of glass-top tables to the right runs the length of the long narrow room. I dump my backpack on the floor, and take a seat at one of them, wondering if he'll kick me out if I don't buy something to eat.

I pull out my journal. I can't shake the feeling of that ferry ride, plunging into the sea, plunging into darkness. For five hours I was a whale in rough seas and had no trace of seasickness. And I'm still swimming. Even though I sit a kilometer from where we docked in a small darkly lit coffee shop at a table with a red and white plaid tablecloth covered by a sheet of glass, I still swim the sea. I still rock, I still roll. I don't know that I've ever had such vivid images of a primordial time, and this one while possessed by the spirit of Poseidon during those hours of self-imposed blindness.

Finally, the perpetually eating Greek and the smell of food overcomes me. I walk to the glass counter and look at the pots of food sitting in the dark recesses of the metal cabinet, most with little left in them, large chunks of pale broiled chicken, something resembling eggplant, noodles and beef stew. I have the stew and some of that firm Greek bread I've been missing. My bill comes to 900 dr, no tax, no tip. The price you see is the price you get.

★

By four in the morning, the ferry is a half-hour late, and I'm still in the coffee shop waiting it out. I've had time to think over my last ferry ride, and am apprehensive of what I'll encounter on the way to Μιτιλίνι. Nine people now wait with me, drinking coffee from small, clear glasses. Three more dressed in suits enter through the front door, carrying briefcases and letting in the cold. The coffee shop is filled with cigarette smoke and the jabber of Greek. Outside, the taxis have staked out their territory in the darkness, and cars and trucks wait in the wings to board the ferry, which is not yet in sight. The long beams of flashlights stab the darkness and reflect from large puddles.

A mad scramble for the door brings me to my feet, and at the same time, I hear the ferry horn bellow, a call from the depths of darkness. It's a wonderfully reassuring sight, a huge ferry, the largest I've seen. Shortly, I'm inside the hold, up the stairs, and waiting at a reception desk to buy a ticket. It's the plushest ferry I've been on, deep-carpeted floors, sparkling mirror-lined walls, well-dressed crew. I'm so tired. I sit on my backpack in front of the desk, my head in my hands, eyes closed, wondering if I'll get a chance to sleep before we get to Lesbos.

When I finally make it into the passenger compartment, I throw my hiking jacket on the clean carpeted floor between a row of seats, put my black sweater on top of it, and lay my head on the sweater. Sweet oblivion.

★

Two hours later, I'm brought back to life by the loudspeaker telling those of us who are staying in Lesbos to prepare to disembark. I'm surprised it's already day, bright light coming through the row of windows on the sides of the ferry. Yet the sky is overcast, heavy clouds sagging pregnantly.

CHAPTER 19: Lesbos.

I step out into the cold, wet world skirting the aggressive cars and trucks exiting the ferry. The morning light, which seemed so bright from within the ferry, is gloomy, somber. The city of Mytilene lies a half-kilometer away, beneath misty wisps of fog curling down from heavy pillows of black clouds that hug the hills. Orange-tile roofs spread along the horseshoe cove and up the adjacent mountains. But the primary color of Mytilene is blue, the azure deeps of the cove merging with turquoise boats at dockside.

I lumber toward the center of town, looking for a hotel, but only see closed travel agencies and restaurants. The two-lane dockside street seethes with automobiles and motorbikes. This is rush hour in Mytilene, at 25,000, the largest town on the island.

Lesbos, which has a total population of 90,000, was built-up by volcanic eruptions before separating millions of years ago from the Turkish coast. It is the third-largest island in the Aegean, after Crete and Euboia. It is triangular shaped, the apex tilted to the northeast. Two deep-set bays protrude inland, one in the middle of the base of the three-sided island. The other is an inland bay, with a five-kilometer strait for an inlet, that thrusts into the island's eastern apex. The entrances of both bays are difficult, and the small but more-accessible bay here at Mytilene, on the eastern coast next to Turkey, is used by commercial traffic.

Lesbos, "the jewel of the Aegean," is one of the most beautiful and fertile areas in Greece, noted for its wine, grain and olives. Its inhabitants raise sheep, mules and cattle. The island's prosperity has always been favorably affected by its location in the northeast Aegean, on the trade route to the Dardanelles. Historically the island's inhabitants trace their lineage back to the Aeolians of Boiotia Nome, the land of Oedipus. Many also claim to be descendants of Agamemnon. These ancients came here in 1050 BC, during the great migration following the Trojan War. Lesbos had been a Trojan ally, and was sacked many times by Achilles.

When I reach the center of the cove, I walk away from the dock, across the gridlocked street, and stop before a white, modern building with glass doors and marble entryway, the Hotel Sappho. I quickly learn that a room will cost me

Lesbos

5000 dr ($20.83), not within my budget. A room in the Hotel Lesbos next door is even more expensive. Rain starts again, large drops rippling puddles.

Looking for a place to hide from the rain, I enter a dark tunnel through buildings along the frontage road, and exit into a world of pedestrians, on a street overshadowed by balconies. I've found the center of town, and it's as if I've come to the land of umbrellas, their taut river of domes filling the street before me. Motorbikes aggressively pick a path, using the penetrating barks of their horns. A market opens its doors, and black-haired men in dark clothes emerge to stack boxes of vegetables and fruit, carrots, potatoes, onions, eggplant, apples, bananas. The bloody-aproned proprietor of a meat market shouts his specials, standing among hanging sides of beef and boxes of slick smelly fish. When a competitor shouts back, he raises his arms and elevates his tirade. Women are everywhere, old, young, middle-aged. My stomach growls at the smell of cinnamon and yeast from a bakery next door. Mytilene is a gorgeous, drenched little city.

I'm anxious to get a room. Although I want to see Mytilene, my immediate concern is getting to the northern and western parts of the island, where Achilles went on a rampage. I fall in line with the umbrellas, looking up a side street for a pension. I stop in front of an electronics store, the proprietor standing out front. "Δωμοτια?" (room) I ask. He seems concerned, as if I've suggested some grave undertaking. He wants me to repeat my question, then his face lights up. He motions to come with him, and after a few steps, he points at a side street, holds up one finger, motions to the right. I take this to mean to go one block then turn right. "Ευχαριστω," I tell him, and chug up the incline.

One block off the noisy thoroughfare, the narrow street becomes quiet and jammed with parked cars. After turning the corner, I see nothing at first, then spot a small sign in English, "PENSION." The door is unlocked, but the entryway is dark and uninviting. I see no reception desk. I crank up my courage and take the winding stairway to the right, climbing through the dark. On the second floor, a deserted counter, cloaked in darkness, hides in a far corner. A lone bell sits on top.

After a couple of rings, I hear a commotion behind a door, and a man staggers out in a T-shirt and no shoes, his hair mussed and fly unzipped. We wrangle through the language barrier, and he disappears into his room, comes back with shoes on, and a key. We mount two more flights of stairs, and exit to a balcony overlooking the street. He opens a sliding door to the room. It's dark, run-down and smells of mildew, but has all the requisites, a bed, a private bath. We go back downstairs, and I pay for one night.

When I return to the room, I discover it has no lights, no heat, no hot water. I complain to the proprietor, but he looks defeated, says the whole building is like that. "Οχι φως," (no light) he says. I'm not sure if he means temporarily or permanently. The place does have light switches and light bulbs, so I have some hope. As I unpack, I hear the soft-throated warbling of pigeons on the windowsill, the only window, small and opaque, high up on the wall of my tiny, dark room.

I'm still rocking and rolling from the ferry ride to Chios. Seems like a week ago, but I still feel the cyclic pressure of waves tossing me about, the surge, release, surge, release. Two hours of sleep on a ferry isn't much, but I've no time to waste. I grab a cinnamon roll and a donut at the bakery and look for a motorbike rental agency, leaving a trail of sugar granules in my wake. The rain has stopped for now, and I'm taking a chance on getting caught in a downpour, but I may not have long on this island before I have to catch a ferry back to Athens.

I head west on a motorbike that has more pep than I would like, up into the green hills out of Mytilene. The first time I gun it, it almost jumps out from under me. The wet asphalt road hisses beneath me, and I use one arm to raise my jacket zipper to keep out the cold. The hills are rocky and covered with brown grass, their tops capped with deep-green trees. Even the silver-leaved olives come closer to true green. As I crest the hill, I pull to the side of the road to take in the view of Yeras (Prize) Bay spread out below, a large emerald lake with its small Aegean entrance obscured from here. The motorbike putt-putts like a high-powered lawnmower. Puffs of clouds stand around me, and the mist has covered my glasses. I put them in my shirt pocket.

I descend to the small village of Kentro, at the edge of the bay, and follow the road around the end of the hotel-lined waterfront, then start up into the rocky hills again. Just as I crest the ridge and can see the huge expanse of Kalloni (Beautiful) Bay, I run into a squall of large raindrops, and pull to the side of the road, where I shut off the motorbike and frantically scramble through my daypack for my black umbrella. While listening to the patter of rain over my head, I take in the expanse of water before me. Kalloni Bay, eight kilometers wide and seventeen long, is lined with small orange and white villages. The lake's surface shudders in the rain, as a bright streak of sunlight falls across it.

Following the decimation of the population during the flood of Deucalion,[382] the local race on Lesbos was re-founded by the ancient king Makaras, who had five daughters: Mytilene, Issa, Antissa, Arisvi, and Methymna.[383] He founded and named a city for each. Methymna married a man from Aeolia named Lesbos, who, through his marriage, became king, and named the island for himself. During the Trojan War, the Greeks wreaked havoc on the island, Achilles plundering its cities one by one, but when he came to Methymna, even the greatest warrior of all time came up short.

Lesbos

Methymna is on the northern tip of the island, where I'm now headed. When the squall stops, I kick the starter a couple of times, and the motorbike roars to life. At the head of the bay, I turn north through the crossroads town of Kalloni, where I'm enveloped by a dense fog that gives the buildings a ghostly presence. Here's where the road leads on west to the birthplace of the poetess Sappho, which I will visit this afternoon, weather permitting. But for now, I'm on my way north. As I exit the town, I pass a man on a donkey carrying a heavy load of goat fodder. Just before noon, I enter the outskirts of Methymna, my first destination.

I'm struck by the imposing castle sitting on a mountain overlooking the bay. Its square buildings are different from any I've seen in Greece. They are not made of white stucco, but of gray stone. The motorbike shakes like a jackhammer over the steep cobblestone streets, as I descend to the coast.

As Achilles fought outside the city walls of Methymna, a young woman named Peisidice watched his unsuccessful siege from the city's walls.

> Peisidice beheld Achilles,
> Fighting in the foremost ranks,
> Exultant in his killing joy:
> And Aphrodite, Goddess of the bloom,
> Made mad her agitated heart for him.
> She raised her hands into the yielding air
> In supplication for his love.[384]

Peisidice was the daughter of the king of Methymna. She sent word by her governess to Achilles that, if he would marry her, she would open the gates to the city. Recognizing a good deal when he saw one, Achilles readily agreed.

> She welcomed then the army of the Greeks,
> Within her fatherland,
> Levering apart the city's gates.
> Dared to behold with her own eyes
> Her parents slain by sword and women dragged
> In slaves' chains at his command to ships...[385]

But Achilles found Peisidice's act of betrayal repugnant, and never intended to fulfill his promise. He had his men stone her.

A daughter betraying her homeland is a common theme in Greek legend. Ariadne helped Theseus when he came to Knossos to kill her brother, the

361

Minotaur. And Briseis, Achilles' concubine over whom he and Agamemnon argued at Troy, and who had watched Achilles kill her father and three brothers, loved Achilles, and was consoled by the promise of being married to him. The vision of the hero in action is irresistible to some women, and comes with the promise of a new life in a new land.

But Lesbos' women were known for their beauty, not betrayal. Although Briseis, Achilles' concubine, was not from Lesbos, the girl who temporarily took her place, when Agamemnon took Briseis from him, was. That night as Achilles slept, the girl from Lesbos slept on one side of him, with his male companion on the other:

> Achilles slept in the corner of his well-built hut, and beside him lay a woman he had brought from Lesbos, Phorbas's daughter, beautiful Diomede. Patroklos lay down on the opposite side. He too had a woman...[386]

This was a cozy little foursome, when you realize the relationship between Patroklos and Achilles was sexual.

When Agamemnon finally relented and gave Briseis back, he included:

> ...seven women skilled in excellent handcraft, women from Lesbos: when he Achilles himself captured well-founded Lesbos I Agamemnon chose them out for their beauty surpassing all the company of women.[387]

The boxy buildings of Methymna are multistory structures of gray stones, topped by pyramid-shaped, orange-tile roofs. The square windows on the flat surfaces stare out expectantly. My motorbike blasts the silence, as I let off the accelerator and coast down the path to the beach.

Methymna is also the site of an event that occurred even farther back in the mists of time, one concerning the death of Orpheus, the ancient minstrel who lived in Thrace. Orpheus was the son of Apollo and the muse Kalliope and was the first named among Jason's shipmates on the Argo. Apollo taught him to play the lyre, and he was wonderful at it:

> Men say that he by the music of his songs charmed the stubborn rocks upon the mountains and the course of rivers. And the wild oak-trees to this day, tokens of that magic strain, that grow at Zone of the Thracian shore, stand in ordered ranks close together, the same which under the charm of his lyre he led down from Pieria.[388]

Lesbos

Orpheus married Eurydice, a Thracian lake nymph. But on their wedding day, as she fled from a rapist, she was bitten by a snake and died in the Vale of Tempe, the land of the healing centaur, Cheiron. Orpheus was so grieved over her death that he went into the Underworld to retrieve her. Singing while strumming a lyre, he charmed Persephone and Hades:

> And with his words, the music
> Made the pale phantoms weep: Ixion's wheel
> Was still, Tityos' vultures left the liver,
> Tantalus tried no more to reach for the water,
> And Belus' daughters rested from their urns,
> And Sisyphus climbed on his rock to listen.
> That was the first time ever in all the world
> The Furies wept. Neither the king nor consort
> Had harshness to refuse him, and they called her,
> Euridice.[389]

Hermes was sent to retrieve Eurydice, and as the three of them ascended from the Underworld, Hermes instructed Orpheus to lead the way and not look back, or she would stay in Hades. Orpheus obeyed the command, but as they drew near the entrance, he could no longer hear Eurydice's footsteps and grew suspicious of Hermes. Desperate to verify she was still following, he looked back at the last second, and to his everlasting grief, saw she had, indeed, been right behind him, but had already turned to descend into the Underworld once again.

Orpheus' sorrow over Eurydice didn't subside, and he never again sought the companionship of women. He met his death on a Thracian mountaintop in northern Greece, at the hands of the maenads, the female votives of Dionysus. His indifference to women had enraged them. Just as some Christian saints, such as St. Francis of Assisi in 1224 AD, received the stigmata of Jesus, so Orpheus suffered the fate of his patron deity, Dionysus. During an orgiastic rite, the maenads dismembered Orpheus' body, as Dionysus had been by the Titans, gathered the pieces, and burned them, all but the head, which they threw into a river along with the lyre:

> ...the Hebrus River took the head and lyre
> And as they floated down the gentle current
> The lyre made mournful sounds, and the tongue murmured
> In mournful harmony, and the banks echoed

Lesbos

The strains of mourning. On the sea, beyond
Their native stream, they came at last to Lesbos
And grounded near the city of Methymna.[390]

Orpheus' head was still singing, and the sea waves gently stroked the lyre when it ran aground here on the beach. The locals buried the head, but it still wouldn't shut up, and became famous as an oracle. This offended Apollo, who stood over the site and pronounced, "Cease from the things that are mine, for I have borne enough with thy singing."[391] Thus, the minstrel and prophet were finally silenced.

But Orpheus was more than even this. He was a gentle man who lured sheep and wild beasts to lie down together, definitely not a hero in the traditional Greek mold. A religious cult grew up around him following his death.[392] His hymns were sung during Demeter's Mysteries. Orphism, with its emphasis on music, had a strong influence on Pythagorean philosophy of the 6th Century BC. Pythagoras' experiments with music, and the subsequent discovery of the octave and numerical ratios, led directly to the discovery of mathematics. Thus, music, through the influence of Orpheus, came to occupy a mysterious place in Pythagoreanism.[393] In turn, the virtues of self-sacrifice and moderation, from both Orphism and Pythagoreanism, reappeared later in Christianity.

At the edge of the sea, I stop the motorbike, shut off the motor, and descend to the water's edge. The deserted beach is rocky, the large, gray stones making walking difficult. The larger rocks have been collected and stacked back from the beach, creating pebbled areas for the summertime sunbathers. I'm alone on the beach today, listening to waves swish at the shore. I turn to look up the mountain at the gray-faced buildings, and the castle towering over the coast.

My time is short, and I grab a bite to eat at a store in the town square, bread and cheese, and set out again on the road south, back to the crossroads at Kalloni, where I take the road west through a small fertile valley with a patchwork of vineyards. The mountain road winds on forever, the rocky hillsides becoming bleaker. The grass is brown, with only a tinge of new green. A few kilometers from the southwestern coast, I enter the mountain town of Eressos, the birthplace of Sappho in 630 BC.[394] She wrote poetry in the form of long lyrics. She must have caught the voice of Orpheus. Perhaps she had his lyre.

While Homer's epic poetry is filled with war and murder, Sappho's poetry is of a strikingly different spirit. Her poetry has been discredited and destroyed through the ages because many consider her a "lesbian" poet, even though she was married and had a child called Cleis, who was named for Sappho's mother.[395] Christians have been particularly hostile to her sexual lyricism. The following is

Lesbos

the only complete Sappho poem in existence:

A Prayer to Aphrodite

Immortal Aphrodite, Zeus-sired and deathless,
Break not my heart with ache and anguish,
you beguiling goddess, I pray you, come hither!

As once before did you come, hearing my voice from afar,
you listened, and leaving your father's golden house
in your yoked chariot, you came,
the fast-beating wings of your fleet sparrows
coursing the mid-air over the dark earth.
Suddenly near me, bright-eyed and smiling, deathless,
you asked what had befallen me, why I had called you,
what my mad heart then most desired.
"What fair thing would you now lure to love you?
Who wrongs you, Sappho? If now she flees you,
soon shall she follow; she, scorning your gifts now,
soon shall she be the giver; and an unwilling loved one
will soon be the lover."

Now, even as then, come and release me
from bearing this love pain,
and grant all my heart's desire,
you, yourself, be my ally.[396]

Sappho's poetry was so popular in ancient Greece that she was considered the tenth muse. Much of her poetry was sung at weddings.

The buildings of Eressos have the stucco walls and orange-tile roofs I'm used to seeing here on Lesbos. The view of the countryside from Eressos is spectacular, a ravine off to the west, and to the south, rolling hills with orchards and farms.

My daughter used to send her poetry to me so I could print it out on my computer. Following her disappearance, one poem took on a new depth, and reveals her state of mind at the time. Like Sappho's, my daughter's poetry was meant to be accompanied by music. In 1982, prior to my departure for San Diego, she wrote the poem. It's entitled "To Stay." Here's the last verse. I imagine her strumming her guitar and singing:

Lesbos

I saw him smile again today
His face so young in the dying day
And I remembered how we used to play
Him tickling me 'til I got away
And bothering me 'til I screamed for him to get away
And I wonder "Will he ever go away?"
No, he's forever here...
        forever here with me to stay.

The following year, I left her in Phoenix and moved to San Diego.

After a few minutes of sightseeing, I travel on south to the coast, to the beach at Skala Eressos. This is touted as the most beautiful and cleanest beach in the Aegean. It's much different than that at Methymna, and is covered with fine sand and stretchs along the southern coast for one and a half kilometers. The eastern portion of the beach is reserved for nude sunbathing, but I have no compulsion to remove my clothes. My lone companion on the beach today is a fisherman casting far out into the sea.

I stop my motorbike three blocks from the beach, at the chapel of Agios Andreas, St. Andrew. I remember back when I was on my way to Ithaca, I saw the casket containing Andrew's head in the church at Patras. This church is smaller and older, built in 1886 over the ruins of the original one, which was from the 5th Century AD. St. Andrew could very well have stopped here on his way to Patras. He spent some time along the Black Sea, spreading the word of Jesus among the pagans. The church is closed today.

I wonder about all these heads roaming about Greece. First back in Thebes, Pentheus' head came home on his mother's thyrsus, then St. Andrew's head that had been in exile in Rome for 400 years, and now Orpheus' head floating from Thrace to Methymna, singing all the while.

I'm in a daze from lack of sleep, and after a short time walking the cobblestone streets, I'm back on my motorbike, traveling the ninety kilometers of winding road back to Mytilene.

★

It's evening when I reenter my room, delighted to find that the light switch works. I also have hot water. I go for a volta just a half block from the pension, down Ermou Street. Outside, it's motorbike city, Greek testosterone flowing through the streets in gushing streams. The cyclists perform wheelies, and verify their masculinity by blasting through crowds of women and kids. I see stars, and watch a full moon rise in the east through white clouds. It's been a full month

Lesbos

since I saw the Halloween moon from the cliffs of Santorini. In one of the shops, I hear a few bars of "Little Drummer Boy." Christmas is upon me. One week from today, at 4:45 in the afternoon, I'll board the plane in Athens for the flight to London, where I'll have a fourteen-hour layover before my flight to Denver. After I get back to Boulder on the 9th of December, I'll be home for a week, then fly to California to spend Christmas with my family.

I wake in the middle of the night, dreaming of my daughter when she was a baby. She's sick and has one eye closed by infection, a gummy substance festering across it. My wife and I are negligent in not taking her to the doctor because we're too busy with our jobs. My heart fills with guilt over my negligence, and with sympathy for my baby girl. How could I have neglected the well-being of one of her beautiful brown eyes? I hold her to me with a desperate sorrow. I drift off again, realizing that this event never happened, and wondering if the dream has been triggered by my recent focus on my daughter's disappearance.

An Airplane rumbles overhead, on its way to the Lesbos airport just a few kilometers southeast of here, the first passenger plane I've heard since I left Athens two months ago. The sounds of going home.

Another of my daughter's poems was written in 1983 after I moved to San Diego:

> And again I am a horse
> With no limits—only freedom
> And a sense of tranquility
>
> For days on end I ride the wind
> Having no one to answer to
> And no place to be
> Just one alone and free

The poem was written the year after I left her in Phoenix and moved to San Diego. She was sixteen. Her love of horses is coupled here with her strong yearning for freedom, a normal teenage feeling, but one she responded to in a radical way, an affliction she may have caught from her mother and me.

After the futile day of searching for my daughter in Phoenix, and learning she had probably run away with several other girls, I returned to San Diego, anxious to see if she was waiting on my doorstep. I held an image of her sitting on the welcome mat with her back braced against my front door. That image evaporated as soon as I reached my apartment late that night and saw she wasn't there. I slept anxiously hoping the phone would ring and bring word of her, but it too was silent.

The next morning, I went to the local mall, and returned with my first phone answering machine. It was Saturday, but I went to work anyway. We didn't let a weekend get in the way of trying to get our Shuttle payload back on schedule. I spent just long enough at work to have our company quality inspector, who was overseeing the subcontract at Grumman on Long Island, fired. He had been causing no end of trouble, and accused one of our young engineers of sabotaging our hardware.

Sunday I spent at home sitting by the telephone. Late that evening, I called my ex-wife in Phoenix to see if she had heard anything. When I told her I believed Cyndi had run off with four other girls, she was surprised. So I told her about Bear and how grown up everyone said Bear was. My ex-wife scoffed. "Cyndi is Bear," she said. "It's been her nickname for the past year."

Not only did I have renewed concern for Cyndi's safety, but I was also forced to face how far apart she and I had drifted.

Her mother also told me that Mary was probably Vicki, the girl who had tried to burn her parent's home to the ground. "Vicki must be back in town," she stated emphatically. "Cyndi is with her. They may still be here in Phoenix, unless they've gone to Florida."

That proposition sent a new wave of fear through me. "Florida?" The possibility she could have gone that far away set a chill through me.

"Sure. Vicki and Danielle went to Florida when they ran away together a year ago. Danielle returned a few months later, but Vicki's been on the run ever since. I just know she came back for Cyndi. I can feel her in the air."

"So three girls are missing instead of five," I said.

"No. Just two. One of Cyndi's friends saw Danielle in downtown Phoenix this afternoon. But if I'm wrong and Vicki's not with her, Cyndi is alone."

The next morning I went to work with my suitcase packed. That afternoon, I made the trek across the Mojave Desert to Phoenix again, this time by car. I was determined to stay until I found her.

1 Dec, Wednesday

A lightning flash through my tiny opaque window momentarily lights my dark room, followed nine seconds later by a sharp clap of thunder, Zeus at work on Lesbos three kilometers from here. I lie in bed in the dark, listening as the light patter of rain on the rooftop progresses to a torrent. I rise late but unusually tired, still feel a little of the rocking motion from my ferry ride two nights ago.

I walk to the travel agency to see when I can get a ferry to Peiraias. The agent I talk to is arrogant and unresponsive, takes offense when I ask if he speaks

English, tells me tonight's ferry is the only one today, and refuses to speculate when the next might arrive. I've got a choice. I can stay here and take my chances, or be on the one to Peiraias at six this evening. "You buying a ticket, or what?" he asks. He pushes his chair away from his desk, exposing a withered left leg, a brace and heel support. He sneers, then snorts a joke about me to the man next to him.

I walk off to think about what to do, go out the door and walk around the dock, trying to resolve whether I want to go on to Peiraias tonight or spend another day here. The weather is a factor. I would like to go north along the eastern coast of Lesbos to the town of Thermi and the ruins of a Bronze Age settlement, but I'm tired of being out in the cold.

In the small plateia next to the dock stands a tall statue of beautiful Sappho, a lyre resting on her left arm, majestically looking out to sea as if to welcome incoming sailors. What we know of Sappho seems to cast a different impression of her physical presence from that depicted by the statue. According to a late 2nd or early 3rd Century AD papyrus, "In appearance she seems to have been contemptible and quite ugly, being dark in complexion and of very small stature."[397] This mean-spirited description seems to have been overly influenced by a darkness in the perceiver's heart.

Though Sappho was born in Eressos, she lived most of her life here in Mytilene. She was exiled to Sicily for awhile, and one story tells of her death as a suicide over her unrequited love for a man named Phaon. Sappho supposedly jumped from the Leucadian Rock on the southern tip of the island of Lefkadia just north of Ithaca.

While considering my traveling dilemma, I visit the 16th Century Byzantine church of St. Therapon, not far from my pension. The church sits on the ruins of the ancient School of Sappho. Here, she taught Lesbian and Ionian nobility, and was said to have pupils from Colophon, Manto's town just northwest of Ephesus. Perhaps Sappho was influenced by Manto's verses, as was Homer.

The church is a couple of blocks off the main street, an imposing sight, its three silver domes dominating the city's landscape. The front of the church is tan, with huge, recessed double doors. I push them open, walk into the quiet entryway that opens into a cavernous, echoing interior. I allow my eyes to adjust to the dark. I feel out of place with my hiking jacket and boots. A gigantic chandelier hangs from the domed ceiling. The church is almost deserted, only one old woman sitting in a seat to the right of the aisle. When my camera shutter clicks, she turns to stare at me like I've committed an abomination.

I leave the church, and walk the coastline north to a Byzantine castle sitting on top of the ruins of a Bronze Age settlement. In ancient times, this was the center of the city. Mytilene itself was a tiny island then, but is now connected to the main island by a causeway with harbors on each side.

The sky is overcast, with occasional sprinkles, as I walk the castle wall with two "wild" overly friendly dogs, and over the objections of several others, who want to eat me. These wild dogs seem to come in two varieties: those desperate to befriend you, and those who'd rather get their jaws about your throat.

My walk takes me by a statue, a Lesbian (island) version of the Statue of Liberty. She is not as big as that given to America by the French, but stands them in good stead here, on the coast of the beautiful island.

The sun breaks through the heavy clouds, turning the Aegean turquoise blue, the sea and sky reflections of each other. The small psychedelic boats docked in the harbor sparkle in a brilliant wetness. The city of Mytilene has become insufferably beautiful, the orange-tile roofs glowing like a kiln's hot coals. Off in the distance, I see a ferry at dock. I walk to the end of the dock, where the ferry is moored with gigantic ropes. It floats quietly, snuggled against the cement dock, a huge anchor chain emerging from a hole in the prow to fall vertically, and disappear into the dark water.

The dock is fenced, but the gate is open, and I walk alongside the ferry, its white surface towering above me. The dock is strangely silent and deserted. I see no hands on deck. This must be the ferry to Peiraias that leaves tonight. The name on the side is the "Sappho," a beautiful white beast with a passenger compartment the size of a large hotel. Atop the cabin, a lone mast with a single cross member, much like Christ's cross, proudly faces forward.

I walk farther away from the center of town where the fishing boats dock. I like these makeshift structures in outlying areas, where ordinary Greeks dock their little boats. The rain returns as a downpour, and I make my decision. I could stay until tomorrow and go north along the coast to some of the most interesting ruins on Lesbos, but I really feel an urgency to try to get to Aulis.

I go back to the travel agency and buy a ticket to Peiraias. We'll leave at six and sail all night, reaching Peiraias at six in the morning. I'm taking the opportunity to do something I've not done before on my journey. I'm going first class, and will have a cabin and bed.

Now that I've made my decision, the sun comes out again. I walk the city some more, seeing a beautiful, whitewashed church with walkway to match, and an archaeological dig.

I spend the rest of the day visiting the archeological museum, which has Mycenaean artifacts from around the island. I've wanted to see an ancient theatre north of Mytilene, but I'm simply too tired to make the walk. A consuming tiredness and undeniable urge to sleep has enveloped me, as if the energy I've consumed on my entire journey has suddenly come due.

I go back to the travel agency and sit on the sofa in the waiting area, listening through the open door to traffic whiz by on the wet street out front, trying to ignore a heated argument going on behind the counter. I sit on a couch in a large room filled with working employees. A short fence separates me from them at their desks. What the argument is about, I haven't a clue. Greeks really know how to argue. Shortly, the argument ends, and one of the men, the loudest, leaves with two women. Greeks argue and shout at each other, then walk off with no hard feelings. If I heard an argument that loud in the States, I would get the hell out of there for fear the man would return with an automatic weapon.

★

I sit on my bed in my first-class cabin aboard the good ferryboat Sappho, writing in my journal. My cabin is at the end of a long narrow hallway, and walking down here, I felt a tinge of claustrophobia at being so far from an exit. The room is small, with orange walls, mustard floor and white ceiling. The door to the antiquated, but adequate, bathroom is on the left wall, just past the head of my bed. The door is latched open to keep it from banging about. It latches fine in the open position, but will not stay closed when I use the toilet. I'm against the wall in bed "Γ" (gamma, equivalent to "C"), which also makes into a sofa. Two bunk beds are against the opposite wall. The beds are small and made up in white sheets, white pillowcases, and with a folded brown blanket at the foot.

St. Paul spent a short while here in Mytilene in 52 AD.[398] I've completed a swipe of the islands visited by Paul on his third missionary journey; Rhodes, Samos, Chios, Lesbos. I've visited them in the reverse order he visited them.

Another man has just joined me. He's Greek, a jolly little fellow with liquor on his breath. He wears a blue sports coat and has a black leather bag he throws on his bed. Years ago, he was with the Greek commercial fleet, and has been to Norfolk, Virginia and Corpus Christi, Texas. He's a smallish man with glasses and a large nose, balding and a little overweight. Speaks a bit of English. He goes out again, trusting me not to go through his leather bag. It has many compartments, and weighs, I'm guessing now, about six pounds. A very interesting bag with lots of zippers and a shoulder strap. Soft black leather. Hermes whispers over my shoulder that it would be most interesting to see what's inside.

Helen and Menelaus were also here in Lesbos. They were conversing with the aged Nestor following the Trojan War, trying to decide the best way home. Nestor, prince of charioteers, tells of the meeting:

Menelaos, the red-haired captain,

caught up to us at Lesbos
while we mulled over the long sea route, unsure
whether to lay our course northward of Khios [Chios],
keeping the Isle of Psyria off to port,
or inside Khios, coasting by windy Mimas.
We asked for a sign from heaven, and the sign came
to cut across the open sea to Euboia
and lose no time putting our ills behind us.[399]

Tonight, we'll follow that same course sailed by Helen and Menelaus 3200 years ago. As for war, Sappho had her say about it and Helen's motive for running off with Paris in the first place:

The Most Lovely Thing

Some say an army of horsemen, infantry, or a fleet of ships is the fairest thing on the face of the black earth, but I say it's the one you love. This is easily understandable to everyone, for she who far surpassed the beauty of all, Helen, left her noble husband and went sailing far away to Troy, and thought nothing of her child or dear parents. Aphrodite led her away for love, which reminds me of Anactoria, who is not here. Her lovely way of walking, and her bright, sparkling face I would rather see than Lydian war-chariots and well-armed infantry.[400]

I step out on deck to bid farewell to rain-soaked Lesbos. It's dark out now, the city lights beautiful along the waterfront and where they climb into the hills. The weather is cool but we've had no rain since I bought my ticket this afternoon. "The vessel is ready to sail," the Greek woman says over the loud speaker in three different languages.

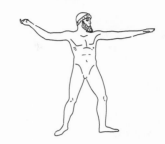

CHAPTER 20: Sounion.

I peek out the window as the walls of the cabin begin to creak; sure enough, we're on the move, the dock lights falling away behind us. This will be my last and longest voyage by ferry, my first overnighter. I sit on my bed, hoping the chubby Greek will return, so we can talk some more. When he doesn't, I shower and walk the long, tunnel-like hall to the lobby, search the ritzy dining room, cocktail lounge. He's nowhere in sight.

I go out on deck and stand at the rail, staring at the evening lights of the island floating past, the brimy smell of the sea lofting toward me. During the siege of Troy, Locrian Aias raped Priam's daughter, the princess Cassandra, on the steps of Athena's temple. Athena was so enraged by the sacrilege that, even though she had supported the Greeks in their siege of Troy, she joined forces with Poseidon to scatter the Greek ships upon their return home. Poseidon, who had staunchly supported the Greeks during the war, turned vengefully against them once he saw Troy burn. He and Apollo had built the walls around the city. He agreed to help Athena wreak havoc on the returning ships for desecrating her temple. Evil days came upon the Greeks, and they fought amongst themselves. Agamemnon and Menelaus argued. Some mustered their ships with Menelaus on Lesbos, others with Agamemnon. Odysseus at first sailed with Nestor, then had second thoughts and went back to join forces with Agamemnon. They all sailed the same part of the Aegean I'm sailing tonight, but few of them would see home again.

Odysseus was gone from Ithaca for twenty years, ten at Troy and ten blown about the Mediterranean trying to get back to home. Odysseus had reached mid-life, somewhere in his early forties, when he left Troy. I'd also just turned forty when I started my wandering, after my wife left. After losing all but one ship, Odysseus came to the island of Aeaea, off the west coast of Italy, where the goddess Circe lived. Seeing that Odysseus was in over his head with the goddess, Hermes came to his great grandson and told him how to deal with the spellbinding goddess so as not to be tricked by her drugs and magic. She had already turned his men to swine. Odysseus tells of his encounter with Hermes:

Sounion

...Hermes met me, with his golden wand,
barring the way—a boy whose lip was downy
in the first bloom of manhood, so he seemed.
He took my hand and spoke as though he knew me...[401]

Odysseus obviously didn't know Hermes was his great grandfather. Hermes was still young with a downy lip, even though Odysseus had entered midlife. Hermes knew that Odysseus, without proper protection, would fall under Circe's evil spell and never leave her island. He gave Odysseus instructions on how to deal with her, specifically stating he must not decline the offer of her bed. When Circe saw Hermes had protected Odysseus from her spells, she took him to bed, and cared for him and his men for an entire year.

My second marriage was reminiscent of this episode in Odysseus' life. I was irresistibly drawn to a young woman, and eventually, married her. Perhaps I was still trying to replace my ex-wife, trying to tie myself to something substantial to keep from floating. I had entered a state where I felt I had no internal reference, that I was losing contact with who I had been. But some part of me thrived on this state of liminality and demanded a new identity, one more closely aligned with who I was, perhaps the person I was becoming before I had the confrontation with my father. Chaos reigned. Everything inside me was being reordered. I no longer knew myself, and experienced an anxiety that culminated in hot flashes of anger, eventually ending in the panic attacks in the Alps.

When I moved from Phoenix to San Diego, my new wife refused to go, and requested a divorce. As with Odysseus and Circe, we were only together a year, two years if you count the one we lived together before getting married. I took my new wife's suggestion as a godsend, jumped at the chance, and have never regretted it. I've learned to live in a transient state, one that's brought me here to Greece, this home on the road.

Finally, Odysseus' men grew restless for Ithaca, and Odysseus went to Circe to see if she would tell him the way home. She said he could only learn his fate from the blind seer of Thebes, Teiresias, who had died years before. Odysseus would have to descend into the Underworld.

Following Circe's instructions, Odysseus sailed a dark ship without a helmsman, out of the Mediterranean to the abyss of Ocean running around the world, to the crumbling homes of Death where no sun shines. Shrouded in darkness, he dug a trough in the black earth, and while facing inky Erebos, slit the throats of a black ewe and a black ram, and as swarms of ghosts hovered about, filled the trough with sacrificial blood. He prayed with all his heart to the faint dead. From the great depths, the rapt shade of Lord Teiresias came from the darkness, carrying a golden staff to sip from the rich black blood. After sipping the crimson broth, he prophesied to Odysseus of his journey home.

While in the Underworld, Odysseus also learned of his mother's death. She had been alive when he left Ithaca, and seeing her soul among the other shades was devastating. He allowed her to drink, and she too spoke:

> ... my mother stirred,
> moving to sip the black blood; then she knew me
> and called out sorrowfully to me: 'Child,
> how could you cross alive into this gloom
> at the world's end?[402]

Odysseus asked her how she died, what had sent her to the undergloom? She first told him of his father, how he lived the life of a recluse, sleeping among the slaves on a bed of leaves, his heart aching for Odysseus. Then she spoke of herself:

> So I too pined away, so doom befell me,
> not that the keen-eyed huntress Artemis with her shafts
> had marked me down and shot to kill me; not
> that illness overtook me--no true illness
> wasting the body to undo the spirit;
> only my loneliness for you, Odysseus,
> for your kind heart and counsel, gentle Odysseus,
> took my own life away.[403]

Odysseus was overcome with sadness and wished to hold her:

> I bit my lip,
> rising perplexed, with longing to embrace her,
> and tried three times, putting my arms around her,
> but she went sifting through my hands, impalpable
> as shadows are, and wavering like a dream.[404]

Unlike Odysseus' mother, my mother was the one who encouraged me to leave home. After I quit college, she was pleased that I got married, and supported my wish to join the Air Force. The woman, who rarely left home and was too nervous to drive an automobile, encouraged me to set out on a life of adventure.

My father was a different story. After spending the summer farming with him, he was disappointed to see me leave. My older brother had made the same decision a couple of years before. In the years to come, my two younger brothers would also farm with him for a while, then leave, unable to get along with him. It broke his heart. His dream of seeing us all farming as one large clan was never to be. Life drained from him, and he became sullen and remote. He took up the bottle and visited the local bars, a trap he had vowed never to fall into. Eventually he came out the other side of the drunken tunnel. Finally, one of my brothers returned to farm again, and forged a workable partnership with him.

Perhaps it's my guilt talking, but I've always felt I was the one he really wanted to stay. If I, like Odysseus, had descended into the Underworld, I wouldn't have met the soul of my mother pining away for my return, but that of my father, the man who came within the squeeze of a trigger of murdering me.

★

I go to bed early, lie awake, feeling the long, loping strides of the ferry gently rock me. I drop off to sleep, worrying how I'll get from the dock in Piraeus to the airport south of Athens to stow my backpack. At the airport, I plan to put a change of clothes and some toilette articles in my daypack, and strike out for the temple of Poseidon at Sounion on the southern tip of Attica.

Sometime during the night, the Greek wakes me while entering the cabin. He tiptoes into the bathroom, then slips into bed. Shortly he's snoring. I lie awake, listening to the soft hum of the ferry motor superimposed on the sea's long song, and think of my daughter. Suddenly, the door opens to that space of terror within me, panic. I feel claustrophobic. It's the monstrous snoring of the man two meters away, the close walls, the long hall to the outside world, the gently-rocking sea that has me trapped aboard this vessel, trapped within myself, the madness going on inside my own head. Images of death flower in the graveyard of my thoughts.

I control my breathing, take deep breaths and exhale slowly. To divert my thoughts from cascading images of the dead, I exert all my mental effort in plotting my itinerary for the next couple of days. I think of my pending visit to Sounion, and the night I'll spend in Chalkis, the town closest Aulis where the Greeks mustered their forces before sailing to Troy, and where Agamemnon sacrificed Iphigenia.

Then comes a dream of a motorbike accident. The accident occurs on a bend in a road, a wide sweep on an incline. Three motorbikes are involved with bodies strewn along the landscape. I hear no sounds, no screams, no wails, no

376

anxious voices, just silence. First, I run to a baby girl. She's bloody and has an eye missing from its socket. The situation is far beyond my capability to help, and I'm engulfed in feelings of inadequacy.

I wake again, still anxious, on the edge of some terrible hysteria.

My car ride across the Mojave Desert to search for my runaway daughter was at night. Off to the south, blinking in and out of sight behind saguaros and Joshua trees, I saw the lights of homes across the border in the badlands of Mexico, and I arrived at my son's apartment in a daze of midnight anxiousness. The next morning, I roamed the streets of Phoenix in a desperate search for her friend, Danielle. That afternoon, after hours of fruitless searching, I went into a screaming rage. My daughter's life hung in the balance, and I was wasting my time in this endless search for a teenage derelict, who probably couldn't help me anyway.

At sunset, I went back to north Phoenix to find Troy, the leader of the New Age church. He was a baby-faced young man in his mid-twenties, and as he stood before me in dirty pants and T-shirt, he looked tired and frustrated himself. Three other young men milled about in the background. I explained that I was Cyndi's father and needed to get in touch with her.

He was unimpressed. "Look, Mister Sheppard, I don't know anything about your daughter," he told me with convincing disinterest and increasing anger. "I've had a hard day, and I don't need your problems."

I was desperate. Troy was my last hope. I didn't know where to go from there. I felt whipped and started to cry. "If I could only get word to her that she doesn't have to run, that she's not a fugitive. If Bear is in trouble, I want to help."

Troy changed. A look of fresh energy came over him. His face softened. Calling my daughter "Bear" had worked a miracle. "You really are concerned about her, aren't you?" He sounded puzzled, as if it wasn't possible for a father to care for his daughter.

I was all choked up and couldn't answer.

"Look, Bear left with Vicki five days ago. I don't know where they went, but Danielle might. I'll take you to where she lives.

Cyndi had always been an animal lover. When she was learning to crawl, it was ants, crickets and spiders. As she grew older, goldfish, gerbils, and hamsters found their way into our home, and we had many disastrous episodes with rabbits and wounded birds. I remember a little green snake smacking water from a spoon. Later, it was dogs and cats. When she graduated to horses, we gave her riding lessons, but drew the line at buying a horse. She had an unexcelled collection of plastic horses, which I still have boxed in storage. When we moved to Colorado, she spent hours watching the deer that came into our yard in the evenings, to eat from our garden and flowerbed. She was a mistress of all things wild. I found out later, her nickname had come from her collection of teddy bears.

A few minutes later, Troy and I parked our cars at the edge of a ravine, and walked down a dead-grass embankment to an old dilapidated shack. It reminded me of the makeshift home we lived in after our home burned when I was a kid. He knocked at the screen, then pulled it open, motioning me to follow him inside.

The three people didn't acknowledge us, just kept talking. Finally, Troy got their attention. One was a man about my age, brown graying hair and full beard, sipping a can of Coors. An aging hippie, I thought. The woman had obviously just come from work. She still wore heels and a dress, and looked about nervously at the cluttered living room. Through the doorway, I saw the kitchen stacked to the ceiling with dirty dishes. Both of them looked tired and old beyond their years.

The third person in the room was the sixteen year old I was looking for, Danielle. She was dressed in a cycling stretch suit. Her hair was golden brown, and fell in ringlets about a beautiful face. Troy spoke to her. "This is Bear's father," he said, motioning to me. Danielle looked up and a winning smile spread across her face. "Yeah," she said. "He looks just like her."

2 Dec, Thursday

The low rumble of the ferry motor wakes me at five AM, and I dress quietly so as not to wake my roommate. I ask a man at the reception desk what time we'll get into Piraeus. "Τι ωρα Πειραιος" I ask. He replies, but I have no idea what his words mean. I thank him and walk off. I feel much better than I did last night, but still on the edge of something dark. If this had happened at Delphi, my journey would have been over.

I walk out on deck, which is dark and enclosed by green wood walls with huge hinged windows that swing in and upward. Some have been opened to expose the night air, and a cold brisk breeze blows through, the ferry slicing swiftly through the dark sea. I stand, arms akimbo at the wood rail, trying to startle myself awake, and grateful for the expanse before me to allay the claustrophobia. I listen to the dull roar of the motor forcing us forward. To starboard, the southern tip of the long island of Euboea, called Cape Caphareus, presents a dark face. This coast is where most of the Greeks returning from the Trojan War lost their lives, so close to home.

Sounion

All the isles
And mainlands round were lashed by leaping seas
Nigh to Euboea, where the Power divine
Scourged most with unrelenting stroke on stroke
The Argives. Groan and shriek of perishing men
Ranging through the ships; started great beams and snapped
With ominous sound, for ever ship on ship
With shivering timbers crashed. With hopeless toil
Men strained with oars to thrust back hulls that reeled
Down on their own, but with the shattered planks
Were hurled into the abyss, to perish there
By pitiless doom...[405]

I breathe in the fresh air as Cape Caphareus floats out of sight in the dark behind us, and the lights on the tip of Attica, Cape Sounion, come into view. Scattered lights of homes sprinkle the shore. Sounion is the very tip of the Attic peninsula, and the magnificent setting for the temple of Poseidon, lord of the sea and bringer of earthquakes. Sounion is where Menelaus and Helen were blown off course and then spent seven years trying to get back to Sparta. The ferry rounds the cape and heads north along the western coast of Attica. The lights of airliners rise up from darkness, conjuring themselves from the Underworld, bright, blinking sparks of life rising into the dark sky.

This darkness and rocky shoreline bring to mind an event that occurred in the 1st Century AD, shortly after the crucifixion of Christ. It's a dark story concerning the freedom-seeking human spirit. The story is about the death of Pan and according to Plutarch, was told by Epitherses, a teacher of literature:

... Epitherses was once sailing to Italy on board a ship carrying merchandise and a large number of passengers. In the evening, off the Echinades, the wind dropped, and the ship drifted close to Paxi.[406] Most of them were awake, and some were still having their after-dinner drinks. Suddenly a voice was heard from the island of Paxi, calling out for someone named Thamous. It was amazing. Thamous was the Egyptian helmsman, whom few of the passengers or crew knew by name. Twice he was summoned, and did not reply. At the third call, he answered. The voice then grew louder. "When you reach Palodes", it cried, "announce that Great Pan is dead." ...they were all amazed when they heard this, and discussed among themselves whether it would be best to obey or to let the matter rest and not get involved. Thamous decided that if there was a wind, he would sail quietly by, but if there was no wind and the sea was calm in the area, he would announce what he had been told. When they arrived off Palodes, there was no wind and no swell. So Thamous looked out from the stern towards the land and cried, just as he had been told, "Great Pan is dead!" Scarcely had he spoken, when a great cry of lamentation and surprise arouse, not of one voice but of many.[407]

The death of Pan was grievous to immortals and mortals alike because, of all the gods, no other had been so universally loved. But all the gods had been under attack for some time. Even during Sophocles' day, the people no longer heeded them. Sophocles was an evangelist of sorts. His plays were a call to the return to worship, a battle he lost. Since Pan means "all," symbolically, all the Greek gods had died, and man, the creation of Christ-like Prometheus, had at last been freed into the hands of the Christian God in accordance with Prometheus' prophecy. Christian legend says that Pan died on the day Christ was crucified.[408]

But some maintain that the gods are immortal, and our awareness of their presence has only been suppressed in man's great striving for freedom. The primary obstacle to man's freedom is the sacred. And in what some have termed the "Post Christian Era," we've become a non-religious society. The fall of religion is in many ways chronicled by the rise of mankind's arrogance. I'm reminded of the statue of Liberty I saw at dockside on Lesbos and that tremendous structure in New York City given to us by the French. We've learned to sail the religious sea without a helmsman, as did Odysseus on his way to the Underworld. All this, signaled by the death of Pan.

When I get back to the cabin, the Greek is up and gone. While I'm packing, the steward knocks on my cabin door to make sure I'm up. I make a final pass through the cabin to gather any overlooked possessions, then, humped under the weight of my backpack, I make the long trek along the tunnel-like hall and down the flights of metal stairs. While waiting in the oppressive, bitter-cold hold for the gangway to lower, trucks belch clouds of carbon monoxide, and a great commotion erupts from the ferry: the rumble of the engine, the scream of machinery, the bang, whir, whine, chatter, and squeal mixing with the excited shouts of dock men. In my state of hypersensitivity, it's like all the madness of the world turned loose upon the ship. I take a deep breath and start forward.

It's still dark outside. I walk through the dim glow of dock lights, the flurry of passengers bumping into me, the chaos of arrival. Cars come from everywhere, herds of taxis. I find the bus station, but in spite of Let's Go's directions, I can't locate the bus to the airport. I'm lost and feeling disillusioned. Am I to become incapacitated here on the last stages of my journey? Suddenly, a young man appears out of the dark, asks if he can help, and then directs me to a bus stop close by. He stands and talks to me for a while, as if to calm me, then disappears into the crowd. I wait, sitting on my backpack in the dark across the street from a kiosk, contemplating who it was that had just come to my rescue. He was like an angel, and then I realize what I've just said. Hermes was the angel, the messenger of the gods. He was the protector of travelers.

A heavy, overcast sky masks sunrise, the pale morning light gradually seeping into the space around me. A taxi stops, and the driver asks if I want a ride. When I say no thanks, he replies that no busses will go to the airport this morning because of a strike. I repeat my no thanks, and he drives on to leave me downhearted and questioning. But ten minutes later, a minibus arrives, and as the dim light of morning slowly becomes day, I listen to creaking bus noises and the whiz of morning traffic on the way to the airport. I feel better in the van, finding comfort in the sound of the heater running and the hum of the city coming to life.

The international airport (East Terminal) looks newer than I remember when I arrived two months ago. I wonder if they've cleaned it up since the deluge of summer tourists, or if my expectations have changed? I walk south to a white flattop storage building, slip a couple changes of clothes, toilet articles and film into my daypack, and repack my backpack for its stay in storage. Then I walk to the arrivals lounge and have a cup of coffee, sit where I sat when I first came to Greece, and plot my last week of travel.

I sip the hot brew while looking through the huge glass windows to the runway, where the Olympic Airlines planes streak by, watch ferries and fishing boats in the Saronic Gulf. The haze is thick under full cloud cover. Even though it's light, I've yet to see the sun.

While sipping the deep, rich coffee, I remember when I first came to Greece, sitting here with the Americans who were to board a cruise boat that morning. I've fully recovered from my bout aboard the ferry, and think how fortunate I am to have traveled Greece on my own. I've been lonely, but now I'll be home in less than a week. I have a great sense of accomplishment. I don't feel like the same person who set foot here two months ago. But now it's off to the temple of Poseidon. I'll be traveling down the coast of Attica, the Apollo coast, to Sounion.

I take the shuttle to the west terminal (domestic), stand at the side of the road for forty-five minutes in the cold drizzle, only to watch the orange-and-white bus slip past without even slowing. For some reason, I believed if I waited under the orange "Sounion" sign, the bus would stop. Not so in Greece. I'll have to wait another hour in the gloomy weather. Hermes let me down this time. Sometimes Hermes makes his contrary presence known through such trickery.

I walk to the sparkling Olympic Airways terminal and have a small pizza. I'm travel-worn in my scruffy clothes, and everyone else looks spiffy in their dark suits, sports coats and tight dresses. The building glistens as though it's been spit-shined. I walk back into the cold and wait the remaining part of the hour. This time, when I see the bus to Sounion, I wave my arms and step out in front of it.

The Apollo Coast from Athens down to Cape Sounion is replete with small peninsulas jutting out into the blue waters of the Saronic Gulf. Traffic quickly thins once we're out of Athens, and a village appears suddenly as the bus rounds turns in the road, its sparse buildings riddled with signs for gyros, souvlaki, ice cream. As with everywhere else in Greece, the abandoned, partially complete construction of apartment complexes, homes and businesses casts a desolate feeling over the landscape.

The bus rounds a corner to the south, the land flattens, becomes chalky clay covered with scrubby bushes, and suddenly, there's Sounion, temple columns perched on the edge of a cliff. The tourist center is under renovation. I'm the only visitor to the windswept site, and wonder if anyone is manning it at all. I knock at a small building at the entrance, and two young people huddled inside swing open a wood window to accept my money.

I walk up the paved walkway to the high-rising, dramatic headland. This is the most desolate site I've visited. Menelaus and Helen made an unscheduled stop here on their way back home to Sparta, before they were swept out to sea, when their helmsman died suddenly. Homer tells the story through the words of Nestor:

> ...when we came off Sunion Point in Attika,
> the ships still running free, Onetor's son
> Phrontis, the steersman of Menelaos' ship,
> fell over with a death grip on the tiller:
> some unseen arrow from Apollo hit him.
> No man handled a ship better than he did
> in a high wind and sea, so Menelaos
> put down his longing to get on and landed
> to give this man full honor in funeral.[409]

The temple of Poseidon rests majestically on a cliff at the edge of the sea, the threshold of the Cyclades, a magnificent site for the grave of Menelaus' helmsman. Colossal marble columns tower skyward above the coastline. It's a quiet temple standing high above the sea. This is a temple to the god who prevented Odysseus and Menelaus from going home. Sounion is Poseidon's most famous temple, but even here, Athena haunts him. A scattering of stones from her temple is only a few meters from it. But the site is a strange wasteland, barren of the archaeological activity that I've see at most other sites. No dig, no stone walls, no cobblestone streets of an ancient city, just hard packed earth two kilometers from a tiny coastal village. Brush on the mountain has been burned off, as has been much of the surrounding countryside.

In antiquity, Sounion was an important landmark for those sailing to and from Attica. The coast here has been settled since the Bronze Age. This particular version of the temple was built in 444 BC, at the same time as the Parthenon on the Akropolis in Athens. Actually, more recent research indicates that the temple probably originally belonged to Apollo instead of Poseidon. This would make considerable sense, because, according to Homer, an arrow from Apollo killed Menelaus' helmsman as they rounded the Cape on their way back to Ithaca.

I sit on a large slab of marble, looking across the Aegean at a small island in the distance, with the sun peeking through a cloud. The sun glistens off the rippled water's surface. I see two fishing boats, one large and moving slowly through the water, the other small and stationary, floating aimlessly between the island and me. A gusty breeze buffets me from the west.

With Phrontis buried, Menelaus took to sea again only to be blown off course: "... Zeus who views the wide world sent a gloom over the ocean, and a howling gale came on with seas increasing, mountainous, parting the ships..."[410] The winds of Zeus blew Menelaus and Helen to the coast of Crete, where they shipwrecked on a reef. They floundered in Egypt, visiting many places along its coast, many now attested to locally, even if they are little more than local wishful thinking. Menelaus and Helen wandered for seven years before once again returning to Sparta. Still, they made it home three years before Odysseus, and hosted Odysseus' son Telemachus when he came searching for news of his long lost father.

★

Mid -afternoon, I sit on the steps beside the tourist center down the hill from the temple, with the banging and clanging of workmen renovating the building, awaiting the bus to Markopoulo and Chalkis, writing in my journal. The wind here at Cape Sounion rakes this stark landscape with huge gusts. Suddenly, a wave of sand descends on me, all over my journal, down the back of my neck. I rise to see what gust could have caused this, but realize it's the workmen. They've swept sand from the rooftop down on the steps where I'm writing. Another wave of sand sends me running from the building. A man stands on the edge of the flat roof, waving his arms at the realization of what he's done. A great gush of apologetic Greek comes from him. Another man comes to stand beside him, laughing.

Finally, the bus to Markopoulo.

We travel up the east coast of shadow-shrouded Attica, turn inland through trees and small villages. As I pick out our route on my map, the man sitting next to me speaks to me in Greek. I believe he's asked where I'm going. I tell him, "Χαλκις." He doesn't understand, so I tell him, "Μαρκοπουλο, Χαλκις." He understands Markopoulo but is confused about Chalkis. I show him my map. "Οχι, οχι Chalkis," he says, "Χαλκιδα" (Halkitha). I drag out another map that has the names in Greek, and sure enough he's right. The name of the town is listed as Halkitha. "Μαρκοπουλο, Χαλκιδα," I tell him. He looks at me again with bewilderment. "Μαρκοπουλο, Αθνα, Χαλκιδα." He points to my map, indicating I must go to Athens before Halkitha. He shouts something at the bus driver, and a great commotion results, including several passengers. Everyone has an opinion. Turns out he's right again. I can't get a bus in Markopoulo for Halkitha. I must go to Athens first. "Λιοσσον Σταθμος," he says. This is not good news. He's telling me I have to go to the bus station on Liosson Street, Terminal B. I hoped to be in Halkitha before nightfall, but now I might have to spend the night in Athens. Not a pleasant thought.

Just before Markopoulo, the bus stops. Up ahead, a flatbed truck, loaded with fresh-cut timber, blocks the road, and a crowd has gathered. Another bus, stopped in the opposing lane, blocks my view. We pull forward to pass the timber truck. Suddenly, pandemonium breaks out inside the bus. Women behind me start shouting and run to the front, crowd to the windows. The bus moves forward a little more, and I looked over the edge of the road down into a culvert. A woman screams. A man lies on the ground spread out face down shaking, heaving as though he's crying. I see a car, twisted and upside down in the culvert, smoke billowing from it. Several men stand at the edge of the road looking down at him. The accident is as fresh as a butchered animal. Two women stand a few yards from the injured man, but no one goes to him. All are frozen with horror.

And then I see it, what has turned these people to stone. At the side of the road where the car went over the edge, lying on his back on a hill of fresh dirt, is a dead man, face pointed to the sky. His unmoving, badly damaged body has turned the men to zombies, and given the women inside the bus a raving, screaming madness. It's a primordial scene, blood-drenched carnage.

My desire to help is overwhelming. I had emergency first aid while in the

Air Force. I grab my daypack and move into the aisle, as the bus starts forward again. I shout at the driver to stop. "Στασι!" I yell, but a woman scolds me and motions for me to get back in my seat. This is my worst nightmare. For decades, I've dreamed of coming upon an automobile accident with bodies littering the landscape and not being able to get to the victims. Finally, it's happened, as if all those dreams have converged at this one instant in my life.

The bus moves swiftly through villages, zipping along the streets. The driver turns on the radio, and music fills the bus, but it can't soften the image of the wreck, the young man in Levis lying in the road, with no one to help him or cover his dead companion.

Where the bus drops me off in Athens, I have no idea. I fiddle with my map for a while, checking street signs, find I'm somewhere north of Syntagma. I walk for half an hour through failing light, construction, traffic, dark, drab buildings, still shaken from the accident. The failing sun casts an eerie glow over the dilapidated buildings, and I descend within myself, lost in thought. In the fading light of the streets of Athens, dark shapes mill about like mythical images.

As darkness takes command of the city, I arrive at Terminal B, where I got lost two months ago and ended up out in the country. The terminal is cold, wind-blown and consumed by darkness. I buy my ticket for Halkitha, and have only five minutes before the bus leaves. I'll arrive late, but at least I won't have to spend the night in Athens.

★

The dome light casts a dim glow, barely breaking the darkness inside the bus, and outside, a thin sprinkle of sparkling lights spreads along the coast of Euboea and across the black water of the strait of the Euripus. Euboea is a long, thin island paralleling the coast of Attica and Boiotia. Between the island and the mainland stretches the blackness of Evoikos Bay to the north and south. Here, in the center of the island, on a small peninsula jutting out from Euboea towards Attica, lies the ancient city of Chalkis. It occupied a commercial and strategic position in Greek history, and ranked among well-known cities like Thebes, Megara, Corinth, and Argos.[411] Where the two shores pucker to kiss each other, the Euripus Bridge spans thirty meters of dark water, and on the Euboian side of the bridge lies modern Halkitha, where the ancient city of Chalkis was located. Water changes directions in this narrow channel as often as fourteen times a day.[412] Just south of this strait, on the mainland side of the gulf, lie ruins of the ancient village of Aulis, where the Greek fleet mustered its forces before sailing to Troy, where Agamemnon sacrificed his daughter. I don't yet know how I'll get to Aulis, whether it'll be possible to walk, or if I'll have to find some means of transportation. I've decided to go to Halkitha to see if I can find a way. Hermes hasn't let me down yet.

Just to the north, on this the Attica side of the Euboian Sea, is Locris, the home of Locrian Aias, who raped Cassandra. Athena demanded[413]that the Locrians send two sacrificial maidens a year to the temple of Athena at Troy for 1000 years.[414] Trojans came out to meet the maidens as they arrived, and tried to stone them. If they escaped death, they served as Trojan slaves within Athena's temple. Maidens who were killed were not buried, but cremated, and their ashes thrown into the sea.[415]

The bus descends the hilly countryside, turns east, and the city of Halkitha comes into view, a sparkling array of city lights reflecting in the gulf. The bus crosses the rattling, shaking bridge into the hillside city, the windows of tall, multistory buildings glowing down upon us, streets filled with the roar of motorbikes, hordes of milling people.

CHAPTER 21: Aulis.

I walk the dark, crowd-strewn streets of Halkitha, trying to find a hotel and remembering that this is the city where Aristotle retired in 322 BC to mourn the death of his pupil, Alexander the Great. I round a corner, and run smack into a forest of Christmas trees and stacks of decorations. After no longer living with my children, Christmas has lost its magic, but on this journey, I've found it again. My stay on Patmos and visiting the home of the Virgin Mary at Ephesus has had a profound effect on me. I simply glow inside when I think of Christmas in California with family. I like Halkitha, even though it has the motorbikes and horns of all Greek cities.

I finally find a room in an old hotel, with an old man behind the desk and an even older, cadaverous man helping him. They creak about like gigantic praying mantises. But what is so strange about my room is the two sets of huge French double doors: one I entered by, and just opposite them, on the far side of the room, the other set leading to a minuscule second-floor balcony through which noise from the street enters unabated. I feel as though my bed is in an entryway.

I unpack, still reeling from the images of injury and death I saw on the road today, on top of which are now superimposed fleeting images of Santa Claus. After unpacking a few things and showering, I walk through the cool evening air to the dock to watch the dark, fast-moving water between Euboea and Boiotia. In Euripides' play *Iphigenia at Aulis*, the Chorus of Women was from Chalkis. They'd come to see famous Agamemnon, Odysseus, Menelaus, Achilles. I imagine their excitement the night before they made their trek south along the coast to Aulis, the anticipation of witnessing a great event. After returning to my room, I undress and lie in bed, thinking that no great event will occur tomorrow at Aulis, just the arrival of one more traveler, who will pay homage and move on.

Finding Danielle was my first break in solving the mystery of my daughter's disappearance, but my good fortune was dampened when I learned that Danielle was even more mystified than I. And she was mad. Vicki and Bear had run off without telling her.

Aulis

After getting the two of us together, Troy left to play nursemaid to the rest of his misfits, and Danielle and I went outside to talk. I sat on a log, and she sat on an old tricycle. Sitting astride the tricycle facing me, she seemed a precocious child. She told me she lived with the woman, who rented the home, and took care of her house, swept the floors and washed the dishes, for room and board. The bearded man was not the woman's husband but her boyfriend. Danielle confessed that she was more than a little behind in her duties. Then she told me about Bear.

As I listened to Danielle talk about Cyndi, I realized that a big change had come over my daughter in the two years I had lived apart from her. She had assumed a rather motherly role toward the less fortunate of her classmates and other young girls like Danielle, high school dropouts. Cyndi had brought them home with her. Danielle had lived with Cyndi and her mother for a few months. Vicki, after her father beat her, also came to live with them. That was Cyndi's connection with Troy, who was running an unofficial home for wayward kids. That was the reason she had a following.

When Danielle told me how much she admired Bear, I got a glimmer of hope, that maybe my decision to leave Cyndi with her mother in Phoenix had not been such a bad idea after all. Her mother was a social worker. Apparently, some of her spirit had rubbed off.

That evening before I left, Danielle took me into her bedroom, and from her closet, retrieved a sweater from among many other items Cyndi had given her. The sight of my daughter's sweater was like seeing a glimmer of her. I held the sweater to me, searching for a warmth that would mean she was still alive.

Danielle told me she would help me find Bear. "Bear is the best friend I've ever had," she said, obviously searching for words to say something difficult. "I'm glad you're looking for her. I like Vicki, but she can be really hard. When we ran away together last year, we hitchhiked to Florida. This may scare you to hear it, but you should know. We caught rides with truckers. Some things that happened to me, I still can't talk about. You should be concerned about her," she said with a look beyond her years. "If they do what we did, she is in danger."

After several months on the run, the police had caught up with Vicki and Danielle in Miami, and sent them home. No one accompanied them, and Vicki exited the plane in Dallas. Danielle, tired of running, appreciated the free ride back to Phoenix.

Danielle said she would talk to some of her friends, and I left her standing in the dark outside the dilapidated home. She seemed reluctant to see me leave, and I was reluctant to go. As I climbed the side of the ravine back to my car, I wondered if it was because she had found a father in me, and I had found a daughter in her. My drive to my son's apartment was full of prayers for my daughter's safety, and horrible visions of what she could be experiencing at the hands of truck drivers. This was when I confronted myself about my faith that God would protect her, and found it seriously lacking. The reality of the situation was what came to the forefront. I've never felt so alone in the world, so abandoned. It was as if God was dead.

In 429 BC, a great plague devastated Athens. It occurred during the Peloponnesian War, when all of Attica was brought within Athens' walls for safety. The crowding and resultant unsanitary conditions created a fertile breeding ground for disease. According to Thucydides, the 5th Century BC historian, the devastation brought with it unprecedented lawlessness and loss of respect for the gods:

> No fear of god or law of man had a restraining influence. As for the gods, it seemed to be the same thing whether one worshipped them or not, when one saw the good and the bad dying indiscriminately. (II, 53)

Within this atmosphere, Sophocles wrote *Oedipus Tyrannus*, the plague being the impetus of Oedipus' search for the murder of Laios, and the driving force that would not let him back off once he realized the result would be his own ruin. Perhaps no parallel exists between this widespread tragedy and my own desperate search for my daughter, my fear for her life. But the hand of God did seem to me to be indiscriminate, and no appeal on my part convincing enough to ensure His interference on her behalf. It wasn't a total disbelief in God, but a rather dramatic realization that I was on my own on this one. I'd always questioned the nature of reality, but in this instance, I had no trouble differentiating it from that of the world of the divine. Everything I knew about God paled in comparison to the necessity for me to act to save my daughter.

The next day when I returned, Danielle was gone. I searched for her all morning, a growing sense of powerlessness coming over me. But that afternoon, just as I was about to give up, I found her on her bike, coming home. She had been on a long training run for an upcoming race. "You need to meet more of Bear's friends," she told me.

She took me to the home of one of Cyndi's classmates, Sue. Sue was not pleased to see us, and mad at Danielle for bringing me. She refused to talk to me at first, but after several minutes of Danielle's coaxing, Sue reluctantly took me into her bedroom. She had several of my daughter's teddy bears, and shoebox after shoebox of letters from friends. Sue claimed Bear and Vicki had left her home with two guys from a rock band. She didn't know the guys because they were from out of town. She cast suspicious glances at me as Danielle pulled bits of information from her. Danielle fed her several names, and finally got a confirmation.

Danielle turned to me, "Two guys from LA," she said. "I know them, but there's no way to get a hold of them. They're always on the road." Sue said the guys were only dropping Bear and Vicki off somewhere in town, but claimed she didn't know where. "A truck stop?" asked Danielle. But Sue clammed up, and it was useless to question her further.

Some of what had happened the day Cyndi disappeared became apparent. She had stripped her bedroom of everything valuable to her, stuffed animals, private correspondence and musical equipment. Sue had picked her up at home soon after Cyndi's mother left for work. When the two guys from the rock band came to pick up Cyndi and Vicki at Sue's, they didn't have room for all of her stuff, and she had to leave much of it behind. But it also indicated that Cyndi didn't fully realize what she was getting into.

I gathered up all of Cyndi's belongings and took them with me. Danielle wanted to know what I was going to do with her letters. I said I was reluctant to read them, because they were private. I have always had a great respect for my children's right to privacy, and would never even consider reading them without her approval. "Don't be so pure," said Danielle. "Read them. Bear's life may depend on it."

That evening, I went back to my son's apartment, sat at his kitchen table, opened a shoe box, and forced myself to do something I considered unethical. But Danielle was right. If her private letters contained a clue to her whereabouts, I had to find it. Hour after hour I poured over the letters, skipping those containing only personal matters, and reading with intense interest those to and from Vicki. Apparently, Vicki had returned Cyndi's letters to her, so I got both sides of their correspondence. One of the most startling discoveries was that both girls were great writers. The "Valley Girl" dialect was high-octane and super-literate.

As the hours passed, though much of what they had to say to each other was in code, a story unfolded. My daughter had been in continuous contact with Vicki, who wrote to her under several assumed names during the year after she ran away. After Vicki separated from Danielle when she exited the plane in Dallas, she spent several weeks there, then drifted to Los Angeles. In a letter mailed during early December, Cyndi suggested that the two of them meet in San Diego when she came to visit me.

A chill went up my spine as I remembered the Christmas Cyndi came to visit, the strange knock at the door late in the evening, her leaving with an unknown kid and returning during the wee hours of the morning, our heated argument. I realized, that on that night she had met Vicki, and they must have planned Cyndi's disappearance four months later. I was lucky she came home at all.

At the time, Vicki was living with her boyfriend and his family in San Bernardino and desperate for money. I read the few remaining letters with increasing urgency, begging Cyndi to tell where they planned to go when she joined Vicki. But the answer I was looking for wasn't in the letters. I was left with several addresses at which Vicki had stayed during the past year, and that of her last boyfriend, in the town of Highland close to San Bernardino.

The next day, I had lunch with Danielle, and told her how little I learned from the letters. We ate at the Good Earth because she, like Cyndi, was vegetarian. She knew Vicki's last boyfriend, and had a telephone number in Highland. We called, but got no answer. She said she would try to get in touch with them during the next few days. I told her I was leaving for San Diego as soon as we finished lunch. The next day, I would drive to Highland.

During the night, in the hotel at Halkitha, I dream of a vertical poem, supposedly written by John Lennon, and wake myself laughing:

ENCYCLOPAEDIA
D
O
N'
T
W
A
N
T
GOAT

In my dream, the visual image is of a goat eating an encyclopaedia, sort of an irreverent approach to learning. I can't contain my laughter. John must be sending news of Pan, the goat god.

As sleep gradually overcomes me again, I think of the temple of sacrifice I'll visit tomorrow and the time I first witnessed a sacrificial ritual on the farm. The "high priest" conducting the ceremony was my father. He was unusually agreeable that morning, and kept me beside him, the better to observe the proceedings.

My parents had talked it over and decided I was old enough to watch the slaughter of the young bull. When he was a calf, I had fed him from a bucket, with a rubber teat that he sucked and butted like it was his mother's udder. I fed him a mixture of her fresh, foamy milk and tan licorice-smelling powder. And now that he was near-grown and had stubby horns out each side of his board-flat head, the adults swung aside the old wood gate and drove him out of the pasture into the large dirt yard in front of our home. My mother stood to the right, outside the kitchen door, still in her apron. My uncle closed the wood gate, shutting off the young bull's retreat, and my older brother stood to the left, should he break for the corrals. My father, standing directly in front, completed the silent box and stopped the young bull with his head held high, nostrils flaring and snorting.

Without animosity, my father raised the pistol and fired a shot between the young bull's horns, shot him in the forehead with a silver pistol. The dust flew when the bullet popped, and the bull shook his head as if to ward off a pesky fly, as if the sting had nothing to do with us at all.

I stood with my elbows out a little from my sides, marking the calmness of the day, the angle of the sun, and the methodical arrangement of the killing by the adults. I edged closer to my father, as he raised the pistol one more time and shot him right between the eyes. The young bull turned his head to correct the terrible thought raging inside and a front leg betrayed him, so that he stumbled momentarily. The other followed, and he kneeled, paused in that pose for a moment, then went limp all over.

My father slit the hide between the bull's leg bone and tendon with a pocket knife, inserted a small, white cotton rope, and my uncle hoisted him by the back ankles to the rafters of the old shed, so he hung head down with large, dull eyes. Then, my father made a small slit at each jugular so the bull's fresh blood poured in two small streams off his chin and puddled in the soft powdery dirt, much as Odysseus had done in the Underworld to lure the soul of Teiresias, a tribute to the Earth goddess to whom all beings return. I didn't realize it then, but the bull is especially sacred to Gaia.[416]

I was twelve at the time, and remember not wanting to turn thirteen, a little younger than Iphigenia when she was sacrificed at the site I'll visit tomorrow. After the bull my father killed was bled, the carcass went to the butcher, where it was dismembered, and we all consumed him, T-bones, rib-eyes, sirloin. The fact that I associated myself so closely with the young bull made it seem a little like I had also died that day. Something about me was lost, and I was never the same, but since visiting all the temples on this journey, I now see my parents' actions in a different light. In ancient Greece, sacrificial animals were frequently used in initiation ceremonies as a surrogate for the initiate, who underwent a rite of passage. On ancient Crete, Dionysus was the bull god, and during rituals Cretans tore bulls apart with their teeth.[417]Dionysus was the twice-born god, and he was torn apart by the Titans, prior to being resurrected as the god of madness. In my case, the sacrifice could be viewed as a ritual, in which I died as a child and was reborn a young adult. The ancient Greek cults seem to tell us the transition cannot occur without experiencing trauma.

3 Dec, Friday

Early in the morning, I walk down the street from the hotel, and rather apprehensively, enter a barbershop. I've needed a haircut for some time, but have been putting it off, hoping to make it back to Colorado. Last night, I caught a glimpse of my reflection in a window, and decided it was time to get the locks chopped. This is not a place for women. I sit with three other men, waiting my turn. It's much like the barbershops in the States, or perhaps as they used to be, swivel chair, toilet paper around the neck, cologne, powder. Afterward, I smell as though I've just gotten out of bed with a woman. I feel so domesticated to Greece.

After walking around a plataea, I take a walk out on the waterfront to get a look at Halkitha, a rather impressive array of expensive hotels spread along the water's edge. I see the bridge connecting Euboea and Attica in the distance. I notice in my guidebook that Halkitha has an archaeological museum, and wonder if someone there can tell me how to get to Aulis.

I finally locate the museum, across from the police station on Venizelou Street. I enter through an iron gate beside a hut, where a gorgeous blond with long flowing hair and a persistent smile sells tickets. I wonder if she's really Greek with all that fair skin and natural-blond hair. I ask if she speaks English, and she tells me sheepishly that she speaks only a little.

I'm not sure of the pronunciation of "Aulis" in Greek. It's spelled Αυλις, and the 'αυ' is pronounced equivalent to the English 'av' in Modern Greek and 'au' in ancient Greek. So I try both on her, adding that Aulis is where Agamemnon sacrificed his daughter. Her eyes light up. "Iphigenia!" she exclaims. Through bits of English and Greek, I learn of a train station on the mainland just across the wood bridge, where I should catch the train to the first stop, "Στενο," Steno. I should get off there, cross the tracks, and follow a dirt road past a cement factory. I'll find a sign marking the location. "Not much there," she says.

★

At noon, I cross the bridge to the Attica side and sit in the train station, a large brick building at the beginning of the line. The tracks start and stop here. I wait for my train to Steno, which will arrive at 12:15, so the rumor goes. The large waiting room echoes with voices and footsteps on the slate-tile floor.

Agamemnon was not the strong-willed, decisive man you'd expect to be in charge of a large army. He was ambitious, but clearly in over his head. He had gotten on the bad side of Artemis, because he killed a deer sacred to her and boasted that he was a better shot than the goddess. Because of this sacrilege, she calmed the winds at Aulis so the Greeks couldn't sail. Through the high priest Chalcis, Artemis demanded that Agamemnon sacrifice his eldest, most beautiful daughter, Iphigenia, upon her altar, or they would never sail to Troy.

Artemis, here on the east coast of Attica, was the nature goddess, the mother of all things wild. As a virgin goddess, she was:

> ...the divine spirit of sublime nature, the lofty shimmering mistress, the pure one, who compels delight and yet cannot love, the dancer and huntress who fondles cubs in her bosom and races the deer, who brings death when she draws her golden bow, reserved and unapproachable like wild nature, and yet, like nature, wholly enchantment and fresh excitement and lightning beauty. This is Artemis.[418]

The train comes, a slow-moving chain of passenger cars. A horde of people exit and another horde get on. I sit opposite an old woman with gray hair and glasses, who looks up at me and smiles as the train starts moving. We travel in silence, with the sea to our left and the rocky mountains growing to our right, as if to squeeze the train off the hillside into the water. The train snakes along the crooked track. "Αθηνα?" the woman asks, wanting to know if I'm going to Athens. "Στενο," I reply. She gets wide-eyed, "Στενο?" she asks, obviously upset. I think maybe I've said something wrong, possibly offended her. To my alarm, she calls the conductor, says many things to him very rapidly. He leaves quickly for the front of the train, and immediately it starts to slow. The woman has saved me. The train had no intention of stopping in Steno. If she hadn't told the conductor, we'd already be past it. Hermes, ever at the ready.

I get off the train alone, out in what seems like the middle of nowhere. It's cold and overcast, and the ground damp. I stand next to an old, rust-red, brick building, watching the train disappear around the bend. I wonder how I'll ever get back on the train if it doesn't ordinarily stop here? The brick train station is locked, and looks as though it's been locked a long time. Away from the tracks to the west, the weedy ground rises, and two old shacks with chickens and dogs lie between the station and a blacktop road further up the hill. I hope I'm not stranded.

Just as the woman at the museum told me, a dirt road runs along the other side of the tracks, beside a tall cyclone fence around a cement factory. I cross the tracks and walk south along the dirt road, as instructed, with the cyclone fence to my left. Beyond the cement factory, the road is lined with trees and tall dead grass. A small, badly polluted harbor appears. Walking along this sandy road, I remember the words of Euripides' Chorus of Women from Chalkis in his play of Iphigenia:

> To the sandy beach of sea-coast Aulis I came after a voyage through the tides of Euripus, leaving Chalcis on its narrow firth, my city which feedeth the waters of far-famed Arethusa near the sea, that I might behold the army of the Achaeans and the ships rowed by those god-like heroes; for our husbands tell us that fair-haired Menelaus and high-born Agamemnon are leading them to Troy on a thousand ships in quest of the lady Helen...
>
> Through the grove of Artemis, rich with sacrifice, I sped my course, the red blush mantling on my cheeks from maiden modesty, in my eagerness to see the soldiers' camp, the tents of the mail-clad Danai, and their gathered steeds...
>
> I beheld the offspring of Laertes Odysseus, who came from his island hills, and with him Nireus, handsomest of all Achaeans; Achilles next, that nimble runner, swift on his feet as the wind, whom Thetis bore and Chiron trained; him I saw upon the beach, racing in full armour along the shingle, and straining every nerve to beat a team of four horses...[419]

No throngs of an army here today, no blushing maidens visiting the site. Aulis is still, damp, a heavy silence imposed by thick clouds. All I see is a couple of homes, no village. Just a rabid dog, who stands at the edge of his yard, threatening to eat me. I wonder if this is really the right location. The woman at the museum mentioned a plaque of some sort, or a sign on a building at the cement company, but I can find nothing. Pausanias described the site as he saw it in the 2nd Century AD:

> Where the Euripose cuts off Euboia from Boiotia... is AULIS... There is a SHRINE OF ARTEMIS here, and white stone statues, one carrying torches, the other shooting... They still keep in the temple what is left of the trunk of a plane tree mentioned by Homer in the Iliad. The story is that the Greeks at Aulis could not get a breath of favorable breeze, but then suddenly a stern wind got up, and everyone sacrificed what he had to Artemis, male and female victims alike: ever since it has been traditional that any victim is acceptable at Aulis. They point out the spring where the

plane tree grew, and on a mound near by the bronze floor of Agamemnon's tent... Not many people live in Aulis, and those who do are potters...[420]

Seems even less of a village than when Pausanias was here. Any confidence I had of finding the actual site where Agamemnon sacrificed Iphigenia has evaporated. I'm in a deserted industrial area, with no sign of a historical monument. I walk on up the road, past a house on the left, a little wood shack sitting among trees. Two dogs growl and pull at their chains, and at a small white lifeless house with a wood fence, a small dog with a squeaky voice follows me up the road, barking at my heels. I keep shooing him away, fearful he'll nip me. Further on, another cyclone fence encloses a field of dead grass, and that's it. Beyond is the asphalt road south. Nothing here. Even worse even than I anticipated.

As I turn back, I spot it, a sign on a tall pole. In the grass field I just passed, a small archeological dig lies beneath a large evergreen tree. Then, I see more ruins on the other side of the tree. The closer I get, the more stones and walls become visible. I sound out the Greek letters on the sign, ΝΑΟΣ ΑΥΛΙΔΕΙΑΣ ΑΡΤΕΜΙΔΟΣ (TEMPLE AULIDEIAS ARTEMIDOS). The temple of Artemis is inside the fence! I never imagined that the woman at the museum was telling me they had excavated the temple, the very spot where Iphigenia was sacrificed.

But it's fenced. I'll not be able to get a close look. And then I see a hole in the fence, one large enough for me to crawl through. The archeological dig is much larger than I thought, perhaps covering three or four acres. It's as if the site was hidden by magic and is slowly materializing before my eyes. My gloomy walk has turned into a glorious event.

I'm standing on the spot where Agamemnon, the seer Chalcis, and Iphigenia stood. Ruins of the stone altar are still here. The small, unimpressive bay I passed on the way here is the Bay of Aulis, where one-thousand ships awaited favorable winds to sail to Troy. Achilles raced the team of horses along the dirt road I just walked. Today, the ruins are quiet and moody, dark and brooding. Homer, through the words of Odysseus, also described the site in *The Iliad*:

> One day, just when the ships
> had staged at Aulis, loaded, every one,
> with woe for Priam and the men of Troy,
> we gathered round a fountain by the altars,
> performing sacrifices to the gods
> under a dappled sycamore. The water
> welled up shining there...[421]

Aulis

I sit on the cold stone altar, light mist falling. A tall evergreen grows at the edge of the temple today, leans inward, just as Odysseus saw the dappled sycamore and Pausanias saw the plane tree, shading it from cloud-filtered sunlight. Two stone statues stood before the altar when Pausanias was here, one carrying torches, the other a bow and arrow.[422] I hear the whish of passing cars on the nearby road, but the overriding sound is the rumble of the nearby cement factory, belching fumes skyward.

When Agamemnon was told he would have to sacrifice Iphigenia, at first he refused, sending word to disband the army. But his brother Menelaus protested, and he and the wily Odysseus' convinced Agamemnon to commit the crime. Agamemnon then sent a message to Klytemnestra, telling her to bring Iphigenia, under the pretext of marrying her off to Achilles, a lie not even Achilles himself knew about. But during the night, Agamemnon had second thoughts, and wrote a countermanding letter to Klytemnestra. Menelaus stopped the messenger before he got out of camp and accused Agamemnon of thinking "crooked thoughts, one thing now, another formerly, and something different presently."[423] Agamemnon stood his ground, insisting he would not sacrifice his daughter, and was about to send the messenger on to Mycenae, when Klytemnestra and Iphigenia arrived. The word got out about the marriage, and gradually, the entire plot unraveled, but the Greek army wouldn't let Agamemnon back out of the sacrifice.

Iphigenia, who was initially excited about her marriage to Achilles, was devastated when she learned of her father's plot. Klytemnestra was enraged. Once events were set in motion, the sacrifice couldn't be stopped. Agamemnon had lost control, and couldn't face his daughter:

...when king Agamemnon saw the maiden on her way to the grove to be sacrificed, he gave one groan, and, turning away his face, let the tears burst from his eyes, as he held his robe before them.[424]

According to Euripides, after Iphigenia's initial resistance, she relented, and went willingly to her own sacrifice:

O my father, here am I to do thy bidding; freely I offer this body of mine for my country and all Hellas, that ye may lead me to the altar of the goddess and sacrifice me, since this is Heaven's ordinance. Good luck be yours for any help that I afford! and may ye obtain the victor's gift and come again to the land of your fathers. So then let none of the Argives lay hands on me, for I will bravely yield my neck without a word.[425]

Aulis

Klytemnestra refused to witness the murder, and afterward, a messenger came to tell her of the miraculous event. Iphigenia's life had been spared at the last second, when Artemis substituted a hind, a red deer; much as God sent an angel to stay the hand of Abraham raised to sacrifice Isaac, and substituted a calf:[426]

> ...the priest Calchas, the seer, seizing his knife, offered up a prayer and was closely scanning the maiden's throat to see where he should strike. ...when lo! a sudden miracle! Each one of us distinctly heard the sound of a blow, but none saw the spot where the maiden vanished. Loudly the priest cried out, and all the host took up the cry at the sight of a marvel all unlooked for, due to some god's agency, and passing all belief, although 'twas seen; for there upon the ground lay a hind of size immense and passing fair to see, gasping out her life, with whose blood the altar of the goddess was thoroughly bedewed.[427]

But the words of the messenger fell on deaf ears. Klytemnestra didn't believe for a second that Artemis had whisked Iphigenia away and substituted a deer in her place.

> She scoffed at him and spoke instead of Iphigenia:
> O daughter, of what God stolen art thou?
> How shall I bid farewell to thee?—how
> Know this for aught but a sweet lie, spoken
> To heal the heart that for thee is broken?[428]

Klytemnestra harbored a hatred for her husband from that day forth, and killed Agamemnon with an ax when he returned from Troy.

Following her disappearance, Iphigenia reappeared as a priestess of Artemis living in Taurus east of Troy, a peninsula in the Black Sea now known as the Crimea. Artemis had whisked her away at the last second, and placed her among the Tauri. There she "was taught the inhospitable law of their horrible kettles, in cutting up men for meat."[429]

After Klytemnestra killed Agamemnon, their only son, Orestes, returned from being raised in exile, to murder his mother in revenge. As penance for having killed his mother, Orestes went to Taurus, under the instructions of Apollo, to retrieve "an image of the goddess Artemis, which fell from heaven."[430] While stealing the heavenly statue, Orestes found his sister, Iphigenia, and both of them tried to escape but were caught by the Tauri. Athena interceded on their behalf, and told Iphigenia of her fate:

> ...Iphigenia, thou must keep her Artemis' temple-keys at Brauron's hallowed path of steps; there shalt thou die and there shall they bury thee, honouring thee with offerings of robes, e'en all the finely-woven vestments left in their homes by such as die in childbirth.[431]

The ruins of the Brauron temple of Artemis are a few kilometers down the Attic coast from here, just east of Markopoulo, where a collapsed cave has been identified as the tomb of Iphigenia.[432] Maidens from Athens practiced bear rituals at the site. A girl, when she was to go from maidenhood to a young woman, would make an offering of her own hair at the tomb of Iphigenia. It was a symbol of the death of herself as a maiden and her rebirth as a young woman, just as Iphigenia had been sacrificed and resurrected. The maidens were required to perform a "bear" ritual prior to getting married. During this ritual, they symbolically became bears,[433] an animal sacred to Artemis. In this myth, a bear is substituted for the sacrifice of the maiden. Girls between the ages of five and fifteen attended the temple for training. They wore a short saffron, honey-yellow chiton and danced the "bear" barefoot, with their hair down about their shoulders.[434]

The connection between the bear ritual and my daughter, Bear, is so obvious that I look at my Greek dictionary to see if her name, Cynthia, might also have a Greek equivalent. The transliteration of Cynthia is Κυνθια. The closest word is Κυνθος, Kynthos, the name of the hill on Delos where Artemis was born. On impulse, I check my handbook of Greek mythology for "Cynthia." Sure enough, Cynthia has an entry. The name comes from Kynthos and is an epithet for Artemis, the goddess to whom Iphigenia was sacrificed. Another rather startling coincidence.

Artemis was the essence of feminine freedom, the goddess who "disappears into the distance. The Argives regularly celebrated her departure and her return."[435] As caretaker of all young creatures, she was especially the nurse of children,[436] and benefactress of orphaned daughters.[437]

All my daughter's activities before running away are symbolic of Artemis' influence. Even both her given name and her nickname are epithets of Artemis. I sit, staring into the foggy mist, trying to digest this powerful relationship between myth and the reality of our lives, and a little shaken at how Iphigenia's myth has seemingly infiltrated the lives of my daughter and me.

A light mist falls, a sign that the time to leave the temple of Artemis has come. On my walk back, I stop to view the Bay of Aulis. Now that I know the Greeks mustered their ships here, I take a better look. The bay is small and deeply recessed into the coast of Boiotia, its mouth almost closed. The water is murky white, chalky from the cement factory that hovers over it. The water stands calm, the stillness that was Iphigenia's bane. It's deathly still now, badly polluted.

Standing here before this murky bay, I'm suddenly anxious to get back to Athens. The legend of Iphigenia is so closely related to the myth of Persephone that I must go to Eleusis where she reappeared. This is the story of another father, Zeus, giving up his daughter for the sake of others, and the mother, Demeter, resisting all the way, as did Klytemnestra.

I walk the sandy road and re-cross the tracks to the deserted train station. A light rain falls. I wonder if the train will stop for me, or will I be stranded here? After a short wait, I see its tall shape emerging from around the bend on its way to Athens. I feel small, insignificant. I imagine myself trying to stop a train in the States. But as I raise my hand, it slows. In Greece, I have the power to stop a train.

After saying good-bye to Danielle at the Good Earth, I returned to San Diego, another lonely trek across the badlands of the Mojave Desert, arriving home late that night. The next morning, as I packed to leave for Highland, Danielle called. She had talked to her friends in Highland, and they said they knew nothing of Vicki or Cynthia. "They wouldn't lie to me," she said. "Bear is not there."

When I hung up the phone, a wave of quiet desperation engulfed me. My every lead had evaporated. I went back to work the next morning and tried to concentrate on getting our spacecraft ready to fly on the Space Shuttle. I had my own war to fight, getting hardware delivered and shipped to Kennedy Space Center.

I realized that Cynthia was dead.

CHAPTER 22: Eleusis.

In the evening, I sit on my bed in the Hotel Couros in Athens. I decided to return to Plaka, where I stayed when I first came to Greece two months ago, but this time, I've taken a quiet hotel off the main drag. I hear a motorbike, but the sound is distant and muffled. Hotel Couros is a large brick building, but old inside. The halls are narrow and echo with the sounds of footsteps and voices. Our community bathroom, just outside my door, could qualify as an archaeological dig. A dark-green heat radiator sits against the wall, but the nice young man at the front desk said that they will not turn it on until next month.

I have so much left to do here in Athens. I must see Eleusis, where in antiquity the divine ritual of the Mysteries was held. Life-giving, death-bringing Demeter was perhaps the most powerful of the goddesses. She brought Zeus to his knees, and she did it without the use of force. When I came to Greece, I had no plans to visit Eleusis, but all the problems concerning my daughter's disappearance surfacing have brought the myth of Demeter and Persephone with them. And also, I must see Colonus. Oedipus died there. On my last day here, I'll do nothing but catch the bus to the airport and board my flight back to the States. My ticket is still carefully tucked away in my security pouch around my neck. I'll have another twelve-hour layover in London, and I'm not looking forward to it.

★

I wake several times during the night, cold and fighting for more cover. I have a nightmare about another Space Shuttle disaster: a giant explosion on the launch pad, a fireball, screaming.

4 Dec, Saturday

Church bells from every direction, a chorus of divine peals heralding a new day. The bell in the church next to the hotel clangs, a sharp, shattering sound, followed by silence. I arise later than I would have liked, feeling tired and stiff, and convinced not to tolerate another freezing night of sleeplessness in Hotel

401

Eleusis

Couros. Even stacking all my clothes on top of me wasn't enough. I check out and walk to Hotel Phaedra, where I stayed when I first arrived in Greece two months ago. The man behind the counter, with the aristocratic presence and easy smile, recognizes me immediately, says he's glad I'm back. He assures me that my room will be heated.

The sun gradually warms me, dissolving my stiff-jointed sluggishness. Bright sunlight streams between tall buildings, zebra-striping Plaka's deep shadows, on my walk to the temple of the Olympian Zeus. Athens has changed in the two months I've traveled Greece. It's cooler, and both the traffic and exhaust have mellowed. Hadrian's Arch cuts a striking presence without the fumes and din of traffic. This morning, I start my quest for the sites involved in the ancient Mysteries of Demeter. If the lives of Oedipus and Laios are the Rosetta Stone for the myth of men and the male half of civilization, the Mysteries constitute the great myth of women and the feminine side of civilization.

As in the legend of Agamemnon and Iphigenia, Demeter's story is of the disappearance of a daughter. The connection between the myths of mortal Iphigenia and the goddess Persephone define the parallel between mortal and immortal existence. The events of Iphigenia's life were literal in that they concerned her death as a maiden and her rebirth as a young woman. The events of Persephone's life were symbolic of all death and rebirth into the Afterlife. The two girls were on opposites sides of the gulf forever separating mankind and the gods. The religion of the ancient Greeks and that of modern Christianity are one long statement of the attempt of the gods to explain mortal life to mankind, and to bridge the communication gap between us and them, the gulf forever separating mankind and the gods. I'm reminded of Michelangelo's painting on the ceiling of the Sistine Chapel, depicting God reaching forth his finger to touch the finger of Adam.

A large, circular wall with many gates surrounded ancient Athens. The sites leading to Demeter's Mysteries are strung along a line cutting the city in half, from the southeast to the northwest. The first site attended by the initiates was to the southeast, outside the city walls and next to the temple of Olympia Zeus, where I am now. This temple was the first I visited when I came to Greece back on October 3rd. This ground was also sacred to the Earth goddess, Gaia,[438] although it's rarely recognized now.

As I enter the site, I'm still struck by the colossal marble columns of Zeus' temple in the middle of the open field. This was also where the last waters of the Great Flood ran, through a two-foot split in the ground. But Zeus' temple is not what I've come to see this morning. I walk south through scattered pines, one bare trunk weaving a lazy S before donning a dense-green cloud of pine needles. A recent rain has settled the dust. I walk to the chest-high stone fence bordering the southern edge of the site and peer over the edge. In front of me lies what's left of the bank of the ancient Ilissos River. The river is no longer visible. It was diverted underground in 1956-67,[439] and the riverbank excavated. It's a ghostly underworld presence now, Styx-like.

This is the ancient district of Agrai. The name Agrai comes from the goddess Artemis Argrotera, which means wild, country-loving. A temple by that name was located just across the river. The area was congested with buildings in Plato's day but is now sandwiched between the stone fence and Αρδιττου (Ardittou Street), which traverses the old riverbed.

In Plato's *Phaedrus* dialogue, Socrates, on one of his few excursions outside the city walls, and Phaedrus, a friend of his, walked barefoot along the bank of the delightfully-clear Ilissos to the shade of a tree, where they sat cooling their feet in the cold water. A gentle breeze blew as they discussed the nature of love. Socrates described the setting:

> Upon my word, a delightful resting place, with this tall, spreading plane, and a lovely shade from the high branches of the agnos a willow like tree. Now that it's in full flower it will make the place ever so fragrant. And what a lovely stream under the plane tree, and how cool to the feet! ...And then too, isn't the freshness of the air most welcome and pleasant, and the shrill summery music of the cicada choir! And as crowning delight the grass, thick enough on a gentle slope to rest your head on most comfortably.[440]

The bank of the Ilissos has deteriorated significantly from that described by Socrates. The hard-packed earth is hardly a place to rest your head. Maidens also drew their prenuptial bath water here at the Killirrhoe Spring,[441] and this is where the Athenians crossed the Ilissos.

The reason I've come here is that this is the site of a great purification ceremony attended by the initiates to Demeter's Mysteries, which took place twenty kilometers east of here at Eleusis. The ceremony was held in the month of Anthesterion, the month of flowers (our February), and took place in the Metroon on the south bank of the Ilissos.[442] The purification ceremony, called the Lesser Mysteries, was for those of unintelligible speech (non-Greek speaking) or murderers, who could not attend the great spiritual Mysteries at Eleusis without purification.

The first and most famous person purified at Agrai was Heracles (Hercules to the Romans), the great hero and native of Thebes, who had killed many men. To be purified of the murders, he had to be cleansed and experience a symbolic death and rebirth. Heracles used a pig, Demeter's favorite animal, to symbolically represent himself. For purification, he bathed with the pig in the cold February water of the Ilissos then sacrificed it. The pig died in his place, similar to the deer dying in Iphigenia's place at Aulis. He ate the pig, thus completing identification with the animal, which put him in a symbolic state of death. He was then allowed to see what mortals were forbidden to see. He was shown an infancy basket with a great snake coiled about it. The basket contained sacred objects signifying rebirth. Thus, he had symbolically died, and returned to infancy. In this purified state, he was ready to learn the mystery taught at Agrai.

The mystery was kept secret and is still not known today. We do know it was about Demeter and in particular, Persephone, her daughter who disappeared into the Underworld. The cost of purification at Agrai was fifteen drachmes, a little over six cents (American) today, but ten days' wages in antiquity.[443] Even slaves could attend provided they were citizens of Athens and had the fee.

When Socrates and Phaedrus left the bank of the Ilissos, as I'm about to do, Socrates recited the following prayer to Pan:

> Dear Pan, and all ye other gods that dwell in this place, grant that I may become fair within, and that such outward things as I have may not war against the spirit within me. May I count him rich who is wise, and as for gold, may I possess so much of it as only a temperate man might bear and carry with him.[444]

Socrates lived the true spirit of the Mysteries, because they were spiritual and not associated with wealth or power.

A year and a half after attending the Lessor Mysteries at Agrai, the initiates were permitted to attend the Greater Mysteries at Eleusis, which occurred over several days and also started here in Athens. The initiates of the Greater Mysteries assembled in Athens[445] on Boedromion 14th (late September). Boedromion 15th, the first day of the Greater Mysteries, was called "agyrmos," or "gathering," which also included a sacrifice.

Just as the initiates had bathed in the Ilissos in the Lesser Mysteries, they again bathed with piglets, but this time in the Saronic Gulf. This occurred on Boedromion 16th, when the Hierophant commanded, "Initiates to the sea!" and was followed by a procession to the coastal town of Phaleron, just south of Piraeus. After returning, they sacrificed and ate the piglet. The following day, the rites were picked up at the Asklepion, a sacred temple at the foot of the Akropolis, where I'm now headed.

After a quick bite of lunch at the same street-side restaurant where I had the stuffed eggplant back on October 3rd, the first day I was in Greece, I take a hike to the foot of the Akropolis. The air has warmed, but shadows are forever long this late in the fall. On the west side of the theatre of Dionysus, up the pine-speckled hill close to the cliff rising to the Akropolis, lie the ruins of the temple of Asklepios, Apollo's son and god of healing. This is the reason Asklepios is a part of the Mysteries.

Originally Asklepios, whom I've encountered in Epidaurus, Kos and Pergamon, was mortal even though he was the son of Apollo. Cheiron, the centaur who taught him the art of healing, raised him. With the help of Athena, who had given Asklepios the resurrecting blood from the Gorgon Medusa, Asklepios learned to heal the dead. Zeus was concerned that Asklepios might make the race of humans immortal, and killed him with a lightning bolt. Apollo promptly made Asklepios immortal. Asklepios, as a god, was closely associated with Demeter and the Mysteries, because the Mysteries provided a process whereby the souls of mortals were made immortal.

The Asklepion was built in 420 BC when Asklepios was brought from Epidaurus to purify Athens after the plague had ravaged it from 430 through 426 BC.[446] The plague killed slave and aristocrat alike, even Pericles, the leader of the Athenian state, who died of it in 429. Birds of prey that dined on the rotting carcasses died also.[447] Asklepios came to Athens in the form of a snake. Sophocles was caretaker of Asklepios while the temple was being built, selected because of "his reputation for uprightness and religious scrupulosity."[448]

The Asklepion, here next to the theatre of Dionysus, is actually two temples, the first built in 420 BC and the other around 350 BC. The old temple had four rooms, a temple with an altar, and a spring with a square cistern. The rites of the Great Mysteries continued here on Boedromion 16th, which was called "Epidauria" in commemoration of Asklepios' arrival, and was for late arrivals, as had been Asklepios. On this day, the god of the Underworld, Hades, assumed the form of Asklepios, the god of healing. In his snake aspect, Asklepios was himself associated with the Underworld, herbs, plants, and all things that spring from the earth, and so closely related to Demeter, giver of all vegetation sprouting from the earth.[449] Thus, the healer and physician, who could even resurrect the dead, merged with the Lord of Death.

I climb the slope next to the Akropolis cliff, walk the tourist-packed earth through pine trees to an assembly of granite stones. His temple, like all those of antiquity, lies in ruins. It was literally built into the cliff of the Akropolis, the large, stacked stones forming retaining walls. The site is now a jumble of stones with a shallow cave recessed even further into the side of the cliff.

The sun is already nose-diving in the west, reflecting brightly off the vertical surfaces of buildings. I feel its radiant energy from the heat-absorbing Akropolis cliff. This fall sun is bashful, rising late, hanging close to the southern horizon all day, and setting early.

The procession to the Asklepion was followed by a major sacrifice and all-night celebration. The following day, Boedromion 18th, was a day of rest. Sacred objects were also used in the ceremony and were brought under escort to the Athens Eleusinion. The Eleusinion was just south of the Agora, another site I missed two months ago, but one I'll visit today. On Boedromion 19th, the initiates escorted the sacred objects from Athens back to Eleusis, and on Boedromion 20th, the great procession of initiates walked to Eleusis, both processions starting from the Eleusinion, just south of the Agora.

I walk east of the Akropolis, past the hotel and along Adreanou Street where the smell of gyros and seafood greets me, past the Roman Agora, and eventually to the southeast entrance of the ancient Greek Agora, where I enter. Here, near the entrance at the side of the street, lie the ruins of the Eleusinion. I stand in the shadow of the Akropolis, the sun eclipsed by a marble monolith, stand on the ground where the initiates gathered for the walk to Eleusis. The purpose of their walk was to have their souls saved by a goddess whose image was that of a young girl. Several thousand people made the walk: young, old, women, men, children, even slaves. I imagine a great commotion as they heard the signal to proceed, the shouts of thousands.

Mylonas, the classical scholar who collaborated in the excavation of Eleusis, describes the procession:

> Iacchos and his priest were at the head; then came the priests and the panageis, the all holy, priestesses of Demeter bearing the Hiera sacred objects...Then came the officials of the state, the theories of other cities and foreign representatives, then the mystai initiates on foot--men and women and children with their sponsors, then those in carriages, and finally the pack animals forming the end.[450]

I exit the Agora, cross the bridge over the train tracks running along its northern edge, the same path followed by the procession, watch a slow-moving train clippity-clop along the shallow ravine. I walk through the Monastiraki district, past the taverna where, two months ago, JoAnn and I sat talking of my pending journey through Greece, seemingly an eternity ago. She was a new acquaintance then but now seems a long-lost friend.

The procession came through the Agora, along the Sacred Way, cutting a diagonal path through the maze of buildings and temples, and then on east to the Dipylon ("with two gates"), where it exited the city through the Sacred Gate to Eleusis. The wall surrounded the entire ancient city of Athens, and the Dipylon was the double-gated main entrance through it. The adjacent gate led to Plato's academy, where he founded his famous school of philosophy.

I walk north to Hermes Street, west to the ruins of the Dipylon. On the outside of the city walls was the Kerameikos, the Potters Quarters, which served as the city cemetery as far back as Mycenaean times, the age of Theseus. The site is now located in an industrial zone, gray buildings lining dirty streets, but the ruins are several meters below ground level, which isolates them from the hubbub of traffic. A couple of scraggly cats skirt my path to hide at the foot of olive trees and oleander bushes.

In ancient times, an inscription to Pan had been cut into a well by the Dipylon. It read as follows: "O Pan, O Men, be of good cheer, beautiful Nymphs, rain, conceive, overflow."[451] The theologian Hyppolytus believed these words to be the secret of the Mysteries, and according to Proclus, the Neoplatonist scholar of the 5th Century AD, the following words were spoken during the Mysteries: "... they gazed up to the heaven and cried aloud 'rain,' they gazed down upon the earth and cried 'conceive.'" The words may well have been a part of the Mysteries, but they could in no way have been the essence of the ceremony. To have revealed the secret of the Mysteries at the Dipylon would have been a sacrilege punishable by death.

I sit on a bench among pieces of ancient walls, walkways, marble statues, and with the Acropolis far in the distance. The sun tries, successfully at times, to break through the cloud cover. I like the homey, maple-treed atmosphere, golden leaves falling about me and scattering on the pebbled ground. A giant cypress stands to my right, its trunk enveloped in a deep-green, bushy bonnet. Between trees, I see stone steps, walls, monuments, and buildings, all ruins from a time when the initiates of the ancient Mysteries walked through here on their way to Eleusis.

This is as far as I plan to walk. Tomorrow morning, I'll pickup the Sacred Way by catching the bus and traverse the twenty kilometers to Eleusis along the freeway.

★

I sit on my bed in the hotel with all my clothes stacked on me to hold in my body heat, trying to remember more about my daughter's disappearance. After the call from Danielle telling me Cyndi was not in Highland, I had nowhere to turn. Since I had read Cyndi's letters, I knew a great deal about her private life during the past year, and yet I had no idea where she was. I went back to work the next morning, still embroiled in the mystery of her disappearance. I knew she hadn't been kidnapped and wasn't on drugs, but still had no idea why she ran off two months before she was to graduate. Was she hitching with truckers? Why didn't she call? Was she alive?

I still regretted leaving her years before, and all my guilt surfaced. Why did I believe it would be best for her to stay with her mother in Phoenix? She needed her father, needed more than a weekend telephone relationship with him. I had sacrificed her for my career. I wanted to be optimistic, but could not override the growing realization that she was dead. It was a subconscious fear, a subterranean daemon of terror that poked his head into my consciousness during unsuspecting moments of quiet.

Work was a bubbling cauldron. We were in final systems testing prior to shipping the spacecraft to Kennedy Space Center. Grumman, who was building additional hardware for us, was also ready to deliver. I made a quick trip to their Long Island facility to observe crucial, last-minute testing. I remember sitting in Kennedy International Airport awaiting my return flight while writing a quick postcard to Danielle as I heard the call to board. Little did I realize, I had spent the last few days in the neighborhood of the answer to all my concerns.

5 Dec, Sunday

In the early morning, I walk north of the Akropolis to Plateia Eletherias, a couple of blocks northeast of the Dipylon, the ancient gate through the city wall, to catch a bus to Eleusis. I feel closed off this morning, old and irritable. The low angle of the fall sun makes for long shadows and, together with the dinginess of the sidewalks and streets, adds to the greasy look. I sit up front, next to the bus driver. The murmur of voices settles into the soft swish of the bus along the asphalt.

The Mysteries were the most important religious rites practiced in antiquity. The ancients believed the existence of Greece depended upon the rites, and that they held the entire human race together.[452] Eleusis seems like the focal point of my journey, as though it has been one long circular pilgrimage to Eleusis.

The word "mystery" comes from the ancient Greek "μυστηριον," mysterion, meaning a religious truth known only by revelation, and one that never could be fully understood by mortals. Although it originally applied to the many mysteries practiced throughout ancient Greece, and particularly the Greater Mysteries at Eleusis, the word also came to describe Christian sacraments. In the same way that the Mysteries were the reenactment of Demeter's search for her daughter, the life of Jesus is a mystery now reenacted in the Christian sacraments, which symbolize the spiritual path to everlasting life.

The Mysteries were not about big egos, power and glory. To its credit,

Eleusis did not participate in the Trojan War.[453] But they were about death. The Mysteries were very old, originating in Crete, and may even have come to Crete from Egypt. They are closely connected with the worship of Isis.[454] Crete, and particularly Knossos, during 14th Century BC, fell under the influence of mainland Greece, the Mycenaeans. Then, King Minos ruled Crete, and Theseus ruled Athens. During this time, most likely, the Mysteries came from Crete to Eleusis. Perhaps Theseus' descent into the Labyrinth to kill the Minotaur, and Persephone's descent into the Underworld, are symbolically related.

The initiates' procession to Eleusis started here in Athens and was the beginning of the reenactment of Demeter's search for Persephone after she was abducted. They left Athens at the Eleusinian at the foot of the Akropolis, walked through the Agora, as I did yesterday, along the Sacred Way to the Dipylon, and there they exited the city walls. A statue of torch-bearing Iakchos, the alter ego of Dionysus,[455] led the throng, the procession chanting "Iakchos! Iakchos!" When they came to the bridge over the Kephisos River, just outside Athens, a group of men and prostitutes, disguised in masks, were waiting to ridicule the procession, make obscene gestures, and shout insults and obscenities, all as a part of the ritual.

Some scholars believe that the Homeric "Hymn to Demeter" is the "libretto" to Demeter's "opera" at Eleusis. According to the "Hymn," which was written in the 7th Century BC, after Persephone disappeared, Demeter wandered aimlessly and without food for nine days, trying to find her daughter. Then, she went to see the sun god, Helios, whom she heard had witnessed Persephone's disappearance. Helios told her that Hades had abducted Persephone with the approval of her father, Zeus. Demeter was enraged at Zeus and withdrew from the assembly of Olympian gods. She was grief-stricken and assumed the form of a rag-clothed crone, dressed in a veil and dark robe, and wandered the land of mortals until she came to Eleusis, where she sat near the Maiden's Well.

Demeter was still at the well grieving when the four daughters of King Keleos found her. Not realizing she was a goddess, they complained of the tough life imposed on mortals by the gods.

> "...what the gods send us, we mortals
> bear perforce, although we suffer;
> for they are much stronger than we."[456]

Impressed by Demeter's demeanor, the daughters took her home with them to meet their mother, Metaneira, who also complained of our lot in life.

Eleusis

"...we mortals bear perforce
what the gods send us, though we be grieved;
for a yoke is set upon our necks."[457]

Demeter, as if in response to all of this complaining, agreed to raise Metaneira's child, Demophoon, and while carrying out her duties, decided to make him immortal. She anointed him with ambrosia and buried him in the glowing coals of the hearth to burn away his mortality, a more intense form of the "fires of life" complained about by Metaneira and her daughters. But one night, Metaneira spied on Demeter, caught her with Demophoon in the fire, and shrieked in fear. Demeter jerked the child from the hearth and admonished all mortals as ignorant and incurably foolish. Then, she revealed herself as a goddess and requested they build a temple where she would introduce her rites, the Mysteries.

Perhaps this request of the goddess points to the secret of the Mysteries: the revelation of the "fires of life," the purification process leading to immortality. She was telling the citizens of Eleusis not to fret. Life's tribulations and suffering have a purpose. They are the path to everlasting life.

I'm reminded of Job in the Old Testament, the good man who suffered at the hands of God for no reason, and also of a quote from Jeremiah:

Is not my word like as a fire?
saith the Lord; and like a hammer
that breaketh the rock in pieces?[458]

Perhaps this also casts a new light on the plight suffered by Oedipus, who had unwittingly killed his father and married his mother. The gods had subjected him to the "fires of life" that we all must experience before we find our way into the afterlife.

When the procession of initiates from Athens finally reached Eleusis that evening, the women danced around the Maiden's Well, and sang through the night. The following day, the initiates rested until evening, when they witnessed the epiphany of the Mysteries.

As the bus approaches Eleusis, off to the south, I see the glistening waters of the bay and the island of Salamis, which, except for the narrow straits on each side, blocks Eleusis from the rest of the Aegean. In antiquity, the island sheltered Eleusis from sudden attack by pirates or a hostile fleet, and provided a quiet harbor for commerce.[459] Eleusis was annexed by Athens because of its strategic location, just off the road that ran between Attica to the east and

410

the Peloponnese to the west. The lone road north through the mountains to Thebes[460] started here at Eleusis.

Elefsina, today's little industrial town surrounding the ruins of Eleusis, has an oil refinery, cement factory and shipyard that form the ugly, metal skyline, along with a forest of TV antennas protruding from roofs of artless, square buildings. A recent shower has settled the perennial dust cloud, for which the site is famous. I crossed the outskirts of Eleusis six weeks ago, when I drove to the Cleft Way where Oedipus killed Laios.

The Sacred Way provides entrance to the archeological site as it did 2500 years ago, ending at a marble-paved courtyard before the entrance. Two large gates, called the Great and Lesser Propylaea, provided entry to the sacred complex. Chariots could drive through the Great Propylaea but were turned back by the smaller, more limiting gate. It's a sprawling site, larger than I expected, and a jumble of paved pathways, exposed floors, and tumbled blocks of stone and marble. I also see remains of the ancient walls that enclosed the sanctuary. Standing above it all, a hill blocks my view of the Bay of Eleusis. Occupation of the hill, where King Keleos' palace stood, stretched back to the 3rd millennium BC.

Since all the buildings have been destroyed and the Mysteries abandoned for fifteen hundred years, I'll be able to go anywhere I choose, but such was not the case in antiquity. Anyone who entered the sanctuary surreptitiously did so under the threat of death. Two young men, who attended the ceremony "by mistake" and gave themselves away by asking questions, were executed.

I follow the Sacred Way through the scant remains of the two gates. Off to the right, I see the foundation of a wall that blocked the initiates' view of one of the most sacred locations at the site, a cave that was the entrance to the Underworld. This is where Persephone was abducted, and where she later reappeared. The collapsed cave is now a shallow recess in the side of the mountain. The Mirthless Rock, where Demeter sat in mourning after learning that Hades had abducted her daughter, is just in front of the cave. The initiates viewed Demeter there, wailing out her sorrow.

After Demeter learned that Hades had kidnapped Persephone, she remained apart from the Olympian gods, went into mourning and refused to allow anything to grow on Earth. She would have destroyed the human race if Zeus had not intervened. He sent golden-winged Iris, female messenger of the gods, the angel, to request Demeter return to Olympus. But dark-cloaked Demeter refused, even when all the other gods and goddesses went to Demeter offering beautiful gifts.

Here, we see who really contains power in the world, the cloak finally removed to expose the primal essence of the gods, and it's Demeter, a manifestation of Gaia, the Earth goddess. Demeter no longer allowed anything to grow upon the Earth, and all things, including mankind, would have died.

Finally, Zeus relented, sending Hermes, guide of souls in the Underworld, to tell Hades, ruler of the dearly departed, to release Persephone. This, Hades readily agreed to do, but asked Persephone to eat one pomegranate seed, before she returned to the light. She did so, and thus ensured her return to the Underworld for four months of every year, becoming not only goddess of the Earth, but also Mistress of the Underworld.

I walk to the temple of Demeter, the Telesterion, a large, paved, rectangular area where the initiation ceremony took place. Inside the Telesterion, a forest of columns supported the upper floor, none of which remain. Around the periphery of the Telesterion, stone steps, with a seating capacity of three thousand, lined the rectangular building. The steps still exist, for the most part. The southern edge protruded into the side of the mountain. In the center of the Telesterion was the Anaktoron, the Holiest of Holies.

The Anaktoron was a small, rectangular structure with only one doorway where the throne of the head priest, the Hierophant, stood. This is where the real mystery, the epiphany, was presented to the initiates. Throughout the centuries, the shape of the Anaktoron and its location never changed, even though the Telesterion, which housed it, had been enlarged many times to accommodate the increasing number of initiates, as the sacred sanctuary gained in popularity throughout the Mediterranean.

The intriguing debate continues among scholars as to what actually took place at the Anaktoron. We do know that the epiphany was a viewing, not a verbal message. Until the viewing, the initiates were blindfolded, possibly to simulate blindness, and led about in the dark. As the sacred ceremony approached the epiphany, the initiates were permitted to view the Sacred Objects that the priests had taken to Athens, and then returned with the procession. Perhaps they were artifacts passed down generation to generation from Mycenaean times.[461] One of them may have been a golden ear of grain. Then, the Hierophant sounded a gong, summoning Persephone from the Underworld, as the throng of initiates, sometimes numbering in the thousands, filed into the Telesterion. Suddenly, the Anaktoron was bathed in a blinding light.

Mylonas quotes a passage from Stobaios that describes the journey of the soul just before death, which he relates to the experience of the initiates to the Mysteries:

The soul has the same experience as those who are being initiated into great mysteries... at first one wanders and wearily hurries to and fro, and journeys with suspicion through the dark as one uninitiated: then come all the terrors before the final initiation, shuddering, trembling, sweating, amazement: then one is struck with a marvelous light...[462]

No initiate ever told what he witnessed, but several eyewitnesses on the outside of the sanctuary reported seeing intense flashes of light. One such account, as reported by Herodotus,[463] occurred during war, after all of Attica had been evacuated and Eleusis deserted. During the battle of Salamis, in 480 BC, the Athenian exile, Dicaeus, heard a divine voice, and saw a dust cloud caused by 30,000 invisible initiates. Since all of Attica was evacuated at the time, he believed that the initiates were ghosts. This event occurred on the eve of the sea battle that resulted in disaster for the invading Persian forces.

Other witnesses report a nativity scene, Persephone having given birth to a Divine Child while bathed in intense light. The Hierophant officiated at the throne of the Anaktoron, "under the great fire."[464] Fire births are not unusual in Greek mythology, as evidenced by Apollo rescuing the infant Asklepios from his mother's funeral pyre at Epidaurus, and the birth of Dionysus, when Zeus killed Semele with a lightning bolt, then rescued the divine child from the smoldering corpse.

It's not difficult to conclude that the Divine Child of the epiphany at Eleusis was born in fire, as Demeter had tried to make Demophoon immortal by putting him in the hearth. Also, the sacrificial pig that represented the initiate was cooked prior to being eaten. Archeologists have found fire marks on the terrace dating back to Mycenaean times. It could be that the initiates stood dumbfounded as Persephone, goddess of Death, gave birth in an eruption of fire so severe it was visible for miles around.

In a similar ancient story recorded in the 2nd Century AD,[465] the birth of Jesus occurred in a cave, and was accompanied by a great silence where no wind blew, streams ceased to flow and time stopped.

> The child himself Jesus, like the sun, shone bright, beautiful, and was most delightful to see, because he alone appeared as peace, soothing the whole world. In that hour, when he was born, the voice of many invisible beings in one voice proclaimed "Amen." And the light, when it was born, multiplied, and it obscured the light of the sun itself by its shining rays.[466]

I walk back through the entryway to the Telesterion, but go off to the left, up a flight of stone steps ascending the hill, to a terrace where a temple of

Eleusis

Persephone once stood, proceed on up the mountain to an even higher terrace where a small chapel now stands, the Chapel of the Virgin Mary. The presence of this modest structure overlooking the entire site is no coincidence. For local residents, the cult of Demeter and Persephone survives as belief in the Holy Virgin, a startling revelation providing insight into the reason Christianity was absorbed so quickly into Greece, when even most Jews wouldn't accept it.

I climb to the top of the mountain, the view opening to a vast expanse containing the Bay of Eleusis and the large island of Salamis, four kilometers away. A line of red and white fishing boats stretches along its northern shore. It's almost noon, yet the sun is low on the horizon, its rays warm on my face.

If the Zeus religion didn't epitomize what we know now as divine love and forgiveness, the Mysteries at Eleusis did. They were the remnants of the Earth goddess religion. The origin of Demeter's name is ambiguous. In the ancient Greek version of her name, Δημητηρ, the prefix, Δη, meant either earth or corn, and μητηρ meant mother. So her name meant either "earth-mother" or "corn-mother,"[467] and she was viewed as one of the many manifestations of Gaia, the Earth goddess. Her spirit gave birth to the Neolithic Age, the discovery of crop cultivation that ushered in agriculture. Demeter gave grain to one of the Kings of Eleusis, Triptolemus, and taught him how to sow the seed. This was the beginning of agriculture, right here in the fields about Eleusis. Her daughter, Persephone, was a ghostly presence, representing both death and resurrection. Persephone was so feared, her name could not be spoken in public. Those who attended the initiation were comforted and given hope in the Afterlife.

The belief in the Afterlife goes back to the dawn of man, before the coming of the Cro-Magnons to Europe.[468] The Orphics, possibly the most ancient of Greek religions, and later, the Pythagoreans believed the soul is trapped in the human body, that the body is a prison. The Mysteries were a demonstration of the liberation of the soul. In the Afterlife, those who had witnessed the Mysteries, a baptism of sorts, went to the Elysian Fields with the gods. The meaning of the Mysteries in the 5th Century BC is revealed in a fragment of a Pindar poem:

> Blessed is he who hath seen these things before he goeth beneath the hollow earth; for he understandeth the end of mortal life, and the beginning of a new life given of god.[469]

Socrates describes the epiphany of the Mysteries, as he witnessed it:

> ...then were we all initiated into that mystery which is rightly accounted blessed beyond all others; whole and unblemished were we that did

celebrate it, untouched by the evils that awaited us in days to come; whole and unblemished likewise, free from all alloy, steadfast and blissful were the spectacles on which we gazed in the moment of final revelation; pure was the light that shone around us, and pure were we, without taint of that prison house which now we are encompassed withal, and call a body, fast bound therein as an oyster in its shell.[470]

The ancient Greeks believed that Socrates' oyster, the seed of our immortal soul, must be nurtured during this lifetime for it to be reborn in the next. During the ceremony, the initiates were shown a barley ear, which symbolically represented the seed, the divine part of the initiate that became the divine child in the afterlife. Planting was equated with impregnation.[471] The planting of the seed, a burial in the Underworld, resulted in new life, a rebirth as a divine child in the Elysian Fields. Persephone was the silent goddess of Death, goddess of the Underworld, and also the gateway to the Afterlife. Part of the revelation at Eleusis was that Demeter and Persephone were one,[472] the same goddess, and thus, constituted the bridge from mortality to immortality. Christianity then replaced the mother/daughter myth with the Father/Son myth, Jesus being the bridge to eternal life.

Viewed in this way, a woman's body is a mystery, an earthly metaphor of Demeter and Persephone, and therefore, sacred. Demeter's search for Persephone is the search for self, just as Oedipus' search for the murderer of his father was a search for himself.

Who was the Divine Child born to Persephone in this flash of fire at Eleusis? He was Iakchos, whose name the initiates had shouted during the procession to Eleusis. Iakchos was the alter ego of Dionysus, the twice-born god who had mated with his own mother to give birth to himself. He was the god of indestructible life, born in blinding light, wrapped in an animal pelt. Dionysus signified that we are our own fathers. Our lives are a fathering process for the immortal child we will become.

All of these elements are also present in the legend of Oedipus, the twice-born man who was the "son" of Dionysus. I now realize that the story of Oedipus is closely related to the myth of the Earth goddess, of Demeter and Persephone. It's the male side of the story, the confrontation with the father, and the doubling back on our lives to begat ourselves. Sophocles knew this. His last play, *Oedipus at Colonus*, written just before his death at the age of ninety, was set at a site sacred to the Earth goddess and Demeter. It was about Oedipus' death and rebirth into the Afterlife. My next stop is the setting of that play, Colonus, in northern Athens.

Eleusis

I leave the hill, walk back down the slope, through the ruins, along the Sacred Way to the bus stop. I stand in the shade of a tree and wait, looking back at the sacred archaeological site. Nothing lasts forever, and this was true of the Mysteries also. After holding the world together for two thousand years, the Mysteries faded as Christianity gained favor in Greece. The temple of Eleusis was officially ordered closed, and the rituals prohibited in 392 AD by the Roman emperor Theodosios I.[473]

While waiting for the bus, I think about Oedipus, who experienced a severe form of this "purification by fire," having unknowingly killed his father and married his mother. Oedipus, as a grumpy Job,[474] could no more have prevented his fate than he could have prevented his own birth. I know I couldn't have prevented what happened between me and my father, my own brush with disaster, nor my marriage to a woman much like my mother. We all survived the events, and they opened up my life in ways that led to accomplishments beyond my own dreams. But my life has disintegrated in the last few years, and that disintegration seems to have also been built into the very fabric of those events. So was the disappearance of my daughter.

After all my attempts to find Cynthia came to naught, my world collapsed. I had lived alone since I moved to San Diego, and Cynthia's disappearance left me with a consuming grief. I was listless at work and unengaged, found myself staring at the walls, even when confronted with astronaut safety issues. I was lethargic, my gloomy apartment stacked to the ceiling with the accumulating debris of my life.

Two weeks after she disappeared, I received an evening telephone call from her mother, my ex-wife. The initial sound of her voice sent an Arctic chill through me. But then I heard her say, "Cyndi called. She's okay and has a job."

I couldn't talk. I simply fell against the wall and cried.

Cynthia had called Sue, the girl who last saw her before she left Phoenix. We still didn't know where she was living. A few of days later, I called another of her friends, and learned that she had also talked to Cynthia. She didn't know where Cynthia was either, but had a telephone number for the pay phone on the street outside where she worked. The area code was 212, New York City.

Just as Iphigenia had reappeared at the edge of the Black Sea, the edge of the known world to the ancient Greeks, and Persephone had returned from the Underworld, Cynthia had reappeared at the edge of the continent, three thousand miles away.

My daughter's disappearance was a death of sorts, as was Persephone's descent into the Underworld. And I still have dreams of my daughter dying, as if her death actually occurred. And in a sense, she did die. The ritual of Iphigenia at Aulis, where girls left a lock of hair, signified the death of the maiden and her rebirth as a young woman. When my daughter resurfaced, she was no longer a little girl, but she wasn't married. Her nature was more closely related to that of Artemis, the virgin goddess of all things wild.

During the weeks of this journey, I've developed a theory of why my daughter's disappearance affected me so, when her mother was relatively unaffected. My confrontation with my father resulted in a death of sorts, the death of the life I was living. The path I had chosen for myself, one of literature and philosophy, abruptly changed. I joined the Air Force and became a man of war, as suggested by my Athena-like mother. When my daughter was born, she resurrected this softer side of myself, and her disappearance felt as if I had lost myself again, as if I had died. My search for her was a search for self, as had been Demeter's search for Persephone.

A bonding occurred between my daughter and me while she was still a baby, when her mother became ill and was hospitalized for three months. I had just started a new Air Force assignment in Oklahoma City and was not performing well. We provided support for the B-52's flying missions over North Vietnam. I was still unsure of how I felt about the war, and strongly disagreed with the mass killings caused by bombing the North. Providing support for the planes that were causing so much death and destruction bothered me. Uncertainty filled my life, and I felt as though I was under siege from all directions. It was my kids and me against the world.

My wife's lengthy stay in the hospital left me listless and grief stricken. Her health was very bad, and I wondered if she would ever return. During that time, I took care of our kids, our five-year-old son and two-year-old daughter. I cooked all our meals, washed the clothes, the diapers, and dressed them in the mornings before I went to work, dropped them off at the babysitter, read them bedtime stories in the evening. Our hardship forged a close bond between us. For a while, I was their mother and father, and I've never lost the way I related to them then.

★

Back in Athens, I walk north to Omonia Square, the center of the modern city. Streets spread out in all directions from the traffic circle, all of them clogged with frantic vehicles. The refugees from Bosnia have made this part of Athens unsafe, and my guidebooks suggest keeping a tight hold on packs and avoiding talking to anyone. I run into the largest mass of people I've ever seen, an open-air flea market. Vendors line both sides of the street, selling secondhand junk, antiques, carpets, shirts, jewelry, cartons of motor oil, oil filters, apples, oranges, big bunches of bananas, chestnuts, ties, scarves, pants, belts. Hordes of people fill

Eleusis

the streets, all dark-haired, olive-skinned Greeks, the machine-gun Greek filling the air with a cloud of conversation punctuated by shouts, questions, demands, orders, imperatives, and exclamations. Traffic tries to creep down the center of this jammed street, trucks, taxies, the perennial motorbike. All in conflict, all trying to negotiate a path through the crowded world.

At first I think the flea market is localized to one block, but as I push and shove my way through the crowd, I look south and see an ant trail of people looming far in the distance, all the way to the Acropolis. I follow the street through the swarm to Plaka, where I turn aside when I reached Adrianon Street and return to my hotel.

★

Before sleep, I lie in bed complaining to myself about the mosquito bites I received six weeks ago in Corinth. The bites still haven't healed. I have scabs, knots under the skin, and they itch. Is this a lifetime affliction?

Tomorrow I'll try to find Colonus, where Oedipus met his mysterious death.

CHAPTER 23: Colonus.

6 Dec, Monday

I wake before sunrise and lean against the headboard with my clothes on, the covers pulled to my chest. I have two blankets on my bed, plus my running jacket and sweater spread over them. The heat is on, but I'm still cold.

I rise early to look at a map of Athens, planning my search for Colonus. In addition to the modern map, I have a copy of an ancient map of Athens that I got from the University of Colorado library before I came to Greece. A continuous oval-shaped wall, one kilometer by one-and-a-half kilometers, encircled the ancient city. The Akropolis was a little off center, to the southwest. It shows the district of Colonus as being just inside the north wall, south of the Acharnian Gate, three quarters of a kilometer north of the Akropolis. From my modern-day map, this is Σοφοκλεους Οδος, Sophocles Street.

★

I walk Adrianou Street to the Monastiraki district, then take Aiolou Street north of the Akropolis to Hermes Street, the shopping district. I laugh to myself, realizing they've named the street through the shopping district for the prince of thieves. I know a few streets back in the States that could be aptly named for Hermes. Except for the Greek heritage evident in the appearance of the people, I could be in downtown Denver. The buildings are tall and well-built, modern, the store windows displaying women's and men's clothes, dresses, skirts, shoes, suits, all now with a Christmas touch, a twist of mistletoe, a twig of holly, a miniature Santa.

I hear a shout coming through the cool morning air and look around to see who's causing the commotion. I spot an old man sitting up against a building at the edge of the sidewalk, an old blind man with his legs folded underneath him, his alms bowl on the cement between his knees, arms outstretched. He shouts, "Καλιμερα! Καλιμερα!" Good morning! Good morning! He spews more words I can't understand. His expression is aggressive, chiding, overwrought, his manner demanding, calling the people to him. His entire face shrinks in around his naked eyepits, as though the vacuum left by the absent eyeballs forcefully sucks his wrinkled face into the void, something like Oedipus must have looked after gouging out his eyes with Jocasta's broach. To accentuate the effect, he doesn't wear a patch. His muss of gray hair covers his forehead, and he wears loose khaki pants and shirt. The clink of coins in his cup punctuates the many voices of the crowd. I give him a wide berth, as if afraid he'll strike me.

But I run into another beggar, a once badly burned, middle-aged woman, blond, flashing gray eyes. She sits, legs stretched out in front, leaning against a cement column with the hem of her soft feminine skirt pulled to her crotch so I can see her brown and white scars, which go so deep that they've eaten into her flesh and disfigured her legs. She pulls the front of her blouse open, exposing more and more of her burned, disfigured breasts, pulls the large masses of flesh from within the twin-pouched bra, fondles them to ensure I see that her nipples are burned off. Her nose is artificially pugged, eyebrows gone, ears only stubs. She displays the wares of her trade, the display case that is her body. She calls out desperately for money in a shrill, shrieking voice. I feel ashamed for thinking lofty thoughts yesterday about the "fires of life" that this woman has so literally experienced. My revelations now seem trivial.

No, this isn't Denver. I walk away from all this, not knowing whether to cry out of pity or laugh at the burlesque nature of the sight. Finally, it's two dirty children that bring my feelings to a conclusion, and I cry a little, get a few sobs out to break loose the choking knot inside. The children, perhaps four years old, sit on the sidewalk with their little tin cups, their faces artificially smudged. Even they have the unmistakable mark of the actor, chewing their fingers and trying desperately to cry, but not quite making it.

I walk north, looking for the street called Σοφοκλεους, Sophocles, overcome with disillusionment at the brutality of life, turn west down a street that has been cordoned off and covered with a corrugated tin roof. Underneath the dark enclosure, meat marketers shout their specials while standing among red slabs of hanging beef, huge chunks of flesh on table tops, kidneys, livers, joints. And then pork, complete hog heads with pointed ears and lolling tongues, fish, large fish, small fish, octopus, squid. The death and mutilation reminds me of the dead man I saw at the side of the road near Markopoulo. Hordes of people bump into me, men in bulky blazers, women in heavy coats, crowding, shoving; and the meat cleaver coming down, Whack! Whack! Whack! as it cleaves thick chunks of flesh under rows of sparkling lights.

Sophocles Street is a mass of modern buildings. I can find nothing to identify with Colonus, so I walk to the National Archaeological Museum to see if someone there can tell me where to find it. Inside, at a reception desk, I talk to a young woman. She's all smiles, while telling me that Colonus is located northwest of the train station. I pull out my map of the city. "There," she says.

Colonus

"It's still called Colonus." "Is that where Oedipus died?" I ask. "No one knows for sure," she replies. Where do these gorgeous women come from? This young lady wasn't here when I visited the museum two months ago.

I'm too tired and hungry to walk to Colonus now, and soon I find myself sitting in a Wendy's restaurant in downtown Athens, eating a Big Classic with cheese, a small order of fries, and a cup of American coffee with two creams and three sugars, really soaking up the "Greek" culture. I sit on the mezzanine filled with a horde of roughhousing Greek teenagers. I've come to this American restaurant to start my reentry into our culture, smooth over the shock I anticipate.

When Oedipus, in old age, came here at the end of his blind wanderings, his oldest daughter, Antigone, was with him. Some twenty years had lapsed since he learned he had killed his father and married his mother. His other daughter, Ismene, came to Colonus on horseback with news of an oracle and of the impending war between his two sons, who were fighting over the throne of Thebes. Ismene also had trouble finding Colonus. "The sufferings I bore in seeking where you were living, father, I will pass by; I would not renew the pain in the recital."[475] She had serious business. Her brothers were at war with each other and seeking an alliance with Oedipus because an oracle from Delphi had stated that whatever land was home to Oedipus' grave would fall under divine protection. The welfare of Thebes depended upon Oedipus' grave being on Theban soil.

Eteocles, who was then the king of Thebes, had sent his uncle Creon, dead Jocasta's brother, to coerce Oedipus back to Thebes. But Oedipus, with the news of the oracle brought by Ismene, saw through his charade. When Oedipus wouldn't go back with him, Creon abducted both Ismene and Antigone. But Oedipus had befriended Theseus, king of Athens, and he sent an army to retrieve the girls.

Polyneices was the next to come after Oedipus, and his words upon seeing his father for the first time in years resurrect the sight of the old blind man I saw this morning on the streets of Athens, an echo of old, blind Oedipus in his final days, when he sat begging in this same town over 3200 years ago. Polyneices was taken aback by the old man's appearance, much as I was by the blind man this morning, and agonized about it to his sisters:

> Ah me, what shall I do? Shall I weep first for my own sorrows, sisters, or for my aged father's, as I see them yonder? I have found him in a strange land, an exile here with you two, clad in raiment of which the foul squalor has dwelt with that aged form so long, a very blight upon his flesh—

while above the sightless eyes the unkempt hair flutters in the breeze; and matching with these things, it seems, the food that he carries, hapless one, against hunger's pinch.[476]

Oedipus was forever Oedipus, still the same old moaner and groaner, protesting his fate and proclaiming his innocence, as he had since learning that he had killed his father and married his mother. But here, he revealed a new hatred, that for his sons. Instead of becoming the mediator between these two hot-brained young men, realizing the destructiveness of their behavior and trying to turn them in a new direction, Oedipus expressed his animosity. Polyneices had cast Oedipus out while he was king, and Eteocles didn't call Oedipus back when he assumed the throne. Oedipus was not in a forgiving mood, and instead put a curse on both of them.

By the time I finish lunch, it's mid-afternoon and too late to walk to Colonus. I decide to wait until tomorrow and make a fresh start early in the morning. I slip past the hordes of pseudoamerican teenagers, out of the Wendy's, and down the street to Hotel Phaedras.

★

I stand out front of the hotel in the cool evening, looking down on the Byzantine church in the recessed courtyard, where two months ago a monk posed as I took his picture. A wedding crowd has gathered before the Church of St. Catherine. A video camera man, floodlights, and a sudden rush of well-dressed people signal the arrival of the bride's car, her father driving, her mother in the passenger seat. The wide-eyed bride, dressed in white and sitting in the backseat between two dark-suited men, hides in a mountain of flowing fabric. The crowd quickly disappears inside the church.

I stand outside the door, wishing I could see inside, when a smiling woman appears beside me, grabs my arm, and pulls me just inside the door. The church is small and elaborately decorated. The crowd, now seated and shrouded in darkness, is packed into the small room. Up front, the bride and groom appear in bright light. The priest, dressed in his finest sacred raiment, approaches them. The smiling lady, who has made me privy to this private scene, gently pushes me back outside and pulls the door closed behind her.

An hour later, the crowd reappears and mills about the courtyard. The newlyweds have escaped through the back exit. I have a good, solid feeling for them, their family and friends, getting married within the walls of a six-hundred-year-old Byzantine church, all under the watchful glow of the Acropolis.

On my next trip to Long Island, I made a pass through Manhattan. I didn't go there to see a Broadway play or the bright lights. My rental car was a big problem, and when I finally found a parking garage, the cost was ten dollars an hour. Strawberry's, where my daughter had found a job after a week on the run, was on Park Avenue. I saw my runaway daughter standing among the racks of women's clothes, helping a woman with a dress. She turned toward me and smiled, looking so bright-faced and healthy. I finally got to hug her. After all my worry and concern for her, it was her turn to worry about me. She told me not to walk the streets alone. "This isn't San Diego, Dad. This is the Big Apple, and you have to watch your step." Very motherly, I thought.

That evening, after she got off work, we had dinner downtown at the English Pub. We had shepherd's pie and sipped shandies afterward. The little girl I once knew was gone, and in her place was this young woman, Bear, congenial but guarded with her father, definitely defiant at times, worldly. She had been on her way to London, she said, but fell in love with New York City. She was offended that I thought she had hitchhiked. She had hocked everything, electric guitar, amplifier, keyboard, and bought two plane tickets for herself and Vicki. Vicki got a job as a waitress the day they arrived; it took Cynthia a week to get the job at Strawberry's. She had to take a lie detector test to get her job. She lied her way through it.

She turned hostile when I asked about college. She said she had learned from my decision to leave her with her mother in Phoenix and go to San Diego to work on the Space Shuttle project, and also from her mother leaving me, that sometimes you had to shake yourself up, take that big chance. But that night, she was dressed in black and admitted to dabbling in witchcraft, not a devil worshiper, mind you, but definitely on the fringe of something scary. She wouldn't discuss it. Like Persephone, she had retained a touch of the Underworld. My concern for her returned, but now accompanied by disappointment.

She showed me the City. I met her friend, Vicki. The two of them were living in an attic in Flushing. Before I caught my flight back to San Diego, I dropped her off there. As I walked away from her, I felt her death returning. I turned to look back at her, but she had already turned away, receding into a world I've never understood.

Even tonight, lying here in bed in Athens, a part of me still believes she's dead.

7 Dec, Tuesday

I wake well before dawn with a comfortable sleepiness, knowing that tomorrow will be a day of traveling. I'm going home. Today, I'll walk to Colonus where Oedipus met death. According to Sophocles, Colonus had a religious significance. It contained an entrance to the Underworld and was home to the

Furies. But, as the young lady at the Museum told me yesterday, no one knows the exact spot where Oedipus died.

I pull out my city map to plot my walk north. I notice Greek words at the green circular spot on the map that the young lady at the museum yesterday identified as Colonus, Λος Ιππειου, Κολωνου. With the aid of my dictionary, I translate these words as "Hill of the Horses, Colonus." I turn to Sophocles' play and read old, blind Oedipus' inquiry of a citizen of Colonus, when he first came there. Oedipus asked him where they were:

> As much as I can tell you, I will tell.
> This country, all of it, is blessed ground;
> The god Poseidon loves it; in it the firecarrier
> Prometheus has his influence; in particular
> That spot you rest on has been called this earth's
> Doorsill of Brass, and buttress of great Athens.
> All men of this land claim descent from him
> Who is sculptured here; Colonus, master horseman,
> And bear his name in common with their own.
> That is this country, stranger: honored less
> In histories than in the hearts of the people.[477]

Since the man, Colonus, was a master horseman, and the park I'm visiting this morning is "Hill of the Horses," the site just might be what I'm looking for. Poseidon was said to have fathered the first horse there. He fell asleep on a rock (Mother Earth), and his semen fell on it, which then gave birth to the first horse.[478]

I hear the garbage truck outside, see its flashing yellow light on the drapes. The loud voices of men float into my room, a trail of fading voices.

★

I walk through dingy streets, cutting a crooked path through the city. I pass car repair shops, tire shops, construction sites. Rubble fills the space between dilapidated buildings, everything coated with a layer of exhaust, dust, grime. Athens has been populated as far back as Neolithic times and is constantly fighting decay. I come to a set of railroad tracks and balk. No obvious crossing, and I'm the only pedestrian among the hordes of cars. I scurry across anyway.

On the other side of the tracks, I pick up Ioanninon Street and go north. My pulse quickens as I approach Colonus. The streets are wider, less dingy, less crowded, cleaner. To get here, I've walked only through industrial areas, but Colonus is residential, tree-laden. If this is the land of the Furies, they've mellowed through the millennia. Up ahead, the dark, fettered shape of treetops sticks above roofs. I see a park and approach an intersection with a kiosk. A cloud of bird chatter drifts toward me. I walk past the kiosk and into the park along a stone walkway, the sun's rays blocked by a covering of green leaves. The park is on a large hill covered with trees. Underneath the foliage, tree trunks glisten like chocolate.

At the edge of the walkway, curbs enclose tilled earth. Recently planted seedlings stand awkwardly, and vines twine around tree trunks. The path becomes steeper, and as I come to the top of the hill, the trees open to bright sunlight and a children's sand-covered playground, a red teeter-totter, a swing, the gangly wood structure of a climbing maze. I walk along a stone-covered courtyard, past the playground to an overlook of the city, red-domed Byzantine churches pocking the ocean of tan buildings.

Within the confines of a prickly, wrought-iron fence are monuments that shine brilliant white in the morning sun, surrounded by shadows, much as the statue of the horseman, Colonus, must have in antiquity. They mark the tombs of two archaeologists,[479] Carl Otfried Muller (1797-1840), a German scholar who looked upon the classical past "as a world of human experience to be brought into an organic relationship with the present,"[480] and Francois Lenormant (1837-1883), who was a French professor of archaeology, interested in Mediterranean civilizations. His father was also a distinguished archaeologist.[481] But this isn't what I'm looking for. If Sophocles lived and died here, surely the Greeks commemorate the spot with something. I walk to another iron railing where the hill drops away.

Suddenly, I'm overlooking a small theatre with a large semicircular stage and a flat conclave. Finally, I'm satisfied. Surely, this theatre is a tribute to Sophocles. I sit on a short stone wall overlooking the theatre, overlooking Colonus, open my book of Sophocles plays, and read *Oedipus at Colonus*. I've come here to be initiated into the mysteries of Oedipus.

But before I get past the first few lines, someone addresses me in Greek, and I look up to see a withered old man standing over me, his bright eyes investigating my foreignness. I understand little of his Greek, something about "Οιδιπους" (Oedipus). He points to his own eyes and repeats "εδο" (here) several times. I show him my book, open to *Oedipus at Colonus*. He's delighted, asks me where I'm from in halting English, and when I tell him, "United States," he expresses great pleasure, and says something about him being in Canada long ago, and how he used to speak English but has lost the ability. I tell him Colonus is very beautiful, "Ωραια πολι," I say, and he excitedly waves his arms indicating the land hereabouts, expressing his pleasure to me in words I have no hope of understanding, but their essence comes through loud and clear. After a while, he moves on, speaks to another Greek gentleman nearby about the "Αμεριχανος" (Amerikanos).

Again, I open my book of Sophocles' plays to *Oedipus at Colonus* which Sophocles wrote at the age of ninety, during the last year of his life. The play was first performed five years after his death and was staged by his grandson.[482] While Sophocles was writing the play, his sons rebelled against him and tried to prove him to be an imbecile, so they could relieve him of business matters. In his defense, Sophocles read the following ode,[483] which describes and praises Colonus, and is from the play in progress. A citizen of Colonus addresses Oedipus:

Stranger, in this land of goodly steeds thou hast come to earth's fairest home, even to our white Colonus; where the nightingale, a constant guest, trills her clear note in the convert of green glades, dwelling amid the wine-dark ivy and the god's inviolate bowers, rich in berries and fruit, unvisited by sun, unvexed by wind of any storm; where the reveler Dionysus ever walks the ground, companion of the nymphs that nursed him.

And, fed of heavenly dew, the narcissus blooms morn by morn with fair clusters, crown of the Great Goddesses Demeter and Persephone from of yore; and the crocus blooms with golden beam. Nor fail the sleepless founts whence the waters of Cephisus wander, but each day with stainless tide he moveth over the plains of the land's swelling bosom, for the giving of quick increase; nor hath the Muses quire abhorred this place, nor Aphrodite of the golden rein.

And a thing there is such as I know not by fame on Asian ground, or as ever born in the great Dorian isle of Pelops—a growth unconquered, self-renewing, a terror to the spears of the foemen, a growth which mightily flourishes in this land—the gray-leafed olive, nurturer of children. Youth shall not mar it by the ravage of his hand, nor any who dwells with old age; for the sleepless eye of the Morian Zeus beholds it, and the gray-eyed Athena.

And another praise have I to tell for this the city our mother, the gift of a great god, a glory of the land most high; the might of horses, the might of young horses, the might of the sea.

For thou, son of Cronus, our lord Poseidon, hast throned her in this pride, since in these roads first thou didst show forth the curb that cures the rage of steeds. And the shapely oar, apt to men's hands, hath a wondrous speed on the brine, following the hundred-footed Nereids.[484]

Colonus

Needless to say, Sophocles was acquitted of being an imbecile.

Many of the features of Colonus described by Sophocles 2400 years ago still apply today. Colonus is a pleasant oasis in a sea of noise and fumes. I hear children's voices echo from the school yard close by, even as I hear the bell to bring them back indoors, but it's all quickly overlaid by the sound of a jack hammer. The hill is covered with olives, pines, deciduous trees, and bushes, their deep bright color, a testament to the rich earth.

But Colonus was also a land to be feared. When Oedipus and Antigone first found a place to rest, one of the citizens of Colonus, to Oedipus a stranger, came to them worried about where they sat:

> STRANGER:...quit this seat, for you are on ground which it is not lawful to tread.
> OEDIPUS: And what is this ground? Sacred to what deity?
> STRANGER: Ground inviolable, on which none may dwell; for the dread goddesses hold it, the daughters of Earth and Darkness.
> OEDIPUS: Who may they be, whose awful names I am to hear and invoke?
> STRANGER: The all-seeing Eumenides the fold here would call them; but other names please in other places.[485]

The other name for the Eumenides was the Furies, those vengeful deities who drove Orestes insane.

My shadow keeps forming and dissolving as clouds intermittently block the sun's rays. The stone where I sit is cold. The air is cool, but here comes the sun again. I feel its heat on my back.

I now turn to the description of Oedipus' death, or disappearance, as it may be more aptly described. Theseus was the only one permitted to see Oedipus' death, and Oedipus told Theseus he was to pass this knowledge along to only one person. Oedipus gave Theseus specific instructions:

> But for mysteries which speech may not profane, you shall mark them for yourself, when you come to that place alone; since neither to any of this people can I utter them, nor to my own children, dear though they are. No, do you guard them alone; and when you are coming to the end of life, disclose them to your heir alone, and so thenceforth.[486]

In this way, Oedipus created his own mysteries at Colonus, as Demeter had her Mysteries at Eleusis. The mysteries of Oedipus would provide protection for Athens. As Ismene told Oedipus shortly after she joined him, the land containing his grave would be protected, "By force of your wrath, when they take their stand at your tomb."[487] That which had destroyed him in this life, his wrath when he killed his father, would be his asset in the Afterlife, as protector of Athens. Having treated his sons as he did, it's fitting that he would descend to the land of the vengeful Furies.

Although Oedipus was blind to this world, he was no longer blind to the next. The old blind man led his daughters and Theseus to where he was to die, "the sheer Threshold bound by brazen steps to earth's deep roots."[488] He spoke as he led them: "This way, here, this way, for this way doth guiding Hermes lead me, and the goddess Persephone of the dead!"[489] Antigone and Ismene fetched water from a spring for a drink offering, and in doing so, they came to this very hill where I now sit, which was sacred to Demeter, another definite connection with the Mysteries: "And they went to the hill which was in view, Demeter's hill who guards the tender plants..."[490]

Irritated by Oedipus' prolonged farewell to his daughters, Zeus called him to the task at hand, "Oedipus, Oedipus, why delay we to go? You tarry too long."[491] Finally, Oedipus said good-bye to his daughters and led Theseus to the site. A messenger tells what he saw:

> ...when we had gone apart after no long time we looked back. Oedipus we saw nowhere any more, but the king Theseus alone, holding his hand before his face to screen his eyes, as if some dread sight had been seen, and such as not might endure to behold. And then after a short space we saw him salute the earth and the home of the gods above, both at once, in one prayer.
>
> But by what doom Oedipus perished no man can tell save Theseus alone. No fiery thunderbolt of the god removed him in that hour, nor any rising of storm from the sea; but either a messenger from the gods, or the world of the dead...[492]

Just as at Eleusis, the epiphany at Colonus, the mystery of Oedipus' disappearance, was kept secret.

In my trip through Greece, I've encountered both the ancient Greek gods and Christianity, and in particular the words of St. John on Patmos, the Apocalypse. Since Oedipus was such a vengeful man and, at death, went into the land of the Furies, I wonder if there might be a connection between the words of John and Oedipus' death here on the Hill of Horses. What happened to Oedipus? Could it be that he jumped astride that pale horse and road it into darkness? Was Oedipus the "Death" John saw?

Sophocles died shortly after completing *Oedipus at Colonus*, in 406 BC. His funeral train was said to have been guarded by Dionysus, god of theatre himself. Sophocles was a member of an Asklepios cult. When Asklepios, the god of healing, came to Athens in 420 BC to purify the city after the great plague, he came in his usual form, a snake. Sophocles took the snake into his home for safekeeping, while the Asklepion at the foot of the Akropolis, which I visited two days ago, was being built. After death, Sophocles was worshipped locally as the god Dexion, the Receiver, in recognition of his caretaking of the snake.[493]

In the years to come, citizens of Colonus erected a shrine that Pausanias saw when he came through in the 2nd Century AD. He also told of the destruction of the site by the Macedonian general Antigonos during the 3rd Century BC:

> The citizens of Colonus show the place called Kolonus of the Horses, where they say Oedipus entered Attica....they show you an altar of Poseidon of Horses and Athene of Horses and a hero-shrine of...Theseus and Oedipus and Adrastos. Among the damage Antigonos did to the country side in his invasion was to fire the grove of Poseidon and the shrine.[494]

On my way back from Colonus, I walk southeast to the train station, then south to a slim walkway over the tracks, where I look down upon an old black locomotive, a life-size version of one I got under the Christmas tree as a kid. I continue on through the flea market again, turn a corner, and suddenly, I'm face-to-face with Santa. He sits astride a sleigh pulled by two stuffed reindeer. His costume is the most authentic I've seen, and the children crawling in and out of his lap are having a great time. So is the old American watching them.

A change has come over me in the last few days. I'm no longer a traveler or a tourist, but a man displaced in another country and needing one last look at this glorious city.

★

At sundown, I walk up the side of the mountain to the foot of the Acropolis, walk alongside whitewashed homes and small streets, and ascend the Areopagos, Ares Hill, to overlook Athens. Beautiful buildings fill the valleys and hillsides below. Athens is a city of building stacked on top of building, a sprawling metropolis with an organic homogeneity, an ocean of tan buildings and dark-island peaks. I've never seen anything like it, and must admit I've fallen in love. I know she has her problems, but my God, what a city!

I've come here to think about Orestes' acquittal of murdering his mother.

Colonus

In Aeschylus' play, *The Euminides*, Apollo defends Orestes. Apollo's defense is that Orestes did not kill his mother, that true motherhood does not exist:

> The mother to the child that men call hers
> Is no true life-begetter, but a nurse
> Of live seed. 'Tis the sower of the seed
> Alone begetteth. Woman comes at need,
> A stranger, to hold safe in trust and love...[495]

At Delphi, the most sacred site in the Greek world, Apollo seized the sanctuary from Gaia, Mother Earth, by force. Here on the Areopagos, his attack on her was complete. He stripped her of motherhood. Thus, the disenfranchisement of women in ancient Greece was complete.

The problem with Apollo's agricultural analogy is that it ignores the genetic contribution of the woman during conception. This perception is a cornerstone of western thought, the tenet of a patriarchal society, subtle remnants of which exist today. The metaphor of a man sowing his "seed" is particularly telling in light of the Greek view of the earth as the Earth goddess, Gaia. Perhaps before the Neolithic age and the coming of agriculture, the female was seen as the source of all life, everything coming from the body of the female. But as agriculture, planting and sowing, became a way of life, man related his own semen to seed. To sow seed, man first splits the earth, penetrates it just as he penetrates a woman's body during sex. Thus, the idea of Apollo's flawed metaphor came to be.

Apollo's defense of Orestes, based on this agricultural analogy, was the death of the great Earth goddess. To the ancient Greeks, women were only the incubators for men's babies. They divested the female of motherhood. Thus, women give up their surname when they get married, and we trace family genealogy along the line of fathers. The Earth goddess, whose temples I saw replaced all over Greece, was finally dealt the death blow here on the Areopagos. Apollo uses the birth of Athena as proof. He says Athena was born of father alone:

> There have been fathers where no mother is.
> Whereof a perfect witness standeth nigh,
> Athena Pallas, child of the Most High,
> A thought-begotten unconceived bloom,
> No nursling of the darkness of the womb,
> But such a flower of life as Goddess ne'er
> Hath borne in heaven nor ever more shall bear.[496]

Colonus

To avoid divine wrath, I'll attribute this remark to the author, Aeschylus, instead of Apollo. Athena had a mother, Metis, the most wise of all gods and goddesses. Zeus conned her into becoming small and swallowed her. Metis was pregnant with Athena at the time. Her birth occurred when Hephaestus split Zeus' head, but it was not a true birth, only a liberation.

Even Athena participated in the charade. Orestes fate was to be decided by the council of judges on the Areopagos, this hill where I now sit and where murderers were tried. After both Apollo and the Furies presented their cases for and against Orestes, the judges cast their lots. But the vote was a tie, and Athena, who presided over the trial, cast the deciding vote. Since she was born of father alone and always took the side of men, she cast her vote for acquittal and freed Orestes.

Thus, Orestes was acquitted on false grounds. Klytemnestra was his mother. All mothers are true mothers. The father is a partner in conception, not the source of life. Our entire civilization, civilizations all over the world, are based, in part, on this lie. This disenfranchised not only women, but also discredited the feminine element of men, and reinforced the masculine element in women. Modern woman is cast in the mold of Athena.

A stiff breeze has cleared the air, and as the dying rays of sinking sun kiss the sides of buildings, I descend from the hill named for the god of war.

On January 28, 1986, nine months after my daughter's disappearance and resurrection, I made another of my many trips to Kennedy Space Center for flight-team training, so I could man one of the spacecraft ground consoles during the Shuttle flight. We had a short layover in Dallas to change flights and as I exited the plane, I heard a comment from someone on the concourse. "...there was a fireball, and it fell into the ocean..." I had been too busy with preparations for our own Shuttle launch to pay much attention to Challenger that morning. But upon hearing these words of a stranger, I knew immediately what had happened, and also knew our project would be canceled. The payload we were building was too dangerous to survive the scrutiny that would certainly follow a Shuttle disaster.

I continued on my flight to Orlando and drove to Cocoa Beach, listening to the continuing news coverage on the rental-car radio. I cried all the way. The disaster had consequences beyond the professional impact, personal consequences. I had consciously moved to San Diego for a job on the most challenging project confronting the aerospace industry to try to prevent a Shuttle disaster. But one had occurred anyway. I had sacrificed my daughter for nothing.

I again had the feeling I had been shown something, taught a difficult lesson, and that someone somewhere was having a good belly laugh at my expense. Man received his inventiveness, cleverness from Prometheus, who was a Titan, that race of gods who came before Zeus and Apollo. A Titan's way of dealing with the world was not one of enlightenment but one of inventiveness, a more primitive form of intelligence. Prometheus gave this inventiveness to man.

Zeus didn't think much of it. He realized Prometheus' inventions would leave a trail of new misery for men.[497] After he discovered Prometheus had given men fire, Zeus roared with laughter,[498] realizing the evil it would bring. I had sacrificed my daughter to work on a Space Shuttle contract, and I heard an echo of Zeus' laugh after Challenger exploded. But the laughter of Zeus is not malicious. Our tragic flaw comes from the desire to be like the gods. Zeus seems to be also pulling for us. Our attempts to be heroic, reaching beyond our limitations, trying to deny our fate, result in disaster and cause his spontaneous laughter.

And on this journey through Greece, I've come to view the events surrounding, not only my daughter's disappearance, but also those of the confrontation with my father, in a different light, one not shrouded by guilt and blame. It seems our lives at times parallel the old myths. Whether we observe them or not, the processes of cult are ever-active. We experience the "trial by fire" and are unconsciously initiated into the Mysteries.

Modern psychology has placed the human experience very close to myth: "...we are, in soul, mythical beings. We emerge into life as creatures in a drama, scripted by the great storytellers of our culture."[499] We had better watch this phenomenon closely, because, when our lives parallel myths, we are drawn toward disaster.[500] But even if we don't reenact the myths literally, we still experience them internally, feel as though the tragedies literally occurred. I still can't get beyond the feeling that my daughter is dead. This is the cult process.

I've worked on hardware now sitting on the surface of Mars; stood at the bottom of a missile silo, looking up at a the long missile cylinder with a multi-megaton warhead that could destroy our world sitting on top, the unleashing of Prometheus' gift of fire on an unimaginable scale; stood on the launch pad at KSC, climbed aboard the Space Shuttle to peer inside the cargo bay. Because of Prometheus, the human race has become godlike. But Mary Shelly's *Frankenstein, The Modern Prometheus*, shines like a beacon across the millennia between us and the ancient Greeks. Her novel is the perfect metaphor for 20th Century man's arrogance. The scientific mind has indeed created a monster in our own image, reached the pentacle of arrogance. Our godlike posturing would have been punished swiftly and severely in antiquity.

Colonus

While walking back to my hotel, my journey drawing to a close, I wonder where I shall go now? What path shall my life take? I feel that I've led my life mimicking Sophocles' guard in *Antigone,* when he comes to the king bearing bad news:

> My liege, I will not say that I come breathless from speed or that I have plied a nimble foot; for often did my thoughts make me pause and wheel round in my path to return. My mind was holding large discourse with me: "Fool, why are you going on to your certain doom?" "Wretch, tarrying again? ..." So debating I went on my way with lagging steps, and thus a short road was made long. At last, however, it carried the day that I should come here to you; and though my tale is nothing yet I will tell it. I come with a good grip on one hope—that I can suffer nothing but what is my fate.[501]

He's so modern, full of indecision and doubt, so afraid. It's as if Sophocles looked into the eyes of this character and saw 2500 years into the future, into the heart of modern man.

What path shall I choose to end my lengthy unemployment? I no longer feel I'm in control of my life. Perhaps the feeling of control I had in the past was an illusion. Now I feel that my fate is in the hands of another. As Jesus told his disciple Peter:

> Verily, verily, I say unto thee,
> When thou was young, thou girdedst
> thyself, and walkedst wither thou
> wouldest: but when thou shalt be old,
> thou shalt stretch forth thy hands,
> and another shall gird thee, and carry
> thee whither thou wouldest not.

★

This evening I feel purposeless. I eat dinner at a local restaurant, a big piece of roast beef in brown sauce, boiled potatoes with rice, and a tiny bottle of Greek wine, retsina, which tastes a little like paint thinner. Later, I have an ice cream served by the gorgeous brunette at the crepe shop I so frequently visited when I first came to Athens, my first love, so to speak. But I feel lost. I've spent my evenings over the past ten weeks planning the next day's activities, where to go, what to see. This evening I have nothing to plan. And once again, I'm alone.

Colonus

I wonder about the loneliness of Oedipus' youngest daughter, Ismene, the only member of her family to survive. Her mother committed suicide when she was a child. Just after her father/brother died his strange death at Colonus, her two brothers killed each other, and not long afterward, Antigone died in a last-ditch defense of the rites of the Earth Goddess. That would make Thebes a lonely and desolate city for Ismene. The Greek poets don't address her fate. She was gentle and timid, a sensible, down-to-earth young woman who seemed bewildered by the heroics of her family. She poses the question of her own fate to herself after her father's death:

Ah me unhappy! Friendless and helpless,
where am I now to live my hapless life?[502]

I think of Ismene in the days following that turbulent time as a self-imposed exile in some obscure township where no one knew she was a member of that infamous family. I see her married with children, possibly a great storyteller, singing her poetry to her grandchildren and great grandchildren, telling of Oedipus and Antigone, keeping the legends alive. I see her old and withered, sitting with her feet to the fire, wrapped in a gray blanket, staring into the glowing coals. Perhaps Ismene told her tales to Teiresias' daughter, Manto, and they eventually became some of Homer's best lines. Perhaps, Ismene alone escaped to tell it all.

If Ismene and Antigone represent two of the three feminine presences of Oedipus' quaternion, where is the third? Am I missing a part of the Rosetta Stone? Perhaps the answer to this question lies in Demeter's Mysteries. According to Plato's view of the Mysteries, we spend our lives nurturing a pearl that is the human soul, which will be reborn into the Afterlife. It is a ghostly presence, but always a part of us. My guess is that this pearl represents the remaining, undetectable feminine aspect of Oedipus' personality, his soul.

8 Dec, Wednesday

All is quiet in my room and outside Hotel Phaedra, on the day of the Feast of the Immaculate Conception, my last morning in Greece. I lie between the covers, on top of which I've spread my running jacket, my army-green long-sleeved shirt, black pants and black sweater, to hold in the heat. I try to contain my excitement. I'm going home.

I rise feeling energetic, younger than my years, and walk to Syntagma to catch a bus, only to learn that a strike started this morning. Finally, a man standing next to me, waiting for a shuttle bus, speaks to me in English. He's an

American from Parker, Colorado, an engineer on business here in Athens. He suggests I walk with him to the Hilton where he's staying. He'll get us a taxi to the airport. We can split the fare.

The Hilton is a little nicer than the hotels where I've stayed, echoing foyer, glass doors, plush red carpet, mirrored walls, a vaulted chamber large enough for a blimp, a swimming pool. I wait in the lobby for him to get his suitcase, trying to reenter a world for which I no longer feel suited. We talk in the taxi on the way to the airport, and I end up at the wrong terminal. I split the taxi fare to the East Terminal with an American couple on vacation from Saudi Arabia, where they both work.

I retrieve my luggage from storage, relieved to be reunited with the first volume of my journal and my forty rolls of film. I change clothes behind a row of storage shelves and repack my backpack.

★

In the early afternoon, I sit at the departures terminal, awaiting my flight to London. The modern waiting room seems sterile after all the ruins I've visited. I check my security pouch and find that I still have $200 of the $2500 in traveler's checks I brought with me on this journey.

Perhaps I'll never find what was going on inside me when my father loaded the deer rifle, but my journey has been far from a failure. Zeus would have looked down on me and smiled for coming 7000 miles to look for something I brought with me. "Before Zeus, the laughing onlooker, the eternal human race plays its eternal human comedy."[503]

I've learned that, as a result of the death of the Earth goddess, Oedipus and his family define our entire masculine society. His mother died, having taken her own life, an event similar to Athena putting the finishing touches on Gaia. In his mother's absence, old blind Oedipus wandered the countryside, wallowing in self-pity, raging and cursing his sons, while his daughters flitted about in his service. The modern woman is either like his daughters, or like Athena, the goddess born of a father only, and although she has the wisdom to guide all civilization, she devotes herself to the service of only the masculine, even the masculine part of herself.

My daughter's life was a mystery to me, and it is no coincidence that, through trying to understand our problems, I've discovered Demeter and Persephone and have been introduced (dare I say initiated?) into the Mysteries. We now have little understanding of the true feminine spirit. To uncover it, we must search for the Earth goddess, for Hera, Artemis and Aphrodite, search for the elements of them within us all. Within them, we'll find the ruins of our complete selves and begin the restoration. Perhaps that's the true purpose of developing a personal mythology. Here in Greece, I've begun this process, and perhaps that's where I'll eventually find the feelings I suppressed when my father turned to the deer rifle to solve the problems between us. It's as if the feminine part of my nature died in that one instant, and remains hidden behind the mask of Dionysus. I didn't accomplish the task I came here to perform, but perhaps I've awakened enough of my suppressed self to make the recovery possible.

I've found more than my own mythology. A personal mythology gives us a tool to think about and consider our lives. The fact that it is an ancient art demonstrates that it's a natural characteristic of the mind. But it's only a tool. Life for me was like a bad suit: it never quite fit. I'd never found that center from which every life projects. I had to pick up my life and shake it until I fell out. My daughter learned that early in life. Though thirty-two years late, I finally woke up. It took a trip to Greece. Through this personal mythology, I've finally centered myself.

When I look back on it, I realize that my own motivation for having a family, and in particular, a career was a sense of myth. When I pulled alerts in ICBM silos, stood at the bottom of the silo looking up at that long, sleek, shiny shaft that could end civilization as we know it, I was reveling in the male myth of our civilization. The ancient Greeks destroyed theirs several times. The first occurred around 2000 BC, and the second 1000 BC following the Trojan War. Classical Greece destroyed itself during the Peloponnesian War. We almost destroyed ourselves during World Wars I and II. The pull toward war has always been an overpowering impulse for men, the unleashing of anarchy an irresistible part of the male psyche.

But the cure for all of this violence may have manifested itself between wars, in 1922 with Women's Suffrage, and during World War II when women took over the workforce to build ships, submarines and planes to support their men, who were off killing each other. Women, through the influence of Athena, are the bringers of civilization, and men, through worshiping Ares, the great destroyers. Oedipus was not just a descendent of Kadmos from Tyre. He was also a descendent of the Sparti, the sown-men, a descendent of the dragon, and thus of Ares himself. All men have the irresistible pull toward anarchy, the thrill of destroying a civilization. But women have now entered the scene in force for the first time in the history of the world. This is the single most important fact that determined the outcome of the Cold War, that enabled it to reach a conclusion peacefully. The nature of civilization is changing through the feminine influence.

We take the shuttle to an airplane parked on a cement pad next to the runway, and as I enter, I'm greeted by a beautiful British Airways hostess with

Colonus

the most delicious English accent I've ever heard. Christmas carols coming over the intercom fill the interior of the warm plane, "It's Beginning to Feel a Lot Like Christmas." Much laughter and good-spirited joking. I enjoy the crowding, the closeness of people. Now they're playing, "I've Got My Love to Keep Me Warm." I can't quit smiling.

We taxi. A great sunset is occurring in Athens. The bright rays peek from under a cloud and glisten off the Aegean, a swipe of blazing light across the sea and toward us. We wait while a plane lands, its two propellers blurred circles. We move into position for our ground run, taking off to the north.

The acceleration pushes me back in my seat. What a glorious feeling to be going home. The lightness as the plane leaves the ground. Higher now, out over the water, ferryboats, fishing boats, the sun rising above the horizon to vanish behind a cloud, the Aegean rippled like corrugated metal, a glassy washboard. Two flattop tankers directly below, one sparkling white, the other a deep rust. We bank to the right. Helios has set fire to Athens.

EPILOGUE

During mornings in California, while home visiting my parents at Christmas, I sat on the love seat in the living room listening to the sounds of my mother cooking for her two men. My father read the morning paper, while I wrote letters to those I met on my journey: Letizia in Italy, Alan in Kenya, and Sarah in Australia. I heard my mother scrape the brown gravy from the cast-iron skillet, the click of china, the clunk of the pan of biscuits against the table top, the smell of bacon, her call to breakfast.

I gave a three-hour slide show and the whole family came, even my arthritis-crippled aunt. I had to repeat it the next day for my uncle. My parents watched both times, spellbound by the Greek countryside, and gushing questions about the ruins of the ancient civilization.

During my days there, I mostly stared out the front window at a green field, where a flock of snow-white egrets gawked through alfalfa like animated Christmas toys, long question-mark necks. Now and then, one spread its wings to loft like a white kite buffeted about by a breeze above the deep-green field. The far edge of the alfalfa disappeared into the fog shrouding farmhouses and barns.

My son came down from San Francisco. I was pleased to have him with me for the holidays, but still felt the loneliness of my daughter's absence, she a continent away in New York.

Christmas Eve, the four of us got into the old two-seat pickup for the short drive to my brother's new home. I remember sitting in the cramped backseat with pies surrounding me, chocolate meringue, coconut cream, wafts of pumpkin pie rising from one in my lap, another on the seat beside me, another yet on the floorboard, and stuffing in a pot ready for the turkey.

The most lasting image of my father was when we passed out presents, the kids shouting and laughing through piles of wrapping paper. He sat in a straight-backed kitchen chair, three presents in his lap like gift-wrapped tumors. When asked why he didn't open them, he said, "It's not Christmas yet." And it wasn't. It was Christmas Eve. But for him, Christmas joy had been overridden by some sad memory. Did he still worry about what had happened between us years ago?

Epilogue

I'm not sure he even remembered it. More likely, he simply longed for the days when his parents were alive, and we all had Christmas at their home.

One evening after returning to Colorado, I read Beryl Markham's book of barnstorming around Africa in the '20s and '30s, *West with the Night*. My pulse quickened at her description of being attacked and almost killed by a lion when she was a child. The unnaturally domesticated lion roamed a neighbor's land and was tame, had never made a kill. But one day, he spotted lighthearted Beryl singing and running through a hot-dirt field and had a change of heart. After knocking Beryl to the ground, the black-mained lion, affectionately named Paddy, stood over her roaring, paws buried in her back. Her description of the experience contains some of the most moving lines I've ever read:

> The sound of Paddy's roar in my ears will only be duplicated, I think, when the doors of hell slip their wobbly hinges, one day, and give voice and authenticity to the whole panorama of Dante's poetic nightmares. It was an immense roar that encompassed the world and dissolved me in it.[504]

Her neighbor, who'd witnessed the attack, charged the lion and the lion charged the neighbor to protect his fresh kill, thus releasing Beryl and allowing her to escape. Her last words were of sympathy toward the lion: "He was a good lion... and I cannot begrudge him his moment," she wrote.[505] Upon reading these words, I put the book down, and quite unaccountably, cried.

Then I went to buy a ticket to a movie I was to see later that evening. Spielberg's *Schildler's List* had just been released. When I returned home with ticket in hand, I was still sad, a magnificent hurt in my chest. I continued having flashes of the scene from Beryl Markham's book, the image of Beryl facedown on the ground with the lion standing over her, she his fresh kill, the neighbor rushing to her rescue. The scene kept coming to me with waves of unbearable anguish. And I wondered, Why should I relate so strongly to an image of Beryl Markham, on the threshold of being eaten by a lion?

Suddenly, the year was again 1961. I was face down on the bed in my parents home, my father in the bedroom loading the deer rifle. My hands opening and closing on the cold stiff sheets. I was the fallen child, he the lion roaring over his fresh kill. Again, I heard my mother's footsteps as she charged into the room.

Wave upon wave of unbearable grief coursed through me like the waves that night on the beach at Matala, Sophocles' ebb and flow of human misery. I had finally found the feelings, the grief, I had not felt thirty-two years before. They were hidden beneath the image of a girl, undoubtedly the suppressed feminine part of myself, who appeared as my mysterious imaginary companion

Epilogue

when I was eight years old the night our home burned. She was the only safe place I knew to hide my feelings.

AFTERWARD

May 1999

I now live in the aftermath of my Greek experience, watching as it continues to ripple through my life. Recently I moved from Colorado to New Mexico, where I now write in an old home built by my grandfather, much of which he constructed from discarded bomb boxes from World War II. I've decided against returning to engineering and just finished a novel set in ancient Greece. I'm drawn ever deeper into a world two thousand years gone. I feel as if, while in Delphi, I fell into that abyss.

My father passed away May 12, 1999. My sister-in-law called to tell me, my brother too sad to talk. Our father had been progressively deteriorating the last two years, suffering from the bone marrow disease myelophybrosis. The week before, he'd fallen in the morning while trying to get up from the kitchen table and broken three ribs. Or at least he believed he'd broken them. As I learned later, he never went to the doctor.

I'd called him that Sunday to see how he was doing and talked to him awhile. He sounded well enough, but made some curious comment just before we hung up about this being "the end," as he was apt to do the preceding months. Yet this comment was more final somehow, though none of us thought his time had come. I couldn't quite make out his last words. His voice was raspy and weak over the phone.

The next morning, I received a call from my brother saying that our father was in the hospital. He'd gone in on emergency not long after talking to me and was really in trouble. His blood pressure had dropped precipitously, blood-sugar 9, lower than anyone had ever heard of for a living human being. His body was filled with infection.

A little later, my uncle called to say he'd gone into a coma. The word "coma" sent a flash of fear through me. Never had I heard the word applied to a member of my family. I thought about trying to get a plane flight home, but later that day, he stabilized and began to improve. They sent my mother home for the night.

But she received a call at four in the morning saying he'd taken another turn for the worse. His kidneys had failed. He lapsed into another coma and died at one in the afternoon.

I'd wanted to be there when he went. I'd fantasized about how I would hold his hand and tell him how much I loved him. My words would be the last he'd hear. But I was 1,700 miles away in Carlsbad. My brother was the one who held his hand, felt his life falter and slip away.

I caught a plane for California, and the morning of the viewing, I went to my arthritic aunt's home and helped her negotiate the few blocks in her motorized wheelchair. She'd been the only one he'd told he loved before he died, and she'd told him that she appreciated him saying that. She'd not known. He'd been more of a father to her than a brother, she said, as he'd been to everyone.

We had to enter the funeral home by a side door into the casket room, and when I opened it, light spilled onto the grieving family members inside: my mother, brothers, sisters-in-law, my nieces and nephews and their kids. The door slammed, quenching the light and enveloping us in darkness. I was immediately overcome by grief and slumped onto a bench. After I recovered a little, I went to the casket, where my mother was crying softly and rubbing him with her hands.

A silent prayer gushed from me unbidden. I couldn't quit thanking God for giving him to me as my father. Over and over, I gave thanks. But I never saw his face. He had a glow about him there in the dim light, and his hidden features suddenly showed through. I looked into the face of an angel.

We held the service at the cemetery, the spring winds bowing trees, grass bright green with new growth. The Masons, whose order was founded by ancient stonecutters, conducted the ceremony, him having achieved the 32 Degree and the Scottish Rite. I found the ritual surprisingly meaningful, lots of words about sacrifice and everlasting life, symbolized by the lambskin and evergreen wreath draped over his casket. The words were so familiar that it startled me. It was as if they'd come from the Mysteries at Eleusis.

That night back at home, I sorted through the few books my father kept, until I found the only one connected with the Masons, titled, *Morals and Dogma of the Ancient and Accepted Scottish Rite*, by Albert Pike, Grand Commander 1859-1891. I opened it and thumbed through a few pages, and there it was:

Though Masonry is identical with the ancient Mysteries, it is so only in this qualified sense: that it represents but an imperfect image of their brilliancy, the ruins only of their grandeur...

Afterward

My father had tried to get me into the Order years before, while I was in high school, but as with so much he tried to pass along, I rejected it. We all have our own paths to truth. Our life together on this planet had been a series of near misses. We had skirted both tragedy and communion, and it wasn't until I attended his funeral that I finally came to realize the full connection between us, how we'd traveled similar paths. I had studied the ancient Mysteries; but as a farmer, a man of the earth, and a Mason, he'd lived them.

In August, my mother came to visit me in Carlsbad. One evening as she was about to go to bed, there in the old home built by her father and mother, she told me that not long before my father died, his mother came to him in a dream. He tried to tell my mother what his mother had said but broke down and just couldn't. Later he went to see his sister, my invalid aunt whom I'd assisted in her wheel chair, and tried to tell her, but couldn't then either.

And that's where it stood at the time he died, this saddest of all sad things still weighing on him with no way to let it out, and leaving us with nothing but our own speculation. My mother said she thought probably his mother had told him that he would be with her soon, but somehow I can't believe that was the central issue. I imagine something more ominous, as is my nature. At any rate, God evidently didn't want the content of the dream told, but left a mystery. I'll not divulge even my own private thoughts on the subject, since, if I was to be right, I would be revealing that which God has deemed unspeakable.

THE END

ENDNOTES

1 From Thornton Wilder's Introduction (1955) to: *Sophocles', Oedipus The King*, translated by Francis Storr, Norwalk: The Easton Press, 1980, page 16.

2 Kaplan, Robert D., *Balkan Ghosts, A Journey Through History*, New York: St. Martin's Press, 1993, 273.

3 Whitman, Cedric, H., *Sophocles*, Cambridge: Harvard University Press, 1951, page 20.

4 Kerenyi, C., *Dionysos, Archetypal Image of Indestructible Life*, tr. by Ralph Manheim, Princeton: Princeton University Press, 1976, page 284.

5 Ibid., page 132.

6 Kerenyi, Karl., *Athene, Virgin and Mother in Greek Religion*, tr. by Murray Stein, Dallas: Spring Publications, Inc., 1978, page 2.

7 Hesiod, *Theogony, Works and Days, Shield*, tr. by Apostolos N. Athanassakis, Baltimore: The Johns Hopkins University Press, 1983, page 36.

8 Pausanias, *Guide to Greece, Vol. 1, Central Greece*, tr. by Peter Levi, New York: Penguin Books, 1971, page 69/70.

9 Mehling, Dr. Marianne, editor, *Athens and Attica*, New York: Prentice Hall Press, 1986, page 65.

10 Letters, F. J. H., *The Life and Work of Sophocles*, New York: Sheed and Ward, Inc., 1953, page 8/9.

11 Ibid., page 1.

12 Plutarch, *Plutarch's Lives*, "Theseus," tr. by John Dryden, ed. by A. H. Clough, New York: Modern Library, 1992 (~1700).

13 Ibid. Note: Many ancient Greeks heroes had two fathers. Frequently, a god and a mortal man would lay with a woman on the same night and an ambiguity would arise as to who the father really was. The individual would then have both a heavenly father and a mortal one. In Theseus' case, they were the god Poseidon and Aegeus, the king of Athens.

14 Kerenyi, C., *The Gods of the Greeks*, New York: Thames and Hudson Ltd., 1951, page 155.

15 Hesiod, page 68.

16 Herodotus, *The Histories*, tr. by Aubrey de Selincourt, New York: The Penguin Group, 1954, page 430.

17 Segal, Charles, *Oedipus Tyrannus, Tragic Heroism and the Limits of Knowledge*, New York: Twayne Publsihers,1993, pg. 31.

18 Sophocles, *Sophocles, The Three Theban Plays*, tr. by Robert Fagles, New York:

Endnotes

The Penguin Group, 1982, page 233.

19 Demakopoulou, Karie and Dora Konsola, *Archaeological Museum of Thebes, Guide*, Athens: Archaeological Receipts Fund (T. A. P.), 1981, page 10.

20 *The Homeric Hymns*, tr. by Apostolos N. Athanassakis, Baltimore: The Johns Hopkins University Press, 1976, page 21.

21 Nonnos, *Dionysiaca*, Vol. I, tr. by W. H. D. Rouse, Loeb Classical Library, Cambridge: Harvard University Press, 1940, page 165.

22 Ibid., page 165/6.

23 Demakopoulou, page 54.

24 Ibid., page 52.

25 Homer, *The Odyssey*, tr. by Robert Fitzgerald, Franklin Center: The Franklin Library, 1978, page 126/7.

26 Chadwick, John, *Linear B and Related Scripts*. Linear B was the ancient Minoan script, which was deciphered by the Englishman Michael Ventris in 1953. He proved that the Bronze Age civilization spoke Greek. See also *The Decipherment of Linear B* by John Chadwick.

27 Knox, Bernard, *The Heroic Temper, Studies in Sophoclean Tragedy*, Berkeley: University of California Press, 1964, page 79/80.

28 Sophocles, *The Complete Plays of Sophocles*, tr. by Sir Richard Claverhouse Jebb, ed. and with an introduction by Moses Hadas, New York: Bantam Books, page 117.

29 Pausanias, *Description of Greece*, tr. by Peter Levi, New York: The Penguin Group, 1971, Vol. 1, page 360/1.

30 Sophocles, The Complete *Plays of Sophocles*, page 121.

31 Ibid., page 129.

32 Demakopoulou, page 23.

33 See the essay "Oedipus Revisited," by James Hillman in *Oedipus Variations*, by Karl Kerenyi, and James Hillman, Dallas: Spring Publications, 1990, page 122.

34 Kerenyi, C., *The Gods of the Ancient Greeks*, tr. by Norman Cameron, New York: Thames and Hudson Ltd., 1951, page 254.

35 Ibid., page 258.

36 Euripides, *Euripides*, Vol. III, tr. by A. S. Way, Cambridge: Harvard University Press, Loeb Classical Library, 1912, page 7.

37 Kerenyi, C., *Dionysos, Archetypal Image of Indestructible Life*, tr. by Ralph Manheim, Princeton: Princeton University Press, 1976, page 114.

38 Sophocles, *The Complete Plays of Sophocles*, page 84.

39 Ibid., page 84.

40 Pausanias, page 344.

Endnotes

41 Lewis, Neville, *Delphi and the Sacred Way*, London: Michael Haag Ltd., 1987, page 83.

42 Kaplan, page 273.

43 Callimachus, *Callimachus, Hymns and Epigrams*, tr. by A. W. Mair, Cambridge: Harvard University Press, 1921, page 119.

44 Apollodorus, *Gods and Heroes of the Greeks, The Library of Apollodorus*, tr. with intro. and notes by Michael Simpson, Amherst: University of Massachusetts Press, 1976, page 147.

45 Hesiod, *Theogony, Works and Days, Shield*, translated by Athanassakis, Apostolos N., Baltimore: The Johns Hopkins University Press, page 83.

46 Apollodorus, page 157.

47 Kerenyi, C., *Zeus and Hera, Archetypal Image of Father, Husband, and Wife*, tr. by Christopher Holme, Princeton: Princeton University Press, 1975, page 43.

48 Apollodorus, page 32.

49 Aeschylus, *The Complete Plays of Aeschylus*, Franklin Center: The Franklin Library, 1978, page 339.

50 *The Homeric Hymns*, tr. by Apostolis N. Athanassakis, Baltimore: The Johns Hopkins University Press, 1976, page 25.

51 Ibid, page 19.

52 Kerenyi, C., *Dionysus, Archetypal Image of Indestructible Life*, tr. by Ralph Manheim, Princeton: Princeton University Press, 1976, page 209.

53 Farnell, Lewis Richard, *The Cults of The Greek States*, Vol. III, Oxford: The Clarendon Press, 1907, page 1.

54 Pausanias, *Description of Greece*, tr. by Peter Levi, New York: The Penguin Group, 1971, page 466.

55 Aeschylus, *Aeschylus*, Vol. I, tr. by H. Weir Smyth, Cambridge: Harvard University Press, Loeb Classical Library, 1922, page 385.

56 Fontenrose, Joseph, *The Delphic Oracle*, Berkeley: University of California Press, 1978, page 198.

57 Plutarch, *Selected Essays and Dialogues*, tr. by Donald Russell, Oxford: Oxford University Press, 1993, page 55.

58 Kerenyi, C., *Dionysus*, 1976, page 207.

59 Fontenrose, page 4.

60 Plutarch, *Moralia*, Vol. IV, tr. by F. C. Babbitt, Cambridge: Harvard University Press, 1936, page 183.

61 Diodorus Siculus, *The Library of History*, tr. by C. H. Oldfather, Vol. III, Cambridge: Harvard University Press, 1939, page 29/31.

62 Plutarch, *Moralia*, Vol. IV, page 55.

63 Ibid, page 62.

Endnotes

64 Ibid, page 74.

65 Andronicos, Manolis, *Delphi*, Athens: Ekdotike Hellados S. A., 1976, pg. 10-12.

66 Fontenrose, page 196/7.

67 Since I wrote this, further research and experimentation has been conducted. The "fumes" did exist. See *The Oracle*, by William J. Broad, New York: The Penguin Group, 2006.

68 Fontenrose, page 5.

69 Fontenrose, page 208.

70 Kerenyi, C., *Dionysus*, page 211.

71 Ibid, page 215.

72 Ibid, page 223.

73 Otto, Walter F., *Dionysus, Myth and Cult*, tr. by Robert B. Palmer, Dallas: Spring Publications, 1965, page 207.

74 Pindar, *Pindar*, tr. by Sir John Sandys, Cambridge: Harvard University Press, 1915, page 63.

75 Fontenrose, page 4.

76 Ovid, *Metamorphoses*, tr. by Rolfe Humphries, Bloomington: Indiana University Press, 1955, page 50.

77 Hesiod, *The Homeric Hymns*, Athanassakis, pages 38.

78 Ibid, page 46.

79 Nonnos, *Dionysiaca*, Vol. III, tr. by W. H. D. Rouse, Cambridge: Harvard University Press, 1940, page 313.

80 Hesiod, *The Homeric Hymns*, Athanassakis, page 29.

81 From "The Acts of Andrew" in *The Other Bible*, ed. and introductions by Willis Barnstone, San Francisco: HarperSanFrancisco, 1984, page 460.

82 St. Mark, 1:17.

83 St. Mark, 13:24-6.

84 From "The Acts of Andrew" in *The Other Bible*, ed. and introductions by Willis Barnstone, San Francisco: HarperSanFrancisco, 1984, page 461.

85 Kerenyi, C., *The Heroes of the Greeks*, tr. by H. J. Rose, New York: Grove Press, Inc., 1959, page 77.

86 Homer, *The Odyssey of Homer*, tr. by Robert Fitzgerald, Franklin Center: The Franklin Library, 1978, page 401.

87 *An Intermediate Greek-English Lexicon*, Oxford: Oxford University Press, 1995 (1889), page 544.

88 Hesiod, *Theogony, Works and Day, Shield*, tr. by Apostolos N. Athanassakis, Baltimore: The Johns Hopkins University Press, page 21.

89 Homer, *The Odyssey of Homer*, page 266.

Endnotes

90 Ibid, page 267.

91 Ibid, page 32.

92 Ibid, page 75.

93 Ibid, page 75/6.

94 Ibid, page 354.

95 Ibid, page 446.

96 Ibid, page 462.

97 Ibid, page 483.

98 Tripp, Edward, *The Meridian Handbook of Classical Mythology*, New York: Meridian, 1970, page 403.

99 Pausanias, *Guide to Greece*, tr. by Peter Levi, New York: The Penguin Group, 1971, page, 216.

100 Guthrie, W. K. C., *Greeks and Their Gods*, Boston: Beacon Press, 1950, page 111. Note: These are the usual twelve. Here at Olympia, Hephaestus, Demeter and Hestia were replaced with Kronos, Rhea and Alpheios (Guthrie, page 112).

101 Ibid, page 111.

102 Karpodini-Dimitriadi, E., *The Peloponnese,* Athens: Ekdotike Athenon S. A., 1984, page 177.

103 Pausanias, *Guide to Greece*, Vol. 2, tr. by Peter Levi, New York: The Penguin Group, 1971, page 247.

104 *The Homeric Hymns*, tr. by Apostolos N. Athanassakis, Baltimore: The Johns Hopkins University Press, 1976, page 48.

105 Kerenyi, C., *The Gods of the Greeks*, tr. by Norman Cameron, New York: Thames and Hudson, 1951, page 96.

106 Ibid, page 97.

107 Kerenyi, C., *Zeus and Hera, Archetypal Image of Father, Husband and Wife*, tr. by Christopher Holme, Princeton: Princeton University Press, 1975, page 123.

108 Pausanias, *Guide to Greece*, Vol. 2, pages 248-55.

109 Ibid, page, 226/7.

110 Ibid, page, 199.

111 Ibid, page 245.

112 Levi, Peter, *The Hill of Kronos*, New York: E. P. Dutton, 1981, page 58.

113 Pausanias, *Guide to Greece*, Vol. 2, page 246.

114 Pindar, *The Odes of Pindar*, tr. by Sir John Sandys, Cambridge: Harvard University Press, 1915, page 63.

115 Pausanias, *Guide to Greece*, Vol. 2, page 239.

116 Brown, Norman, *Hermes the Thief*, Great Barrington: Lindisfarne Press, 1990 (1947), page 103.

Endnotes

117 Ibid, page 8.

118 *Encyclopaedia Britannica*, Vol. 16, Chicago: University of Chicago, 1965, page 944.

119 Pausanias, *Guide to Greece*, Vol. 2, page 259.

120 Ibid, page 345.

121 Kerenyi, C., *Zeus and Hera*, page 133.

122 Pausanias, *Guide to Greece*, Vol. 2, page 345.

123 Guthrie, *The Greeks and Their Gods*, page 269.

124 *Berlitz Travelers Guide to Greece*, ed. by Alan Tucker, New York: Berlitz Publishing Company, Inc., 1993, pages 125-129.

125 Pausanias, *Guide to Greece*, Vol. 2, page 275.

126 Ibid, page 279.

127 Kerenyi, C., *The Gods of the Greeks*, tr. by Norman Cameron, New York: Thames and Hudson, 1951, page 173.

128 *The Homeric Hymns*, tr. by Apostolos N. Athanassakis, Baltimore: The Johns Hopkins University Press, 1976. page 62/3.

129 Ibid, page 63.

130 Hillman, James and Wilhelm Heinrich Roscher, *Pan and the Nightmare*, Dallas: Spring Publications, 1972, page 23.

131 Kerenyi, *The Gods of the Greeks*, page 174.

132 Hillman, *Pan and the Nightmare*, page 22.

133 Kerenyi, *The Gods of the Greeks*, page 95.

134 Pausanias, *Guide to Greece*, Vol. 2, page 462.

135 Hillman, *Pan and the Nightmare*, page 53.

136 Kerenyi, *The Gods of the Greeks*, page 64.

137 Ibid, page 24/5.

138 Levi, Peter, *The Hill of Kronos*, New York: E. P. Dutton, 1981, page 89.

139 Pausanias, *Guide to Greece*, Vol. 2, page 9/10.

140 Fitzhardinge, L. F., *The Spartans*, London: Thames and Hudson, Ltd., 1980, pages 9-14.

141 Alcman, *Greek Lyric, Vol. II, Anacreon, Anacreontea, Choral Lyric from Olympus to Alcman*, tr. by David A. Campbell, Cambridge: Harvard University Press, 1988, page 379.

142 Fitzhardinge, *The Spartans*, page 13.

143 Alcman, *Greek Lyric*, Vol. II, page 455.

144 Sappho, *Greek Lyric, Volume I, Sappho and Alcaeus*, tr. by D. A. Campbell, Cambridge: Harvard University Press, Loeb Classical Library, 1982, page 171.

145 Plutarch, *Moralia*, Vol. IV, tr. by Frank Cole Babbitt, Cambridge: Harvard University Press, Loeb Classical Library, 1936, page 307.

146 Aristophanes, *The Complete Plays of Aristophanes*, tr. by Jack Lindsay, New York: Bantam Books, 1962, page 328.

147 Pausanias, *Guide to Greece*, page 40.

148 See Levi's comment in Pausanias, *Guide to Greece*, tr. by Peter Levi, New York: The Penguin Group, 1971, page 69/70, note 178.

149 Fitzhardinge, *The Spartans*, page 24.

150 Pausanias, *Guide to Greece*, page 69.

151 Pindar, *The Odes of Pindar*, tr. by Sir John Sandys, Cambridge: Harvard University Press, 1915, page 565.

152 Pausanias, *Guide to Greece*, Vol. 2, page 456.

153 Aeschylus, *The Complete Plays of Aeschylus*, tr. by Gilbert Murray, Franklin Center: The Franklin Library, 1978, page 266.

154 Ibid, page 322.

155 Ibid, 330.

156 Otto, Walter F., *Dionysus, Myth and Cult*, tr. by Robert B. Palmer, Dallas: Spring Publications, 1965, page 91.

157 Ibid, page 140.

158 Aeschylus, *The Complete Plays of Aeschylus*, tr. by Gilbert Murray, Franklin Center: The Franklin Library, 1978, page 334.

159 Letters, F. J. H., *The Life and Work of Sophocles*, New York: Sheed and Ward, 1953, page 235.

160 Apollodorus, *Gods & Heroes of the Greeks, The Library of Apollodorus*, tr. and with an intro. and notes by Michael Simpson, Amherst: University of Massachusetts Press, 1976, page 72.

161 Iakovidis, S. E., *Mycenae-Epidaurus*, Athens: Ekdotike Athenon S. A., 1993, page 12.

162 Ibid, page 21.

163 Pausanias, *Guide to Greece*, Vol. 1, tr. by Peter Levi, New York: The Penguin Group, 1971, page 167.

164 Iakovidis, S. E., *Mycenae-Epidaurus*, Athens: Ekdotike Athenon S. A., 1993, page 12.

164 Ibid, page 34.

165 Ibid, page 35.

166 Aeschylus, *The Oresteia*, tr. by Robert Fagles, New York: Bantam Books, 1975, page 144.

167 Pausanias, *Guide to Greece*, Vol. 2, page 456.

168 Acts, 18:13.

169 Pausanias, *Guide to Greece*, Vol. 1, page 134, note 16.

170 Hillman, James and Wilhelm Heinrich Roscher, *Pan and the Nightmare*,

Endnotes

Dallas: Spring Publications, Inc., 1972, page 34.

171 *Encyclopaedia Britannica*, Vol. 7, 1965, page 462.

172 Hesiod, *Theogony, Works and Days, Shield*, tr. by Apostolos N. Athanassakis, Baltimore: The Johns Hopkins University press, 1983, page 18.

173 Karpodini-Dimitriadi, E., *The Peloponnese*, Athens: Ekdotike Athenon S. A., 1984, page 27.

174 Landels, J. G., *Engineering in the Ancient World*, Berkeley: The University of California Press, 1978, page 182/3.

175 Diodorus Siculus, *Diodorus Siculus*, Vol. I, tr. by C. H. Oldfather, Cambridge: Harvard University Press, 1933, page 299.

176 Euripides, *Bacchanals*, lines 757-8.

177 Aeschylus, *The Complete Plays of Aeschylus*, translated by Gilbert Murray, Franklin Center: The Franklin Library, 1978, page 223.

178 Kerenyi, C., *The Gods of the Greeks*, tr. by Norman Cameron, 1951, page 97.

179 Pausanias, *Description of Greece*, Vol. 1, tr. by Peter Levi, New York: The Penguin Group, 1971, page 414.

180 Hesiod, page 71.

181 Kerenyi, *Gods*, page 96.

182 Euripides, *Euripides*, Vol. III, tr. by A. S. Way, Cambridge: Harvard University Press, 1912, page 347.

183 Sophocles, *The Oedipus Plays of Sophocles*, tr. by Paul Roche, New York: Mentor, 1991, page 44.

184 Iakovidis, S. E., *Mycenae-Epidaurus*, Athens: Ekdotike Athenon S. A., 1993, page 127.

185 Euripides, *The Plays of Euripides*, tr. by Edward P. Coleridge, Franklin Center: The Franklin Library, 1984, page 195.

186 Acts, 18:18.

187 Callimachus, *Callimachus, Hymns and Epigrams, Lycophron, Aratus*, tr. by A. W. Mair and G. R. Mair, Cambridge: Harvard University Press, 1955, page 87.

188 *Mediterranean Europe On a Shoe String*, Berkeley: Lonely Planet Publications, 1993, page 422.

189 C. G. Jung, *The Spirit in Man, Art, and Literature*, tr. by R. F. C. Hull, Princeton: Princeton University Press, 1966, page 81/2.

190 Sophocles, *The Complete Plays of Sophocles*, tr. by Sir Richard Claverhouse Jebb, ed. and with an intro. by Moses Hadas, New York: Bantam Books, 1967, page 130/1.

191 Pindar, *Pindar*, tr. by Sir John Sandys, Cambridge: Harvard University Press, Loeb Classical Library, 1919, page 563.

Endnotes

192 Callimachus, *Callimachus, Hymns and Epigrams, Lycophron, Aratus*, tr. by A. W. Mair and G. R. Mair, Cambridge: Harvard University Press, 1955, page 85.

193 Homer, *The Odyssey of Homer*, tr. Allen Mandelbaum, New York: Bantam Books, page 121.

194 Plutarch, *Plutarch's Lives*, Dryden tr., ed. and rev. by Arthur Hugh Clough, New York: The Modern Library, page 12.

195 Kerenyi, C., *The Gods of the Greeks*, tr. by Norman Cameron, New York: Thames and Hudson, page 130.

196 Hesiod, page 36.

197 *The Homeric Hymns*, page 16.

198 Ibid, page 18.

199 Doumas, Christos, *SANTORINI, a Guide to the Island and its Archaeological Treasures*, Athens: Ekdotike Athenon S. A., page 10.

200 Ibid, page 12.

201 *Baedeker's Greece*, New Jersey: Prentice-Hall, page 236.

202 Herodotus, *The Histories*, tr. by Aubrey de Selincourt, London: The Penguin Group, 1954, page 320.

203 Plato, *Timaeus and Critias*, translated by Desmond Lee, Middlesex: Penguin Books Ltd., page 135.

204 Ibid page 37.

205 Ibid, page 38.

206 Doumas, page 127.

207 Herodotus, page 320.

208 Ovid, *Metamorphoses*, tr. by Rolfe Humphries, Bloomington: Indiana University Press, 1955, page 54.

209 Heracles was assigned ten labors as a result of murdering his own sons in a fit of rage. As penance, the oracle at Delphi told him to perform whatever Eurystheus, king of Mycenae, might request. Eurystheus assigned ten labors (some say twelve) for Heracles. (Apollodorus, page 92).

210 Wood, Michael, *In Search of the Trojan War*, Oxford: Facts on File Publications, 1985, page 98.

211 Marinatos, Dr. Nanno, *Crete*, Athens: D. & I. Mathioulakis, 1986, page 15.

212 Ibid, page 23.

213 Ibid, page 65.

214 Ibid, page 143.

215 Ibid, page 93.

216 Chadwick, John, *Reading the Past, Linear B and Related Scripts*, Berkeley: University of California Press, 1987, pages 17-21.

217 Paul, page 188.

Endnotes

218 Euripides, *The Plays of Euripides*, tr. by Edward P. Coleridge, Franklin Center: The Franklin Library, 1984, page 329.

219 Sophocles, *The Oedipus Cycle*, tr. by Robert Fitzgerald, New York: Harcourt Brace Jovanovich, Inc, 1976, page 146.

220 Kerenyi, Carl, *Dionysos Archetypal Image of Indestructible Life*, tr. by Ralph Manheim, Princeton: Princeton University Press, 1976, page 105.

221 Apollodorus, *Gods and Heros of the Greeks, The Library of Apollodorus*, translated with introduction and notes by Michel Simpson, Amherst: University of Massachusetts Press, page 221.

222 Homer, *The Odyssey*, tr. by Robert Fitzgerald, New York: Doubleday & Company, page 225.

223 Pindar, *The Odes of Pindar*, tr. by Sir John Sandys, The Loeb Classical Library, Cambridge: Harvard University Press, 1919, Olympian Ode VII, page 77.

224 Hesiod, *Theogeny, Works and Days, Shield*, tr. by Apostolos N. Athanassakis, Baltimore: The Johns Hopkins University Press, 1983, page 35.

225 Ibid., page 35.

226 Pindar, page 75.

227 Ibid, 75.

228 Hesiod, page 36.

229 Homer, *The Odyssey*, tr. by Robert Fitzgerald, Chicago: Encyclopaedia Britannica, 1961, page 61/2.

230 Ibid, page 63.

231 Ibid, page 67.

232 Ibid, page 73.

233 Ibid, page 74.

234 Ibid, page 74.

235 Pausanias, *Guide to Greece*, Volume 2: Southern Greece, tr. by Peter Levi, New York: The Penguin Group, 1971, page 70.

236 Goodspeed, Edgar J., *Paul*, New York: Abingdon Press, 1947, page 188.

237 Erdemgil, Selahattin, *Ephesus*, Istanbul: Net Turistik Yayinlar A. S., 1993, page 107.

238 Kominis, Athanasios D., general editor, *Patmos, Treasures of the Monastery*, Athens: Ekdotike Athenon S. A., 1988, page 11.

239 Bournis, Archimandrite Theodoritos, *"I was in the isle of Patmos ..."*, Athens: (no publisher listed), 1988, page 31.

240 Bowra, page 51.

241 Bowra, page 59.

242 Aeschylus, *Aeschylus*, Vol. 1, tr. by Herbert Weir Smyth, Cambridge:

Harvard University Press, 1988 (1927), page 227.

243 Scythia and the Caucasus mountains where Prometheus was bound are on the northeastern coast of the Black Sea.

244 Aeschylus, page 215.

245 Revelation, 1:9-11.

246 Revelation, 1:12-16.

247 Revelation, 21:1.

248 Revelation, 21:27.

249 Se the Wikipedia entry for quaternion.

250 Aeschylus, page 298/9.

251 1 Samuel 17:42.

252 Aeschylus, page 257.

253 Aeschylus, page 255/7.

254 Hesiod, *Hesiod, Theogony, Works and days, Shield*, tr. and with an introduction and notes by Apostolos N. Athanassakis, Baltimore: The Johns Hopkins University Press, 1983, page 68.

255 Aeschylus, page 237/9.

256 Aeschylus, page 225.

257 St. Matthew, 27:46 and St. Mark, 15:34.

258 *The Homeric Hymns*, tr. by Athanassakis, Apostoleo N., Baltimore: The Johns Hopkins University Press, 1976, page 2.

259 Ulysses is the Latin name for Odysseus.

260 Jupiter is the Latin name for Zeus.

261 *Athens News*, ed. by Nikiforos Antonopoulos, Athens: Yannis Horn, Tuesday, 16 November 1993.

262 St. John, 26, 27.

263 Brown, Norman O., *Hermes the Thief*, Great Barrington: Lindisfarne Press, 1990 (1947), page 6.

264 Erdemgil, Selahattin, *Ephesus*, Istanbul: Net Turistik Yayinlar A. S., 1993, page 84-6.

265 Ibid, page 98.

266 Ibid, page 21.

267 This story appears in "The Acts of Paul, Paul in Ephesus," from *The Other Bible*, general ed. and with intros. by Willis Barnstone, San Francisco: HarperSanFrancisco, page 453.

268 Erdemgil, page 106.

269 Pagels, Elaine, *The Gnostic Gospels*, New York: Vintage Books, 1979, page xiii.

270 Ibid, page xv.

Endnotes

271 Pausanias, *Guide to Greece*,Vol. 1, tr. and intro. by Peter Levi, New York: Penguin Books, 1971, page 230.

272 Erdemgil, page 8.

273 Pausanias, page 231.

274 The Acts of John, page 421.

275 "... the city of the Ephesians is a worshipper of the great goddess Diana Artemis, and of the image which fell down from Jupiter Zeus." Acts, 19:35.

276 Erdemgil, page 30.

277 *The Other Bible*, ed. and introductions by Willis Barnstone, San Francisco: HarperSanFrancisco, 1984, page 420/1.

278 Bournis, Archimandrite Theodoritos, *"I was in the isle of Patmos ..."*, Athens: (no publisher listed), 1988, page 19.

279 Ibid page 13.

280 Callimachus, "To Artemis," from *Callimachus, Hymns and Epigrams, Lycophron, Aratus*, tr. by A. W. Mair and G. R. Mair, Loeb Classical Library, Cambridge: Harvard University Press, 1921, page 61.

281 The following is taken from "The Infancy Gospel of James (The Birth of Mary)," published in *The Other Bible*, ed. and with intros. by Willis Barnstone, New York: HarperSanFrancisco, 1984.

282 Ibid, page 386.

283 Ibid, page 388.

284 Ibid, page 392, Note 1.

285 Ibid, page 389.

286 *The Glorious Koran*, tr. by Marmaduke Pickthall, New York: Alfred A. Knopf, 1992 (1909), page 310.

287 See page 180.

288 Erdemgil, page 119.

289 Jung, C. G. and C. Kerenyi, *Essays on a Science of Mythology*, Princeton: Princeton University Press, 1963 (1949), page 19.

290 Zimdars-Swartz, Sandra L., *Encountering Mary, from La Salette to Medjugorje*, Princeton: Princeton University Press, 1991, page 5.

291 Ibid, page 7.

292 Sophocles, *The Complete Plays of Sophocles*, tr. by Sir Richard Claverhouse Jebb and ed. with an intro by Moses Hadas, New York: Bantam Books, 1967, page 78.

293 Zimdars-Swartz, page 8.

294 Ibid, page 51.

295 Erdemgil, page 119.

296 Zimdars-Swartz, page 19.

Endnotes

297 Hesiod, *Hesiod, Theogony, Works and Days, Shield*, tr. with an introduction and notes by Apostolos N. Athanassakis, Baltimore: The Johns Hopkins University Press, 1983, page 36.

298 Zimdars-Swartz, page 267.

299 Pausanias, *Guide to Greece*, Vol. 1, tr. with an intro. by Peter Levi, New York: The Penguin Group, 1971, page 231.

300 Finley M. I., *Early Greece, The Bronze and Archaic Ages*, New York: W. W. Norton & Company, 1981 (1970), page 8/9.

301 The Black Sea was called the Euxine in antiquity.

302 The Don River was called Tanais in antiquity.

303 The Dniester River was called Borysthenes in antiquity.

304 The Danube River was called Ister in antiquity.

305 Guthrie, W. K. C., *Orpheus and Greek Religion*, Princeton: Princeton University Press, 1952 (1993), page 26.

306 Bosporus means "Cow's Ford" and was named for Io, ancestress of Argos, Thebes and Crete, and obsession of Zeus. She rejected him and, as protection, was turned into a cow by Hera. She was forced to wander throughout Greece. She crossed into Asia at the Bosporus and visited Prometheus at the far edge of the Black Sea while he was chained to the cliff.

307 *Encyclopaedia Britannica*, Vol. 22, Chicago: The University of Chicago, 1965, page 505.

308 From Lycophron's "Alexandra," in *Callimachus, Hymns and Epigrams, Lycophron, Aratus*, tr. by A. W. Mair and G. R. Mair, Cambridge: Harvard University Press, 1921, page 323.

309 Homer, *The Iliad*, tr. by Robert Fitzgerald, Franklin Center: The Franklin Library, 1974, page 233.

310 From the introduction to: Quintus Smyrnaeus, *The Fall of Troy*, tr. by A. S. Way, Cambridge: Harvard University Press, Loeb Classical Library, 1913, page v.

311 Pausanias, *Guide to Greece*, Vol. 2, tr. and with an introduction and notes by Peter Levi, New York: The Penguin Group, 1971, page 455.

312 Homer, *The Iliad*, page 47.

313 Sevinc, Nurten, *Troia*, Istanbul: A Turizm Yayinlari Ltd. Sti., 1992, page 9.

314 Homer, *The Iliad*, page 47.

315 Ibid, page 147.

316 Ibid, page 46.

317 Ibid, page 168-170.

318 Ibid, *The Iliad*, page 329.

319 Sevinc, page 13.

Endnotes

320 Phrygia is the name of northwestern Asia Minor (Turkey).

321 Apollodorus, *Gods & Heroes of the Greeks, The Library of Apollodorus*, tr. and an intro. by Michael Simpson, Amherst: University of Massachusetts Press, 1976, page 173.

322 Finley, M. I., *Early Greece*, The Bronze and Archaic Ages, New York: W. W. Norton & Company, 1981, page 9.

323 Sevinc, page 26.

324 Wood, Michael, *In Search of the Trojan War*, New York: Facts On File Publications, 1985, page 30.

325 Quintus Smyrnaeus, *The Fall of Troy*, tr. by Arthur S. Way, Cambridge: Harvard University Press, Loeb Classical Library, 1913, page 555.

326 Ibid, page 559/561.

327 Ibid, page 557.

328 Sevinc, page 24.

329 Quintus Smyrnaeus, 609.

330 Revelation, 2:13.

331 Revelations, 2:14.

332 Bayraktar, Vehbi, *Pergamon*, Istanbul: Net Turistik Yayinlar A. S., 1987, page 78.

333 (deleted)

334 Thomas, Dylan, *Dylan Thomas, Collected Poems*, 1934-1952, New York: New Directions, 1957, page 10.

335 Kerenyi, C., *The Religion of the Greeks and Romans*, New York: E. P. Dutton & Co., 1962, page 182.

336 Ibid, page 16.

337 Ibid, page 11/12.

338 Diodorus Siculus, *The Library of History*, Vol. III, tr. by C. H. Oldfather, Cambridge: Harvard University Press, Loeb Classical Library, page 307.

339 Guthrie, W. K. C., *Orpheus and Greek Religion*, Princeton: Princeton University Press, 1952, page 1.

340 *The Orphic Hymns*, tr. by Apostoleo N. Athanassakis, Atlanta: Scholars Press, 1977, page 43.

341 *The Homeric Hymns*, tr. by and with introduction and notes by Apostolos N. Athanassakis, Baltimore: The Johns Hopkins University Press, 1976, page 3.

342 Iakovidis, S. E., *Mycenae-Epidaurus*, Athens: Ekdotike Athenon S. A., 1978, page 130.

343 *The Orphic Hymns*, page 89.

344 Kerenyi, C., *Asklepios, Archetypal Image of the Physician's Existence*, tr. by Ralph Manheim, New York: Bollingen Foundation, 1959, page 56.

Endnotes

345 Pausanias,Vol. 1, page 157.

346 Kerenyi, C., *Asklepios*, page 56–59.

347 Bayraktar, page 93.

348 Pausanias,Vol. 1, page 174.

349 Dothan,Trude and Moshe, *People of the* Sea, *The Search for the Philistines*, NewYork: Macmillan Publishing Company, 1992, page 10.

350 Ibid, page 47-9.

351 1 Samuel; 17:5-7.

352 Finley, M. I., *Early Greece, The Bronze and Archaic Ages*, NewYork: W. W. Norton, 1981, page 69.

353 Ibid, page 87.

354 Diodorus Siculus, *The Library of History*,Vol. III, tr. by C. H. Oldfather, Cambridge: Harvard University Press, Loeb Classical Library, page 29-31.

355 Apollodorus, *Gods & Heroes of the Greeks, The Library of Apollodorus*, tr. and with an intro. and notes by Michael Simpson, Massachusetts: The University of Massachusetts Press, 1976, page 271.

356 Dothan, page 216.

357 Ibid, page 216.

358 Ibid, page 217.The Dothan's point out the ambiguous language of Genesis 49:16, "Dan shall judge his people, as one of the tribes of Israel."

359 Dothan, page 215/6.

360 See the introduction by Alexander Wilder, M. D., in *The Eleusinian and Bacchic Mysteries*, by Thomas Taylor, San Diego:Wizards Bookshelf, 1987, page XVII.

361 I Corinthians 2:7.

362 I Corinthians 15:37-8, 44.

363 EVA stands for ExtraVehicular Activity, an astronaut space walk.

364 Kerenyi, Karl, *Zeus and Hera, Archetypal Image of Father, Husband and Wife*, tr. by Christopher Holme, Princeton: Princeton University Press, 1975, page 155/6.

365 Kyrieleis, Helmut, *The Heraion at Samos*, published in Greek Sanctuaries, New approaches, ed. by Nanno Marinatos and Robin Hagg, NewYork: Routledge Inc., 1993, page 130.

366 Kerenyi, Karl, *Zeus and Hera*, page 152.

367 Kyrieleis, page 129.

368 Pausanias, *Guide to Greece,Vol. 2,* Southern Greece, NewYork: The Penguin Group, 1971, page 425.

369 Kyrieleis, page 135.

370 Kerenyi, Karl, *Zeus and Hera*, page 105.

Endnotes

371 Ibid, page 108.

372 Avagianou, Aphrodite, *Sacred Marriage in the Rituals of Greek Religion*, Bern: European Academic Publishers, 1991, page 1–18.

373 Homer, *The Odyssey*, tr. by Robert Fitzgerald, Franklin Center: The Franklin Library, 1978, page 59.

374 Homer, *The Iliad*, tr. by Robert Fitzgerald, Franklin Center: The Franklin Library, 1979, page 497.

375 Kyrieleis, page 125/6.

376 Barnes, Jonathan, *Early Greek Philosophy*, New York: The Penguin Group, 1987, page 82.

377 From a statement by Proclus as quoted in Alexander Wilder's introduction to *Eleusinian and Bacchic Mysteries*, by Thomas Taylor, San Diego: Wizards Bookshelf, 1987, page XVIII.

378 Kerenyi, C., *Prometheus, Archetypal Image of Human Existence*, New York: The Bollingen Foundation, 1963, page 20.

379 *The Homeric Hymns*, tr. by Apostolos N. Athanassakis, Baltimore: The Johns Hopkins University Press, 1976, page 20.

380 Ibid, page 79.

381 Letters, F. J. H., *The Life and Work of Sophocles*, London: Sheed and Ward, Inc., 1953, page 41.

382 Diodorus Siculus, *The Library of History*, tr. by C. H. Oldfather, Vol. III, Loeb Classical Library, Cambridge: Harvard University Press, 1939, page 319.

383 Lesbios, P., *Lesbos*, Athens: Sotiris Toumpis, 1989, page 4.

384 From a poem by Apollonius Rhodius as quoted in *Parthenius, Erotika Pathemata*, tr. by Jacob Stern, New York: Garland Publishing, Inc., 1992, page 45.

385 Ibid, page 45/6.

386 Homer, *The Iliad*, tr. by Martin Hammond, New York: The Penguin Group, 1987, page 180.

387 Ibid, page 168/9.

388 Apollonius Rhodius, *Argonautica*, tr. by R. C. Seaton, Cambridge: Harvard University Press, Loeb Classical Library, 1912, page 5.

389 Ovid, *Metamorphoses*, tr. by Rolfe Humphries, Bloomington: Indiana University Press, 1955, page 235.

390 Ibid, page 261.

391 Guthrie, W. K. C., *Orpheus and Greek Religion, A Study of the Orphic Movement*, Princeton: Princeton University Press, 1952, page 35.

392 Ibid, page 264.

393 Ibid, page 220.

Endnotes

394 From the introduction to *Greek Lyric I, Sappho and Alcaeus*, ed. and tr. by David A. Campbell, Cambridge: Harvard University Press, Loeb Classical Library, 1982, page xi.

395 Ibid, page 5/7.

396 Author rendering from various sources.

398 Acts, 20:14.

399 Homer, *The Odyssey*, tr. by Robert Fitzgerald, Franklin Center, The Franklin Library, 1978, page 44.

400 Author rendering from various sources.

401 Homer, *The Odyssey*, tr. by Robert Fitzgerald, Franklin Center: The Franklin Library, 1978, page 190.

402 Ibid, page 210.

403 Ibid, page 211/2.

404 Ibid, page 212.

405 Quintus Smyrnaeus, *The Fall of Troy*, tr. by Arthur S. Way, Cambridge: Harvard University Press, 1913, page 603.

406 Paxi is a small island in the Ionian Sea north of Ithaca and just south of Corfu.

407 Plutarch, *Selected Essays and Dialogues* (Oracles in Decline), tr. by Donald Russell, Oxford: Oxford University Press, 1993, page 27/8.

408 From Robert B. Palmer's introduction to Walter F. Otto, *Dionysus, Myth and Cult*, tr. by Robert B. Palmer, Dallas: Spring Publications, 1981 (1965), page ix-x.

409 Homer, *The Odyssey*, tr. by Robert Fitzgerald, Franklin Center: The Franklin Library, 1978, page 48.

410 Ibid, page 48.

411 Bakhuizen, S. C., *Studies in the Topography of Chalcis on Euboea*, Leiden: E. J. Brill, 1985, page xiii.

412 *Greece*, Claremont-Ferrand: Michelin Tyre, page 83.

413 Fontenrose, Joseph, *The Delphic Oracle*, Berkeley: University of California Press, 1978, page 131.

414 Apollodorus, *Gods and Heroes of the Greeks, The Library of Apollodorus*, tr. by and with intro. and notes by Michael Simpson, page 274.

415 Hughes, Dennis D., *Human Sacrifice in Ancient Greece*, London: Routledge, 1991, page 169.

416 Farnell, Lewis Richard, *The cults of the Greek States*, Vol. III, Oxford: Clarendon Press, 1907, page 11.

417 Guthrie, W. K. C., *The Greeks and Their Gods*, Boston: Beacon Press, 1950, page 45/6.

Endnotes

418 Otto, Walter F., *The Homeric Gods*, tr. by Moses Hadas, Boston: Beacon Press, 1964 (1954), page 81/2.

419 Euripides, *The Plays of Euripides*, Vol. 2, tr. by Edward P. Coleridge, Franklin Center: The Franklin Library, 1984 (1952), page 333.

420 Pausanias, *Guide to Greece*, Vol. 1, tr. and intro. by Peter Levi, New York: The Penguin Group, 1971, page 347/8.

421 Homer, *The Iliad*, tr. by Robert Fitzgerald, Franklin Center: The Franklin Library, 1979 (1952), page 40.

422 Pausanias, Vol. 1, page 347.

423 Euripides, page 336.

424 Ibid, page 372.

425 Ibid, page 372.

426 The connection between the two myths is rather famous. See Lubeck, Maria Holmberg, *Iphigeneia, Agamemnon's Daughter*, Stockholm: Almqvst & Wiksell International, 1993, page 7.

427 Euripides, page 372.

428 Euripides, *Euripides*, Vol. I, tr. by Arthur S. Way, Cambridge: Harvard University Press, Loeb Classical Library, 1912, page 149.

429 Nonnos, *Dionysiaca*, Vol. I, tr. by W. H. D. Rouse, Cambridge: Harvard University Press, 1940, page 437.

430 Euripides, *The Plays of Euripides*, Vol. 2, page 289.

431 Ibid, page 325.

432 Dowden, Ken, *Death and the Maiden*, New York: Routledge, Inc., 1989, page 25.

433 Ibid, page 26.

434 Hughes, Dennis D., *Human Sacrifice in Ancient Greece*, New York: Routledge, 1991, page 181.

435 Otto, page 82.

436 Diodorus Siculus, *The Library of History*, tr. by C. H. Oldfather, Cambridge: Harvard University Press, Loeb Classical Library, Vol. III, page 295.

437 Otto, page 88.

438 Pausanias, *Guide to Greece*, Vol. 1, tr. by Peter Levi, New York: The Penguin Group, 1971, page 52.

439 *Athens and Attica*, ed. by Dr. Marianne Mehling, New York: Prentice Hall Press, 1986, page 113.

440 From Plato's "Phaedrus Dialogue," tr. by R. Hackforth, in *The Collected Dialogues of Plato*, ed. by Edith Hamilton and Huntington Cairns, Princeton: Princeton University Press, 1961, page 478/9.

441 *Athens and Attica*, page 113.

Endnotes

442 Foley, Helene P., *The Homeric Hymn to Demeter*, Princeton: Princeton University Press, 1994, page 66.

443 Foley, page 66.

444 Plato, *The Collected Dialogues of Plato*, page 525.

445 The following discussion follows Kerenyi, Eleusis, and Kevin Clinton's "The Sanctuary of Demeter and Kore at Eleusis," in *Greek Sanctuaries, New Approaches*, ed. by Nanno Marinatos and Robin Hagg, London: Routledge, Inc., 1993.

446 Hammond, N. G. L., *A History of Greece to 322 BC*, London: Oxford University Press, 1967, page 450/1.

447 Thucydides, *The History of the Peloponnesian War*, (no translator identified), Franklin Center: The Franklin Library, 1978, page 105.

448 Whitman, Cedric H., *Sophocles*, Cambridge: Harvard University Press, 1951, page 11.

449 Farnell, Lewis Richard, *The Cults of The Greek States*, London: Oxford University Press, 1907, page 32.

450 Mylonas, George E., *Eleusis and the Eleusinian Mysteries*, Princeton: Princeton University Press, 1961, page 254.

451 Ibid, page 270.

452 Kerenyi, C., *Eleusis*, page 11/12.

453 Mylonas, page 29.

454 Diodorus Siculus, *The Library of History*, tr. by C. H. Oldfather, Loeb Classical Library, Cambridge: Harvard University Press, 1933, Vol. I, page 95–97.

455 Kerenyi, C., *The Gods of the Greeks*, tr. by Norman Cameron, New York: Thames and Hudson, 1951, page 274.

456 Hesiod, *The Homeric Hymns and Homerica*, tr. by H. G. Evelyn-White, Cambridge: Harvard University Press, 1914, page 299.

457 Ibid, page 305.

458 Jeremiah, 23:29.

459 Mylonas, page 24.

460 Ibid, page 23.

461 Kerenyi, C., *Eleusis*, page 111.

462 Stobaios, IV, p. 107 (Meineke) as quote by George E. Mylonas in *Eleusis and the Eleusinian Mysteries*, Princeton: Princeton University Press, 1961, page 264.

463 Herodotus, *The Histories*, tr. by Aubrey de Selincourt and revised by A. R. Burn, New York: The Penguin Group, 1954 (1972), page 544/5

464 Kerenyi, C., *Eleusis*, page 92/3.

Endnotes

465 From "A Latin Infancy Gospel: The Birth of Jesus," in *The Other Bible*, ed. by Willis Barnstone, San Francisco: HarperSanFrancisco, 1984, page 405.

466 Ibid, page 406.

467 Farnell, Lewis Richard, *The Cults of the Greek States*, Vol. III, Oxford: The Clarendon Press, 1907, page 29/30.

468 Knox, Bernard M., *The Heroic Temper, Studies in Sophoclean Tragedy*, Berkeley: University of California Press, 1964, page 98.

469 Pindar, *The Odes of Pindar*, tr. by Sir John Sandys, Cambridge: Harvard University Press, Loeb Classical Library, 1915, page 593/5.

470 Plato, "Phaedrus," by page 497.

471 Guthrie, W. K. C., *The Greeks and Their Gods*, Boston: Beacon Press, 1950, page 211.

472 From C. Kerenyi's essay, "Epilegomena," in Jung, C. G., and C. Kerenyi, *Essays on a Science of Mythology, The Myth of the Divine Child and the Mysteries of Eleusis*, tr. by R. F. C. Hull, New York: The Bollingen Foundation, Bollingen Series XXII, 1949, page 181.

473 Ζιρω, Δημοσθενης Γ., Η Κυρια Εισοδου του Ιερου της Ελευσινος, Αθηναι: Αθηναις Αρχαιολογικη Εταιρεια, page 297.

474 See the essay by Meyer Fortes, "Oedipus and Job," in *Sophocles, Oedipus Tyrannus*, tr. and ed. by Luci Berkowitz and Theodore F. Brunner, New York: W. W. Norton & Co., page 47; and Knox, Bernard M., *The Heroic Temper, Studies in Sophoclean Tragedy*, Berkeley: University of California Press, 1964, page 146/7.

475 Sophocles, *The Complete Plays of Sophocles*, tr. by Sir Richard Claverhouse Jebb, ed. and with an intro. by Moses Hadas, New York: Bantam Books, 1967, page 228/9.

476 Ibid, page 250.

477 Sophocles, *The Oedipus Cycle*, tr. by Dudley Fitts & Robert Fitzgerald, San Diego: Harcourt Brace Javanovich, 1939, page 85.

478 Kerenyi, C., *The Gods of the Greeks*, tr. by Norman Cameron, New York: Thames and Hudson Inc., 1951, page 186.

479 Gartner, Dr. Otto, *Baedecker's Greece*, tr. by James Hogarth, Englewood Cliffs: Prentice-Hall, Inc., page 91.

480 *Encyclopaedia Britannica*, Chicago: The University of Chicago, 1965, Vol. 15, page 981.

481 Ibid, page 947.

482 Segal, Charles, *Oedipus Tyrannus, Tragic Heroism and the Limits of Knowledge*, New York: Twayne Publishers, 1993, page xiv-xv.

483 See Cicero's essay, "On Old Age," in *Cicero, The Basic Works of Cicero*, tr. and ed. by Moses Hadas, New York: The Modern Library, 1951, page 135.

484 Sophocles, *The Complete Plays of* Sophocles, page 237.

485 Ibid, page 221.

486 Ibid, page 256.

487 Ibid, page 230.

488 Ibid, page 257.

489 Ibid, page 256.

490 Ibid, page 257.

491 Ibid, page 258.

492 Ibid, page 258/9.

493 Whitman, Cedric H., *Sophocles, A Study of Heroic Humanism*, Cambridge: Harvard University Press, 1951, page 11/12.

494 Pausanias, *Guide to Greece*, tr. and with an intro. by Peter Levi, New York: The Penguin Group, 1971, Vol. 1, page 89.

495 Aeschylus, *The Complete Plays of Aeschylus*, tr. by Gilbert Murray, Franklin Center, The Franklin Library, 1978, page 369.

496 Ibid, page 370.

497 Kerenyi, C., *The Religion of the Greeks and the Romans*, tr. by Christopher Hume, New York: E. P. Dutton, 1962, page 193.

498 Hesiod, *Theogony, Works and Day, Shield*, tr. by Apostolos N. Athanassakis, Baltimore: The Johns Hopkins University Press, 1983, page 68.

499 Hillman, James, and Karl Kerenyi, *Oedipus Variations, Studies in Literature and Psychoanalysis*, Dallas: Spring Publication, 1991, page 101.

500 See Murray Stein's Postscript on "Hephaistos," in *Facing the Gods*, ed. by James Hillman, Dallas: Spring Publications, 1980, page 82.

501 Sophocles, *The Complete Plays of Sophocles*, page 122.

502 Ibid, page 260.

503 Kerenyi, C., *The Religion of the Greeks* and Romans, page 195.

504 Markham, Beryl, *West with the Night*, San Francisco: North Point Press, 1983 (1942), page 63.

505 Ibid, page 67.

Bibliography

Ancient Texts - Translated

Anacreon, *Greek Lyric, Vol. II, Anacreon, Anacreontea, Choral Lyric from Olympus to Alcman*, tr. by David A. Campbell, Cambridge: Harvard University Press, 1988.

Aeschylus, *Aeschylus*, Vol. 1, tr. by Herbert Weir Smyth, Cambridge: Harvard University Press, Loeb Classical Library, 1988 (1927).

_____, *The Oresteia*, tr. by Robert Fagles, New York: Bantam Books, 1975.

_____, *The Complete Plays of Aeschylus*, tr. by Gilbert Murray, Franklin Center: The Franklin Library, 1978.

_____, *The Complete Plays of Aeschylus*, Franklin Center: The Franklin Library, 1978.

Apollodorus, *Gods & Heroes of the Greeks, The Library of Apollodorus*, tr. and with an intro. and notes by Michael Simpson, Amherst: University of Massachusetts Press, 1976.

Apollonius Rhodius, *Argonautica*, tr. by R. C. Seaton, Cambridge: Harvard University Press, Loeb Classical Library, 1912.

Aristophanes, *The Complete Plays of Aristophanes*, tr. by Jack Lindsay, New York: Bantam Books, 1962.

Barnstone, Willis, ed., *The Other Bible*, San Francisco: HarperSanFrancisco, 1984.

Barnes, Jonathan, *Early Greek Philosophy*, New York: The Penguin Group, 1987.

Callimachus, *Callimachus, Hymns and Epigrams, Lycophron, Aratus*, tr. by A. W. Mair and G. R. Mair, Cambridge: Harvard University Press, 1955.

Campbell, David A., ed. and tr., *Greek Lyric I, Sappho and Alcaeus*, Cambridge: Harvard University Press, Loeb Classical Library, 1982.

Cicero, *Cicero, The Basic Works of Cicero*, tr. and ed. by Moses

Diodorus Siculus, *The Library of History*, tr. by C. H. Oldfather, Loeb Classical Library, Cambridge: Harvard University Press, 1933, Volumes 1-12.

Euripides, *Euripides*, Vol. III, tr. by A. S. Way, Cambridge: Harvard University Press, Loeb Classical Library, 1912.

_____, *The Plays of Euripides*, tr. by Edward P. Coleridge, Franklin Center: The

Bibliography

Franklin Library, 1984.

Herodotus, *The Histories*, tr. by Aubrey de Selincourt and revised by A. R. Burn, New York: The Penguin Group, 1954 (1972).

Hesiod, *The Homeric Hymns and Homerica*, tr. by H. G. Evelyn-White, Cambridge: Harvard University Press, 1914.

_____, *Theogony, Works and Days, Shield*, translated by Athanassakis, Apostolos N., Baltimore: The Johns Hopkins University Press.

Homer (Unknown), *The Homeric Hymns*, tr. by Apostolos N. Athanassakis, Baltimore: The Johns Hopkins University Press, 1976, page 48.

_____, *The Iliad*, tr. by Robert Fitzgerald, Franklin Center: The Franklin Library, 1979.

_____, *The Odyssey of Homer*, tr. Allen Mandelbaum, New York: Bantam Books.

_____, *The Odyssey of Homer*, tr. by Robert Fitzgerald, Franklin Center: The Franklin Library, 1978.

Nonnos, *Dionysiaca*, Volumes I–III, tr. by W. H. D. Rouse, Cambridge: Harvard University Press, Loeb Classical Library, 1940.

Otto, Walter F., *Dionysus, Myth and Cult*, tr. by Robert B. Palmer, Dallas: Spring Publications, 1965.

_____, Walter F., *The Homeric Gods*, tr. by Moses Hadas, Boston: Beacon Press, 1964 (1954).

Ovid, *Metamorphoses*, tr. by Rolfe Humphries, Bloomington: Indiana University Press, 1955.

Parthenius, *Erotika Pathemata: The Love Stories of Parthenius* (World Literature in Translation), tr. by Jacob Stern." New York: Garland Publishing, Inc., 1992.

Pausanias, *Description of Greece,* Volumes. 1 & 2, tr. by Peter Levi, New York: Penguin Books, 1971.

Pindar, *The Odes of Pindar*, tr. by Sir John Sandys, Cambridge: Harvard University Press, Loeb Classical Library, rev. 1919.

Plato, *Timaeus and Critias*, tr. by Desmond Lee, Middlesex: Penguin Books Ltd., 1965.

_____, *The Collected Dialogues of Plato*, ed. by Edith Hamilton and Huntington Cairns, Princeton: Princeton University Press, 1961.

Bibliography

Plutarch, *Moralia*, Vol. IV, tr. by Frank Cole Babbitt, Cambridge: Harvard University Press, Loeb Classical Library, 1936.

_____, *Plutarch's Lives*, Volumes 1-2, tr. by John Dryden, ed. by A. H. Clough, New York: 1992.

_____, *Selected Essays and Dialogues*, tr. by Donald Russell, Oxford: Oxford University Press, 1993.

Quintus Smyrnaeus, *The Fall of Troy*, tr. by Arthur S. Way, Cambridge: Harvard University Press, Loeb Classical Library, 1913.

Sappho, *Greek Lyric, Volume I, Sappho and Alcaeus*, tr. by D. A. Campbell, Cambridge: Harvard University Press, Loeb Classical Library, 1982.

Sophocles, *The Complete Plays of Sophocles*, tr. by Sir Richard Claverhouse Jebb, ed. and with an introduction by Moses Hadas, New York: Bantam Books, 1967.

_____, *The Oedipus Cycle*, tr. by Robert Fitzgerald, New York: Harcourt Brace Jovanovich, Inc, 1976.

_____, *The Oedipus Plays of Sophocles*, tr. by Paul Roche, New York: Mentor, 1991.

_____, *Sophocles', Oedipus The King*, translated by Francis Storr, Norwalk: The Easton Press,

_____, *Sophocles, Oedipus Tyrannus*, tr. and ed. by Luci Berkowitz and Theodore F. Brunner, New York: W. W. Norton & Co., 1970.

_____, *Sophocles, The Three Theban Plays*, tr. by Robert Fagles, New York: The Penguin Group, 1982.

Thucydides, *The History of the Peloponnesian War*, (no translator identified), Franklin Center: The Franklin Library, 1978.

Tyrpanis, Constantine A., ed. and tr., *The Penguin Book of Greek Verse*, New York: The Penguin Group, 1971.

Works by Scholars

Avagianou, Aphrodite, *Sacred Marriage in the Rituals of Greek Religion*, Bern: European Academic Publishers, 1991.

Brown, Norman, *Hermes the Thief*, Great Barrington: Lindisfarne Press, 1990

Bibliography

(1947).

Pagels, Elaine, *The Gnostic Gospels*, New York: Vintage Books, 1979.

Segal, Charles, *Oedipus Tyrannus, Tragic Heroism and the Limits of Knowledge*, New York: Twayne Publishers, 1993.

Taylor, Thomas, *Eleusinian and Bacchic Mysteries*, San Diego: Wizards Bookshelf, 1987.

Whitman, Cedric H., *Sophocles, A Study of Heroic Humanism*, Cambridge: Harvard University Press, 1951.

Dowden, Ken, *Death and the Maiden*, New York: Routledge, Inc., 1989.

Farnell, Lewis Richard, *The Cults of The Greek States*, Volumes I-VI, Oxford: The Clarendon Press, 1907.

Finley M. I., *Early Greece, The Bronze and Archaic Ages*, New York: W. W. Norton & Company, 1981 (1970).

Fitzhardinge, L. F., *The Spartans*, London: Thames and Hudson, Ltd., 1980.

Foley, Helene P., *The Homeric Hymn to Demeter*, Princeton: Princeton University Press, 1994.

Fontenrose, Joseph, *The Delphic Oracle*, Berkeley: University of California Press, 1978.

Guthrie, W. K. C., *The Greeks and Their Gods*, Boston: Beacon Press, 1950.

_____, *Orpheus and Greek Religion*, Princeton: Princeton University Press, 1952 (1993).

Hammond, N. G. L., *A History of Greece to 322 BC*, London: Oxford University Press, 1967.

Hughes, Dennis D., *Human Sacrifice in Ancient Greece*, London: Routledge, 1991.

Kerenyi, C., *Asklepios, Archetypal Image of the Physician's Existence*, tr. by Ralph Manheim, New York: Bollingen Foundation, 1959.

_____, *Athene, Virgin and Mother in Greek Religion*, tr. by Murray Stein, Dallas: Spring Publications, Inc., 1978.

_____, *Dionysos, Archetypal Image of Indestructible Life*, tr. by Ralph Manheim, Princeton: Princeton University Press, 1976.

Bibliography

_____, *The Gods of the Ancient Greeks*, tr. by Norman Cameron, New York: Thames and Hudson Ltd., 1951.

_____, *The Heroes of the Greeks*, tr. by H. J. Rose, New York: Grove Press, Inc., 1959.

_____, *Prometheus, Archetypal Image of Human Existence*, New York: The Bollingen Foundation, 1963.

_____, *The Religion of the Greeks and the Romans*, tr. by Christopher Hume, New York: E. P. Dutton, 1962.

_____, *Zeus and Hera, Archetypal Image of Father, Husband, and Wife*, tr. by Christopher Holme, Princeton: Princeton University Press, 1975.

Knox, Bernard, *The Heroic Temper, Studies in Sophoclean Tragedy*, Berkeley: University of California Press, 1964.

Landels, J. G., *Engineering in the Ancient World*, Berkeley: The University of California Press, 1978.

Letters, F. J. H., *The Life and Work of Sophocles*, New York: Sheed and Ward, Inc., 1953.

Lubeck, Maria Holmberg, *Iphigeneia, Agamemnon's Daughter*, Stockholm: Almqvst & Wiksell International, 1993.

Zimdars-Swartz, Sandra L., *Encountering Mary, from La Salette to Medjugorje*, Princeton: Princeton University Press, 1991.

Ζιρω, Δημοσθενης Γ., Η Κυρια Εισοδου του Ιερου της Ελευσινος, Αθηναι: Αθηναις Αρχαιολογικη Εταιρεια.

Works by Psychologists

Hillman, James, ed., *Facing the Gods*, ed. by James Hillman, Dallas: Spring Publications, 1980.

_____ and Karl Kerenyi, *Oedipus Variations, Studies in Literature and Psychoanalysis*, Dallas: Spring Publication, 1991.

_____ and Wilhelm Heinrich Roscher, *Pan and the Nightmare*, Dallas: Spring Publications, 1972.

Jung, C. G. and C. Kerenyi, *Essays on a Science of Mythology*, Princeton:

Bibliography

Princeton University Press, 1963 (1949).

_____ and C. Kerenyi, *Essays on a Science of Mythology, The Myth of the Divine Child and the Mysteries of Eleusis*, tr. by R. F. C. Hull, New York: The Bollingen Foundation, Bollingen Series XXII, 1949.

_____, *The Spirit in Man, Art, and Literature*, tr. by R. F. C. Hull, Princeton: Princeton University Press, 1966.

Archaeology

Andronicos, Manolis, *Delphi*, Athens: Ekdotike Hellados S. A., 1976.

Bayraktar, Vehbi, *Pergamon*, Istanbul: Net Turistik Yayinlar A. S., 1987.

Broad, William J., *The Oracle*, New York: The Penguin Group, 2006.

Chadwick, John, *The Decipherment of Linear B* , Cambridge: Cambridge University Press, 1958.

_____, *Reading the Past, Linear B and Related Scripts*, Berkeley: University of California Press, 1987.

Demakopoulou, Karie and Dora Konsola, *Archaeological Museum of Thebes, Guide*, Athens: 61 Archaeological Receipts Fund (T. A. P.), 1981.

Dothan, Trude and Moshe, *People of the* Sea, *The Search for the Philistines*, New York: Macmillan Publishing Company, 1992.

Doumas, Christos, *SANTORINI, a Guide to the Island and its Archaeological Treasures*, Athens: Ekdotike Athenon S. A, 1989.

Erdemgil, Selahattin, *Ephesus*, Istanbul: Net Turistik Yayinlar A. S., 1993.

Iakovidis, S. E., *Mycenae-Epidaurus*, Athens: Ekdotike Athenon S. A., 1993.

Karpodini–Dimitriadi, E., *The Peloponnese, Athens*: Ekdotike Athenon S. A., 1984.

Lesbios, P., *Lesbos*, Athens: Sotiris Toumpis, 1989.

Marinatos, Dr. Nanno, *Crete*, Athens: D. & I. Mathioulakis, 1986.

_____ and Robin Hagg, editors, *Greek Sanctuaries, New approaches*, New York: Routledge Inc., 1993.

Mylonas, George E., *Eleusis and the Eleusinian Mysteries*, Princeton: Princeton

Bibliography

University Press, 1961.

Sevinc, Nurten, *Troia*, Istanbul: A Turizm Yayinlari Ltd. Sti., 1992.

Travel Writers

Kaplan, Robert D., *Balkan Ghosts, A Journey Through History*, New York: St. Martin's Press, 1993.

Lewis, Neville, *Delphi and the Sacred Way*, London: Michael Haag Ltd., 1987.

Levi, Peter, *The Hill of Kronos*, New York: E. P. Dutton, 1981.

Mehling, Dr. Marianne, editor, *Athens and Attica*, New York: Prentice Hall Press, 1986.

Wood, Michael, *In Search of the Trojan War*, Oxford: Facts on File Publications, 1985.

Reference Works

An Intermediate Greek-English Lexicon, Oxford: Oxford University Press, 1995 (1889).
Bakhuizen, S. C., *Studies in the Topography of Chalcis on Euboea*, Leiden: E. J. Brill, 1985.

Tripp, Edward, *The Meridian Handbook of Classical Mythology*, New York: Meridian, 1970.

Miscellaneous Works

Pickthall, Marmaduke, tr., *The Glorious Koran*, New York: Alfred A. Knopf, 1992 (1909).

Thomas, Dylan, *Dylan Thomas, Collected Poems*, 1934–1952, New York: New Directions, 1957.

Bournis, Archimandrite Theodoritos, *"I was in the isle of Patmos ..."*, Athens: (no publisher listed), 1988.

Goodspeed, Edgar J., *Paul*, New York: Abingdon Press, 1947.

Bibliography

Kominis, Athanasios D., general editor, *Patmos, Treasures of the Monastery*, Athens: Ekdotike Athenon S. A., 1988.

Markham, Beryl, *West with the Night*, San Francisco: North Point Press, 1983 (1942).

Index of Ancient Greek Names

Abraham 19, 243, 261, 274, 398
Acamas 314
Achilles 44, 120, 232, 301, 304, 305, 307, 308, 309, 310, 311, 313, 314, 318, 321,
    322, 326, 328, 329, 345, 348, 351, 358, 359, 360, 361, 362, 387, 395, 396,
    397
Adrastus 157, 158
Aegeates 70, 71, 72
Aeneas 313
Aeschylus 11, 17, 148, 430, 431, 446, 450, 451, 453, 454, 464, 465
Aethra 18, 217, 314
Agamemnon 8, 9, 73, 86, 94, 95, 102, 120, 121, 122, 125, 126, 127, 131, 132, 133,
    134, 135, 148, 194, 210, 217, 237, 267, 268, 305, 307, 308, 313, 315, 318,
    322, 329, 330, 338, 339, 353, 358, 362, 373, 376, 385, 387, 393, 394, 395,
    396, 397, 398, 402, 461, 469
Agenor 193, 217
Aias 314, 373, 386
Aias of Locris 314
Alexander the Great 59, 283, 313, 387
Althaemenes 221
Andrew 19, 70, 71, 72, 74, 190, 283, 366, 447
Androclus 328
Androgeus 195
Andromache 309, 314, 318, 321, 322
Anna 162, 165, 171, 294
Antigone 34, 37, 38, 46, 168, 421, 427, 428, 433, 434
Antissa 360
Aphrodite 21, 98, 111, 120, 141, 142, 143, 172, 216, 225, 255, 285, 286, 308, 361,
    365, 426, 435, 459, 467
Apollo 27, 29, 40, 41, 43, 47, 50, 53, 54, 56, 57, 58, 59, 60, 64, 66, 67, 68, 69, 75,
    98, 103, 113, 117, 127, 128, 141, 142, 144, 145, 151, 154, 155, 156, 165, 172,
    173, 174, 188, 193, 198, 238, 250, 270, 290, 295, 305, 307, 310, 311, 323,
    326, 330, 356, 362, 364, 373, 381, 382, 383, 398, 405, 413, 430, 431, 432
Areios 322
Ares 18, 22, 29, 30, 98, 100, 303, 308, 328, 429, 436
Argeia 157, 158
Ariadne 172, 173, 199, 200, 204, 211, 216, 361
Aristotle 9, 128, 387
Arisvi 360
Arkesilaos 307
Artemis 98, 111, 113, 116, 119, 126, 154, 155, 165, 172, 173, 174, 216, 224, 237,
    286, 289, 290, 291, 292, 296, 299, 302, 329, 342, 343, 348, 349, 351, 375,

473

394, 395, 396, 398, 399, 403, 417, 435, 455
Asklepios 155, 156, 232, 326, 327, 328, 405, 413, 429, 457, 458, 468
Asterios 212
Astyanax 314
Athena iv, 13, 14, 18, 21, 22, 29, 49, 53, 66, 67, 79, 80, 82, 87, 98, 111, 115, 119,
     120, 127, 133, 153, 223, 224, 225, 255, 297, 307, 308, 309, 311, 314, 315,
     325, 330, 373, 383, 386, 399, 405, 417, 426, 430, 431, 435, 436
Atlas 182
Atreus 86, 102, 131, 133, 134, 168
Atropos 248
Autolykos 75, 76
Battus 75
Bia 240
Briseis 305, 362
Calchas 147, 148, 330, 398
Calypso 79
Cassandra 311, 314, 330, 373, 386
Castor 119, 120
Catreus 217, 221
Centaur 155, 267, 317, 344
Chalcis 394, 395, 396, 460, 471
Chariclo 49
Charon 266
Cheiron 155, 232, 326, 363, 405
Christ 19, 58, 71, 233, 238, 240, 242, 246, 273, 295, 321, 370, 379, 380
Chryseis 305
Chrysippus 47, 50, 57, 94, 106
Cleis 364
Cleito 182
Clotho 248
Cocalus 217
Codrus 328
Coronis 155
Creon 38, 167, 421
Critias 181, 182, 183, 452, 466
Cybele 290, 322, 329
Cyclops 21, 79, 284
Cynops 238, 239, 250, 270, 290, 330
Daedalus 194, 196, 199, 200, 217
Damesistratos 150, 151
Dardanus 303, 313
David i, ii, 154, 252, 259, 260, 285, 328, 449, 460, 465
Deimos 308

Index of Ancient Greek Names

Delilah 331
Demeter 98, 104, 111, 248, 266, 267, 322, 323, 324, 326, 342, 364, 400, 401, 402, 403, 404, 405, 406, 408, 409, 410, 411, 412, 413, 414, 415, 417, 426, 427, 428, 434, 435, 448, 462, 468
Demetrius 286
Demophoon 314, 410, 413
Deucalion 360
Deukalion 53
Dexion 429
Dicaeus 413
Diodorus 58, 329, 446, 451, 457, 458, 459, 461, 462, 465
Diodorus Siculus 58, 329, 446, 451, 457, 459, 461, 462, 465
Diogenes 142
Diomede 362
Diomedes 307
Dionysus 11, 12, 15, 40, 41, 42, 59, 60, 113, 118, 122, 129, 145, 148, 152, 155, 171, 188, 198, 199, 204, 216, 323, 324, 325, 327, 363, 393, 405, 409, 413, 415, 426, 429, 436, 446, 447, 450, 460, 466
Dirce 34, 36, 39, 42, 150
Dryope 112
Dryops 112
Echion 30
Eileithyia 173
Electra 126, 127, 128, 134
Ephorus 118
Epigoni 46, 158
Epistrophos 307
Epitherses 379
Erichthonius 22
Eris 120
Eteocles 36, 37, 38, 40, 46, 47, 101, 157, 158, 328, 421, 422
Eumenides 427
Euripides 11, 17, 42, 151, 387, 395, 397, 445, 451, 453, 461, 465
Europa 29, 34, 179, 188, 193, 194, 201, 209, 210, 212, 217, 329
Eurydice 363
Eurystheus 131, 452
Fates 108, 244, 248
Furies 122, 127, 128, 129, 145, 153, 187, 190, 231, 237, 296, 363, 424, 427, 428, 431
Gaia 38, 53, 54, 60, 67, 98, 100, 110, 111, 115, 198, 216, 392, 402, 412, 414, 430, 435
Goliath 252, 328, 329
Gorgon 131, 405

Index of Ancient Greek Names

Hades 73, 78, 79, 82, 103, 164, 197, 216, 217, 266, 267, 327, 363, 405, 409, 411, 412
Hadrian 6, 20, 402
Hekate 324
Hektor 44, 309, 310, 314, 318, 321, 328
Helen 22, 24, 85, 86, 90, 94, 95, 101, 118, 119, 120, 121, 126, 127, 133, 216, 217, 220, 221, 222, 223, 224, 227, 231, 302, 303, 305, 307, 309, 311, 313, 314, 315, 318, 321, 348, 371, 372, 379, 382, 383, 395
Helios 221, 223, 224, 229, 324, 409, 437
Hephaestus 20, 21, 22, 40, 98, 100, 195, 223, 240, 348, 431, 448
Hera iv, 21, 41, 42, 98, 100, 101, 103, 104, 111, 116, 120, 139, 146, 149, 152, 154, 173, 198, 322, 342, 346, 347, 348, 349, 351, 435, 446, 448, 449, 456, 458, 469
Herakles iv, 195, 197
Hermes 21, 42, 60, 61, 67, 68, 70, 75, 76, 79, 90, 92, 93, 95, 98, 102, 103, 112, 120, 123, 230, 235, 248, 255, 264, 266, 276, 277, 284, 363, 371, 373, 374, 381, 382, 386, 394, 407, 412, 419, 428, 448, 454, 467
Hermione 121, 127, 318, 321, 348
Hesiod 9, 49, 78, 82, 150, 173, 206, 329, 444, 446, 447, 451, 452, 453, 454, 456, 462, 464, 466
Hestia 98, 284, 448
Hippocrates 232
Hippodameia 101, 102, 103
Homer 8, 9, 21, 34, 35, 37, 64, 69, 75, 76, 80, 85, 89, 93, 169, 206, 224, 283, 285, 301, 303, 304, 307, 309, 311, 312, 313, 329, 330, 334, 348, 356, 364, 369, 383, 395, 396, 434, 445, 447, 452, 453, 456, 459, 460, 461, 466
Hyacinthus 117
Hyperion 224
Hyppolytus 407
Iacchos 406
Idomeneus 217, 307
Ilus 312, 313
Iphigenia 126, 134, 397, 398, 399, 400, 402, 404
Isaac 19, 243, 261, 274, 398
Isis 321, 409
Ismene 34, 37, 38, 46, 421, 428, 434
Issa 360
James 232, 445, 449, 450, 455, 463, 464, 469
Jason 232, 302, 303, 323, 362
Jesus 19, 20, 29, 54, 71, 190, 232, 233, 238, 239, 242, 250, 260, 261, 273, 283, 287, 288, 294, 295, 297, 324, 341, 363, 366, 408, 413, 415, 433, 463
Joachim 294
Jocasta 24, 37, 40, 41, 47, 50, 73, 108, 120, 149, 151, 157, 158, 167, 248, 420, 421

Index of Ancient Greek Names

John 6, 16, 19, 51, 165, 213, 219, 223, 226, 228, 232, 233, 235, 236, 237, 238, 240,
    242, 243, 246, 250, 251, 270, 273, 283, 284, 286, 287, 290, 291, 295, 296,
    297, 299, 321, 330, 342, 343, 391, 428, 429, 444, 445, 447, 448, 450, 451,
    452, 453, 454, 455, 463, 466, 467, 470
Kadmos 29, 30, 34, 35, 36, 39, 41, 179, 188, 193, 206, 217, 220, 312, 329, 436
Kalliope 323, 362
Kalypso 213
Kekrops 13
Keleos 409, 411
Kerberus 78, 79
Klonios 307
Klytemnestra 73, 121, 122, 126, 127, 132, 133, 134, 149, 305, 315, 397, 398, 400,
    431
Kratos 240
Kronos 98, 100, 103, 143, 150, 164, 221, 240, 282, 349, 448, 449, 471
Kythereia 143
Labdacus 50
Lachesis 248
Laertes 75, 86, 395
Laios 24, 33, 37, 40, 41, 43, 44, 47, 50, 52, 56, 57, 58, 63, 65, 94, 105, 106, 118,
    145, 149, 150, 151, 152, 155, 167, 168, 179, 188, 337, 389, 402, 411
Laodamas 47
Laxias 57
Leda 118, 119
Leitos 307
Leto 172, 173
Locrian Aias 373, 386
Lysimachus 283, 290
Machaeon 326
Maia 75
Makaras 360
Manto 47, 50, 57, 58, 68, 101, 290, 303, 329, 330, 369, 434
Mary Magdalene 283, 287, 288, 291
Medea 131, 303
Medusa 14, 405
Megapenthes 231
Melanthus 328
Membliarus 179, 188
Menelaus 86, 94, 95, 118, 120, 121, 127, 131, 194, 217, 220, 221, 222, 223, 224,
    225, 227, 231, 302, 307, 313, 314, 315, 318, 321, 322, 328, 329, 348, 371,
    372, 373, 379, 382, 383, 387, 395, 397
Menestheus 307
Metaneira 409, 410

Index of Ancient Greek Names

Methymna 360, 361, 362, 364, 366
Metis 13, 21, 223, 431
Miletus 225, 289, 290, 293, 329
Minos 131, 164, 172, 193, 194, 195, 196, 197, 199, 201, 205, 212, 217, 221, 266, 289, 409
Minotaur 164, 172, 195, 196, 199, 200, 201, 202, 212, 217, 221, 362, 409
Mopsus 303, 329, 330, 331
Muses 49, 116, 255, 426
Myrtilus 102, 131
Mytilene 225, 358, 359, 360, 366, 369, 370, 371
Neaera 75
Nemesis 118, 244
Neoptolemus 311, 314, 318, 321, 322, 326, 348
Nereids 227, 426
Nestor 371, 373, 382
Nikostratos 231
Nireus 395
Nymphs 78, 79, 80, 81, 82, 87, 135, 407
Odysseus 8, 14, 35, 61, 65, 66, 67, 73, 75, 76, 78, 79, 80, 81, 82, 85, 86, 87, 88, 89, 90, 94, 95, 96, 106, 120, 135, 141, 157, 164, 172, 197, 213, 217, 224, 266, 284, 285, 307, 311, 315, 329, 351, 373, 374, 375, 376, 380, 383, 387, 392, 395, 396, 397, 454
Oedipus 1, 8, 12, 15, 24, 25, 26, 27, 28, 30, 31, 32, 33, 34, 36, 37, 38, 39, 40, 41, 42, 43, 44, 46, 47, 50, 52, 53, 56, 57, 58, 63, 64, 65, 73, 80, 94, 95, 100, 101, 105, 107, 108, 120, 133, 134, 138, 140, 141, 142, 144, 145, 146, 147, 148, 149, 150, 151, 152, 153, 155, 157, 158, 167, 168, 179, 181, 188, 190, 210, 221, 248, 266, 291, 296, 301, 329, 331, 334, 336, 337, 358, 389, 401, 402, 410, 411, 415, 416, 418, 419, 421, 422, 423, 424, 425, 426, 427, 428, 429, 434, 435, 436, 444, 445, 451, 453, 463, 464, 467, 468, 469
Oenomaus 102
Orestes 121, 122, 126, 127, 128, 129, 130, 133, 134, 139, 153, 231, 237, 296, 302, 318, 322, 398, 427, 429, 430, 431
Orpheus 197, 303, 323, 325, 362, 363, 364, 366, 456, 457, 459, 468
Ouranos 143
Pan 98, 110, 112, 113, 114, 122, 129, 145, 148, 379, 380, 391, 404, 407, 449, 450, 469
Pandora 14, 21, 255
Paris 94, 120, 121, 136, 214, 217, 221, 222, 224, 302, 309, 310, 311, 314, 328, 372
Pasiphae 194, 195, 201, 217, 221
Patroklos 362
Paul 18, 20, 72, 141, 142, 147, 161, 209, 220, 225, 229, 232, 233, 283, 286, 287, 295, 299, 307, 312, 329, 342, 355, 371, 451, 452, 453, 454, 467, 471
Pausanias 14, 101, 103, 109, 115, 139, 150, 305, 347, 395, 396, 397, 429, 444, 445,

Index of Ancient Greek Names

        446, 448, 449, 450, 451, 453, 455, 456, 458, 461, 464, 466
Peisidice 361
Peleus 120, 310, 322
Pelops 101, 102, 103, 105, 106, 131, 426
Peneleos 307
Penelope 73, 87, 90, 92, 94, 120, 351
Pentheus 42, 74, 148, 366
Pergamus 318, 322
Pericles 356
Persephone 197, 216, 248, 266, 267, 324, 363, 400, 401, 402, 404, 409, 411, 412,
        413, 414, 415, 416, 417, 423, 426, 428, 435
Perseus 75, 131, 167
Peter 71, 190, 232, 433, 444, 445, 446, 448, 449, 450, 451, 453, 455, 456, 461, 464,
        466, 471
Phaedrus 403, 404, 461, 463
Phaon 369
Phobos 308
Phorbas 362
Plato 9, 128, 181, 182, 403, 407, 434, 452, 461, 462, 463, 466
Podaleirius 326
Polyduces 119, 120
Polyneices 36, 37, 38, 40, 46, 157, 158, 179, 301, 328, 421, 422
Polyphemus 79, 284
Polyxo 231
Poseidon 98
Priam 44, 85, 86, 309, 311, 313, 314, 373, 396
Priapos 112, 285
Prochorus 238, 242
Prometheus 21, 239, 240, 250, 254, 255, 257, 260, 303, 380, 424, 432, 454, 456,
        459, 469
Proteus 227
Prothoenor 307
Pythagoras 265, 353, 364
Pythia 54, 58, 59, 64, 121
Rakios 329
Rhadamanthos 205
Rhea 98, 248, 349, 448
Sappho 9, 301, 345, 358, 361, 364, 365, 369, 370, 371, 372, 449, 460, 465, 467
Serapis 321
Simon Peter 71
Sinon 311
Sisyphus 75, 76, 141, 363
Skhedios 307

Index of Ancient Greek Names

Socrates 9, 403, 404, 414, 415
Sophocles 9, 11, 12, 17, 18, 28, 37, 44, 108, 151, 168, 210, 336, 356, 380, 389, 405,
    415, 419, 420, 423, 424, 425, 426, 427, 429, 433, 439, 444, 445, 450, 451,
    453, 455, 459, 462, 463, 464, 467, 468, 469
Sphinx 27, 30, 31, 39, 47, 49, 57, 107, 108, 220
Stobaios 412, 462
Tantalus 363
Teiresias 37, 43, 47, 49, 50, 58, 68, 73, 181, 197, 217, 266, 290, 303, 329, 374, 375,
    392, 434
Telchines 164, 184
Telemachus 87, 106, 224, 383
Telephos 301, 307, 317, 318, 326
Telesphorus 327
Thamous 379, 380
Theras 179, 181, 188, 296
Thersander 46, 158, 179, 301, 318
Theseus 8, 18, 22, 23, 24, 53, 119, 131, 148, 150, 157, 158, 162, 164, 167, 172, 173,
    195, 196, 197, 199, 200, 204, 211, 212, 216, 217, 290, 303, 314, 328, 329,
    361, 407, 409, 421, 427, 428, 429, 444
Thetis 120, 164, 310, 311, 395
Thucydides 389, 462, 467
Thymoites 328
Tlepolemos 231, 307
Triptolemus 414
Tros 303, 313
Tyndareus 118, 119, 120
Uranus 98
Virgil 313
Xanthus 330
Zeus iv, 6, 8, 9, 13, 21, 22, 29, 34, 41, 42, 53, 54, 59, 60, 61, 67, 75, 79, 98, 100,
    101, 103, 104, 107, 112, 115, 117, 118, 120, 126, 128, 131, 149, 150, 154,
    155, 156, 164, 168, 173, 179, 193, 194, 197, 198, 199, 201, 205, 209, 212,
    216, 217, 221, 223, 224, 227, 240, 248, 250, 253, 255, 260, 266, 290, 292,
    295, 298, 301, 308, 315, 322, 323, 324, 325, 326, 327, 347, 349, 368, 383,
    400, 401, 402, 405, 409, 411, 412, 413, 414, 426, 428, 431, 432, 435, 446,
    448, 449, 454, 455, 456, 458, 469
zoë 41
Zoë 216

6251316R0

Made in the USA
Lexington, KY
02 August 2010